Sebastian de Grazia

MACHIAVELLI IN HELL

Sebastian de Grazia, political philosopher and writer, is
the author of *The Political Community; Of Time, Work
and Leisure;* and *Machiavelli in Hell,* which won the
Pulitzer Prize for Biography in 1989. His most recent
book is *A Country with No Name.*

Machiavelli in Hell

(1469–1527)

Sebastian de Grazia

MACHIAVELLI IN HELL

VINTAGE BOOKS

A DIVISION OF RANDOM HOUSE, INC.

NEW YORK

FIRST VINTAGE BOOKS EDITION, JANUARY 1994

Copyright ©1989 by Sebastian de Grazia

All rights reserved under International and Pan-American Copyright Conventions.
Published in the United States by Vintage Books, a division of Random House,
Inc., New York, and distributed in Canada by Random House of Canada Limited,
Toronto. Originally published by Princeton University Press, New Jersey, in 1989.

Library of Congress Cataloging-in-Publication Data
De Grazia, Sebastian.
Machiavelli in hell/Sebastian de Grazia.
p. cm.
Includes index.
ISBN 0-679-74342-1
1. Machiavelli, Niccolò, 1469–1527. Principe.   2. Machiavelli, Niccolò, 1469–1527—
Contributions in political science.   3. Machiavelli, Niccolò, 1469–1527—
Ethics.   4. Florence (Italy)—Politics and government—1421–1737.   I. Title.
[JC143.M394D4   1993]
320.1—dc20   92-50594
CIP
Manufactured in the United States of America

To Jay Gordon Hall

Contents

Machiavelli in Hell

"And then whoever sees the devil truly
sees him with smaller horns and not even black"

IRREVERENT AND ON THE GO

> I myself did not hear the sermon,
> for I do not use such practices.
> —Letter to Vettori
> 19 December 1513

N O O N E, so far, has called Niccolò Machiavelli a bigot.

From the start let us refer to him as Niccolò. That is the way he refers to himself at the onset of a personal crisis that so shook him he doubted who he was. And that is the way to salute great men—by their first names. Dante is Italy's greatest poet, Niccolò her greatest writer of prose. Also, in these times names are in flux: Niccolò signs himself in several ways and his correspondents address him with these and several more. He favors the Tuscan style, as it appears on the preface to his *Art of War*—Niccolò Machiavegli.

To continue, no one accuses Niccolò of being a bigot. He is not a devout man. He does not attend mass as often as some of his contemporaries. More often than not he relishes the role, enjoyed by university students, of one who can be counted on to tell off-color stories about popes and priests. In his play *Clizia* he mentions Friar Timothy, a personage in an earlier play of his, the *Mandragola*.

HUSBAND: And one cannot go to anyone but Fra Timoteo, who is
           our family confessor and a real saint, and has already
           performed miracles.
WIFE: Which?
HUSBAND: What which? Don't you know that through his prayers
           Lady Lucrezia . . . who was sterile became pregnant?
WIFE: Great miracle, a friar makes a woman pregnant!
           A miracle it would be if a nun made her pregnant!

This one exchange also manages at the same time to advertise and make fun of our playwright's previous comedy.

Once the wool guild of Florence asked Niccolò, who at the time was on an official mission to a nearby convent, to secure them a preacher for Lent. At news of this request, Francesco Guicciardini wrote that giving him this errand was like asking a confirmed pederast to pick out a beautiful and wanton wife for a friend. Such was opinion, particularly of this friend, of Niccolò's attitude toward the clergy.

The role of flippant anticlerical is not uncommon. One can see it played to the hilt by Guicciardini (who, by the way, often salutes his friend as "Maclavello") in just this exchange of letters over the Lenten preacher. But Guicciardini's anticlericalism is fierce. "Before I die I want to see . . ." he wrote, "the world freed from the tyranny of these pernicious priests." Niccolò does not include any such wish among his fondest desires. Though he advances sharp criticism of the church and its prelates, the anticlericalism he affects is studentesque. He relishes shocking the sanctimonious. (In jest, friends threaten to drag him from home to the cathedral to make a vow.) He dislikes those who parade "under the cloak of religion."

At those sharp points in his career when accusations against him were encouraged, when a rival faction wanted him removed from office, or when a new regime put him to torture on suspicion of conspiracy, what we know of the charges does not include blasphemy. Foes—and friends, too, half jokingly—may accuse him of being a dyed-in-the-wool republican or, on the contrary, of catering to Medici rulers, of roaming too long in too many foreign countries, of speaking ill of the Florentines, of being a bastard's son, of reading too many books, of being impractical, of being ribald, a lackey, an intellect, a sodomite, a philosopher. Socrates was accused of impiety; not Machiavelli, not even with trumped-up evidence. The most his enemies can say is that while he does not lack faith, there is not much to spare.

The Machiavegli family had property in and around Florence, where they had been active in politics, providing that city with a number of republican magistrates. One of them, a distant relative, a decade before Niccolò saw the light of day, had opposed the rise of a regime "of the few." In order "to give a start to that government of terror that they had begun with force, [these few, through their picked magistrates] exiled Messer Girolamo Machiavelli" to Avignon. Upon his breaking exile they declared him a rebel. Niccolò will further record of him in the *Florentine Histories* that "going about, circling Italy, raising princes against his country," he was captured through the treachery of one of the lords of the Lunigiana, "conducted to Florence, and put to death in prison."

Another distant relative, but one who should not and indeed does not appear in the *Florentine Histories*, was Chiovo di Gherardino Machiavelli. Some seventy years before Niccolò's birth, as a youth, he had been arrested for breaking and entering and theft, to which he confessed. The court commuted the penalty of death or mutilation to a fine, in consideration of his destitute parents and sisters, his military service, and the many worthy deeds his Machiavelli ancestors had done for Florence.

Niccolò's paternal grandfather, Niccolò di Buoninsegna, died a bachelor. On his deathbed he legitimated a natural child, Bernardo, as his son and charged a brother with raising him. This Bernardo, our Niccolò's father, administered the modest family estate (not always managing to stay in the black) and was evidently a man for good conversation. He had connections among literary men in the Florentine Chancery and Medici circles. Schooled in law, he was enrolled in a most powerful Florentine society, the lawyers' guild. Niccolò's mother, Bartolomea Nelli, had some literary leanings too, apparently, and composed lauds and hymns to the Blessed Virgin, dedicated to her third child and first boy, Niccolò. One suspects that as first male child he did not suffer from lack of attention. One also suspects that he was let out to nurse: the Machiavegli are members of the wet-nursing class.

BOY INTO MAN

A *Book of Records*, really an account book that his father kept, spanning ages six to eighteen in Niccolò's young life, reveals that at seven he was sent to his first teacher, at eleven he was placed with a "maestro of abacus who is to teach him the abacus," and at twelve he was well into Latin literature: "Niccolò does the Latins." School expenses included "for the fire [for heating], 9 soldi 8 danari, and for the benches [for sitting], Niccolò gave [the maestro] 6 soldi." His Latin teacher was both a priest and a member of the lawyers' guild, with connections in Chancery and literary circles, and Niccolò's more specialized education begins with him.

Among the more well-known books bartered for, bought, or borrowed that Bernardo had at home at various times between 1474 and 1487 were Aristotle's *Ethics* and fragments of the *Topica*, Cicero's *Phillipics, de Officiis* and *de Oratore*, Ptolemy's *Cosmography* ("I record that this day, eleventh of May, I brought back . . . Ptolemy, that is, the *Cosmography* without tables"), Boethius's *On Divisions*, on loan from the convent of Santa Croce (in the *Mandragola* Niccolò, playing on the first two vowels of his name to suggest an ox, will describe the husband as "a doctor who learned a lot about law in Boethius"), the Justinian Code and Digest, Macrobius ("I lent [the chaplain of San Giovanni] a Macrobius of mine on the *Dream of Scipio* and *On the Saturnalia*"), and *Italy Illustrated* and *The Decades* of Flavio Biondo.

Much learning, many scholarly favorites, many quotable ancients are in these volumes. And, yes, one should not omit another item in particular. Bernardo notes in his account book that he had been given printed sheets of Livy from the printer "as reward for my labors" in making an index of "all the cities and provinces and rivers, islands, and mountains mentioned in the *Decades* of Livy." He gave the sheets to a binder. "My son Niccolò," age 17 [to whom Bernardo was giving many errands of increasing responsibility], delivered to the binder in partial payment at a special price "a barrel of vermilion wine." Given this errand and the household traffic in books, it is not surprising that Niccolò courses through life with his saddlebags stuffed with books and that Livy becomes "our Titus Livy" and "our historian."

All this adds up to not much: childhood and youth pass with little to show. A brother (his one and only brother as it turns out) is born when he is six; his mother dies when he is twenty-seven; and to date no letters to or from him exist to mark such events. The gap in the record is unfortunate. As Niccolò himself observes in his great work, *Discourses on the First Decade of Titus Livy*, "it is very important that a boy of tender years begin to hear the good or bad said of a thing, because it must of necessity make an impression and through that thereafter rule [his] way of proceeding in all the rest of his life."

In default of other resources, Niccolò's plays and verse offer some help. The play *Clizia* gives a sense of what home life may have been like. The wife soliloquizes on the change of her husband's daily routine since he lost his head over the young Clizia, ". . . he used to be a man grave, resolute, circumspect. He disposed his time honorably. He rose at a good hour in the morning, heard his mass, provided for the day's meals; afterward if he had business in the square, in the market, [or] at the magistrates', he did it; when he did not [have such business], either he went off with some citizen engaged in honorable discussion . . ." ('honorable discussion' may have included literary encounters; wives could not be expected to know about such things) or, the wife continues, "he withdrew to the house in his writing room where he assembled his writings [and] put his accounts in order; afterward he dined pleasantly with his brigade [of family] and, [having] eaten, reasoned with the son, cautioned him, led him to understand men, and with an example or two, ancient and modern, he taught him to live." If Niccolò's father 'heard his mass' each morning (it seems unlikely), his daily schedule in this particular differed from what was to be his son's. If his father's teachings recommended the imitation of ancient and modern examples, his son's did likewise; the combining of ancient and modern examples in *The Prince* reaches artistic pitch.

The honest wife goes on: "When the evening came, [the bells of] Vespers found him in the house; he stayed a little with us at the hearth if it was winter; afterward he entered the writing room to look over his business; at three hours [after sunset] he supped cheerfully."

This monologue may contain not only a bit of biography about Niccolò's father, but autobiographical elements, too, about the author. The ins-and-outs of the writing room have special significance for Niccolò's own habits, and the soliloquy as a whole presents an idyl of family love, security, and education. "This order to life was an example to all the others of the household, and everyone was ashamed not to imitate it; and thus things went ordered and happy. But afterwards when this fantasy about that [Clizia] got inside him . . ."

Let us leave the afterwards for another occasion, except for one little exchange that shows the husband in a less than reverent attitude toward church services.

HUSBAND: Where are you going?
WIFE: To mass.
HUSBAND: And this is even Carnival time. Think what you'll be
         doing when Lent comes around!

The Machiavegli lived off farm and rental properties rather than off trade and banking or the professions. Bernardo for some reason did not practice much law, and when he did he accepted gifts or goods in barter as remuneration. Niccolò, when out of a job, will admit that he knows how to discuss "neither the art of silk nor the art of wool, neither of profits nor of losses." To political and military changes all over the world his ears prick up: they hear less of the gradual economic shifts, the growth of competition from northern cities, the trends, mainly declines, in Florentine international trade and banking. He has broad economic ideas of his own, however, and will elucidate them, particularly as they pertain to military and political affairs. And when economic changes are clamorous, he does not ignore them. Lorenzo the Magnificent, under whom most of the Medici banks floundered or failed, "was as far as trade goes most unsuccessful. . . . So that he . . . leaving aside mercantile industries turned to landed property as stabler and firmer riches."

Looking again at the gap in information about Niccolò from boy to

. . . the literary side of his education . . .

young man, we can think of many events that were then taking place in the region, events that may have left an impression.

The book errands Niccolò runs for his father and the literary side of his education would make him aware of the birth of the printing houses—if not that of Aldo Manuzio in Venice in 1495, at least that of Filippo Giunta in Florence in 1497, a bookseller to Bernardo and Niccolò's own publisher-to-be. The construction of most of the great churches and *palazzi* (the great residences and other imposing buildings) occurred before he was born or too early to count as events in his life. Palazzo Pitti was begun in 1435 before he was born, but it stands there across the street from where he lived, and he will signal its political significance in his *Florentine Histories*. Palazzo Strozzi, on the other hand, was begun in 1489 when Niccolò was twenty: some thirty years later he would dedicate the *Art of War* to "Lorenzo di Filippo Strozzi, Florentine Patrician," who had become his friend and patron.

Of the many contemporary dramatic events (excluding pageants, games, and special festivities) that one could select simply for suggestive value, we may note four that Niccolò would later put to pen and paper: the Pazzi conspiracy of 1478, the battle of Poggio Imperiale in 1479, the death of Lorenzo de' Medici in 1492, and the entry of Charles VIII of France into Florence in 1494.

MOMENTOUS EVENTS

Niccolò is nine years old when the first event occurs—the Pazzi conspiracy. We may take a moment before glancing at the other events to look at it more closely. It displays some of the extreme features of Florentine turbulence and may have turned sour from the start a subject that our author is going to be concerned with and implicated in for much of his life: conspiracies, a subject that is not, he warns, one "to pass over with brevity."

"Of all the other Florentine families at that time in Florence the Pazzi for their riches and nobility were the most resplendent." Supported in many ways by the Pope, they were the closest rivals to the Medici among Florentine banking families. After 1466 the running of "the state was restricted all to the Medici who had taken such great authority [that] it was better for those who were discontent either to bear with patience that way of living or, if they wanted to eliminate it, to try to do so by way of conspiracies and secretly." Even "Giuliano de' Medici complained many times to his brother Lorenzo [older by five years and destined to be known as the Magnificent], saying he feared that for wanting too much of things, they [the Medici] would lose everything." Lorenzo, "hot with youth and power," did not listen. Feeling themselves pushed to the wall, the Pazzi formed a conspiracy. After several meetings they "decided that they must not defer putting [their plan] into effect, for it was impossible, being [already] known to so many, that it would not be discovered. They therefore determined to kill [Lorenzo and Giuliano] in the cathedral church of Santa Reparata where, the cardinal being present, the two brothers would come according to their habit." One of the conspirators, a seasoned captain who had the task of killing Lorenzo, said that "his courage would never be enough to commit so great

[9]

an excess in church and to accompany treachery with sacrilege. This was the beginning of the ruin of their enterprise." They were constrained to replace him with two of their supporters who lacked armed experience. They then determined that the attack would take place at the moment "when the priest who was celebrating High Mass in the temple took Communion." With joking and youthful talk, the Pazzi and the Medici pretended to be friends as they strolled to the cathedral together, one of the Pazzi trying, as he put a comradely arm about Giuliano, to feel whether he was wearing an armored corselet. "When the killers were ready then, some by the side of Lorenzo, where because of the crowd in the temple they could stand easily and without suspicion, and the others together with Giuliano, the destined hour arrived." A dagger passed through the chest of Giuliano, who "after a few steps fell to the ground" dead. One of the Pazzi threw himself on the body and "blinded by fury," stabbing wildly, stabbed himself deeply in the leg and had to retire from the fight. Lorenzo, but slightly wounded in the throat, "defended himself with his own weapon" and with the help of friends escaped into the sacristy.

While all this was going on, another phase of the plot was unrolling in the Palazzo della Signoria, or Palazzo for short, the seat of government. There the archbishop of Pisa, a fellow conspirator of the Pazzi, was trying to seize the stronghold with his men. (Niccolò narrates these events not as an eyewitness but as a mature historian with a sure knowledge of intimate detail. When he comes to describe what is happening at the various doors, windows, stairs, floors, and exits of the Palazzo, we should note that the Chancery in the Palazzo was later his headquarters for the many years he served as Florentine Secretary.) "The greater part of these [men of Pazzi] shut themselves up in the Chancery by themselves, because its door was so designed that closing it, it could not be opened except by help of the key, from the inside as well as from the outside."

With the Archbishop and two more conspirators hanged and dangling from the Palazzo windows, and with others thrown out from the upper stories while still alive, "all the city was up in arms . . . all over the city the name of Medici was shouted, and the limbs of the dead were seen either stuck on the points of weapons or dragged through the city; and everybody with words full of anger and deeds full of cruelty hunted down the Pazzi. People already took over their houses, and Francesco [the Pazzi who had disabled himself and was lying in bed] was taken out of the house naked as he was and, led to the Palazzo, was hanged alongside the Archbishop and the others."

"There was not a citizen, armed or unarmed, who did not go to Lorenzo's house in that [hour of] need, and everybody offered himself and his sustenance to him . . ." Would this include Bernardo, Niccolò's father? And was Niccolò, the boy, an eyewitness to some of these dreadful acts? Or was he quickly shunted behind closed, bolted doors? Or were both father and son at the villa that fateful Easter Sunday. Bernardo's account book has no entry for the day. On Monday, an entry records the sale of one of his oxen.

There is one thing neither he nor his son can avoid seeing over the next fifteen years, to wit, the alfresco paintings, on the walls of the Captain's Palace adjacent to the Palazzo, of the swinging bodies of the conspirators. They follow a tradition of so-called defaming paintings, portraits of wanted persons who had fled and escaped capital punishment. Usually, fugitives were painted upside down, hanging from the gallows by a foot. In the Pazzi case, several departures from tradition occur. Over eighty men are hanged in a couple of days, including the archbishop clothed in episcopal robes and miter. Men of good family, and there are many such among them, were normally decapitated rather than basely hanged. These men, however, are not only hanged, they are hanged out of palace windows rather than from gallows. They had not, moreover, been allowed the final rites given to condemned men. And the paintings of the chief conspirators are not drawn of wanted men but of men already captured, strung up and twisting in the wind. Lorenzo gives the commission to paint these figures to Sandro Botticelli, who executes the job in three months. Seven figures are shown hanging by the neck, one (who was never caught) hanging by a foot. For each figure Lorenzo writes an epitaph. (Only after Lorenzo's death and the overthrow of the Medici are these paintings canceled out.)

One other conspirator is not there hanging from the Palazzo windows in person, and that is the one who actually knifed Lorenzo's brother. There is a picture of him, however, and under it Lorenzo writes:

> I am Bernardo Bandini a new Judas
> Homicidal traitor in church was I
> Rebel to await a cruder death.

Bandini had fled to Constantinople. Lorenzo persuaded the Sultan to extradite him, and not much more than a year after the plot he has the pleasure of seeing him outside the Captain's Palace dangling at the end of a rope, dressed as a Turk. While he is still hanging, Leonardo sketches him, noting in script the colors of the Turkish garb.

"That this case should not lack for some extraordinary example," Nic-

*While he is still hanging, Leonardo sketches him, noting in script
the colors of the Turkish garb.*

colò will write of the head of the Pazzi family, "Messer Jacopo was first buried in the tomb of his ancestors; then, taken from there as if excommunicated, he was buried alongside the city walls; and then, pulled by the noose with which he was hanged, he was dragged naked through the whole city; and afterward, so that he could not find his burial place in earth, by the same ones who dragged him around he was thrown in the Arno river, whose waters then were at their highest. Truly the greatest example of fortune was to see a man from so much riches and the happiest condition fall with so much ruin and much shame!"

The word 'extraordinary' at the beginning of the above paragraph, an important term for Niccolò, is used here in the restricted sense of portentous. Evidently, many took the heavy rains falling into the swollen Arno as a sign of God's wrath on seeing Jacopo buried in hallowed ground, because one of the Pazzi, just before being hanged, had been heard to invoke the devil.

Though he will write of the Pazzi conspiracy as a mature man, when the event occurred he was a boy living in the paternal house three blocks or so from the Palazzo, on the other side of the Ponte Vecchio. Also living at home were two older sisters and a brother, Totto, younger by six years. Nearby, within the area of a square block, were many other relatives. Any happening in the center of the city or its ceremonial routes was certain to reach the family's eyes and ears, old and young, in minutes. These "grave and tumultuous events" were "so terrible that it seemed as if the temple might be destroyed."

There remained to the dead Giuliano, continues Niccolò in the *Florentine Histories* where the plot is most fully recounted, "a natural son who, a few months after [his father] was dead, was born and called Giulio, who was replete of that virtue and fortune that in these present times the whole world recognizes and that by us, when we shall come to deal with present-day things, God giving life for it, will be amply shown." (As Niccolò writes these words, the natural son Giulio has grown up to become Pope Clement VII and the patron of our historian, who will dedicate to him these same *Florentine Histories*.)

The military aftermath of the Pazzi plot was a campaign directed against Florence by armies collected by the Pope and the king of Naples. The battle and successive actions of Poggio Imperiale, in 1479, the second of the four events earlier singled out, form part of the campaign. Bernardo, Niccolò's father, notes in the account book beforehand that troops moving to the defense "passed through Sant'Andrea," the site of their country villa. Goods were sent into Florence. A year later a succinct entry appears, "I record that on day 7 of September 1479 [the battle of] Poggio Imperiale was lost." He sends all hands away from the villa, and further records that on 22 November a captain on the Florentine side who had lodged "in my houses from the first of the present until now, left Sant'Andrea with his troops." (Three years later Bernardo will find himself up there fixing the ceiling of one of these houses "wrecked by the soldiers.")

The debacle of Poggio Imperiale fills "the king's soldiers with booty and the Florentines with fear," Niccolò would write. Mercenary troops were so sluggish and undisciplined that "the turning of one horse's head or rump gave victory or defeat."

Just prior, Florence had been afflicted by a grievous plague: "all the citizens to flee death withdrew to their villas [in the countryside]." Once the rout occurred, those whose villas were situated in the valleys connected with the Poggio Imperiale side of town (these would include Niccolò's father), having fled the plague with their possessions, now turned about and "immediately as best they could, not only with their children and goods but with their workers, fled to Florence." Bernardo's *Book of Records* notes that in May of 1479 he sent the children away from Florence to the nearby Mugello with relatives of their mother, to escape the plague. A month later an entry begins: "I record that this day 30 June I came back [to town] from the villa sick." Niccolò's father had caught the plague. He arrranges for the fearfully administered medical treatment, recovers, and pays the doctor's bill. No debt to God recorded in this account book, no exclamations over the beauty of book bindings or the pilfering of soldiers. The entry on his illness appears simply to record the money he lays out for treatment. Other relatives all about are sick and dying and are making last wills and testaments.

The next in this chronicle of events that are sure to have affected Niccolò is the natural death of Lorenzo de' Medici. He had ruled Florence from the time Niccolò was turning ten, a time of dawning political consciousness. Now he is a young man of twenty-three, nearly twenty-four, which is soon to be the minimum age of citizenship. The young man must have felt the aura of Lorenzo on his own growing interests. Lorenzo was a statesman of renowned skill, a liberal patron of brilliant men of letters, a stalwart of the vernacular, and a poet of grace and power. The fascination that great men of the world can generate was there to feel in Lorenzo de' Medici. Niccolò will write that the Florentines for the last five years of his reign lived "in the greatest happiness." At his death "all the citizens and all the princes of Italy" mourned. The portents were extraordinary: they warned of the beginning of the end for Italy.

The fourth event stigmatizes the year 1494 as a black date in the periodizing of history: the entry into Florence of Charles VIII of France. With lance poised on thigh like a conqueror, he "took Italy with chalk"

. . . *he "took Italy with chalk"* . . .

in the first new wave of "barbarian insolences." (All that Charles's men had to do during the invasion was to mark with chalk whatever houses they wanted for billeting.)

What has happened is that Lodovico Sforza of Milan (whose ambition, our historian will say, Lorenzo had satisfied and braked), feeling himself threatened by an unfriendly Naples and an uncertain Florence, becomes "the prime mover" of Italy's ruin. He induces Charles VIII to assert his rights to the kingdom of Naples, in effect calling in "the barbaric peoples" and starting the rash of expeditions into Italy that leave her prostrate, "raced over by Charles, preyed on by Louis, forced by Ferdinand, and vituperated by the Swiss." Niccolò's serious works never shake off this nightmare of degradation and imminent ruin. His *First Decennial*, a ten-year chronicle, opens with that date: "one thousand and four hundred ninety-four [years] from the time that Jesus first visited our cities and, with the blood he lost, extinguished the diabolical sparks." Even in the two most important of his three comedies, in their first act he gives 1494 its pivotal significance.

Amid the uproar of Charles's march toward Florence, Lorenzo de' Medici's son Piero, his successor, surrenders Florence's prized strongholds, including its outlets to the Tyrhennian sea, Pisa and Leghorn, and promises to pay a heavy tribute. Outraged, the Florentines take arms, Piero flees, a deputation arranges better terms with Charles, and new legislation, shaped in significant measure by a Dominican friar, Girolamo Savonarola, changes the constitution. From the behind-the-scenes rule of a powerful banking family, Florence becomes a republic uplifted by a powerful preacher.

We consider Charles's entry into Florence to be the final event in this chronicle because by now the gap in information is behind us. The next great happening in Florence is the rise and fall, excommunication, executing, and burning of Fra Savonarola. A prophet unarmed, Niccolò will write, and "he went to his ruin." But the date is now 1498, Niccolò is twenty-nine and standing ready to step into public office. We begin to have news of him. Once the friar is dead, the theocratic enthusiasm of the republic subsides. Within a month Niccolò, elected by the republic's Grand Council, undertakes his post as chancellor (or secretary) of the Second Chancery, and within a month after that, also becomes secretary to the Ten of Liberty and Peace, an executive committee for military and external affairs.

ON THE JOB

Had the program of his early education continued, Niccolò would have proceeded with a legal and literary curriculum, as he no doubt did, and

. . . Fra Savonarola . . . a prophet unarmed.

arrived at a thorough grounding in the law and the great Latin authors. Disabilitated perhaps by a tax indebtedness of his father, he never attained membership in the lawyers' guild. He managed nonetheless to obtain a high government post, one usually reserved for lawyers. When we first find him in this office, he seems to have had just the right preparation. He takes the place of a man of experience, he can write a chancery hand, he uses the correct abbreviations and phrases, takes minutes, composes letters, prepares reports.

On the job, Niccolò's instructions might come in sundry ways, from the chancellor of the First Chancery or from The Ten or from another committee or from the head of government, the Gonfalonier. By and large, as secretary of the Second Chancery, his work keeps him at a writing table and at domestic, including territorial, matters; as secretary to The Ten it puts him on horseback as envoy to various countries. The two areas, internal and external affairs, are in any case closely meshed. Niccolò's responsibilities are not precisely described nor is any distribution among them stipulated. Nor do the offices and executive committees always have the same names, duration, functions or rules. Having already been screened for adequacy of preparation and acceptability of political views by his election, Niccolò is quickly recognized on the job for his talents and put to use by the chief magistrates (as a body, the Signoria) of the republic for increasingly important tasks—whether as *Cancellarius* or as *Secretarius* does not decisively matter. Though never granted the title of ambassador—the letters of introduction he carries present him variously as "our envoy," "our citizen," "our secretary"—he often bears the responsibilities of an ambassador and treats with king and pope. Louis XII of France addresses him thus: "Secretary, I have no enmity either with the pope or with anyone." Niccolò will take on this title, with the addition of a distinguishing and justly broad adjective, as the Florentine Secretary.

He assumes his post in the flurry and excitement of a new regime. The Palazzo throbs with dismantling and rebuilding. Due to all the reconstruction going on, some to symbolize the more secular and republican character of the new government, some to accommodate new personnel and business, more later to provide for the new head of government and his family who decide to live in the Palazzo, the work space of the Second Chancery and of Niccolò and his colleagues within it is shifted about considerably. They find their most permanent location in all likelihood on the top floor of the Palazzo, their windows overlooking the square toward a monumental lineup of buildings—the Bargello, the Arte della Lana, and the Duomo.

Niccolò seems rarely to limit himself to the particulars of his special

They find their most permanent location in all likelihood on the top floor of the Palazzo, their windows overlooking the square toward a monumental lineup of buildings—the Bargello, the Arte della Lana, and the Duomo.

assignments, especially when on trips abroad. He interests himself in more general problems, he speaks about them to ministers, courtiers, and counselors, he delves into the history and customs of the place, he observes, compares, analyzes, notes. On occasion he takes time to write analytic summaries for his superiors—a practice he will recommend to new ambassadors—or sometimes to draft short papers with his own ideas and conclusions. The latter he does at the request of relatives, superiors, or friends—or for his own future use. In the tradition of officials in the Chancery, he preserves some of his papers for future use and also tries his hand at literature. Whenever the job can spare a few moments, he lights a few literary fuses. They sputter, throw out sparks, but never reach the charge.

When he takes over his post as secretary, hardly does he sit down to a writing table in the Palazzo when the government begins packing him off on missions. Apparently he has a hand in initiating these travels. Colleagues are not happy in his absence because the work grows heavier and has to be differently organized; it puts them under the orders of others, and the office in general falls apart. One day in October of 1502 his assistant Agostino Vespucci angrily wrote him a letter in Latin, and several days later followed it with a postscript taking it all back. The letter reveals something of his feeling about working under Niccolò. "I would want to have in the chancery no superior other than you." This, though, is not the point. Vespucci taxed him with constantly leaving friends and colleagues in the lurch at the office and dashing away somewhere. "You see therefore where it leads to, this spirit of yours so avid for riding, running here and there, and racing off. I shall blame you and no other if some incident happens." A Vespucci accusing someone of wanting to roam! His key words sound like a physician's description of symptoms in Latin: *equitandi, vagandi ac cursitandi*.

ACTIVE LIFE, QUIET LIFE

Niccolò is a tireless man. Energy characterizes him, perhaps from childhood. In *The Ass*, a long tale he told in tercets years later, our poet, seemingly to no great advantage to the narrative (although we should reserve judgment, for he never finished the work), inserts the story of a young Florentine of good family, afflicted with a steadily worsening malady. His father had him visited by philosophers and doctors whose "thousand remedies of a thousand reasons" were a waste of time. The disease was "that he ran through the streets at any place / and at any time without regard." Finally the father resorted to a charlatan who promised to heal him. "And he put a hundred perfumes to his nose /

drew blood from his head, and then / it seemed to him to have the running remitted." For a month he seemed cured, "But one day, [having] arrived at Via Martelli, / where one can see the length / of Via Larga, / his hair began to rise." Seeing that straight and spacious street laid out ahead, he let his coat drop to the ground and said: " 'Here not [even] Christ will hold me', and ran off." By choosing Via Larga, the poet may be alluding to political architecture, the "regal habitations . . . works and actions" of Cosimo de' Medici and the "new streets to be filled with new buildings" ordered by his grandson Lorenzo. Backed up by the church and piazza of San Lorenzo, Via Larga with Palazzo Medici on the corner, became a stretch of Medici territory.

The cautionary tale of *The Ass* makes of the runner's disease a vain struggle of education against "our mind," which is tied to "habit or nature." When the central story itself at last begins, the time is spring: "between the one and the other horn / the sun of the celestial ox flares." For rhyming purposes the poet employs the word *ox* to stand for Taurus, the celestial bull, Niccolò's own zodiacal sign: born 1469, May, day three, hour four, minute unknown.

We take leave of the young man and his incurable malady: "while he lived, he always ran."

༄

NICCOLÒ'S present is the heyday of navigators and explorers. A member of the Vespucci family, we noted above, is one of Niccolò's assistants in the Chancery. When news of Amerigo's discoveries reach Florence, torches burn outside the great palazzi for three days and nights. Once, at the beginning of his *Discourses* on the histories of Titus Livy, Niccolò alludes to the great explorations. His own explorations, evidently, are to be no less rewarding and fearful. He is entering on a path not yet tread by anyone, seeking new ordering principles, "to find new modes and orders," a political phrase pointing to reform measures and new constitutional dispositions. To venture on this path is "no less dangerous" than "to seek unknown lands and seas." The wake of great men of the past—Livy may have been the first he met—draws him irresistibly. Along this course he awakens to a new and noble love. It is a strange kind, a love of country infused with a love of life and people, of language and woman, of God and heroes. A bewildering sentiment.

To proclaim this love, to make it turn true for others as well as for himself, Niccolò invents a new moral reasoning and, more, redimensions the world, visible and invisible, balancing heaven and hell and making room for a different earth.

. . . Taurus, the celestial bull, Niccolò's own zodiacal sign: born 1469,
May, day three, hour four, minute unknown.

He has more than one way of persuading people. If the serious vein is not enough, he will try the comic. If the public does not laugh at his tales, Niccolò will be glad to stand them a drink. But if they do laugh—and they unhinge their jaws laughing—laughter brings them closer to the truth and makes it easier for them to see what he sees and love what he loves, and in reverse, it helps convince our author that he is right.

All forms of Niccolò's writings will turn up in the pages to come. For convenience we can list some of them now, including the chief works, and assign them dates of composition. The more definite dates appear in parentheses; those in brackets are tentative.

First Decennial
(1504)
A chronicle in verse of events in Florence and Italy in the decade 1494 to 1504.

Second Decennial
(1514)
A successive chronicle covering the years 1505 to 1509; unfinished.

The Prince
(1513–c. 1515)
A treatise on politics.

Discourses, or *Discourses on the First Decade of Titus Livy*
(1513–1517)
Writings on politics utilizing the first ten books, mainly, of the Roman historian.

Belfagor, or *The Devil Who Took a Wife*
[1517]
A fable.

The Ass
[1517]
An unfinished fantasy in terza rima about metamorphosis.

Andria
[1517]
A comedy, *The Girl from Andros*, by the Roman playwright Terence translated into the vernacular.

The *Mandragola*
(1518)
A play.

The Life of Castruccio Castracani
(1520)
A short biography.

"Discursus," or "Discourse on Florentine Public Affairs after the Death of the Junior Lorenzo"
(1520)
A proposal for a new constitution.

Art of War
(1521)
A book in dialogue form.

Florentine Histories
(1520–1525)
A history from 375 to 1492.

Clizia
(1525)
A comedy based on *Casina* by the Roman playwright Plautus.

"Exhortation to Penitence"
[1525–1527]
A sermon to a confraternity.

Dozens of small pieces will be quoted, mainly letters, minor political writings, several official reports, and verse—carnival songs, sonnets, epigrams, serenades.

Various casts of characters appear: family, friends, statesmen, captains, loves and cuckolds, popes, cardinals, kings and emperors, patrons, nobles, commoners, great poets, men and women of history, and the persona of plays and stories. The settings are various too: the streets and squares of Florence, the monumental Palazzo della Signoria, the courts of princes, foreign and Italian, the dungeon where Niccolò is tortured, his house and farm in the Tuscan hills, the gardens where literary men gather, the gardens where his plays are performed. Here is one scene.

1513

December. Dusk settles early. We are in a lone hamlet astride the ridge of a hill, about seven miles from Florence. One street divides the few houses. The bells of vespers ring. A door opens. We hear a loud exchange of good nights. Niccolò is taking leave of the tavern where he gamed and poured the afternoon away. He walks to his house next door, opens and steps inside the receiving hall, soiled still from road and field, smelling a bit of poultry and hay. ("Give my regards to the chickens," his friends tease in letters.) The house is quiet, wife and children upstairs. He turns toward the writing room. He had spent part of the morning there with the bills and records of a working farm; there also he had admitted one hired hand to listen to his grievances against another and rebuked a tenant farmer for not keeping in repair the cart he lent him. He opens the first door to the writing room and steps into the passageway. He opens the other door directly in front of him. He can see and feel the fire in the fireplace ahead glowing discreetly. He takes off his country clothes and footwear

He walks to his house next door . . . .

"I enter the ancient courts of the men of antiquity . . ."

and puts them in a closet in the wall on the right. He takes out and puts on his courtly robes and slippers. He opens the closet door to the left and washes in the stone washbowl there and dries himself. Straightening up, he stands still for a moment, takes a deep breath, and crosses the doorstep into another world. First to the writing table. (Light is not a problem but he is forty-four years old. His younger friend, Vettori, complains about beginning to have difficulties already. "I cannot read much due to my sight's being diminished by age.") He warms his hands over the brazier alongside, takes a sliver of wood, ignites it, lights a lamp . . . "I enter the ancient courts of the men of antiquity where affectionately received by them I pasture on that food that alone is mine and for which I was born, where I am not too timid to speak with them and ask them about the reasons for their actions; and they in their courtesy answer me; and for four hours of time I feel no weariness, I forget every trouble, I do not fear poverty, death does not dismay me; I transfer all of myself into them. . . ."

In the distance the bells of Complin sound. Niccolò snuffs the lamp, crosses back over the threshold, and retires. In the morning he rises with the sun.

A rare theme, surely, and a great one. Niccolò crosses a divide to where the ancients dwell; he joyfully mingles with them, conversing, questioning, learning: a widely diffused solar myth and literary motif, a hero's journey to the otherworld.

"Take on the complexion of the dead." Such were the words the oracle laid upon Zeno, who took them to mean, "Study ancient authors." No doubt, journeys to the otherworld have some connection with primitive and ancient cults of ancestors and the dead; so also, however, does a love and admiration of antiquity or a belief such as Niccolò's in the didactic value of the past. The historian's craft as a whole does not escape this tie. For historical and other reasons, the past so fascinates Niccolò that he becomes an habitué of the otherworld.

We shall return to the country scene more than once, and to this description of it that draws aside the curtain on his writing habits, imaginative faculties, and interest in crossing the threshold.

Out of the sedentary sessions in the confines of the writing room, Niccolò "composed a little work." He was to refer to it as "our treatise 'On the Prince'." Some five years later comes another genre entirely, the *Mandragola*, a comedy that ranks with the world's masterpieces. The prologue contains a novelty, "The composer" (elsewhere he is "the author") appears onstage and delivers himself of a few brief personal stanzas. He confesses to the public that he turns to playwriting because of his political ill-fortune,

> for elsewhere he has not
> a place to turn his face:
> for he has been barred
> from demonstrating with other works another virtue,
> there being no reward for his labors.

Florence is a small city, some might say. But it is better to take Niccolò's own words on the subject, and whenever possible to take the background of those words, too, in his own words. Niccolò says that Florence is one "of the big cities." Big it is, then. Big city or small, many in the select audience know that some five years earlier the author had fallen from favor. There is more in the prologue to listen to.

> And if this material is not worthy,
> for being light, even
> of a man who wishes to appear wise and serious,

excuse him with this, that he contrives
with these vain thoughts
to make his wretched time smoother.

No longer Secretary, Niccolò has time of his own. No meetings to attend, no letters and documents to draft, no horsebacking to foreign courts. He hates the very thought of such inactivity. Forced out of politics, Niccolò writes about politics; unsuccessful in writing about politics, he turns to writing of a less serious kind. Gradually, he grows to like getting away from the city, it seems, though he never admits it, and goes back to his villa to write. And the idea of inactivity in his doctrines of sloth, temporizing, and indolence will assume a major negative role. He holds it to be "a great and continuous malice of fortune" that forced inactivity as a public official on him at age forty-three. That it was instead a boon of providence never dawns on him.

Our author does not deny he has a talent as playwright. Else why ask an audience to look and listen? His great talent, though, is for politics. He does not have to say outright that politics, not only in his opinion but in any true order of values, is more important than playwriting. All he has to do is to associate *wise and serious* with the one, and *light, vain, and not worthy* with the other, and the thing is done.

Plays, letters, songs, tercets, histories, dispatches, theological discourse—but let us first turn to *The Prince*, an undeniably serious work.

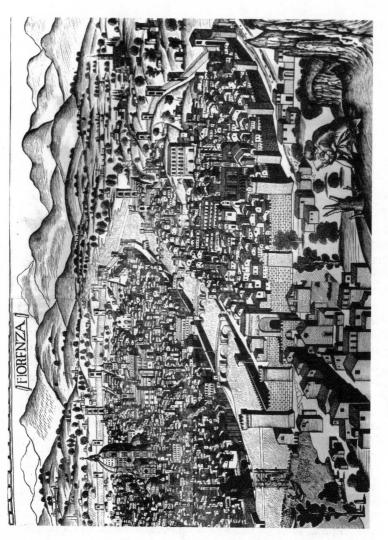

FIORENZA

Niccolò says that Florence is one "of the big cities." Big it is then.

GOD'S FRIENDS AND MACHIAVELLI'S

> . . . nor was God more a friend
> to them than to you.
> —*The Prince*

O DD PASSAGE in an odd chapter by a not particularly religious
man. The epigraph is from the twenty-sixth chapter of *The Prince*.
The twenty-sixth is the last chapter of that famous book. The author has
laid down all the distinctions, rules, and conclusions he intends to for-
mulate for the time being. Finally now, loudly and clearly, he tells us the
purpose of these rules—to save Italy from the deep trouble she is in.

Juxtaposing the plight of the Israelites in Egypt, of the Persians
among the Medes, and the scattering of the Athenians, he declares with
a passion that had begun to stir in Chapter XII, that Italy is more slave
than were the Hebrews, more servant than the Persians, more dispersed
than the Athenians. The chapter, as he titles it, is an "Exhortation to
Take Italy and Free Her from the Hands of the Barbarians." The cry to
liberate Italy from invaders had been raised earlier by Italy's two greatest
poets—Dante (1265–1321), in the sixth canto of the *Purgatory*, and Petrarch (1304–1374), in the song "My Italy." Even popes, every now and
then, as they extended or defended their temporal presence, had spoken
as the voice of Italy and, as Julius II did, sloganized for the deliverance
of Italy from servitude. Out with the barbarians!

Some of the language of the last chapter differs sharply from the rest
of the book. In the covering letter to *The Prince*, Niccolò had remarked
that he used an unadorned rather than an ornamental language. The
distinction is an ancient one going back to the Greek philosopher Theo-
phrastus and (closer to our author) to Cicero, Roman statesman and
orator. A plain, or dialectical, style is supposed to be suited for factual
discourse; a grand style for emotional expression. Unlike many others,
Niccolò remarks, "I have not decorated [this work] with blown-up cadences or turgid and magnificent words or any other preciousness or
extrinsic ornamentation" because "I wished that each thing [in the

work] honors it, or that only the variety of the material or the gravity of the subject makes it appreciated." This last argument—the gravity of the subject—is the same argument that Augustine uses in his rhetorical treatise, *On Christian Doctrine*, in counseling would-be expositors of scripture. Niccolò uses plain style so elegantly that he sets an unattainable standard for future generations of those whose task it will be to discover and write about facts.

As a stylist he may well have wished to keep his tone down throughout—and he more or less does so for twenty-five chapters. In the twenty-sixth he rings out the call to arms. Here, unveiling an unsuspected skill in prophetic language, he approaches the grand style. Not that as a writer he can be cut up and tossed into two bins, one plain, one grand. It is not literary practice to hit the peak of the discourse at the start. Chapter XXVI comes at the end. Whenever we can assign a rhetorical explanation to a question of style, we should give it weight: Chapter XXVI as a peroration has force.

In this powerful final chapter Niccolò, one, portrays Italy as a country enslaved and vituperated, two, looks for hope to the Medici house, and three, introduces God into the argument. He did all three before, in earlier chapters: one, in Chapter XII, two, in Chapter XI, and three, in Chapters XXV, XII, VII, and VI, in passages already quoted or to be quoted later. Why does he here, there, and elsewhere have to introduce God at all? He is not a theologian. One can understand that when trying to reproduce popular speech, in plays and stories, he may have to use the exclamations, vocatives, and interjections of the piazza. "Oh, God, what will happen then?" "God help me!" "May God do him evil!" "Oh, God, this old age . . . !" "For the love of God!" Could not our author write at least his political and military works without mention of God? Evidently not. His remarks are not trivial. The references to the divine in *The Prince* comprise significant metaphysical and theological statements, with political bearings just as significant.

Chapter XXVI mentions God about a half-dozen times, but the passage chosen as epigraph—'nor was God more a friend to them than to you'—is the most uncommon. This phrase, even as it stands, is so important as to affect the basis of Niccolò's political and moral philosophy. Before examining its broader significance, we may see whether it has a history that throws some light on the way he uses it.

'To them' refers to Moses, Cyrus, and Theseus, who led their people out of trouble—the virtuous Moses, the great-spirited Cyrus, and the excellent Theseus. (Niccolò praised them also in Chapter VI.) 'To you' refers to the one "in whom [Italy] might at present have more hope." The following remark, "in your illustrious house with its fortune and virtue, favored by God and by the Church, of which it is now prince," identifies the Medici family. The Medici Cardinal Giovanni had recently been elevated to the pontificate as Leo X. Niccolò mentions him by name in Chapter XI of *The Prince*.

The 'you', both a singular and plural pronoun, may refer as well to the one or another person to whom the author intends to present his work. The first intended addressee, according to Niccolò's letter of 10 December 1513, before *The Prince* is finished, is another Medici: "I address it to His Magnificence, Giuliano" (not the one who was assassinated in the cathedral, but his nephew, the brother of the new Pope), now residing in Rome. Since Niccolò has had previous contact with Giuliano, this may be the place to consider his relation to him and to the others whom he may have had in mind for the 'to you' part of the phrase we have under scrutiny.

❧

THE events of five years, of 1512 to 1517, are crucial. They are crucial for the sufferings they imposed on our author. They are also pivotal, and may show us some of their connections to what came before and after. The language our author uses to deal with these events may also be helpful when we begin to encounter the terms of his political and moral ideas.

In September 1512 the Florentine republic headed by the Gonfalonier-for-life, Piero Soderini, falls. In November the succeeding government, as recorded in the Latin of the Chancery, did strike off, deprive, and totally remove Nicolaum domini Bernardi de Machiavellis from the most important office of his life, the one he had held since the start of his career, for which he was known as the Florentine Secretary. It also put him on the carpet concerning his handling of funds, imposed a bond of one thousand gold florins, barred him access to the Palazzo, and forbade his leaving Florentine territory and dominion for a year.

Niccolò now believes that Giuliano may help him. Though he had been Secretary under the republic rather than under the Medici, his position was not uncompromisingly anti-Medicean. And in one critical preliminary to the return of the Medici to Florence in 1512, Niccolò had acted as intermediary. Francesco Vettori, with whom he had worked as an aide on ambassadorial missions, was his friend, stood as godfather to one of his children, and possessed a villa as Niccolò did on the same side of Florence, though farther toward Siena and much grander. Vettori's brother, Pagolo, was one of the many citizens "of the most noble of this city" who, coming "armed to the palazzo . . . to force the Gonfalonier [the head of government] to leave, were persuaded by some citizens to do no violence but to let him leave as agreed. And so the Gonfalonier accompanied by [the citizens] themselves returned home," and the next night he was led to Siena.

Niccolò's *Florentine Histories* does not arrive at the events of 1512. The best account in his own hand is that of a letter, from which the above quotation was taken, addressed sometime after his dismissal, to an unknown gentlewoman (not a Florentine) of highest rank. She had conveyed to him, evidently, a desire to understand what had happened. Vettori, long afterward, writing as a historian about the same events, adds a detail. The Gonfalonier "immediately sent Niccolò Machiavelli, Secretary of the Signoria, to find Francesco Vettori [that is, the writer himself]." Vettori went to the Gonfalonier "right away and finding him alone and fearful, asked him what he wanted done. The Gonfalonier replied that he was disposed to leave the Palazzo if he could be sure not to be injured . . ."

The Florentine Secretary would not have been thought of for this delicate mission, nor would he have accepted, had he not some friendly connections among those Medici supporters who together with Giuliano himself had secretly gathered in Vettori's villa and on 31 August 1512 erupted into the Palazzo. Afterward, Niccolò kept in touch with some of them. Justifiably then, he might have had some hope of keeping his post or receiving a new one under the Medici. Almost everyone else had remained on the job. His secretaryship had not been a post that necessarily required taking an anti-Medicean stand. The letter to the high noblewoman refers to the Medici as "the friends of your most illustrious Ladyship and my patrons." It closes saying that the city of Florence "hopes to live not less honored with the help [of these magnificent Medici reintegrated in all the honors and ranks of their ancestors] than it lived in times past when the happiest memory of the magnificent Lorenzo, their father, governed."

The Secretary's implacable foes had not been the Medici. During his tenure he had made many enemies of some of the influential patricians who constituted a political group known as the *optimates*. In a memorial to the Medici composed about the time of these critical events—another indication that he thought himself acceptable in the Medici house—Niccolò distinguishes and tries to separate the Medici from the optimates, an effort we shall examine in a later chapter.

Any hope that he might obtain another, comparable post, however, is dashed when four months after his dismissal a plot against the Medici is discovered. Into the new regime's hands has fallen a piece of paper listing eighteen to twenty possible supporters of a plan to assassinate either Cardinal Giovanni or Giuliano. On the list is Niccolò's name. The conspirators and compilers of the list, two idealistic and ingenuous young men, are quickly taken. With a "Wanted" proclamation out for him, Niccolò presents himself. He protests his innocence, is thrown in prison, and put to torture to extract information.

THE PRISON SONNETS

Three sonnets addressed to Giuliano bear the scars of prison. Two of them, set within prison itself, may be called "The Prison Sonnets." Whether Niccolò actually sends them to Giuliano is not known, but they, better than anything else, describe his internment for one short month, 12 February to 12 March 1513, while the executioner's axe waits outside the door.

> I have, Giuliano, a pair of shackles on my legs
> with six hoists of the rope on my shoulders:
> my other miseries I do not want to talk about,
> as this is the way poets are to be treated!

How can he call himself a poet? In the broadest sense, he is a poet for being a literary man in a literary position. To be a man of letters, that is, to read and write Latin, is a requirement of office. Chancery officials are expected and encouraged to produce works of literary quality, sooner or later, either in their spare time or in their retirement. Our poet produced his verse chronicle, the *First Decennial*, in 1504, a product "of fifteen days," the brief stretch of time "conceded me for such leisure." The poem was published (with his office helpmate Vespucci's moral and material support) and given currency by being quickly plagiarized; a lawsuit was initiated against the culprit, thus certifying Niccolò as the true author. This work and perhaps ones already composed and circulated in manuscript entitle him to use *poet* in a more restricted sense.

Poet also is a good word to use because as a youth Giuliano himself had written verses. Niccolò's father Bernardo had through a friend, the former First Chancellor, enjoyed some contact with Medicean cultivated society. So a later literary exchange between Niccolò and the ten-year-younger Giuliano is not unlikely.

Let us continue with the first of the Prison Sonnets.

> These walls exude lice,
> sick with the heaves no less, that [are as big as] butterflies,
> nor was there ever such a stench in [the massacre of] Roncesvalles.

Roncesvalles is the village in the Pyrenees where, in the *Song of Roland*, the Saracens ambushed the rear guard of Charlemagne's army. 'These

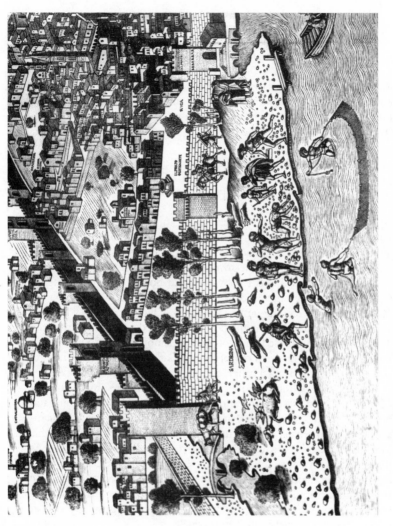

Sardinia, on the Arno, . . . where dead horses and mules are skinned and left behind with other carrion to be picked over by the buzzards or washed downstream.

walls' are those of the Bargello, the Florentine palazzo where tortures and executions are performed, which the poet now calls his "dainty inn."

> or among those groves in Sardinia,
> as there is in my so dainty inn;
> with a noise that sounds just as if at the earth
> Jove was striking lightning, and all Mount Etna [too].

Sardinia, on the Arno, is the area outside the walls, just past the western end of Florence, where dead horses and mules are skinned and left behind with other carrion to be picked over by buzzards or washed downstream.

> One man is being chained and the other shackled
> with a clatter of keyholes, keys, and latches;
> another shouts that he is [pulled] too high off the ground!

Apparently, under this legal interrogative torture, the same as applied to our poet, it is possible to communicate with the torturer, the officials, and others present, even about the correct limits of the procedure.

The form of torture is the *strappado* or, more familiarly, the rope. Your wrists are tied behind your back and bound to a rope hanging from a pulley. The other end of the rope is pulled down and you are hoisted up to the ceiling, arms yanked up behind, your body turning almost horizontally, its weight borne by twisted arms and shoulders. Then the rope is released and you plunge almost to the floor, the halt virtually tearing your arms out of their sockets. The process is then repeated, four times being a rough average for interrogative purposes.

In his earliest political writings Niccolò never underestimates the fear of force and pain as a consideration in politics, punitive operations, and war: "And I say again to you that without force cities do not save themselves." His experience with torture did nothing to divert him from this idea. In later works, the fear of pain is given increased responsibility. As his doctrine develops, law and treaties, the moral correction of men, oaths binding them to their word, all will depend on sanctions and the threat and memory thereof. A generalized statement on pain and punishment will appear in *The Prince*: "fear [of the prince] is held by a dread of punishment that never abandons you."

Soon after he walks out the prison doors, Niccolò writes Vettori that he conducted himself creditably under torture, better than he believed he would. "I want you to have this pleasure out of these troubles of

DOMENICO BECCAFVMI P.^e

"... fear [of the prince] is held by a dread of punishment that never abandons you."

mine, that I have borne them so straightforwardly that I myself love myself for it." Soon he can refer to the torture without circumlocution. On receiving bad news from Vettori he writes back, "This letter of yours dismayed me more than the rope." That Niccolò can mention it so soon, and suggest an equality between disappointment and the pain of torture is a healthy sign; he means these words to be taken at least in part as bravura. Similarly with a remark months later when he is living in his country house and Vettori invites him to Rome for a visit Niccolò courteously and humorously declines: "I should fear that on my return I might think that I was dismounting at home and be dismounting [instead] at the Bargello." He adds, "I beg you to resolve this fear for me, and then within the given time I shall in whatever event come to find you."

The Sonnet moves toward conclusion.

> What disturbed me most
> was that close to dawn while sleeping
> I heard chanting: "Per voi s'ora."

"For you we are praying": the prayer chanted by priests for the souls of those condemned to die, in this case the two conspirators whose list put Niccolò in jeopardy and whose decapitation is imminent. Granted that the execution took place in the Bargello, to have overheard the priests praying for them signifies that Niccolò is being held there too, available for execution himself. As he afterward notifies his nephew, "it is rather a miracle that I am alive because my office was taken from me and I was about to lose my life . . ."

One can understand that Niccolò might have felt uncharitable toward the two young conspirators going to their death, and to anyone connected with the prison, jailed and jailors alike. He had been sought like a criminal, thrown in prison, tortured, and put in line for the executioner's block.

The sonnet ends,

> Now they can go their own way;
> if only your mercy may turn toward me,
> good father, and these criminal bonds be untied.

'Good father' may seem strange directed by an older to a younger man and a prince-like ruler. Niccolò's plight is desperate to the point of confused identity. So runs the second sonnet to Giuliano:

> In this night, begging the Muses
> that with their sweet zither and sweet poems
> they, to console me, should visit
> Your Magnificence and make my excuses,
> one appeared who upset me,
> saying: "Who are you who dares call me?"
>
> I told her my name, and she to torment me
> hit me in the face and shut my mouth for me,
> saying: "You are not Niccolò . . .
> because you have your legs and heels bound together
> and stay there chained up like a lunatic."
>
> I wanted to give her my reasons:
> and she responded and said: "Go to the devil
> with this shirtsleeve comedy of yours."
>
> Bear her witness,
> Magnificent Giuliano, for high God,
> that . . . I am I.

In between the three dots above is a name. In full the line reads thus: "that I am not Dazzo but I am I." Dazzo refers to the family name of Andrea Dazzi who bore a reputation—evidently so, if Giuliano could be expected to know of it—for grand aspirations and little talent. The line may be read: 'I am I'.

The third sonnet to Giuliano closes thus:

> Let opinions go,
> Your Magnificence, and feel and touch
> and judge with your hands and not with your eyes.

What Niccolò seems to be asking is: Do not look past me just because of what people say, those people who "take good bites . . . out of me," thin as I am. Grasp who I am. You know me.

He seems to be doing more than asking Giuliano to remember the contact they may have had during the Gonfalonier's flight from office. The literary recognition to which the word *poet* refers may be to any private literary exchange of the poet-patron or poet-poet kind, or merely to the fact that Niccolò was now addressing Giuliano in sonnets.

At all events Niccolò is confident of Giuliano's good favor. He writes Vettori in Rome: "His Magnificence Giuliano will be coming there, and you will find him naturally disposed to please me." This new leader of Florence, many believed, was to become like his father, Lorenzo the

Magnificent, a patron of poets and lover of the arts. The term *good father* is sometimes used for a patron, and the sonnets do play on the poet-patron link.

. . .

Florence, though frequently at odds with Rome, sometimes ferociously as in the Pazzi conspiracy, is tied to the church in many ways not entirely spiritual, such as the handling of papal funds by Florentine bankers, or by the system of benefices and church livings that for centuries has increased the income and power of the Florentine patricians, resources that cannot easily be reached or cut into by unfriendly regimes. (The Machiavegli's too had enjoyed benefices for centuries, and a few remaining to Niccolò's side of the family were increased through the efforts of his younger brother, the priest Totto. When Totto dies in 1522, several of his small but not negligible benefices devolve on Niccolò.)

On 11 March 1513 Giovanni de' Medici, son of Lorenzo the Magnificent, becomes Pope Leo X. Among the Medici family and followers the news of the election of a Medici pope, hard on the heels of the return of Medici power in Florence, causes wild excitement and a four-day celebration during which little could be heard above the noise of firecrackers, bells, and cannons. The popular, miraculous Madonna lodged in the church of nearby Impruneta was brought into Florence in joyous procession. The conjunction now of Medici rulers in Rome (Leo X and Cardinal Giulio as his right-hand man) and in Florence (Giuliano and Lorenzo) promises closer ties, indeed a domination: Florence would be supervised by Rome. In the amnesty that Leo X granted upon his elevation, Niccolò is unshackled and released from his 'dainty inn'. "I have got out of prison," he writes Vettori, "amid the universal happiness of this city."

Nine months later, at the end of 1513, Niccolò writes that he had composed and nearly completed *The Prince*, and is addressing it to Giuliano. For one reason or another he does not send the book. Doubts assail him. He had debated with another friend whether it was a good idea at all "to give it or not to give it" to Giuliano and "if it were a good idea to give it, whether it was good that I take it to him or that I send it there. [On the side of] not giving it what made me doubtful was that it might not even be read by Giuliano and that this Ardinghelli [Giuliano's secretary in Rome, who Niccolò suspects is hostile to him], somehow by presenting the book as his own, might receive honor out of this my latest effort. [On the side of] giving it, what impelled me is the necessity that drives me, because I am consuming myself and cannot stay this way

. . . the news of the election of a Medici pope . . . causes wild excitement and a four-day celebration during which little could be heard above the noise of firecrackers, bells, and cannons.

a long time without becoming contemptible through poverty . . ." Then comes a select metaphor. "I would have that these Medici lords begin to adopt me, if they have to begin by having me roll a stone." Sisyphus has a particular torture in hell: he is eternally bound to roll up a hill a rock that once at the top always rolls down again. Note, however, that Niccolò in this pasage twice used the verb *begin*. They may begin to adopt him like Sisyphus, but not keep him at it eternally.

A few months thereafter when it becomes clear that Giuliano is not coming back to rule Florence, Niccolò writes the same friend, this time about another potential prince, Lorenzo de' Medici—the nephew of both Giuliano and the new Pope.

> I do not want to leave out news of the way the Magnificent Lorenzo conducts himself, which has been up to now of [such] quality that he has filled the whole city with good hope; and it seems that everyone begins to recognize in him the happy memory of his grandfather. Because His Magnificence is solic-itous in his tasks, liberal and grateful in audience, slow and serious in reply. His way of conversing is of a sort . . . that has no proudness in it; nor does he mix it up in a way that through too much familiarity breeds small reputation. With the young he keeps the same equal style that does not alienate them from him or give them courage to commit any youthful insolences. In sum, he makes himself both loved and revered rather than feared. . . . [In his house there is] great magnificence and liberality, yet he does not depart from civil living.

Probably a postscript to a letter to Vettori, this is a short note without opening, closing, or signature, but not without purpose to its fulsome praise. "I thought to describe this to you, because from my testimony you may have the pleasure that we all have . . . and you can when you have occasion, testify to it on my part to His Holiness of our Lord."

A half year or so previously in studying the Pope's aims, Niccolò had observed to the Florentine ambassador to Rome that the Pope had "brothers and nephews without a state [to rule over]." Vettori from his vantage in Rome confirms that "Leo X in any case thinks of giving states to Giuliano and Lorenzo." Niccolò thinks of sending *The Prince* to Lo-renzo, and composes a covering letter accordingly, the last part of which reads: "Desiring therefore to offer myself to Your Magnificence with some testimony of my devotion to [Your Magnificence], I have not found among my personal property anything that I hold dearer than or esteem so much as the knowledge of the actions of great men . . . which I, having . . . now reduced [it] to a small volume, send to Your Magnif-icence. . . . Take, then, Your Magnificence this little gift with that spirit in which I send it; which if by [Your Magnificence] it is diligently considered and read, you will recognize in it an extreme desire of mine, that you may reach that greatness which fortune and your other qualities promise. And if Your Magnificence from the apex of his highness sometimes will turn his eyes to these low places, he will know how much I bear undeservedly a great and continuous malice of fortune." All this could have been written as well in a covering letter to Giuliano.

The letter is not couched in the prevailing style of fawning courtiers, of those "always used to addressing their works to some prince," as Niccolò remarks in the dedicatory letter of the *Discourses*, as though he had never written that one for *The Prince*. Perhaps he never intended that the covering letter to Lorenzo be preserved or attached as it is now to the manuscript as a permanent appendage. What it and the postscript (and a poem of uncertain date called "Pastoral") do though, is illustrate a frame of mind in which Niccolò, firm republican though he is, finds himself under special circumstances idealizing a leader.

He is not so enamoured of Lorenzo as to think him alone capable of what he hopes the 'you' in Chapter XXVI of *The Prince* will do. It is in 'your house' that our author repeatedly rests his hopes. Lorenzo proves a disappointment. He does not extend the former Florentine Secretary a helping hand. The leadership he begins to display is autocratic.

．　．　．

When Niccolò hears (the time is now early 1515) that Leo X has tagged his brother Giuliano for rulership of what might be formed into a single new state by uniting several duchies and cities of northcentral Italy, he bursts with enthusiasm. (Some such prospect had been exciting him since the days of Pope Alexander VI and his son Caesar Borgia (Duke Valentino) over more than a decade ago. "Let us pass to the pope and his duke. . . . [E]very man knows what their nature and appetite is," Niccolò wrote in one paper of 1503 and made it more explicit in another one several months later: "[Caesar Borgia] aspires to the imperium of Tuscany as [being] nearer and more disposed to being made into a kingdom with the other states he holds . . ." This region would make a good, strong, and secure state, Niccolò now writes Vettori, "if in the beginning it is well-governed. And to want to govern it well, one must know the quality of the subject. These new states, occupied by a new ruler have . . . infinite difficulties. . . . So whoever becomes prince of them must think of making one same body of them." There follows a paragraph of rules for dealing with the difficulties, parallel to rules found in *The Prince*. Giuliano, if he is going to live in Rome instead of in the new state, would be wise to appoint a president over the whole dominion.

The post should go to Pagolo, Vettori's brother, who already is slated to be governor of one of the cities. In 1502, Caesar Borgia had appointed a president for his newly conquered region of the Romagna with excellent results. "I would always imitate the works [of Caesar Borgia] were I a new prince," Niccolò writes.

Our author is ignoring what he had narrated in Chapter VII of *The Prince* about the fate of this president in the Romagna. The omission indicates how carried away our political thinker is by the idea of a central Italian "lordship . . . beautiful and strong," ruled over by a Florentine through the medium of a Florentine lieutenant who would be counseled, as one might expect, by a Florentine advisor. Chapter VII, though, reveals dramatically that after the president, Ramiro de Lorqua, had done his job, Caesar Borgia had him laid out in the town square early one morning, butchered. To anyone who had read that chapter, the thought might occur, especially to a brother, whether this is to be Pagolo's fate too. Perhaps our author trusts that Pagolo's brother, Francesco, did not read the copy of *The Prince* that he had sent, or possibly he has not yet written this story or did not include it in the portion of the manuscript he had sent his friends.

Pagolo was close to Giuliano. Indeed, he may have interceded with him two years earlier for Niccolò's release from prison. Niccolò now writes Francesco, "I talked with [Pagolo]. He liked the idea, and will figure out how to further it." Francis I, new king of France, did *not* like the idea, Leo X dropped the plan, Giuliano lost the prospect, so did Pagolo, and another of Niccolò's "castles in the air" evaporated. Even had the plan gone further, his chances for employment were not good: word had come down from Giuliano's secretary, Ardinghelli, sniffing Pagolo's scent—"this must be an invention of Paulo [Pagolo] Vettori"—and advising Giuliano in the words allegedly of the Cardinal de' Medici, "not to get involved with Niccolò." The use of the first name either by the cardinal or by Giuliano's secretary is suggestive. As soon as our poet was released from prison he wrote Vettori: "Keep me if it is possible in the memory of Our Lord." Again we hear an echo of earlier communication with the Medici. Niccolò had written to Giovanni de' Medici (now Leo X) after the Gonfalonier had fled, helpfully pointing out the risks the Medici would be taking if they sought too resolutely to get back property lost to them after 1494 when they went out of power.

TOTALLY WRECKED

The confusion of identity that first appears in Niccolò in "The Prison Sonnets" has a second phase. The accusation—'You are not Niccolò'—

issued from the swift blows of dismissal, imprisonment, and torture. Exit from prison brought relief—"it is over." But a series of blows over the two or three years just reviewed, from about 1513 to 1515, as the consequences of dismissal rolled in and as each surge of hope dropped down to nothingness, pound him on the head in slow succession, clouding his identity again.

Losing his job meant not only that Niccolò would have much less income. Relatives and friends could or would do nothing to help him. Totto, on learning that his brother was imprisoned, had sent off a dispatch rider to Vettori to beseech help. Vettori could do nothing. The names of relatives, of other Machiavegli, although their houses neighbor his in country and town, appear infrequently in correspondence. His perquisites, too, went down the drain. The favors he could do for friends and relations, these were gone, the company and standing he enjoyed with them dissipated. Gone too are those rarer pleasures that Vespucci, in the letter quoted in the previous chapter, hinted at: "I believe, by Hercules, that there [at the court of Borgia] you are held much in honor; the duke himself and all of the courtiers pay you favor, they praise you as a prudent man, they gather around and flatter you."

Connected to the loss of income and honors is something more profound. Niccolò's image of his place in the world takes form from the figures of Florentine Citizen and Secretary, the titles he would identify himself with a half-dozen years later (when he is back in the good graces of the government), on the title page of the only full-scale work published in his lifetime—"Proem by Niccolò Machiavelli, Citizen and Florentine Secretary, to the Book of the Art of War."

To be deprived of Florentine citizenship and removed from Florentine office changed Niccolò's relation to his native land. Now a noncitizen confined to Florentine territory, he is more like a subject. This is not a crisis in body, but in spirit. It cannot help but affect the ideas of the onetime Secretary, a man who is about to write grand and grave treatises on politics. If, as Secretary, Niccolò was a Florentine citizen, a Florentine official, and a poet, as "quondam secretary," out of grace with the Medici regime, all is lost or threatened. His identification as a Machiavegli is itself limited. The reduction appears in the beginning of the third Prison Sonnet where the poet sends Giuliano a present of thrushes, "so that His Magnificence might remember a little of poor Machiavello."

What else in a name? The name the Muse calls in question and the one our author clings to on the verge of death, is a Christian name, part of the naming custom of his branch of the family, given to him at baptism on day two of his life. Despoiled of all else conveyed by a name, he refuses to give up "Niccolò."

The former Secretary makes his dismissal and the attendant ugly events the pivot of his life. After these, his life is to be something left over from what went before. "All that is left of life to me I acknowledge [to come] from the Magnificent Giuliano and your [brother] Pagolo," he writes Vettori on being released from prison, and closes with, "thus we go on . . . enjoying this rest of life that to me seems to be dreaming." Another letter to Vettori a month later reaffirms that "I acknowledge [as due to your family] all that to me remains." Most revealing of all is a note the Ex-Secretarius makes while classifying at home some of his past official papers. On the cover page of one, a brief of 1506 for the formation of a militia, there is an insertion before and after the title, in Niccolò's handwriting but written with a different ink. Before the title he has inserted the date "1512," the year of his fall from grace, and after it he has added the docket in Latin, "After everything was totally wrecked."

We saw Niccolò later place hope in the Pope, in Giuliano, and in Lorenzo. We did not see the ensuing despair. Indications appear mainly in correspondence, at first with Vettori, then with his nephew, Giovanni Vernacci, over a period in which letters thin out and news of Niccolò drops off. It is still early in this history of sorrow (6 April 1513) when he writes Vettori: "I cannot believe that if my case is managed with any skill that I cannot succeed in being adopted for something, if not for benefit of Florence, at least for benefit of Rome and the pontificate; in which case I should be less suspect . . . if [only] His Holiness of Our Lord might begin to adopt me . . ." He quotes from Petrarch's *Rime*, evidently from memory: "For if sometimes I laugh or sing, / I do it because if not this I do not have a / way to vent my bitter weeping."

On 10 June 1514 a number of other despairing themes appear in a letter to Vettori: "So I am staying thus among my lice [in this village], without finding a man who remembers my service [to Florence] or who believes that I might be good for anything." This is the motif of ingratitude, a lamentable vice on which he composes a poem and to which he will give a top rank in his catalogue of deadly sins. "But it is impossible that I can stay long this way . . . and I see . . . that I will be forced one day to get out of the house and place myself as tutor or secretary to a constable, if I cannot do otherwise, or stick myself in some deserted land to teach writing to the young, and leave my brigade [of family] who may [as well] count me dead; they could do much better without me because I am an expense to them." Here are themes of impotence, divestiture of family, and abandonment by society, mixed with some self-pity, quickly canceled. "I do not write you this because I want you to take either disturbance or trouble for me but only to unburden myself and not to write anymore about this matter, as odious [a subject] as can be."

Finding it hard to face such misery, friend Vettori takes a month and a half to respond: "you seemed to me afflicted beyond measure."

That summer things improve: Niccolò writes Vettori that he has fallen in love with a lady living nearby. But by 20 December 1514 gloom redescends. "I do not think I shall ever be able to do good either to myself or to others." Vettori replies that he has shown a couple of Niccolò's letters on foreign affairs to the Pope and two cardinals, one of whom is Giulio de' Medici, and "all marveled at the intelligence and praised the judgment." Nothing but words, yet the good opinion of highly placed men cannot but help him, says his friend. A month later Niccolò learns of the Giuliano project for northcentral Italy and his hopes soar over mountains, only to fall to earth in a crash.

. . .

Soon afterward, Vettori leaves his post as ambassador to Rome and returns to Florence to follow the fortunes of the Magnificent Lorenzo. Niccolò's great intense correspondence with Vettori is at an end. Only a few of Niccolò's letters now come to light, mostly to his beloved nephew, the son of his sister Primavera, a young man in whom Niccolò seems to confide more freely than in any other person. In them the theme of self-confusion reappears. If I have not written, pens Niccolò, blame it on "the times that have been and [still] are of a sort that have made me myself forget myself." A few months later, Niccolò reassumes the family he had earlier had the notion of leaving, "fortune has not left me other than relatives and friends," only to scuttle them again in another couple of months, in a repetition, too, of the motif of impotence: "as for me, I have become useless to myself, to relatives and to friends."

Sixteen months go by. Meanwhile, the Magnificent Giuliano dies. Niccolò writes his nephew again to excuse his not writing. "But being reduced to staying in the villa for the adversities I had had and [still] have, I stay sometimes a month without recognizing myself . . ." Neither the flown Muse, nor the dead Giuliano, nor he himself recognizes Niccolò.

We have seen the thought of leaving home and family cross Niccolò's mind. Rejected by politics, he in turn rejects politics. He looks on his going to the country house to live—"reduced to the villa" he calls it—

as witness to his alienation from politics. "Excuse me for being alien in spirit to all these [political] goings-on . . ."

Niccolò had made a draft of this letter in which he stresses his anti-political mood more strongly still. "And though even I have vowed not to think any more of things of state to reason about them, as my coming to the villa testifies, and to have fled conversation [about them] . . ."—Vettori's political queries in a previous letter had quickly succeeded in re-arousing interest—". . . nevertheless, to respond to your question, I am forced to break every vow . . ." Then, more than a year later, when writing that he has fallen in love, Niccolò again rejects politics. "I have left the thoughts of things grand and grave; reading of ancient things no longer delights me, or to reason about the modern . . . I have never found [in the things of state] anything but harm, and in these [of love] always good and pleasure. Keep well."

Though Vettori pulls him back into political discourse once more, perhaps after the love affair is over, the antipolitical temper is not yet broken. When finally he begins to re-enter literate society in Florence, he is composing *The Ass*, the most antipolitical of his works. He announces the composition in a letter to a new correspondent. "I have read this day *Orlando Furioso* by Ariosto, and truly the poem is wholly beautiful and in many places wonderful. If you find him there [in Rome] greet him for me and tell him that I am sorry only that he, having remembered so many poets, left me out like a prick, and that he has done to me in his *Orlando* what I shall not do to him in my *Ass*." Niccolò never mentions Ariosto in *The Ass*, probably because he never finishes the poem, and that is the last of his openly antipolitical mood. But once again, we may note, Niccolò is thinking of himself as a poet—one to be compared with the very best. Things must be looking up. The date is 1517.

One more possible reaction to the miseries of the 'totally wrecked' period, similar in kind to turning his back on politics, the rejecting of the rejector, is Niccolò's drawing away from Florentine allegiance, not in the way of disloyalty, but in the diminishing of his love for it as his country. Before the spiritual crisis of these years, Niccolò had already begun to look outside Florence for a solution not simply to Florence's, but to Italy's problems. He became convinced that Florence was a weak republic, unable to cope with the papacy and large foreign countries like France and Spain. The *First Decennial*, the publication written in 1504, is less about Florence than about Italy. "I shall sing of Italic troubles . . ." He praises the man, Alamanno Salviati, to whom he dedicates the work, for helping Italy by maintaining liberty in "one of her first limbs," namely, Florence. In *The Prince* he now goes much further. By devoting the whole of Chapter XXVI, the last of the book, to an appeal to free Italy, and by calling it an exhortation, he invites readers to consider the appeal as the ultimate purpose of the entire book.

Something sustains him in these bleak years, perhaps his robust, energetic constitution. The Pope and Lorenzo give him nothing, a child is born and dies in three days, a love affair comes and goes, Giuliano departs this vale, hope after hope is pricked—'he has not a place to turn his face'. Except downward. He plies the pèn he almost never lets go of. *The Prince*, the *Discourses*, several short poems, and *The Ass* jump to life on paper.

Niccolò does not take stock of the many things these hard years taught him. He does acknowledge picking up one lesson—caution. In what way was he so incautious as to be imprisoned and tortured? It seems unlikely he had said anything to anger the Medici. After the flight of the Gonfalonier but before our poet's imprisonment, his writings about the Medici were addressed to them or their supporters. They contained remarks hostile to the patrician families, who were enemies of the Soderini republic and now were competitors of the Medici for power. True, the Medici may have thought some of the remarks too kind to the ex-Gonfalonier, but only the optimates, rather than the Medici, would likely have been so angered as to make Niccolò the victim of "this persecution," as Vettori calls it. One of the men whose name appears with Niccolò's on the list of possible conspirators had confessed under interrogation that "He [Niccolò] said that it appeared to him that this state would not be governed without difficulty because it lacked someone to stand at the tiller, as had Lorenzo [the Magnificent]." Whatever the reason for his troubles, Niccolò writes that "I trust I shall not run into [trouble] any more both because I shall be more cautious, and because the times shall be more liberal and not so suspicious."

ॐ

TO address or make a gift of or dedicate a work to someone does not necessarily mean that it is written for that person alone. In any such case a letter or memorial would be appropriate. That our author had the Medici in mind as readers is clear from his addressing their house at more than one point in the body of *The Prince* itself, most emphatically in the last chapter. That he wished to find employment with them is obvious from numerous letters, of which some of the most important are quoted above. The two things, the book and the employment seeking, however, have a narrow interface. A book is only one way, and that not too sure, of obtaining employment. Niccolò reasoned that his employment chances were limited to the Medici, in Rome or Florence. He did not think that they would not employ him unless they received or read the work. While he undoubtedly once intended to give the book to Giuliano, and afterward wrote a dedicatory letter to Lorenzo, in the end he may have sent it to neither one.

The Medici are not the only ones who can read the language our author writes in, and understand or profit from it. Although without question much in *The Prince* fits the possibility mentioned earlier of a papal-Florentine, central Italian state, it applies to many other, widely variant possibilities as well. Niccolò advertised the book and offered it as accreditation for employment in only two places—the letter to Vettori speaking of Giuliano as addressee and the covering letter to Lorenzo. None of his other entreaties for employment mention the book, not even when so pertinent as in the Giuliano project.

A work as long as *The Prince* also has one so far unmentioned addressee—the printer, to whom, due to his father's literary passion, Niccolò is no stranger. Furthermore, our author has already published his first verse chronicles. And to pinpoint another audience, when Niccolò writes of *The Prince* to his friend Vettori, "if ever any whimsy of mine pleased you, this should not displease you," he adds, "and by a prince, most of all a new prince, it ought to be well received." He considers Giuliano to be a new prince, explicitly, and also Lorenzo, presumably, but who knows how many new princes the future holds?

DIVINE FRIENDSHIP

So much for the pronouns 'them' and 'you' in the phrase '*God more a friend* to them than to you.' The 'God more a friend' part, attuned to the rest of this chapter, rings religious bells. It needs to be situated, its semantic possibilities, if not exhausted, at least explored. Knowing more about its background one might be better able to grasp what having God as a friend entails.

The late second and third centuries saw the emergence of the Christian church and the spread of the fame of martyrs. Christians called the martyrs "friends of God." By the end of the third century, in the Roman world religious leaders arose to form a spiritual counterpart to temporal authorities. These leaders, mostly bishops, were also called friends of God. In the fourth century, on the eastern fringes of the Christian church, Saint Anthony began the line of celebrated ascetics, holy men whose sufferings, exertions, and devotion testified of closeness to the divine. Like their martyred antecedents, these men too were friends of God. Not only the power of the Christian church in this world and beyond, but also its architecture and art evolved around the commemoration and worship of these various friends of God.

Once the year A.D. 1000 came and went, the appellation, friend of God, seems to have resurged to attach itself to the extraordinarily pious and faithful believer and more properly, as in the early centuries of the church, to the rare and marvelous person of saintly nature with leadership or mystical qualities—a Bernard of Clairvaux or a Meister Eckhart. In the thirteenth and fourteenth centuries there were some groups, notably in Germany and Switzerland, in regions along the upper Danube and the Rhine, that called themselves friends of God. Niccolò, in his days, as envoy, had journeyed near these lands, but the days of the *Gottesfreunde* were before his time. Yet, to bring the phrase up to date in those regions, we need merely note that the eighty-fourth of the Ninety-Five Theses (1517, in Latin) by a contemporary, Martin Luther, refers to "friendship with God." In the Italy of the fourteenth century, Petrarch in his reflections "On the Solitary Life" wrote of the secluded souls who are the friends of God. Niccolò reads his poetry. In the fifteenth century, "friend of God" might appear in an occasional sermon. Fra Girolamo Savonarola used the phrase, "friendship of God," from the pulpit of San Marco in Florence, and here the scent gets stronger, for Niccolò heard him preach there.

The friend of God, then, has a long history, longer than that of the Christian church. Plato uses the phrase. Epictetus applies it to himself: "I, Epictetus, was the friend of God." Niccolò is a student of paganism and Christianity and of their differences, and of early Christian religion, too, to judge from the remarks he makes about the founder of Christianity. The historical "friend of God" and his own 'God more a friend' in *The Prince* are not the same, however, and the variance, sometimes ambiguous, sometimes subtle, calls for scrutiny.

The use of "of" in "friend of God" (*amico di Dio, amicus Dei*) conveys a certain direction of sentiment, moving from human to supernatural being: mortal → God. The *of*-genitive construction can be ambiguous, however, and interpreted either way or both: mortal ⇆ God. Even when taken in the one-way sense, mortal → God, when God's feelings are thus not involved, a presumption of reciprocity may exist. A friend of God, wishing to please God, does do what he thinks God wishes him to do, and therefore the presumption might well be that God reciprocates his friendship. As Simeon Stylites atop his column bowed to God one thousand times, many in the crowds of spectators obviously believed that these heroic devotions were pleasing to God and that therefore He was pleased or friendly with Simeon. This ambiguity cannot be eliminated from the *of*-genitive in the phrase "friend of God." The use in English of the *s*-genitive as in "God's friend" [a construction Niccolò does not have to worry about] conveys sentiment in the direction of superhuman to human, God → mortal, principally but not unequivocably. It also can be interpreted as the reverse.

The epigraph from *The Prince* leaves no ambiguity. The preposition "*to*" makes it clear. 'Nor was God more a friend *to* them than *to* you.' One need not question the direction of sentiment. It goes, God → man.

Among Greek and Roman families, heroes, and cities, having one or more gods as patrons or as personal guardians is a relationship not infrequently encountered. In Plato's *Republic* the true poet or the just man may be a friend of the gods or of God—from the context it is not always clear—or dear to the gods, a phrase appearing also in Latin literature, notably in Horace. In the play entitled *Andria*, Niccolò translates into vernacular a comedy of Terence, *The Girl from Andros*. The last scene has one character assuring another that he alone is "loved by the Gods." Here again the direction surely is, Gods → mortal. Another case appears in the preface to Book II of the *Discourses*. Our author writes of the capable youth of the day and hopes that among them may be someone "more loved by Heaven." The direction of sentiment here is the same as in the Greek and Latin examples.

In the *Florentine Histories*, consigned to Pope Clement VII in 1525, Niccolò's last book, we find that Lorenzo the Magnificent "was loved by fortune and by God to the highest degree." In this work our historian adopts the ancient practice of quoting historical leaders fully, although their speeches can hardly be expected to have always been recorded word for word. In one instance, the spokesman for the Milanese people who were angered and disillusioned by the treachery of Count Francesco Sforza, condottiere and later duke of Milan, appears before the count and condemns his action. God, he warns, "will not want to be a friend of wicked men." The count counters that God would demonstrate through the outcome of the war which of them might be "more His friend." Here, some context is needed to show that the direction is reversed: count → God. God will choose the count rather than the Milanese people as His friend because, as the count clarifies, of the "greater justice" with which he has fought. God will reveal that he, the count, is more a friend to God than are the Milanese. We took note earlier of the inextricable connotation, though not the necessary inference, that God in such cases reciprocates the friendliness, in this instance by giving victory to the count.

So while the phrase 'God more a friend' is clearest as to direction and comparison, it obviously is not the only expression by which Niccolò in preferential terms links men, God, and friendship or affection. In general, the sentiment is exclusive and sometimes discriminating in amount, regardless of the direction. Not everyone, but some are, or one is, the singular or greater recipient of divine love or friendship.

Is it possible to decipher the passage to mean that God is a friend to nobody, that just as He did not befriend Moses, Cyrus, and Theseus, He will not befriend you? This would be hard to sustain in light of the specific references to God's speaking to Moses, to God as Moses' teacher, to the possibility of God's loving certain men, and many others yet to be cited. Or is it possible that since God was not more a friend to Moses than to you, He could have been less a friend to Moses than He is to you? Logically, this interpretation could be made of our author's statement but, again, the possibility can barely be entertained in light of the grace with which He crowns Moses.

Now, this unusual phrase, 'God more a friend,' may also reflect Niccolò's republican background. In the equality of citizens, a republic is like a band of friends. Christ as friend was not an uncommon expression. Christ used the term in parable, "Friend, go up higher," or to a disciple, "Friend, wherefrom art thou come?" The society of Christian believers was often called *respublica christiana*, a usage broached by Augustine in *The City of God* and employed by Niccolò himself in the *Discourses*. But were God a republican, He would be a friend to all citizen-believers, and they to Him as well. Niccolò's 'God more a friend' is discriminating.

TALKING WITH GOD

In the Old Testament one can learn about the Lord who picks friends selectively. Exodus 33:11 reads, "And the Lord spake unto Moses face to face, as a man speaketh unto his friend." The Latin Vulgate that our author would have read or heard preached gives the last phrase of this passage as *ad amicum suum*. This, then, and not a line out of Plato or an early Christian martyr or a late medieval preacher would seem to be the phrase that Niccolò recast into the telling 'God more a friend.' And not a republicanizing god, but the hero-loving Lord of the Old Testament would be the model.

Niccolò's other heroes, whose deeds "seem not discrepant from those of Moses," are, as noted, Cyrus and Theseus. (Romulus, who appeared in the first lineup in Chapter VI of *The Prince*, does not appear in Chapter XXVI, where Niccolò sets out to nominate to whom God is more a friend, perhaps because to Romulus, as he mentions in the *Discourses*, "the authority of God was not necessary.") There are only a few whom the Old Testament itself so favors as a friend of God, most notably Abraham and Moses. Cyrus is not overlooked. Commended for liberating the Jews from the Babylonian captivity, he is the Lord's annointed, *pastor meus*. So Niccolò has a biblical base for considering Cyrus, too, to possess God as a friend. Theseus, who has no biblical authority, he cites last.

Earlier, in another context of *The Prince*, in introducing David, our author speaks of the Old Testament as one of his sources. "I want also to bring back to memory a figure of the Old Testament . . ." In the *Discourses* he affirms that Moses was forced to kill numberless men, if one "reads the Bible sensibly." True enough, one need only back up in the Book of Exodus to a passage just preceding "unto his friend" to find chapter and verse (32:27–29). The Levites killed three thousand brothers, friends, and neighbors on orders of Moses.

These few references may suffice to show that Niccolò acknowledges the Old Testament as a source, advises reading it for historical facts such as the quantity of men killed at a given time at the instance of a given man, and takes this man and others like him to be but men, however great—"nevertheless they were men." Without questioning the divinity of the Lord or the allegorical teachings of the Bible, he is attributing literal historical value to the Old Testament just as he might do with Livy or any other classical historian. In almost the same words, in the *Discourses* he advises reading history sensibly.

The very phrase in Exodus of the Lord's speaking as a man to his friend appears in the *Summa Theologica* of Thomas Aquinas, the great philosopher and theologian, who misquotes it as "a friend to his friend," thereby emphasizing however, the reciprocity of God's friendship with Moses. When scripture states that He spoke face to face, Aquinas continues, this is to be understood as expressing the opinion of the people, who thought that Moses was speaking with God, mouth to mouth.

Savonarola, an older contemporary of Niccolò, was also reputed to have spoken with God. This man, for a flash of a half-dozen years, transformed the lives of all Florentines—Fra Girolamo Savonarola, Dominican friar from Ferrara, prior of San Marco in Florence, eloquent preacher, legislator, virtual dictator of Florentine morals and manners, reformer of religion and daily life (mothers took their babes back from wet nurses to suckle them themselves), learned burner of vanities (carnival masks, improper books and paintings), denouncer of papal and Medicean corruption, republican theocrat, initiator of a Franco-Florentine alliance, prophet of death and disaster, universal millennarian visionary, brandisher of a spiritual and temporal sword of God. Rarely have Florentines been so strung out with piety and religious fervor. The air was heavy with groans, hymns, and incense. It is no wonder that if there is a man toward whom Niccolò's writings remain ambiguous, it is Savonarola.

*. . . if there is a man toward whom Niccolò's writings remain ambiguous,
it is Savonarola.*

Before being hanged and burned as a heretic and schismatic, Savonarola denied that he had in any particular way spoken with God or that
God had spoken with him—in a confession signed on the rack. Released
from pain, he denied his denial. "I have denied You, I have denied You,
I have denied You out of fear of torture!"

Shortly after the friar's execution, in the changeover of government
that ensued Niccolò, twenty-nine years old, entered public service.
Other good evidence exists that he was not regarded as a follower or
sympathizer of the Savonarolian party. A few months earlier, he had
gone to church (the practice he says he does 'not use') to hear the

preacher expound Exodus. Apparently he had been asked by the anti-Savonarolian former Florentine ambassador to Rome to give an eye-witness account of the friar's performance in the church of San Marco. (The request and the response also hint that Niccolò had just been presented as a candidate for the Chancery post.) He sent the ambassador a neat summary of two of the friar's sermons, but it was not until years later in the *Discourses* that he brought up the subject of the friar's speaking with God. The existence of the Deity or His ability to converse is not in question. Niccolò simply is not sure that the friar ever talked with Him. "The people of Florence . . . were persuaded by Friar Girolamo Savonarola that he talked with God. I do not wish to judge whether it was true or not, for about one so great a man one should speak with reverence; but I do say that infinite numbers believed it . . ." Out of respect for 'one so great a man', a phrase he uses also in praise of Cosimo de' Medici, "FATHER OF HIS COUNTRY," he withholds judgment.

About the great Hebrew prophet, Niccolò offers no such doubts. Moses "must be admired for that grace alone that made him worthy of speaking with God." This passage, too, derives from Exodus (33:17), where God says to Moses, "For thou has found grace in my sight." So do other biblical phrases in the last chapter of *The Prince*: "extraordinary events without example, conducted by God: the sea has opened; a cloud has shown you the way; the rock has poured forth water; here it has rained manna . . ."

The expression 'God more a friend' runs back to the pagan and biblical "friend of God." Niccolò's phrase is original and stronger: it commits the affection of God unmistakably. Evidently this is the way he wishes to put it. To certain men—one of the Medici or a new prince or whoever will take up the banner of Italy's redemption—he is promising God as a friend.

Why is it so important that these men have God for a friend? A lot hinges on who God is.

"extraordinary events without example, conducted by God: the sea has opened; . . .

the rock has poured forth water; . . ."

THE HEAVENLY HOST

> Stay in good with Christ
> and scoff at the saints!
>
> *—Clizia*

HAVING GOD as a friend seems a preferment not lightly to be dismissed. The friend of the gods, Plato writes in *The Republic*, may be supposed to receive from them all things at their best. Moses, Niccolò writes, "had so great a preceptor" as God Himself and received spoken orders from Him.

Nowhere does our author discuss at length his conception of God. Scattered about his writings, though, like poppies in a field of chick peas, are many references to God. Together they form an unmistakable likeness. Niccolò's God is the creator, the master deity, providential, real, universal, one of many names, personal, invocable, thankable, to be revered, a judge, just and forgiving, rewarding and punishing, awesome, a force transcendent, separate from but operative in the world. The quotations to follow and others later that reveal the author in light, dark, and serious moods, will establish these and other divine aspects and relationships.

GOD AND THE SAINTS

On the occasion of the visit of the duke of Milan and his court, Niccolò notes in the *Florentine Histories*, the city of Florence witnessed an unprecedented exhibition, for during the Lenten fast, "that court of his without concern for the Church or for God fed itself totally on meats." This, as will be seen elsewhere, is a characteristic passage about God: it simply takes His existence for granted. God is not a product of men's imagination, thinking, superstition, desire, or needs. "All the unhappy are wont to hope [for the help of God]," Niccolò remarks earlier in the *Histories*, but God is no hallucination because of it. Men without "fear of God" have "no faith in other men," the author declares in *The Prince*, but God is neither more nor less real because of them. Niccolò does not deck God out in snappy metaphors, as he does fortune and other supernatural forces. He discourses about God always in the conventional reverent attitude.

In a poem in tercets, "On Ambition," he speaks of God the creator of the universe and man. "God had just made the stars, the sky, the light, the elements, and man / dominator of so many beautiful things." Of greater length is the "Exhortation to Penitence," a piece written for a religious occasion, conserved in his own hand, carefully composed, probably late in life, for delivery to a confraternity. Lay confraternities, almost all of religious orientation, play an important part in the civil and social life of Florence. Niccolò urges his "honored fathers and greater brothers" to consider "the benefits we have received from God." "Do you not see how much toil the sun endures to make us part of its light, to give life with its power both to us and to those things that have been created for us by God?" Thus "everything is created for the honor and good of man, and man is created only for the good and honor of God." The Creator fashioned a man-centered world and a God-centered man.

Niccolò, leaping from one historical period to another, with ancient, Christian, modern, and recent illustrations, assumes that God then and there, whatever He was called, is the same God as here, now, and hereafter. The Zeus of the Greeks, Yahveh of the Jews, Dominus of the Vulgate Bible, Jupiter of the Romans, are one to him. The God of Numa, of Lycurgus, Solon, or Agathocles, is the same universal *Dio* or *altissimo Iddio*. God, who was a friend to Moses, was also a friend to Cyrus and Theseus, and would be a friend, too, to a new prince. Moreover, Niccolò monotheizes God. The plural gods that Livy's Romans stand in awe of are the same as Niccolò's singular God.

The tendency to reduce the quantity of deities shows up early in Niccolò's career. Once, he ghostwrites a speech to be read by a high official at the solemn seating of a new magistrate. Beginning with a tale, told in Virgil's *Georgics* and Ovid's *Fasti*, the address (its identifying title is "Allocution Made to a Magistrate") tells of the first age of humanity, when men were so good the gods did not hesitate to descend from heaven to come join them. As vice grew on earth, the gods gradually went back up to heaven. The last to leave was Justice, driven up finally by the stench. Reluctant, however, to abandon men, Justice every now and then—sometimes here, sometimes there—continued to alight on earth. After praising Justice for his benefits to kingdoms and republics, Niccolò changes the divinity to a virtue. "This virtue alone is the one that among all others pleases God." Quoting a few lines of Dante from the *Purgatory*, he calls them golden and divine verses through which one sees "how much God loves justice and mercy." His final urging to the new judge and the assembly is that they be so just and impartial that Justice "will return to live in this city." But in getting to that point he had transformed the gods into God and Justice the god into Justice the virtue, the one most pleasing to God. We see in this protestation of justice an example of the Florentine's literary adaptation of pagan deities, his syncretizing bent, and his view of God as the lover of justice and mercy.

Though God be one alone, there are literary nuances in the names of other gods that a writer and poet does not wish to give up. In a short poem of uncertain date, full of allusions to pagan mythology, Niccolò attempts a pastoral, a genre familiar especially in classical times, often a paean to a prince. In it our poet sings of his unidentified hero's being created by God, but earlier in the poem he invokes Phoebus, "O sacred Apollo," and "O Jove god." Of all Niccolò's verses, this is the most uninspired. Other literary works, and letters as well, citing the myth and poetry of classical antiquity also refer frequently to pagan deities, major and minor. In the beginning of *The Ass*, the antipolitical poem he left incomplete, the one that began with the story of the young man who could not stop running, the poet tells how, lost in the wilds, he met a beautiful woman, a damsel of the goddess Circe. She, like Dante's Beatrice, acts as his guide (but, by contrast, gives him no chance to sublimate his love: she quickly takes him to bed). He appeals to the Muses for help, and proceeds, "Fine, arched, and black were her eyebrows / because in fashioning them all the Gods were present / all the heavenly and supernal councils / . . . I do not know who made that mouth: / if Jove with his hand did not make it himself . . ." Pagan muses and pagan gods.

Our author does not neglect Jesus Christ. In a letter to a friend, a Florentine man of letters, Niccolò charges that Pope Clement VII, by letting himself be caught off guard and virtually imprisoned in his fortress, had made so tangled a mess "that even Christ could not straighten it out." The situation was desperate, the dangers were great, Niccolò's feelings high—to get such an outburst from him. The expression about Christ, however, consists of a Florentine saying, as does a similar expression we read in *The Ass*. Unable to resist a wide open stretch of street, the youth with a compulsion to race dropped his cloak to the ground, crying out, 'Not [even] Christ will hold me here.'

In the *First Decennial* another mention of Christ dismisses the fascinating, controversial Caesar Borgia: a Spanish general, el Gran Capitan, "laid on him the weight that a rebel against Christ deserved." The *Discourses* mentions Christ in a different context, commending Saints Francis and Dominic for upholding "the example of the life of Christ." The

"Exhortation to Penitence" declares that, "Upon this [love] is founded the faith of Christ." For its part, the comedy *Clizia* associates Christ's name with the proverbial idea that the master god is the one that counts: 'Stay in good with Christ and scoff at the saints.' Christ in the celestial kingdom is linked to the saving of souls, but only once—in the "Exhortation"—and not in an active role, whereas elsewhere therein men anticipate judgment in fear and awe of God. In our author's writings, not counting the opening and closing of letters, Christ will be found a dozen times, God more than a hundred. Niccolò is not Christocentric. Nonetheless, when in the *Discourses* he will write of the founder of Christianity, Christ's importance will become clear.

As for Christian saints, the four that seem most important are Saint Francis, Saint Dominic, Saint Jerome, and Saint Paul. Niccolò mentions Saint Gregory, Saint Benedict, Saint Peter, Saint Zanobio, and the rarer saints Hillary, Puccio, Blaise, Clement, Romulus, John Gualberto of nearby Vallombroso, and a few others. In the opening of the *Mandragola*, where the lover has just arrived from Paris, we learn about Saint Cuckold, "the saint most honored in France." Otherwise, the saints hardly exist. Mary, the Holy Spirit, saints, gods—most of them do not interest Niccolò except, perhaps, in a literary way. "May God help me, and Our Madonna," implores Lucrezia, the heroine of the *Mandragola*. Or in an official way. The language of official papers and bills insures that in Niccolò's capacity as Florentine Secretary he will frequently invoke the names of Saint John the Baptist, the patron saint, and the Mother Madonna. And as historian he may feel obliged to register the words of historic figures: the duke of Milan, whose courtiers visiting Italy one Lenten season stuffed themselves with meat, was later killed in Milan, his body pierced by the short, sharp knives of three conspirators. He fell, "unable to do or say anything exept call on the name of Our Lady in his aid." Our historian had previously noted in the *Florentine Histories* that "many signs of his future death occurred."

SPEECH AND FAITH

The language of household and piazza, fondly reproduced in Niccolò's plays and stories, redounds with "Pray God that . . . ," "God save you," "O God, perform this miracle . . . ," "In the name of God," and many other such expressions. The mere reproducing of such formulas of thanks, augury, witnessing, imprecation, and the like, does not necessarily signify that he believes that God responds fully or in part to personal invocation or that these phrases reflect other than widespread usage. One of his characters in *Clizia* posts a limit to what one can ask of God. "Oh, crazy old man! He wants God to hold hands in his dishonesties!"

So deeply entrenched is the taking of the Deity's name in crisis that a moment of shock will bring the disbeliever born of generations of skeptics to ejaculate: My God! Once the tremor of piety passes, he recovers his balance. Niccolò's formal observance of ritual will be covered in a subsequent chapter, but his informal practice in the invocation of God may be looked at now, where we may expect to find instances, in letters to family and friends.

A god who can be a friend, "like a man to a friend," as Exodus puts it, has human qualities. God, like man, can be called upon, prayed to, and thanked. In personal letters Niccolò will occasionally close with the customary "May Christ watch over you," or something similar. Typically, the usage is reserved for correspondence with family, intimates, and clergy. Writing letters to relatives, he may mark the conventional cross in the upper left hand, followed by "In the name of God" and the date, and close with the conventional, 'May Christ watch over you', or the less conventional, "May Christ watch over you indeed," or "May God conduct you [safely]." To his friend Vettori, he may open with "Jesus Maria." In another he ends with the thought, "Our archbishop at this hour must be dead; may God have his soul and all of his [family]." To a son, Niccolò the father closes with, "May Christ watch over all of you." Family members writing him also use orthodox signs. His son, Guido, destined for the clergy, writes to him marking "Jesus" on the upper left of the page, ending with, "May Christ watch over you, and keep you in prosperity," another common closure in letters. His wife, Marietta, writing in her one extant letter to him begins with "In the name of God, day 24 [Nov. 1503]," and closes with "God be with you, and watch over you."

Such expressions in such contexts can easily be perfunctory, a linguistic habit without much fideistic import. Habit, rites, or ceremony, however, as ritualists and liturgists insist, may also house faith and the springs of action. A less automatic usage is often met with in times of great sorrow, the death of father, mother, brother, or children. We have no letters to preserve these events in Niccolò's life.

The six months or so after his dismissal as Florentine Secretary were a time of deepest danger, narrow escape, and great loss. Our poet in his distress, or relief, invoked God. We can illustrate this simply by adding a few more words to some of the passages from letters quoted in the previous chapter: "grace of God, it is over" (13 March 1513); "I pray God . . . to be able to be grateful to you for it because I can say that all that is left of my life to me . . ." (18 March); "and I was about to lose my life, which God and my innocence saved for me" (26 June); "I feel all right in body, but bad in everything else . . . And no other hope remains to me but that God may help me, and up to here he has in fact not abandoned me" (4 August). The latter two of these letters are to his nephew, Giovanni Vernacci, the others are to his friend Vettori.

PROPHETS AND PORTENTS

Thus far we have contemplated God and the saints; we have not canvassed the entire range of supernatural powers and beings. There are references to fortune and occult forces in our author's writings, both literary and political.

The "sage might command the stars and fates," Niccolò reflects in a draft of a letter of 1506 to his friend Giovani Battista Soderini, nephew of the Gonfalonier, but "one does not find these sages." Yet he did not cease looking for them. Perhaps it was listening to Savonarola that stirred his taste for prophecy and the interpretation of celestial signs. *The Prince* faults Savonarola for blaming Italy's woes on men's sins, but credits him, as does the *Discourses*, with prophecy: the woes predicted did come. "And without moving myself from home to prove this, everyone knows how much was [truly] predicted by friar Girolamo Savonarola before the coming of King Charles VIII of France to Italy."

The chance of hearing prophecies seems to be about the only thing that draws Niccolò of his own accord near a church. The prophetic mood of all Florence was exacerbated in the decades after 1494. Here is a report to Vettori late in 1513.

One finds in this, our city, magnet for all the pitchmen of the world, a friar of Saint Francis who is half hermit, who on account of his greater credibility in preaching, assumes the profession of prophet; and yesterday morning in Santa Croce where he preaches, he said "many things great and wonderful." That before much time passed, so that those who were ninety years of age would be able to see it, there will be an unjust pope created over a just pope, and he will have false prophets with him and will create cardinals and divide the Church. *Item*, that the king of France would be annihilated and someone of the House of Aragon would predominate in Italy. Our city would go up in flames and sacking, the churches would be abandoned and ruined, the priests dispersed, and for three years there would be no divine services. There would be dying and greatest hunger; in the city there would not remain ten men, in the farms there would not remain two. That there has been a devil for eighteen years in a human body, and said mass. That well over two million devils were unleashed to be administrators of the above affair, and that they used to enter into many dying bodies, and they did not let that body putrefy, so that false prophets and clerics might resuscitate the dead, and be believed.

One might have thought that the fame of such a man might have pulled Niccolò into the nave to listen. The Franciscan was prophesying in the church of Santa Croce, where the Machiavegli were buried. Niccolò's retailing of the friar's prophecies as quoted above provides the background for the epigraph to Chapter 1 above, that he himself did not hear the sermon, as he did 'not use such practices', "but I heard it recited thus by all of Florence."

Niccolò considers himself expert in matters of state, in the movement of men toward political aims, yet finds himself thinking about theology and natural philosophy, too. *The Prince* and certain letters reveal that he studies the art of the state by reading ancient history and reflecting on its relation to his own experience in politics, foreign affairs, and war. He learns about heaven in much the same way, although he does not say so, and in addition by reflecting on passages of the Bible, on the prose of great theologians like Augustine and Thomas Aquinas, on the stirring lines of prophetic poets like Petrarch, prophetic preachers like Savonarola, or late philosophers like Marsilio Ficino, and, as we have just seen, by seeking, hearing, and rubbing elbows with men who claim to prognosticate from heavenly signs. From one of the last letters of his life to his patrician friend Guicciardini, one hears that Niccolò has been in Modena for two days where, "I met up with a prophet who said with witnesses that he had predicted the flight of the Pope and the vanity of the enterprise, and also says that evil times have not all passed, in which the Pope and we [too] will greatly suffer."

Niccolò's attraction to theories of spiritual intervention does not on the one hand liken him to superstitious savages or on the other make him attractive to adherents of Lucretius or his master, Epicurus. Some of the most attractive philosophical theories of the day in Florence, in particular those of Pico della Mirandola (Niccolò esteems him highly) enoble nature and spirit worship by enfolding it in the love of God.

The republican Romans took augurs solemnly. This at times gave military leaders problems. "The ancient captains had a worry of which [captains] today are almost free, which was to interpret auguries unlucky to their objective; because if an arrow fell on an army, if the sun or moon darkened, if an earthquake came, if the captain in mounting or dismounting fell from the horse, it was interpreted in a sinister way by the soldiers and generated in them such fear that, coming to the fray, they would have easily lost it. And therefore as soon as a similar incident happened, the ancient captains demonstrated the reason for it or reduced it to a natural cause. Caesar, falling on getting off ship in Africa said, 'Africa, I have taken you'."

Our military expert (for these remarks come from the *Art of War*) gives Christianity credit for its war on superstituion. "And many have rendered [similar] explanation for the darkening of the moon and for earthquakes; which things [interpreted thus] in our times cannot happen, both because our men [today] are not so superstitious and because our religion by itself wholly removes such opinions."

Niccolò ridicules the idea that demons take possession of human bodies. The last few items he took from the Franciscan friar above are but passing examples. The belief in demonic possession he thinks worthy of a story well told and amusing indeed—*Belfagor*. He locates the tale in ancient Florentine history on the presumption that nowadays such superstition about a demon would be held to be, as he titles the piece, "a fable" of the devil who took a wife.

He satirizes astrologers, too. Astrological imagery appears here and there in his writings, notably in *The Ass*, but not nearly on a par with allusions to pagan deities or spirits. A carnival song addresses "gracious and lovely women" and makes fun of their fears. "Every astrologer and fortune-teller has scared you." He laughs at "these empty rumors" of "a horrid and strange period that threatens each land with / plague, flood and war, tempests, earthquakes, and avalanches / as if the world were already ended."

ASTRAL SPIRITS

Niccolò ridicules belief in demonic possession and in the alarms of astrologers. There are true prophecies and portents, however, that have been told by poets, priests, and philosophers, and there are true portents that have been read by everyone. The *Discourses* contains a chapter titled, "Before Great Happenings Signs Come That Prognosticate Them or Men [Come] Who Predict Them." Niccolò confesses: "How it comes about I do not know, but it is clear both from ancient and modern cases that never does any serious misfortune befall a city or a province that has not been predicted either by divination or revelation or by prodigies or by other heavenly signs." Others, he thinks, should discuss and explain the cause of such events, but he goes ahead to speculate that, "Still, as some philosophers would have it, since this air is full of intelligences who by natural virtues foresee future things and have compassion for men so that they may prepare defenses, it could be that they warn them with such signs."

Spirits appear in many of our author's verses in both classical and

Christian guise. One song, "On the Blessed Spirits," takes the form of a warning and a plea for peace.

> Blessed Spirits are we
> who from the celestial seats
> have come here to reveal ourselves on earth
> . . . since it is full pleasing to our Lord
> that [men] lay down arms and stay in peace.

Here, their relation to God is so close that the blessed spirits might be called angels.

Friendly spirits seem to exist and wish to help men prepare a defense against disaster. Yet, heaven and fortune seem to take priority over such spirits, and at times may hide all signs of impending events, blinding anyone who may interfere with their designs. They may thus seem unfriendly to men, but this is not necessarily so. Heaven or fortune may have an ulterior strategy, as fortune had when it made Rome great. "One knows this well from [Livy's] text how, that in order to make Rome greater and to lead it on to that future greatness, fortune judged it was necessary to batter it . . . but did not want to ruin it altogether." (This perverseness and inscrutability of fortune warrant treatment in a later chapter.) And the heavens, every now and then through catastrophe, give the world a new start.

> As for causes [of disaster] that come from heaven, they are those that extinguish human generation and reduce to a few the inhabitants in a part of the world. And this is brought about either by pestilence or by hunger or by an inundation of waters. And the most important of these, because it is more universal, is the last . . . when all lands are filled with inhabitants so that they cannot live there or go elsewhere because all places are occupied and filled, and when craftiness and human malice has come as far as it can come, it is necessary that the world be purged in one of the three ways, so that men, having become few and battered, may live more comfortably and become better.

The concept of overpopulation is clearly present. That of the extinction of humanity is not. In *The Ass*, Niccolò brings up providence ("that providence that maintains the human species") and in the *Discourses* he states that even in floods, rude men from the mountains will save themselves and from the purge will come the health "of the human generation."

If you wait long enough or look ahead far enough, then, you will see that these aerial bodies, these floating intelligences, this heavenly disposition, this inscrutable fortune—all bearing intentions seemingly harmful in the short run—may prove to be salutary in the long haul. The only dark forces, in both the long and the short run, that Niccolò mentions are the two Furies in the terza rima poem, "On Ambition." At the time of Cain and Abel,

> an occult power that nourishes itself in the sky
> between the stars which that circling encloses,
> to human nature hardly a friend,
> to deprive us of peace and put [us] in war,
> to take away from us every quietness and every good,
> sent two furies to live on earth.

The Furies thread a passage back through Rome and Greece to ancient Persia's eschatology.

The seeds sown by these two pests fill the world with Envy, Accidie, Hate, Cruelty, Pride and Deceit, War and Death. The evil permeates the world upon Adam and Eve's leaving the Terrestial Paradise of the Garden of Eden, and thus forms part of the Fall, penetrating the breasts of men, transforming the "human mind," becoming "natural instinct." Fallen man turns into that matter that has to be shaped and reshaped, with as much aid as possible from the forces of God, heaven, fortune, and even the intelligent ethereal bodies, who at times, to hold off the Furies, it would seem, and to save mankind, may have to wreak catastrophe on the world.

Thus drenched in celestial design, natural phenomena lack neutrality or indifference. They have a purpose directed toward human phenomena. They warn men with portents, caress some, burn up others like straw dogs. If an individual stands in the way, fortune kills him or renders him incapable of opposition. God and the celestial forces have before them tactics and strategies comprehending individuals, communities, and the entire human species.

. . .

Niccolò, on the look-out for prophecy, cannot let any change go by without understanding what it signifies for men. In common with alchemists and scientists, he thirsts for knowledge of the physical world. But he is their partner only insofar as natural phenomena impinge on men. There is much about prophecy and signs to which our author confesses ignorance, but he is sure of the friendly warning intent of portents and the providentiality of disasters.

In the *Florentine Histories* (though the event seems to have no special political or military significance) Niccolò traces a two-mile-wide hurricane as it passes in August of 1456 from Ancona to Pisa, ravaging the countryside surrounding the hamlet of Sant'Andrea where he was then writing. "It seemed that God Himself wished to take up [arms], so great was the storm of winds . . . pushed by superior forces, either natural or supernatural . . . God wished without doubt to threaten rather than punish Tuscany: because if so great a storm had entered in a city . . . it would have made that greater devastation and scourge that one can conjecture in one's mind. But God wished that this bit of example might for then suffice to refresh among men the memory of His power."

Niccolò repeats the lesson of portents by including in both the *Discourses* and the *Florentine Histories* the death of Lorenzo the Magnificent. "And how from his death the greatest ruins would be born, Heaven then showed many most evident signs; among which the highest summit of the temple of Santa Reparta [the cathedral] was struck by lightning with such fury that a large part of the pinnacle was wrecked, to the stupor and wonder of all." The last sentence of the *Histories* confirms that "once Lorenzo was dead, those evil seeds began to be born that . . . ruined and still ruin Italy."

Niccolò records yet another portent. "Everyone knows even now how, a little before Piero Soderini, who had been made Gonfalonier for life by the Florentine people, was chased out and deprived of his rank, the Palazzo was similarly struck by a lightning flash." Our author does not mention that that same lightning presaged for him (the Gonfalonier's right-hand man, and thrown out of office soon after, too) the beginning of that troubled span of years 'after everything was totally wrecked.'

By introducing spirits Niccolò adds with one hand what he subtracts with the other. He reduces the saints, yet augments the heavenly host. The sky he paints is thick with aerialists. In this, the ethereal part of his theology, the relation of deities, their super- or subordination, and the extent of their cooperation are not always easy to make out. Still, such evidence as there is, appearing both in what our author calls his light and his grave works, is sturdy. That all portents are subject to God, for instance, can be glimpsed in a remark made to Vettori: "From here, there is nothing to tell you except prophecies and announcements of bad times; may God, if [the prophets] tell lies, annihilate them; if they speak truth, may He convert it into good." That the spirits emanate friendly portents can be estimated from the several texts already drawn from the *Discourses* and *Florentine Histories*. That fortune is subject to God can be seen in a sentence from *The Prince*, in that last chapter where the proviso to be a friend of God is introduced. The sentence is about

Caesar Borgia, referred to dramatically as "someone." "And even though up to this point some gleam of light may have shown itself in someone to judge that he might have been ordained by God for [Italy's] redemption, yet one has seen afterward how, in the highest course of his actions, he was reprobated by fortune." The 'yet one has seen' refers to Chapter VII of *The Prince*, which shows Borgia to have suffered "an extraordinary and extreme maliciousness of fortune."

The composition of the quoted sentence is interesting. To convey its meaning it relies less on structure than on contrast of moods, subjunctive in the first clause, indicative in the second, so that the uncertainty of God's ordainment is stressed and the certainty of fortune's reprobation made crystal clear. At the same time, the words associated with the action of the participants take on strict theological import—the unusual 'reprobated' by fortune, 'redemption' by Caesar Borgia, 'ordained' by God. Among the things God may do for a friend is to destine him, as He must have destined Moses, Cyrus, and Theseus, to set a people free.

.   .   .

Of these teleological beings that interrupt natural events, God is the least active but the great strategist; heaven or the heavens, usually a weak, paganized variant of God, comes next; fortune, the perverse, the most active, the hardest to understand, follows closely; and astral forces do their amiable best with presages. Thus might they appear sitting for a pantheonic portrait.

In this chapter, to discover just how important it is to have God as a friend, we began to look at what Niccolò's idea of God is and to consider what relation the parade of saints and spirits might have to it. He knows God exists, he pays some attention to Jesus Christ and the saints, he is convinced and curious about other supernatural beings. These last he does not try to incorporate, order, and refine into formal religion (as a hagiographer might) at the expense perhaps of excluding credences and half-beliefs that much of humankind may hold. He includes them without sorting them out.

Though he is not so promiscuous as the characters in his plays in taking the Lord's name, Niccolò's conception of God holds unexpected richness. A variety of the Deity's qualities have appeared in this chapter; others will appear later. Not yet in play in their complexity are our author's ideas of God's arching purpose or of His relation specifically to friends, to men of politics, men of the church, and others, and to the afterworld.

Niccolò's God of "infinite goodness" has the moral loftiness of

Cleanthes' "O God most glorious, called by many a name." He is in no way a God indifferent to man. *Altissimo Iddio* is just and merciful and loves men who are just, merciful, and charitable to their neighbors. This noble and orthodox portrait, what morality does it inspire in our author, and does it inspire the generality of men to walk the same path?

THE WAY OF EVIL

Oh, fine!
As if God granted graces
for evil as for good!
—*Mandragola*

FEW WOULD hold that Niccolò is a moral absolutist. Yet he never questions that there is good and evil. Authentic norms exist. We are "enveloped in the laces of sin," he grieves in the "Exhortation."

Niccolò thinks of himself as a good man. The previous chapter touched on his rather conventional religious practice and faith. As for family, he may not be the world's best provider: to listen to him, he barely keeps a roof over the house and the wolf away from the door. His last words of advice given in a family letter, are, "Live happy and spend as little as you can." He may not have been the world's most faithful husband; on the other hand, he cannot boast of 1,003 conquests in his native land alone. He has a few handfuls of love affairs but, as Friar Timothy says in the *Mandragola*, these are sins that "wash away with holy water." By existing evidence, his affection for his wife is constant, as it is for his children. The same last family letter, written to his son Guido (the youngest, Totto, was still nursing), reads, "Greet [your mother] mona [madonna] Marietta, and tell her that . . . I have never had such desire to be in Florence as now. . . . Just say . . . that she should be of good cheer." The letter closes affectionately, "Kiss Baccina, Piero, and Totto [named after the uncle who died a few years before], if he is there [that is, if he is not out at the wet nurse's], about whom I should appreciate learning whether his eyes have healed." Then, a perennial parental complaint: "And remind Bernardo [the eldest son, named after the grandfather], to whom fifteen days ago I have written two letters and I have no reply to them, that he had better behave himself. Christ watch over you all." Guido answers that from his father's letters to his mother they learned that he had bought a beautiful little chain for Baccina [or Baccia, a nickname of Bartolomea, so named after her grandmother] who now "does nothing but think about this beautiful little chain, and prays God for you, and that He will make you return soon." His wife is still sending him his clothes, washed and mended. "Mona Marietta greets you and sends two shirts, two towels, two caps, three pairs of socks, and four handkerchiefs. And prays that you return soon, and we all together [do, too]."

When he recalls his fifteen years of service to the republic Niccolò sees his poverty as attesting to his good faith. He writes this to Vettori, who did some of the same kind of work himself and knew what opportunities for corruption did exist. Slightly more than a year before, after the fall of the Soderini republic, the new regime had put Niccolò on the carpet and interrogated him on his accounts but found nothing to charge him with. Although Niccolò sometimes had to handle large sums for disbursements in the field, his own salary and resources were small, so small that once he had to write his superiors and threaten to sell his horse (government issue) if they did not send him the money to get back home. After all, he points out to Vettori, "one should not doubt my word, as, having always kept faith, I do not need to learn now to break it; and whoever has been faithful and good for forty-three years, which years I have [to my age], should not be able to change [his] nature."

Once, a young man just embarking on a diplomatic career as ambassador to Spain sought Niccolò's counsel. The ex-Florentine Secretary, who had never reached the grade of ambassador though he often had the responsibility of one, writes a memorandum for him, full of hard-won advice that would profit any young aspirants for the post. The memo assumes from the start that the commission would be held by someone "who is good," and proceeds with the technicalities of protocol, intelligence gathering, and tact. At one point he makes an ethically dubious suggestion, recommending that the ambassador in reporting his own judgment to his superiors use these words: "Considering, then, everything that has been written, the prudent men that one finds here judge that this and that effect has to follow."

To disguise one's own judgment, no matter how prudent, as the words of anonymous others, does seem questionable, at least until one notes Niccolò's reason. Apparently, among ambassadors this was less a departure from truth than a simple code or stylistic device, like the editorial "we." Niccolò can be seen using it himself in his dispatches, and it does take the self-centered sting out of the "I." He explains it thus: "your judgment in your [own] mouth would be offensive."

Niccolò, like everyone else, sometimes uses good and bad in the sense of right and wrong. One day, writing to Vettori on the international situation, he prefaces his remarks with: "I believe it to be the duty of a prudent man at all times . . . to favor good and oppose bad in time . . ."

The context later makes it clear that he is talking of the immediate opportunities and perils lying before the new Pope Leo X. Different from this sense of good and bad are the sketches of himself as a good man that appear in the preambles to the first and second books of the *Discourses*. In the first sketch he describes himself as "driven by that natural desire that was always in me to work, come what may, for those things that I believe bring the common benefit . . ." The theme of the second concerns the adverse circumstances that hinder the author's actually bringing about benefit—"it is the duty of a good man to teach to others that good which, because of the maliciousness of the times and of fortune, you have not been able to accomplish [yourself] . . ."

Niccolò the moralist writes of himself as a good man, urges others toward right conduct, and recognizes it as his duty to teach good. His language blossoms with the flowers of ancient moral philosophy: virtue, nature and the nature of man, choice, necessity, mind and soul, to name several.

Himself good, others are not necessarily the same. It is not difficult to discover his views of mankind. The problem is to select and order them in some conventional fashion. They are too numerous for all to be presented. Many seem to be similar, but given his talent for expression, they do not always express a similar value. That same talent, furthermore, enables him to make moral judgments so subtly that one can hardly be sure to have located them all or appreciated their significance. This chapter gathers his more general judgments and begins to sketch the moral background to that portrait, introduced in the previous chapter, of God most high, taking first Niccolò's views of man's place in the order of things and of what makes him different from other sentient beings and proceeding then to what constitutes the nature of this particular being and his society.

FALLEN MAN

. . . and man is created only for the good and honor of God, who gave him speech that he could praise Him, gave him his face turned not to the earth like the other animals but to the sky that he could constantly see him, gave him hands that he could build temples, make sacrifices in his honor, gave him reason and intellect that he could speculate and know the greatness of God . . .

Think therefore how all the things made and created are made and created for the benefit of man.

These passages are from the "Exhortation to Penitence." Similar themes appeared already in the previous chapter. Man was created by and for God, and the beautiful world was created by God for man's dominance and pleasure. The essence of man is his possession of the word, upright posture, religiously creative hands, and reason. These differentiate him from all other living things. Indeed, all the things made and created in the world—the immense space of the earth, the animals, the plants and grasses—bend providentially to the honor and good of man.

So much for man's place in the world and for his essence. What then is the nature of men-creatures? The broadest view is that they are "readier for evil than for good." In one form or another, that view appears in *The Prince*, the *Discourses*, and the *Florentine Histories*. In the religious phrasing of the "Exhortation," it runs thus: "Highest God knew how easy it was for man to slip into sin." Such statements have profound significance for Niccolò's moral and political philosophy. Obviously something has happened to man since his loving creation for the good and honor of God, as dominator of a beautiful world made for his benefit.

Let us go back to the creating of man and thence pick up the chronology—the fall of man, human nature, free will, the origins of society and the state. We may find therein some explanation of man's inclination toward evil.

. . .

In addition to the "Pastoral," Niccolò wrote four fairly short poems in terza rima, one apiece on ambition, ingratitude, fortune, and occasion, each a topic that he rarely lets out of sight. The most powerful of these verses is the one titled "On Ambition." God had just made the stars and sky, light, the elements, and man ('dominator of so many beautiful things') and just quelled the pride of the angels and chased Adam out of Paradise, who with "his woman" became a rebel "for the taste of an apple." Cain and Abel were living happy by their labor, in their poor dwelling with their father, when an occult power in the sky, "hardly a friend to human nature," sent two furies to live on earth in order "to deprive us of peace and put [us] in war, / to take from us every quietness and every good," and to loose the pest and poison of sins in the world. The quiet and *dolce vita*, of which "Adam's house" was full, fled along with peace and love. The poison penetrated Cain, arming him against his good brother. Thereafter evil grew and multiplied.

In the poem, "On Ingratitude," one finds a similar but abbreviated account, without the story of Adam and Eve. When the stars and heaven took a dislike to the glory of mortals, Ingratitude was born, the daughter of Greed and Suspicion, nursed in the arms of Envy. Ingratitude's poison ever after rests in the breast of princes and kings and taints with perfidy the heart of all people. *The Ass*, too, reports the change in man and in his condition upon the appearance of evil in the world. Ambition and greed cancel the goodness in hands and speech. No other animal has a more fragile life or a greater desire for that life or a more confused fear or greater anger. The "Exhortation" narrates a breaking away from the purposes for which God created man: "that tongue made to honor God curses Him; the mouth through which one is to take nourishment he makes into a sewer and a way to satisfy the appetite and stomach with delicate and superfluous food; those thoughts of God he converts into thoughts of the world; that appetite to preserve the human species becomes luxury and much other wantonness." Toppled from his blessed state, man, it appears, is a different creature.

At times, to read Niccolò, it would seem that lapsed men and the world they inhabit are unchanged and unchanging. None of nature's parts, including mankind, has changed "in motion, order, and power from what they were anciently." At other times we read that things are in flux: "generally and particularly, times and things often change." On one hand Parmenides, on the other Anaximander. What our author does not straighten out is that the unchanging nature men exhibit is one of variability within wide limits. Within these not fully specified but historically exemplified limits are appetites, humors, the intellect, and other variables.

The view may be briefly presented thus. In the beginning God created the world and man, and men are part of nature. Niccolò in listing nature's parts includes the sky, the sun, the elements, men. Second, man's original nature changed, and since then men's nature remains fixed: "in all cities and in all people there are those same desires and those same humors, and . . . they are there as they always were." Third, within men's unchanging nature there are those appetites, humors, reason, imagination, and dispositions he speaks of, but distributed among men unevenly. "I believe that as nature made men diverse faces, so did she make them diverse intellects and diverse imaginations." Fourth, in addition to a common nature, men have particular natures. Men are not able "to command their nature." Each one's behavior differs from the others'; that is, there is variation within the species because of the unequal distribution. *The Prince* maintains that "one cannot deviate from that to which nature inclines you," and "one sees that men, in the things that lead them to an end, which each has before [him], that is, glory and riches, proceed there differently: the one with caution, the other with dash; the one through violence, the other through skill; the one with patience, the other with its contrary." And fifth, within individuals, behavior varies at different times, inasmuch as the promptings of nature, in appetites, humors, and so on, do change and can be fulfilled in more ways than one. They have "other appetites, other pleasures, other considerations in age than in youth." The *Discourses* further argues that "human appetites [are] insatiable, as having from nature the power and wish to desire everything . . ."

Whenever one's particular nature and its distribution of appetites is not involved in a particular circumstance, the range of flexibility increases: one can then be "disposed to turn as the winds and variations of fortune command." In case four above, you are lucky if the times call for impetuous action and you happen to have an impetuous nature. If, though, you happen to have a cautious nature, you go to your ruin. Case five permits you a wider range of response in certain areas: you can swim with either current. If bad luck puts you in yet another current, one you cannot negotiate, a cross-current, then, however, you still go under. Niccolò points out these difficulties in Chapter xxv of *The Prince*, as he does in the draft of a letter of speculations to his friend, G. B. Soderini, which concludes that "that [man] is happy who matches his way of proceeding with the times, and that [other], on the contrary, is unhappy who by his actions turns himself against the times and the order of things."

So far, there seems to be no moral perspective. Even the insatiable appetites would only make for movement or change; in itself, this change would be neither good nor bad.

MORALITY AND CHOICE

Another passage from the *Discourses* approaches the question of morality more generally: "Men act either out of necessity or out of choice." Without pausing for nuances in such an assertion, we may simply recall that it fits the position of both Aristotle and Augustine that only with choice can an act be moral. It also fits the moral assumptions of the Justinian Code, as Niccolò's superiors in the Florentine government once pointed out to one of their ambassadors while reminding him that "every sin is sin inasmuch as it is voluntary."

If men have freedom of choice or free will, they may enlarge the possibilities in their nature by exercising it. Twice toward the end of *The Prince*, Niccolò raises the question of free choice. In Chapter xxv he submits that "our free choice has not ceased to be," and in Chapter xxvi he affirms that God does not want "to take away our free choice." So when he versifies about the evil seeds of the Fall or declares that men are readier for evil than for good, a moral potential remains. A disposition to evil may be inborn; it is a disposition, a tendency, a proneness, never fully fixed or determined. Because Niccolò acknowledges choice and free will and uses the words *good* and *evil*, the acts that these terms encompass are at least in part humanly willed and subject to moral judgment. It may be difficult for men to resist their wicked tendencies and easy for them to flow into sin; doctrinally, at least, they still have the choice of resistance, of control, of good acts.

However man fell from his original state, he landed on a new plateau as a different man, a rather malevolent creature with free will and with a human nature now always composed of the same formula—a volatile paste.

The poem, "On Ambition," takes the biblical account of the Fall up to the murder of Abel by Cain, "the first violent death in the world and the first bloodied grass!" The temporal sequence resumes in the *Discourses* where, to narrate the world as we know it and the way men came together, Niccolò turns to non-biblical accounts of the beginning of the world, when men lived "dispersed in the likeness of beasts." He doubts that the world is eternal, as some philosophers (possibly those stemming from the Arab, Averroës) would have it, and believes false that it goes back 40,000 or 50,000 years, as the histories of Diodorus Siculus would have it. Instead, he takes from Polybius's *Histories* the dateless tale not of the origins of the world but of society.

Niccolò's rendering of this account runs thus: Before men built their cities, they lived "dispersed in many and small parts" and could not live securely against those who preyed on them. In defense they drew together (moved collectively to action or else moved by someone among them of greater authority) and chose a place that was more convenient to live in and easier to defend. Defensive impulses thus brought men to their first banding together. Niccolò does not explain how the attacking "enemy" itself came to be banded together or in what the "greater authority" of leaders consisted.

This account appears in the very first chapter of the *Discourses*. The second chapter narrates another account of human origins, starting from "the beginning of the world, the inhabitants being few." As population increased, they drew themselves together and "to defend themselves better, they began to look among themselves for [the one] who was the most robust and of stoutest heart, and they made him like a chief and obeyed him." Once again the problem of defense is key, and it now seems that authority was granted for strength and courage.

In both these versions men banded together not because they have speech and reason, hands and upright posture. A life together was not due to their essence. Others, not wolves, but of their own species, preyed on them, and they defended themselves by association. Both accounts derive from Polybius. In the first, Niccolò's topic is the origin of cities; in the second, how to explain variations in government. Polybius put much care into his narrative. The same cannot be said of our author's abridgement and revision. As a writer on the state he may have felt he needed an account of the beginnings of the world of men with which to start the *Discourses*, and the account being passed around at the time in intellectual circles such as the Orti Oricellari, which Niccolò frequented, was that of Polybius.

The discourse turns to the development of morality and justice. "From this [obeying of a chief] was born the knowledge of honest and good things, different from the pernicious and criminal: because, on seeing that if one harmed one's benefactor hatred arose from it and sympathy, [too,] among men [arose for the injured party] . . . , and on blaming the ingrates and honoring those who were grateful, and on thinking further that the same injuries could be done to them, [these early men] . . . undertook to make laws, [and] to order punishments against those who transgressed: wherefrom came the knowledge of justice."

From the making and obeying of a chief, it would seem, came awareness of good and evil. From men's gratitude and ingratitude in relations with him and with each other, and from a disposition to put themselves in another's place, came laws and punishments and the understanding of justice. Polybius wrote of ingratitude too, but within the family; and of a benefactor also, but not of a particularly political one. Niccolò narrows the field, making the understanding of good and evil and of justice the result of political experience. And unlike Polybius, who wrote of justice issuing from a sense of duty, our author speaks of it in almost procedural terms—laws and sanctions.

To continue with the story, as a result of their awareness of justice, when choosing a ruler, men no longer backed the most energetic but "the most prudent and most just." Once this first, rudimentary republic changed, once a prince rose to rule by succession instead of by election, good government began to fall to pieces as his heirs began immediately to degenerate. Over time a series of different forms of government emerged, sowing and harvesting a crop of vices that include greed, ambition, and the stealing of women.

By attaching these beginnings of the world and the men in it to Eden and the Creation, one might conclude that, in suffering the Fall, man became brutish. The Polybius-Machiavelli accounts depict men as living in pre-political brutishness. Preyed upon and resisting and preying in turn, choosing a leader, praising and condemning the grateful and ungrateful, stirred by sympathy, men dimly made out morality and justice

[78]

and their value, only to succumb to a series of vices that Niccolò's earlier verses identified as evil disseminated at the Fall, and his *Florentine Histories, The Prince*, and the *Discourses* identify as the evil-readiness of men's nature.

SOURCES OF MORAL CODES

The sources of Niccolò's span of vices are not always the same, and they merit some attention. They seem related to Christian religion or, better, to particular elements within it. Familiar with Matthew, our moralist does not rely on the Sermon on the Mount. Familiar with Exodus, he does not list the Ten Commandments. He waters at other oases. True, when he speaks in the "Exhortation" of "all the evils, all the errors of men," he does link them to the first two commandments: "Though they are many and are committed in many ways, nonetheless they can be divided in two parts: the one to be ungrateful to God, the other to be enemy to one's neighbor." This critical juxtaposition of God and neighbor is based on Matthew 22:37–39 and on Mark 12:30–31 as well, where (in the Douay translation) Jesus says, " 'You shall love the lord your God with your whole heart, and with your whole soul, and with all your mind.' This is the greatest first commandment. The second is like it: 'You shall love your neighbor as yourself '." But when Niccolò comes to detail component evils and errors, he draws on other sources.

In his tercets, "On Ambition," as our moralist laments of avarice (or greed) and the Furies, who filled the world with envy, accidie (or sloth), hate, pride, cruelty, and deceit, his mind hovers over the familiar seven deadly sins—of which Thomas Aquinas made capital and which Dante incorporates in the *Inferno*—pride, envy, sloth, avarice, anger, lust, and gluttony. If we may equate ambition with covetousness or avarice (as Niccolò himself often does) and exchange hate for anger, there are only two substitutes in the list. Lust and gluttony give way to two politically more important entities—cruelty and deceit.

Still other negative moral terms appear. In the *Discourses* our author adds "suspicious" to "ambitious" as adjectives of "the nature of men." He mentions "suspicion" in other contexts of vice. For example, in the poetry of "On Ingratitude," Ingratitude "was the daughter of Avarice and Suspicion," and in the prose of the *Discourses*, "this vice of ingratitude is born out of avarice or suspicion." Again in the *Discourses*, speaking of the tyrant of Perugia, who was unable to be all evil, Niccolò judges him in terms that never convey other than a condemnation—guilty of "incest and a notorious parricide." In *The Ass*, the pig, advocate of the animal world, puts lust in "that life of yours you [men] esteem so highly," using the word as a deadly sin (*lussuria, luxuria*). In that life, venomous ambition and greed also run their course.

Our moralist is not presenting a view over all of ethics. He brings to the fore only those morals that engage the immediate context. Even so, the shapes of evil are so many and metamorphic, as saints Simon and Anthony testify, that one cannot hope to exhaust the negative ethical positions he reveals or implies. Three of them, however, are more important: ambition, ingratitude, and cruelty. Each shows up with notable frequency and intensity in Niccolò's varied genres and his groupings of sins, faults, and bad qualities. Each, too, appears not simply in contexts of blame but undergoes special analysis in poetry and prose.

ON AMBITION AND INGRATITUDE

"Men Leap from One Ambition to Another," a chapter title in the *Discourses* begins. Ambition associated with greed is closely related to lusting after and jockeying for personal power. Every man hopes "to climb up, oppressing now this one, now that." Ambition "is so powerful in human breasts that no matter to what rank they rise it never deserts them. Even the "noblest writers [of the history of Florence] . . . fooled themselves and showed that they knew little of the ambition of men . . . ," the *Florentine Histories* states. As a 'natural instinct' associated with greed, "Ambition ruling everywhere" infects the human mind. From the time of Cain, the violence of ambition cuts into the arteries of states and spurts out in civil bloodshed and war. "From ambition come those wounds / that the dead regions of Italy bear."

Ambition as a separate immoral entity shows up in the sonnet just quoted that bears its name. Ingratitude, too, shows up separately in a sonnet of its own. As our poet often joins ambition to avarice, he couples ingratitude with envy, and places it even deeper than ambition into political settings. These tercets, wherein the poet borrows directly from Roman writers or indirectly from Savonarola who also preached against ingratitude and envy, give an orderly description of the vice. They single out, as its worst example, the acts of "the man [who] never remembers / nor rewards the benefit but . . . / tears and bites his benefactor." Though ingratitude "lives in the breasts of princes and kings," it is greater in republics, where the people rule, for ingratitude "delights the more in the heart of people when [the people] is lord." Scipio Africanus is our poet's central figure, Scipio so saddened and embittered by "this common vice / aimed against him" that he voluntarily left "the ungrateful hospice." He took no revenge but "just did not wish" to be buried in Rome, "to leave to his country those bones / that she did not deserve to have," thus closing "the circle of his life . . . / outside of his fatherland nest."

In the beginnings of civil life narrated in the *Discourses*, the ungrateful were already there. Niccolò spends three chapters in that work on "this vice of ingratitude." Their titles are, "For what reason the Romans were less ungrateful than the Athenians to their citizens," "Which is more ungrateful, a people or a prince," and "What methods a prince or a republic should use to escape this vice of ingratitude; and what [methods] a captain or citizen [should use] in order not to be oppressed by it." Continuing to link it to greed, and now also to suspicion, Niccolò reverses the opinion of his poems that it is greater in a ruling people than in a prince, "for peoples never used [ingratitude] out of greed, and [they used it] out of suspicion much less than princes, having less reason to be suspicious . . ." Rome, which proved less ungrateful than Athens, nevertheless had the one bad example of Scipio. In these pages our author explains that the actions of Cato the Censor and the magistrates against their great general were due to fear of the authority extraordinary triumphs would confer on one man and that their suspicion of him might be excused because it was justifiable fear for the republic. They were afraid of hero worship.

The *Florentine Histories* reports plentiful instances of political ingratitude. Taking the decade 1378–1387, a time of popular unrest and uprisings and counteractions, we find Giorgio Scali, about to be beheaded: "in front of that people who shortly before had adored him," a multitude in which there was "no faith or gratitude whatever"; Michele di Lando, exiled: "for his good works his country [was] not at all grateful"; Benedetto Alberti, exiled, died at Rodi: "his bones were brought to Florence and buried with greatest honor by those who, when he was alive, persecuted him with every calumny and injury." This handful of pages indicates also how the ethics and related maxims, traced mainly in Niccolò's earlier writings, spread throughout his last great work.

Alongside ingratitude, the evil of envy plays its part in these strife-filled years. Gaining the city of Arezzo was at least one happy event for the Florentines and it set off many celebrations. The splendor and magnificence of those of the Alberti family went too far, outshining all others. "Worthy of any prince," they aroused against that family "much envy," which later for Benedetto Alberti became the "cause of his downfall." The evil of ambition has its role, too. In "the division [between the people and the plebs] already started . . . by the ambition of the Ricci and the Albizzi . . . at various times afterward the gravest consequences followed." While remarking the occurrence of these sins, Niccolò does not hide his indignation at the men who commit them. For instance, in the new government there were two men, called Tria and Baroccio "of so vile and disgraceful a state that they made men's desire grow to free themselves of so much shame." Our moralist also exemplifies the lessons of *The Prince*, drawing them from the mouths of historical actors like Benedetto on the eve of his banishment, bidding sad farewell to his assembled relatives: "I do not wonder, nor should you wonder at this, for it always happens like this to those who, among many bad [men], wish to be good."

In *The Prince* a compact ethical description of men begins thus: "For men one can generally say this . . ." The first sorry trait is "that they are ungrateful"; then follow the others: that they are "inconstant, simulators and dissimulators, fugitives from danger, greedy of gains." Worst of all, the "Exhortation" laments, man is ungrateful to God. Ingratitude is more than a fault: it is a sin, for man's greatest sin is 'ingratitude against God.' The offense of "ingratitude against God is the greatest." It leads inevitably to man's second great sin, enmity to his neighbor. "Those who are ungrateful to God, it is impossible that they not be enemies to [their] neighbor." The *Art of War* puts it as a question. "How can those who scorn God respect men?"

The passion in these outbursts against ingratitude, envy, and ambition, suggests autobiography. Our political philosopher may identify in these sins of mankind the causes of the fall of republican government in Florence, of his own downfall, and then of people's avoiding him who once sought him out. It was men's envy that toppled the Gonfalonier Soderini, Niccolò's supporter and chief executive of the republican government, and toppled Savonarola before him. "The one as much as the other of these two were ruined, and their ruin was caused by not knowing how nor being able to conquer this envy." Men's envy threatened Moses, sent Savonarola to the scaffold, and Soderini to his ruin. Moses was "forced . . . to kill infinite [numbers of] men who [were] moved by nothing other than envy," Savonarola's "sermons are full of accusations against the sages of the world . . . for thus he called these invidious [ones]." Soderini thought that with time, with goodness, with luck, with favors, and without scandal, violence, and tumult (the Ex-Secretarius Florentinus records in the *Discourses*), he could "extinguish this envy."

At the opening of the tercets on ingratitude, our poet writes that he seeks by singing "to draw from my heart / and block that pain of adverse happenings / that runs behind my furious soul"; the subject of his verse will now be how years of service may be lost, "as if one sows seeds in sand and water." In truth, who else but the Florentine Secretary has spent fifteen years during which he "neither slept nor played"? Who else has been 'loyal and good for forty-three years'? And who afterward, like the Roma Scipio, gets from the hands of compatriots his reward—"prison, exile, slander, and death," not to speak of torture? The closing lines of this poem are as bitter and anti-political as those to be found in *The Ass.*

> So it happens that often one toils in serving,
> and then for his good service brings back
> miserable life and violent death.
> Therefore, Ingratitude not being dead,
> everyone must flee the courts and states:
> for there is no shorter road to lead man
> to weep over what he wished for, once he got it.

Niccolò did more than his share of weeping 'without finding a man who remembers my service.' His heroine in *The Ass* confirms as much: "Among modern people and among the ancient, / she began, no one ever bore / more ingratitude or greater toil."

ON CRUELTY

There seems to be no autobiographical tinge, however, to Niccolò's discussion of the third vice, cruelty. If he sees himself at all in Scipio, he also realizes that the general was not cruel but, if anything, too kind. There are no apparent signs of cruelty in Niccolò's letters. Unfortunately, we know little of his dealings with subordinates; almost all his extant correspondence is with equals or superiors. At any rate, no contemporaries of whatever rank report him to be cruel or mean. The last letter to his son Guido suggests personal gentleness, and this not even to men but to a little mule gone crazy. It should not be tied up the way people tie up the crazy, writes Niccolò the father. "I want you to let it loose . . . take off the bridle and halter and let it go where it wants to in order to feed itself and get rid of its craziness. The country is wide, the animal is small, it cannot do any harm."

Guido, like his uncle Totto, took on an ecclesiastical career, and tried his hand at letters and translation. Ludovico, another son, was of violent temper. More than once his father had to help bail him out of difficulties with the authorities for brawling. Bernardo was more tractable. His father, about to assume a new post late in life, as chancellor of an ad hoc commission to shore up the walled defenses of Florence, writes about it to his friend, Guicciardini, adding, "I am having one of my sons help me."

The closest thing to personal combat Niccolò ever threatens is not physical but verbal contest, as in the prologue to *Mandragola*. "Yet if someone thinks, by speaking badly [of the author], to catch him by the hair . . . I warn him and say to this fellow that [the author] too knows how to bad-mouth [others]." But he does not really care about the contest. "But let us let him go ahead to speak ill of whomever he wants to."

Cruelty, unlike ingratitude, does not appear in Niccolò's broad generalizations upon men's nature. Unlike ingratitude—and ambition, greed, suspicion, and deceitfulness, which seem to be staples of human nature—cruelty appears to be derivative, an infection from an open wound like envy, yet so common that it distinguishes the species. So observes the pig savant in *The Ass*: "Only man kills, crucifies, and despoils another man."

People as spectators or in mobs sometimes appear to have an atavistic impulse to share in blood-letting or to be mesmerized by cruelty, as by the serpent's gaze. When Caesar Borgia had his president of Romagna, Ramiro de Lorqua, "a man cruel and prompt," killed, he had him placed one morning "in the square at Cesena in two pieces, with a piece of wood and bloody knife alongside." Our reporter's language here is arcane. Why a piece of wood? If it was a block of wood or a butcher's block, why not say so? What does 'in two pieces' signify? If beheaded or split in two or quartered, why not use those words? Was the body cut across at the waist? Although Niccolò does not say *cut* in two pieces, the presence of the knife suggests that it was cut. With what kind of knife? How does one cut a body in two with a knife? Why not an axe or cleaver or saw? Perhaps some unknown symbolism of the Spanish Borgias lodges in this description. Perhaps the staging represents a re-enactment of Ramiro's own style of cruelty, a tit-for-tat. In a later chapter when we return to this scene under a different light, some of these questions will reappear.

The report in *The Prince* is powerful, but strange. It leaves no doubt though, of the effect on spectators. "The ferocity of such a spectacle left those people satisfied and stupefied at the same time." The power to purge hatred belongs to our author's theory of the spectacle. Caesar Borgia, he claims, wished "to purge their minds" of hate, an echo of the Aristotelean theory of tragedy.

Another scene, this from the *Florentine Histories*: a mob has gathered in the square demanding of the tyrant besieged in the Palazzo that two officials and the not yet eighteen-year-old son of one of them be turned over to summary justice. The son's youth and innocence did not save him from the fury of the multitude: "those that they could not wound alive, they wounded dead; not satiated with tearing them with steel, they lacerated them with their hands and teeth. And so that in the vendetta they might satisfy all the senses, having heard first their cries, seen their wounds, touched their torn flesh, they wanted still to savor the taste, so that when all the outside parts [of their senses] were satiated with it, those of the inside they satiated too." The furor saved the remaining offical: "for the multitude fatigued in the cruelty against these two, forgot the other one."

There are some kinds of people specifically addicted to cruelty. Tyrants as a class are cruel. The *Florentine Histories* bears witness to, among others, the duke of Athens, the besieged tyrant above, and the duke of Milan, the one who, cut down by conspirators, cried out to Our Lady for help. Soldiers, too, as a class, may be cruel. The cruelty of their soldiers gave the Roman emperors problems. The troops wanted their emperors to be insolent, cruel, and rapacious, notes *The Prince*, so that they could "give vent to their [own] greed and cruelty." The "most cruel and rapacious" emperors were Commodus, Severus, Antoninus, Caracalla, and Maximus. Only Severus, "a new prince," was able to keep from being killed. The others were sooner or later dispatched because of their "many cruelties," "cruel and bestial spirit," or "ferocity and cruelty so great and so unheard of."

In his remarks about imperial troops, Roman emperors, and tyrants, cruelty is despicable. Niccolò does not often give examples of particular acts that are cruel in themselves. Cruelty to large numbers of men, however, wrings from him the superlative, cruelest. In *The Prince* he states that there can be "no more miserable or rare example" than Ferdinand of Aragon's "pious cruelty" in ridding Spain of the Muhammadans. The instance of Philip of Macedon in the *Discourses* is also instructive. History discloses that he shifted men bodily from region to region as herdsmen shift their herds. Our author considers this a horror. "These methods are the cruelest and the enemies of every way of life, not only the Christian but the human; and any man ought to flee them, and to wish rather to live as a private person than as king with so great a destruction of men." Niccolò here acknowledges a moral law that goes beyond the community of the faithful, a norm common to humans everywhere.

So great a destruction occurs also when entire peoples and their families move from one place, forced either by hunger or by war, and go in search of a new location, not to rule it but to settle in it and drive out or kill its inhabitants. When a prince or republic assaults a region, "it is enough to kill [in opposing forces] only those who command"; but when these populations assault they "must kill everyone, because they want to live on that which the others were living on." A war involving a migrating or invading population "is cruelest and most terrifying." Great human destruction also may be wreaked without shifting populations. The cruelty of Antoninus Caligula involved large numbers of men: "his ferocity and cruelty was so great and so unheard of for having, after infinite particular killings, killed a great part of the people of Rome and all of that of Alexandria . . ."

Chapter VIII of *The Prince* narrates two instances of "infinite treacheries and cruelties." The chapter, as its title indicates, focuses "On Those Who Reach the Princedom by Crimes," namely, in a manner "criminal and nefarious"—strong and rare words that suggest the utmost villainy, especially *nefarious*, which connotes acts that are impious or contrary to human or divine laws. One instance involves Oliverotto da Fermo, who in the classical manner of Xenophon's *Anabasis*, murdered his whole company of guests in a banquet ambush, the principal target having been his uncle, who had reared him. Disingenuously, our reporter ends the paragraph on another banquet scene thus: "one year after the parricide [was] committed, he [Oliverotto] along with Vitellozzo, whom he had had as maestro of his virtues and crimes, was strangled"—on orders of Caesar Borgia.

Teacher and pupil gasping out their life together. Surely Aristotle in the *Politics* showed no such moral nicety or requital in his giving of rules for tyrants.

Agathocles, the other and prime example of the chapter, was a man of "savage cruelty and inhumanity." His crimes exacted death not simply from large numbers—namely from all the senators and all the rich— what hangs a millstone from his neck was his putting his "own citizens" to death. Agathocles transformed Syracuse from a republic with citizens into a monarchy with subjects. Though he credits Agathocles with courage and determination, Niccolò charges him on five counts. "Still one cannot call it virtue to kill one's citizens, betray friends, be without faith, without compassion, without religion." The language of these five vices—so they may be called, for our moralist gives no indication here that they are anything but vicious—intimates what he will make clearer in the *Discourses* with regard to Philip of Macedon, that the norms that tyrants break are natural, human, and divine. Such may be the way of evil, as opposed to the "way of good" that some men take to form not a kingdom or a republic but "an absolute power which by the authors [of politics and history] is called tyranny."

❧

T H I S chapter made inquisition into the ethics of Niccolò Machiavegli, moralist, to see whether they are consonant with his just and merciful high God. It traced in diverse texts some important constituents of his political philosophy—fairly conventional, paganizing, Christian ideas of the essence of man, his creation and fall, his human nature once fallen, his coming together with other men and their banding into political organization. At some point, presumably after the Fall, although no precise moment is mentioned, God lets men have free will or choice. The freedom to act for good or evil makes their actions liable to moral judgment, and our author does not refrain from judging them. Ingratitude, ambition, envy, greed, cruelty, mass dislocations and killings, tyranny, parricide, impiety and betrayal, and incest he recognizes for what they are: full-blown evil. And the answer to our inquiry would seem to be, yes: God, too, would recognize in these the way of evil.

Niccolò cannot be found to speak irreverently of God. The same cannot be said for his writings about the church and churchmen. Though divinity and morality are typically established in a church, church and religion are not the same. Niccolò has a church practice of his own and a religious doctrine branching out in many, perhaps unexpected, directions.

CLERGY AND COUNTRY

Ah monks! To know one is
to know them all.
                    —*Mandragola*

BORN ON 3 May 1469, Niccolò is baptized the next day in the baptis-
tery of San Giovanni; dead on 21 June 1527, he is buried the next day
in Santa Croce.

His children are duly baptized; we can assume that he and his family
receive the sacraments at the hands of the clergy at least at birth, marriage, and death. His last will, 27 November 1522, chooses "as tomb of
the body, the sepulcher of the ancestors" in the Franciscan church of
Santa Croce and, as the custom goes, makes a bequest to the cathedral
of two pounds and of "one pound toward the building of the [city]
walls"—neither miserly nor overly generous contributions to the spiritual and temporal provinces.

Niccolò is not in the habit of going to mass, a masculine lapse hardly
worthy of note. Vettori, in a letter describing daily life in Rome, claims
that he himself is "religious, as you know," and twits his friend: "On
feast days I hear mass, and do not do as you, who sometimes lets it go."

A little more than this can be learned about Niccolò's church practice.
A letter from a relative sent to him in Rome reports, "you have had a
fine and lively son [Bernardo], who today was baptized with honors, as
your station requires." His station was then that of Florentine Secretary.
Most of the rest of the letter talks about church livings possibly available
to Niccolò's younger brother, the priest Totto. Given the Secretary's
cultural setting, it would have seemed at least eccentric, and more certainly scandalous, were not all such rites to take place according to
schedule. A career of government and foreign service, hedged as it is
with religious ceremonies, would require that one be a communicant.
By breaking with the religious rigor of Savonarola, Florence did not
break with instituted Christianity and its rites; actually, it had rid the
Pope of an infuriating, excommunicated adversary, and brought itself

closer to establishment ritual. Had Vettori given a ducat for each time his friend's station required him to participate in a religious ceremony, Niccolò would have been able to bequeath a few more pounds to Santa Croce.

. . .

In *The Prince* and *Discourses*, Niccolò discusses certain aspects of religion at length and quite systematically. His writings allude to Greco-Roman and Muhammadan as well as to Judeo-Christian history and sources. Let us be clear which religion our political philosopher cleaves to. For Niccolò, all religions great and small are false; the exception is Christianity. He sometimes refers to it as "our religion," or the religion that shows us "the truth and the true way," echoing the gospel of John's "the way, and the truth."

Conceived as a faith, Christianity is the true faith. Conceived as a church, Christianity is an instituted religion, the Roman church, "head of our religion," professing to embody the precepts of God and Christ. Conceived comparatively, religions or sects are different ways of worshipping the same one highest God and, as such, worthy of respect. (Niccolò's views here recall those of the fifteenth-century theologian and philosopher, Nicholas of Cusa.) In any church, the faith professed and ritually enacted by its religious leaders or clergy may or may not coincide with that of the founder of its religion. Moreover, various aspects of the beliefs and observances of false religions may be similar to Christianity, the true faith.

The Prince and *Discourses* criticize the church for its corrupting of Italians and its foreign policy. Owing to the "criminal examples" of the Roman Curia, Italy "has lost all devotion and religion. . . . So we have with the Church and the priests, we Italians, this first debt: to have become irreligious and mean." Fierce irony. Those people who are "closer to the Roman church, head of our religion, have less religion." If you want to see the truth about this right away, Niccolò satirizes, take the Roman court and "send [it] to live in the lands of the Swiss." You would see "that in a short time the criminal habits of that court would make more disorder in that country than could possibly arise from any other event at any time whatever."

The church has played a dog-in-the-manger role in Italy. "So that all the wars made by the barbarians in Italy after these times [the eighth century], were for the most part caused by the pontiffs, and all the barbarians that inundated [Italy] were most of the time called in by them." Itself the possessor of states and temporal power, but not strong or virtuous enough by itself to unite Italy, the church has prevented other Italian states from bringing the land to obedience under one republic or prince, as transpired in France and Spain, it not having been "able to occupy the whole of Italy, nor having allowed anyone else to occupy it."

Below the popes fall the prelates and, according to Niccolò's diagnosis in *The Prince*, Italy's prelates have been as harmful as its princes. Thus the powerful Orsini and Colonna barons of Rome "will never be at rest as long as they have cardinals, for [these two clans] nourish factions, both in Rome and outside it . . . so from the ambitions of the prelates, the discords and conflicts between the barons are born." The *Discourses* charges prelates and "the heads of religion" not just with dishonesty but with disbelief in the judgment of God: "and so they do the worst they can, because they do not fear that punishment [of God's] that they do not see and do not believe in."

Anticlericalism is nothing to write home about, nor has it been for the last one thousand years. Wherever there existed a hierarchical, privileged clergy, a current of scorn and hatred could be felt running through numbers of students, scholars, physicians, lawyers, the commercial classes, and the aristocracy. Recall Boccaccio's tale upon tale of women, money, deception, and priests. The epigraph for the present chapter incorporates a saying popular in many lands. Henry VIII knows it as: "Monks! Know one and you know them all." Nor is criticism of the church's foreign policy anything new. Dante and, after him, the scholarly Marsilius of Padua had blamed the papacy for Italy's civil wars and foreign invasions.

No one is about to brand Niccolò a heretic. His position in the community is firm. No record shows that any relative or friend was ever cut off from the church. Cardinals are still his friends and are going to write him letters of recommendation or stand as godfather to a son; popes are still going to give him jobs, ask that his plays be performed, commission his writings, or listen to his views on military affairs. In writing to his son, Guido, a few months before his death, Niccolò boasts a bit to convince the boy of the importance of study: "besides the great friendships I have, I have made a new friendship with Cardinal Cibo [papal legate to Bologna], and so great that I myself marvel at it, which will redound to your benefit, but you must learn . . ." In the last decade of his life, our author will find more support for his ideas and works in popes and cardinals than in Florentine public officials.

Niccolò is not a priest-hater. Strictly speaking, his position is not anticlerical: it is better described as reform clerical. It is not indiscriminate. He admires some popes for certain things, and some clerics, notably St. Francis and St. Dominic, whom he credits with rejuvenating and main-

*. . . Niccolò will find more support for his ideas and works
in popes and cardinals
than in Florentine public officials.*

taining Christianity against the worst efforts of prelates. In his comedies, he pokes fun at clergy and laity both—at the everyday invocation
of the deities and saints, at popular belief in the frequency and pettiness
of divine intervention, at clerical cupidity, concupiscence, and insistence
on cult observance without care for true faith or belief. Listen to Friar
Timothy in a monologue from the *Mandragola*, act 5, scene 1:

> And I waited to pass the time in various things: I said matins, I read a life of
> the Holy Fathers, I went in church and lit a lamp that was spent, I changed
> the veil of a Madonna that performs miracles. How often I have told these
> brothers that they must keep her clean! And then one wonders that devotion
> is lacking. I remember when . . . Nowadays no one does these things, and
> then we wonder that things get cooled off. Oh, what tiny brains these broth-
> ers of mine have!

As Niccolò discriminates good and bad priests and prelates, so he
distinguishes bad ceremonial practice from good theory. In *The Ass*, he
puts the subject abstractly.

> Indeed necessary are prayers
> and full crazy is he who forbids the people
> ceremonies and their devotions
> because from them in truth it seems that one harvests
> unity and good order, and on that
> then depends fortune good and happy.

In some other ways, Niccolò seems a religious conservative. Unlike
Marsilius of Padua, he does not bother to deny the papacy's divine connection. He does not disapprove of the church's temporal power; he
disapproves of the inept use of it. In Chapter XI of *The Prince*, "On
Ecclesiastical Principalities," he stresses the advantages a history of spir-
ituality confers on ecclesiastical states. Since he writes not of papal but
rather of ecclesiastical states, he may wish to include those of the Holy
Roman Empire (which he wrote of after two missions to the Emperor
Maximilian I in 1508 and 1509), those where the prince is a prelate. These
"spiritual princes" or "ecclesiastical princes," to use our envoy's language, "alone have states and do not defend them; subjects, and do not
rule them; and their states, though undefended, are not taken; and the
subjects though not ruled, do not care, neither do they think to nor can
they alienate themselves from them." (Later in *The Prince*, Niccolò also
admires the kingship of the Sultan, probably having in mind the cali-
phate, which "is similar to the Christian pontificate" where, though the
prince may be new, he is received when elected "as if he were" a hereditary lord and has "none of the difficulties" of a new princedom.) Setting

aside ecclesiastical states generally, our author switches to "the church in the temporal [sphere]." While he blames the church for a divisive foreign policy in Italy, he views with pride the temporal efforts of Pope Julius II and Pope Alexander VI and his son Caesar Borgia, who so armed the pontificate that "a King of France trembles at it." To such "greatness" has the church come in the temporal sphere. He is outraged whenever it does not show enough temporal force, decisiveness, and courage to unite parts of Italy in fighting off barbarians. In one of his infrequent personal appearances in the contemporary or fresh examples he gives in *The Prince*, Niccolò narrates that Louis XII's adviser told him at Nantes that the Italians did not understand war. Our Secretary retorted that "the French did not understand the state," otherwise they would not have let the church grow so powerful in the temporal sphere. The dispatch Niccolò slips into the courier's pouch on 21 November 1500, when the interview is first reported does not mention this tilting.

BLESSING OF WEAPONS

Approving of the church's use of temporal power if used expertly and for the benefit of the church and Italy, of censures "together with arms, mixed with indulgences," he approves also of the church's lending its spiritual power to the state's temporal power in a joining of forces. Often he blends the two in the arena of military power. We may wish to consider now this part of Niccolò's thought and work at a point where he first joins it with religion and ceremony, in "Purpose of the Military Forces." One of his earliest pieces, an example of those several small political writings he drafts during his secretaryship, this particular paper was written six or seven years before *The Prince*. In it Niccolò first proposes to secure "arms of one's own" and "to mix [with them] something of religion." In the single word *arms*, he conceptualizes military forces, their recruitment, organization, discipline, equipment, and payment.

From the beginning to the end of his career, the Florentine Secretary is immersed in military affairs. His customary short title is misleading: it fails to convey how many of his missions and reports in fourteen years of office are substantially military. He is Secretary of the Ten of Liberty and Peace, the panel of magistrates dealing with war and foreign affairs. He recruits and trains troops, conducts operations and negotiates treaty terms in the field, and advocates military ideas in written reports, letters, and in person wherever he can, to republicans, princes and prelates, all leading to the publication in 1521 of the *Art of War*, a timely success that gives him a greater reputation for military than for political writing and rivals his fame as a playwright. From spring 1526 to spring 1527, in the fight of the League of Cognac against the invading forces of the Holy

Roman Emperor, the Pope, the Florentine government, and the lieu-tenant-general of the pontifical army all use Niccolò with and for their military forces on various missions of advice, reporting, and evaluation. In this period, he undertakes also to inspect the fortifications of Flor-ence and to make recommendations for improved defense. His report accepted, he is appointed chancellor of a new commission, the "Five Administrators of the [City] Walls," his last official post.

Our author's first source for the association of military affairs with religion is a Roman historian whose volumes he pored over in the pa-ternal homestead ever since he first learned to read Latin and on whom he based the great work we call the *Discourses*, titled in full, *Discourses on the First Ten Books of Titus Livy*. That work relates arms to religion via oath-taking, sacrificial ceremonies, the kinds of persons to emulate, and in general, the education toward virtue of the citizen and soldier. After being cashiered, in the phenomenal period of great writing at his house in the country, Niccolò does some great reading as well, learning much more about these same subjects from another classic, Polybius's *Histo-ries*. He has material in more recent history, too. Florence utilized com-munal militia in the thirteenth century, and in the fifteenth century it armed its farmers in the face of invasion. A few years before Niccolò became Secretary, the Florentine republic sought to raise infantry in the countryside to meet the French invasion of 1494, and he hardly begins to work in the Palazzo when the republic again, on an ad hoc basis, has to raise countryside militia in defense of its territory.

Extending his knowledge through travels on various legations, Nic-colò learns in France of the franc-archers, sees in Forlí the "good, loyal infantry" of Caterina Sforza, hears on all sides reports of Swiss citizen-soldiers, and in Romagna knows at first hand of good, native infantry raised not by a republic but by a prince, popularly known as Valentino, namely, Caesar Borgia—in his youth a cardinal, in his prime the duke of Valentinois and of Romagna. On one legation to Caesar Borgia in 1502, the Secretary works alongside the then bishop, and future cardinal, Francesco Soderini (brother of the Gonfalonier Piero), whom he con-verts to his views of the militia and enlists as a stalwart in the struggle for Florentine military reform. Niccolò soon begins to write and speak openly about a militia, crystalizing his ideas in a proposal for its forma-tion. He quickly becomes identified as its most ardent advocate.

1506–1507

The Florentine Secretary, now thirty-seven years old and in full swing, composes the brief he had hoped for several years to write. The full title he put on it a half-dozen years later is "The Purpose of the Military

Forces, Where One May Find Them and What Must Be Done." It proposes statutes to govern the recruiting, equipping, payment, command, and discipline of native infantry and explains why such legislation is necessary. The brief is couched, as was probably requested of him, in the form of a letter or memorandum by a strong supporter who wants to pass it around among his colleagues to gain further support, and in the best of cases, to draw up from it a future statute. Niccolò's rhetorical strategy is to underplay the novelty and controversy inherent in the enterprise, for it aims at arming thousands of men within Florentine territory.

Florentine practice of the time is to hire its major military forces through condottieri, professional captains, leading their own troops. Niccolò's experience with such mercenaries is bad already. In the midst of the campaign to take back Pisa in 1499, the Florentines had to arrest their condottiere for treason and then to try, condemn, and decapitate him. With the events surrounding the case the Florentine Secretary had his hands full. Later, he himself is at the front where Gascon and Swiss mercenaries, sent to aid Florence by Louis XII, are in mutiny. Later still, he joins a legation to the French court to help explain to the king what happened.

It was the refusal of these mercenary troops to enter a breach in the Pisan walls that may have convinced Gonfalonier Soderini and others in the government to try out a scheme of levying countrymen. The Secretary is sent off to raise troops in the valley known as the Mugello. Although called back to Florence to depart with a legation to Pope Julius II at the end of summer, he keeps in touch with the recruiting and training of troops and the politics of choosing a commander. The trouble is, as he will diagnose in *The Prince*, that in Italy, with the growth in temporal power of the church and the rise of republics, there are priests and citizens but no soldiers: "those priests and those other citizens not used to knowing about arms began to hire foreigners."

The Gonfalonier, struggling with the patrician families who oppose the project and the choice of commander for it, utilizes "Niccolò mio" on his return in an effort to calm their fears. The unfortunate result is that some of them now consider the Secretary to be Soderini's puppet. They had already held Niccolò in mistrust and condescension for his nonaristocratic and republican background. Their hostility—he would call it their envy—will pursue Niccolò throughout his government career and beyond. And the nub of his proposal—the militia—will agitate his detractors for years to come. They had reason to fear. They were afraid of arming the people, afraid of a commander who might use those troops in internal Florentine politics, afraid of a Gonfalonier-for-life

In the end the bill ... passed ... a success for the Secretary ...

(for to such an office was Soderini elected) who might use commander
and troops to impose a tyranny on Florence.

In the end the bill is framed (Niccolò's hand in it is evident) and
passed on 6 December 1506—a success for the Secretary—and men from
the countryside are swiftly drafted and trained. That very same winter,
one can just visualize the scene in the square of the Palazzo, Niccolò's
first body of infantry, pikes, crossbowmen, and musketeers—with their
white doublets under resplendent breastplates, and their stockings divided lengthwise in white and red—line up, maneuver, and march to
sound of fife and drum.

To our immediate purpose is the way in which Niccolo's suggestion
about blending in religion to make recruits more obedient is carried out
in the actual statute. After a statement of purpose, the bill does it by
providing and ordaining "with the name of God omnipotent and of his
most glorious mother, madonna Saint Mary-Always-Virgin, and of the
glorious precursor of Christ, John the Baptist, advocate, protector and

patron of this Florentine republic." The new magistrature, the Nine of the Florentine Ordinance and Militia, whose seal is the image of St. John the Baptist, must in the presence of the city magistrates, having "first heard the mass of the Holy Spirit, from time to time accept and swear said office in the same manner as the [highest officials] accept and swear their office."

This much politico-religious ceremony is customary. As for the soldiers themselves, Niccolò carries out the intention of his memorandum to introduce religion as follows. The day after the soldiers have passed in review, the commissioner must hold

> a solemn mass of the Holy Spirit performed in a place where the assembled [troops] can hear; and after said mass, the deputy must address them with those words that are proper in similar ceremony; afterward [he must] read them what and how much has to be observed and give them solemn oath of it, making them one by one touch by hand the book of the sacred Gospels; and before such oath-taking, must read them all the capital punishments to which they are subject, and all those warnings that will be ordered by said officials in conserving and confirming their union and loyalty, adding weight to the oath by all those obigatory words of soul and body that are the most efficacious to be found; and this done, they are to be dismissed and to return to their homes.

From his memorandum, the draft of the bill, and the bill itself, and from pertinent correspondence, Niccolò reveals that even before he writes *The Prince* or the *Art of War*, he is convinced of the importance not simply of arms, but of arms of one's own, of something akin to a militia, and of religious oaths and other ceremony in securing its loyalty and obedience. In the *Art of War*, he throws the lesson back to history: "Very valuable, in keeping ancient soldiers [properly] disposed, was religion and the oath that one gave them when they were led to military service . . . which many times, combined with other religious forms, made every move easy for ancient captains, and would always do so, where religion is feared and observed." Having 'arms of one's own' integrated with religion is an objective our military theorist will never abandon.

. . .

From these texts there are some literary observations also to be made, two of which can be mentioned now. One concerns the genesis of Niccolò's style. In his memorandum, as well as in some other early political writings, the universal generalization appears. Niccolò reminds the reader that the communication had been requested and that he will respond, but adds that he is going to do so "a bit from on high." He shows immediately what this means by going beyond the Florentine case to include the whole world and all history: "everyone knows that whoever says empire, kingdom, principality, republic, whoever says men who command, beginning with the first rank and descending even to the master of a brigantine, says justice and arms."

Also in this writing, Niccolò's powerful stylistic device of the either-or choice appears. Discussing how to organize the troops so they cannot do harm, he writes that they "can do harm in two ways: either among themselves or against a city." Each of these two he then divides in two subcategories, from each of which he selects the more pertinent and divides that one further in two.

Both stylistic elements are refined in our author's later and greater works and penetrate his political analyses, as in his preference for a two-fold classification of governments (republics and principalities) over the classical Greek preference for a triad (monarchy, aristocracy, and polity, or others similar). Niccolò much prefers to divide by two than by three.

The second observation to make is biographical rather than stylistic. The Secretary's personal identification with the militia gives him some of the hardest work of his life—horseback-riding here and there, in the Florentine dominions, in the cold of winter on snow-covered mountain roads, setting up troop levies—and gives him his first taste of glory: credit for the performance of the troops before Pisa. A letter of congratulations from a colleague in the Chancery reports on the city's delirium on 8 June 1509. "Here it is not possible to express what happiness, what jubilation and joy, all this people has received at the news of the recovery of that city of Pisa. Every man in some way is wild with exultation; there are fireworks all over the city, even at 21 hours; think of what they will do this evening at nighttime." It ends with a postscript: "I swear by God, so great is the exultation that we have, that I would make you a Tullian [a eulogy worthy of Cicero] . . ."

The victory of native militia is heightened by contrast with the defeat of mercenary troops ten years before at the same Pisa. Later, Niccolò's advocacy of native troops will, in 1512, present him with a different spectacle—the sack of Prato by the Spaniards, let in by the ignominious flight of the militia, a disaster that renders the fall of the Soderini republic immediate. Little matter that the troops were few and poorly equipped, demoralized and badly officered through the neglect of the Gonfalonier's government. The ex-Secretary, in a letter to a noblewoman describing the events, writes of "the cowardice that was seen in our soldiers at Prato." but at that moment he does not wish to criticize the ex-Gonfalonier and thus appear to be turning against his former protector. Niccolò is not an ingrate. His mature judgment on the rout appears in the *Art of War*: wise men should not measure the utility of the militia from its having "lost once." Rather, as one loses, one can win and "remedy the reason for the loss." Little matter, too, that the succeeding regime will attempt a derivative plan for its own militia—except that while managing his farm in Sant'Andrea and restively awaiting the pleasure of the newly restored Medici regime, it may have encouraged Niccolò to make the subject a major theme of *The Prince*.

But before all that, while still Secretary, jaunty with alertness, enthusiasm, and the support of the Gonfalonier and his politically ambitious family, Niccolò openly criticizes government policy. "Of justice you do not have much," he writes in the "Purpose of the Military Forces," referring to Florentine rule over its dominions, "and of arms, nothing at all." He knows that this memorandum of his is to be read by friendly eyes. Later, in drafting the bill itself, which will be scrutinized by hostile eyes as well, he writes that "your republic is with good and saintly laws well instituted and organized for the administration of justice and that there is missing only the providing of oneself with arms."

. . .

Our writer of hundreds of letters, drafts, and dispatches can turn vinegar into honey when discretion calls for sweetness. Yet, quite clearly, he is going beyond his role of Secretary. Openly the partisan of the government, openly the trustee of the Gonfalonier, Niccolò is not wading in politics, he is in it up to his ears.

From this experience he may have derived a lesson in prudence. Among the last chapters of the *Discourses* there is one that seems to be inserted with little thought of those before and after. It carries the title, "What Risks Attend Making Oneself the Leader in Counseling a Thing, and the More It Has of the Extraordinary, the Greater the Risks One Runs."

The chapter itself is unusual. It follows our author's normal procedure of taking illustrations from history and arguing from men's nature and habits of reasoning: "All the bad that comes of [any advice] they impute to the author of the advice; and if it comes out well, he is commended for it. But by far the reward does not counterweigh the harm." Yet, untypically, it follows no discernible order in the *Discourses*, shows little or no dependence on texts from Livy (which our writer is supposed to be discoursing on), consists of an exotic substance—advice to an advisor—and, most unusual, describes the horns of the dilemma but does not seize them. "It is, then, most certain that those who advise a republic and those who advise a prince are put in these straits: that if they do not advise without prejudice the things that to them seem useful for the city or for the prince, they are lacking in the duty of their office; if they do advise them, they enter in danger of [their] life and of the state . . ."

One might expect that Niccolò, just as he would counsel any country caught between more powerful belligerents not to stay neutral, would—having thus posed the dilemma—urge the advisor to seize on one or the other horn. Instead he settles for the bull's broad, flat forehead. The advice is rare and worth quoting at length.

> And thinking about how they might escape either this infamy or this danger, I do not see any other way but to take the things with moderation, and not take any of them for one's [own] project, and to give one's opinion without passion, and without passion to defend it with modesty: so that if the city or the prince follows it, [it or he] follows it voluntarily and it does not appear that they are dragged into it by your importunity. When you act this way, it is not reasonable that a prince or people would dislike your advice, [because] it is not being followed against the will of many [others]: for danger is present where many [others] have opposed [the advice], who will then in case of an unhappy outcome join to ruin you. And if in this case [of your moderation] that glory is missing that one acquires in being the only one against many [others] in advising a thing when a good result happens, there is in exchange two benefits: the first, absence of danger; the second, that if you advise a thing modestly, and because of opposition your advice is not taken and because of the advice [given by others] some harm results, you receive from it greatest glory. And though one cannot enjoy the glory that one acquires from damage to your country or prince, yet it is to be held in some account.

~

WE leave now those early writings and experiences and the facets of biography they illumine. As yet, we have barely scratched the surface of that mortal god—the visible church and its man-administered religion. Confined no longer to practical politics, the suggestion of blending into the militia something of religion leaps onto the pages of the *Discourses* transformed into a doctrine: lacking religion, you cannot rule without harsh force, keep men to their oaths, make the guilty shameful, put a fighting army in the field; you cannot have political virtue. Niccolò's examples in the *Discourses* are taken mostly from Roman history. From the beginning, Roman republicans had an enduring faith. To maintain it, their leaders would go so far as to exploit superstition.

Our historian does not accuse the great figures of Judaism and Christianity of manipulating popular religious belief. Moses did talk with God; so, perhaps, did Joan of Arc and Fra Savonarola: on them, Niccolò makes no judgment. As for the claim that Numa, founder of the ancient Roman religion, was on familiar terms with a nymph, Numa "simulated." Religious belief and ritual are essential, whether or not a particular religion is false or its practices superstitious. Disbelievers are "apt to perturb every good institution."

A false religion, like the Roman pagan one, is better than none, so long as it worships God and is incorrupt. Without recourse to God and religious devotions, a state cannot be built or stand or be virtuous. Numa, "finding a savage people, and wanting to bring it to civil obedience with the arts of peace, turned to religion as something fully necessary to wish to maintain a civilization, and constituted it in such a way that for centuries there was never greater fear of God than in that republic." Its citizens "feared much more to break their oath than the laws, as they respected the power of God more than that of men."

The state must have law and arms; law and arms must have religion. "For, where there is religion, arms can be introduced easily," Niccolò writes. "And truly, never was there an ordainer of extraordinary laws to a people who did not recur to God . . ." As doctrine, this is newer and more significant than anticlerical and anti-Curial barbs. All states, if they wish to remain incorrupt, must "above every other thing keep the ceremonies of their religion incorrupt and keep them always in their veneration, because one can have no greater indicator of the wreck of a land than to see the divine cult scorned."

Niccolò holds that today the church's paradigms—its norms of conduct, the model of man it upholds as pleasing to God—are wrong. Contemporary standards Niccolò holds mark a deterioration of Christian ideals. "If that religion had been maintained by the [secular] princes of the Christian commonwealth as it had been ordained by the giver of it, the states and Christian republics would be more united, happier by far than they are." In more detail, "Our religion has glorified humble and contemplative men more than the active. It has placed the highest good in humility, abjection, and in scorn for human things: that other [the ancient Roman] religion placed it in greatness and spirit, in strength of body, and in all the other things apt to make men the strongest. And if our religion asks that you have strength in yourself, it wants you to be more ready to suffer than to do something strong."

Moreover, Christian ceremony is lukewarm. (Here Niccolò's criticism in the *Discourses* adds to that quoted earlier from the *Mandragola* where he satirizes ceremonial formalism.) Our sacrifices are "more delicate than magnificent," whereas ancient sacrifice was magnificent, "full of blood and ferocity" and the killing of animals. Niccolò then contributes a proposition to what we shall later examine as his theory of staging: the values aroused in rites turn men to their likeness. The "spectacle, being terrifying, made men similar to that."

According to Plato, Socrates' very last words were, "Crito, we ought to offer a cock to Asclepius. See to it, and do not forget." The sacrifice of a rooster may not be terrifying, but it is bloody. Moses' peace offering of oxen in Exodus—Moses, who takes blood from the basin and sprinkles it on the altar—or the immolation of oxen depicted on Roman reliefs, would be more to Niccolò's liking. The Crucifixion conceived as sacrifice is bloody enough but, in time, the church through its representations thinned the blood of its rites, creating a delicate ceremony: the bread and wine of the Eucharist—"This is My Body, This is My Blood"—and in its interpretations cast the passion as a humble, not a heroic, narrative. Such might be Niccolò's view, and the distance that words like "Blessed Sacrament" and "Host" have come from blood, oath, and sacrifice, supports his view of a mellowed conception. Christianity wants action and got contemplation, wants boldness and got meekness, wants agents and got patients.

THE PROPHECY

And whoever considers the foundations [of the Roman church, head of our religion], and sees its present use, how diverse it is from them, would judge it to be, without doubt, close either to ruination or the scourge.

The 'scourge' is prophetic and Savonarolian language—"the scourge of God." Niccolò, thus takes his turn at prophecy. Heavenly castigation may be about to fall on the church. By way of temporal context, the prophecy comes more or less as Niccolò is finishing the *Discourses*, Martin Luther is casting his Ninety-five Theses, and Henry VIII (though "Defender of the Faith" against Luther) is challenging Pope Clement VII over who shall be head priest of England. Each in his own way, Henry VIII of England, Louis XII of France, and Maximilian and Charles V of Hapsburg and the Holy Roman Empire, all are seeking more and more to limit the power of Rome by raising issues of spiritual-temporal jurisdiction, of sects and errors in the church (as Charles V is later to put it in a letter to Clement VII), and of the nature of the authority of the pope.

To tell the truth, the way Niccolò uses the phrase, church of Rome intimates something more than historical knowledge of the separation of Christian Byzantium or of nearly a century of an Avignon Pope. There is a religious intensity elsewhere—in the virtuous peoples of Germany, and particularly "in the lands of the Swiss, who alone today are peoples that live both in religion and military institutions according to the ancients . . ."—that is not that of the prelates of Rome. What Niccolò senses in Germany and Switzerland is a deeper religious fervor, and in France, possibly a royalist or more nationalist Gallic clergy. He has no optimism about the church of Rome's headship. Saints Francis and Dominic have saved it up to now. In just what way its punishment would come in the future, Niccolò does not prophesy. As Florentine envoy, he does not remain in foreign countries long enough to observe specific schismatic possibilities.

In June 1520, Leo X replied to Luther on the doctrine of penance, and this and ensuing events may have come to Niccolò's attention. Luther burned the papal bull and the canon law, Leo X excommunicated him, and Charles V, with the Edict of Worms, put his doctrines under the Imperial ban. It was not until a half-dozen years later, when Charles himself prepared to descend on the Italian peninsula with German forces called *landsknechts* and rumors of their animus against Rome started to circulate, that the term *Lutheran* began to be heard in Italy with rising frequency. (The *landsknechts*, originally German medieval pikemen, had been remodeled by Maximilian to match Swiss infantry and tactics.)

Niccolò, at the pontifical camp with Guicciardini (then the Pope's lieutenant and general of the army), writes his young son, Guido, to tell his mother not to worry, that "I will be there before any trouble occurs." The son writes back that "We do not worry anymore about the landsknechts because you have promised to want to be with us, if anything happens. So mona Marietta does not worry anymore." The *landsknechts* pass by Florence and head for Rome, together with Spanish contingents. The Sack of Rome begins. Overnight, the word *Lutheran* gains currency and richer significance. Two weeks later, Niccolò dies.

So much for religious prophecy.

MORAL BETTERMENT

The model of man the church upholds has perverted Christianity for all us Italians. For Niccolò, that the church can do this shows how important it is to the state as an educative force among the people. What makes people weak, he believes, "is the diversity of our education from the ancient, founded on the diversity of our religion from the ancient." The education Niccolò speaks of is not for reading, 'riting and 'rithmetic, or music, or the crafts of wool, wine, and banking, but for conduct. One must agree that, given a lack of state schools, religion would seem to be the one institution able to put an imprint on all children and their families.

Today's corrupt education is due "without doubt to the cowardice of the men who have interpreted our religion according to indolence and not according to virtue." Blame falls not on the people but on these leaders of religion. Without their "teachings and so false interpretations," people could be educated in virtue.

Virtue is teachable, then; men are morally educable. In spite of their slipping into sin, it is possible for them to be held upright and uplifted. True Christianity, or any religion that worships God, can educate them to goodness. These possibilities shed a brighter light on the human nature Niccolò portrays. Good teachers can make men better.

If moral education rests with religion, its tutors must be the clergy. This would appear to follow, unless the state has a teaching apparatus of its own, and even in that case, state-employed teachers in moral education would have to be inspired by or somehow related to the worship of God. Worship of a prince is uncertain and as short-lived as the prince himself, whereas the institutions of religion are ancient.

The possibility that public schools or other character-forming institutions may be capable of reaching down through the population seems not to enter Niccolò's mind. The monopoly of moral education by clerics may seem orthodox, but one must not forget that this is a reformed clergy that one looks forward to, a clergy to whom forming the character of citizens can be safely left. The educational methods of religion, in Niccolò's purview, should rely mainly on paradigm and ritual. Accordingly, the offices of preceptors would consist in upholding great models and in performing sacrifices and other rites whose meaning accords with the ideals symbolized by the great models.

These doctrines—that human nature can be modified by moral education and that virtue is generally teachable—carry the implication that under proper circumstances virtue may be so widespread as to characterize not just an individual, great or small, but also an institution or a country as a whole. In fact, our world historian proposes a fixed-quantity theory of the world's virtue:

And thinking how these things proceed, I judge the world to have always been in the same way, and there to have been in it as much of good as of evil; but [I judge] this evil and this good to vary from land to land, as one sees by that amount of news one has of those ancient kingdoms that varied the one from the other, because of the variations in customs, but the world remained that same one. Only there was this difference, that where [the world] had first lodged its virtue in Assyria, it gathered it in Medes, then in Persia, so that it came to Italy and to Rome; and if after the Roman Empire there has not followed an empire that lasted, nor one where the world kept its virtue together, one sees it nonetheless to be dispersed in many nations where one lived virtuously; as was the kingdom of the Franks, the kingdom of the Turks, that of the Sultan [of Egypt], and today the peoples of Germany, and before that, the Saracen sect that made so many great things and occupied so much [of the] world, after it destroyed the oriental Roman Empire.

The virtue of the world is fixed in quantity, but divisible and shifting.

Later in the *Discourses*, Niccolò adds the educational element to the theory. "This virtue and this vice, which I said one finds in one man alone, one finds also in a republic." It depends "on the education in which you have been nourished," and "what one says of one alone, one says of many who live in one same republic together."

The possibility of teaching and of acquiring virtue individually and collectively, lessens the impact of men's evil disposition as described in the previous chapter and prompts another look at human nature according to our author.

It is easy to go wrong in gauging the range of Niccolò's moral propositions. When he writes that 'of men one can generally say this: that they are ungrateful, shifty, simulators, and dissimulators', and so on, he may or may not then and there bind this conclusion in time and space. We may take note of whether he speaks of *man* or *men*, the first perhaps referring more precisely to man's essence, as in the "Exhortation," the second to human nature, innate or modified, as in the *The Prince* just quoted. If the latter, we may ask, All men? Anywhere? All of the time? The answers may be found in the immediate context or in an earlier or later text in the same work or in another work or, most difficult to reconstruct, it may be found in an elision, that is, a witting or unwitting omission of a common assumption.

In the above quotation, the immediate context does limit the statement to a particular, frequent relation of men to a prince, in which they follow the leader for his favors, not for love of him, a relationship of bought friendship: "because the friendships that are acquired with a price, and not with greatness and nobility of spirit, are purchased."

Another example approaches the good possibilities in men's nature. When our author concludes in *The Prince* that "men as a whole judge more with their eyes than with their hands," he has already restricted the proposition to 'men' and 'generally.' He goes on immediately to narrow the specification: "because to see belongs to everyone, to feel to a few." At least a few will judge with their hands. The context of the passage about 'ungrateful, shifty' men makes a distinction in time or circumstance: men act differently "while you [the prince] are favoring them" or "when the need [for them] is far off; but when [the need for them] approaches . . ." This distinction still shows the bad side of men. Later, in the last chapter, our moralist throws the light to their good side. When they look on someone as savior of their country, their love of country and faith in the leader make them good: "Nor can I express with what love he will be received in all those lands . . ." In still other cases, weak or corrupt leaders leave men's good possibilities untouched, as illustrated (Niccolò notes) by the recent poor showing of Italian troops in battle.

Keeping such caveats in mind and proceeding, we may thus far count religion and leadership as factors in the moral improvement of men. There are others: good military organizations or "good arms," which emphasize proper recruiting and motivating of soldiers, and good laws, which include the customs and morals that the original constitution or principles of the people nourish and that religion supports and arms insure. To demonstrate the interdependence and relative importance of religion, arms, and laws, Niccolò sometimes strings them together in various combinations. In *The Prince*: "there cannot be good laws where there are not good arms, and where there are good arms there must be good laws." In the *Discourses*: "so that if one were to debate over which prince Rome was more obliged to, either Romulus or Numa, I believe that Numa would be the one to obtain first rank . . ." because 'where there is religion, arms can be introduced easily.'

Another major factor in maintaining the morality of mankind is necessity, which comprehends austerity and poverty. Without the means to be corrupt, people cannot corrupt themselves. Without riches, they cannot luxuriate. Law and custom may keep them at a level of republican poverty whereby the people are poor and the country is strong. Adversity may be brought about by men or by heavenly phenomena. People may be humbled and reduced to poverty by catastrophies of one sort or another—defeat, plague, flood, fire, and famine. Chastened, they return to simple and sturdy virtue. So reads that chapter in the *Discourses* on what made the Roman Republic "more perfect." Men "work nothing well if not out of necessity; but where choice brims over and where license is found, everything fills up with confusion and disorder. Thus it is said that hunger and poverty make men industrious and the laws make them good."

Customs and morals support and are supported by law. "And where something works well by itself without the law, the law is not necessary; but when the good custom is lacking, the law is immediately necessary."

Somewhat differently put: "as good customs to maintain themselves need laws, so laws to be observed need good customs."

Niccolò cites these different factors sometimes as institutions, sometimes as persons, sometimes as concepts. He refers to laws as justice or as the legislator or, implicitly as legal punishment or as the ideals sought by constitutional or customary law. They interlap and sustain each other. Thus, laws as sanctions imply the use of force or arms, and arms as organized force imply ordinances or laws, so that it is impossible to lay them in a linear sequence like religion → arms → customs and morals → laws. Laws without arms are soap bubbles. With the support of good customs, law may need less, yet needs at least some, armed sanction. And arms without religion will have difficulty in securing the morale and discipline of arms-bearers. For Niccolò, then, law is not self-nourishing. Apart from an ecology of custom, arms, and religion, it withers on the vine.

Bernardo Machiavelli was trained in law and Niccolò, his son, knows the law in much of its technicality—procedural, contractual, bill-drafting, inheritance, statutory, customary, natural, canonical, constitutional, Roman, international, and of political succession. Religious and political lawgivers win his greatest admiration, but he shows no great interest in discussing who should rule according to law. He advocates republican rule, rule by more than a few and by more than one family while not underestimating the advantage of rule by king or aristocrats with hereditary status. And he favors law above the inconsistency of men. In the *Florentine Histories*, a saddened statesman about to go into exile speaks a sympathetic piece: "I shall always esteem it not much to live in a city where the laws do less than men, because that fatherland is desirable where [your] possessions and friends can be securely enjoyed, not where they can be easily taken from you, and friends for fear of themselves abandon you in your greatest necessity."

Rulers should obey the law they themselves have made or supported. Savonarola violated this rule, thereby showing himself to be ambitious and partisan and ruining his reputation. The title of the chapter in the *Discourses* that recounts this incident begins, "It Is a Thing of Bad Example Not to Observe a Law [that is] Made, and Most of All by the Author of It. . . ." The chapter itself unwinds the theme: "I do not believe that there is a thing of worse example in a republic than to make a law and not observe it; and all the more when it is not observed by whoever made it." Note, however, that according to our jurist, the law, man-made (not divine or natural), should be obeyed by lawmakers not because it is something divorced from private interest or because its ceremonial enactment has magical power, but because abiding by it sustains a leader's reputation and sets good example. Earlier, Niccolò explained that such reputation and example are important because they lend law authority and inviolability, thereby enabling people to live under it securely, which is what the great quantity of them want. The kings of modern France are "bound to infinite laws" that comprehend the security of all the people, and "they cannot dispose otherwise than [whatever] the laws ordain." When the people see that "no one may break such laws, they begin in short time to live secure and content."

❧

LET us retrace some of our footsteps. By losing divine essence, man lost an original nature and obtained a human nature of evil tendency but capable of moral choice. The rest of nature does not have this choice, nor is it exposed to evil as men are: choice allows men either to succumb to their impulses toward ingratitude, ambition, cruelty, luxury, and other vices, or to regulate them. Men can become good voluntarily by following right examples and by loving justice, the laws, virtuous citizens, and high-minded leaders, or be kept good by the constraints or necessities born of poverty, adversity, custom and law, force, and the fear thereof. Moral education has thus negative and positive sides: it reins in appetites with pain or the threat of it, with awe of God or fear of men's punishment; and it inspires imitation, love, commiseration, or shame. If these inducements are present over long periods, human nature may build up a resistance to evil that will hold over short periods of lack. As a general rule, however, if ever these ingredients are lacking, the soufflé collapses.

Thus, save in Niccolò's accounts of the beginnings of mankind, there seems to be little evidence of lengthy moral growth, development, or progress. Men are born with an evil-readiness; good religion, arms, and laws, good leadership, harsh necessity, or adversity make them better. Without these, the run of men return to evil in short order. They have no steep hill to climb to moral perfection, no brake on the chute to corruption.

The brief Polibianizing accounts of men's beginnings do seem to reveal a slight trend toward moral improvement. Men are able to put themselves in another's place. This capacity enables them to see where their needs or interests are common and on that basis to work out together a system of defense, morality, law, punishment, and justice. Also, men were born equal enough among themselves to make one of their number 'like a chief' and to obey him, and to proceed from a criterion of sheer strength in their choice of him to one of prudence and justice.

LAW AND CHOICE

Choosing to follow good example or to love justice still seems to be a moral act. Keeping to the good path out of constraint or necessity seems to deprive the act of voluntary, and therefore of moral, quality.

In saying that laws make good men, Niccolò may not be excluding the possibility of making men good by idealizing or defining for them certain good acts which they then choose to follow. This is the import one gathers when *The Prince* states that there are "two ways of combat, one with laws, the other with force. The first is proper to man, the second to beasts." In this passage, because Niccolò juxtaposes force and laws, he intends law in a sense that excludes coercion or sanctions; and if, as it seems, he is borrowing this contrast of man and beast from Cicero, then he has in mind a more elevated sense still—moral or natural laws; and because he uses *man* rather than *men*, he may be suggesting that law, in this sense, is proper to man in his essence. Force governs the relation of animals. Animals, unlike men, are innocent in their use of force, one assumes, having retained their original, divinely bestowed natures. "[God] made to be born [on earth] so many animals . . . for [man's] benefit," the "Exhortation" affirms. "We are greater friends to nature," reproves the pig, defender in *The Ass* of the animal against the human world.

Generally, however, Niccolò spends more time on a different possibility that not only the word *men* points to (in the phrase, "the laws make men good"), but also the word *make*. The intended sense here is *to constrain* or *to force*, a meaning that deprives the word *good* of its voluntary or subjectively moral quality. *Good* here refers to a good measured by the conformity of acts to the promulgated standard of the laws. By this interpretation, men conform to the legal norm not because they make it or choose it, but for fear of sanctions if they violate it.

Our jurist-turned-playwright illustrates this neatly in the *Mandragola* through remarks made by Nicia, Lucrezia's woolly-brained husband. At the time of the play, the criminal tribunal in Florence is called "The Eight," after the Florentine practice of abbreviating its government entities by the number of magistrates they contained. (When Niccolò, to create a militia, proposed a new bench of magistrates, The Nine, it had to be approved by the Ten.) Nicia, advised to administer a deadly infectious potion to a stranger, refuses at first, exclaiming that "it's a case for The Eight. I don't want to get in trouble over it." Then he agrees to go ahead with the plan, "but above all, no one must know, for love of The Eight!" Nicia is made good by the laws; he thinks he has no choice.

Once he has choice, once he thinks he can avoid the penalty, he reverts to immorality.

Punishment, poverty, adversity, or necessity leave little or no choice. Those responsible for these events or conditions—God, the heavens, legislators—in their own diverse ways make men perform good acts. In doing this, the acts of those responsible are moral; the constrained, conforming acts are non-moral. In the case of a republic where more than a few participate in ruling, the choice and the morality adhere to citizens in their lawmaking.

When those responsible for domestic lawmaking are faced with a foreign crisis, where their decisions are constrained by the force of others, then their moral choice, too, in full or in part, is taken away, as was Florence's in the quarrel between pope and king over the Council of Pisa. "Among private persons, faith is kept by laws, writings, and pacts; among rulers it is kept only by arms." This, the Florentine Secretary postulates in one of his early political writings, "Words to Speak on Providing Money, Given a Bit of Proem and Excuse." He composes it in the spring of 1503 as an introduction to a speech probably to be made by the Gonfalonier himself, on the necessity of finding additional sources of funds, ultimately by taxation of all property, including the ecclesiastical. Niccolò's part of the speech consists in clarifying the necessity for arms if one is to have a choice in foreign affairs and not lose one's liberty to invaders. In the telling, Niccolò reveals why he is not much interested in the question of who should rule according to law. Laws domestic or international are but words written in legal language, unless rooted in the rich soil of common customs, authority, religion and arms. In foreign affairs, where the nutrients are thin, good faith is 'kept only by arms'; but this, then, is not law.

Niccolò does not write much about bad laws. Presumably, they would be constitutional or other laws that do not fit the fundamental laws or principles or customs of the people, or are weak or unenforceable laws, or laws that instead of bridling men's evil tendency give rein to it. The laws (our author usually elides the word *good*) bridle or rein or correct the evil disposition of men, put "a bit in their mouths that corrects them." By means of the good laws made by one or more men, other men keep to good acts by necessity, by the fear of sanctions. Law, by coercing, removes moral choice, and, by being good, restores republican equality in simple living. This resolves the paradox in the remark: "one sees there to be greater virtue wherever choice has less authority."

It follows from the compelling or necessitating element in legal sanctions, that some men, those who create laws or fiats or similar restraints, may have to make moral choices of greater consequence than the rest. This predicament includes the prince or legislator. What can a church or clergy do to help this man who has these greater moral choices to make?

Not much evidently. Church or clergy may grant absolution or indulgences for morally dubious acts, but Niccolò does not consider these as viable or desirable possibilities. When Caesar Borgia, the Pope's son, had Oliverotto and Vitello strangled, Niccolò in a short paper wrote, describing the event, "Description of the Way Used by Duke Valentino [Caesar Borgia] in Killing Vitellozzo Vitelli, Oliverotto da Fermo . . ." et al. The Florentines "sent Niccolò Machiavegli their secretary" on a mission to the duke. The last paragraph reports that "words worthy of their past life were not used by any of them, because Vitellozzo prayed that the Pope be supplicated to give his sins plenary indulgence and Liverotto, weeping, shifted all guilt for the injuries done the Duke onto Vitellozzo" (the 'maestro of his virtues and crimes', *The Prince* later calls him).

A prince, on his own, can try to make amends by good works or philanthropy, as the cruel Agathocles of Syracuse did in later life. Such effort at remedy, however, need not pass through the clergy. Like anyone else, surely, the prince can invoke God. Niccolò does that himself from time to time, and in the *Florentine Histories*, he reports cases in which rulers invoked God to help them and to show the justness of their actions. They needed no sacerdotal class to do this.

The "Exhortation" seems to be the only place where Niccolò recommends that men of ruling caliber invoke the divinity. He proposes penitence for everyone, and may have in mind the sacrament of penance, although he does not mention it in this context. In the *Mandragola*, he does have the confessional in mind when cautioning that "these priests are worldly wise, astute; and it is understandable, because they know both our sins and theirs." This is not a criticism of the institution. Elsewhere, we have read, he praises saints Francis and Dominic for their confessional work among the people and the preaching that helped restore Christianity to its original ideals. In the "Exhortation" his exemplars are two—Peter and David—and they repent without benefit of clergy: they confess their sins and contrition directly to a forgiving God. "I have . . . called to you, O Lord, misericordia." For this class of person, at least, Niccolò's doctrine may be a form of contritionism, holding that repentence without priestly intermediation is sufficient for absolution.

Peter may be considered a religious figure; David is a major military and political hero, second only to Moses. Drawing from Samuel, Paraleipomenon, Luke, and the Psalms, Niccolò paints him in *The Prince* as an Old Testament figure who fought with his own arms; in the *Discourses*, as "without doubt a man most excellent in arms, learning, and judgment," whose policy as king deserved to be sung; in the "Exhortation," as prophet and sinner, taking as text, Psalms 50:3 and 129:1, recalling David prostrate on the ground, crying out "Misere mei, Deus."

The sins for which David cried out to the Lord are those of adultery and murder and lust. They are acts that a prudent prince should never commit—Niccolò disapproves on practical grounds of a prince's taking the women of others—yet they are not sins issuing from David's political goals. Many a private person, male or female (read Boccaccio again), has committed adultery and homicide out of lust or love. This does not sound like the kind of princely moral difficulty that worries our author. "Discreet and wise" opinion in *The Ass* holds that to ruin a kingdom it is "not enough" to have committed "some carnal sin."

There are some things in which religion may help the prince as well as the people. He, too, must be active and bold and have active and bold men at his side and for his models; the teachings and rites of religion will help form his character. Yet Niccolò is not seeking men of sheer energy. To catalyze virtue in both prince and people something else is needed, a directional code for all that energy.

The church of Rome has the wrong code. Our tractarian's criticisms of that church—of its deformed ideals, corrupt prelates, ruinous foreign policy, tepid ceremonialism, and educational failure—all involve damage to country. "For were [these base religious leaders] to consider that [our religion] permits us the exaltation and defense of [our] country, they would see that it wishes that we love and honor her and prepare ourselves to be such that we can defend her."

It is *country* that religion should help.

❧

1517–1520

Niccolò breaks through the grey clouds of his fall from grace. Had not Circe's damsel promised that "times happier than ever" would return to him? Henceforth, there are no more complaints about fortune's mistreatment. A new kind of life lies ahead: not politics, but new writings, new friends, new rewards. The first clear sign of it is a letter he wrote at the end of 1517 to a friend in Rome. "I know that you find yourself there all day long together" with a group of mutual friends, "and you remember little of us poor unfortunates here, dead of cold and of lack of sleep." (In winter, Rome compared to Florence is warm.) "Still, in order to seem alive, we [friends here] get together sometimes, and we discuss that trip to Flanders with such efficacy that it seems we are [already] on the way, so that of the pleasures that we shall have, we have already consumed half."

Niccolò is planning a pleasure tour! With a group of new friends! What news do they have of Flanders? Three years later another friend, one of the would-be Flanders tourists, goes to Rome and reports to Niccolò: "I have talked of your particular cases with the Pope and, in truth, for whatever much appears, I found him optimally disposed toward you." He speaks also in Rome with Cardinal Giulio about a commission for Niccolò to write the annals or history of Florence, telling the cardinal of "our company" of friends in Florence, too, and of how much they value Niccolò "for [his] intelligence and judgment." Lastly, "I spoke [to him] of your comedy," the *Mandragola*.

Our author has emerged from rural isolation, going down from the Tuscan hills to the city and across the river to frequent the walled gardens of the Rucellai family, the Orti Oricellari, which we may call for short "the Orti" or "the gardens." There over a period of several years he finds those younger friends and admirers, 'our company,' and where other men of letters come together under the wing of Cosimo ("Cosimino") Rucellai. The gatherings apparently have no precise political scope; most of the regulars are not part of the Medici government, yet are of high enough social standing to frequent the Medici. Niccolò carries down with him there some of the thoughts he entertained while composing the *Discourses* and the *Art of War*. The *Discourses* are addressed to a fellow-frequenter, Zanobi Buondelmonti, and to Cosimino. Niccolò says to them in thanks, "You have forced me to write what I never of myself would have written."

In these get-togethers, Niccolò receives comment, criticism, and encouragement from his closest friends. When he is away, they urge him to return as soon as possible "to us, your friends." He submits for their comments his experimental biography, *The Life of Castruccio Castracani*. "There is a part [of it]," one of them answers, "that does not have the vivacity and grandeur that one would ask of so great a man." They urge him to write the history of Florence: "It seems to all of us that you must put yourself with every diligence to writing this history." By the end of 1520, Niccolò has a suggested wording: "for years etc. with salary etc. each year with the obligation that he should be held to write the annals or else the history of the things done by the state and city of Florence, from that time which may seem to him more appropriate, and in that language either Latin or Tuscan that he may wish. [signed] Nicholaus Machiavelli."

. . .

Soon after Cosimino dies the reunions at the Gardens die too. In the same year, 1519, Lorenzo de' Medici (to whom as second choice *The*

Prince's covering letter was addressed) also dies suddenly, throwing the whole question on the table again: How was Florence to be ruled—as a republic, by the Medici, and if the latter, in what way and by which of them?

Pope Leo X, himself a Medici, the son of Lorenzo the Magnificent, designates as ruler of the Florentines his cousin, Cardinal Giulio di Giuliano de' Medici (who later becomes Pope Clement VII, patron of Raphael, Michelangelo, and Niccolò). The cardinal takes over control of the city. He asks a few select persons to state their individual views on how Florence could best be governed in the future. Among these is our political philosopher.

Niccolò submits a paper entitled, "Discourse on Florentine Public Affairs after the Death of the Junior Lorenzo," which we shall call "Discursus" for short, an absorbing lesson in constitution drafting and the stubbornness of Niccolò's republicanism. His readers, he knows, are members and supporters of the Medici house. "[His Holiness] would desire to find a constitution whereby his authority in Florence might remain great, and [his] friends might live securely." He approaches them with utmost candor. But "Your Holiness and the Most Reverend Monsignor . . . having to pass away [someday] and wishing that a perfect republic remain . . ." Niccolò's constitution, "this republic of mine," will insure this. Florence's traditions, moreover, go that way: a thesis he has argued strongly in *The Prince*. Of all forms of government, a long-standing republic is hardest to change. Here he lends the thesis a broader moral cast: changing a form of government, when it is suited to the form it has long had, "is difficult, inhuman and unworthy of anyone who wishes to be held merciful and good."

Toward the close of the work Niccolò states the connection of morality, religion, and state thus: "I believe that the greatest good that one can do, and the most gratifying to God, is that which one does for one's country." This is at the heart of his credo.

❧

NICCOLÒ ducks the theologian's cowl: he denies knowledge of the supernatural. Yet he informs the church of its deviation from Christ, prophesies a scourge, tells the Pope what pleases God most. Theological sallies like these put the church on the theological defensive in relation to the state.

He follows a long anticlerical tradition in Italy and Europe. He avoids going to mass as much as possible. He criticizes the cupidity, lechery, short-sightedness, and petty opportunism of the priesthood, and the faithlessness of the prelates who crowd the Roman Curia. He holds neither Pope nor prelates in awe, nor does he approve of the long-term effect of the church's military and political policy.

But he does not challenge the existence of the papacy (the office, as opposed to particular incumbents), the priesthood, or the sacerdotal use of temporal power. He discriminates good clerics from bad, good policy from bad. He acknowledges the advantage popes have of combining spiritual and temporal resources. In moral education, he appreciates the singular reach of the clergy and the means of ritual and example at its disposal. He accepts Christianity as the true religion, but insists that the restoring of its church calls for a God-fearing clergy, blood-thirstier sacrificial rites, a foreign policy aimed at Italian unity in the face of barbarians, and a return to the active and patriotic principles of Christianity and to Christ as its head.

Other religions, too, are the moral educators of their peoples. In Niccolò's comparative and syncretic outlook, religion involves a claim, true or false, of a relation with God. It claims to identify God, reveal what He can do, teach what He likes and dislikes, through rites and paradigm. Pagan religions did this; so does Christianity.

One could look back on Niccolò's anticlericalism and dismiss it as juvenile irreverence. But it would be a mistake to take this view, to add to it the fact that he challenges neither the existence of clergy, papacy, and church, nor their extension into the political world, and then to conclude that all of his views on the relation of church and state are conservative.

Niccolò stands in no awe of the sacerdotal class, from the pope down to the lowest friar, for a number of possible reasons: his family's ecclesiastical connections; the long conflict, reenacted in Florentine history by the Guelf and Ghibbeline factions, between Emperor Frederick II and popes Innocent III and Gregory IX; the Florentine Secretary's association with a government whose policy is sometimes pro-, sometimes anti-papal, and with a city that has twice in his lifetime been interdicted or, as the city magistrates would phrase it, "out of the Church's lap," and might then instruct its ambassador to arrange his words so as on the one hand to satisfy "what His Holiness wants" and on the other to be not so humble and supplicant to seem "a species of subjection." (When Florence was interdicted by the Pope in reprisal for the Medici's extermination of the Pazzi and their allies in 1478, the Tuscan bishops issued their own decree excommunicating the Pope. A new printing press in Florence provided copies that were sent throughout Europe with the title: "Counter-excommunication of the Florentine Clergy against the Highest Pontiff Sixtus IV.")

His lack of reverence for popes and archpriests extends to their person, to his entertaining the possibility of their being done bodily harm, or their being killed or taken captive. Niccolò knows the history of attempts on the pope. In the summer of 1510, he suggests to the court of the king of France that "to keep a curb on the pope, one does not need so many emperors, nor to make so much noise, because the others in the past who have made war [on a pope] have either deceived [him], as did Philip the Fair, or they have closed [him] up in Castel Sant'Angelo by means of his barons, the Orsini and Colonna families, who are not so spent that one cannot find a way to re-fire them." He once remarks in a letter to his friend Vettori that "all the things that have been, I believe, can be [again]; and I know that one has seen pontiffs flee, be exiled and persecuted, and suffer the extreme penalty, as [have] temporal lords, and [all this] in times when the Church in the spiritual [sphere] had more veneration than today."

The *Florentine Histories* narrates an event of more recent history. A hundred years before Niccolò was born, an attempt was made on Pope Nicolas V by a Roman citizen, Stefano Porcari, learned, noble by blood, "but much more for excellence of spirit," who for his share of glory wished "to take his country out of the hand of prelates." He failed. The Pope had him and many of his companions taken and killed. Someone might hold Porcari's intention to be laudable, our historian concludes, but everyone would blame his careless planning. Similar undertakings, if they have "in themselves some shadow of glory in the thought, have almost always certain harm in their execution." Though a cardinal is channeling money for these *Florentine Histories*, and they will be dedicated to him as Pope, our historian lets his admiration for Porcari's objective creep in.

With greater pleasure does he contemplate the dispatching of prelates in the *Discourses*. He narrates a case (where he himself was present) in which Pope Julius II's party could and should have been liquidated. The circumstances were these: after his early recruiting for the militia, he is sent on a mission. "Niccolò," his instructions of 25 August 1506 begin, "you will go on horse as far as to Rome to find His Holiness the Pope." This is his second assignment to the court of Rome; the first having been in the winter of 1503–1504. He now accompanies the campaign of Julius II, who marches at the head of a party of prelates and troops to oust tyrants from the church's lands in central Italy. The Pope enters Perugia "unarmed," putting himself in the fully armed hands of the tyrant Giovampagolo Baglioni. The tyrant leaves town without resistance, to the amazement of Niccolò, who earlier in the day had written of the event that if harm did not fall on the Pope and his cortege, "it will be because of Baglioni's good nature and kindness." In the *Discourses*, he revises his judgment, writing that the tyrant was so evil a man—he slept with his sister and murdered cousins and nephews right and left—that he could not have "abstained [from the deed] out of either goodness or conscience." The real reason was his cowardice, and that he missed the chance of eliminating his enemy at one fell swoop, there being with the Pope "all the cardinals with all their delights," and he missed also the chance of "perpetual fame" for having been "the first to demonstrate to the prelates how little one should esteem those who live and reign as they do." The object of his scorn is less Julius II, for whom he bears little affection, than the prelates, for whom he bears none.

Turning to juridical and moral, rather than physical, threats to the pope, there, too, Niccolò is familiar with pertinent events, both as historian and as envoy. He knows much of the fifteenth-century history of the religious councils that had been contending that the pope is not a monarch, but a delegated ministerial head whose authority rests finally with the community of the faithful or their representatives gathered in council.

When Niccolò was Secretary, the foreign policy of his government was based on an alliance with France, but on terms not so strong as to provoke papal anger. Lorenzo the Magnificent had faced this choice too, and had also chosen the king over the pope on the basis of calculations Niccolò adumbrates in the *Florentine Histories*. It appeared to Lorenzo that alliance with the king was more stable and safe, "because the shortness of life of popes, the variations in the succession [to the papal throne], the small fear that the Church has of princes, [and] the few scruples that it has in taking sides work so that a secular prince cannot wholly trust in a pontiff, nor can he securely link his fortune to him. Because whoever is ally of the pope in wars and dangers, will in victories have company and in defeats be all alone, for the pontiff is sustained and defended by the spiritual power and reputation."

Niccolò was present himself at the disastrous schismatic Council of Pisa in 1511.

1510–1511

The king of France presents Florence with a small bill for his friendship, on the part of "the Emperor, my good brother, we and other Christian princes, together with a good number of cardinals." He requests that Florence, "for the love of God, peace of Christianity, usefulness and reformation of the Universal Church," allow a council to take place in "your city of Pisa." Committing a ghastly blunder—Pope Julius II was ill, apparently to the point of death, and the Florentines banked on it—the republic agrees. In response, the Pope invokes an ecumenical council himself at Rome, and puts Pisa and Florence under interdict and censure. For the Florentines, this meant that the clergy, on penalty of suffering excommunication itself, could not sound church bells for divine offices and, when holding offices, had to close church doors, could not confess anyone who was not on point of death, could not administer supreme unction, could not proceed with or without the cross to bury the dead, and could not accept the dead in hallowed ground. Clergy outside the borders of Florentine suburbs could not permit entry to their church of Florentines or of anyone living within the suburbs.

The Gonfalonier, in instructions for the first legation to France, had reminded Niccolò that "if the Pope as a friend is not worth much, as an enemy he hurts a lot."

To extricate itself from the papal squeeze, the government puts most of its ambassadorial resources to work and sends "our Secretary" on a gallop to Pisa, Milan, and the court of France to plead with dissident, mainly French, cardinals and bishops and with His Most Christian King, Louis XII himself, not to provoke Julius II and the Spaniards into military and naval action and not to insist on holding the council in Pisa. (Louis, during Niccolò's first mission to the court of France, told him that if crossed, he would "persecute [the Pope] in his state and in his person, and [would] believe himself to be excused both to the whole world and to God.") On 2 November 1511, Niccolò returns to Florence, then on 3 November hastens to tumultuous Pisa, where the council is starting, taking three-hundred troops with him to help keep order. Though focused on Florentine foreign aims, the instructions and dispatches to and from the government, its ambassadors and agents, and "our nuntius, citizen, and secretary," indicate clear understanding of the motives for the creation of the council, of the participants and absentees, and of its weaknesses from the start.

The council opens officially in Pisa and soon shifts to Milan (Niccolò deserves some of the credit for the shift), but the damage is irreparable, and the aftermath of this episode in the struggle of Louis XII and the Gallic clergy against Julius II shears the republic of allies. Florence is done for. Now it is, in our political philosopher's words, a special type of republic subject to different rules and great limitations—a weak republic.

CHALLENGE TO THE CHURCH

Having seen Niccolò's intimacy with the problems provoked by the conciliar controversy, one may sustain that his attitude toward physical and other threats to the pope evidences disbelief in the sacred person of bishops and in the apostolic succession. "And to whoever might reply that the Pope, for the veneration of his person and for the authority of the church, is in another category and will always have a refuge to save himself, I should respond that such reply merits some consideration and that one can find some foundation in it. Nevertheless, it is not to be counted on; actually, I believe that, wishing to be well-advised, it is not to be thought of . . ." As for refuge, if he does not side with France, the pope can, if defeated, "go to Switzerland to die of hunger or to Germany to live in despair or to Spain to be defrauded and sold."

Our theologian does not take the conciliar line, however, that the consent of the faithful or their gathered representatives is necessary to lend authority to the pope, that the use of force—widely accepted as the distinguishing feature of the secular arm—lies outside the pope's reach, or that simony and indulgences are the mark of papal corruption. Niccolò makes a different thrust at the authority of the church. He treats the pope as the exceptionally short-lived, all-too-fallible, rector or head, de facto, of the Christian church, whose powers are not limited by spiritual/temporal distinctions, but whose greatest strength lies in his reputation as legitimate pastor of a spiritual or ecclesiastical state.

In his message to the government on the election of Julius II, Niccolò writes:

Magnificent Lords: I advise your lordships in the name of God that this morning the Cardinal of San Pietro in Vincula has been pronounced the new pontiff, may God make him a useful pastor for Christianity. Farewell. First day of November 1503

Servant Nicholò Machiavegli, Secretarius
Rome

The pontiff is 'sustained and defended by the spiritual power and reputation,' he writes in the *Florentine Histories*; ecclesiastical principalities are "sustained," he writes in *The Prince*, by "the ancient institutions of religion," in this case, the institutions of the true religion. The pope is the head of the church, de jure, only in as much as he acts not for personal or family gain but for the welfare of church and country, according to the foundations or principles laid down by Christ, the giver-founder of Christianity.

In this view, our political philosopher does approach a conciliar thesis, that Christ—not the pope—is the true or essential head of the Church. We have seen the accusation in the *Discourses*: that dishonest prelates and heads of religion have not maintained religion as given by Christ. This is a grave charge. Niccolò pits the spiritual authority of the

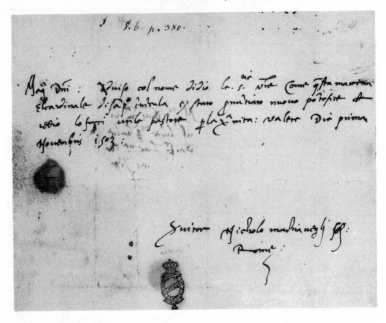

". . . the new pontiff, may God make him a useful pastor for Christianity."

founder against the institutional trappings of the church. Whenever the teachings of the church deviate from Christ and God's religion, by implication, the papacy is illegitimate and its reputation false; popes, prelates, and clergy have lost their spiritual authority.

Our author, in effect, turns the tables on Augustine. In *The City of God*, the great bishop puts the state on the defensive by charging that without justice states are but great robber bands. Niccolò now puts the church on the defensive by accusing it of corrupting its spiritual message. The church has deformed the founding principles of Christ and has lost its right to teach.

From an irreverent wordsmith who recommends mixing the militia with something of religion, Niccolò becomes prophet of the scourge of God, and the *Discourses* becomes a fundamental work in the political theory of religion. "Therefore the princes [that is, the heads] of a republic or a kingdom must maintain the foundations of the religion they have; and having done this, it will be an easy thing for them to keep their republic religious, and in consequence, good and unified." He is compressing the duality of church and state.

In the later "Discursus," Niccolò is more radical still. He shifts from the church and religion to God, Himself, affirming to popes and cardinals that the deeds of great men of state are 'the most gratifying to God.' The significance of this phrase is greater than that of 'God more a friend' in establishing God's preference for those who do good for their country.

It is country that religion should help, and it is God who wishes this.

If God wishes it, one can understand that the church should reform itself to teach us to love, exalt, and defend our country and that the church that does not do so is in danger. But why does God wish this, and why should He look with highest favor on those who do great deeds for their country? What is country that one should defend, honor, and love it? Love it?

THE FOOL OF LOVE

The soldier dies in a ditch,
the lover dies in despair.

—*Clizia*

NICCOLÒ DOES not spout poetry on request, but he is in love. He is fifty-six years old, and if he cannot write poetry, he will serenade. (In the past, he has offered serenading services to friends.) The woman he is serenading now, on his own behalf—"Love, I feel my soul / burn in the fire where / I burned happy . . ."—is Barbera, a well-known singer.

> If with your sainted preciousness,
> Love, you can see to it that always
> I seem to her to have lived in this fire,
> I shall be so happy
> that under the crudest hardships
> my living will be joy and dying will be a game
> and always my song
> will call her lord and you my god.

He plans to stage her with her chorus between the acts of his comedy hit, the *Mandragola*, when it opens in Faenza.

৶

WITH the help of friends in the Orti, Niccolò had broken his country isolation. At last he seemed to be in the good graces of the Medici, who still ruled Florence. In 1522 another plot against them was discovered, its origins traceable to the Orti. This time, Niccolò's ignorance of the whole thing was immediately clear, but, soon after, these gardens were closed, leaving our Niccolò again without intellectual intercourse. A year or so later, however, we see him more and more in the milieu of a wealthy kiln-owner called "the Kilns-man," who owns a villa with ample gardens across the Arno River, outside the gates of Florence, not as cultivated an environment as the Rucellai Gardens, but a generous one with a greater variety of people in attendance. It is on the side of town closer to his country house and closer to his family neighborhood in town, where he grew up and lived while Secretary, in property he still owns. Here at the Kilns-man's, toward the end of 1523, Niccolò meets Barbera, the popular young singer.

At the moment, on business away from Florence and "Barberaland" (so a chum calls it) he asks friends to look out for her. "You asked me for your love of her to give Barbera kisses, with her permission," writes Filippo Strozzi, himself no slouch at womanizing, "but not having been able to obtain it, I have not yet been able to kiss her; and then I thought it over, that you in fact did not want me to get that far, having imposed such a difficult condition, wherefore I do not thank you much for such generosity, having recognized in it a subtle miserliness."

Via the Kilns-man, our lover complains to his beloved that she does not write him; she replies through the same medium that by her silence she was playing a little trick to test whether he loved her and that she desires him back in Florence as soon as possible because it seems that when he is there she sleeps tranquil and secure (a remark betraying a rather lengthy intimacy). The Kilns-man, in reporting to Niccolò, adds prudently, "Now, you know her better than I do: I do not know whether to believe everything she says."

Guicciardini twits his friend about this amour: ". . . although her name denotes cruelty and pride, she has gathered to herself (about which I wish to keep to what you say) as much kindness and piety as would spice up a city."

❧

NICCOLÒ, at age thirty-two had married Marietta Corsini. One letter from her to him away in Rome, repays quoting in full. The only letter in existence from her to him, it illustrates conjugal love, tells us something about her literary level, and contains the few clues we have to what our hero looked like. The year is 1503. They have been married nearly two years.

In the name of God, day 24 [November]
    Carissimo Niccolò mio. You make fun of me but you're wrong, that I would feel better if you were here. You know how happy I am when you're

down here; and even more now that I have been told there is such a great plague up there, imagine how reassured I am, because I do not find rest day or night. This is the happiness I have of the baby boy [about two weeks old, the first son, named Bernardo after the grandfather]. However, I beg you to send me letters more often than you do because I have not had other than three. Do not wonder that I have not written because I could not, because I have had a fever up to now. For now the little boy is well, he looks like you [a friend says, "he is your spitting image: Leonardo da Vinci could not have portrayed him better"]: He is white like snow, but he has a head that seems like black velvet, and he is hairy like you [another friend writes that he looks "like a little crow, he is so black]; and since he looks like you, to me he is handsome, and he is lively [so] that it seems like he has been in the world for a year, and he opened his eyes before he was born, and put the whole house full of noise. But the little girl [Primavera, the first child] is feeling ill. I remind you to come back. Nothing else. May God be with you, and watch over you. I am sending you an undershirt and two shirts and two handkerchiefs and a towel, that I am sewing here for you.

Your Marieta in Florence

To the end, the exchanges between Niccolò and Marietta, seen mainly through the letters of children and friends, bespeak affection if not love.

Betrothal arrangements do not guarantee love. It may come at first sight or later or not at all. Of major concern is the dowry. Niccolò's parents are dead when he marries, but we may be sure that the dowry and other arrangements were negotiated by members and agents of the Machiavegli and Corsini families. There is a correspondence with Francesco Guicciardini, who has four young daughters, that exhibits another role in our author's repertory.

Machiavelli the matchmaker holds that the wise policy is to marry the first daughter well, that the others will benefit from it. Guicciardini replies that he is afraid of putting the first in paradise and the others in hell. Niccolò dismisses this pessimism with a quotation from the *Paradise*, sending Guicciardini scurrying for a copy of Dante. He then tackles the problem of a large dowry for the first daughter, proposing that his friend write the Pope for help and disclosing that His Holiness had contributed 4,000 florins, one-half of the dowry, for a daughter of Filippo Strozzi, and 2,000 ducats for the daughter of Pagolo, Vettori's brother. "I should write a letter . . . and having made a [suitable] preamble, I should show him what your condition is, and that you find yourself without male children but with four females, and how you think it is time to marry one . . . and constrain him and burden him with the most efficacious words you know how to find, to convince him how important you think the thing is . . ."

These letters about matchmaking, an art on which Niccolò had spent no little thought, indicate that *love* need not be mentioned in choosing a fiancé.

Nor does one find *love* often used in connection with wives, siblings, children, or other kin. A case in point is Niccolò's brother, Totto, some six years younger, who became a priest. His letters do not speak of their affection; they usually deal with business matters, most often of the possibility of benefices, but with the sureness that banks on fraternal aid and love. Totto seems to have given most of his share of the family property to his brother. He dies in 1522, and in that year, Niccolò makes his second and last will. We hear nothing of fraternal grief, except a consolatory letter written to him by a friend while his brother was ill. He later names a son Totto.

The executed will names Donna Marietta, "his dear spouse," guardian of the children until each of them reaches age nineteen, and leaves her a farm and farmhouse, two houses, one small, as repayment of her dowry (which was an attractively large one), along with lifetime usufruct of the country house they had lived in. Then, before proceeding to bequests to the sons, he provides for his one unmarried daughter, Bartolomea (the Baccina he had bought a little gold chain for), "200 gold-minted florins for her dowry," a modest sum compared to the pope's contributions mentioned earlier. When she was a child, her father had invested for her a sum calculated to provide her with an honorable dowry at age of marriage (normally seventeen). Moreover, he stipulates in the will that she is to receive "three gold-minted florins" a year for food and clothing until she marries. The male heirs, her brothers, are charged with attending to these provisions and to take care of her dowry if, at the death of the testator, the amount calculated for it had not yet matured.

❧

ONCE, Niccolò, perhaps in a mood of fun and experiment, jotted down some rules for a world turned upside-down. As a piece of writing it does not jell; he leaves it unfinished and uneven. It is called, "Rules for a Pleasure Party." One rule: Wives may remove their husbands from the premises by giving them purgatives if they "do not do their duty." In the Machiavegli household this 'duty' does not atrophy. At age fifty-five, two years before he dies the last child is born.

Away from home for any length of time and without a wife to pay the marital debt to, Niccolò may find himself in difficulty. While on a mission to Emperor Maximilian, he writes a friend a graphic account of his unhappiest experience of the flesh. The date is 1509, he is forty years old, the place is Verona.

Damn it, Luigi; and see how much fortune in the same affair gives men different results. You having fucked her, the desire to fuck her came upon you [again] and you want another go-around; but I, have been going around here many days blind for scarcity of matrimony. I found an old woman who washed my shirts, who lives in a house that is more than half below the ground level, nor can one see a light there except for the entrance, and I passing there one day, she recognized me and, greeting me warmly, said to me that I might be pleased to come into the house a little, that she wanted to show me some beautiful shirts, if I wished to buy them. So, new prick that I am, I believed it, and, arriving inside, I saw in the gleam a woman. . . . This ribald old woman took me by the hand and bringing me to her said, "This is the shirt I want to sell you, but I want you to try it first and then pay for it." I, timid as I am, everything filled me with fear; still, remaining alone with her in the dark [because the old woman left the house immediately and shut the door] . . .

Hag laundress-procuresses and hag prostitutes lying in wait for lusting young men! Indeed. The friend to whom Niccolò is writing is Luigi Guicciardini, older brother of the historian-to-be, Francesco. Their family lives in a big, new palazzo across the street from Niccolò's modest dwelling in town. Luigi had encouraged his friend to give rein to whimsy in writing, and Niccolò had replied earlier that he was thinking all the time of doing just that. (He did dedicate his impassioned tercets, "On Ambition," to Luigi.) Whether true or false, all or in part, the tale is a popping concoction—one part merchandise, one part sexual appetite, and other parts thrown in from ancient and regional jars.

Francesco Vettori, ambassador to the papal court in Rome, the friend who describes himself as "religious" and says he goes to chapel every morning, once wrote Niccolò that "on reflection this world is nothing but love, or, to speak more clearly, lust. . . . Nor do I know what is more delightful in thinking or in doing than fucking. And philosophize each man as he wants, this is the pure truth, which many understand thus but few say it."

To hear Niccolò tell his own story of lust, there was nothing delightful about it. For Vettori, *lust*, 'to speak more clearly,' must have meant *sexual urge consummative with a proper object of desire*. Niccolò himself does not utter *lust* in the same breath as *love*. In reply to his friend's coarse remarks, he versifies delicately of Love's sweet chains. For Niccolò, what more likely makes the world go round is love . . . when he is in the mood for love poetry.

❧

IN the fall of 1510 the Secretary is sent to the court of France to help loosen the vise on Florence, caught between Louis XII and Julius II. While off-duty, he (now forty-one years old) consoles himself with Jeanne, whom he evidently calls "Janna." A friend writes that he was waiting to see Niccolò in Florence, where "by the grace of God and then of Janna, you may be led back safely, and on your arrival here you will perhaps see Riccia again." In Florence, Niccolò resorts often to the company of Riccia. He tells in one letter of trying to steal a kiss from her "on the wing." She pouts: "these wise men, these wise men, I do not know where they live." He and his friends sometimes spend time on holidays—even just after 'everything is totally wrecked'—in the company of "some girls, to regain [their] strength." A zealous preacher once complained to the straight-faced Niccolò that the prostitutes of Florence "wag their tails more than ever."

(The carefree attitude toward lovemaking, though, is destined to end. Syphilis has arrived and is taking giant strides. Many physicians are busy experimenting with mercury in various forms. High government officials are soon to die of the disease, which was quickly discovered to be venereal. Joking in the Chancery with the word *chancre* begins to be not quite so funny.)

While passing the time in Faenza much later, awaiting decisions of the irresolute Clement VII, our correspondent met "Maliscotta," for Francesco Guicciardini writes that after Niccolò left, she spoke worthily of him and "highly praised his manners and entertainments," and "I assure you that if you return here you will be welcomed well and perhaps caressed better." Guicciardini at the time was president of the papal state of Romagna. To judge from Niccolò's possibly seeing Maliscotta again, from her language, and from his about her, she is not a whore. She, Janna, and Riccia are more likely honest courtesans or women of good company who offer the possibility of enjoyable bedding, plus enjoyable conversation before and perhaps even afterward.

From Rome, while still ambassador to the papal court, Vettori reports—in the same breath as that chiding Niccolò for letting mass go sometimes, whereas he hears it faithfully—that he has a courtesan now who comes there often herself. She is "very reasonable in beauty, and in speaking, pleasant. I have another in this place, though it is solitary, a neighbor that you would not dislike; and though of noble parentage, she takes on an occasional job."

If it is not a contradiction in terms, such relationships might be subsumed under carnal love, but Niccolò, in writing of them, does not use *love*, and that is the word we are looking for in this chapter, eventually in the phrase, *love of country*.

Under favorable circumstances, carnal desire can lead to love. At the end of *Mandragola*, the heroine has yet to make the transition. In one grand plot of deceit involving all the characters—husband, mother, priest, and all the others except Lucrezia—the whole play has been leading up to a lover's bedding with her. Now, on that long-panted-after first night, the lover Callimaco tells her of the ruse, and "when she had tasted the difference there is between my laying and that of Nicia" (her husband), she, after a few sighs, falls in with him and instructs him how to continue deceiving her husband and how to come and go "constantly and without suspicion." But not a word of love. Earlier, Callimaco, whom the author describes as having "signs and traces of the honor of gentleness," had poured out his desire for Lucrezia in a notable monologue. "I can hardly stand, because from every side so great a desire to lie once with her assails me that I feel everything changed in me from head to foot: my legs shake, my innards follow suit, my heart unhooks itself from my chest, my tongue grows mute, my eyes are dazzled, my brain spins."

Some might say this is much desire and little love. Still, there is more here than a list of limbs and organs. Callimaco's sentiment—individualized, concentrated, and persistent—idealizes Lucrezia and wraps her in sexual tenderness. Speaking of his "love," he ends by promising to marry her . . . whenever the Lord decides to dispatch her aging husband. (Boccaccio would have had the two of them plotting to dispatch the husband themselves.)

When Niccolò started living in the country, he went in the morning to a fountain carrying a book—Dante, Petrarch, Tibullus, Ovid—and "I read of their passions and their loves, remembering my own . . ." Within a year he falls in love romantic, with a lady of rare and suave visage living nearby. A love affair in a rural area close to home creates problems. Yet the fifty years he is "already near to" do not bother him, "nor do the harsh roads tire me, nor the darkness of the nights frighten me. Everything seems easy to me, and to [her] every desire, no matter how different and contrary to that which should be mine, I conform. And though I seem to have entered great trouble, yet I feel in it such sweetness . . ." The creature in question—he writes Vettori, "so gracious, so delicate, so noble" (he never mentions her name)—may have been a friend's sister whose husband had deserted her to live in Rome, or she may have been an invention, just to show his friend that Niccolò, isolated up there in the country, has a love to write about, too—not merely a past love, but a present one holding him "with nets of gold stretched among flowers." That friend needed no convincing. At times he had seen Niccolò "in love" and he realized "how much passion" love aroused in him.

The greatest and last love (of which we have knowledge) and one that created some scandal is the affair of Barbera. She is unquestionably of flesh and blood, and her full name is Barbera Raffacani Salutati. We began this chapter with her: "At Barbera's Request" is the title of the poem. Niccolò's play *Clizia*, too, may have been written at her urging (supported by the Kilns-man), as were the special songs added to the *Mandragola*.

Guicciardini, teasing about Barbera, writes, "you are a lover of all women." Niccolò seems to be attractive to women. Is he handsome? No one seems to notice. Reading into Marietta's letter, we gather he is not *bello*. They had been married only two years, she obviously loves him dearly, and they have just had their first baby boy; yet she does not convey that the baby's father is handsome by objective standards. Since the baby looks like Niccolò, she writes, 'to me' he is handsome. Apparently, he is not remarkably thin or fat or short or tall. He must be rugged in constitution, else he could not ride horse day upon day, back and forth, over hill and down valley, in heat and snow, on one mission after another. He is energetic: we already know that. His counsel for love would be the same as for politics: "I believe, believed, and always shall believe that what Boccaccio says is true," he writes Vettori in a letter of the winter of 1513–1514, "that it is better to do and regret than not to do and regret." He is brave: to face up to some of the toughs he is dealing with—Caesar Borgia is a conspicuous example—requires physical courage; to propose recruiting and training a militia, and then to form it himself and all but put it on the battlefield, requires moral courage. Above all, he is the life of the party. His letters from the field keep his mates at the Chancery "dying of laughter," and when, for his republican sins, the powers that be inhibit his free access to Florence, his brigade

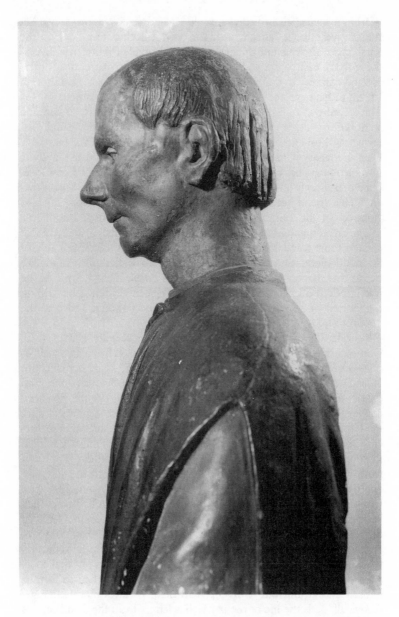

Niccolò seems to be attractive to women. Is he handsome? No one seems to notice.

of friends miss him and complain that there is no one around to get a party going. Strength, energy, bravery and the gift of fun, one hazards, are not qualities typically unattractive to women. And what is it Maliscotta praised so highly of him? His 'manners and entertainments'.

But love is more than love of women. There is love of family, too, as we have already seen. His affection for his nephew Giovanni illustrates a wider circle of family love, as we recognized in an earlier look at Niccolò's perils, in prison and afterward. As a loving uncle, he confides easily to his nephew, even about his low moods.

> Carissimo Giovanni, You never write me of not having received my letters without driving a knife in me . . . I have heard from several [persons] of your troubles. I thank God, that they have calmed down and you remain alive . . . I am yours. May Christ watch over you.
>
> > Day 15 of February 1515
> > Niccolò Machiavegli in Firenze

There is also love of a friend. Niccolò writes to Guicciardini with the sincerity "that the love and reverence I bear you commands." There is love for a new prince, singled out in a letter to Vettori: "and all the love" that people bore him, "which was great, considering the newness." And there is love of country. One of the last captions of the *Discourses* reads: "That a Good Citizen for Love of Country Must Forget Private Injuries." There seems not to be love of the state or love for the state.

Of *amour-propre*, the whole human species is guilty. The reproof comes from the formerly human, now animal, world of *The Ass*, in the words of the wise pig. "Your own love so greatly deceives you that you do not believe in any good outside of the human essence and value."

Love of one's neighbor, love of God, and Christian love sometimes take the name of charity (Latin *caritas*), distinguished thus from love of family, friends, and women. "This, my fathers and brothers, is that which alone is worth more than all the other virtues in men, this is that of which the church has so fully spoken: that he who has not love [*caritas*] has nothing." Our theologian goes on to describe this love in the phrases of Paul.

Then there is the love of exercise of the mind. Though he rarely puts it in so many words, one cannot deny Niccolò's love of ideas, of the mind, of the search for truth and wisdom. "And so marvelous did it seem to me / that I wanted to discourse with myself / of the varying of mundane things" he confesses in *The Ass*. He loves the life of action, too, though he never says so explicitly, and he urges it on all good men, but the preparation indispensable for right action is knowledge. We shall return to this subject in greater scope but cannot let the occasion pass without recalling that our Niccolò has read trunkloads of books, documents, and manuscripts. He reads while rusticating, he reads while on the run or on horseback legations. In the covering letter of *The Prince* he talks of things he has "lengthily cogitated." In the letter of 10 December 1513, he tells of seeking in history the "reasons of" actions and of spending 'four hours of time' each night in profound thinking "on this subject" of principalities, of years of "study of the art of the state." In the *Discourses*, he sides with reason and rejects authority and force. "I do not judge nor will I ever judge it a fault to defend any opinion with reasoning, without wishing to use either authority or force." Throughout all his writings one senses the power of a passion for learning, reading, comparing, analyzing, distinguishing, mediating, generalizing.

WOMEN AND POLITICS

Niccolò's passion for stir and study swirls around politics. "Not knowing how to reason about the art of silk or about the art of wool [two of Florence's greatest industries], or about profits and losses [one of Florence's greatest contributions to civilization is double-entry bookkeeping], it is necessary that I reason about the state, and I must either make myself keep quiet or reason about it." The food on which he pastures, that is his alone, is the history of men of state, ancient and modern, their lives, writings, and deeds. We know, however, that this same Niccolò, when in love with the lady in the country, abandons reasonings about the state. There seems to be some relation between love of woman and love of politics.

The premium men in these times set on woman's love and honor makes it a political factor. A chapter of the *Discourses* bears the heading, "How One Ruins a State Through Women." Here and in the chapters on the creation of the Roman Decemvirate and on conspiracies, Niccolò recalls historic cases. His conclusion: Of all matters affecting the honor of men, to deprive them of the honor brought by their women or to dishonor their women outright is politically the most dangerous. In the *Florentine Histories*, without mentioning the point, he provides an illustration. He begins the modern history of Florence with its first civil split. A young cavalier breaks his word with one girl to marry another, thereby tearing the city in two, with respective families and their allies on opposing sides. The scene in which the mother of the second girl gets the already affianced young man to inspect the merchandise recalls

Niccolò's hag-procuress of Verona. "Seeing messer Buondelmonte coming toward her house alone, she went down, and behind her she led her young daughter, and as he passed, she put herself in his way, saying, 'I am most truly happy that you are to take a wife, even more as I have saved for you this daughter of mine'; and pushing the door ajar, she showed her to him. The cavalier, seeing the beauty of the girl . . . lighted up with such ardor to have her that, not thinking of his troth or of the injury that he would do by breaking it, or of the evils that the broken pledge could bring him, said, 'Since you have saved her for me, I would be ungrateful, being still in time, to refuse her'."

Niccolò approves of Aristotle's placing the violation of woman and the breaking of marriages among the principal causes of the downfall of tyrants. This part of Aristotle shows, as our author's examples in *The Prince* and *Discourses* do also, in what esteem men then held woman's honor and love. Elsewhere in the *Politics*, Aristotle claims that women upset not tyrannies alone, but also republics like Sparta, by their addiction to luxury and ease and their corrupting of the homefront while their men were away at war. Lycurgus (one of Niccolò's exemplars) tried to bring them in line but failed, Aristotle says. Though this side of women deals with the corruption of states, a theme dear to our author, he does not pick up the possibility of their potential damage to the republican form of state.

In the letter about his lady-love in the country, Niccolò indicates by his own behavior that love of woman may compete with passion for politics and perhaps may be a superior attraction, or at least a solace. Sometimes he hints at the competition in humorous terms. In January of 1526, absorbed in tracking the march of the Emperor's forces in Italy, he nevertheless ends a letter by reminding Guicciardini that "Barbera is there" and asking that he do whatever he can for her, because "she gives me more to worry about than the Emperor." Sometimes he hints at it in politico-religious terms like "glory" and "grace." When Guicciardini relays Maliscotta's compliments, Niccolò replies: "This morning I received your letter in which you inform me in how much grace I stood with Maliscotta, of which I glory more than anything else I may have in this world."

The Ass, too, exalts woman and puts the pursuit of her love above politics. In this work, the poet, left alone, spends the day in contemplating the affairs of the world. The sound of a horn announcing his beloved's return makes him realize "that every other thing was vain except her of whom I was made a servant." Niccolò leaves this poem unfinished. He hardly discusses the ass that the title prefigures. Among the formerly human animals who do appear, is the wise pig, and with its words the work ends on the highest antiactivist note Niccolò ever hits. The porcine savant advises our hero thus: "And if among men there is anyone who seems a god, prosperous and happy, do not believe him too much, for I live happier in this mud where without worry I bathe and roll over."

All things considered, our poet would prefer not to wag his tail in the mud. That we occasionally bump into contradictory views should not disconcert us. His thought responds to health and age, to the way family and finances are going; it changes with what he reads and with whom he talks. His thought changes with thought—that absorption and intentness of mind he mentions in various writings already within our range—*The Ass, The Prince*, the *Discourses*, the 10 December letter to Vettori; it varies with whether the public applauds his latest writings, and with whether he is in or out of work—or in or out of love.

Love of woman seems to be a force withdrawing men from politics; if interfered with, it becomes a danger to civil life. Niccolò has no positive political role for women in a republic or any other form of government. He considers them neither as run-of-the-mill political actors, citizens or subjects, nor as potential for the country's infantry or militia. He reports of French troops that once their first fierce charge is resisted, they become cowards like women. He repeats more than once Livy's own repeated judgment of the Franks: they charge the fray like supermen and slacken off worse than women. Callimaco, the lover in *Mandragola* thinks that women are easily discouraged. Just before his monologue on love, he pulls up on his bootstraps, saying to himself, "Do not get yourself down, like a woman."

An anonymous and rare poetess of the fourteenth century wrote

> Keep quiet, O males, . . .
> Women know how to wield the sword,
> they know how to rule empires.

Niccolò would doubt the truth of the second line, yet not of the third. He recognizes without prejudice the merit in women as rulers, never imputing sexual differences in political capacity. The *Discourses* ranks Dido, the legendary founder and queen of Carthage, alongside Aeneas and the founders of Marseilles, while *The Prince* quotes Virgil's *Aeneid* to define her as a new prince. In the *Mandragola*, Ligurio, the middleman, a character without romantic interest in the heroine, Lucrezia, contrasts her with her spouse. "I do not think that there is in the world a more stupid man. . . . She is a beautiful woman, wise, well-mannered, and fit to govern a kingdom." High praise.

To glance at historical women, the ruler of Forlí —Madonna Caterina or the Madonna of Forlí (1463–1509)—is mentioned in both *The Prince* and *Discourses*, and in the *First Decennial* and the *Florentine Histories* as well. Conspirators had already assassinated her husband and taken her and her children prisoners; they needed, they thought, only to occupy the fortress. The castellan refused to unbolt the gates. Promising her captors that if they let her go in, she would induce him to open up, Madonna Caterina left her children behind as hostages. Once inside, she appeared on the walls, spat on the assassins, threatened them with fearful revenge, and, crying out that she still retained the means to make other children, she raised her skirts and showed them her gentials. The conspirators fled.

This beautiful and remarkable woman touched on Niccolò's career in the beginning and the end. While he is still new on his job as Secretary he is sent as envoy to her court. A friend in the office asks him to bring back a picture of her. Later, one of her sons becomes a famous condottiere, Giovanni delle Bande Nere, and on him, in 1526, Niccolò pins hope for the defense of Italy against Charles V. Signor Giovanni, sad to say, fell in battle in a desperate attempt to keep the *landsknechts* from crossing the Po River.

Niccolò cannot resist adding to the *Florentine Histories* the sixth-century story of Queen Rosamunda. Alboin, king of the Longobards took her as prey, killed her father (the defeated ruler), made a drinking bowl of his skull, and wedded the daughter. One day, drunk with wine and victory, Alboin insists that she drink out of the macabre goblet. Bent on revenge, she exchanges bed places with her handmaid, sleeps with that girl's lover, a young Longobard nobleman, and threatens afterward to expose him to her husband as her violator unless he kills her husband first, which he does. They had to flee the country, however. Still later, in another plot, she tries to kill her consort in favor of another. She prepares a cup of poisoned wine and offers it to him after his bath. He drinks half of it, senses the rush of poison, and collects enough strength to force the rest down her throat. Theatrically, they fall over each other, dead.

Joanna I of Naples (1326–1382), dispatched her husband, which does not seem to perturb our historian. She in turn was dispatched by her brother-in-law. Her daughter, Joanna II of Naples (ruled 1415–1435), was the amorous widow whose favorites, successors, designates, and rival claimants kept Italian ambassadors dancing to a jig that many historians looked on with disfavor. Our historian treats her at length and with respect. In both *The Prince* and *Florentine Histories*, he hints that her sex might have created military difficulties for her, but not that she was inferior to men in political capacity. Being a woman, weapons do not suit her well, but neither do they suit priests and businessmen. (Madonna Caterina had finally to surrender to Caesar Borgia.) Joanna fought one battle after another with males, sometimes bested, more often besting them, never giving up her throne.

NICCOLÒ'S HEROINES

Women in history aside for now, the romantic loves and ideals of Niccolò, since they figure prominently in letters, plays, and verse, invite renewed attention. For one thing, they glance downward, from life to death, to the depths of hell. His song to Barbera claims that 'dying will be a game' that his soul burns in fire. In the Roman poet Ovid, whom he knew and used well, the theme, serious and satirical, of dying for love is strong. In the thirteenth century, the theme appears among the courtiers of the King of Sicily and Holy Roman Emperor Frederick II, and in his own verse, in the earliest version of the Italian language. "O alas! . . . the leaving of my lady . . . indeed it seems I died."

In Niccolò's *Serenade*, an object-lesson (derived from Ovid's *Metamorphoses*), a youth who kills himself for unrequited love first insists, "I die content." In *Andria*, the play Niccolò chooses to translate from Terence, the young lover threatens to die from moment to moment. In *Mandragola*, Callimaco, the young lover, consoles himself with the thought that the worst that this frenzy of love, this misery of hope and fear, this distress of spirit can ever lead him to is death and hell, and waits for the news that will keep him alive or kill him. Apparently, a lover when happy says, "I want to die for happiness." Our playwright must have noticed this, for he gives that line to Callimaco. Whereupon the unromantic Ligurio asks in an aside to the audience: "What kind of people is this? That one there, first out of happiness, then out of misery, wants to die in any case." Juxtaposed here is the perspective of the one in love who means what he says, and of the not-in-love observer who recognizes the malady and laughs.

Lovers, for their loves, not only die, they go to hell. Half of a half-dozen carnival songs that Niccolò composed at various times versify about lovers, dying, hell, and heaven. "Ladies, . . . do not send them to the cursed kingdom: for whoever provokes the damnation of others, to a like punishment heaven condemns her."

These loves and lovers, they glance upward, too. Callimaco's beloved Lucrezia shows him how. "A celestial disposition wanted it this way and

I am not up to refusing what heaven wants me to accept." Whereupon he hears the call of sainthood: "I find myself the happiest and most contented man in the world ever, and were this happiness not to cease through death or through time, I would be more blessed than the blessed, more a saint than the saints."

So at the top, through a zigzag unknown to Plato, appears the classical divine. "Whoever does not experience, Love, / Your great power, hopes in vain / Ever to make true trial / Of what is heaven's highest value." Niccolò the serenader promises that his song will always call Love his God—*te mio Dio*.

The Ass, where one finds the richest fantasy of physical womanhood, describes the poet's servitude to Circe's damsel. What does she look like? There are so many beautiful women. Who do we know that looks like her? Who expresses her spirit? Ghirlandaio's *Giovanna Tornabuoni*, Botticelli's "Flora," Leonardo's *Lady with an Ermine*? Most possibly Flora: "a woman full of beauty but fresh and leafy showed herself to me with her tresses blonde and ruffed." Niccolò's madonna, his duchess, his woman, is tall and gentle, with thick, curly, golden hair, the one with fine, arched black lashes and a mouth fashioned by Jove. She takes him by the hand, he abandons himself in her arms, she kisses his face ten times or more. Our hero blushes, feels like a new bride in the sheets alongside her husband, until his damsel taunts him with, "Am I made of thistles and thorns?" and pulls his cold hand under the coverlets and runs it over her body. "Blessed be your beauties / Blessed the hour when I put / foot in the forest . . ." Wrapped in angelic loveliness and pleasure, he tastes the end of all sweetness "full prostrate on her sweet breast."

Long might we dally in this bower of Apuleius, Dante, and Petrarch, but it must not detain us. It is not our poet's only conception of woman. He has some crusty views, too. Take the song at the end of act 3 of *Clizia*:

> The one who offends woman
> Wrongly or rightly is mad if he believes
> through prayers and weeping to find mercy in her.
> As she descends in this mortal life,
> with her soul she brings along
> pride, haughtiness, and of pardon none;
> trickery and cruelty accompany her
> and give her such help
> that each enterprise increases her desire;
> and if contempt bitter and ugly
> moves her or jealousy, she acts and handles it:
> and her strength exceeds mortal strength.

Certainly, this is not Niccolò's heroine, not his damsel of Circe. In his verses and plays, mean or stupid or unsympathetic women rarely appear, and never as the heroine. The heroine is so good she hardly has more than three lines to utter. A mean or stupid side to women may be found in the heroine's mother compromising with morality or in the wife avenging herself on her husabnd. The song above from *Clizia* reflects on the behavior of a wife, Sophronia. Likewise in *Belfagor*, the author makes sport of that special class of women—former objects of love, perhaps, now objects of fear, more fearful than Lucifer—wives. While not flattering, neither are these occasional harshnesses nearly so devastating and thorough as those of the great Roman poet Lucretius. Nor are they portraits, like the damsel of Circe, of the woman one would love to love.

(In the verse opening this chapter, for ready comprehension, the "him," wherever it appeared, was changed to "her." Niccolò follows the courtly convention of conceiving the lady as the lover's "lord.")

LOVE PAIRINGS

The metaphorical pairing of love and divinity recalls other love-pairings that might well be worth brief consideration at this point. The literature of political philosophy often draws parallels between love of country and some other love. Aristotle in the *Ethics* proposed the love of friends for each other. Niccolò in the *Art of War*, which urges that citizens should love one another, uses that parallel in a eulogy of his friend Cosimino Rucellai: his name will "never be remembered by me without tears, having known in him those qualities that may be wished for by friends in a good friend and by one's country in a citizen." Niccolò treasures the love of friends but recognizes its limits. Greater love has no man than laying down his life for his friends, surely, but Niccolò observes that in almost all tests, the love of one's own skin is greater. "One does not find anyone willing to go to a certain death." He cautions would-be conspirators that those of their trusted co-conspirators, "who for love of you would go to their death," might number "one or two." Then follows the lonely observation: you deceive yourself "most of the time in the love that you judge a man bears you."

The Florentine Secretary may not always have been so despairing of the people around him. Back-stabbing politics, especially in the Soderini republic, may have helped bring Niccolò to this bleak view. When he was away on missions his good friend and colleague Biagio Buonaccorsi would report the goings-on in the Chancery. Once he had to inform Niccolò of moves by some of the Secretary's adversaries to exclude him from holding public office. "You have so few who wish to help you," Biagio writes. Now, "don't go out and make the presupposition, as you usually do, that I see everything black."

Love in conspiratorial friendship seems, for Niccolò, to be similar to love for a new prince, for whom also there are risks to take, and both loves are related to the use of the term as a political policy, as a way of treating subjects or citizens, allies or conquered populations, a use current in political circles to refer to acts of placating, cajoling, honoring, favoring, enriching or rewarding, particularly in contrast with acts of force, coercion, or punishment.

The use of this contrast appears early in Niccolò's career, in a fragment of a paper delivered to his superiors in 1499, called "Discourse on Pisa." Of his recorded political reflections it is the first to be autonomous, to go beyond the daily writing tasks of the Chancery. Not that his literary talent was not immediately seen in passages of his official letters and dispatches, passages that could not have been dictated by his superiors. This is the first paper in which he attacks a single problem in political and military theory—the reconquest and holding of a subject city. The means he sets forth are "either force or love, as would be either to recover [the city] by siege or [to act] so that it comes into your hands voluntarily." *Love* is a policy that hopes to evoke voluntary political cooperation.

The antithetical pairing becomes important in *The Prince*, where it takes the form of *love* versus *fear*. "Out of this a debate is born: whether it is better [for a new prince] to be loved rather than feared." If he has to choose, it is much more secure to be feared rather than loved, for though a prince can regulate punishment, he cannot regulate love— "men love at their own choice," not his. In this context Niccolò sets the passage about what 'one can say of men generally: that they are ungrateful', and so on, identifying this love of a prince as friendship of a particular kind—bought friendship. The love available to a prince who has not, then, the love to which fear is preferable, is a bought friendship.

Friendship is not necessarily between men only, or between women only. Riccia may be a friend of Niccolò, even though (when he has no other place in Florence but hers to stay in) she calls him "house pest." She "opens for you when you wish," Vettori says, reminding him that she has great faith and compassion for him, unlike other women who, most of the time love the fortune and not the man, and when fortune changes, so do they.

Homosexual love has also been coupled with love of country. Phaedrus in Plato's *Symposium* proposes that only lovers are willing to die for one another. Were an army to be made up of soldier-lovers, they would never quit ranks or throw away their arms, would choose to die many times over, rather than behave shamefully in front of their lovers. Tyrants fear the love of such friends; experience has shown (Phaedrus continues), that the power of unity that lovers enjoy, if set against tyrants, can topple them from power.

Though Niccolò's military writings discuss what kinds of love or fear might hold the soldier fast and fierce in battle, they never seek it in homosexual affection in the ranks. Not that pederasty is unfamiliar. Niccolò has homosexual friends. Several of his wonderful storytelling letters of the winter of 1513–1514 detail some of their comings and goings, telling us how common a theme homosexuality is. In one, Niccolò confirms that his leaning is in the opposite direction. Vettori in Rome had been complaining of his houseguests and their discordant tastes. They had driven his usual pleasures out the door. Niccolò writes back that with such a scene of austerity, perhaps he ought to appear there to clarify things, for "I lay hand on and cater to women." On seeing the cheerless house he would say, "Ambassador, you must be sick; I don't think you're having any fun; here there is no boy, here there are no girls; what kind of a fucking house is this?"

There was one Florentine who, on the disappearance from the scene of Fra Savonarola, moralized, "Thank God, now we can return to our sodomy." That was not Niccolò; it was one of the city's highest magistrates.

Male-female sodomy, too, appears in Florentine literature, although Venice may wish to contend for primacy in that particular practice. While Niccolò was Secretary, an anonymous accuser brought charges of male-female sodomy against him to The Eight. "One notifies you Lords Eight that Niccolò . . . fucked Lucretia, called Riccia, in the ass. Send for her and you will find the truth." The charge was dismissed. The accusation did not damage Niccolò and Riccia's friendship. Ten years later he is still trying to steal a kiss from her. Now that we know her correct given name, we have one more possible source for the choice, by an association of opposites perhaps, of the name Niccolò's chaste-until-the-last moment heroine in the *Mandragola*—Lucrezia. In the play itself, Niccolò treats this particular sexual practice ingenuously. Scene: outside the confessional. A widow has just given the priest some money to say the mass of the dead every Monday for her husband.

WOMAN: But do you believe he's in purgatory?
FRIAR TIMOTHY: Without doubt!

WOMAN:	I do not know about that. You know also what he used to do to me sometimes. Oh, you, how much he hurt me with that! I kept away from it as much as I could; but he was so insistent. Uh, dear God!
FRIAR TIMOTHY:	Do not doubt, the clemency of God is great; if man does not lack the will, the time to repent will never be lacking him.
WOMAN:	Do you think the Turk will pass this year through Italy?
FRIAR TIMOTHY:	If you do not say your prayers, yes.
WOMAN:	Faith! May God help us with these deviltries! I have a great fear of that impaling.

More commonly, the literature of political philosophy and religion, by analogy, links love of mother, father, and home to love of country or God. (Plato in *The Republic* and Aristotle in the *Politics* exploit these analogies.) To depict the ideal relations of countrymen the most frequent metaphor is fraternity. *Brother* and *sister* occur frequently in Christian religious orders alongside *father* and *mother*, usages one sees reflected in the "Exhortation." The aligning of politics and religion also occurs, commonly in mottos and slogans like, *For Church and Liberty!* or *For God and Country!* Socrates in the *Crito* carries out the parents/country metaphor in a long passage, part of which reads: "it is impious to use violence against either your father or your mother, and much more impious to use it against your country."

The *Florentine Histories* picks up related varieties of the metaphor. Relating how the people of Milan rebuked Francesco Sforza for trying to make himself duke of the city by turning their own weapons against them, Niccolò writes: "You, yourself, will judge yourself worthy of that punishment that parricides deserve." In Florence, Niccolò notes, Cosimo de' Medici is called 'Father of his Country'. In 1469, he continues, Piero de' Medici speaks to the leading citizens of Florence: "So, this country of ours has given us life, why do we take it from her? She has made us victorious, why do we destroy her? She honors us, why do we vituperate her?" Niccolò writes all the above passages late in life, but earlier, his poem "On Ambition" expresses *country* in phrases like "the fatherland nest" and "paternal soil."

The *Discourses* recalls episodes of Roman history where fathers (Brutus and Manlius) had to kill sons for the safety of the republic. Actually, these were not so much instances of family metaphors as of the conflict between two great systems of allegiance—family and state—instances where the Romans chose state over family.

Niccolò is not a sloganeer. Plato and Aristotle are not pamphleteers. They do not blow their metaphors through trumpets. One expects to find great figures of speech in them because the emotion of love of country is powerful, although not existing anywhere in the same kind or degree. From person to person—modified by age, sex, personal traits, status, adversity, and prosperity—from parochialism to world empire, from petty suzerains to representative republics, that love varies. Each affection is different, and whenever it changes, a sentiment persists in which there is both something recognizably old and something excitingly new. In describing a new unknown, even a new blend of old and new, like a mixed state, a tried and true solution is to take recourse in figures of speech, in analogy and metaphor.

As Plato and Aristotle use more than one figure of speech in speaking of country, so does Niccolò. Turning back a bit, we may appreciate more fully that our author's concoctions in verse of love of woman waft the flavor of servitude, bondage, vassalism. They taste of Ovid's *Amores*, of ecstasy before the Madonna, of the *chanson de geste*, of the courtier's lyrics.

Songs and serenades bind our humble, faithful, adoring suppliant to the beloved heroine as her servant. Send him through hell, haughty lady, and if he returns prostrate before your throne, drip him a drop of grace. Phrases like "I die and burn" dot many of the ballads, songs, and snatches of the day, but other phrases appear as well. The verses of Poliziano and Lorenzo the Magnificent do not typically settle on a single woman: they usually bask in nymphs.

❧

RESPONDING to Vettori's crude conclusion that fucking makes the world go round, our poet sings of that young archer and thief, Love, who has put "such strong chains on me that I wholly despair of liberty, nor can I think of any way I may have to unchain myself; and even if fate or some human device should open to me some path for getting out of them, perhaps I should not wish to enter on it; so do I find those chains, now sweet, now light, now heavy, and they make a tangle of such a sort that I judge I cannot live contently without this kind of life." In chains he is free.

One example more: Niccolò's renewing of the theme of vassalage:

> Believe me who knows him: that man loves
> you more than his life, and you only he wants,

> you only he desires in this world and longs for,
> and seeks nothing else under the sun:
> that man calls himself your servant in everything,
> of you only he speaks, you only he honors and cherishes:
> you are his first love, and if you wish,
> to you he has dedicated all his years.

From such love as this we can move more directly to a parallel with love of country. Imagine that the word *you* in the above "Serenade" refers to one's country and that the words *first love* refer to love of that country. Suppose we should wish to compose an allegory of love of country and in it should wish to make a defense of Niccolò Machiavegli. We could use these lines without changing a word. Take that Italia now, as he describes her in *The Prince*—lost without a guide, without direction, seized by savages, beaten, disrobed, lacerated, enslaved, praying God to send someone to rescue her from barbarous cruelties and dishonor, searching the horizons for sight of someone to take her and raise her banner aloft.

What scene is this? Is it Perseus, the sea-monster and the virgin Andromeda bound to the rock? Is it the king's daughter tied there, dressed as a bride? And on horse, lance poised for the dragon, is that the Christian knight, St. George?

What to make of it? It could be one of those intramural games of figures of speech played by poets and tractarians. The lines of Petrarch that gave Porcari, the would-be assassin of the Pope, hope for Italy (and Niccolò quotes him in the *Histories*) go like this: "Above Mount Tarpeio, my song, you will see a cavalier that all Italia honors." Our author is open to so many literary currents, eddies, and whirls—the varieties of Greece and Rome, the historical, juridical, biblical, Arab, feudal, Sicilian, Provençal, Tuscan, Florentine, and on and on, not to mention the parlance of palace, court, and piazza. Once, in connection with his affirming in effect the parable of the beam and the mote, he writes Vettori, "I could adduce in example Greek, Latin, Hebraic, Chaldean things and go as far as the land of the Safi and of Peter John [Persia and Arabia] to adduce them for you if domestic and fresh examples did not suffice." Of all disposable models, he adopts the "Love, I am your servant" theme for abstract discourse in letters about love and for objects of love like the damsel of Circe, and for his lady-in-the-country, fictitious or not, and for Barbera who without doubt exists in the flesh and has captured his heart.

It may also be that these love themes—love for a regal lady whose grace the lover must have, that binds him to her in unquestioning service, that sends him hell-bent to save her or to gratify her whim, that enobles the lover and his sacrifices—these themes of the knightly poet-musicians of the eleventh to fourteenth centuries, of that literature variously and uncertainly called courtly love, love-service, or chivalric love, it may be that they attract our author for other than love affairs or technical experiment or fashionable literary choices.

We began this journal of Niccolò's loves because *love* is a word he uses to refer to sentiment for country, an ancient usage, transferring the term from concrete persons and things to the abstraction of country. The catalogue of objects of love and affection, ranging through spouse, offspring, kin, friends, courtesans, God, and oneself, contains two in which "dying for" is prominent and honorable in itself: the unswerving love-service of woman and of country. The directions in which this love-pair leads are complicated and at times puzzling.

Man's interest, passions, loves, and fears shape cornucopia out of which pour endless symbols and representations. The spill of permutations is sometimes startling to our prosaic eyes and ears. *Mary* can stand for a hundred different things in church, state, family, business, or sport. Savonarola preached that she had greater power in governing the world than any saint, and had been assigned power over Florence specifically. Mary may also be the troubadour's Lady, Florence's Madonna of Impruneta, and Niccolò's Italia. Nothing exhibits the possibilities so brazenly as the marble pair in the Vatican, sculpted and signed by the youthful Michelangelo, the popular "Pieta." There Mary, in the eye of the beholder, is virgin or mother or bride, frozen beautiful and young. The freshly wounded or dead man on her lap is, or could be, Christ the soldier or the soldier of Christ. In other eyes, he is virgin or mother or bridegroom.

The family metaphor of community may be most popular in political imagery; it may also be used with other metaphors, and it may be supplanted when circumstances put different calls on less prosaic minds. Niccolò must urge taking any risk for country. The family-country pair may appeal more strongly when there is a threat to identification with country—one belongs to one's family-country no matter what. Protection is what you offer, coverage like that which Mary in the many paintings of the Madonna of the Cloak or the Madonna of Mercy provides with her mantel. "Under the shadow of Mother Church," reads a coin struck by Clement VII. When risks for country are what you urge, the lady-country pair may quicken the pulse more—to die for that lovely lady, your country.

THE ALCHEMY OF LOVE OF COUNTRY

Niccolò may be groping for new metaphors for love of country, for the secret formula of an alchemy. Certain ingredients are at hand. Language helps. He appropriates Dante's linguistic definition of *Italia* (which ignores Spain): "every part of the world where the 'sí' sounds." In the tongue of that land *Italia* takes the feminine gender, as do the names of most other countries. History helps, too, and geography: Roman history identifies Italy as an entity, and ancient geography at least as far back as Cicero considers Italy to be a geographic unity, the peninsula separated from the north by the barrier of the Alps. This reveals a difficulty: a political ingredient is lacking. Italy is not politically "united as it was at the time of the Romans."

Over the preceding centuries, with the rise and fall of condottieri and tyrants, of communes and oligarchies, with unsettling patterns of rule and succession, with ever-present threats to the maintenance of political power, each city-state seemed to be someone's or some family's personal but nondurable possession. When Lorenzo the Magnificent writes to other rulers for aid, he pleads that he is in danger of losing *his* state. Each ruling group, aware of its feeble claims to authority and legitimacy, offers commissions to artists or digs to find roots in the past. In Florence, one of the strongest of stimuli to the search for ancient manuscripts and Roman relics was the need to strengthen the republic's claims to be descended from republican Rome.

Many of the separate Italian city-states, small though they are alongside nations, built their own forms of allegiance around princes and principalities. In republics, political symbolism typically celebrated antityrannical methods such as assassinations and antimonarchic concepts such as liberty. Representations, often stylized regimes rather than the state itself. In Florence, figures of both sexes serve in the political iconography of the ins and outs of republican and Medicean regimes. David and Judith are two Old Testament figures in Florentine art seized on to represent Florence and the republic. Popular sentiment embraces the Lady of Impruneta, a Madonna painted on wood in the late thirteenth or fourteenth century, which is housed in the baptismal church of nearby Impruneta, not far from where Niccolò owns a wood, and brought into the city by the authorities whenever great triumphs occur or disaster—drought, pestilence, assault—threatens. She stands not for a particular regime, but for Florence as a whole; her entrance and procession follows the hallowed foundation boundaries of the city. In gender, though patron saints may be masculine and may as such represent the city, as Saint John the Baptist and, in an earlier epoch, Saint Zanobio, Florence conceived as herself, apart from partisanship, is feminine—the lovely lady, daughter of Rome.

One of the great Florentine Chancellors, Coluccio Salutati, used both ancient literary sources and Roman architectural remains to prove that Sulla's Roman veterans founded Florence. Other great Chancellors extolled Florence's architecture as evidence of their country's political superiority. The old palace—the Palazzo della Signoria—is another symbol of Florence as a whole. When it was being built, the commune and people of Florence (so reads a document of 1299), wanted a temple more beautiful than any other in Tuscany. The building of the Duomo, the cathedral of Florence (now Santa Maria del Fiore, earlier Santa Reparata, and still occasionally called that by Niccolò), completed in 1463, surpasses it. Brunelleschi's cupola high in the heavens is the cosmos centered in Florence and covering an empire of the peoples of Tuscany. The cupola, whose construction still contains undeciphered secrets, presents indisputable evidence of Florence's hegemony—artistic, scientific, and theological no less than political—over the rest of Italy, a hegemony like that of Athens over Greece, over the world and the ancients even, for the Duomo, in the opinion of architecturally sophisticated Florentine men of letters, excels the Pantheon or the Hagia Sofia.

Less grandiose than the Duomo and the Palazzo, but no less beautiful, is Florentine sculpture. At the base of these artworks, for patriotic motives, inscriptions sometimes appear. The base of the marble, *David the Prophet*, sculpted by Donatello (who might be titled the iconographer of Florence) and moved to the Palazzo della Signoria in 1416, bears a message in Latin: "To those who bravely fight for country the gods will lend aid even against the most terrible enemies." (Inscriptions are usually voted on by existing authorities, but sometimes a sculptor will make his own contribution.) Donatello's *St. George*, free-standing in an exterior wall niche of the Church of Orsanmichele, originally in marble, a battle-ready warrior-saint, looks the part of Florence's and Niccolò's ideal militiaman, upright, incorrupt, and high-minded. Underneath, more at eye level, at the base of the original niche, stretches the divinely sketched, *schiacciato* strip of George, the horse, the lance, the dragon, and the helpless, praying virgin.

Now to return to Niccolò's own words. We observed in the previous chapter that after the 1494 walk-through of Charles VIII, followed by

Underneath . . . stretches the divinely sketched, schiacciato strip of George, the horse, the lance, the dragon, and the helpless, praying virgin.

the 1510 mission to the Council of Pisa, he begins to look on Florence as a weak state. Belief in Florence's glorious political destiny, of a future fated to outstrip the cultural world must appear to him as the rosiest optimism. He closes the *Art of War* with thin hope, urging youthful listeners, if they agree, to help and to counsel their rulers along the lines he taught them. He does not want them to despair, "because this land seems born to resuscitate dead things, as one has seen in poetry, painting and sculpture." This is a faint reprise of the theme of the great literary Chancellors of Florence, his predecessors—Bruni, Salutati, Marsuppini—and even so, Niccolò uses the general term *land* or *province* instead of the name *Florence*, leaving open the possibility that he wishes to indicate a region of greater size. He appreciates the power that great houses exude but seems to see that power redounding to the glory of single great families, not to Florence and her fabulous political destiny. The palaces that Luca Pitti had built are "all proud and regal," and the one built by Brunelleschi known as Palazzo Pitti, across and down the street from where Niccolò grew up, was "much larger than any other up to that day built by a private citizen."

That masterpiece, the Duomo, is to Niccolò part of the efforts by Florentines "to adorn their city." Like his predecessors, he does acknowledge the genius of the builder, "a most excellent architect named Fillipo di ser Brunellescho, of whose works our city is full, so that it was deserving after his death that his image in marble be placed in the principal temple of Florence with letters at the base which, to whoever reads, still bear witness to his skill." Yet Niccolò gives the great work of the cupola no imperial significance. He had the opportunity to do so, for in the *Histories*, he recalls that the Florentines managed to get the Pope to consecrate the new temple: "for greater magnificence of the city and the temple, and for greater honor of the pontiff, a stand was made running from Santa Maria Novella, where the Pope was living, up to the temple that was to be consecrated . . . all covered above and around with the richest draperies, along which came only the pontiff with his court, together with those magistrates of the city and citizens who were designated to accompany him; all the rest of the citizens and people placed themselves in the street, in houses, and in the temple to see so great a spectacle."

Once, our author mentions the Duomo as a sign of parochialism. In the *Mandragola* he has Ligurio nettle Nicia, the husband, for not being a man of parts: "you're not used to losing the Cupola from sight."

The claims that the Florentine republic had a special descent from the Romans seem to have eroded. In the account of the city's origins in the *Histories*, our historian of Florence brushes them aside. "I think therefore that it was always called Florenzia for whatever reason it was so named; and so, for whatever reason it had its origin, it was born under the Roman empire [not Republic]; and in the times of the first emperors it began to be recorded by historians." The *Discourses* label Florence's beginnings under the empire as "servile"; the effects of so low an origin have never and can never be overcome.

There may be some truth to what his enemies were alluding to when he was Secretary, that he finds too much fault with Florence. Niccolò admits that, "It is true . . . I am contrary, as in many other things, to the opinion of [Florentine] citizens." One thing is clear: he is not much interested in the city's claim of a special republican origin. He seems to be on the trail of larger game.

Such ingredients of political symbolism as we have assembled can be put to work in the service of small or large states. Europe contains as political actors sizeable monarchies and small city-states in various stages of expansion and contraction. Symptomatic of the times, the word *country* or *patria* becomes elastic. The same music can be set to different words. What can be transposed from Rome to Florence can be transposed from Florence to Italy.

We cannot go much further into the intricacies of a shifting iconography. The most we can do now is indicate lines of possible development out of a mélange of elements. Whatever Niccolò's larger game may be, it would seem that without a doctrine of special origin or descent he is left without authority for rule and allegiance that such a doctrine might support. In the stress he puts on the value of and need for preserving ancient ways, he seems aware of the lack.

In the essay he composes for the greater part late in 1510, "Portrait of the Affairs of France," based on missions to the French court, the Secretary observes that the people there hold "their king in great veneration," and he gives much credit for popular allegiance to the institutions of primogeniture and, in particular, "the Crown, going by succession of blood-line." In *The Prince*, for all his commitment to new principalities and provinces, Niccolò never denies the benefits of possessing ancient or hereditary institutions, be they of the church, a ruler, custom, law, or tradition. For a new ruler, "in hereditary states, accustomed to the blood-line of their prince," it is "enough just not to stray from the institutions of their ancestors." And "the ancient institutions of religion" are what sustain ecclesiastical principalities. They "have been of such power and quality that they keep their princes in the state no matter how they proceed or live."

Summing up toward the end of *The Prince*, Niccolò uses the hereditary prince's secure rule as a standard for the value of the whole latter part of the treatise. "The above-written things, prudently observed, make a new prince ancient and render him immediately more secure and firm in the state than if he had been of ancient lineage in it." One could quote this line as a selling point for the book.

Niccolò's same appreciation for the ancientness of institutions appears in his grand formulation in the *Discourses* that "all things of the world," in order to live as long as the course ordained by heaven, must return to the principles governing them at their origins. He presents this idea as a law of nature governing all bodies, pure and "mixed," under which he includes states, religions, and other organizations. Drawing heavily on his favorite Roman historian, Livy, he locates these principles and origins in religion, justice, fundamental customs, and constitutional laws and explains that the original principles of organizations, must have had "some goodness in themselves through which they might recapture their first repute and their first increase." Leaders and laws, before corruption goes too far, must induce a return to these fundamental traditions and observances. If they fail to do so internally or, as he says, intrinsically, the only chance for an organization is that their return be pressed on them extrinsically by some external blow, some event, a defeat or disaster, that threatens their corporate existence and forces them "to take greater account of their virtue." Several pages later, Niccolò repeats with greater force a warning to be found also in *The Prince*. "May princes know then that they begin to lose [their] state at that hour in which they begin to break the laws and those customs and usages that are ancient and under which men have lived for a long time."

LORD, LIEGE, LOVER, BELOVED

Niccolò, it would seem, tries to make up for the lack of a doctrine of descent or legendary or mythic past by enjoining a new prince—who would feel the lack most—from disturbing ancient principles, customs, laws, morals, and religion. The weakness in this purely negative approach is that if ancient doctrines and legends related to allegiance, religion, and morals are already corrupted or gone, there is nothing left for a new prince to leave undisturbed. The weakness will be clearest when the new prince tries to move men into the field of arms and warfare, of low pay and high risks. Niccolò seeks and finds a doctrine, or perhaps better, he already has it, in a sentiment, love of country.

Niccolò in his political writings does not use the phrase "We Florentines." Nor does he speak of "We Tuscans," although he does at one point in *the Prince* write of Tuscan as "our language"; and in the contract proposal he drafts for the commissioning of the *Florentine Histories*, he gives himself the option of writing the work in the Latin or "the Tuscan tongue." He does, however, write of "We Italians" or "We in Italy." Moreover, laying aside his official correspondence as Florentine Secretary, one constantly runs into the word *Italia*. By comparison, *Firenze* takes a distant second place. One finds Italia's preeminence even in the *Florentine Histories*, which he says will more than those books of his forerunners concern itself with domestic affairs. The opening of this last great political writing of his does not speak of Florence as a country but as a city, with one notable exception, and that in a recall of times past when its citizens could and did think of it as their country. Our author's first published writing, the *First Decennial*, enjoyed considerable success and was immediately pirated. We have learned of its Italic emphasis. The opening of the *Second Decennial* also, which he began ten odd years later but did not finish, announces, "I shall sing" of events on "the Italic site."

The word *Italic* forces itself on us most insistently in the last chapter of *The Prince*, a chapter of starbursts that demonstrate Niccolò's skill in metaphorical pyrotechnics. The startling changes of language these few packed pages present include a shift into Old Testament imagery and a heightened animation of Italia. They also present a radical change in the character of men. True, the disposition of men was open to spiritual improvement from several sources before, but our author seemed more intent on its lean to the side of badness. Moreover, he generalized often for all men (within limiting contexts, of course); now he restricts himself to the character of Italians only. The chapter title announces a concentration on Italy: '. . . Take Italia and Free Her . . .'

The Italians in this chapter appear to be new men. Niccolò includes them certainly in his earlier characterizations of *men*, where Italians, if not worse, are as bad as others. Whereas, they once ran away whenever danger peeped round the corner, now they march as perfect troops. "One can have no more loyal nor truer nor better soldiers." They have lost their envy, they no longer seek to line their own pockets or save their own skins; they exhibit obstinate fidelity and piety and obedience.

Whence this transfiguration? The chance for improvement we have seen thus far lay in true religion, good customs and morals, laws, arms, leadership, the rigors of adversity. With good leadership one might hope for overnight improvement, but Italy is weak in leadership, "because those that know are not obeyed, and everyone thinks he knows." None of the other elements, furthermore, offer quick moral conversion. Good arms, for instance, take time to institute and to work their beneficent influence on laws, religion, and men. The equation still lacks a factor.

In the last chapter of *The Prince*, though, Italia shows that she is "all ready and willing." And here Niccolò pens the lady-in-peril passage. Italia had to be disrobed and beaten and in danger of her honor for this readiness to appear.

Who is to rescue Italia, to raise the banner as "she prays God to send someone to save her from these cruelties and barbarian insolences"? The dragonslayer. Who appears also as the Messiah (our author intersperses the chapter with passages from Exodus—including 'God more a friend', and words like 'manna', 'redeem', 'redeemer', and 'redemption'). Who appears also as the new prince. "It seems to me that so many things concur in favor of a new prince that I do not know what time was ever more fitting than this." The dragonslayer, messianic new prince. *He* is to take Italia and free her from the hands of the barbarians.

We have already heard popes and princes crying out to free Italia from barbarians. They cried out, particularly when it suited the current international policy of their particular states. Ambassadors on all sides exploited the call to free Italy from foreigners but the appeal moved rulers and their envoys only when it suited their particular strategy. In a situation of indifference, other things being equal, they preferred to see Italians rather than foreigners ruling the other Italian city-states. In 1454, not long before Niccolò is born, Venice, Milan, Florence, and a few other Italian states formed the Italic league. It was, relatively, not a bad time to be born and grow up. *The Prince* describes the equilibrium then prevailing. Italy was "under the rule of the pope, Venetians, King of Naples, duke of Milan, and Florentines. These rulers had to keep two principal concerns: the one, that a foreigner did not enter Italy with arms; the other, that no one of themselves occupied more state." This was before 1494, when "Charles King of France passed through Italy," and a new surf of foreign soldiers began to roll in.

To find impartial appeals to free Italia one must look to the noble poets. Only they, independent of ongoing political maneuvers, cry out to all Italian rulers. It is a noble poet whose stirring lines Niccolò quotes at the close of *the Prince*.

> Virtue against the fury
> will take arms; and may the fighting be short:
> because the ancient bravery
> in Italic hearts is not yet dead.

These lines are part of Petrarch's "Italia Mia." The full canzone in which they appear is called, "The Rulers of Italy." That Petrarch is addressing the rulers of Italy does not appear in the lines Niccolò selects. In contrast, Niccolò is not asking anything of the rulers of Italy. He knows better. He berates princes at every turn for ruining Italy through their politics of ambition and division.

When officials, ambassadors, and courtiers talk about the unity necessary to free Italy, it is to come about through actions agreed on by the city-states. When *The Prince* talks about it, it is to come about through the deeds of a new prince. He might be found in an existing or embryonic prince. Perhaps he is a member of the Medici family of Florence; one of them at the time of Niccolò's writing is Prince of the Church; another, the ruler of Florence. Even without so suitable a combination, a Medici pope alone should forecast a pro-Italian and pro-Florentine policy. The Medici are good possibilities, and there may be others. The new prince may be found in the bulrushes.

But by himself he cannot liberate Italia. "Heads without tails die out quickly," Niccolò writes Vettori. His appeals to liberate Italy further differ from those of pope and prince, and of poets, too, by reaching farther, beyond them, to the men or the citizens whom he must press into the ranks. Without them, without those who for love of country will die in a ditch, a prince new or old, with money new or old, is not enough. The new prince will *not* be alone. He will have the support of the people, Niccolò foresees in *The Prince*. "Nor can I express with what love he would be received in all these lands that have suffered from these external floods [of barbarians]; with what thirst of vengeance, with what obstinate fidelity, with what piety, with what tears. What doors would be closed to him, what peoples would deny him obedience? What envy could oppose him? What Italian would deny him allegiance?"

To join prince and people in one body our author evokes an organic metaphor. He calls for a "head" of the redemption, and encourages him: "Here in [Italy] there is a great virtue in the limbs, when it is not lacking in the heads." To the same end he metaphorizes the philosophic distinction between matter and form. The occasion exists, the matter—the people, the material of the state—is ready and waiting for "someone prudent and virtuous to introduce [the proper] form into it." Again, what people is he referring to as these virtuous limbs or this matter aching to be formed? Hitherto he has not described the people of Italy as notable for their good qualities.

An intense, deep, working love of country for Italia, a fervid Italianism, is what Niccolò counts on in the last chapter of *The Prince*. Love of country is not something one learns as a general learns strategy in warfare. Its pervasiveness may be what leads Niccolò to say off-handedly, "Love of country is caused by nature." There must be an atavistic form of the sentiment that one may possess and yet be unaware of. This, it seems, is part of the reason for the occurrences here of the term *Italic*. The word triggers associations with the Italic League, the Italic Kingdom of Odacre and Theodorus, the Italic War of the rebels against Rome who called their capital Italica, the *jus italico* or right of citizenship granted by Rome to the Italian populations after the Italic War, and the Italics, the ancient peoples of the peninsula.

The Italians may be descended from the ancients after all. In their Italic hearts the ancient bravery is not yet dead. "It is necessary therefore to prepare for these arms in order to enable Italic virtue to defend oneself from outsiders." When in the opening of the *Florentine Histories* Niccolò writes that he will treat of "Italic" events as well as Florentine, he denotes events that go back at least to Roman times. When in the closure of *The Prince* he writes of "Italic virtue" (joining the two words that Petrarch gave separately), he connotes a virtue that has roots in antiquity, a capacity and will to do good for country that have never died out, that can be re-evoked—given historical readiness.

We may now be in a better position to understand the metamorphosis of Italians, from bad or vice-disposed to good or virtue-disposed. Intrinsically, even given wise internal rulership, there was no chance of a return to the original or fundamental principles that alone could save Italy. Its people and institutions were corrupt and inept; its princes, too. The alternative was extrinsic, an external accident, a force from outside. The barbarian floods provided the extrinsic blow that forced Italians to take a look at themselves, "to take greater account of their virtue," of the moral superiority of their ancient origins.

The shock revives love of country in Italic hearts. "Wishing to know the virtue of an Italian spirit, it was necessary that Italia be reduced to the terminal [condition] she is [in] at present." Out of readiness, occasion is born. Occasion is a goddess, Niccolò versifies in tercets of the same name; her head is bald in back, so that once she passes, we cannot grasp her from behind. While we waste time talking and busying ourselves with useless thoughts, we do not comprehend that, whoosh! she has slipped through our fingers.

"One must not, therefore, let pass this occasion so that Italia, after so long a time, might see her redeemer." From the Italic peoples arises the prince, a new prince, because reborn in him, too, is Italic virtue, that 'greatness and nobility of spirit' that scorns 'bought friendship' and counterfeit love, that "high intention" that distinguishes a Caesar Borgia from an Agathocles. Italians now salute him. A leader, a people, as one, to redeem beautiful Italia, enoble her and, through this arcane alchemy, enoble themselves, too,—lord, liege, lover, beloved.

Niccolò sees this Italianism as a poet-prophet sees. No one knows better than he that republican rulers do not show it. As Florentine Secretary, he is present often enough at meetings of the city's politicians; as envoy he is told often enough what line to take. No one knows better than he that the principalities and princes do not have the Italic spirit either. There are, to be sure, examples of their beginning to take to heart the accusations that, by asking for foreign military aid, they betray Italy. Ludovico il Moro, duke of Milan, who originally appealed to Charles VIII to bring troops into Italy and then tried to get other Italian states to join him in ridding Italy of Charles's successor, Louis XII, is reported to have been remorseful. "I confess I did great harm to Italy, but I did it to save my position. I did it unwillingly." And if phrases like "Italy must be governed by Italians," "the common good of Italy," "the liberty and independence of Italy," and "the need of all Italy" are frequently heard in the discourse of courts and councils, they must carry some weight. In these times of invasion, apparently even ordinary people of the city-states sing songs about "la bella donna Italia." Soldiers at the battlefront sometimes chant at the camp of foreign troops, "Italia, Italia!"

Sentiment for country does exist in the peninsula below the Alps. Not enough, of course. Niccolò cannot complete the synthesis of love for country nor foresee its future among the countries of the world. Even so, there has to be more to his formula, and there is more, as we shall continue to see, than the unswerving love-service of country. Yet we should not ignore the possibility that these love themes do find their way into popular sentiment.

As love can deny nothing to love, so love can deny nothing to country. The transposition we made earlier from the "Serenade" to an allegory of love of country applies not only to Niccolò but to any lover of country today. The persistence and power in these figures of love-speech, themselves originating in the political setting of courts, invite future scholarship. For Niccolò, the challenge is now.

Like the martyr dying for his Lord, so the heroic warrior would shed his blood for his Lord. Lords must have the love of vassals, else who will fight and die for them? Countries, too, need those who will shed their blood for them. Throughout his life, Niccolò insists that no one is going to fight and die for country, not nobles, nor priests, nor captains, nor soldier bought, begged, or borrowed from others. No. No one except her own countrymen. You cannot pay men to do what lovers of their country will do.

Bought or borrowed soldiers, *The Prince* declares, "have no other love or other reason to hold them firm in the field except a bit of salary, which is not enough to make them want to die for you."

The *Discourses* teaches 'That a good citizen for love of country must forget private injuries' and insists that "any citizen who finds himself in the position of advising his country" must remember that "where one deliberates wholly of the health of one's country, there should fall no consideration whatever of either just or unjust, kind or cruel, praise-worthy or ignominious."

The *Art of War*: "And in what man ought the country to find greater faith than in he who has to promise to die for her?"

The *Florentine Histories*: "so much did those citizens then value [their] country more than [their] soul." (Presumably *one's soul* is a religious term.) This passage refers to the Florentine "Eight Saints," who in the fourteenth-century War of the Eight Saints defied the Pope and the interdict, took away the goods of the local churches, forced the clergy to celebrate offices, and let the unanointed corpses pile up in the streets like uncollected garbage.

And in one of the last letters, Niccolò exclaims to his old friend Vettori: "I love my country more than my soul." Certainly this declaration can and does mean willingness to suffer anything for one's country—shame, torture, mistreatment, dishonor, exile. It can and does mean willingness to lie, cheat, and kill, to do evil for one's country, thereby forfeiting one's soul. It can and does mean dying for one's country and—if necessary—going to hell for her.

The code of love rests intact: the lover bound to his lady's service, to suffer her whims, her rejections, bound to champion her honor, to save her from dragons, bound to go to hell for her.

> Women, knights, arms, loves,
> Courtesies, bold deeds I sing.
> —Ariosto, *Orlando Furioso*, 1516

Is this then why the citizen should be ready to die for his country, because in some mysterious way she is his Lady, and he owes her a succession of otherwise pointless adventures? Or are there better reasons?

Chapter 7

THE POINT OF IT ALL

... to the perfect and true end.
—*Discourses*

NICCOLÒ'S WORDS about love would drill a hole through a wall. He says so himself. No doubt about it: when writing about love poetical and when not himself in love, Niccolò, like Ovid, sometimes has tongue in cheek.

There are three things that make people laugh, our playwright theorizes: you cannot do it with "serious and severe" speech. You have to represent persons who are foolish, or ill-spoken of, or in love. But . . . love of country never makes a man ridiculous. Indeed, he should suffer being laughed at, if it would help his country.

So, if we cut this connection between love of woman and love of country, if we dig up the substratum of courtly love, scratch out the troubadour's metaphor, what are we left with? If we say we are not interested at the moment in such imaginary things, what do we find of truth, a mindless state-worship? If we say as brusquely as he has said to himself, "this metaphor does not help me anymore," we may ask, why should one man, or two, or ten, or ten thousand, or ten million die for country? Again, what is country that one should love it and die or suffer any ignominy for it, that God should favor it?

In the language not of love lyrics but of political philosophy, we want to ask what is Niccolò's conception of the design, the highest purpose, or ultimate end, of one's country or of the state; or whether he had no such conception. The question in abstract form may receive many answers. It need not have one answer alone: a number of answers may fit together, or be operating in conflict, or not in conflict but at different times or levels. For as much as may be supposed, country or state may have no design or purpose whatever. Any end given it by the political writer may be a pretence, a sophistical fiction. Moreover, the end for which country exists may be different from the reason that one participates in politics. To judge from the sorrow Niccolò expressed at being out of politics, when in it he must have enjoyed it. Political activity may be a means to a livelihood, too, to listen to his worryings about poverty; and to still another end, the fulfilling of a duty, out of which much pleasure in politics may result. Participating in politics, for our author, may combine the pleasurable with the useful and the good. These biographical questions should not divert us, however, from confronting the teleological issue. Of the thing called country, what is the ultimate end, or as our political philosopher phrases it, 'the perfect and true end'?

To approach the answer, many critical areas of Niccolò's political thought must first be sorted out. How are country and state related? Is the state the end in itself? Or is the end to be one particular form, perhaps a republic? Is defense or peace the end? Can it possibly be war? Is it expansion or unity? Happiness or the common good? Is the ultimate purpose equality, or civil tranquility? Is it liberty and wealth, or justice? What is the point of it all? These queries will lead us to canter over a lot of territory familiar to political philosophy.

COUNTRY AND STATE

Niccolò writes a lot about country and state. Country is state when considered particularly and possessively as one's own country, as in the rule that must be remembered "by any citizen who finds himself [in a position] to counsel his country." Our author has need also of an abstract term, because of the propensity we observed earlier for making universal propositions. The state, for him, is country considered abstractly, as "Italy was divided into several states."

These two terms appear in many other senses as well, especially *the state*, which Niccolò uses so often as to give it a prominence in political philosophy comparable to the *polis* and *respublica* of the ancients. The meanings given above, which are as complementary as the abstract is to the particular, are those most important to his political philosophy. The very first noun of *The Prince* is the word *state*, and the very first sentence defines it in a dramatic interior clause here italicized: "All states, *all dominions that have had and have imperium over men*, have been or are republics or principalities."

The drama, which would be lost without literal translation, lies in two Latin terms preeminent in the political, legal, and military writings of Rome, the Holy Roman Empire, and the Italian city-states: *dominion*, a domain or territory, and *imperium*, the right or authority to command. The definition locates the constituents of a state in three nouns. A state has all three—a dominion, an imperium, and men. It is a special case of dominion (the *definiens*): one that is held by rightful (for which can be substituted just, lawful, or authoritative) command (which from its military antecedents contains a strong sense of sanctions or force) over men (who are located in the territory and obey the commands—laws, orders, rules, decrees—as rightful).

Dominion asserts its meaning in the terms of the sentence imposed on Niccolò in November 1512, after being let out of prison. He is not exiled; on the contrary he is confined, *in territorio et dominio florentino per unum annum continuum*. Six months later he writes Vettori in Rome that he would go there to see whether the Pope was at home, "if I could get out of this hole of the dominion."

The term *imperium* draws strength from its key position in the early struggles of Italian city-states to free themselves from the Holy Roman Emperor, struggles in the name of liberty that took legal form in the disputes of jurists of the fourteenth century over whether imperium took its authority from law or from fact. If the judicial part of the state is contained in the authority and command senses of the word, the ethical and affective parts rest in the imperium's position over men.

Men are the matter or material of the state and given form by imperium. Niccolò appropriates the philosophic (Aristotelian and scholastic) concepts of matter and form and applies them to the people and imperium of the state. His writings, especially *The Prince*, often embody imperium in a prince like Moses or another 'prudent and virtuous one' who when occasion offers him the matter, namely, a readied people, is able 'to introduce [the proper] form into it'.

Imperium is 'over men' because they obey not alone for its threat and use of force but also for its rightfulness. Germany, for instance, writes Niccolò, is "compartmentalized into the Swiss, into republics called free lands, into princes, and emperor. And the reason that among so much diversity of ways of life wars are not born, or if they are born they do not last long, is the very insignia of the emperor; who though it happens that he may not have forces, nevertheless he has among them such reputation that he is a conciliator for them, and with his authority, interposing himself as a mediator, he at once extinguishes every discord."

The position of *state* as *definiendum* at the opening of *The Prince*, its concise description in an appositive clause (the defining of terms is not a common practice; dictionaries are not at hand), and the drama of the *definiens*, herald that the term *state* is a linguistic innovation about to take a conceptual place in the work, as in the following statement from *The Prince*: "The principal fundaments that all states have . . . are good laws and good arms."

This brief description of an abstract concept—Niccolò never speaks of love of state as he does of love of country—foretells its importance but not its highest purpose or end, except in implying that it is consonant with the authority or rightfulness of imperium. In its particularistic form as one's country, it is something one should exalt and defend, love and honor; in that form, at least for the sentiment it should evoke, the state must be of great value.

There are several other meanings of the *state*, the most important of which often omits the article. Niccolò frequently employs it in a related, shorthand usage, which may be confusing, to refer to the imperium or command sector alone of the state. Thus, "he was still the leading captain of Italy and [because he was] not in possession of [the imperium of a] state, whoever was in [possession of the imperium of a] state had to fear him, and most of all the Duke." A rebuke of one Florentine citizen to another in the conspiratorial year of 1466 illuminates the contrast between state as *imperium* or the command sector and *country* as object of love: "this game that you play will deprive our country of its liberty, deprive you of the state and your substance, deprive me and the others of [our] country."

This variant of *state*, used when indicating the given person, party, or group who holds the pertinent offices in the command sector, moves easily into the sense of party or regime. "The Ghibellines . . . awaited only the occasion to retake the state." To cite the case of the change in regime that threw Niccolò out of office, among the intentions of the Spanish army was "to change the state in Florence"; to this the people should never have agreed, for by agreeing they gave up "the preservation of their state," that is, the preservation of a state that they had controlled. The same variant is also used sometimes to refer simply to the leaders or rulers of states: "men who did not have states but were like captains for hire [with their troops]," or "out of the ignorance of those who held states." At other times Niccolò will refer to the regime as the state's rulers, while keeping the term *state* in its meaning as country: "Those who governed the state of Florence from 1434 up to 1494 . . ." Sometimes he will wish to emphasize one or another of these various elements of imperium and will do so by mentioning it separately. "Whoever acquires imperium [here, internal, command *in fact*] and not [military] forces together [to defend it from external threat], goes to ruin." Or he may wish to stress the *in law* and *in fact* aspects of imperium and dominion located in a textual network like *the state*. The terms are so close in common usage that he will not infrequently exchange one for another. Or our author may play with a piazza usage of *state* by having a character in a comedy employ it. In the *Mandragola*, Nicia uses it to signify influence or a position in the government, "Whoever does not have the state will not find even a dog to bark at him." At other times he will take a usage not his own but absorbed from Roman historians. For instance, conceptually it is important that he keep the term *republic* to signify the form of state he prefers, a state governed by more than just one or a few; yet in transposing from Livy, Cicero, or others, he may use the term as they sometimes did, to mean a state of whatever form. At rarer times he may cite a usage explicitly not his own. Referring to the above-mentioned men who governed the state of Florence from 1434 to 1494, namely the Medici and their supporters, he adds, "They said . . . that it was necessary to retake the state every five years, otherwise to hold it was difficult; and they called retaking the state, putting that terror and that fear in men."

❧

AFTER the defeat of the militia and the sack of the nearby town of Prato by Spanish troops and upon the threat of an uprising in Florence, the Gonfalonier of Justice for Life, Piero Soderini, fled. Niccolò had not yet been removed from his office as Secretary. Although the Medici now had the upper hand, there was doubt that they would be able to keep it should the grand families unite to oppose them. In this period Niccolò wrote a short memorial known traditionally as "To the Palleschi." The Palleschi were the supporters of the Medici, on whose coat of arms appeared a varying number of balls or *palle*, at this time, six. The memorial illustrates Niccolò's early usage of the two main meanings of the state: as the state entire and as its imperium portion, the latter particularly in the sense of a regime's holding of imperium. Although there is no direct evidence, Niccolò probably sent the paper to some of the Medici family and their supporters, with the opening words: "Note well this writing."

We may see in it if we wish one of his first efforts to ingratiate himself with the Medici and an attempt to avenge himself on the optimates. The hostility of these grandees was to pursue him for years and his was going to pursue them, as we shall see later, in written form. The memorial is more important as Niccolò's first presentation of himself in the role of the impartial political counselor, one who has no partisan objective. It offers us also his first analysis of domestic politics rather than of the foreign affairs treated in previous short writings. He begins by advising the Medici that they should carefully examine the aim of those who wish to deprive Piero Soderini of his reputation with the people. They will find that "this gang" is not motivated to do "good for this state." Here the meaning of state is that of the abstract sense described earlier, the whole country.

By placing himself alongside the good of the state, Niccolò attests to his lack of personal or partisan bias. The opponents scheme, for "their own selves," to win favor with the populace by whom they are and have hitherto been hated. This egoistic tactic of the grand families would not help the Medici, "nor those who wish to stick with them through good times and bad." It seeks to deprive them of the favor of the people that they now possess. "I say again that to find fault with Piero [Soderini] does not bring reputation to the state of the Medici." Here the use of *the state* signifies a particular regime's possession of imperium. And finding the Medici on the side of the people, our political advisor confers on them the motive of doing good for the state, thus hinting why he aligns himself without prejudice "to the good of the Medici." Having erected this structure, the nonpartisan counselor can in his political analysis attack with justification this crowd of "enemies of Piero" (and of Niccolò), namely, the aristocratic families who "whore between the people and the Medici."

As would-be counselor to the Medici, Niccolò's advice is: Open your eyes. Do not let the self-serving optimates deceive you into helping them find popular favor. Since the people now hate them, they are weak and should be kept weak so that they will cling to the regime. Win and keep the people for yourself, for your regime and for the good of the country. *The people* here indicates those who have modest political privilege—in large measure, medium and small businessmen, artisans, merchants, money dealers, and proprietors. In Florence, the optimates themselves are mostly of such origin, too, but their success has been so great and long standing that in one way or another they have taken on the aura of a titular nobility.

In the "Discursus" a decade later, where Niccolò sketches a constitution for Florence, he will take the same perspective of a political advisor—now much more expert—who, because he has settled for himself that the good of the regime reflects the good of the country, can again counsel the Medici without prejudicing his concern for the common good. The Medici Pope's authority will increase, he writes, his friends will be honored and secure, and the "community of citizens" will "have reason most evident to be content."

❧

GETTING back to the problem of how to determine the purpose or end of the state, the possibility exists that the state, in the full sense of country rather than of imperium alone, or of regime, may come to ruin or be destroyed, by conquest, war or anarchy. By looking into cases where the state is destroyed, we may get some idea of what purpose the state serves.

In the "Discursus," which is addressed to the Pope, Niccolò alludes to the possibility of civil war in Florence—"from which may God guard [us]"—and declares, "I want to make a prognostication . . . Think, Your Holiness, how many deaths, how many exiles, how many extortions would follow upon it; [enough] to make the cruelest of men, not to mention Your Holiness who is most pious, die of grief." The author is writing about dangers that lurk in any attempt to transfer power where there is no orderly succession. Struggling to win imperium, men tear at each other's throats. The approach he takes is to imagine or call up from history or memory, cases in which the state's imperium disappeared, leaving license or anarchy or no state at all.

In these cases, the collapse of the state comes about through the collapse of imperium. A state may also be destroyed by depriving it of dominion or by depriving the state of its third element—men or population—or by separating men from their native territory. These cases, too, draw the expression 'cruelest' from our philosopher of politics. With similar expressions, we recall, he excoriates the acts of Philip of Macedon, who bodily "shifted the men [of various countries] from land to land." Such methods are cruelest, anti-Christian, inhuman. Wars of conquest that dispose of enemy commanders and not infrequently, it may be supposed, of the heads of conquered regimes, may be cruel, but wars that involve a migrating population and the killing off or driving out of all the inhabitants of the invaded state, are 'cruelest and most terrifying'. The cruelest things happen to men, it appears, if their state is lost, whether by destruction of its imperium, dominion, or population.

An equally fundamental approach to the question, and one often relied on by political philosophers when wishing to show what the end of the state is, consists of describing its real or imaginary origins, how things were before men ever organized into a state, when they lived in a state of nature. The *Discourses*, we may remember, begins with an account of the genesis of states. In Chapter 2 of that work the most general statement follows, narrating how men lived scattered like beasts and how, growing in number, they drew together and made one 'among themselves' as head, 'the better to defend themselves'. We marked this passage earlier, when considering the origins of mankind and morality, and noted that the account is indebted to Polybius's *Histories*. Since Niccolò does not read Greek, he must have studied the work in translation, where the Roman *respublica* was substituted for the Greek *polis*, following Cicero's lead, and so Niccolò turns here to *republic*, interrupting his newer usage of *state*.

We also noted earlier that this story of origins does not seem to interest him much. He gives it new and important twists, as he does almost any literary source he lays his hands on, but he does not mention or praise Polybius, as for example he does "Thucydides, Greek historian," or Plutarch, "a most serious writer." He does not project men's status or rights on the basis of the narrative, or defend the republican form of government as stemming from the original equality of men, or elaborate a doctrine of consent from their first choosing of a chief, or take account of the innate faculty of sympathy to explain the existence of the state, or justify war by citing men's earliest resort to defense. His moral philosophy rests on man's essence and its degeneration; his political generalizations seek and rely on men as they act throughout history, as they have been and are, not as they may once have been in a hypothetical prehistory.

WAR AND PEACE

One thing men had at their beginnings as men, it seems clear, and have always had and still have, is a need to defend themselves. The findings of Niccolò's two approaches to the state—as viewed through its ruin and through its origins—suggest that men associate in a state for defense and that without their constant military protection of that state they are doomed.

"Without armies, cities do not maintain themselves but come to their end. The end is either through desolation or through servitude." The Secretary continues: "Go out of the house now, and consider what you see around: you will find yourself in the midst of two or three cities [Lucca and Siena] who desire your death more than their life. Go farther beyond, go out of Tuscany, and consider all Italy: you will see it spinning around under the King of France, Venetians, Pope, and Valentino [Caesar Borgia]."

These remarks are from an early paper of Niccolò's entitled, "Words to Speak about Raising Money, Given a Bit of Introduction and Excuse." For short, we may call it "Words to Speak." He prepared it in an oratorical, yet intimate, style, probably at the request of someone who wished to speak to legislators on the urgency of raising more revenue to meet the dangerous military situation of the spring of 1503. It is another of those several papers he wrote while on the job, which were so important in the evolution of his style and ideas.

Political units that call themselves independent or free but exist at the mercy of others, are servile states. Strictly speaking, they are not states at all, but the dominions of others. They may have a formal or titular imperium but must do what others command, directly or indirectly, or perish. Italy, Niccolò writes in *The Prince*, "has been governed for many years by mercenary arms," and has been either their servant, or, as he writes in the *Discourses*, "the servant of foreigners." And, he narrates in the *Florentine Histories*, "in the end the way was opened again to the barbarians, and Italy put back in their servitude."

If not servitude, then desolation. The passage from "Words to Speak" that comes to the fore now is that in which Niccolò reminds his fellow citizens what an enemy army recently did to Firenzuola, a nearby town: "You began to feel the deserts of your obstinacy; you saw your houses burned, goods stolen, your subjects killed, taken to prison, your women violated, your possessions torn apart, without your being able to provide any remedy." These are the deserts of not being able to defend one's dominion.

In outrage and grief, the tercets "On Ambition" portray life and death in a make-believe state:

> Turn your eyes here whoever wishes to see
> the troubles of others, and look again whether yet
> the sun ever saw so much cruelty.
>
> One weeps for the dead father and one for the husband,
> that wretched other, from under his own roof,
> is to be seen dragged out beaten and naked.
>
> O how many times, the father holding close
> in his arms the son, with a single blow alone,
> the breast has been sundered of one and the other.
>
> That one abandons his paternal soil,
> accusing the cruel and ungrateful Gods;
> within, his family full of grief.
>
> O examples never having existed in the world!
> Because one sees every day many births
> born out of the wounds of their womb.
>
> Behind her daughter full of troubles
> the mother says, "To what an unhappy wedding,
> to what a cruel husband have I brought you!"
>
> The ditches and water are dirty with blood,
> full of skulls, legs, and hands,
> and other limbs torn and cut off.

Rapacious birds, forest animals, dogs
are then their paternal graves:
O sepulchers crude, ferocious and strange! . . .

Wherever you turn your eyes, you see
the land full of tears and blood,
and the air of shrieks, sobs, and sighs.

Crushing defeat in war, especially in a total war of migrating populations, and the loss of statehood, through anarchy or reduction to weakness and servility, swamp people in man-made catastrophes. The horror begins with unrestrained violence, inflicted by foreigners or by one's own—yesterday's—countrymen. The frightfulness of anarchy is due to the loss, with the loss of the state, of the moral restraints and uplifting influence of law, religion, custom, and leadership. If law is proper to man, if the law makes those men good to whom it is no longer proper, the consequence of the disappearance of law—not law written on stone or paper but law sustained by arms, custom, and religion—is apocalyptic.

Niccolò's grief over the horrors of war—and "God does not like it"—might lead one to think that the obverse of the coin is inscribed PAX, that if violence and rapine are consequences of statelessness, the ultimate end of the state must be peace. Unfortunately, the problem is not that simple. War is inescapable. It is rooted in the cardinal vice of ambition, as the poem above laments, ambition that pushes princes and peoples into a headlong race for private gain, fame, and power. Ambition pulls one into its vortex by a primitive relation of men and tools: "Between an armed and a disarmed man," observes *The Prince*, "there is no proportion whatever." And states act with the same passions as men. The "Words to Speak" warns that "every city, every state, must regard as enemies all those who can hope to be able to occupy its own [territory], and from whom it cannot defend itself."

The need for a common defense against other men, according to Niccolò (and Polybius), arises at the dawn of mankind and remains day and night. In the face of current evidence on all sides and in the history books, it is childish to cry out, "Peace!" As he is settling down to the writing of *The Prince*, he quotes in Latin to his friend Vettori, Savonarola's rendering of Ezeckiel. "I believe the Friar who used to say, Peace, Peace, and there will be no peace."

There will be no peace because there cannot be peace. States cannot stay for long as Italy stayed for awhile, "balanced in a certain way," so that they fear no other state while at the same time no other state fears them. Niccolò's acceptance of war as a fact of life is clear in all his serious writings. "One does not remove war" or escape it, *The Prince* says, "one postpones it to the advantage of others." One of many chapter headings in the *Discourses* that exemplify his matter-of-fact attitude reads, "Whether It Is Better, Fearing to Be Assaulted, to Charge Out to War or to Wait for It." In a letter to Guicciardini of 15 March 1526, he prognosticates," I estimate that in whatever ways things proceed, that [there will] have to be war, and soon, in Italy." War, the hell that it is, the gore that it trudges in, at best can be held to a minimum only by preparing yourself to fight.

Readiness for war is not easy to maintain. The Christian clergy is not meant to fight on the battlefield; and regrettably for the republican government of Florence, the business classes have no military inclination: they believe that the solution is to hire foreign mercenaries to fight for them. Worse yet, the wealthy are often unwilling for their own defense to open their purses. The proem of the *Florentine Histories* recalls that in the war against the Duke of Milan a century earlier, the Florentines spent three-and-one-half million florins and then went on to wage war against Lucca. But they were the Florentines of a century ago. Now, in the "Words to Speak," like a popular storyteller who in a few effective lines strikes a moral, Niccolò recounts an oriental tale. "And many of you must remember when Constantinople was taken by the Turk [1453]. That emperor foresaw its ruin. He called together its citizens, not being able with his ordinary armies to provide against it; he exposed the dangers to them, showed them the solution, and they made fun of it. The siege came. Those citizens who first had small regard for their lord, once they heard the artillery sound within their walls and the rumble of the enemy army, ran crying to the emperor, with their skirt-laps full of money, who drove them away, saying: 'Go and die with that money, since you did not want to live without it'." So, men of substance lose their liberty, money, lives, their loved ones' lives—to those who are ready and willing to fight.

Niccolò, who bewails the horrors of war, urges Florentines (in the concluding line of the *First Decennial*) to reopen their ancient "temple of Mars." He spends most of his career in military matters and risks advocating a militia. He insists in the second book of the *Discourses* (based on Livy's accounts of Rome's wars), that war is fought, "with steel and not with gold," that "gold is not enough to find good soldiers, but good soldiers are easily sufficient to find gold." Or as he restates it in the *Art of War*: "Men, steel, money, and bread are the sinew of war; but of these four the first two are the most necessary, because men and steel find money and bread, but bread and money do not find men and steel." Again the relation of men and tools.

Citizens may open their purses; that is still not enough. For they may empty their purses in order to acquire territory by buying off its defenders. "It would take long to narrate how many lands the Florentines and Venetians have bought; after which one has seen the disorder and how the things that they acquire with gold they do not know how to defend with steel." The Roman republicans "never acquired lands with money, never made peace with money, but always by virtue of their arms."

Or citizens may buy soldiers to defend their bought territories. Money may hire captains and troops and pay for the horses and engines, the drums and guns of war. In the end they will turn the weapons you bought against you. This is the conclusion that leads Niccolò to shun mercenaries and to seek a vast military reorganization, first of Florentine and later of pontifical forces, based on a trained and willing militia.

Citizens must be themselves prepared to fight. Again, in the proem to the *Florentine Histories*, he recalls that the city was able to raise 1,200 horse and 12,000 infantry—"from its own citizens." This happened more than two centuries ago. Perhaps the one sentence most indicative of Niccolò's preoccupation with war readiness appears in *The Prince*: "A prince therefore must have no other objective or other thought or take anything for his craft, except war . . ."

Military preparedness confers benefits other than defense. Niccolò's advocacy of the militia contemplates arming large sectors of the population and, as part of what he calls 'good arms', subjecting them to military discipline. The obedience and orderliness of good arms (or good military organization) predispose to law and order, and the danger of combat strengthens the need for religion. In turn, the civil benefits of good religion and lawfulness support good arms. This we learned earlier.

Good arms for preparedness against outsiders, moreover, make up part of good laws at home, the part of enforceability. For the enjoyment of domestic peace, law and order, and prosperity may slip into corruption and license. The evil disposition of men, their ambition, envy, and violence, lie underneath, occult, but close to the surface. So, "should [a republic] not have an enemy outside, it would find him at home, as seems to happen necessarily with all large cities." Without the jaws of force, the law would have no bite. Without the constraints of good laws enforced by good arms, the reins of evil disposition would snap, 'imperium over men' disintegrate. Peace can be a dangerous period for a country. There are "those evils that tend to generate themselves more often than not in peacetime," Niccolò notes in the *Florentine Histories*, and more emphatically in the *Discourses*: "were heaven so benign that a city had not to make war, it would happen that indolence would make

Peace can be a dangerous period for a country.

[the city] either effeminate or divisive, which two things together, or each by itself, would be the cause of its ruin."

Tipped at times by metaphors of growth, he seems almost—but not quite—ready to say that a state should keep growing, that once it stops growing it begins to wither. Such is the tenor of his remark in the *Discourses* that a country in which freedom prevails has two ends, one to acquire dominions, the other, to keep itself free, or, later in the same work, that "it is impossible that a republic succeed in keeping order and in enjoying its liberty and few boundaries, because if it does not molest others, it will [itself] be molested; and out of being molested will come the desire and the necessity of acquiring." A few complicating historical facts like the conservative policy of long-lived Sparta, keep him from an expansionist position. Rome, for an example of an expanding state, "lived free four hundred years," he observes in the *Art of War*; the non-expanding state, Sparta, lived eight hundred. Each "was armed."

Yet other problems turn Niccolò to an appreciation of war readiness and military expansion. "It has always been, and always will be, that great and rare men in a republic are neglected in peacetime." Indignant, they become restless, troublesome, warmongers. One solution is "to keep citizens poor" (a policy that requires later elaboration), so that they can "neither corrupt themselves nor others" with undeserved riches. The alternative is to "organize the country for war so that it can always make war," and thus always has room for military leadership. Reasoning thus, Niccolò finds that an aggressive or acquisitive, expansionist or simply militarily prepared foreign policy may busy giddy minds, shake the bleary-eyed and drunk, occupy the spirited, and keep all vigilant for liberty. He puts narrow limits to the policy in the *Art of War*: "make war willingly to have peace, and seek not to disturb the peace to have war."

Niccolò is not a militarist at heart. A republican, he holds with civilian control of the military. He has an idea of what the citizen-captain and soldier should be: what they were in republican Rome, where "the captains, content with triumph, returned to private life with desire; and those who were soldiers put [their] arms down with greater desire than they had picked them up, and each one returned to his trade around which he had arranged [his] life." The types Niccolò meets with nowadays do not exemplify civilian control but the servility of a country without its own soldiers. As soon as some one becomes a soldier, "he immediately changes not only [his] dress, but he deforms himself from every civil manner in customs, usages, in voice and in bearing . . ." To keep to ordinary bearing and words does not seem fitting "to the one who wants to scare other men with a beard and with swearing."

The day-to-day predicaments of Florence and Italy do most to keep Niccolò focused on expansion and unification. He rebukes the church, we recall, for Italy's disunity, for Italy's not coming to obey "one republic or prince, as has happened in France and Spain." Larger states, even a single larger state, can better cope with the ever more powerful and aggressive monarchies of Spain and France, with the invaders of Italy, who have already reduced its city-states to non-states, to states without imperium. The small states cannot remain free while the big states march over them, take them with chalk, dance like elephants among chickens. It is not that Niccolò dislikes smallness in itself. But "in the present day / each city lives secure / by having not even six miles around." He reflects on this in *The Ass* and recalls that, "To our city [of Florence] no scare gave / Henry [VII of Luxemburg, the Holy Roman emperor]: at that time [1312] with all his force / when he had captured the boundaries up to the [city] walls; / and now that it has its power spread / around and has become great and vast, / it fears everything, not just big armies."

Growth or expansion, for Niccolò, must be stimulated "by virtue or by necessity." States have an optimum size or equilibrium to attain. "For that virtue that suffices / to support one body when it is alone, / is not enough to hold up greater weight."

Small as they are, it is all but impossible for cities to remain free: "a prince should have enough state to support himself, if need be, by himself." Recognition of this strikes Niccolò from all sides, and guides his hand as it pens *The Prince* and *Discourses*. For this, he is intrigued by Caesar Borgia's career of military expansion; to this, his hope for a somehow unified central Italy is pinned, as he gazes at the conjunction in the Medici firmament of a possibly virtuous pope with a possibly virtuous prince; through this, may be explained his interest in new princes; in adding on new states; in having one's own arms and armies; in mixed states, customs, and laws; in confederations; in religious education and syncretism; in population increase—in a Greek word, in *synoekismus*, the amalgamation of several communities into one. As in the Greek view, typically an action accomplished by a single person, so it is, as a succeeding chapter shall show, in Niccolò's view. The most celebrated Greek *synoekismus* was the welding of Attica into one state by one of *The Prince*'s heroes—Theseus. It was "the excellence of Theseus" that brought the scattered Athenians together.

The predicaments of Florence and Italy impassion Niccolò; they determine the direction of much of his political theorizing. Yet, in themselves, they make up but a particular circumstance in the destiny of weak states. The pursuit of unity and expansion that they should envision cannot be considered to be a universal or ultimate aim of the state. Questions of unity and size are not to be defined by big or little but by what size enables a state to keep itself secure, or as he often puts it, to maintain itself. Unity and aggrandizement cannot be ultimate aims of the state; they are subordinates to independence, and independence is nearly equivalent to statehood. Without independence a state expires or is snuffed out with ease.

One can see now that while it is desirable to seek as much peace as possible, to believe in permanent peace is an illusion that brings something worse than war—war plus defeat, sacking, raping, killing of noncombatants, loss of liberty, death of country. Niccolò does not defend war for war's sake, or espouse the policy of regular warfare of the kind his middle–Republican Romans waged, marching out to battle each spring or early summer. Instead, he uses the language of the just war. A just war is a necessary war, a war that keeps worse-than-war as far away as possible. In the last few pages of *The Prince*, and in the *Discourses* and the *Florentine Histories*, Niccolò repeats Livy in confirmation: "Just is the war for those to whom it is necessary, and pious the arms when there is no hope but in arms." As contrary examples, the wars Florence fought with King Ladislao and with Duke Philip were unjust: "they were made to fill the [wealthy] citizens [with riches and power], not for necessity." If necessity impels you to battle, you have the right to war.

To conclude with an observation that may bring these remarks together, Niccolò, when telling the horrors of war, describes the ruin of families, of the fruits of men's labor, and of the lives of noncombatants. The death, wounds, mutilation, and suffering of troops are excluded. The soldier dying with sword in hand, facing his country's enemy, is not a horror; it is a brave and honorable sight. The victim is one thing, the warrior is another.

Peace, yes. "The Blessed Spirits" come down from heaven, Niccolò versifies, to demonstrate that "our Lord would be pleased to the full if [men] would lay down arms and stay at peace." But not peace at the price of further war and defeat and loss of a free country. The *Discourses* quotes in Latin as noteworthy a phrase of the Sannites to the Tuscans: "peace as slaves is heavier than war as free men." Peace and liberty, or independence, are fine together, but basking in the former loses the latter. Unlike other writers of the times, Niccolò cannot for a moment ignore war or look forward to peace on earth, to a concord with war putting it out of sight and mind, nor can he ignore the military and civil benefits of good arms. Permanent peace cannot be a country's ultimate end. It is part of necessity always to keep war in mind. Internally, it is part of necessity always to keep insurrections and conspiracies in mind, and occasionally to proceed to executions; externally, it is part of necessity always to keep war in mind, and sometimes to wage war. One cannot follow the course of "these lazy princes or effeminate republics" who think that the wisest commission they can give their hired captain is "above all else guard himself against coming to battle."

We can hope, however, for periods without active hostilities—if our arms are good enough to act as a deterrent. There are but three periods: (1) peace with danger, (2) war, (3) worse than war. Without readiness for war, there is neither peace nor liberty. The good leader in defending the people has "to love peace and know how to make war." So says the protagonist of the *Art of War*.

HAPPINESS

Another candidate for the ultimate aim of the state is happiness. When accusing the Church of having prevented Italy from attaining unity, Niccolò writes that "truly no province was ever united or happy . . ." unless it achieved a statehood like France and Spain. The word *united* suggests happiness as a group end. It also suggests that the happiness of a collectivity comes not from external goods or possessions but from the unity of the whole. Furthermore, it seems to identify the happiness of persons with that of the collectivity, namely a *provincia*, a nation or land or region—France, Spain, Italy. So far, this follows the Greek identification, as reported by Aristotle, of the happiness of persons with that of the *polis* or state. But Niccolò's *happiness*, unlike Aristotle's, is not the ultimate practical good for mankind. The word seems to play a minor part in his politics, appearing in a collective sense, as the general happiness, often in paired phrases such as 'united or happy'; or "secure and happy" or "ennobled and . . . most happy"; and appearing as the happiness of a single person sometimes in paired phrases associated with fortune: whenever you are at the top of the wheel you are, "for the time being, happy and good."

The happy-fortunate equation appears elsewhere too. In the *Discourses*, Niccolò writes that "the religion introduced by Numa was among the first reasons for the happiness of that city." The sentence goes on quickly to clarify the meaning of this collective happiness as good fortune: "because that [religion] caused good institutions, good institutions make good fortune, and from good fortune were born the happy successes of enterprises." In the proem to the *Florentine Histories*, he speculates that "if Florence had had such great happiness that . . . she might have taken a form of government that would have kept her united, I do not know what state, either modern or ancient, would have been superior." Niccolò's use of a conditional sentence structure in the last quotation indicates that by happiness he means *luck*. One can see that translating it by 'happiness', as above, experimentally, the sentence makes awkward sense.

Niccolò, in the draft letter of whimsies to G. B. Soderini, draws a conclusion: that person is "happy who matches his way of proceeding with the times . . . and truly . . . he would always have good fortune." In *The Prince*, he writes a corresponding passage: "I believe also that one is happy who matches his way of proceeding with the quality of the times, and similarly, that one is unhappy for whom the times discord with his procedure. . . . I conclude therefore that, with fortune varying and men keeping their obstinate ways, they are happy when they are in concord together and when they are in discord, unhappy."

Here we have a triple linkage—fortune, happiness, unity. Most often, it seems, happiness, when applied to a collectivity like the state, does mean lucky and is associated with the subsidiary aim of unity and concord, or with being on the right road to the state's ultimate end, but not with being that end itself. It is not the happiness at which Plato and Aristotle thought the polis aimed, and which, following their lead, Marsilius of Padua proposed as civil happiness and near-contemporaries of Niccolò made part of their own doctrines. Our author does not make happiness prominent even for the state of being in love: the lover is often in despair. Happiness cannot be tossed aside, however, as irrelevant. The term refers to the sensation of pleasure attendant on unity, and in the political sense appears associated with progress toward statehood, independence, and constitutional perfection.

The passage most revealing of Niccolò's conception of happiness as an aim of the state occurs in his opening constitutional arguments of the *Discourses*. "So that one can call happy [read *lucky*] that state that by chance gets a man so wise that he gives [constitutional] laws so arranged that, without need of re-correcting, it can live with them securely." Niccolò has in mind the case of Lycurgus and Sparta. "And contrariwise that city that, not having come across a wise lawgiver [and] having by itself alone to rearrange itself out of necessity, holds some degree of unhappiness [bad luck]. And of these, the still more unhappy [unlucky] is that one that is further distant from the [faultless] constitution; and that one is furthest from it that, with its [constitutional] laws, is completely off the straight path that can lead it to the perfect and true end." Happiness is still good luck and the pleasurable sensation associated with good luck. Rather than the end of the state, it is the good luck and pleasure—"if a republic were so happy . . ."—of being on the right track "to a constitutional perfection." What that perfect end is, we as yet have not succeeded in identifying.

THE COMMON GOOD

The two approaches to the purpose of the state that we have been using, evoking its origins in defense and security and its demise in anarchy, servility, or loss of independence, have revealed not the ultimate, but what may be called the self-preserving, aim of the state. To discover in Niccolò a positive and invariant goal of the state, its ultimate purpose, we may resort to a third expedient of the political philosopher and compare the ends of a good or just state with those of a bad state. As soon as we begin to do this, a net contrast appears.

A bad or unjust state is a tyranny, one ruled for private gain. Most of the time, when there is a prince, "what is good for him harms the city, and what is good for the city harms him. So that immediately a tyranny is born . . . and if by chance there arose a virtuous tyrant . . . no usefulness would come to that republic, but [only] to him." (Niccolò recognizes another ancient sense of tyranny—"an absolute power which by the author is called tyranny," but he uses it less often.) A just state is one ruled for the common good. The virtuous ruler, the new prince, the good citizen, the just war, the great founder-legislator—they all have as their end the common weal or benefit or good.

Niccolò's usage falls in the great Greco-Roman and Christian tradition. The conviction that the state's goal is the common good certainly antedates Plato and moves toward our author in the writings of Thomas Aquinas, in Dante and Petrarch, and in lesser, more contemporary writers. So intimate is the common good for Niccolò that he never troubles to detail it. In speaking about men, it may be expressed as the opposite of a conflicting private aim or simply as the good end: "if the men [involved] have the good end." In propositions about the state, Niccolò most often omits it altogether. Whenever he thus elides or merely implies the state's end, that end is the common good. Once this is grasped, the contexts of many of his passages find a determinate place. Moral and rhetorical texts, particularly, lose much of their equivocality and ambiguity. Often one learns about the common good from the vices and bad examples it is opposed to. Niccolò uses the term when other philosophers might use justice. And whenever he wishes to retain the morality in the word *virtue*, it is more likely than not the morality of the common good.

Moses, Lycurgus, and the other great founders of kingdoms and republics made laws "according to the common good." A less famous legislator, Cleomenes, also was able to do "this good for his country." Any single man who wishes to reform his republic must wish to benefit "not himself but the common good, not his own succession but the country common [to all]." The common good is part of Niccolò's own profession of faith, as observed elsewhere (including in his earliest papers); it is part of why he considers himself a good man and of why he can be an impartial counselor, of why he is willing to face the "envious nature of men" and the attendant "troubles and difficulties" of taking a path "not yet trod on by others." He is "driven," we recall from a previous chapter, by that natural desire to work, come what may, for those things that he believes bring the common benefit "to each one."

What may seem to be a tautology in this last quotation, the phrase 'to each one', may be Niccolò's way of conveying that the benefit is incomplete if it benefits the city or state, say in new roads or new buildings, by helping some of the citizens but not others; or if it helps only the prince and his family or a few legislators or group of administrators supposed to be concerned with the welfare 'of each one'. The common good seeks to benefit each one in some way. The seeming tautology is a slim reed on which to hazard this interpretation, but it is one of the author's rare self-characterizations, and the argument for-the-good-of-the-country versus for-the-good-of-community-members does occasionally appear in Florentine discussions of the common good. Moreover, we shall soon observe another expression of the common good in terms of its member-beneficiaries.

Not only founders and reformers of states but also the new prince will want to honor himself and to do "good for the generality of men." The ideal of that sort of prince can be found in the poetry of Petrarch. Earlier we heard Niccolò quoting some of the poet's lines that moved a young aristocrat to rebel against papal government. The rest of this quotation draws the rebel hero as "a cavalier that all Italy honors, more concerned about others than about himself." And citizens as well as magistrates and rulers should be animated by the desire to do public good. It is part of their virtue, too. When the *Art of War* questions what things of the ancient Romans should be introduced in these times, the answer for citizens is "to love one another, to live without factions, to value the private sphere less than the public."

Niccolò wants to stabilize the judgment of history, it would appear, on a number of personages who killed brothers or sons or fathers for the common good. Romulus is his most important case and, as he is aware, the best-known. "I say that many may judge it a bad example [to set] that a founder of a state, as Romulus was, had killed a brother of his and afterward consented to the death of Tatius the Sabine, chosen by him as his companion in [ruling] the kingdom." Niccolò takes the trouble to explain his unorthodox view. "Which opinion could be true, did one not consider what end induced him to commit such homicide." Romulus's end was "to benefit not oneself but the common good, not one's own succession [of descendants] but the common country." The republic Romulus founded and the "absolute and tyrannical" government he rejected, demonstrate that "in the death of his brother and companion he deserved to be excused."

The exoneration of Romulus's killing of Remus is but one of many shocks our author administers in the name of the common good: Brutus killed his foster father Caesar in "the desire to free [his] country"; Lucius Junius Brutus, "the father of Rome's liberties," executed his own sons for conspiring to restore the monarchy; Manlius had his son decapitated for disobeying the order not to fight outside the ranks. Manlius's way of ruling was "all in favor of the public" and cared nothing for "private ambition." In republics, a leader must show himself to be, like Manlius, "always harsh to everyone and loving only the common good."

Niccolò is opposed not simply to egoism but also to any altruism, whether for friend, sect or party, or family, that would hurt the common good. He urges magistrates "to close your eyes, stop up your ears, tie your hands whenever you have to consider in judgment friends or relatives . . ." He considers those persons who follow a leader bent on personal gain to be partisans rather than citizens. He praises "those citizens" who show that they value "the common utility over private friendship." The word *utility* changes color at his hands: It remains a positive term so long as the utility intended has no ill effect on the common good or is itself the common good; otherwise it becomes a negative term. In a moment of crisis, one of the anonymous citizens of the *Florentine Histories*, "moved by love of country," accuses the opposition infected with "love of [political] parties" of assembling "not for any public utility but for their own ambition" (in contrast to those who meet "for the public good and utility") and of making laws "not for the public but for their own utility." Princes and prelates who favor their families reap indignation. But nepotism as a particular case, if it helps the common good, may have his approval. Caesar Borgia gave his subjects in Romagna "well-being" and "good government"; Niccolò does not blame father Alexander VI for pushing son Caesar ahead.

EQUALITY

Strip yourselves naked, all of you. You will see yourselves alike. Dress yourselves, we, in their clothes and them in ours: without doubt, we, will seem nobles, and they, commoners.

This passage from the *Florentine Histories* is part of an eloquent speech our historian gives to "one of the more daring and more experienced" of "the plebian men" who in 1378 rose to arms and took over the Florentine government for six weeks. The anonymous speaker's audience is composed of the assembled *minute people* (the unskilled workers) and the wool-carders (also known as the *Ciompi*) of the wool guild. The oration contains several maxims drawn from *The Prince* and *Discourses*, and expresses Niccolò's anti-hereditary doctrine of equality clearly. "Do not let that ancientness of blood that they reproach us [for lacking] scare you" the speaker asserts, "because all men, having had one same beginning, are equally ancient, and by nature are made in one [same] way."

Among the arches of the common good strolls our political philosopher's egalitarianism, a good common to everyone. In ancient Rome, early political changes brought forth a regime in which the people "postponed every comfort of theirs to the common usefulness, and governed and preserved private and public things with greatest diligence." But a generation passed and "the children" were no longer "content with civic equality." Wherever "there is great inequality of citizens," he holds in the "Discursus," "one cannot set up a republic." All other forms of state are blemished by various forms of particularism.

The citizens of an incorrupt republic "keep among themselves a peer equality" and are fierce enemies of "lords and gentlemen." As fierce as Niccolò himself. "Those republics where a political and incorrupt way of life is maintained" are "the most hostile to those lords and gentlemen who are in that province; and if by chance some happen to come into their hands . . . they kill them."

Our author wishes to clarify the noun, *gentlemen*. It is a term with newish connotations, its meaning yet unstable, except as applied to Venice where, "all those who can hold administrative office are called gentlemen." Niccolò is going to put his own stamp on it. "And to clarify this name of gentlemen as it stands, I say that those are called gentlemen who, idle, live abundantly from the incomes of their possessions, without having any care either of cultivation or of other effort necessary to [make a] living. . . . Out of this discourse then I draw this conclusion: that he who wishes to form a republic wherever there are lots of gentlemen, cannot do it if he does not first get rid of all of them; and he who wishes to form a kingdom or principality wherever there is much equality, will never be able to do it" unless he derives gentlemen from "out of that equality."

We are hearing an echo of the ancient justification of property by use. Whoever owns property, especially property in land, and does not put it to some good, owns it unjustly. Niccolò himself owns land, but he personally manages its cultivation when he is on the property. Not to care for the land properly, for its produce and animals, its wine and oil, is unthinkable. His son Bernardo, as a young man of twenty-three, anxious about the approach of marauding foreign soldiers, once wrote him: "We beg you to write if the enemies are thinking of coming to do us damage, because we still have many things in the villa: wine and oil, even though we have [already] brought down here twenty or twenty-three barrels." Niccolò not only sells the usual Tuscan farm products like wine ("the wine that you sent us [a message] to sell"), but lumber, too. "In the morning I get up with the sun and take myself to a wood that I am having cut, where I stay two hours to look over the work of the previous day . . ." Supervising the farm aside, Niccolò insists he has to work for a living. If he does not work he is just a costly mouth to feed. We have already heard him complain after everything was 'totally wrecked' that if God did not show himself more favorable he would be forced one day to leave home and to stick himself in some deserted land to teach writing to the young.

Gentlemen exercise no occupation. *Otiose* is an unpleasant word in Niccolò's lexicon. These gentlemen are otiose. We may call them *landed gentlemen*. Our author goes on to define another kind. "These fellows are pernicious in any republic and in any religion; but more pernicious are those who, in addition to the above-mentioned fortune, command from castles, and have subjects to obey them." This second type—which is to be found in the regions of Naples, Rome, the Romagna, and Lombardy—may be called *feudal gentlemen*. They own land and are idle; they are distinguished by possessing castles and the sort of 'imperium over men' that goes with castles. (Caesar Borgia wooed those in Rome from their allegiance to the Colonna and Orsini families, our author notes in *The Prince*, by heaping on them stipends, military commands, and public offices.)

Niccolò next answers a possible objection. "I believe that to this opinion of mine, that wherever there are gentlemen one cannot form a republic, the experience of the Venetian Republic will seem contrary, in which only those who are gentlemen have any rank. To which one answers that this example is not in opposition at all, because the gentlemen in that republic are [such] more in name than in fact: because they do not have great revenues from land holdings, their great riches being based on merchandise and movable property." This third example of gentlemen is a negative case, a class composed of false gentlemen. As they are not real gentlemen, Niccolò favors them. As a group they would have no proper title and he gives them no new one, letting them remain as gentlemen-in-name. We may call this third type, *gentlemen of affairs*. They have no aristocratic title other than gentleman; they have no direct command over men, but they have political influence: their wealth gives them access to political office and honors.

But not their wealth alone. So far, Niccolò's definitions discuss neither heredity nor armed service to a lord as a claim to aristocracy or gentlemanliness. Although elsewhere he does mention these factors, the distinguishing contrasts here in the *Discourses* are confined to political command or jurisdiction versus political influence, property versus no property, real or landed versus personal and city-based property, idleness versus work. The hereditary element can be taken for granted, since the laws of property succession protect family succession to wealth along male lines rather more effectively for real or landed than personal or movable property. There is another distinction, however, brought up elsewhere in the *Discourses*, that the enfranchised, originally resident, moneyed gentlemen of Venice are not few in number but many, so numerous in truth that "the number of gentlemen either is equal to [the un-enfranchised relative newcomers] or it is superior." They comprised nearly a majority, it would seem, and thus Venice, though replete with gentlemen, would still classify as a republic. To contrast families of original inhabitants with "those who came there to live afterward," however, does not brush the Venetian gentlemen with a hereditary stain.

As a republican, Niccolò believes that access to political office and policy should be open to men who are called citizens, not subjects. He is not a democrat in the sense of advocating that such access be granted to all adults, or even to all male inhabitants. He never poses the question. Even if he were to use the phrase *universal suffrage*, and he does not, its meaning would take in not all men, as the term *democracy* connotes, but simply *more than a few*, which is as far as the term *republic* technically commits itself, and which in these days of the Florentine Secretary amounted to about one-fifth of adult male Florentines. Republics can be qualified by the adjectives *popular* (or democratic) or *aristocratic* (or oligarchic) to indicate mainly the greater or lesser proportion of persons with franchise. Niccolò's narration of internal discords in the *Florentine Histories* often illustrates that the aim of the struggles was in part to widen or narrow political access, as in the dramatic uprising in 1378 of the unskilled workers and the wool-carders. They demanded separate guilds—one for wool-carders and dyers, another for barbers, doublet makers, tailors, and similar mechanical trades, and the third for the "minute people"—and representation in the highest legislative organ, the Signoria.

Niccolò's position generally is that access to political office and policy should be open to more men than present statutes provide for. In the *Discourses* he cites with favor the liberality the Romans showed in donating citizenship to foreigners, even when "so many new people [were] born who began to have so much of a part in suffrage" that new (but not insurmountable) difficulties arose. In sketching a new constitution for Florence, he proposes to enlarge the Great Council, which is considered the most democratic of Florentine legislative institutions. He does this in the teeth of the Medici, who had asked for his recommendations, but whose firm policy is to restrict political access to a number of men they can control. Niccolò does make provisional concessions to the present rulers: he asks them to consider themselves—Pope, Cardinal, their family and friends—as but lifetime tenants of Florentine lordship! At the expiration of their term, namely, at the Pope and Cardinal's deaths, lordship would return to the republic. Not an easy thing to propose, but he does it. He tries to take some bitterness out of the gesture. With a graceful bow to mortality, "Arranging thus the [organs of] state, if Your Holiness and the most reverend monsignor were to live forever, it would not be necessary to provide for anything else; but [your] having to be missing [someday], and wishing that a perfect republic may remain . . ."

As he works it out, "I judge it necessary to reopen the hall of the [Great] Council of one thousand, or at least of six hundred citizens, . . ." for "[i]t remains now to satisfy the third and last rank of men, which is the generality of citizens." The other two he here calls the first and middle ranks. The generality "will never be satisfied (and whoever believes differently is not wise), unless one renders them and promises to render them their authority." Unless this many men take part in government, apparently, it is not republican in form. "Without satisfying the generality of men, one never made any kind of stable republic. One will never satisfy the generality of Florentine citizens, if one does not reopen the hall [of the Great Council]; therefore, it is proper, wishing to make a republic in Florence, to reopen this hall, and to render this distribution [of powers] to the generality of men, and may Your Holiness realize that whoever thinks of taking the state from you, will think before anything else of reopening [the hall]. And therefore it is the better move that you open it with secure terms and means, and that you remove from whoever might be your enemy this occasion to reopen it [themselves] to your displeasure, and to the destruction and ruin of your friends."

Dedication to the ideal of the common good and the equality it implies leads Niccolò to make a most intensive study of factions, of "the divisions," "parts," or "sects" that arise within a state and work against the common good, a study of nobles, grandees, optimates, and magnates; the people, the fat and the minute people, the powerful, middling, and low people; men of breeding, of riches, and of industry; the plebs, the barons; landed, encastled, and moneyed gentlemen; the multitude, the generality, the prelates, businessmen, craftsmen and minor craftsmen; the first, middle, and last ranks—to list most of the distinctions he makes and which, as he says, in various countries go "under various names."

One antagonism, Niccolò believes, is found in all cities—people versus the grandees. But each group of the above lengthy list has a different temperament or leaning, a durable cast of mind and feeling, that reveals it to be conscious of others as distinct in honors, belongings, and political power. Often, Niccolò calls the dispositions of these groups appetites or humors, or both: "Because in every city one finds these two diverse humors . . . and from these two diverse appetites comes . . ." They are terms with an ancient and medieval history in medicine and philosophy. *Appetite* is an important word in our author's general theory of human nature, as we learned in Chapter 4 above. *Humor* dates back to the old medical theory of humidity and the body's four fluids (blood, phlegm, yellow and black bile) and may still be used to mean saliva. "Castruccio, [having] gathered a lot of humor in his mouth, spat it all out in Taddeo's face." The term, it would seem, is already a dead metaphor: the variety of verbs Niccolò uses with it often seem to preclude metaphoric extension.

The occurrence of internal divisions Niccolò will explain in some depth, frequently attributing them to desires—for one, to the illimitability of men's desires in general; for another, to their particular desire to preserve what they have, which leads them to want to get more to keep what they already have. These desires and counter-desires ultimately lead back to the deadly sin of ambition. The poem, "On Ambition," it may be remembered, refers to the tendency to regard the good of others as bad and the bad of others as good, as a 'natural instinct', something that requires braking by "law or greater force."

So honors, possessions, and political power cannot fully satisfy men: "human appetites being insatiable, because having from nature the ability and will to desire everything and from fortune the ability to obtain [but] a few of them, there continuously results a malcontentedness with what they possess, and small satisfaction with it." Discontent and desire remain. Those with political power will desire "to dominate" and the others will desire "not to be dominated," or the one will want "to command" and the other "not to obey," and those who wish to acquire are pitted against those who "fear to lose [what they have] acquired," one "who forces" against one "who is forced," and one who "wants to keep the honor already acquired" against one who "wants to acquire [that honor] he has not," those who fear "to lose" against those who wish "to acquire," and those "who have" against those who "desire to have."

Though such divisions always exist, the inclinations, humors, or appetites of any one group may undergo radical change. Niccolò is under no illusion that when the seesaw of politics brings to the top those who want 'not to be dominated', they will keep their temper sweet and humble. He refers to Livy, "where he says that always either the People or the Nobility lorded it and the other was humiliated." We are already familiar with the chapter title that begins, "Men Jump from One Ambition to Another," and ends, "and First They Seek Not to Be Injured, Then They Injure Others." In the *Florentine Histories*, Niccolò will give ample illustration of the insolence and oppressiveness of the plebs who revolted, took power, and ruled, or, as he puts it, "from 1378 to 81 subjugated [the city] with its arrogance."

Likewise, he will treat of the haughtiness and ambition of "the people and, of them, the part most ignoble." A quarter-century before, after the overthrow of the duke of Athens (described in Chapter 4 above), "the cruelest enemy of the name Florentine would have been ashamed of such great destruction." One saw then "through experience" that "the haughtiness and ambition of the grandees was not extinguished [with their destruction] but was taken over from them by our common people." For men on all sides, he generalizes, "it is not enough that they recover what is theirs, but want to take over that of others and avenge themselves."

In all this there is no attribution of cause specifically to economic needs or station. Rather, it seems that if men are in no position to oppress, they try not to be oppressed. If they *are* in a position to oppress, they oppress. What counts is the relative capacity of the groups to oppress, each desiring more or less the same mundane things—riches, honors, political power, possessions—one group having a lot, another having little.

Thus the "stench of the plebs," as well as the "arrogance of the grandees" or of the gentlemen or of any other rank, overpowers whenever it can, however the economic and political bases of each group may differ. The power to oppress affects those who want "to keep the [position of] honor already acquired" as well as those "who want to get that [position of honor] which they do not have." *Honor* here refers to men's status or position built on their possession of the same old things—riches, titles, trappings, office. Thus our author can say more succinctly on the next page of his *Histories* that the main gulf lies between those who want 'to keep' and those who want 'to get'.

Good moralist that he is, Niccolò goes further. Asking which kind of men are the "more harmful in a republic, those who wish to acquire or those who fear to lose the acquired," he asserts without hesitation in a brilliant analysis, that ambition grips more those who possess than those who want to get:

> the one appetite or the other can easily be the cause of greatest tumults. Nevertheless, most often they are caused by those who possess, because the fear of losing generates in them the same desires that are in those that want to acquire; because it does not seem to men that they possess securely that which [a] man has if one does not acquire some more again. And there is more: that possessing much, these with greater power and greater movement can make change [take place]. And there is more still, that their impermissible and ambitious behavior fires the desire of possession in the breasts of those who do not possess, either in order to revenge themselves against them by despoiling them, or in order to enable them to have access to those riches and honors that they see badly used by the others.

From the country, in the summer of 1513, Niccolò writes Vettori of men and states. "And I beg you to consider the things of men as they should be believed and the powers of the world, and mainly of republics, how they increase; and you will see how to men it is first enough to be able to defend themselves and not be dominated by others; from this they rise to offending others and wish to dominate others." They, men and states both, like to taste "the sweetness of dominating."

When he comes to write the *Florentine Histories*, Niccolò says at the start that he is going to pay more attention than preceeding historians of Florence to "civil discords, to intrinsic enmities." "I shall describe particularly, up to 1434, only the things [that] occurred inside the city, and of those outside I shall not say more than will be necessary for the understanding of those inside." While other countries have had one split, "Florence not content with one, had made many." First there were "the nobles among themselves, then the nobles and the people, and at the end the people and the plebs, and often it happened that one of these parts, remaining superior, divided itself in two, out of which divisions were born so many deaths, so many exiles, so many destructions of families than ever were born in any city of which one has memory. . . . [Instead] if Florence had taken the form of government that would have kept it united, I do not know what republic either modern or ancient would have been superior to it."

The civil divisions and natural enmities he laments are not to be mistaken for the tumults he praises in the *Discourses*. "Tumults," the word Niccolò chooses here, consist of internal conflicts that "rarely give birth to exiles, and most rarely to bloodshed." He seems to be indicating commotions of civil protest: "the people together shouting against the Senate, the Senate against the People, to run tumultuously through the streets, to bar up the shops, all the plebs leaving Rome, which things frighten only those who read of them." Such forms of protest do not produce "any exile or violence in disfavor of the common good, but [create] laws and institutions of benefit to public liberty"—provided a country is not already corrupt and its men have "the good end" in view. Then, "tumults" do not harm; "indeed they do good for the republic." They tune the laws more finely.

The occurrence of violent death in these struggles is both indicative and causal of deep discord. As long as there are no deaths, the policy can be to allow people, in a phrase Niccolò repeats, "to give vent to" their anger or mood or bad feeling, a problem that can be handled by authority; if deaths occur, he affirms in the *Discourses* and the *Histories*, sects and their partisans spring up, and the affair gets out of hand. The *Discourses* traces the causal pattern: death in a clash is an "injury by a private person on another private person, which injury generates fear, the fear seeks defense, for defense partisans are sought, from partisans factions are born in the cities, from factions [comes] the [cities'] ruin."

Civil discord and war, in contrast to tumults, loom huge and ominous. They can change the regime, lay the country open to foreign intrigue, and stir up the danger of anarchy. Niccolò states in *The Prince* that in every city one finds these two, appetites "that the people do not want to be commanded or oppressed by the grandees, and the grandees want to command and oppress the people: and from these two diverse appetites comes one of three effects, either a principate or liberty or license." By *liberty* he means a republic; by *license* he means anarchy. Italy today being unbalanced, he continues, "I do not believe that divisions [into factions] ever do any good."

Niccolò's strictures on divisiveness indicate that the equality republican laws provide aims at a balance wherein no citizen can oppress another. He seeks for the concord that ensures the common good. He certainly does not find it among the unhappy fruits of rebellion as the state collapses in discord and anarchy, or in tyranny or absolutism, where by definition the good sought belongs to the tyrant or absolute monarch. Though he be "a virtuous tyrant—no good would result to that republic, but just to him. . . . So that he profits from his acquisitions and his country does not. And whoever would like to confirm this opinion with infinite other reasons, read Xenophon in his treatise that makes up *Of Tyranny*."

Although principates or monarchies are states, and may be good states, as was the Roman empire from Nerva to Marcus Aurelius, if hereditary, dynastic, or family succession is the rule, they are unlikely to be good states. According to Niccolò, the period from Nerva to Marcus was good because it was then that the Roman emperors nominated their own successors by adoption. In any case, while hereditary one-man rule may be legitimate and certainly better than anarchy, while, as we saw in the previous chapter, it may make ruling easier and longer lasting, it can never be the best form of state, which for Niccolò can only be a republic. Only a republic tends to the common good.

LIBERTY: THE FREE WAY OF LIFE

Asking what is the best as opposed to a merely good state, is yet another—a fourth—way political philosophers have of approaching the ultimate purpose of the state. "It is not," our political philosopher writes, "the particular good but the common good that makes cities great. And without doubt this common good is observed nowhere but in a republic . . . it is no wonder then that ancient peoples persecuted tyrants with so much hate and loved the free way of life, and that the name of liberty was so highly esteemed by them."

Niccolò equates republics not only with equality and the common good but with the free way of life as well. 'The free way of life' is a synonym for republic. The word *liberty*, externally, in foreign affairs (as in the struggles of the communes to free themselves from the Holy Roman empire), comes to mean independence of one state from any other, to mean not merely legal liberty but factual, assured by the good arms that enable it to be and stay free. Internally, in domestic affairs, it means a republic where a sizeable body of citizens share the privilege of a king or prince, of an aristocracy or oligarchy, to wit, to legislate by and for themselves. Conflict within the common good arises when some group, for one reason or other, gains enough power to push through particularistic laws or to install partisan officials exclusively. "Those laws they then created were designed not for the common utility but all in favor of the winner." This is holding power not "by laws" but "by sects or divisions, not according to the free way of life, but according to the ambitions of that party that has won."

Aside from comment on particular republican institutions like the tribunate and dictatorship in ancient Rome or the Great Council in Florence, Niccolò rarely discusses what specific freedoms are important to the free way of life. He does talk about the importance of rulers' not breaking their own laws, and in this respect, refers to republican rulers Savonarola and Soderini. He writes also about a republic's offering "honors and rewards because of some honest and determined reasons, and outside of those it does not reward or honor anyone." Niccolò extends this passage of the *Discourses* by observing that "that common utility which one draws from a free way of life . . . is to be able to enjoy his things freely without any fear, to be sure of the honor of women, of that of his children, and to have no fear for himself."

These concerns appear elsewhere in our author's writings. At the dawn of society with which the *Discourses* begins, one man joined with others the better to "have no fear for himself." Physical fear also often keeps men on the path of discipline, obedience, and law-abidingness. *The Prince* concludes that the fear of punishment is ever present. In the same treatise, concern for women appears. When referred to in such contexts, women and their honor may symbolize family security (as here where it is followed by the mention of children), the male kin's possession of and responsibility for female kin, and love and sexual attraction. To be esteemed, a prince should "animate his citizens to pursue peacefully their occupations, both in merchandise and in agriculture and every other occupation of men, and in it the latter [should] not fear to embellish his holdings for fear that they may be taken from him, and that the former [not fear] to open a business for fear of taxes." Fear for one's property, for loss of enjoyment of one's things, takes high priority, and while counseling rulers "above all, to abstain from the property of others," Niccolò warns that "men sooner forget the death of [their] father than the loss of [their] patrimony." Elsewhere he explains that once a father or brother is dead, a change in regime cannot restore him, whereas land once expropriated can indeed be thus recovered. Pater lives on in the patrimony.

In the *Discourses*, Niccolò contrasts the equal freedom of republics with the servile way of life. In true republics, private profit and public profit go hand in hand.

All lands and all countries that are in all respects free . . . derive greatest profit. For there one sees greater population, because of marriages being freer, and more desired by men: because each one procreates willingly those children he thinks he can nourish, not worrying that [his] patrimony may be taken from him, and that one knows not only that they are born free and not slaves, but they through their virtue may become princes [leaders or high officials].

Riches multiply there in greater number, both those that come from agriculture and those that come from the arts [industry]. Because each one willingly
multiplies in that thing and seeks to acquire those goods that one believes
[that once] acquired one can enjoy. Whence it happens that men in contest
think of private and public benefits, and the one and the other come to grow
wonderfully. The contrary of all these things takes place in those countries
that live slavishly: and the more they descend from the given good, the harder
is their servitude.

This is a unique passage. The two paragraphs above, about 'the common utility . . . from a free way of life' came from the first book of the
Discourses. In it Niccolò disclosed that a free way of life grants a freedom
from fear—for one's self, one's property, women, and children. Here in
the second book of the *Discourses* alone he details again a number of
freedoms that internal liberty offers, some new, others overlapping with
the previous ones—of marriage, private property and inheritance, of access to highest elective office, and enjoyment of the fruits of one's industry. He asserts that political and economic freedom generate greater
power and riches, a higher birth rate (a brief excursion into politico-
demographic theory), and more dynamic men. The optimism and ea-
gerness of free men increase both private and public benefits; the loss of
freedom results in their not going further ahead, nor growing in power
or in riches, but most of the time, indeed, always, in their going back-
wards. Remarkable also in this passage is not simply the implication that
private and public benefits do not necessarily conflict, though their seek-
ers may be in contest, but also the force of the assertion that private and
public benefits increase, amazingly, side by side.

As for Niccolò's mention of population, apart from the interesting
suggestion that fertility is voluntary and affected by the form of government, one may note that he is evidently writing of a republic that wishes
to grow. Population had to grow if the state was ever to raise the "fifteen
or twenty thousand young men," troops it had to put together from its
own territories, according to our military theoretician's calculations in
the *Art of War*, whether it wished to expand its dominion or simply to
stay securely free. Certainly in the growth of a state one needs a large
population that can then acquire larger dominions, "because without a
great number of men, and they well-armed, a republic will never be able
to grow." Population also had to expand to make up for past and future
losses to plagues. In referring to the terrible one of 1348, Niccolò compliments Boccaccio: "that memorable pestilence celebrated with such
eloquence by messer Giovanni Boccaccio, in which in Florence more
than ninety-six thousand souls were gone." Plagues occurred in that and
the succeeding century at more or less regular intervals. Niccolò has had

his own brushes with pestilence. Marietta worries about the plague striking her husband when he is away from home. Once while in Rome, toward the end of 1503, he feared he had been exposed to contagion and evidently, no doubt remembering his father's narrow escape, wrote to Florence expressing much alarm. Totto, the priest and younger brother, tried to reassure him, writing back that the contact he had was not that deadly, and ended up preaching to the Secretary, "Be of stout courage, because to lose heart is a thing for children or women." Niccolò's son and nephew, while on business travels in the Levant, also skirt pestilential areas anxiously.

Niccolò's rhapsody on liberty in the *Discourses* does not raise the problem (he cannot raise all problems at once) of keeping luxury from corrupting people: we presume that his policy would entail taxes and perhaps sumptuary and other limits, for he wishes to keep people "equally poor" in a republican simplicity, while enabling the country to be correspondingly rich and strong; well-ordered republics keep "the public rich and their citizens poor." Nor does he raise the issue of military service and preparedness in the midst of the contest for private and public benefits, but we know that his policy insists both on holding down the level of wealth and on maintaining an armed people within a disciplined militia. Nor does he pose here the question of possible conflict between private and public benefit, but we know from his words as quoted above that in any such conflict citizens will 'value the private sphere less than the public', that private gain always will take second place to the public, that equality should be such that no citizen can oppress another. Arms, to take one case, have a vital function—the defense of the common good: "all the arts that are instituted in a political community for the purpose of the common good, all the measures taken in that [community] in order to live in fear of the laws and of God, would be useless if their defenses were not prepared." It would be like having a palace adorned "with gems and gold" but without a roof "to defend [its rooms] from the rain."

Defense, peace, equality, liberty, wealth—whatever ends we choose to consider must eventually, for Niccolò, be related to the common good and, if necessary, restricted to the common good. The long, lyrical passage of the *Discourses* above, in its prizing of riches while omitting the dangers of corruption and private gain, remains curious. Every now and then the *Discourses* does surprise one by introducing material that seems not to fit Niccolò's steady pressure on his major ideas. In this category falls Polybius's *Histories*. In the long passage of the *Discourses* it appears that Niccolò has turned a particular page or two of the writings of his predecessors in the Chancery, most likely of Leonardo Bruni, and was there reminded of their old paeans to Florentine liberty, a liberty that generates energy in its citizens through a promise of public honors and private gain. In preparation for his own histories, Niccolò "diligently read" the writings of "two most excellent historians," Bruni and Poggio Bracciolini (whose ideas of liberty are similar to his), but he may also have looked into them earlier, when he was Secretary or while he was writing the *Discourses*.

Niccolò does not feel obliged to pay earlier Florentine writers or his distinguished predecessors in the Chancery the same respect he gives the ancients. He pays more deference to literary greats of a century or two before, like Petrarch, of whom he has nothing bad to say. Bruni and Poggio, who had also worked in the Palazzo and wrote histories, he criticizes for neglecting the civil discords of Florence; indeed, he intends in his own histories of Florence to correct this deficiency.

This is far from saying that Niccolò does not appropriate in one way or another the ideas of writers chronologically or occupationally closer to him. Concerning liberty, Niccolò generally will take little time to explain how free government benefits men singly and together, materially and spiritually. For the most part he can take the benefits for granted because notable Florentine writers of the thirteenth and fourteenth centuries had amply covered the topic. In the rhapsodical text on liberty he has gone back to their pages momentarily, it seems, and as usual has not left unchanged or unimproved whatever he absorbed or borrowed.

JUSTICE

The end of the state and the only good in itself is the common good. The prince old or new is a good prince insofar as he is an exceptional man working for the common good. In the concept of justice, the procedural and administrative parts—promulgation, impartiality, systems of courts and officers—must also be related to the common good, but the content of justice, what is right, just, and fair, including equality and liberty, is equivalent to the content of the common good. Niccolò does not use the term *justice* often. The "Allocution to a Magistrate," an exception, is built around the word. It conveys to the assembled, most distinguished citizens that justice is not only to defend the poor and powerless, to humble the proud and audacious, to bridle the rapacious and greedy, to castigate the insolent and dispell the violent, but also to generate equality. Typically, however, Niccolò speaks of *the laws*.

Although indebted to Cicero, the glossators, Thomas Aquinas, and Dante, he follows the usage of the great Florentine chancellors—who also worried about the divisiveness of particular interests in a republic. By employing the term *common good* he can rest on the communal or republican substance of justice while keeping his skirts clear of the details of procedural law. The more abstract, rational, and exalted aspects of justice, he treats under the phrases *good law* and *great legislators*, both of whose aims are the attainment and preservation of the common good, which might just as well be termed justice (except perhaps in the technical senses in which Thomas Aquinas distinguishes but also relates the two terms). Niccolò would not oppose justice in the old Greek sense of "to each his own," with its individualistic emphasis. As we have noted, and will note next in a passage from the *Mandragola*, while he prefers the for-the-public-good formula of the Roman lawyers, he occasionally modifies its abstract communal stress.

Our author's good friend, Cardinal Soderini, in writing him, phrases the aim in Latin: "non commodium privatum sed publicum." So comfortable is Niccolò with the ideal of the common good, and so confident is he that others know of it too, that in the *Mandragola* he parodies it. The situation is this: In order to test the moral elasticity of Friar Timothy, Ligurio, the intermediary, approaches him with a fistful of money and a problem: a girl was deposited by her widowed father in a convent "where, either by the neglect of the nuns or by the silliness of the girl herself, she finds herself four months pregnant." The good name of the nuns, the girl, the father, the uncle (who is supplying the money), and the rest of the family is threatened with shame. So fearful is the uncle of scandal that if the pregnancy does not become known, he vows "to give 300 ducats for the love of God." Only Friar Timothy and the Abbess can solve the problem. "How?" the Friar asks. The answer from Ligurio: "by persuading the Abbess to give a potion to the girl to make her abort."

FRIAR: That is something to think about.
LIGURIO: In doing this, look how many good things result: you
          maintain the honor of the monastery, the girl, the
          relatives; you give the girl back to her father, you give all
          the charity that 300 ducats provide; and on the other
          hand, you injure nothing but a piece of flesh not yet born,
          without sensation, that [anyway] in a thousand ways
          might be lost.

Then follows the punch line, the ethic of the common good:

          And I believe that is good that does good for the most
          and with which the most are content.

What we have here is a proposition covering a particular case, in language that would seem understandable and even acceptable to a priest (though it is not a Christian moral rule), an ethic that enjoys a certain currency. Three standards of good must be met. First, that the good actually *does* good. It must be a real, not an opined good. Second, that those to whom it does good are the most or the majority. The quantitative emphasis on *the most* marks it as a republican good (for the most, many, or majority, not for the one or few) and places the phrase alongside Niccolò's seemingly tautological formulation pointed to earlier, 'the common benefit of each one'. Both phrases settle the benefit not on the community considered as an abstract whole, but on its members as individuals (each one) or as superior numerically (the most). And third, that those who benefit from the good should sense it as good. The rule contains a sensed or sensual element: *the most* must be or must feel *content* with this actual good. And *content* here borders on *happy* rather than on *satisfied*.

The humor of the passage follows upon one's succumbing to the obvious sophistry: the rule is misapplied to such a low good and to such a small universe, the few *most*. A handful are overjoyed—the nuns, the girl, her father, uncle, family, those who receive the 300 ducats worth of charity—the rest of the world is uninvolved, the piece of flesh has no sensation.

Niccolò can poke fun at his own writings. We saw him laughing in *Clizia* at the reputed miracles of the same Friar. The phrasing above of the ethic itself, however, is almost technical and not a simple parody, and will recommend itself to us in a later chapter. Up to now we have seen Niccolò chiefly as moralist. In his comments on equality and liberty, war and peace and civil discord, we have encountered the political philosopher. In his strictures on the particular versus the common good and in the formulation of the altruistic proposition above, we glimpse the moral philosopher.

.   .   .

The state, then, aims at the common good. This norm of Niccolò's embraces his absolute vices and virtues. Opposed to the common good are the cardinal egoisms of individuals, private persons, or families, the factionalism of ambition, envy, and ingratitude. Part and parcel of the common good are republican egalitarianism and liberty.

We have already spoken of liberty as freedom from foreign subjection, and of arms of one's own as the means to it, and of unity and arms as the means to independence, and of republican poverty and simplicity and military preparedness as the way to avoid virtue-corrupting riches and luxury, and of expansion both as mean to unify and as cause and result of good arms. In an earlier chapter, we saw also that lawmaking gives men greater moral scope than law-abidingness alone, whence it follows that the more numerous the participants in lawmaking, the greater the moral freedom. This freedom, along with those of private property, inheritance, and marital choice—the *Mandragola* quotes the proverb: "God creates men, and they pair off!"—accounts for the dynamism of peer equality in republics. And since republics, over all other forms of states, provide for this equality and freedom in a common good of the greatest number, a republic is the best form of state.

We seem now to have reached a higher platform. Whether Niccolò presents country as an approximation or contrast to the ideal of republic, as a divine lady, or as the dominion that has imperium over men, he has good reason to insist that whenever one is deciding the very health of one's country, no consideration of just or unjust, of merciful or cruel, of praiseworthy or ignominious, must enter; "indeed, one must defer every other concern in order to follow that alternative that will save her life and keep her freedom." The state has its constitutional perfection, its true and perfect end, in a country where the common good is best observed, that is, in a durable independent republic where law is respected and women honored, where high office is open to all citizens, where social and economic equality obtain, where freedom to enjoy the gains of liberty and industry and to pass them on to one's children is assured—in "a perfect republic," one that will run "the whole course ordained by heaven." This is the point of it all.

Chapter 8

CAN MEN GOVERN?

God does not want to do everything . . .
                    —*The Prince*

I N SPEAKING of the ultimate aim, purpose, or goal of the state, of
its true end, or of the reason for which it exists, in common usage
one has to admit design or will. Whose design or will? Something that
presumably is capable of designing or willing, therefore, something animate, as one understands the term, or anthropomorphic, such as an
individual human's will, a collective will of some sort, a supernatural or
spiritual will, perhaps, or a divine will.

In political philosophy one may ask whether men's purpose or
whether divine, or supernatural or metaphysical purpose is involved in
the state, or both. According to Niccolò, God favors country. Why God
does so should be more understandable now that we know that country
ultimately seeks the common good. In favoring country, God favors the
common good. Do men, too, have part in this goal? Do they will this
end, and if and when they do, can they help achieve it? Can men do
anything at all to help attain their country's perfect and true end or to
reach the direct road that leads to perfection? God may beam benignly
on country and yet keep the whole experience of common good out of
men's hands.

Niccolò himself has considered the last possibility in *The Prince*, and
leans a little in that direction. "And it is not unknown to me that many
have had and have the opinion that the things of the world are in a way
governed by fortune and by God, that men with their reason cannot
correct them, [and] even that they have no remedy at all; and for this,
they can judge that one should not sweat much over things, but let oneself be governed by chance. . . . Thinking about this I sometimes in
some part incline toward their opinion."

That our author brings this up is quite remarkable. When he points
out that 'many have had and have' this opinion, he may be thinking of

[194]

writers, scholars, clerics, and others who praise contemplation, leisure, or the solitary life. By way of examples there are Plato and Aristotle, Epicurus, Seneca, Petrarch, and those of the Christian eremitic tradition. He may also have in mind preachers, some in the church (but not the Dominicans), and others in the government who insist that with fastings and penance one reforms inside and outside, that if one follows the virtuous life of the Christian, God will sort out the political fortunes of this world. Or he may have in mind near-contemporary thinkers like Marsilio Ficino and Pico della Mirandola, who were associated with the Platonic Academy patronized by Lorenzo the Magnificent and took their lead from Plato's writings on the contemplative or theoretical life. Unlike the latter, Niccolò rarely uses derivatives of the Latin *otium* in its positive sense of leisure or contemplation; he selects the negative sense of idleness, indolence, self-indulgence, laziness.

Political philosophers by and large assume that men can achieve at least some success in their political aims; the only pertinent question revolves about what degree of success may be possible. Ethics and politics as practical sciences, according to Aristotle, aim at the good things that can be attained by human action. If the common good is not to be provided in full by God or something other than men, then men can attain it only by their own action. As we have by now grasped, Niccolò stresses the active life. *The Prince* talks about the life, active indeed, of a new prince who from a private station arrives at imperium. The *Discourses* protests that, 'Our religion has glorified humble and contemplative men more than the active'. For affairs of the heart, Niccolò gives the same advice he gives in politics. 'I believe, believed, and shall always believe . . . that it is better to act and regret than not to act and regret'.

NECESSITY AND NATURALISM

Yet there are limits to this action. Our author has already mentioned fortune and God. In a world affected by natural laws there may be other limits. He pays notable attention to two—necessity and political cycles.

In all their actions men are doubtless limited by necessity. He sometimes expresses the concept through the inexorable natural or cosmological laws previously quoted: men are born, live, and die always in the one same order; it is impossible that the sky, the sun, the elements, and men might have varied throughout history; or, generally and particularly, times and things often change. These phrases, reminiscent of Lucretius's "sure law of nature," pose the existence of an order that has to be. Men acknowledge necessity when their preferable course of action has to presume an order contrary to the existing order, that is, a natural impossibility. They then have no choice: they must switch to a less desirable course consonant with the unyielding existing order.

This is but one of a range of meanings. Necessity may refer to the well-known, ordinary, and blameless frailties of the flesh, as sensed in labor, pain, death, cold, and hunger and wonderfully overcome in folk and fairy tales—Table, set yourself!—frailties that deflect human purposes. In a frequent, broad application they go by the name of necessity and are specially important in poverty and adversity. Not only these frailties are part of unchanging human nature but also men's ways of proceeding, their imagination, their character—patience, humaneness, impetuousity, goodness. These latter traits must be granted some degree of flexibility, as we saw in Chapter 4 and shall see again in a later chapter. To nature, Niccolò ascribes not traits restricted to heredity or one's blood line, but rather, traits attributable to one's environment—family, local customs, education, native soil, and language. As a rule, however, 'men are not able to command their nature'. A rarer usage, but well-developed by our author, appears in a kind of syllogistic reasoning. To get from A to C it is necessary to pass through B. To go from A (bad custom) to C (good custom), B (law) is "immediately necessary."

Here another variant deserves singling out for its frequent use in regard to the common good. Necessity may characterize a course of action dictated by one's seeking a goal or ideal, or a good proximate to a more important goal or ideal. Thus, molested by its neighbors, a country will have to face the necessity of conquering and annexing them to keep itself free (a good proximate to the elided common good).

Chapter 5 treated of necessity in various forms as adversity, austerity, poverty, as the cosmic catastrophes of flood, plague, and famine, and as bearing upon custom, law, and moral improvement. The perspective here is somewhat different, that of considering necessity as a possible limit on men's political capacity. But even in the earlier chapter, one could glimpse that Niccolò had turned necessity around to enlist its aid in moral improvement. He does the same thing here, giving necessity a turn for the positive, making it a stimulus to virtuous political action.

The necessity in Niccolò's naturalism, and the naturalism itself, are far from thoroughgoing. The sky, sun, elements, and men that are supposed never to vary, were created by God, he tells us in the "Exhortation to Penitence" and in the poem "On Ambition." God created the world for man's benefit, and He by Himself or through heaven, fortune, and other supernatural beings, continues to exercise His purpose on the natural phenomena therein and on the affairs of men. Moreover, that world contains not merely necessity but—set against it—choice. Niccolò's naturalistic canopy remains narrow and literary, rent with holes.

The idea of necessity in nature serves our author not primarily to instill pessimism about the best laid political plans, or indifference or resignation to an inevitable, necessary chain of causes, but to be able to apply ancient history to modern events and to encourage the present-day imitation of ancient models, for "in all cities and in all peoples there are the same desires and the same humors, and the same as they always were. So it is an easy thing for whoever examines past things to foresee future [things] in each republic and to take those remedies that were used by the ancients, or not finding any used, to think up new ones based on the similitude of events." Interestingly, if history does not have on file the exact solution to a contemporary problem, it lends itself by the suggestiveness of similarity, to devising new solutions. Whereas, if those who read history neglect or do not understand these considerations, solutions both old and new will not appear to them and they will keep on making the same mistakes. Even if some readers do understand, given that "these considerations . . . are not known to whoever governs, it follows that there are always the same disorders in every period."

Since by nature men are the same as they always were and will be, and since in other times and most clearly in the centuries of the Roman republic they were able by their own virtue to establish good republican government, the necessity that accompanies them throughout life cannot be an insurmountable hurdle. One reads about virtuous people in history only to judge "imitation [of them] not only difficult but impossible." Yet the sky, the sun, the elements, and men have not changed and will not change. If virtuous peoples or leaders like Moses, Cyrus, and Theseus—"rare and marvelous" to be sure, 'they were nonetheless men'—if they once could do great deeds, men can do them today also. Their unchanging nature has enough potential, history has demonstrated, for them to solve their political exigencies.

This is not the end of the argument from necessity. Men, although part of the natural world, are not necessitated in each and every act, for men act either by necessity or by choice. The existence of choice eliminates the possibility of a completely necessitated world. Choosing or *electing* (to use the cognate of the term Niccolò pits against necessity) is related to liberty, and as such to free governments or republics. As we saw in the last chapter, Niccolò's position is clear: he glows when he writes about the freedoms republics have. When he writes of choice versus necessity, however, he is thinking chiefly of republics that have been corrupted by peace and ease and are headed toward licentiousness or anarchy, a state of overabundant choice. Along the way he finds an ally not in choice but again in necessity: there is 'greater virtue wherever choice has less authority'.

Given men's nasty disposition, choice more often than not leads them to a bad act. From the view of one man alone, of the individual who acts, the act seems good: measured by a standard that exists outside the norm that Niccolò himself has in mind or takes for granted, the act is bad. If necessity then forces the actor to perform a good act, it amplifies rather than limits the possibility of virtuous political action, which "testifies to what I have said above, that men work nothing well if not through necessity; but where choice abounds, and where one can become licentious, everything immediately fills up with confusion and disorder." Thus, planning a colony on poor soil will keep its inhabitants hard at labor and far from a corrupting luxury.

Niccolò is able to enlist necessity to his side by shifting the judgment from the individual to an often implicit extrinsic norm. One man alone would judge the effect of harsh necessity on himself; Niccolò judges from a collective norm—typically, the common good—where necessity becomes virtuous: "necessity makes virtue, as we have often said." Now he supplants his natural-law conception of necessity with one of special intervention, supernatural in the case of God or the heavens sending down catastrophes, human in the case of law and coercion. In both there is a purpose involved: the constraining and redirecting of men's acts.

The idea of using choice to create a man-made necessity is particularly ingenious, finding its happiest application in constitutional legislation: "how many necessities the laws made by Romulus, Numa and the others constrained Rome to, . . . and kept it full of such great virtue, with which no other city or republic has ever been adorned." In application to individual citizens we may recall the scene in the *Mandragola* where Nicia remains good only so long as he fears the law. *Law*, in Niccolò's phrase, 'the laws make [men] good', refers to law as a good standard and to its attendant force. The effectiveness of force in coercing action to a standard relies on an everyday frailty of the flesh—susceptibility to pain—in a part of human nature that never changes. In effect, Niccolò poses one kind of necessity—the pain threshold of men's nature, against another less compelling necessity, the proneness to evil of men's nature. The second natural trait, we saw in Chapter 5, is not wholly inflexible; certainly not as inflexible as the certain reaction to pain and punishment.

To raise moral tone, men may go beyond the use of force. They may create a doubly synthetic necessity: force to secure conformity to law, and law to create a necessitous environment, as when a city founder selects a difficult site or a general orders bridges and boats burned behind his troops (and there are many military examples of this doubly synthetic necessity in the *Discourses* and the *Art of War*).

After weaving necessity in and out of technical and common usage, the high reaches of natural law, the theology of creation, the teleology of supernatural intervention, the admission of choice, the logic of empirical history, the tension of individual choice versus extrinsic norms, and the double synthesis of man-made constraint based on natural frailties, Niccolò can optimistically conclude that necessity helps men rule virtuously. "At other times we have spoken about how useful necessity is to human action and to what glory they have been led by it, and how by some moral philosophers it has been written [that] the hands and the tongue of men, two most noble instruments to enoble him, would not have worked perfectly nor led human works to that height that they are seen to be led, if they had not been pushed by necessity."

POLITICAL CYCLES

With necessity and naturalism we have by no means exhausted the possible constraints on political action. A number of other things prevent action from being free enough so that men might correct the things of the world with their reason. Men are found in interaction with others who have the same freedom, or lack of it, and who have the same needs and appetites and evil tendencies. This is less a limitation than it is the matter or material within which and out of which they must form the good common to them all. Apart from their nature as men, they have not grown up in a vacuum. They have been reared with families, customs, religion, law, arms, political institutions, and ideals, all of which, if long-existing and well-ordered, may contribute to the common good, but if not, given men's nature, may lead to private advantage and divisiveness. These are things Niccolò well understands and takes account of as both limiting and supporting factors, and in so doing distinguishes his statecraft and stamps it with sophistication. Beyond these, there are two characteristics of the world that he considers at length. Should they exist, they would diminish the range of rational possibilities in working toward the common good. They may be called forces. One is the periodicity of political cycles, the other is fortune. Both are ideas of ancient origins.

One can detect in Niccolò a current of fatalism that inclines him toward the thesis that there is not much to be gained, as he says, in sweating over things, that the way things are and have been, they always will be. We have met with some antipolitical expressions of his, not many, but notable, at various moments in these pages. When he began going down to the Orti he may have picked up and studied a few theories that his younger friends there had encountered: those that had some appeal he may have begun to work into the *Discourses*. That book has more of an air of scholarship than *The Prince*, which by comparison reflects more of the distilled experience of magistrates, government officials, and ambassadors, of courts, chanceries, and palaces. One of these theories may have been that of the origin of states, which we have already discussed at some length; another may have been that of the periodicity of political cycles. Both of them come from the same source, the *Histories* of Polybius, whom Niccolò, without identifying by name, puts in the category of those "who have written on states."

First Niccolò considers the source. "Some others . . ." he writes. As revealed by the extent of his borrowing, first among them is Polybius. "Some others, and wiser . . ." he continues, but not letting the judgment pass without qualification: "wiser, according to the opinion of many." Next he presents the theory: these reputedly wiser others "have the opinion that there are six [instead of three] forms of government: of which three are worst; three others are good in themselves, but so easy to corrupt themselves that they also become pernicious. Those that are good are the three above [principates, optimates, and popular, sometimes called kingdoms, aristocracies, and democracies]; those that are bad are three others that depend on these three, and each of them in a way is like the one it is close to, so that they jump easily from one [form] to the other: because the principates easily become tyrannical; the optimates with ease become a state of a few [oligarchy]; the popular [form] without difficulty is converted in license [anarchy]. So that . . . no remedy can work it out in a way that [any given form] does not slip into its contrary. . . . And this is the circle in which all states that have been governed turn about." Any state from its starting point rings in the subsequent five changes seriatim.

Having presented the theory (note that he calls it an opinion) in much more detail than this of course, Niccolò takes it apart, gently, quickly, wittily: "But rarely do they return to the same [starting] governments, because almost no state can have so long a life that it can pass many times through these changes and stay on its feet." Also another state may conquer it. "I say, therefore, that all six said forms of government are pestiferous, for the brevity of life that is in the three good ones and for the malignity of life that is in the three bad." The fact that he calls them pestiferous indicates that he believes they can and should be avoided, that there is a choice; and indeed there is. Great lawmakers like Lycurgus have recognized the malevolence of the bad forms and chosen instead to create a mixed constitution where all three good forms—monarchical, aristocratic, and democratic—blended together in one and checked each other, "so that the one watched the other." Rome "remaining mixed, formed a perfect state."

Contrary to what Polybius writes, we see, the intervention of men, according to Niccolò, breaks the cycle either by incursions from outside a state or by their enacting a mixed constitution within.

If cycles exist as Polybius would have them, the lessons of history would be restricted to shortening or lengthening the life of a particular form of government already existing, its rise or fall to the next form in the series being practically unavoidable. Were this the case, most of Niccolò's study and experience would be good for little except contemplation. The sort of political action he believes in and calls for would produce but illusory causes and effects. But if men know that cycles exist, might they not jab a stick in the wheels? If they tamper with the cycles, block or moderate their amplitude, or change their serial order, the fascinating eternal inevitability of the theory would be gone. In *The Prince* and *Discourses*, our author often discusses whether to change the form of state of a newly acquired dominion and, if so, how to go about it most expeditiously.

In writing of the origins of the state in the *Discourses*, Niccolò's opening phrase is 'in the beginning of the world'. At another point he entertains and discards the span of forty thousand or fifty thousand years postulated by the *History* of Diodorus Siculus as the age of the world. If there was a beginning of things, there could not always have been cycles. Men originated before cycles. If there are beginnings, there can be ends. Our philosopher of history recognizes ends, too. "It is a thing most true," the third book of the *Discourses* begins, "that the things of the world have an end to their life" and "a course that is ordained them by heaven."

Cycles can wind down, states can be wiped out. In his broadest scanning of history, in the *Discourses*, where Niccolò traces the virtue of states over thousands of years, there is no sign of cycles, as virtue lodges here and there among Medes and Persians, Romans and Franks, Germans and Saracens. Niccolò writes of heavenly chastisements of men throughout history, and he could not easily have been thinking that God coordinates His punishments of men to coincide with cycles, and so He has often to delay punishment or let men go unpunished. "[E]veryone prayed God to give us time," Niccolò says for the benefit of his fellow citizens in "Words to Speak." "I am persuaded that God has not yet castigated us in the way he wishes and that he is reserving for us a greater scourge." God here is taking His own sweet time, not waiting for a turn in cycles.

Divine catastrophes can destroy states completely and even all but obliterate mankind. The greater scourge Niccolò feared was to hit the Florentine republic ten years later, when the Medici took over the city and threw out its Secretary, and another one hit twenty-five years after that, when imperial forces swept down into Italy and wiped the republic out of history.

FORTUNE

The theory of political cycles appears early in the *Discourses* and, in effect, is then discarded. *Fortuna* appears in every major work and apparently can never be discarded. In the pantheonic portrait of Chapter 3 of all the purposeful beings that enter into the affairs of men, fortune is the most active, the hardest to understand, and the most perverse.

Niccolò has so many formulations of fortune, each varying in some way, that one may well despair of presenting them all. It is surely the most serious threat to rational political action. Unable to describe fortune prosaically, carried away by the frustrations it induces, Niccolò pens many figures of speech, some of them conventional—the wheel, winds, stars, games of fortune—some of them among his richest and best conceived—woman, rivers, wheels, and the eagle.

> Have you ever seen in any place
> how a fierce eagle acts
> driven by hunger and fasting?
>
> And how it takes a tortoise up so high
> that the blow of falling shatters it,
> and it feeds itself on that dead flesh?
>
> So Fortune, not so that one may remain there,
> takes one up high, but so that destroying [one]
> she enjoys it, and one cries as one falls.

The eagle is not perverse, it destroys out of hunger. Niccolò breaks off the metaphor, takes advantage of the feminine case of the noun *fortune* to slide over to the female Fortuna, who enjoys destruction for its own sake and who, if she has a hunger, hungers not to feed on fallen flesh but to destroy. While she destroys, the verse hints, she takes pleasure in her victim's cries. Perverse Fortune-eagle enjoys giving pain. We shall in a moment see that under another guise she enjoys receiving it.

Niccolò reveals in the first chapter of *The Prince* that fortune is to be one of his many subjects. He pairs it there with virtue, in the sense of right political action. Dominions are acquired, among other ways, "by fortune or by virtue." The most direct statement on fortune appears in the next to last chapter of that work. There are several other statements that help round out his conception, and we should consider them, too. One is contained in the poem "On Fortune," which is the source of the above verses and which parallels many of his views as set in prose in *The Prince* and *Discourses*. Others appear in particular chapters of the *Discourses*. Prose and poetry interplay throughout.

Niccolò is not alone in believing fortune worth puzzling over. It presents itself as a force in almost every one of the classical and near-contemporary writers and poets he reads most assiduously, from Plutarch and Livy, to Dante and Petrarch, and on to lesser lights closer still to his day. The writers just preceding him are on the whole confident about men's own ability of mind and spirit to conquer adverse fortune. They expand on the nostrum, "Virtue conquers fortune." In Poggio Bracciolini and in the poetry of Poliziano and Lorenzo the Magnificent, doubts appear. Niccolò's trail makes an intricate zigzag pattern, at times marking off more power to fortune, at times less.

As with all his special terms, Niccolò uses *fortune* in many ordinary senses, too, for example, to mean chance or plain dumb luck, as in betting odds, or probability, as in the reasoning that recommended three reformations of Roman ranks in battle: it was improbable that fortune would work against them three times. Or success, as again in writing of the Romans he asserts that all other princes would have enjoyed the fortune they did, had they used the same methods of virtue. Such meanings are infrequent and generally reveal themselves by their lack of purposefulness. Of the various meanings—and we shall touch on several more—the most persistent for an appraisal of political possibilities or of human action is that of fortune as a hypostatized cause of force (like a goddess) or a secularized deity (like a cause of a force) that unpredictably but purposefully determines the outcome of human actions, typically, from the human perspective, in an unfavorable way. Fortuna is the "friend of discords," we read in that chronicle of discords, the *Florentine Histories*.

Fortune's own fortunes have varied through the years. The Romans, early in their history, erected a temple to fortune. They had more of a conception of a Fortuna good and reliable, a goddess who provided divine escort and favorable winds. In Augustine's time the conception was not as widely favorable. The great bishop protested the belief that fortune is a goddess, insisting that a god is always good, not sometimes bad, not perverse or fortuitous. Can it be, he asks in the *City of God*, that when Fortune is bad, she is no longer a divinity but is suddenly changed into a malignant devil? Yet succeeding centuries did not abandon her. Petrarch had complained in his essay on Fortuna that some of his contemporaries exalted her as a diva in heaven. Niccolò puts her in heaven as a diva and more, as a *dea*, too, as more strictly a goddess than a diva. "This inconstant *dea* and fickle diva." Like the Romans, moreover, he places her in a kind of temple, "a palace open on all sides."

Inconstant and fickle, Fortuna cannot be swayed by the worship accorded a normal deity. From an unpredictable goddess, worshippers cannot trust in benefits. She does not wish that "one discerns her powers," in order to demonstrate to the world that she, and not reason, makes men great. She asks not to be worshipped but to be recognized, which is to say, acknowledged as an intermediate yet individual power who passes "through transverse and unknown paths," and whose effects, positive or negative, on individual persons do not necessarily reflect their own personal deserts. Our poet dares to sing of her and hope that she sees him from "up high above everyone," where she "commands and rules impetuously." The poem itself can be seen as an act of worship or acknowledgment but perhaps falls more accurately under the heading of warding off evil, "and may the cruel diva meanwhile turn / her ferocious eyes toward me and read / what I now sing of her and her kingdom."

In treating of fortune, the limits of human perspective should be borne in mind. The pertinent chapter in the *Discourses* carries the following title taken from an observation of the historian Livy: "Fortune Blinds the Minds of Men When She Does Not Want Them to Oppose Her Designs." When there are great things to be accomplished or great destruction to be wreacked, Fortuna chooses men to help her purpose. "And if anyone might oppose it, either she kills him or she deprives him of every faculty of doing any good." That chapter, in adapting to Livy's language, interchanges fortune with "heaven" or "the heavens." Though occult, their purpose is bound up with a higher strategy not of their making, and above heaven and fortune, in Niccolò's divine panoply, there sits God alone.

Even the centuries after Augustine did not completely abandon the goddess. She was still a pagan deity, but Supreme God was above her, and consequently she had to be carrying out His will. Beyond this, the relationship remained indefinite. Dante's *Inferno* refers to her as "general minister and leader." One of Lorenzo the Magnificent's lines calls her "Fortuna ministra di Dio." The language of Florentine citizens as preserved in the records of government meetings around the turn of the fifteenth century shows that their conception, too, was that Fortuna was

God's aide or minister, and that she was to be identified with His direction or wishes. This is more or less Niccolò's position. Although his complaints at times make her out to be the personification of evil in the world, a devil or demon, he also speaks of her in god-like terms. "She is said by many to be omnipotent." Mind that Niccolò himself does not claim she is omnipotent. The reason he gives for belief in her omnipotence, moreover, is inadequate: "because whoever comes into this life, / sooner or later feels her strength." Then he writes, "one knows for sure / that even Jove fears her power." We have seen our poet use Jove before, not to integrate one master deity with another, but to avoid implicating God. He never opposes fortune to God's will. *The Prince*, in a rare juxtaposition, holds (we observed in an earlier chapter) that Caesar Borgia's rejection by fortune—'in the highest course of his action'—implied that he was not ordained by God.

With typical penetration Saint Augustine raised another objection: is it the case that Jupiter sends Fortuna at his pleasure? If so, he alone should be worshipped. There is a further question to be raised. If God sends her at His pleasure, does she ever use her great power for her own purposes? Is she God's obedient servant in full or in part? One presumes that this minister of God sometimes eludes detailed supervision and does things on her own. Such presumption would make the great bishop jump to his feet in further protest; yet without it, men's attempts to oppose Fortuna would be useless and impious. They would amount to opposing God, Whose will she is fulfilling. In Niccolò's writings, Fortuna is more than a delegate or courier. She has character and purposes of her own that men should know and take into account. Her will at times seems almost rebellious. Fortuna, as a captain laments on his deathbed, "wants to be arbiter of all human things." As long as Fortune remains God's powerful and mysterious but full and faithful servant, men could have no complaint against her. It is when she becomes a demiurge and slips into a will of her own that men must seek a remedy.

Now to a closer look at Fortuna as Niccolò pens her.

Fortuna has a wide sphere of acting over "the things of the world." "Power, honor, riches and wealth / stand as the reward: as the punishment and pain, / servitude, infamy, disease, and poverty." This sphere, in its political and moral repercussions of giving and taking states and glory, worries Niccolò. Both good states and virtuous, prudent, and courageous men often fail to get the good fortune they deserve. "She often holds the good [men] under her feet / raises the wicked . . ."

Given the power that fortune wields over men, their chance of attaining political objectives through their virtue, reason, courage and altruistic or patriotic motives does not seem worth betting on. The draft of the letter to G. B. Soderini has it that she "commands men and holds them under her yoke." Niccolò tries to determine what kind of power this is that fortune holds. He knows it is great enough to be involved in the semblance of evil in the world. "And both kingdoms and states she turns upside down / according to what she thinks, and she deprives the just / of the good that she lavishly gives to the unjust." He is more interested in discovering whether in some way men may obtain power over *her*.

This is not an easy question, compounded as it is by the difficulty of distinguishing fortune neatly from other concepts like heaven(s), occasion, and the times. As a deity, fortune is somewhere above, up in the sky. Sky or *cielo* is the same as the word for heaven. The two are distinguishable in most of our texts by the context of purpose associated with heaven-the-deity but not with sky-the-space. One does not say that so-and-so or such-and-such was ordained by the sky. As observed before, in texts where our author follows on Livy's heels, he often equates heaven and fortune and translates *the gods* as *the heavens*. Often, still, he easily couples and uncouples fortune with *occasion* or *the times*. In one sentence we find, "the heavens giving them occasion or taking it away from them . . . ," and in the next, "those occasions that [fortune] extends."

Also Niccolò attaches fortune and occasion to the philosophic matter-and-form proposition mentioned in the preceeding chapter above. For fortune gives the occasion in which a readied matter (the people) presents itself to a possible leader. If he is a virtuous leader, he will seize the opportunity, win imperium or rightful command over them, and introduce form into them, as did "Moses, Cyrus, Romulus, Theseus, and others similar." They received from fortune nothing "but the occasion which gave them their matter [so] to be able to introduce that form that seemed [right] to them; and without that occasion the virtue of their spirit would have been spent, and without that virtue the occasion would have come in vain."

Fortune is often crisscrossed with the times: a title of the *Discourses* reads, "How One, Wishing Always to Have Good Fortune, Must Vary with the Times." Sometimes our author can discuss an action that he elsewhere treats as being subject to fortune simply at the level of being at variance with *the times*. By ignoring fortune, he can leave supernatural considerations out altogether. He does this in a chapter in the *Discourses* with the title, "One Often Obtains by Impetus and Audacity That Which One Would Never Obtain by Ordinary Ways." Times may call for impetuousness or caution. The chapter need not and does not mention fortune. But once Niccolò raises the level of argument to, How is it that some persons are offered the *occasion* or are readied for *the times*? the discourse moves onto the higher plane of Fortuna the deity. One is tempted to combine some of these meanings: fortune (success) consists in having the fortune (good luck) to vary with fortune (the times), none of which would you have were not the occasion extended you by Fortune (the deity).

Niccolò acknowledges that men find it hard at times to distinguish the accomplishments of fortune from their own. "Because the evil that comes to you, / one imputes to her, and if / a man finds any good, / he believes he has it through his own virtue." Niccolò himself is not always sure of the distinction. He attributes events to fortune that he has elsewhere already attributed to virtue, and vice versa. An uncertainty appears in *The Prince* in the case of Caesar Borgia who as he told Niccolò in Rome, went to his downfall because, rejected by fortune, "he had thought of what would happen when his father died, and he had found a solution for everything except that he never thought that on his [father's death] he too would be [ill] near death." Was this the work of fortune or did the duke lack virtue or prudence in not foreseeing the double contingency? Niccolò does not ask the question in Chapter VII where the story is told. He writes that the duke "erred" in his role in electing a new pope and that "this was the cause of his ultimate ruin." The final verdict in *The Prince* is that the duke was 'reprobated by fortune'.

Taking another illustration of Niccolò's uncertainty, the lines in the *Discourses* where virtue is portrayed as fullest in Assyria, then in Medes, and afterwards in Persia, contrast with similar lines in the poem "On Fortune."

> In the first place, colored and tinted,
> one sees how already under Egypt
> the world stayed subjugated and conquered. . . .
> One sees then the Assyrians ascend up
> to another scepter, when [fortune] did not wish
> that that of Egypt dominate [any] longer;
> then [one sees] how she turns happy to the Medes,
> from the Medes to the Persians: and the locks of hair of the Greeks
> she adorned with the honor she took from the Persians. . . .
> Here they show how they were beautiful,
> high, rich, powerful, and how at the end
> Fortune gave them in prey to their enemies.

Niccolò wrote these lines about the time he wrote *The Prince*, and probably before he wrote the virtue passage in the *Discourses*.

However hard it may be to distinguish the influence of fortune from virtue, men, as part of their virtue, of their capacity for prudent and proper action, must know as much as possible about this cruel diva. One should take her "for one's star / and as much as is possible to us, every hour / accommodate ourselves to her variation." Lucky is the man who "grasps a wheel that conforms to her wish." But this is not enough, "because while you are whirled around the rim / of the wheel, she happy and good for the time being / is apt to change the twirls in the middle of the spin; / and you not being able to change [your] person / nor leave the course that heaven gives you, / in midway she abandons you." *The Prince* adds that "if one could change nature with the times and with things, fortune would not change," but 'one cannot deviate from that toward which nature inclines'. And, "having always prospered walking along one path, one cannot persuade oneself to leave it." Thus, both one's particular nature and one's particular leanings prevent one's tagging along with fortune. A "memorable" case happened "in our days and in our country," Niccolò records in the *Discourses*. The chapter ("How One, Wishing Always to Have Good Fortune, Should Vary with the Times") recalls the sweeping from power of his friend and superior, the Gonfalonier-for-Life Piero Soderini, and of himself, too, with the same swish of the broom. Soderini "proceeded in all his things with humanity and patience. He and his country prospered while the times conformed to his way of proceeding; but when afterward times came when it was necessary to break with patience and humility, he did not know how to do it; so that together with his country he went to ruin."

The wheel of fortune cannot be stopped from twirling, not even by nailing it fast. In the *Florentine Histories*, Niccolò reports an event of the mid-fourteenth century. A prominent citizen in the midst of a banquet he was giving received from either a friend or a foe "a silver goblet full of candies," in which a nail was hidden. When "discovered and seen by all the banqueters, [it] was interpreted [to mean] that [the host] was being reminded to fasten the wheel [of fortune]; because fortune having lifted him to height, [the interpretation] could not be other, if [the wheel] followed in making its circle, than drawing him to the bottom. Which interpretation was verified first by his [political] ruin, afterwards by his death."

This one, like other stories in the *Histories*, puts fortune on stage as the punisher of hubris. The present tale has additional interest, recalling that the Machiavegli escutcheon consists of a cross azure, field argent, and four nails, also azure, that stick in the four angles made by the cross. The nails represent the *bad nails* that nailed Christ to the cross. They sometimes appear in devices of families with connections to the Cru-

We do not know who of the family first acquired the cross and nails symbol . . . In his country house, the nails symbol appears in various places: on a chest . . .

sades or the Holy Land as soldiers or pilgrims. We do not know who of the family first acquired the cross and nails symbol or how the family itself came to be called Machiavegli, but in the late thirteenth century one ancestor, a penitent and contemplative, had evidently gone to the Holy Land and at a ripe old age died there in so holy a state that he was counted as one of the blessed. Among the older family appear two first names that are unusual and clearly related to nails—Chiovello and Chiodo. The family last name, which we have seen Niccolò and others spell in various ways, can be broken down into the Latin Mal(i) plus Clavus(-i) or Clavellus(-i) = "bad nail(s)." Niccolò is sure to know that this origin can be put to his family name. What may be his first signed letter, that of 29 April 1499, as Chancellor of the Second Chancery, carries the signature "Nicholaus Maclavellus Cancellarius." Colleagues in the Chancery sometimes address him as "Nicalao de Maclavellis," or informally as "Maclavelle mi." In his country house, the nails symbol appears together with the cross as well as separate from it in various places: on a chest, on fireplaces, and cut into a closet door.

The image of the wheel of fortune antedates Niccolò by millenia. To express his idea of the difficulties of adapting to fortune, he adds more wheels to her iconology and thereby creates a new image. Within her temple many wheels turn, "and these rotate always night and day, / because so wishes heaven with whom one does not quarrel /. . . . / But if one understands and notes this, / he would be happy and blessed who could jump from wheel to wheel." The ideal man as fortune's acrobat.

Sadly, men are not this agile. Fortune is mysterious and volatile, dropping them one day, raising them the next. Depressing though this seems, it gives Niccolò a ray of hope and enables him to urge a more dignified and less acrobatic pose for men.

A man should confront fortune with dry-eyed stoic virtue, and win with glory or lose without shame. "But because crying to a man was always ugly, / at the blows of one's fortune / one should turn a face dry of tears." This stoic counsel is from *The Ass*. A chapter in the *Discourses* displays a similar attitude. Its title: "Strong Republics and Excellent Men Keep in [Every Kind of] Fortune the Same Spirit and Their Same Dignity." At the very end of the *Art of War* the author speaks, as he does throughout, in the well-worn battle dress of the man-of-arms: "had Fortune conceded me in the past a state sizeable enough . . . without doubt either I would have increased it with glory or lost without shame."

At those times when "Fortune wants to do everything herself," the better course is "to keep quiet and not to bother her;" at other times, when "she will let men do something," the moment has come for action. This he writes to Vettori in the famous letter of 10 December 1513. If a prince, or anyone for that matter, goes to his ruin today, he should keep heart; he may prosper tomorrow. The first stance, then, is this: If fortune seems determined to oppose your aims, withdraw but do not give up; wait for the wheels to turn upward, as they eventually do. "Nor does she always bear down on / the one who lies at the bottom of her wheel."

"Wait, Watch, and Hope" is the motto. With it he concludes one of his chapters on fortune in the *Discourses*: "I strongly affirm this again to be most true, according to all the histories one sees, that men can follow fortune and not oppose her; they can weave her warps and not break them. They must surely not give up ever; . . . they must always hope, and hoping, never give up in whatever fortune and in whatever trouble they find themselves."

Personally for Niccolò, fortune is bad fortune. When young or when in love, Niccolò has no complaints. After everything is 'totally wrecked', he feels that fortune has treated him badly. He writes Vettori that he is waiting, in the hope that Fortuna will be ashamed of herself. The covering letter of *The Prince* closes in pathos: "undeservedly I bear a great and continuous malice of fortune." She treats him badly for about five years, after which new vistas open up, the success of the *Mandragola* resounds, and the *Art of War* comes out in print. The proud author is 'Niccolò Machiavegli, Citizen and Florentine Secretary'. His demands on Fortune have increased. Once he would have thought her changed toward him, had she restored him a post at the level of Secretary; now, with improved morale, he hints that, not unreasonably, she might have given him 'a state sizeable enough' to work with.

As for fortune generally rather than personally, the most direct statement appears in *The Prince*. It takes the form of a conclusion, and untypically, a conclusion expressed in quantified terms. "I judge it can be true that Fortune is the arbiter of half of our actions, but that also she lets the other half of them, more or less, be governed by us."

He does not explain whether the half left to us is available without 'sweating' on our part or whether we have to strain to our most virtuous action to win that much. The phrase could also mean that the half left to us comes almost automatically, that whatever more we can do through our virtue may cut into fortune's half.

Having done the utmost to explain Fortuna's power precisely, Niccolò follows this passage from Chapter xxv with a long, attractive analogy.

> I liken her to one of those ruinous rivers that when they are enraged, wreck trees and buildings; they remove earth from this side, they put it on the other: everyone flees before them, everyone gives in to their impetus, without in any way being able to block them. And though [the rivers] are made in this fashion, there remains, however, that men, when times are quiet, take measures, and with banks and dykes, so that [the rivers], growing then [anew], would go through a canal, or their impetus would be neither so wild nor so harmful. Similarly it happens with Fortune, who demonstrates her power when there is not ordered virtue to resist her, and therefore she turns her impetuosities to where she knows dykes and banks have not been made to hold her. . . . And I wish this to suffice as far as having spoken about opposing Fortuna in general.

The simile certainly reveals that men's actions count for something in the struggle against perverse fortune, and the motto of this stance of 'ordered virtue' may be called, "Foresee and Prepare."

We are still left in doubt whether banks and dykes raise the percentage up to a maximal one-half or cut into fortune's half to give us up to an unheard-of 100 percent. It does not matter too much: our author evidently thinks that if we can chalk up to our own control at least one out of every two actions we take, the percentage is encouraging. Surely 50 percent is encouraging when contrasted with the zero percent with which he opened the chapter, with the opinion that men 'have no remedy at all'.

The enraged rivers simile appears also in Niccolò's tercets "On Fortune," as does another, even more attractive, figure of speech in *The Prince*. In the Roman tradition, if fortune has gender it is the female. Niccolò senses this, of course, and succeeds in tossing away the old clothes of "this ancient witch," and in concluding Chapter xxv, turns her out in the smartest youthful ensemble. He wishes to give the most positive ending to this chapter on Fortune. No doubt half a loaf is better than none; and that one should accommodate to, have foresight of, and prepare for Fortune's mood is good advice but not always possible to follow. We have already heard Niccolò describe Fortune as impetuous. He begins to end the chapter: "I judge this well [to be the case]: that it is better to be impetuous than cautious, because . . ." He is about to apply a homeopathic remedy.

> Fortune is woman, and it is necessary, wanting to hold her underneath, to beat her and jolt her. And one sees that she lets herself be conquered by these [who treat her thus] more than by those who proceed coldly; and then always, as woman, she is the friend of the young, because they are less respectful, more ferocious, and with greater audacity command her.

The passage is rare. A quintessential equivalence: Fortune = woman. All at odds with Niccolò's love-service of the lady. He has leapt from the courtier's to the trooper's love. The metaphor, in Latinized and proverbial form—'Fortune is woman'—marks the first appearance in great literature of a theme met with principally in folklore or in the theater of street and square.

There is a Latin saying that "Fortune aids the audacious." Niccolò goes far beyond it. He draws a subtle drama of the sexes.

If Fortune is feminine, virtue (a term with which Niccolò and other writers often pair fortune) is the essence of masculinity. Apart from its Latin derivation from *vir*, or man, and its association with all manly qualities—reason, prudence, military skill, and courage—one of its meanings is manly sexual potency or prowess. Among Niccolò's abundant uses of the word, there is this sense, too. Led to bed by the beautiful damsel of Circe, our hero feels stupid and uncertain, disconsolate, timid and doubtful, "not knowing how open the way was," and like one "who does not hope in his virtue." She teases. "You have so little virtue that these sheets between us make war, and you put yourself so far from me." He creeps closer to her, extending between the sheets a cold hand . . .

> Not in one place did my hand stay;
> but running over her limbs,
> the lost virtue came back firm.

These lines remind us of how far from Niccolò's own gentle way is the roughness he now advocates. Fortune = woman loves impetuosity. Her object is men. She offers power, honor, riches and health "for whomever she bears love." Young men, too, are impetuous, more than old men

"Fortune is woman, and it is necessary, wanting to hold her underneath, to beat her and jolt her."

certainly. To be a cautious youth is difficult, to be a cautious old man is probable. To be impetuous throughout life, as was Julius II, is possible, but only if one's nature and experience mold one that way. So, Fortune = woman's best odds are with younger men. They beat and jolt her.

In the draft of a letter to G. B. Soderini, Niccolò writes that "she is a friend of the young." In *The Prince* he repeats the sentence and prefaces it with a sexual clause: always, "as woman, she is a friend of the young."

(This may be as good a moment as any to note that usually to tell whether Niccolò regards a subject seriously we should be able to find some place where he treats it irreverently, too. Fortuna, he is always saying, is the friend of the young, but in the comedy *Clizia*, the aspirant lover Cleandro, convinced that his seventy-year-old father's plans to bed Clizia are succeeding, cries out accusingly, "This time, you [Fortuna] have been the friend of the old!")

The force men apply to Fortune = woman they can also apply to a man. Were fortune a man, and were men to carry out the same counsel, to wit, to beat and jolt, the reaction might also be submission. But the motive for submission would be to avoid pain and Niccolò would expect something would have to be done to contain, deflect, or purge a more durable reaction—resentment, hatred, and, as an offense to honor, the vendetta: "the offense one does to man," Niccolò writes in *The Prince*, "must be [done] in such a manner that one does not fear the vendetta."

With Fortune = woman it is different. For men she is not an object of love. (This may be what permits Niccolò's use of a motif different from the courtier's.) She is an obstacle to prudent political action who will submit, men believe, to their greater physical force. In truth, she is not coerced; she does not *have* to submit. Unlike men, she *lets* herself be won, because being beaten and jolted please her. The young, in treating and commanding her 'with greater audacity', commit acts that obtain the desired result. But they do not subdue her; they seduce her. Fortune 'lets herself be conquered'. Perversely, she gets underneath.

In the *Discourses*, Niccolò describes "Hannibal in Italy, young and with a fresh fortune." He claims in the poem "On Fortune" that "audacity and youth make a better showing" and that one sees in Caesar and Alexander "how much she likes, / how gratifying to her, one sees revealed, is / the one who jolts her, who jostles her or who chases her down." Still, Fortune did not stay with Hannibal, Alexander, and Caesar. Loss of impetuosity, youth, or virtue is not given as explanation, nor is anything else, and we see again the poet's uncertainty. But in the Fortune = woman metaphor of *The Prince* the uncertainty is gone. Niccolò reaches out for optimism, to find a way for reason or prudence to guide political action, to prevail against a frustrating capricious Fortuna. Here in *The Prince*, the fuller version of the theme ends the chapter happily, and in so doing bridges the gap between cool thought (before action) and hot action (after thought).

In the river simile, the protection against fortune was rational; it was cool thinking, in a period of quiet, about an impetuous, recurring event; it was coming up and acting on the solution ahead of time. The Fortune = woman metaphor suggests the motto of a third stance: "Seize and Throw Her Down."

To advocate impetuous action is to urge acting without cool calculation; Fortuna prefers the impetuous to 'those who proceed coldly'. Niccolò defends impetuous action rationally by claiming its efficacy with Fortuna, a demigoddess, a special nonrational female force in an otherwise more understandable everyday world.

From this flurry over fortune, of mystery and brilliance, we may gather that though himself perplexed, at times sorely, Niccolò wishes us to understand that Fortuna, for all her perversity, for all the pathos of the great and the good in their prideful falls, does leave us, has to leave us, if not an open then a broken field to run.

Neither fortune nor cycles, neither necessity nor naturalism, then, forge unbreakable chains for men's rational pursuit through politics, country, and the state, of the common good.

GOD AND POLITICAL ACTION

Niccolò seems ready in the final chapter of *The Prince* to turn to God. In the next to the last chapter, the one on fortune, he had begun by expressing the opinion of many writers that the things of the world cannot be corrected by men and their reason, governed as they are by fortune and God. For the rest of the chapter, he omits God. When he said that, contrary to the opinion of others, he judges it can be true that 'fortune is the arbiter of half of our actions', he gave no explanation or evidence for the calculation, except in a preceding clause that reads: 'in order that our free choice not be extinguished.' In the final chapter he clarifies this phrase, and gives God's answer to the question, is the world divinely or naturalistically determined, or is there space in it for the free political actor?

We have seen Niccolò locate the purpose of the state in the common good and lay that good as the fundament of his ethics. We have heard him speak of the value of political action and encourage acting in politics for the common good. We have observed his slighting of the theory of eternal political cycles, and more important still, reject the position that fortune and God, in governing the world, leave men nothing to do but get down on their knees and pray.

The original and important passage in the last chapter of *The Prince* affirms this and more: "God does not want to do everything, in order not to take free choice from us and the part of that glory that belongs to us." A flat theological pronouncement: 'God does not want to do everything . . .' It is as if divine legislation had at some time been made and now a ruling is handed down. The sphere of action that God does not want to undertake Himself but leaves to us is causal, not illusory, political action. Were God the only one to govern, men would be deprived of causal power. For Niccolò, men have causal power, most definitely.

Still, this leaves God the option of intervention, directly, or via the heavens or fortune or friendly astral spirits. But the option is limited. It cannot be exercised so as 'to take' from us what already 'belongs to us'. It sounds as if a covenant had been made, when God gave men free will, to the effect that a chance of attaining glory through their own action is part of their birthright. The right, as Niccolò conveys it, will not be taken from us as men. The dignity of men comes from the glory that belongs to them and that they consummate by serving the common good in the political and military life of their country. It would seem unjust of God to take away what belongs to us, and Niccolò's just God would not want to do that.

Henceforth the history of politics cannot be written as if God does not intervene at all—for God does intervene—but as if God intervenes so judiciously that men 'with their reason can correct the things of this world'.

God's decree is part of a great liberating design, loosening men from direct contact with Him in a vast area of reason and energizing them for politics.

THE PRINCE NEW, AND OTHER

SINNERS

> . . . how easy for man to slip into
> sin.
> —"Exhortation to Penitence"

THE DECKS are cleared for action. Country serves the common good, men should love it and work for it and God wishes them to do so.

Chapter 7 began by questioning love of country as love-service of the lady. This chapter begins by questioning love of country as service of the common good. It does this by submitting a vulgarized Epicurean brief. Epicureanism via Lucretius was certainly not unknown to Niccolò.

TO HELL WITH LOVE

Why should one love country above self or soul? We may put the question this way because Niccolò permits no benefit to self when such benefit would detract from the common good. And as we saw in Chapter 6, Niccolò weighs love of country in the lover's suffering torture, mistreatment, exile, and loss of life and soul. To die for country is symbolic of love of country. 'In what man must a country find greater faith, than in he who has to promise to die for her?'

To die for country. An age-old formula. Is the state Niccolò conceives of worth dying for?

If you get yoursef extinguished in the cause, will your lady or your country be saved, helped, freed, glorified, or ennobled? What makes you so sure? If Maximillian or Charles V conquers Italy, will Niccolò become a slave? He may become the emperor's advisor, entrusted with carrying out policies of reform in religion and military forces, two projects close to our reformer's heart. He may wonder why he ever feared for Italy's enslavement. Who knows? Soldiers may all be defeated, humiliated, enslaved, or killed, or victory may fall their way and be worse in the long run than defeat. Useless, all useless. A stubborn sage of the East was once asked in exasperation, If you could help the whole world by sacrificing just one hair of your body, would you do it? Unmoved, he replied: The world will certainly not be helped by one hair.

When they ask you to die for country they usually want you, before getting yourself killed, to kill as many others as possible. These others—foreigners, barbarians, dragons—are they not lives too? Moses was forced for good reason, Niccolò believes, 'to kill infinite [numbers of] men', but were those 3,000 slain brothers, friends, and neighbors not lives? If you are bent on dying to save lives, let your enemy kill you, instead of you him. In that way, you save at least one life—his. "The story of Horatio [at the bridge] is renowned . . ." Just think how many lives Horatio might have saved by letting his first adversary run him through.

You are talking not about lives in general, you may rebut, but the lives of your countrymen. You will gladly give your life to save a thousand fellow men. Good! And to save 999? 320? 43? When those 43 are in the tavern quaffing your praises, where are you? Those who say they care for you more than they do for themselves—children, spouses, brothers and sisters, parents, fellow citizens, friends, lovers, and leaders, whatever the order of priority within the so-called common good—if by your death you deprive them of your company why should they risk your death? And if they do want to risk it, then ask them to die for you and afterward you will sing their praises.

The lover dies to free his lady, a lamé slut. The citizen dies to free his country, a drab of a state. The lover gets no good out of it. Nor does the citizen. He dies for an equality and liberty he cannot experience, a public good from which he is excluded. Well may Niccolò call these words—peace as slaves is heavier to bear than war as free men—a notable phrase. For *free men* substitute *dead men* and see how notable it sounds. So what if Italy is no longer enslaved or vituperated, so what if population increases, if marriages are freely arranged, if your children can become president, if farming and commerce thrive, if everyone obtains the goods they believe they will enjoy when acquired, and if private gain redounds to the public benefit? It all goes on whether you are here or not, and you are *not* here to enjoy any of it. So what if God is pleased with you. You are dead. The love, the laughter, the friends, the *arista*—that dish of pork loin pierced with cloves and garlic and twigs of rosemary, roasted on a spit, that the Council of 1430 convoked in Florence made international—the wines of Poppi, the caviar from Constantinople, the books, the talk that Niccolò revels in—what a logic!—they become a reason to live that is good enough to die for. By dying you deprive yourself of the very things you died to keep, or reach, or enjoy. Your Honors, your possessions, your lady, your common good, and your country are in the same oblivion as you. If this is love of country, to hell with it.

The Epicurean argument is particularly persuasive if one grants that the soul dissolves with the body in the tomb or on the battlefield. But Niccolò makes no such grant. For him there is more than one world.

To start with, God's own existence implies a world outside of mortal existence. In *The Prince* we recall that there is a 'superior cause' contrasted to 'the temporal' and related to God, 'to which the human mind does not arrive'. Or in the "Exhortation": "But let us distance ourselves from these terrestrial things, raise our eyes to heaven, consider . . . those other things that are hidden from us." Further, when Niccolò writes of the world in a generalizing fashion, he typically qualifies it to imply the existence of another world. In the shortest to the longest of his writings, in the earliest to the last of his works, he indulges a penchant for universalizing, for stating propositions valid for all time and place and casting them as natural or historical law by arranging them as preambles to what he is about to say. In the longest of his works, the *Discourses* and the *Florentine Histories*, he develops a style of introducing large sections with reflective proems or prefaces. Drawing on a Latin expression, *res mundi*, he refers to the earthly world of mankind as *the things* and characterizes them as human, or worldly, or earthly. So in the *Discourses* he speaks "of the things of the world" or "the things of men," and in the preface to the fifth book of the *Histories*, of "worldly things." By no means are these or similar phrases found only in the prefaces. They spread through all his works and letters. A number crop up in Chapter 7 above. He may use the prepositional phrase *of the world* ("things of the world"—*The Prince*) or the adjective *mundane* ("the mundane things"—*The Ass*) at any time to reserve the existence of another world. The *Discourses* offers many examples: "the things of the world at all times have their own counterpart with ancient times," "all things of men being in motion," and "how human things proceed."

In these passages Niccolò is not contrasting men with nature or with the physical world. To make that contrast he employs another phrase, *the natural things*. The "knowers of the natural things" are philosophers who speculate loftily about sky phenomena. And rarely does he use the word in a purely geographical sense, as when he refers to the ancient Romans as "those who were masters of the world."

Niccolò ends his "Exhortation" by quoting from one of Petrarch's *Rime*: "repent and know clearly / that all that pleases the world is brief dream." The world that is *not* brief dream is the hereafter, the afterworld of the spirit, the world one enters at the moment of death. In another work of Petrarch, the very poem from which Niccolò quotes the final lines of *The Prince*, there follow lines of warning of that moment:

> . . . death is above your shoulders;
> You are here now: think of the departure;
> Because the soul naked and alone
> has to arrive at that dubious lane.

When Niccolò writes in various places of the fear of God, he refers not to men's fear of God's worldly acts, although he may wish to include some of that fear, too. He refers principally to their fear of what God may do to them in the afterworld. In the *Art of War* he maintains that "the soldiers of ancient times" were kept from error "not only by those evils that they might fear from men but those they might await from God." Those evils might refer to what God would do to them in this world, but the verb *await* implicates a later date, a delay for which there is no reason unless the evils are scheduled for the hereafter.

So far in this book we have talked principally about God's worldly powers and acts, "the power of heaven over earthly things"; we have not yet considered His rule in the afterworld. There, the most crucial of God's acts is a judicial decision. Poets and painters in Florence, Tuscany, and all over Italy, the greatest being Dante and Michelangelo, depict the Judge's judgment.

God is alone in the judgment. Fortuna, whether or not His minister, has no power in the immortal sphere. Her sway is over the things of this world. At most she hopes to be arbiter of all *human* things. As for other possible influences, Niccolò in the speech he ghostwrote on justice early in his career, mentions the successful "intercession of St. Gregory" to place the emperor Trajan, even though a "pagan and infidel," among the elect of heaven. In the fable *Belfagor*, Minos and Rhadamantes, "together with the other infernal judges," are recorded as present in hell. In the *Mandragola* the heroine Lucrezia calls for help on the Madonna, and a widow pays for masses for the dead for a husband said to be in purgatory. The "Exhortation" portrays Jesus Christ at the banquet table. "This [is] that celestial robe [of charity] we must dress ourselves in if we want to be placed amid the wedding feast of the emperor, our Christ

Jesus in the celestial kingdom! This [is] that with which whoever is not adorned will be driven from the banquet . . ." and sent to hell. The banquet table may symbolize the judge's bench; one cannot be sure. But the certainty everywhere in Niccolò's writings is that God is the one to fear, that He has a monopoly on the judgment.

The banquet imagery stands for heaven and hell. We shall survey these two regions with our author in subsequent chapters. At present we may note that though in literary and theological pieces he writes that 'god loves justice and compassion', that He is "clementissimo Iddio," and that 'the faith of Christ' is founded on charity, in political and military works he most often refers to the fear of God. He admires ancient Rome—'There was never greater fear of God than in that republic'—and its citizens who 'feared much more to break their oath than the laws, as they respected the power of God more than that of men'. Wherever in his serious works he espies the absence of fear of God, he decries it. We saw this in the case of the prelates and heads of religion who took advantage of the teachings of saints Francis and Dominic.

The fear of God is related to His justice, for to reward good and punish evil, He must first judge, then prescribe. And the fear that men have is of being punished for evil. The prescribed punishment is hell, that eternal fire. Fulminations from the pulpit illuminate it punctually, lighting up whole sectors of the Inferno of Dante, the great topographer of hell.

INFERNO: Center and profundity of the earth, and place where the rebels against God are bound.

HELL: A nether world in which the dead continue to exist; Hades; the nether realm of the devil and the demons in which the damned suffer everlasting punishment.

Neither in this world nor the next is God indifferent to man. For the next world, it would seem, we have yet to clear the decks.

CATEGORIES OF SINNERS

Who is subject to God's judgment? Everyone. Who commits evil? Everyone. The whole world sins. Highest God, knowing how easy it was for man to slip into sin, "saw that were He to keep to the rigor of vengeance, it was impossible for any man to save himself." Niccolò has said we are wicked, tilted toward evil. In one way or another, as we have seen, all classes of persons do evil. Our author lists their wicked acts in his catalogue of cardinal sins—ingratitude, ambition, envy, greed, hate, cruelty, deceit, lust, luxury, and sloth. Niccolò's poem, "On Ambition," alone implicates Greed, Envy, Accidie, Idleness, Cruelty, Pride, and Deceit: "this evil-sowing having grown, / the cause of evil [having] multiplied, / there is no reason that one repents of doing evil." The remedies that the poet can barely hint at, so overwhelmed is he with sorrow, are the brake of 'law or greater force' and the hope in the "grace [of God] or a better order [of things]." He is a moralist precisely because he puts people to shame, identifies and bewails the evils of the world and tries to correct, and to exhort others to correct them.

Although everyone is sinful, some classes of persons or certain areas of life may be less or more sinful than others. There are two important classes of persons we might consider who, although supposed like everyone else to be in some way a sinner, are presumed to lead a less sinful life and are protected and helped by the community to lead that life. These two classes are the clergy and the female sex. Both are kept away from certain areas of activity that overlap but are distinct enough to be identified as commerce, politics, and war. As long as clerics and women keep off these zones they are at least in theory, inviolate. Should they trespass onto them, they lose their special status. From Niccolò's writings it appears that both these classes nonetheless do evil, but because of the cautions imposed by their special status it is usually evil of minor order. Once they trespass onto the debarred precincts, they suffer the loss of protection and help, and run the risk of greater evil.

The comedy *Mandragola* contains several allusions to clerical wrongdoing. Nicia, the husband, complains of the Church of the Servants of Mary, where his wife Lucrezia, "hearing it said by a neighbor that if she made a vow to hear the first mass for forty mornings [at that Church] she would become pregnant, she vowed and went there about twenty mornings. Would you not know that one of those dirty friars began to hang around her, so now she does not want to go back there." Nicia is indignant. "It is a bad thing, though, that those that ought to set us good examples are made this way. I speak the truth!" Here the wrongdoing is not of engaging in commerce, politics, or war but of one inviolate class attempting to violate another.

In act 4 when Callimaco learns that Friar Timothy has agreed to participate in his scheme to seduce Lucrezia, he rejoices, "Oh blessed friar! I will always pray to God for him." At which Ligurio is moved to sarcasm, "Oh good! As if God granted graces for evil as for good. The friar will want [something] other than prayers!" Callimaco, rendered ingenuous by love, asks, "What will he want?" Ligurio answers in a word, "Money!"

The fact that Friar Timothy will receive money for his help does not

Fulminations from the pulpit illuminate it punctually, lighting up whole sectors of the Inferno of Dante, the great topographer of hell.

mean he is engaged in commerce. He is able to accept the money because of the church's mission of charity and because of the giver's giving the ducats 'for the love of God'. The playwright is satirizing the clear and well-understood ulterior motives for giving and receiving. The clergy sins out of petty greed (the hint is that the friar has small personal uses for the money), but not to enter the territory of commerce, which is reserved to banks and bankers who will handle the dangerous substance on its way to authentic spiritual ends.

Similarly with politics. In the *Florentine Histories* Niccolò quotes a saying of Cosimo the Elder, "States [are] not held with paternosters in hand" (*state* here has the sense of *imperium*). No one knew better than Cosimo—de facto ruler of Florence—that there is some politics in all organizations, the church included. Niccolò, too, knows that the church has its politics. He blames Caesar Borgia for not paying enough attention to it when his father died and the time came for electing a new pope. "Not being able to make a pope to his liking, he could have seen to it so that someone was not pope, and he should never have permitted to the papacy [any] of those cardinals he had offended." Niccolò also knows that some popes have shown "how much a pope [such as Caesar's father] was able to prevail both through money and through [military] forces."

When describing pontifical activities Niccolò refers to money, politics, and the military as "temporal forces." They are of course to be contrasted with spiritual forces, among which are to be counted indulgences, censure, the sacraments, and the paternosters in Cosimo's saying.

Both Niccolò and Cosimo know that elections and politics, wars and banking are not missions of the church. Whenever ecclesiastics raise any of these activities to the plateau of a major objective, they move onto sinning grounds and damage their claim to inviolability. ". . . Pope Julius the Second [went] with his army to Bologna to chase out of the state the house of the Bentivogli who had held the principate of that city for one hundred years." Niccolò contends that Giovampagolo Baglioni easily could have and should have crushed his enemy with one blow. Friar Savonarola ruled Florence and was hanged and burned. The archbishop of Pisa tried to occupy the Palace in conspiracy with the Pazzi and was hanged.

In the last case, the *Florentine Histories* gives both the temporal and spiritual side of the argument. The Florentine citizens claimed that the pontiff "showed himself [to be] a wolf, not a pastor," for "in the company of traitors and parricides" he committed himself to "such great treachery in the temple, in the middle of the divine office, in the celebration of the sacrament, and afterward, because he did not succeed in killing the citizens, changing [the regime of] the state of their city, and sacking it in his way, he interdicted it and threatened and harmed it with pontifical curses." Then Niccolò switches to the other side of the story: "Reasons were not lacking to the Pope to justify his cause either; and so he alleged that it belonged to a pontiff to extinguish tyrannies, oppress the wicked, and exalt the good, which thing he has to do with each opportune remedy, but that it certainly was not the office of secular princes to arrest cardinals, hang bishops, kill, quarter, and drag priests [through the streets], to kill the innocent and guilty without any difference." The temporals charged that the spirituals lost their claim to immunity by turning inviolate territory (the temple) into sinning ground. The spirituals insisted that the temporals violated the protected status of ecclesiastics, and the Pope alleged that he owned the privilege of coursing sinning ground. The Pope wished to have it both ways.

So did others. Many persons high and low took advantage of the immunity of clerical property and dress. Some important families on specially good terms with certain monasteries or churches would for eventual necessity cache arms there. In times of disorder, others put valuables there for safekeeping: "many persons hid their movable property in monasteries and churches." Occasionally, men might camouflage themselves in clerical garb. "This man . . . having no other remedy but to hide or flee, first hid himself in [the church] of Santa Croce, then dressed as a friar he fled to the Casentino." But, of course, the majority did not take advantage of the holiness of religious persons, things, and places. For one, there was the battle-hardened Giovambatista da Montesecco, who refused to take part "in the homicide" of the Pazzi conspiracy, considering it a sacrilege to commit homicide in the cathedral. As a result, our historian relates, the Pazzi had to make do with two substitutes (one of whom a priest), "who by experience and by nature were for such an enterprise the most inept." They failed to kill Lorenzo, fled and hid, and were found, "vituperously killed, and dragged through the whole city."

Getting back to Cosimo's neat saying, 'States [are] not held with paternosters in hand', the words are open to many interpretations, but in the context Niccolò puts them, the meaning seems clear. The saying does not insinuate that there is no morality in politics or that there are no implications for political conduct to be found in the prayer, "Our Father." "Some citizens," Niccolò explains in the *Florentine Histories*, had said that Cosimo "was ruining the city and acting against God by chasing from it so many men of good quality." Cosimo answered with three arguments: that a ruined city was better than a lost city; that two bolts of rose cloth made up a man of good quality; and the third argument, to wit, the saying about paternosters. His enemies used these words "as material to calumniate him as a man who loved himself more than his country and this world more than the other."

The calumny of loving this world more than the other applies most specifically to the saying about paternosters. That word can symbolize not just a prayer or the act of praying, but also prayers often recited or the action of praying constantly, like that of the old man in *Clizia*: "he sticks his head in so many churches and finds and goes to all the altars to mutter a paternoster." The paternoster is the most recited of all prayers and heard in various rites and chains of prayers, notably the rosary. So, Cosimo's saying points out that imperium is not held onto by the chanting of prayers.

What of the phrase, 'paternosters in hand'? One does not usually think of prayers being 'in hand'. The phrase makes a nice example of subtlety in popular speech and at the same time illustrates Cosimo's ease in it. 'Paternoster' refers also to the beads used in reciting a prayer chain. Cosimo did not need to add 'in hand' except to clarify that he had prayer-chanting in mind and to drive home that in chasing out enemies and holding imperium, one should have something 'in hand' too. 'Paternosters in hand' emphasizes the contrast with 'holding states' and insinuates the question, What *should* be held in hand, then?

To hold a paternoster alone is to hold nothing or not enough in hand. One has to hold more than frequent prayers and a rosary; one must hold something that in the circumstances belongs in hand, something actually appropriate to an exercise of imperium or of command—a ban, a law, a sword, or whatever may be useful in driving one's enemies into exile. Money in hand, one daresay, would not be as appropriate, for the contrast seems to consist of praying versus action or, at least, versus a more direct action aiming at results in this world.

The contrast between prayers and something else appears elsewhere. Thus, "I think that persuasions and prayers may help but believe that the [military] facts would help much more." And in deciding what it is that one should hold in hand, Niccolò's remarks about Venice are to the point. The most recognizable symbols of Venice are representations of San Marco holding a book in hand. The book represents study. In the poem "On Ambition," Niccolò writes that "San Marco to his cost and perhaps in vain / learns late that one has / to hold the sword and not the book in hand." More explicitly, in December of 1509, he reports from Verona to his superiors that the Venetians have realized "to their cost that to hold states, studies and books are not enough," for in various places they have begun "to paint a San Marco who, in exchange for the book, has a sword in hand."

An obverse reading of Cosimo would sustain that those who hold paternosters are not holding the sword and thus are properly off limits. The abstention of the priestly class from the use of weapons is an ancient tradition. Serfs were kept from their use for centuries in feudal Europe, although they may have had to house, feed, mount, and do other tasks for the weapon-bearers. They were accorded a protected status that was maintained in varying degrees so long as they stayed away from the dangerous ground of warfare and politics. The merchant class, as trade and travel increased, tried hard to solidify a position for itself as nonusers of weapons. The obvious intimacy of money and politics hampered its efforts. The church, in its concern for the pacific tasks of the clergy and as heir to the powerful arguments of Augustine, scholastic theologians, and canon lawyers, found itself to be the leader in attempts to clarify *jus ad bellum*, the right *to* war, (a problem we have heard Niccolò address in Livian terms, mainly of just cause, right intention, and last resort) and *jus in bello*, the right *in* war that soldiers had in using arms, here particularly what right they had to use arms against certain classes of persons. Secular contributions came largely from feudal and chivalric lord-lady-serf conceptions of princes, lords, and nobles. Complicating factors were the expeditions of the Crusades and the later growth in the military manpower of states. Different views eventually coalesced into a ragged but broad consensus around a noncombatant status for the old, the young, the feeble, clergy, women, and merchants.

The commercial classes exempted themselves from arms but not from politics. The *Florentine Histories* says that Cosimo the Elder was "the most reputed and renowned citizen of the unarmed man [class]." But as for the clergy, so for them: if they tread on political ground they expose themselves to its risks. Neither side in the Pazzi conspiracy argued that the Medici and their followers were unarmed bankers and therefore not to be threatened with weapons.

Those who did have rights and duties in the bearing of arms, and those Niccolò recognizes as having their true profession in soldiering, are the nobles. Italy, in the struggles of its cities against the nobles of the Holy Roman Empire, suffered greatly. The church favored the cities. The conflict brought "almost all of [Italy] into the hands of the church and of some republics, and those priests and those other citizens, not being used to knowing about weapons, began to hire foreigners."

The *Florentine Histories* gives two settings for the change in military capacity of the several groups under consideration, one for Italy, another for Florence. A transitional chapter going from Book I to Book

II reviews the military weakness of Italy. Among the reasons for decline, it identifies "the Pope because arms did not stay well on him, being a man of religion, and the Queen Giovanna of Naples because she was female . . . [and] the Florentines . . . for having extinguished the nobility through frequent civil discords, leaving the republic in the hands of men nourished on merchandise." The loss of military virtue in the decline of the armed nobility and in the rise of unarmed burghers resulted in the employment of foreign mercenaries. For Niccolò, anathema.

Focusing on Florence in the mid-1300s, he writes that in the struggle "the desire of the Florentine people ["to be alone in the government without the nobles participating in it"] was harmful and unjust," resulting in "bloodshed and the exile of citizens." The people triumphed. Among their ranks were the merchants. Afterward, to participate in the government at all, "many of [the nobles] blended into the popular multitude" and pretended to be what they were not. "Out of this came the variations in banners, the changes in titles of families that the nobles made in order to appear to be of the people: so much so, that that virtue of arms and breadth of spirit that was in the nobility was extinguished, and in the people where it was not [in existence] it could not be relit, so that Florence became ever more humble and abject." In the ruin of its noble class Florence had "stripped itself" of fighting quality.

1520–1521

In one of his works Niccolò contrasts the upbringing in an earlier century of a priest with that of a gentleman. He had undertaken at the request of private citizens to go to the nearby city of Lucca to oversee a bankruptcy. Account books were not his forte, but the task was important enough for him to carry the credentials of Cardinal Giulio de'Medici, then actual ruler of Florence and secretary to the Pope and soon to become Pope Clement VII, Niccolò's benefactor. While in Lucca our auditor learned something about the city, wrote a brief paper about it, and also read a little book on Castruccio Castracani. Because he was already contemplating a commission to write the history of Florence and because he had been recently at work on the military questions raised by the *Art of War*, Niccolò chose to compose a short biography, fictionalized and idealized, of this fourteenth-century captain and eventual ruler of Lucca. He wrote it in about a month evidently, and sent it to his friends of the Gardens for comment. The work is dedicated to two of these friends, Zanobi Buondelmonti and Luigi Alamanni, the first of whom, a godfather of one of Niccolò's children, who had just had a child born to himself, replied within a week in the name of the others, too, thus revealing that they had read the manuscript quickly.

Castruccio Castracani in this account is a foundling raised by a canon and destined for the priesthood. He turned out to be, however, "a subject completely unsuited to the priestly spirit." Putting ecclesiastical books aside at about age fourteen, he started to handle weapons. And if he did read once in a while, he liked no readings but those that discussed war and the things done by the greatest men. This shift in direction caused his foster father "inestimable pain and trouble." One day a gentleman—"whose occupation was war"—was chatting with other citizens in the main square and spied Castruccio at play with other boys. Thinking he detected in him "a regal authority," he asked the boy "where he would stay more willingly: in the house of a gentleman who would teach him to ride and deal with weapons or in the house of a priest where he would never hear anything but [divine] offices and masses?" The answer was clear. He went to live with the gentleman. "It is an extraordinary thing to think [that] in the very shortest time he became full of all those virtues and customs that are required in a full gentleman." Comparing the praise Niccolò gives to gentlemen in these texts with the derision he lavishes on them in those quoted earlier, we can see that the passage of a century or two has robbed them of the one virtue that made them true gentlemen—military ability.

Having considered the relation, in Niccolò's judgment, of arms, politics, and commerce to clergy, nobility, and merchants, we are left one more group with a claim to inviolate status—women. They are not to be allowed near the armed forces, not even as camp followers, the *Art of War* decides. Besides, soldiers have not time to think about "Venus." *Effeminate* is a word Niccolò uses often to signify lacking military virtue. He tells the story of the Athenian who asked a Spartan if he did not think the walls of Athens were beautiful, "Yes, if [the city] were inhabitated [just] by women," the Spartan replied. "Let women, the old, children, and the weak stay at home and leave the ground free for the young and the stalwart [males]." Unfortunately, sometimes even when women are not on violent ground they are violated. In the sacking of Volterra in 1472 by Florentines and others, Niccolò records, "neither women nor sacred places were spared." This event prompts from him the statement that 'men are readier for evil than for good', a restatement, slightly modified, of Niccolò's most general characterization of human

[229]

nature, presented in Chapter 4 that men are more prone to evil than to good.

Unless women for dynastic or other reasons happen to find themselves in a princely status as did Dido, Catherine of Forli, and Joanna II, where their behavior is not greatly different from men's, they do not live in the world of politics, commerce, or the military. Their world is one in which relatively small sins are committed, generally, of deceit and carnality. Their domain is the house. Woman is household chores, goes the proverb in *Clizia*. Women are also the domesticators of men. Nicia, the husband of the *Mandragola*, pontificates that without "women in the house" men "live like beasts." His wife Lucrezia's aim should be, according to Friar Timothy, "to fill a seat in paradise [by giving birth to a new creature] and to make her husband happy."

Set in domestic atmospheres, Niccolò's plays reveal that though women can be kept away from arms and politics, their brains, courage, and willfulness, if put to the test, make them anything but helpless dolls. There are forms of wrongdoing other than violence and places for doing them other than the piazza. Household deceit may be used by women on men, as in *Clizia*, or by men on women, as in the *Mandragola*. The measures the husband in *Mandragola* takes to protect his wife are formidable. When they function as they are supposed to, they reduce wrongdoing to relatively small account, even smaller than the 'sins washed away by holy water' of Friar Timothy. But there is always the danger that the lust, the deviousness, and the arrogance of men infiltrate these barriers, as does indeed happen in *Mandragola*.

So much the worse it is when a transgression involves the women of powerful men. Chagrin changes into dishonor and moves into political territory, as in the case of Buondelmonti's breaking of his nuptial vows to the tune of the death of Florence's peace and unity. Niccolò does not want rulers to underestimate the political danger of dishonoring women. "And as one has seen in this history of ours [of Livy], the excess done against Lucretia took the state away from the Tarquins, that other done against Virginia deprived the ten [magistrates] of their authority. And for Aristotle, among the prime causes that he assigns to the ruin of tyrants is their having injured others on account of women, by raping them or violating them or breaking their marriages . . . . I say therefore that absolute princes and governors of republics are not to hold this matter in small account."

When attached to men by blood, custom, or law, as daughter, mistress, wife, or fiancée, women are protected by the honor of their men from the evil of other men. Niccolò insists on the inviolability of women under all circumstances, ranking their untouchability on a plane with property. Less protected are prostitutes and courtesans, whose sexual accessibility is not part of the honor of some male. Nonetheless, the reputed physical inferiority of women as a class keeps them out of the armed forces and morally entitles them, along with other physical inferiors or noncombatants, to exclusion from the use of or subjection to violence, armed or unarmed. Quotations from a couple of letters of instruction sent by the Florentine Secretary to officials outside the city may illustrate these points and also give some of the flavor of Niccolò's domestic government as compared to foreign assignments.

It seems that Alessandro di Mariano from [your jurisdiction], who at present finds himself in the prison of Florence at the instance of the respected Eight of the Guard and Authority in our city, has used one of his servants of eleven years in every way so that she has been ruined; and of this the wife of Cristofano Messo there of your court, and the wife of Lazzaro Magnano, and the woman who is called Pavola have information, [having been] themselves with the said girl, according to what has been referred, washing clothes together at a fountain outside of the Passerina di Colle Gate.

Now because we wish to have full information of all this thing, we wish and command you to have the said three women above mentioned [brought] to you, and similarly said girl, and upon their oath you will have them examined diligently, each one for herself by your cavalier and notary on this case, with the greatest regard and honesty possible to you, so that we have the strict and simple truth of the thing; and once they are examined, you will send us a copy of their words, closed and sealed with your seal, and via a trusted person; and together [with it] you will send us the aforesaid girl accompanied in a way that her honesty be preserved. Do what we command you with the utmost celerity, giving notice on your honor by whom you send said testimonies and who will come with the aforesaid girl.

A similar letter of instruction is in defense of a married woman "who, as we understand, [is] good and of the best family there. . . . [Her husband] has mistreated and [still] mistreats her by keeping a female in the house and under her eyes . . . and she has found it necessary to go out of the house and return to her relatives; and he does not provide her with anything so that the poor woman has scarcely a mouthful of bread, and he with his female enjoys both the dowry of the wife and her inheritance . . ."

Such letters as these typically leave no doubt that the official addressed had better carry out instructions and had better not plead misunderstanding of them. "You understand our mind," is a common closure. "Do what we command you, do not fail."

Warranted or not, the idea is widespread that women are creatures to be shielded. The clergy is protected from harm and from their own wrongdoing by special dress, sometimes by cloistering, and by renouncing the use of arms. Women are similarly protected. Differently from the clergy, however, they are usually shielded by affectionate, customary, legal, consanguineous, and other attachments to particular men.

Though Niccolò supports the inviolable status of clergy and women, he does not envy it. They occupy a low status, one not for him. Those who are barred from politics, or take no interest, cannot or will not attain their full dignity, their share of 'the glory that belongs to us'. Seen in the span of political philosophy, he is resuscitating an ideal of the citizen that thrived in ancient Athens and republican Rome and collapsed under a (in his view) misguided modern Christianity.

Women and priests are protected and kept off the sinning ground of politics, commerce, and war; others—citizens, subjects, soldiers, leaders—tread on it daily. Niccolò does not lump everyone into two heaps, moral and immoral (or nonmoral). Society is too full of shading and varying tonalities. On the other hand, each of these sorts of persons— men, women, children, the old, the infirm, nobles, soldiers, merchants and bankers, subjects and citizens, public officials, kings, gonfaloniers— each has a different status and consequently a different moral position. To arrange such a vast network of relations into some ethical order would be no simple task, and Niccolò has more pressing intellectual and moral problems. In any case, no one should do evil—neither citizen nor prince nor pauper. Yet it is easy for all of them to do evil. And there are a few, we have discovered, who are exposed to greater moral danger. The evil they may have to do is greater than that of any others. As a class these few are unique: the only class to whom our moralist recommends evil, the very one *The Prince* concentrates on and gives a name to—the prince new.

THE PRINCE NEW AND THE ONE-ALONE

We first hear of the new prince (*il principe nuovo*) in that famous letter of 10 December 1513. Niccolò is writing from his country house. He has composed a little work to which he gives the Latin title, "About Principalities." He notes that "it ought to be welcomed by a prince, and most of all by a new prince" (*principe nuovo*). At that moment we have no idea that the phrase *new prince* is to crystallize into a figure. All Niccolò adds in clarification is to be gleamed from the remark that because the work should be welcome to a new prince, he addresses it to His Magnificence, Giuliano. True enough, this man, a descendent of the great de facto rulers of Florence, Cosimo the Elder and Lorenzo the

Magnificent, seems destined for great leadership responsibilities. We traced Niccolò's relation to him in Chapter 2.

The first chapter of *The Prince* does not mention a new prince; it speaks of principalities and classifies them as either hereditary or new. New principalities, in turn, may be newly formed from a different kind of government or else newly acquired and added to a hereditary principality. Niccolò leaves the hereditary category aside, while continuing to analyze new principalities into subclasses. In this way he skews his future topics all in the direction of new principalities. He does not state that he desires to concentrate on them, nor does he give a reason for wishing to do so. The second chapter moves toward an explanation that is clearly announced in the third chapter. "But the difficulties consist in the new principality."

In Chapter III the phrase *new prince* appears for the first time in the book, but in slightly different form, inverted as *nuovo principe*. Although, ordinarily, whether the adjective precedes or follows the noun creates a difference in meaning, in Niccolò's writings the difference often seems to carry little significance, to depend sometimes on sound and rhythm. But in this case he prefers the more unusual form of the adjective preceding the noun (*nuovo principe*) in order to show that a concept somewhat different from common usage is involved. It is almost as if in English (where the rule would be reversed and the force would be greater) one were to use the term *the prince new*.

Here is the way it appears in its first enunciation in *The Prince*: "it is always necessary to harm those over whom one has become prince new, either with cavalry or with infinite other injuries that the new acquisition draws along, so that you have as enemies all those you hurt in occupying that principality; and you cannot keep as friends those who put you there, because of not being able to satisfy them in the way they presupposed and because of not being able to use strong medicines against them, being obliged to them . . ." Thus does Niccolò introduce the prince new and at the same time anticipate special trouble for him. In comparison, in hereditary principalities, as he previously explained, "the natural prince" has less reason and less necessity to injure, wherefore it is inevitable that he be more loved. All he has to do is "not to neglect the order [maintained by] his ancestors, and then temporize with unexpected events."

As the pages of *The Prince* go by, Niccolò more and more can indicate the prince new by way of clauses, as in "one who becomes prince" or "those who are new," by adjectives, as in the *wise* or *prudent* prince, or simply by *prince*, leaving it to the context to distinguish him from the hereditary or "born prince." Chapter 6 begins with the admission that

Niccolò is interested not just in new principalities but also in new princes. He mentions the speaking "I shall do of principalities totally new, both in prince and state." A further dimension of the new prince appears: he becomes "prince from a private [station in life]." Not all new princes need come from private life: an already existing prince can annex another state and, for that new part of his state, become the new prince. His difficulties will then appear outside his old borders, for they will arise within the newly annexed state. By contrast, the new prince who rises from a private station to take over imperium and becomes prince of his own country or of a newly formed principality—his problems at least at the start are within his own borders. Rising from private-to-prince becomes a part of the prince's new image. Of those who have arisen through their own efforts, our author says that the most excellent are 'Moses, Cyrus, Romulus, Theseus, and others similar'.

In Chapter XII of *The Prince*, Niccolò reveals that his having left hereditary princes to one side in Chapter I and having disposed of them systematically in Chapter II, has significance. He now blames these 'born princes' in Italy as the ones who committed sins by leaving Italy to repose "in mercenary arms," defenseless against foreign armies. "And the one who was saying that our sins were the reason, was saying the truth." He is referring to Savonarola. In one of his preachings, the Friar had said that these were the crimes of Italy, Rome, and Florence: their impiety, fornications, usuries, and cruelties. But Niccolò has not yet finished his comment. "But they were not then [the sins] he believed but these that I have narrated; and because they were sins of princes, they too have suffered the punishment for them."

By this time in the work, Niccolò can talk of the prince without qualifiers; the context usually discloses each time, as that above does, whether he means the prince new. Chapter XIV is the first to shift in its chapter title from principalities to prince. "What Pertains to the Prince in the Matter of Military Forces."

Summarizing the whole work in Chapter XXIV, Niccolò writes that 'the above-written things prudently observed make a prince new appear [to be] an old [one] and make him immediately more secure and stable in his state than if he were [hereditarily] aged within it'. The last chapter, the twenty-sixth, opens with the new term, giving it its last enunciation twice in one sentence, and in both its varieties, the more emphatic appearing first. "Having considered then all the things discussed above and thinking to myself whether at present in Italy the times concur to honor a prince new and whether there was material that might give occasion to a wise and virtuous [person] to introduce a form that ought to bring honor to him and good to all men [of Italy], it seems to me that so many things concur in favor of a new prince that I do not know what time was ever more fitting than this." At last the prince new learns of the heroic role he has been groomed to play—the dragonslayer, 'redeemer' of Italy.

Of moment for us in this genesis of a heroic figure is that shortly after *The Prince* begins to carry the word *prince* in its chapter titles comes the revelation that the new prince has a special relation to evil. Chapter XVIII contains the phrase that first appeared almost word for word in the 10 December 1513 letter to Vettori—"a prince, and most of all, a new prince." This kind of prince, the author goes on, is the one who "has the need" to know how to enter evil.

The question arises, why is Niccolò writing of princes old or new if he is such a devout republican? One can try to answer by expanding on some of the biographical events surrounding the composition of *The Prince*. We began to do this in Chapter 1 and shall return to it later. The theoretical answer to the question is this: There are certain times in a state's history, particularly at its formation and in moral or military crisis, when leadership needs to be concentrated in a single person. And if, as is likely, existing leaders or the old princes are worse than useless, the times then concur to honor a prince new.

The prince new is a construction of that masterpiece, *The Prince*. Succeeding works all but drop the phrase from the vocabulary. Except for one twisted echo in the *Discourses*, where it is applied to David as a new king, it would seem that the prince new disappears. What Niccolò does in these later works is to keep to a more traditional, more specific language, one that he used in *The Prince*, too, but overshadowed by the figure of the prince new. Isolating various functions—religion founding, constitution making, state founding or reforming or reordaining—he assigns them to corresponding types of one-man leaders—the religion giver or founder, the lawgiver or legislator, the state founder, the reformer or reordainer, to which one may add the dictator, in the Roman sense of one man legally wielding extraordinary powers for a short period. "And one should take this as a general rule: that never or rarely does it occur that any republic or kingdom is well ordered from the start or reformed wholly new from its old institutions if not set in order by one [person]; indeed, it is necessary that it be one alone who gives the way [to go] and on whose mind any such ordering depends." The beginning of mankind was a time when the dispersed inhabitants gathered together and, seeking among themselves, made one as their head, it may be recalled, and in general, Niccolò recommends, a multitude to act in concert "must immediately from among its own [ranks] make a head . . ."

The various functions to be performed, and the corresponding single leaders, seem to confront situations of life-threatening difference or change. The situation the prince new faces is different from that of the old prince; he has to do things that the old prince had not to do. The founders of religions and states, the legislators, and the reordainers all face circumstances that must be changed. For "there is nothing more difficult to deal with nor more doubtful of success nor more dangerous to handle than to make oneself the head for introducing new constitutions. Because the introducer has for enemies all those who did well under the old orders and has as tepid defenders all those who would do well under the new orders. Which tepidness issues in part from fear of adversaries who have the laws on their side, in part from the incredulity of men who do not truly believe in [fundamentally] new [political] things until they see issue from them a firm result."

Were it a question of maintaining what has already been founded or totally reformed, then the one-man-alone should be set aside. Whatever is established "will not last long if it remains on the shoulder of one [man], but yes, certainly, if it remains in the care of many, and the maintaining of it stays with many." One man to establish the state, many men to conserve it. Just "as the many are not capable of establishing a thing . . . so, once knowing [the good in] it, they do not agree to let it go."

If then there is such a difference between the leadership of one-man-alone (*uno solo*, our author calls him) and of the people, if one is superior to the other, each in different functions, our political philosopher does well to treat of principalities as well as republics, and can do this without impairing his standing as a republican. "And if princes are superior to people in ordaining [fundamental] laws, forming civil ways of life, enacting statutes and new institutions, people are so far superior in maintaining the things set in order, that they without doubt reach the glory of those that set them in order."

Moreover, the actions of new princes and ordainers are like those of a dictator—always in the form of a vital intervention and lasting a relatively short time, perhaps so short as the six months of the Roman dictator but generally not more than a single generation. Sooner or later, these innovators fade away to the republic. Princes have a "short life"; therefore, one cannot consider it "the health of a republic or kingdom to have a prince who governs wisely while he lives, but [rather to have] one who puts it in such order that even with his dying it maintains itself." Moreover, it is difficult to find even two good princes in a row, but a republic has, "because of its way of electing, not only two successions but infinite, most virtuous princes that are the successors of one another: which virtuous succession will always be in every well-ordered republic." When treating of republics, Niccolò will sometimes use the word *princes* to mean elected rulers or eminent citizens who are "numbered among the princes of a city."

THE EXTRAORDINARY AND THE EVIL

The prince new, the founder of religion, the legislator, the sweeping reformer, and "the wise ordainer" have a common problem. Each "must arrange to have authority alone; nor will a man of prudent intelligence ever reproach anyone for any extraordinary action that he might take to set in order a kingdom or constitute a republic." The word *extraordinary* that Niccolò utilizes in various forms to characterize certain acts of the prince or one-man-alone should be singled out. Since the work of those *uno solo* leaders confronts critical circumstances of difference or change, their means range outside the ordinary. To reform an entire country, "it is not enough to use ordinary means, the ordinary methods being [in this case] bad; but it is necessary to come to the extraordinary, as it is, to violence and to arms . . ."

When the situation does not call for extraordinary means, they should be avoided. In the hands of those who have designs on a republic, they should be repudiated. Niccolò da Uzzano, one of the wise speakers in the *Florentine Histories*, knew these "extraordinary means of proceeding . . . perfectly well" and was the "first to dislike the extraordinary ways" both of the Medici partisans of Cosimo the Elder and of those in his own party who wished to destroy Cosimo. Furthermore, extraordinary methods, while necessary to the prince new or the one-man-alone founder or reordainer or redeemer, are counterproductive to a hereditary ruler in his own land, for their deviation from ordinary law and custom may topple his rule at the hour in which he begins 'to break the laws and those customs and usages that are ancient and under which men have lived for a long time'.

Closely related to *extraordinary* is the word *excessive*, which our writer uses at times as a synonym or intensive of *extraordinary*, as in the phrases, "excessive and notable" and "extraordinary and excessive." Also related is the term, "a regal hand," one that wields "absolute and excessive power." Representations of it in regalia show a hand grasping a rod. To create or maintain a republic among corrupt people, "it would be necessary to reduce it more toward a regal state than toward a popular state . . ." This, a circumstance of moral crisis, indicates again that republicans must study principalities, too, "so that those men who cannot be corrected by the laws for their insolence might be in some way bridled by an almost regal power." The power to restrain has to go beyond the ordinary laws; hence the terms *extraordinary* and *excessive*.

Similarly princely in coloration is the phrase "the regal arm." The term carries with it more of a sense of "fullest power," a not necessarily excessive arrogation of the ruler. The regal arm, in turn, is associated with "the majesty of the principate" or the comparable "majesty of the state" of whatever form, *The Prince* mentions. The *Discourses* expands on "the majesty of the ornaments, of the pomp, and of his entourage. So that this pomp can scare you or else through any [sort of] pleasant reception mollify [you]." Of these various terms, the ones with the clearest sense of going beyond legal and customary political limits are *extraordinary* and *excessive* and the metaphoric equivalent *The Prince* uses—'strong medicines'.

Extraordinary may be for the founder or legislator, what *evil* is for the new prince. This is the moment to pick up and begin to look more closely into that menacing text of *The Prince*: "a prince, and most of all a new prince . . . should . . . not depart from the good [as long as] being able to, but [he should] know how to enter evil [for whenever he is] necessitated." These seem to be sharp clauses of absolute morality. The parallel independent clauses separate good and evil, the parallel dependent clauses separate possibility and necessity. Our author certainly does not try to hide a moral connection.

In a briefer, more idiomatic but less exact translation, the two dependent clauses might read: *if possible . . . if necessary* or *if he can . . . if he must*. In the original language they consist of the one word each, *potendo . . . necessitato*. The most literal translation would render them as *being able . . . [being] necessitated*. Any of these versions would better retain Niccolò's effective rhythm, too, but at some cost. The first one-word clause is a gerund, the other a past participle or implied past gerund. The temporal element in the gerund may better be supplied as *as long as* rather than as *whenever*, because state of being ("being able to") denotes on-going capacity rather than discrete intervals. The temporal element in the past participle or past gerund may best be supplied as "for whenever" because it contrasts semantically with the state of being able to and grammatically with the gerund (as well as conforming, semantically again, with its relative clause), inasmuch as knowledge ("to know how") would have to be acquired *before* the moment the prince is "necessitated." An earlier, milder passage in Chapter xv of *The Prince* confirms the sense of acquiring knowledge preparatory to using it; it is necessary for a prince "to learn to be able to be not good, and to use it and not use it according to the necessity."

To tell a prospective new prince that he shall have to enter evil insures that he cannot deceive himself. The passage just quoted is less harsh: it speaks not of *evil* but rather of *not good*. Here and there elsewhere in the book, Niccolò recommends committing acts of dubious morality. He does not identify them with evil or as acts that are often necessary until this passage in Chapter XVIII. The prince, and most of all a new prince, "will often be necessitated in order to preserve the state to work against good faith, against charity, against humaneness, against religion."

We need no sermon to tell us what the implications of these lines are. Similar language—acting without good faith and without religion—appears much earlier in *The Prince* in the five anti-virtues, or vices, laid to Agathocles the Sicilian; but the word *charity*, or *Christian love*, that our author uses now, makes one think of his remarks in the "Exhortations" on loving or being charitable to one's neighbor. 'All the evils and all the errors of men, though they are many and in many and different ways committed, can nonetheless be divided broadly in two parts: The one is to be ungrateful to God, the other to be enemy of one's neighbor'. Working against humaneness and good faith falls in the category of not being charitable. "Those who lack charity," the sermon intones, are "enemies of [their] neighbor," and "he who is not full of religion cannot be full of charity." Whoever does not have this virtue of charity will be "put into the everlasting fire."

There is a catch somewhere. God does not want to do everything. Men have a wide field of reason and a deep pool of energy all ready for correcting the things of this world, for governing, for politics. Along comes our political philosopher and tells the prospective leader that to accomplish the most fundamental tasks he will often be constrained to enter evil. But evil, the prospective leader will have heard, will take him straight down the road to hell.

Is Niccolò going to leave his prince new to boil in the vermilion? "The river of blood approaches . . ." The words are Dante's. Niccolò knows them by heart. He has brought his new prince to the edge. What next? He will not tell him that there is no difference between good and evil or that the difference is one of degree or that a prince new is beyond good and evil. Nor will he say he need not worry, there is no afterlife anyway. Neither will he claim that though there may be another world, there is no divine judgment in it. His way out is different.

It is not an insight gained by suffering through a religious crisis. So far as we can see, Niccolò is not tortured by a thirst for faith. One can imagine his having such a thirst only if one conceives of it as slaked. He did have what is better called a spiritual crisis. It was precipitated by events that shook his relation to his country and his country's relation to morality, religion, and to other governments. It left him doubting he was Niccolò. If there ever were times when he tossed and twisted the night long in a bed of brambles, the period 'after everything was totally wrecked' was one of them.

> I hope and the hoping increases the torment,
> I cry and the crying feeds the tired heart,
> I laugh and my laughing does not pass inside,
> I burn and the fire does not appear outside,
> I fear what I see and what I feel;
> everything gives me new pain;
> thus hoping, I cry, laugh, and burn,
> and have fear of what I see and watch.

We do not know when the poet in his misery composed these eight lines (hendecasyllables in the original). But before and after the crisis, Niccolò comes across strong, apodictic in phraseology, earnest to convert others.

A staunch republican, he is convinced that the times require extraordinary measures taken by one man alone. His republicanism has no theoretical problem accommodating one-generation, one-alone leadership if it will lend life to the republic. But how to reconcile what he calls extraordinary measures or evil with what he calls the way of goodness? We have seen that prayer, penitence, and the church are of little help.

The various parts of his solution lodge in different places—in light and serious writings, in the stories he tells, the expressions he uses, and the plays he composes, in calls to action, in the world he unfolds for the readers' eyes. Perhaps, only once, for one part of his remedy, did he cry out *eureka*! and that will be the part in *The Prince* that sets him among the stars of moral philosophy. The rest of the solution takes shape and finds expression in his observations about men and their portion, and crystallizes in his political philosophy. No tight system, but a generous field of view.

THE TRUTH ABOUT HUMAN THINGS

. . . in this world out of joint . . .
—*Florentine Histories*

THINK NOW how all the things made and created were made and created for the benefit of man. You see first the immense space of the earth which, so that it could be inhabited by man, [God] did not permit to be all surrounded by water but left part of it uncovered for his use. He then made to be born in it so many animals, so many plants, so many grasses, and whatever thing is generated on it, to his benefit: and not only did He wish that the earth provide for the living of that [man] but further commanded the waters to nourish infinite animals for his food. But let us detach ourselves from these terrestrial things, let us raise our eyes to the sky, let us consider the beauty of those things we see . . ." Beyond this "splendor and wonderful work," God gave man speech, a face turned to the sky, hands, reason, and intellect. "You see then with how much ingratitude man rises against so great a benefactor!"

Niccolò finds this world gone bad. He has no complaints against the physical and biological parts of nature—the sky, stars and light, the plants and grasses. He may curse the winter and the north wind for inclemency; he does not blame them. The elements follow a pattern, we have seen, from which they diverge only on supernaturally instigated rare occasions.

MOTION AND IDLING

Let us look at a few propositions Niccolò makes about a different world, the world of men and affairs. (We have met some of them earlier, in different contexts). Our author considers himself knowledgeable in this broad field. He says in the *Discourses* that he has expressed therein how much he knows and how much he has learned 'of the things of the world'. First, "human things are always in motion . . ." He offers in this statement no counterpart to motion, such as rest or inertia: "worldly things [are] not conceded by nature [the possibility of] stopping themselves . . ." Movements within motion can only lead, it would seem, to other movements. And because "all the things of the world . . . [are] done by men," motion as a concept is related to activity and change, terms often used for movement of and among humans, in life and in history.

Next, motion has direction. Constantly in motion, human things "either rise or fall." Movement is contained between two points. It is not an oscillation like that of a pendulum, sideways between the two, or a horizontal periodic thrust forward and back like that of the tides. Nor is it rhythmically or periodically cyclical. It is a perpendicular alternation, over time plotting great variations between two points—one up, the other down.

A like motion appears in the introductory Chapter 1 of the fifth book of the *Florentine Histories*, where the *up* point attains the quality of perfect. When constantly moving worldly things reach "their ultimate perfection, not having further up to go, [they] must descend;" similarly, having gone down "to the last depth . . . they must go up."

This note then turns into a moral refrain. "So always from good they go to bad, and from bad rise to good." Chanting a similar refrain in the *Discourses*, while his eyes sweep the world in time and space, Niccolò has already concluded that there is no preponderance of one over the other. 'I judge the world to have always been in one same way, and there to have been in it as much of good as of evil'.

Our historian applies the up-and-down figure of speech to many sorts of ideas and things—states, persons, whole civilizations, fortune—and employs it in couplets of health and disease, order and disorder, rise and fall, good and bad, recovery and relapse, corruption and redemption.

The various propositions about motion seem to have no antithesis: they say nothing about a point of rest, or stillness or inertia. They say nothing about speed of motion, about going faster or slowing down. But within the stages of up-and-down motion, and elsewhere, too, terms often appear that are opposed to motion: *peace, quiet, tranquility*, and the critical *ozio*—a period characterized by indolence and idleness, indicating that human motion or change or action has decelerated, or lost weight and thrust.

The term "idleness," or *ozio* (or *ocio* as Niccolò elects to spell and pronounce it in verse), has surfaced a number of times, once, for example, as Sloth in a list of sins, but most notably in Niccolò's attack on the indolence of gentlemen. The gentlemen Niccolò dislikes are those who live *oziosi*, the princes he detests rot in *ozio*, the leader he jeers at is the one who remains *ozioso*. Young students on the road to evil are *oziosi*. If heaven were ever so kind to a republic that it kept it from war, '*ozio* would make it either effeminate or divided'. The word has ties with Greek and Roman ideas about leisure and the contemplative (as opposed to the active) life. Our author recognized this in his polemic against interpreting Christianity as a teacher of ozio, a glorifier of 'humble and contemplative more than active men'.

Ozio is more than a term with which to condemn the slackening of motion in people and states. Niccolò often treats it as a pivotal term in the vertical alternation of the affairs of men. The brief quotation above about 'ultimate perfection' appears in the *Florentine Histories*, where the up-and-down motion divides into stages, thus: "virtue breeds quiet, quiet idleness [ozio], idleness disorder, disorder ruin; and similarly out of ruin order is born, from order virtue, out of this, glory and good fortune." You may if you wish, exchange for *quiet*, in a sequence like the above, words like *peace* or *tranquility*. In any case you will soon find yourself bumping into ozio. Similar words precede ozio in descriptions of up-and-down motion, and others like luxury, riches, corruption, disorder, and ruin follow it. Where there is ozio, the world is beginning to spoil. "This way of life then seems to have rendered the world weak and given it in prey to criminal men. . . . And though it appears that the world is effeminated and heaven disarmed, it is due more without doubt to the cowardice of men who have interpreted our religion according to indolence [ozio] and not according to virtue." Of note: Niccolò here employs virtue in the sense of masculine energy, intending it as energetic activity. He thus forms another pair of opposites: *virtù/ozio*. The importance of this binary statement appears also in *The Ass*. "*Virtù* makes the regions tranquil; from tranquility then results *ocio*; and ocio sets fire to countries and towns."

Earlier pages of this book have noticed that ozio almost always appears as a term of disapproval. Niccolò can sometimes be found to use it in the sense of unhurriedness, as in the *Art of War*, in the case of pikemen who killed the enemy at leisure (ozio) and of troops being able to assault a town without haste (oziosamente), but in military matters generally, it would seem that the lesson of the notorious *ozi* of Capua—when Hannibal's troops there encamped abandoned themselves to comforts and ease, letting slip the occasion to march on Rome—lies in the back of his mind.

One noteworthy, almost positive, use of the term appears in the *Florentine Histories*. Niccolò moves it toward its ancient usage again, equating an *honest* ozio with the theoretical life, leisure and contemplation, study, philosophy, and literature: "one cannot corrupt the fortress of armed minds with more honest ozio than that of letters, nor can ozio with greater and more dangerous trickery than this enter into well-instituted cities." He remarks that Cato knew this, and, "seeing how Roman youth began with admiration to follow [the philosophers, Diogenes and Carneades, sent by Athens as ambassadors to the Roman senate], and knowing of the evil that could happen to his country from this honest ozio, provided that no philosopher could be received in Rome."

Aversion to widespread indolence marks that morality of labor and work that we saw Niccolò first apply to gentlemen. He does not celebrate work, nor does he regard labor as the curse that Genesis lays on men. The positive connotations in words about various forms of work suffice to confine it to activities that do not damage the common good. We saw in Chapter 7 above that ownership of property implicates an obligation to work it.

Work is not supposed to make a man rich. It is supposed to keep him in poverty, in an active, not an idle, poverty. The poverty Niccolò intends is not the kind in which you know not where the next meal is coming from, but is a busy one in which you work but never acquire enough surplus to quit working. And so, "well-ordered republics have to keep the republic rich and their citizens poor." We saw in a previous chapter that military readiness and operations also put the idle to worthwhile activity.

Were it not for earlier hints, we might expect poverty to be a conspicuous part of a corrupt world. It is instead a condition of the ideal republic. For, "four hundred years after Rome was built there was the greatest poverty. . . . This poverty lasted up to the times of Aemilius Paulus, which were almost the last happy times of that republic, when a citizen, who with his triumph enriched Rome, nevertheless kept himself poor." (Aemilius Paulus's victory over Perseus in 168 B.C. brought back so much booty that Roman citizens were thereafter relieved of direct taxation.) Cincinnatus worked his little farm with his own hands. The Romans honored poverty: "four jugeri of land were enough to nourish a good and valiant man like Cincinnatus," who when his country was in need became dictator and triumphed as a commander. A jugerum (about an acre) was the amount of land a man and two oxen could plow in one day. Concluding the chapter in the *Discourses* on the dictator's return to poverty, Niccolò writes that "by a long speech one could show how many better fruits poverty rather than riches produces, and how the one has honored cities, countries, sects, and the other has ruined them, were it not that this material has been celebrated many times by other men." He probably is referring to the passages of favorite authors like Plutarch and Xenophon, and certainly of a favorite saint, Francis of Assisi, who by exemplifying the life of poverty helped save Christianity from total corruption.

LIFE ON THE FARM

As political doctrine, a lean citizenry and a fat treasury has Niccolò's approval. As a condition in which one lives, as personal poverty—his own—he is less enthusiastic, and with reason, as one might figure out, for unless everyone is poor, poverty will not be honored. We have heard our author's complaints. He feels the pinch most sharply immediately after the loss of his job as Florentine Secretary. His salary drops to zero. He has to deposit with the government a surety of 1,000 gold florins, some of which he may have to borrow at interest, to insure that for one year he does not leave Florentine jurisdiction. And he has a wife and offspring to support. Once persuaded that a job from the new masters of Florence was not to be hoped for overnight, he packs his family and moves from town out to his villa in the nearby Tuscan countryside. A year later he asks Vettori to intercede with the tax board officials, before whom he has to appear with thirteen and one-half florins for two different taxes: "me, for whom the year goes in 40 florins and I have 90 of them in income or less." Vettori did write, affirming that his friend was poor and worthy, had heavy liabilities, no savings, a small income, and many children. Florentines, among the first to devise an income tax, were among the first to learn to cry poor. Vettori, a far richer man than Niccolò, when presenting his own financial statement sounds poorer.

Villa, one may note, has three major senses, all three of which Niccolò uses in referring to his property at Sant'Andrea in Percussina: (1) property on rural land with a house for the owner's occupancy, (2) the owner's house on that property, (3) an inhabited rural area, a hamlet or village. The meanings are counterposed to urban habitation. Most of the time he uses the first sense, which more detailedly signifies a complex of buildings on land in the countryside capable not only of sustaining its inhabitants but also of producing some farm goods for barter or sale in local markets. Related to the villa's existence is another term, *podere*, a field, variable in size, large enough to sustain a working family of modest proportions.

Tuscany, an ancient region of central Italy, where Florence holds its territories, is one-third mountains, one-third hills, and the rest plains. The soil is thin, much of it rocky and sandy; the climate offers not enough spring rain and too much summer dryness for foraging livestock. Niccolò's farming can be classified as intensive hill agriculture. The swine and ovines outnumber the bovines. He mentions a few horses on the property ("About the other horses") and a mule or two, including the 'little mule' that could not be sent to Monte Pugliano because the grass was not yet regrown there.

In a good year, the farm renders the owners perhaps about forty or fifty barrels of wine, ten or fifteen of oil, forty or fifty bushels of grain and the same of barley, a couple of slaughtered pigs, some cheeses, wool and linen, domestic fowl, rabbits, fruits and nuts—apples, pears, peaches, chestnuts, almonds, walnuts—not to mention hay, wood, and cane, and all garden produce—beans, greens, root crops. Guido, writing from Florence to his father at Forlì in April of 1527, asks to be informed should the enemy *landsknechts* think of approaching, because 'we have many things in the villa; wine and oil, even though we have brought down here twenty to thirty barrels of oil'.

We do not know what terms of labor Niccolò has with workmen on his land. In this part of the country, an old system of tenant farming called the *mezzadria* prevails. It divides the expenses, the produce, and, at times, the management of the land by half. The owners and workers are thus associated in a common interest, the growing and dividing of farm produce, but as the commodities to be divided are scarce, a certain amount of squeezing and cheating on one or the other or both sides slips customarily into the bargain. Workers can also be hired by the season, and contract, verbal or oral, can be made for more or less than the typical 50 percent division, but the basic form of farm labor remains this mezzadria. On the land are the demarcated fields called *poderi*, with their typical living, storage, and other structures. These fields of multiple crops and stock present a patchwork landscape spread over hills, dotted with sparse houses, and dominated by vines and olives.

In comparison to Cincinnatus's four jugeri, Niccolò's holdings do not suffer. He may have to manage the farm himself; he does not do his own plowing. There is no way at present of estimating the area of his holdings at the time when his complaints about personal poverty appear, but he certainly owns all of his father's property. His sister had a dowry but could not inherit real property. His brother was a priest and in 1508 put his half of the inheritance in Niccolò's hands. In the neighborhood of Sant'Andrea in Percussina alone, our author's final will of 1522 disposes of the following possessions:

1. the podere with the owner's residence (called) "La Strada" and with it,
2. the farmhouse for the farmhand and family;

3. a house built on the public road for the administrator of the farming properties;
4. the house at the eight canals, along the Roman Road;
5. a little house at the two canals, adapted for the grape harvest;
6. the house used as a tavern along the Roman Road;
7. the house used as a butcher shop along the Roman Road;
8. the podere (called) "Monte Pagliano";
9. the podere (called) "il Poggio" with its oaks, vines, etc.;
10. two-fifths of the wood (called) "Sorripa";
11. the olive grove at "Vallasi";
12. a little field near Greve;
13. the wood (called) "vallata" in Santa Maria dell'Impruneta;
14. the podere (called) "Fontalla";
15. the oak wood (called) "Caffagio";
16. the wood (called) "Le Grotte."

Nearby, in properties mostly off the main road, were other branches of the family or their heirs. The Machiavegli have been in the area for about two centuries. How they happened to concentrate about half their rural investments at this point of the surrounding countryside remains unknown. The process may have begun with a small property, or with an inheritance, or through a dowry. Other rural properties of theirs exist, dispersed to the west and south along the Val di Pesa. This was the situation reported at the time of the tax report of 1427. There appears to have been no real head of the clan: the properties held by various family members were somewhat small in size. Most of the property in the list above came to Niccolò through his father and brother, Totto, as he declares to tax officials in 1511.

In Florence itself, Niccolò lived in a part of town with an even greater concentration of Machiavegli. Relatives dotted an area called Machiavegli Court. At one time, a tower called Machiavegli Tower was in family hands. In this neighborhood, Niccolò has, as his tax report of 1511 specifies, the house with the little house back of it, on Via di Piaza in the parish of Santa Felicita, the banner-district of Nicchio, and the quarter of Santo Spirito. The house is just across the river from the political center of town. Door to door, Niccolò has to walk about fifty steps to the Ponte Vecchio bridge and about a hundred more to the Palazzo della Signoria, thence up the stairs to the Second Chancery. Across the street, on the nobler side, live friends in the Guicciardini palazzo. A few more meters up is the Pitti palazzo.

In Florence, Niccolò's property holdings seem to remain more or less fixed. When he leaves the city to live in Sant'Andrea he does not sell; he probably lets the property for some consideration, most likely for cash, for, with farm produce as the sole source of income, he is cash poor. The church benefices associated with the family were once impressive, but these had diminished in number and in souls, and some were a source of prestige rather than of cash. Totto, at considerable pains, managed to add a few that eventually went to Niccolò's ledger. At the moment our writer retires to his villa in the country, he is undoubtedly trying to increase his cash crops. He knows he cannot reach the level of his former spending for cash items.

As he takes residence in the country place that he refers to as "this poor villa and tiny patrimony," he writes to Vettori that "being used to spending," he cannot go on "without spending." His chief fear may be that once he has lost his political power and is without two cents to rub together, people will treat him as a no-account. "I cannot stay here a long time without becoming contemptible through poverty." A man of pride, Niccolò can take a lot of punishment, but contempt is hard to bear. At this time, while writing *The Prince*, he deals with becoming "poor and contemptible" and cautions that "among all the things a prince should guard himself against is to be contemptible and hateful."

POVERTY, ACTIVE AND LITERARY

As he writes his great letter to Vettori of 10 December 1513 and tells of his playing cards in the tavern, it sounds as if he were dealing with equals. "After eating I go back to the tavern, where there is the host [and], ordinarily, a butcher, a miller, two kilnsmen. With these I scoundrelize myself the whole day, playing at cricca [card games had come into use over the last century, and Niccolò seems to enjoy playing], at triche-tach [a sort of backgammon], and [here is] where a thousand arguments are born and infinite insults with injurious words, and most of the time one fights over a cent and we are heard to shout from no less [a distance] than San Casciano."

Since the days of Laurentian Florence, the ability to frequent the lower ranks on their own terms, to speak their language, seems to have been viewed by youth of good family as an accomplishment. Before that time the Medici had no need to cultivate it: Cosimó and his forefathers spoke it with naturalness. To be able to speak the language of high and low alike may be attractive to Niccolò as an expression of republican equality, too, and as an expert storyteller, his ear is ever ready to capture the nuances of group and subgroup, class and subclass.

The fact is that in his hamlet, Niccolò is a lord. In Sant'Andrea he cannot easily be held contemptible. His property alone, apart from that of the other Machiavegli in the surrounding area, may well constitute the nucleus of the hamlet. That host of the tavern with whom he plays cards is his tenant, and so is the butcher. In addition to various poderi, Niccolò owns four or five houses on the main road, and they constitute the bulk of this little hilltop village on the postal road to Rome.

In the next sentence of the Vettori letter our correspondent reveals that the idiot country company he keeps is not really his and that he was having fun with the stereotype of the bumpkin. "Thus wrapped up among these lice I scrape the mold from my brain . . ." Earlier in the letter he had mentioned others with whom he deals; their names stand up for themselves—another Machiavegli, two Guicciardini, a Ginori, a del Bene, and "certain other citizens." He speaks also of playing cards four years back "in Antonio Guicciardini's house." So at the villa one takes part in the society of the high and the low.

In the morning, "in one of my woods that I am having cut, I stay for two hours to review the works of the previous day, and to pass the time with those cutters, who always have some mishap at hand between themselves or with the neighbors." Here our correspondent begins to exploit a theme of Cosimo the Elder, that of the villa where the owner does some work with his hands but also cultivates literature. Cosimo's father had bought an old castellated house near Florence, in Careggi, at not quite mid-fifteenth century. Cosimo brought in the architect Michelozzo to convert the house into a palatial type of villa with loggia, courtyard, well, cellar, tower, and walled garden. Here, Cosimo would come out from the city to prune his vines, play chess, and as he put it, cultivate his soul. He would beg Marsilio Ficino to visit and bring his translations of Plato. To this villa, then and later, under Cosimo's grandson, Lorenzo the Magnificent, came the most famous literary and artistic figures of the day. The informally organized Platonic Academy met there to discuss in the presence of Lorenzo subjects like the active versus the contemplative life, the nature of God, and true nobility. On the expulsion of the Medici a few years before Niccolò became Secretary, the villa at Careggi was burned and looted.

Our author's villa has no princely grandeur, but its complex of structures also included a loggia, courtyard, well, cellar, and tower. It lacks the walled garden. We do not know what changes Niccolò makes in the villa to adapt it to his principal residence. At least for some time to come he will not have the resources to make costly changes either exterior or interior; yet even as things stand, there are other literary openings in this property.

He drops the labor theme in his letter to Vettori and picks up literature. "Leaving the wood, I take myself to a fountain and thence to one of my aviaries. I have a book underarm, either Dante or Petrarch, or one of these minor poets like Tibullus, Ovid, and others similar: I read of their amorous passions and of their loves, remembering mine, enjoying myself a bit in this thought." Returning to the house at evening, he holds on to the labor/literature balance and adds a light/serious (love poetry/serious history) contrast as he writes of changing clothes to enter the ancient courts and converse with the men of antiquity. There is a day and night contrast, too, the one for the trivial, the other for the true. In this contrast there may lurk also a real versus imaginary connotation. If so, only the night half is underlined. The Muses come at night.

Vettori once writes Niccolò: "I will pay you for your horse on my return." Niccolò writes back, "As for the horse, you make me laugh to remind me of it . . ." He has spent a good part of his waking life, and probably part of his sleeping life, on horse. He puts his knowledge of the beast to use in *The Art of War*. "It occurs . . . often," he writes,

that a courageous man will be astride a cowardly horse and a coward astride a courageous: whereupon it happens that this disparity of spirit makes for disorder. Nor should anyone wonder that a maniple [unit] of infantry sustains any cavalry thrust, because the horse is a discerning animal and knows the dangers and enters them unwillingly. And if you consider what forces make him go forward and what hold him back, you will see without doubt those that hold him are greater than those that push him ahead, because the spur makes him go forward, and on the other hand either the sword or the pike holds him back. So that in ancient and in modern experience one has seen a maniple of infantry to be most secure, unbeatable, even, by horses. And if you might argue from this that the impetuosity with which [the horse] comes makes it the more furious to hurl itself against whoever wanted to withstand it, to respect less the pike than the spur, I say that as the horse from a distance begins to see that he has to hit the points of the pikes, either he will brake his course himself, so that when he will feel himself [about to be] pierced he will stop himself indeed, or arriving at [the pikes] he will turn to the right or left.

Niccolò's arguments so far are based on the aids and restraints operating on the horse and on what the horse sees, feels, and fears, plus ancient and modern experience. He proceeds to propose an experiment, should anyone care to try a replication. "About which, if you wish to have experience [yourself], try to run a horse against a wall . . ."

At the villa, Niccolò cannot afford the accoutrements of the hunt, an aristocratic sport involving horses, true, but also grooms and other help, pastureland and extensive territory, tack and weapons, hounds, falcons, and the rest. He does go birding at dawn, he relates modestly. Hardly what one would call hunting; nonetheless a sport, and a few tasty morsels. "Up to now I have birded for thrushes with my own hands. Arising before daybreak, I would prepare the [sticky] birdlime [for the snares]; I would go from there further out with a bundle of cages on my back so that I looked like Geta when he returned from the port [loaded down] with the books of Amphitrione; I would get at least two, at the most six, thrushes. And thus I stayed all of September; afterward I missed this sport, even though mean and strange, to my displeasure." From the end of September on, he can no longer bird. The day's schedule now goes something like this: labor, poetry, and light literature, conversing outside the tavern with travelers on the public road, main family meal, card playing, serious literature.

Continuing to look on the literary nuances of Niccolò's proclaimed poverty in these months of austerity, one may detect rosy tints. First there is the theme of the poor poet: Niccolò opens the great letter to Vettori with a quote from Petrarch and peppers the pages with literary references—including Tibullus, the Latin poet well-known for vaunting a literary poverty—at the same time as he eats the meals provided by this humble villa and miniscule patrimony and plays cards for pennies. A variant of this theme is that of the poor public servant and man of letters driven by need to give away his literary product, in this case, *The Prince*, the fruit of years of study and experience. So desperate is he that every little doubt becomes crucial: 'this little work, whether it was right to give it [to Giuliano de'Medici] or not give it . . .'

Then there is the motif of poverty as the ideal educational circumstance from which to rise in life. "I was born poor and learned first to stint rather than enjoy," he confides to Vettori after his dismissal. The assertion reflects stoic and republican beliefs. He writes later in the *Art of War* that all citizens should learn "not to spurn poverty." Moses, perhaps his greatest hero, is the model of the babe in the bulrushes. When Niccolò comes to write the biography of another hero, Castruccio Castracani, he has him found as a baby nestling in the herbs and vines. As we saw before, our author joins this theme to the characteristics of the prince new or extraordinary one-man-alone, who rises from lowly or private station to public greatness.

Yet another literary theme is that of poverty as a witness, as in the poor citizen and public servant whose poverty attests to his incorruptibility: "of my word and goodness the witness is my poverty." This is a rare metaphor. Its ancestor is a short, telling clause in Plato's *Apology*: "I bring the witness, my poverty." Socrates' poverty is witness to something other than his word and goodness: it testifies to his speaking the truth. Niccolò is not claiming this, but rather that poverty testifies to his virtue. The difference reflects a difference in men and in the times. The vividness of the phrase, though, lives in the figure of speech. Had both Socrates and Niccolò said that they were poor, and therefore could not have been dishonest, their phrases would have lost not only meaning but also power and originality. Even then, the similarity would be noteworthy, but that both should choose poverty as their witness indicates a borrowing—somehow, somewhere. At the time of the letter to Vettori, two Latin translations of the *Apology* were in wide circulation, the contemporary one of Marsilio Ficino and the fifty-year-old one of Leonardo Bruni, authors with whose works our correspondent was familiar, and whose translation of this phrase even in Latin are close to Niccolò's own choice of words.

LAW OF NATURE AND HISTORY

We have seen Niccolò moving in and out of poverty and ozio as he might among the trees of his wood as he is having them cut. So long as he works the farm and calls himself poor, his literary efforts are safe from the charge of ozio. Not energetic, active, virtuous poverty, but inert, flabby, effeminate ozio blows the spores of rot over the land.

Ozio, we have seen, signals a turn in the motion of human affairs from up to down. The propositions Niccolò frames around vertical motion are not laws of nature; the nature involved is not that of the physical world, although the laws of nature also prescribe a parallel up-and-down, ceaseless alternation. "You see the stars and heaven, you see the moon," Circe's damsel says to her hero, "you see the other planets go wandering now high, now low without any requiem." Nor do these regularities implicate astrological phenomena, such as those signs and portents mentioned in Chapter 3. "Everyone knows . . . how before the

Moses, perhaps his greatest hero, is the model of the babe in the bulrushes.

death of Lorenzo de' Medici the elder, the Duomo was struck in its highest point by a celestial arrow . . ." Neither do they form theological or supernatural assertions, such as that God does not want to take free choice away from us or that Fortuna is the arbiter of half our actions. They are more like natural laws in the Thomistic view: universally valid, discoverable by reason, implicating the nature and acts of men. But Niccolò's propositions do not prescribe that men should or must act in proper ways; and they apply more to institutions or collective acts of men than to the conduct of single persons. If not as laws of nature, they may be classified as laws of history. Though he uses neither *natural* nor *historical* to refer to them, their context embraces discourse on the nature of history and historical events, which Niccolò commonly Latinizes as *worldly things* or the *human things* of the world.

Our author's interest in making universal historical propositions dates back, we know, at least to his days as Secretary. It brings him to the resounding opening of *The Prince*: 'All states, all dominions that have had and have imperium over men' . . . The propositions of the present group appear mainly in the *Discourses* and to a lesser extent in the *Florentine Histories*. They are related to his assertion of the recurrence of events in history. We first hear that "the world was always in a way inhabited by men who have always had the same passions" in a short, sharp paper written in 1503, "On the Method of Dealing with the Rebellious Peoples [against Florence] in the Val di Chiana." Elaboration appears in the *Discourses*. Anyone who considers present and ancient events recognizes that in all cities and peoples there are "those same desires and those same humors . . . that were there always" and that give rise to "the similarity of events" throughout history. The *Discourses* later refines this similarity to almost a matching of events: "all the things in the world in every time have their own counterpart with ancient times. Which occurs because those [things of the world] are carried out by men who have and always had the same passions, [and so] it must happen of necessity that [those things] come out with the same effect."

In *Clizia*, the playwright as he mounts the stage to deliver the prologue pokes fun at the historian. The case you are about to hear, he explains to the cultivated audience, originally happened in Athens, "but what do you say if the same case, a few years or so ago, happened again in Florence?" He asks the question in order to illustrate his point: "If in the world the same men returned as the same cases do return, a hundred years would never go by before they would find us again together doing the same things as now." Athens is gone now; therefore, the author chooses to recount the Florentine rather than the Athenian case. Besides, he twits the audience (and himself), "those citizens spoke in Greek, and that language you do not understand."

The nonperiodic recurrence in time of analogous or similar events follows from the constancy of men's nature, then, now, and forever. The source and cause of motion and change in worldly things lies in appetites and passions, as well as in the heavens. Adding up divine intervention, Fortune's wheels, and lesser supernatural forces, Niccolò still has that all-important one-half or so of men's actions to account for. He cannot rest content without at least trying to find some explanation for human phenomena in the nature of men.

So many of his points and rules depend on human nature or mind, or breast, or heart, or brains, that it would be surprising not to find that he has a large, pertinent vocabulary at hand. His plentiful terms bear certain relations to each other that he does not take pains to sort out. Chapter 4 above, treating of man's essence, discovered that men were evil-ready and enumerated ambition, ingratitude, cruelty, envy, luxury, and accidie or sloth among their worst vices. Concentrating on men's moral nature and the possibility of improvement, the chapter forewent examination of the implications of this nature when placed in relation to appetites and passions, to choice, and to those aspects of mind, memory, and the senses that the author also writes of. We shall not undertake now to reduce all these terms to a system. It may be helpful, though, to give them the barest arrangement, so that we may understand more about human motion, and particularly about ozio: how it precipitates the corruption of men and states, and why men succumb to it.

DISCONTENT, DISTORTION, DELUSION

In addition to the many names we have seen our moralist use to identify vices and virtues, there are others to describe different faculties of intellect or mind—imagination, memory, habit, knowing, thinking, reason, and prudence. Others fall better under the label of passions—hate, revenge, fear, pain, and love. A related group of terms contains corporeal overtones—appetites, desires, humors. As usual, the terms overlap frequently. In one instance, Niccolò speaks of an appetite for true glory and in another of an appetite for murder.

Appetites and passions can, in his terms, be satisfied or purged, vented, bridled or restrained. They move in attraction or aversion toward or away from certain persons or objects or ideas, among which are rewards, women, beauty, riches, food, drink, self, country, equality, power, health, revenge, liberty, punishment, humiliation, poverty, oppression, contempt. While appetites may be temporarily stilled, they return for gratification anew, as in the recurrent need for food, drink, copulation, and shelter. In the case of some other objects, they may be insatiable.

If men set themselves in motion, the intrinsic cause of the motion is the recurrence and insatiability of their appetites and desires. The pursuit of gratification pushes men to incessant movement; moreover, the impossibility of gratification leads to incessant discontent. Niccolò observes in the *Discourses*, "The cause is that nature has created men in [such a] way that they can desire everything and cannot obtain everything; that desire being always greater than the power of acquiring, there continuously results from it a malcontentedness with what they possess, and small satisfaction with it."

In Chapter 4 above, appetites and desires in themselves seemed neither good nor bad, making only for variousness and volatility, making for the incessant motion just mentioned. Once we consider their objects, they take a deep moral coloration. Given men's nature, the appetites, passions, and desires are apt to be directed in improper ways toward wrong objects. Out issues a preponderance of vices. As in the poem "On Ambition," so in the *Discourses* appetites often converge in the political vice of ambition, the lust for power, and its consequent violence. "Because every time fighting from necessity is removed from [the possibility of] men, they fight for ambition, which is so powerful in human breasts that no matter to what rank they rise it never abandons them." To take an example from the poem, the vice of ambition is a natural instinct that "leads us / by its own motion and passion."

Another aspect of human nature complicates the picture. Men's desires and appetites are not only insatiable and wrongly directed, they are also deceptive. They distort vision, reason, and belief. Nicia, the elderly husband in the *Mandragola*, wanted a male child so badly that he would have believed "a donkey flies." In the *Discourses*, the author warns against believing those who have been chased out of their country. Not necessarily do they try to deceive you; rather, "so great is the extreme desire that is in them to return home, that they believe naturally many things that are false . . ."

The more intense the passion, the wilder the distortion. Niccolò himself had occasion to rue this aphorism that time in Verona when, according to his story, one hag sold him a bill of goods for another hag. To pick up the story where we left it, the pressing sexual urge to couple with a female (he calls it desperate 'lust') blinds him and blunts the senses of touch and smell and makes him disregard fear, and more important, deprives him of a desire to clarify the image. He was willing to let the image remain vague, and let himself clarify it in imagination. The object seemed shy, keeping herself in a corner, he notes. Afterward, his appetite gratified, Niccolò is once more in a steady state of reason and prudence. The desire to know returns to him, he wants his visual and other senses back. "And having done as I did, getting a desire to see this merchandise, I took a brand from the hearth that was there and lit a lamp that was above; hardly did the light take hold that the lamp almost dropped from my hand. Alas! I almost dropped down dead, so ugly was that woman." The rest of the description is too ripe to quote, though it retains a touch of humor: "her mouth resembled Lorenzo de' Medici's, but was crooked on one side and from that side came out some slaver . . ." Enough to say that the sight and smell of her hit Niccolò in the stomach. "I vomited on her. And thus, paid in the money she deserved, I left." Emptied literally or literarily, Niccolò proceeds briefly to discuss his plans to make some money raising poultry.

A horror story of the folly bred of lust. The tale would hardly be worth telling or making up without the underlying moral: the sway of appetite over prudence. Much later in life, Niccolò was to sermonize: "But we are tricked by the libido . . ." Visually, the tale bears the imprint of those old woodcuts that illustrate the encounter of the handsome youth and the hag-bawd who is shown dangling young bait to hook fish. It reveals that recurrent urges can be affected by experience (otherwise the story could not function as a moral tale). "And I bet that place of mine in heaven [he seems quite confident of it], I do not think that while I am in Lombardy lust will come back to me . . ." He does not plan on being there very long in any case.

Differences in age alone—giving rise to 'other appetites, other delights, other considerations'—so deceive men that their judgment of historical events is suspect. "Because men when they get old [are] lacking in force and growing in their judgment and wisdom, it is necessary that those things that in youth seemed bearable and good, then turn out in age to be unbearable and bad." This, together with their insatiable appetites, leads men "to blame present times, praise the past, and desire the future, even though to do this they were not moved by any reasonable cause." In fact, for these reasons, Niccolò doubts himself. "I do not know, therefore, whether I shall deserve to be numbered among those who deceive themselves, whether in these discourses of mine I shall praise too much the times of the ancient Romans and shall blame our own."

Easily deceived, men are dupes. Nicia is not the only one. There is one born every minute. *The Prince* finds men gullible. "And men are so simple and so much do they conform to the needs of the present that the one who deceives will always find one to let himself be deceived." Earlier in this book we saw two masters of deceit, Vitellozzo and Oliverotti, themselves being deceived and strangled for it. These two were military men well versed in political and military deception. In deliberation, in foreign affairs, in military decisions—"In Judging Great Things, How Often False Are the Opinions of Men." Such is the title of one chapter in the *Discourses*. Those who succumb most easily to deception are ordinary people: "to open people's eyes" one has "to descend to particulars." Such is the subject of another chapter of the *Discourses*, while the theme of still a third chapter is that "the people often desire their [own] ruin, so fooled are they by a false image of a good [thing]." In this last case, the difficulty seems to lie with a faulty image. Imagination as a troublemaker for the truth of things, will come up several pages farther ahead.

So, the same credulity that leads most men into the camp of the deceived turns others into their deceivers, into exploiters of that same easy credulity. "And, if in describing the things that happened in this world out of joint, one does not speak of the fortitude of soldiers or of the virtue of captains or of citizen-love of country, one will see with what tricks, with what astuteness and arts, the princes, the soldiers, the leaders of republics behaved . . ." Not intending to leave the recent example of Alexander VI in silence, Niccolò asserts that the Pope "never did anything else, never thought of anything else but to deceive men, and he always found material to be able to do it to." Without fail, his deception took place as he wished, "for he knew this part of the world well."

ENDS AND MEANS

Men need not be exploited by deceivers. They well enough deceive themselves. Concrete examples of self-deception appear whenever men praise or blame an actor for the outcome of a particular act. Men are impressed with what our author calls 'the event of the thing'. They do not look to the attainment of the true end; they do not realize that an event may be a step toward a mere subsidiary or intermediate or even disguised end. Instead, they are impressed by the immediate happening and its visibly successful outcome. As long as the immediate goal is won, they do not accuse the actor of using foul means. On the contrary, they applaud. This is a fact that Niccolò typically indicates with regret. He accuses his own city in particular: "Florence, city . . . that judges [political] things by [their] outcomes . . ."

Appetites and desires press on men holding them back, teasing them forward and about. Again, the delusion affects the multitude most. More confined to everyday exigencies, "the common people are taken in by what seems to be and by the event of the thing; and in the world there is nothing if not the common people." Sad experience will eventually persuade them that "the cause of the illness is the fever and not the doctor."

They are not alone in misjudging the means-end sequence, for "all men in this [are] blind." Niccolò himself may approve a means-end sequence, but it must first meet critical standards. We looked before at his brief for Romulus in the *Discourses*; it may repay another glance.

He begins with, 'It rightly happens . . .' thus conveying at the start that he approves of the proverbial language to follow, something he does not do for any means-end sequence elsewhere. "It rightly happens that the deed accusing him, the effect excuses him; and when [the deed] is good, as Romulus's [was], it will always excuse him." The *him* is not Romulus. Unless we take account of who the *him* is here, it may seem as though Niccolò is tarred with the same brush, that is, approving 'the event of the thing'. The *him* refers to the actor in the previous sentence, to "anyone, who to ordain a kingdom or constitute a republic, used any extraordinary action." Romulus is an example of this generalized anyone. (The meaning of the term *extraordinary* takes the sense unravelled in Chapter 7 above.) Our author quickly makes clear that, "one should reprimand whoever is violent in order to break [things], not the one who is [violent] in order to mend."

Romulus's acts had good results not only in the sense of their working out successfully: by killing his brother he also remained alone as ruler of Rome. This would have been enough for the common people who judge by the event, but for Niccolò, it is critical that the deed not only succeed in being carried out but also have as its final end the common good—or have one's country as the implied instrument and repository of the common good, which end Niccolò often more abstractly expresses as founding, saving, or preserving the state. By quick successive deeds, Romulus demonstrates that "what he did was for the common good and not for private ambition . . ."

We see in this one example that to bring Niccolò himself to justify resorting to extraordinary means, 'the event of the thing' is not enough. Nor is it enough to calculate correctly the cause-effect sequence. There is a moral principle to take account of. Prevailing opinion of Romulus might be correct, we remember Niccolò saying, were one to ignore what end induced him to commit fratricide. The 'event of the thing' should immediately show progress in this proper, ultimate direction before he stamps it with approval: 'It rightly happens . . .'

Desires, appetites, and passions are dangerously deceptive. All deceive the senses and reason, and so does memory. Memory is short and its transmission from one generation to another, faulty. Whenever a form of government changes, say from kingship to republic, one finds a memory gap between those who establish the new form and the succeeding generation. The authority of the new form is lost once "that generation that had established it was exhausted." Regimes topple because one generation does not remember what the previous one suffered and learned and transmitted in principles of law, custom, and religion. Too long a time has passed without concern for fundamental beliefs: "men begin to vary customs and transgress the laws."

The argument appears in the *Discourses* in the chapter titled, "If One Wishes That a Sect of a Republic Live a Long Time, It Is Necessary to Draw It Back Often toward Its Principle." The author clarifies what he means by principle: That is, "that credence that it has at its beginnings," such as republicanism in a state, or poverty in a religion. (From the examples Niccolò gives, it becomes clear that *sect* [a word he often uses to mean any group or organization other than the state] signifies *religious institution*, whereas *republic* takes its broad meaning of a *state* of any form.)

Men slide away from the fundaments of their religious and political communities and need every now and then to be reminded, as Niccolò once phrases it, "to go back toward the target." True of kingdoms and religions, this is true even of republics, where one, following our author, might expect that liberty is never forgotten, "where the public buildings, the places of the magistrates, the insignia of free institutions recall it." Even pain, 'the dread of which never abandons you', which in the form of punishment or correction upholds the law, its memory, too, grows dimmer with time, and "if something does not happen through which one brings back the pain to memory and renews fear in [men's] minds, soon so many delinquents run around that they cannot be punished anymore without danger." 'Those men who used to rule Florence' knew this, evidently. They said it was necessary to retake the state every five years 'and they called retaking the state, putting that terror and that fear [back] in men'.

In presenting this doctrine Niccolò's language sometimes uses a simple lateral direction—drawing back—but since it is associated with the ideas of founding and fundamental principles, it produces a downward echo—drawing back down to fundamentals. One meets also with forward and upward figures of speech. Equally frequent are expressions of being renewed, renascent, and growing. Thus, Rome had to will "that it be born again [be renascent], and being born again, to take new life and new virtue again, and to take the observance of religion and justice anew." To be reborn one must return to one's original sources and drink of them again. One renews "the first faith and the first increase." Going back down to principle brings up green growth, vital energy and upward motion, all of which there was when a country laid its foundations.

Our political philosopher binds the growth metaphor to a heaven-established normal life span, thence to corporeal and medical theory, and to the nature of "all things of the world," meaning all vital or living things or bodies, which he then extends to what he calls "mixed bodies, as are republics and groups." All living things "have an end to their life; but those going the whole course that is ordained them by heaven generally do not disorder the body but keep it ordered in a given way so that either it does not alter or, if it alters, it does so to its health and not to its harm." Those are better ordered and have long life that can be "often renewed." And, he goes on, "it is a thing clearer than light that, without renewing, these bodies do not last." He then brings in the testimony of "these doctors of medicine [who] say, speaking of men's bodies, 'That every day something is absorbed that sooner or later requires a cure'." (Here, as in the *Mandragola*, Niccolò quotes faithfully the bad Latin employed by physicians.) The idea of daily absorbing something does not fit that of daily losing or forgetting something, and metaphorically and theoretically the cure remains that of saving corrupt bodies, simple or mixed, by restoring their beginnings to memory. These restorative measures will be discussed in the next chapter.

For the moment, let us suppose that appropriate action has been taken to recall citizens and their republic to fundamental principle. Niccolò has said that he judges that the world has always had in it as much of good as of evil, but he adds, 'this evil and this good [I judge] to vary from land to land . . . but the world remained that same one'. (Variation within sameness again.) The parade of countries follows, on and off the world's stage, where the bright lights of fortune or virtue shine now on Assyria, now on Media, then on Persia, the kingdom of the Franks, the Turks, the Sultan, and then on the people of Germany. Germany alone, he insists, is not rotten, for "among its peoples this goodness and this religion is still great, which brings it about that many republics live there freely, and [these republics] observe their laws in such a way that none outside or inside dare occupy them." Florence sent Niccolò as envoy twice to the Emperor Maximilian's court, in 1508 and 1509, and though he never got beyond the Tyrol, he wrote three reports on German affairs, remarking the frugality and simplicity of life of the Germans, their concern for the public treasure rather than for their own spending, and "thus they enjoy this rough life and liberty of theirs."

Virtue, it seems, is possible, but not everywhere in the world at once; it is always limited to certain areas at a time. Virtue lodged long in Italy in ancient times, but today "there is nothing to save it from a most extreme misery, infamy, and vituperation;" there is "no observance of religion, or of laws, or of the militia, but they are stained with brutality of every kind." Italy certainly belongs to the rottenest part of this world. It has 'lost all devotion and all religion'. Again, "truly where there is not this goodness one cannot hope for any good, as one cannot hope in the countries that in these times are seen to be corrupt, as Italy is above all others."

Let us further suppose then, that in a given country that has been recalled to principle, the good ingredients of religion, arms, customs, and law are gathered. Why can it not remain virtuous? Why did Assyria, Persia, and Rome drop off the stage? Where does the rot and ruin come in? And it does come in. It is already in, in the backsliding nature of men. Evil seeds lie dormant. As the damp deepens, the seeds sprout. The last of Niccolò's great works, the *Florentine Histories*, ends with the death of Lorenzo the Magnificent and the words, the 'evil seeds ruined and still ruin Italy'.

When "blinded by a bit of ambition" or other passion, "men are easily corrupted and let themselves become of the opposite nature, no matter how good [they are] and well-taught." Contrary nature is the original bred-in-the-bone nature of men to which the superimposed teaching gives way. One cannot bank on permanent moral improvement. Regress is swift. The evil proneness of men cannot be extinguished. Their malice lies hidden, "but then the time uncovers it." "Time," goes the proverb, is "the father of every truth." Men will "always use the malignity of their spirit, at whatever time they have free occasion for it."

Thus far we have touched only on the parts played by lusts, hates, imaginings, and forgettings in deceiving, distorting, and deluding the senses and twisting reason and prudence. Deceptiveness in men's nature is important and our political philosopher is not done with it. But the expression 'free occasion' above reminds us that we have yet to bring in the role of choice. It is a subject discussed before, and here needs but a slightly sharper focus.

Choice has at least two important senses for Niccolò: first, as free choice or will, an integral part of men's nature, as in his statement that

God does not want to take free choice from us; and second, as a circumstance in which men find themselves, one in which necessity or constraint is largely absent. That saying of Niccolò in the *Discourses* puts it nicely: Men act either out of necessity or out of choice. The first, the more philosophical usage, assures that men have a sphere of moral and causal action. The second distinguishes degrees of choice by opposing them to degrees of necessity. Not that the possibility of acts being constrained denies free choice. Instead, degrees of choice and necessity exist, and significant characteristics of human action depend on them.

Whenever men have a choice to make, their wicked nature has free rein. Thus, Niccolò can generalize that men do nothing good out of choice. Many events that people regard as a disaster have an attractive side. They replace choice with necessity, keep hands busy at activities that do not threaten the common good and, in the best of cases, benefit it. In idleness no necessity constrains you, no authority guides you, and the devil finds time for idle hands.

The relation of free choice and evil disposition helps clarify Niccolò's attitude toward idleness, or ozio. When idle, men head in the wrong direction. Idle minds, and youthful hands especially, turn to the corrupting of politics and religion.

One short chapter in the *Florentine Histories* notes the tranquility achieved in the early joint rule of Lorenzo and Giuliano de' Medici and marks the subsequent departure from republican simplicity of the young bloods of the day. "The citizens returned to their usual way of life, thinking to enjoy without concern that state that they had established and made firm. From which was born to the city those evils that are used to generating themselves most of the time during peace, because the youths, looser than usual, in dress, in dining, in other similar lasciviousnesses, spent without limit, and being idle [*oziosi*] consumed their time and substance in gaming and women; and their studies were to appear wise and astute, by splendid dressing and by speech, and whoever snapped at others more skillfully was the wiser and esteemed by more [persons]."

We are back to ozio. Thence to foppery, gluttony, gaming, women, and meanness of speech. To make matters worse, a princely court arrived.

These thus-made customs were increased by the courtiers of the duke of Milan, who together with his wife and with all his ducal court came to Florence to fulfill, according to what he said, a vow, where he was received with that pomp that was due so great a prince and so great an ally of the city. One saw then something at that time not yet seen in our city; it being Lent, during which the church commands that one fasts without eating meat, that court of his without concern for the church or for God, fed itself fully on meat. And because many spectacles were made to honor him, among which in the temple of Santo Spirito there was performed the gift of the Holy Spirit to the Apostles, and because that temple caught all on fire through the many fires that are lighted in similar solemnities, it was believed by many that God, indignant with us, had wished in his anger to show that sign.

To foppery, gluttony, gaming and women, and meanness of speech, we must add unexampled impiety and ingratitude to God.

"If then that Duke found the city of Florence full of courtier daintiness and customs contrary to any well-ordered civic life, he left it much more [so]." In the "Discursus" Niccolò observes circumspectly that the regime of Cosimo and Lorenzo "leaned more toward a principate than toward a republic." From impiety and ingratitude to God, to political decay. As we read above, the evil seeds sown soon thereafter 'still ruin Italy'.

Ozio thus appears in three major senses: as inert ozio versus energetic *virtù*, as licentious ozio versus disciplining *necessità*, and, in a temporal context, as that period in men's lives when choice is overabundant. Two of our author's phrases in the *Discourses* catch the political dangers of overabundant choice in ozio—an "ambitious ozio" and an "ambitious license." Ozio slows men down while offering them superabundant choices; their evil disposition and deceptiveness does the rest. Choices made, they go into motion again, in one direction—downward.

THE NATURE OF THE BRUTE

> O human mind insatiable, alterable,
> shifty, and various and, above every other thing.
> malicious, iniquitous, impetuous and wild . . .

No other great philosopher, no great philosophical school before Niccolò, holds that men are evil-prone by nature or stresses that this evil is magnified and distorted in desire, mind, and perception, and compounded by choice. When we first encountered the affirmation of evil-readiness and when we pursued its reciprocal relation with choice and the appetites, mind, and senses, we did not seek to fix its place in the tradition of political philosophy. Had we done so, we might have been startled by its singularity. Alongside such doctrine, Plato's Thrasymachus in *The Republic* and Callicles in the *Gorgias*, and Thucydides' Athenian envoys at Melos and Corcyrea shrink to spokesmen for bold self-interest, might makes right, and effect follows cause.

Athenians, like Florentines, are men much in motion. Stirrers and travelers, Thucydides and Pericles say of the Athenians, as Petrarch and Guicciardini say of the Florentines—all of them men who have no leisure (*scholia, ozio*) to enjoy whatever they have because they are too busy getting more of it. But they are not as fully occupied with inbred wickedness as Niccolò portrays men. One can find minor writers, their arguments usually traceable to Saint Augustine, advocating monarchical or aristocratic politics because of the nature of men. John of Jandun (philosopher, and associate of Marsilius of Padua) used the exact phrase (in Latin) that Niccolò uses in the *Discourses*. Most men, he writes, are "prone to evil." Ptolemy of Lucca, in completing (and thereby authoring) the bulk of Thomas Aquinas's *On Princely Rule*, based his argument on original sin, stressing the effect of what Niccolò will call 'the event of the thing' in distorting people's perception and reason. On the whole, such writers saw stupid rather than wicked people, and although they covered most men, they made sure their generalizations did not embrace them all.

It may well be that Niccolò comes to his doctrine of human nature through personal observation. Men may be as bad as he says. But he can observe only living men. Yet some of his generalizations apply to men in times past and future. Moreover, contemporary political writers and historians do not subscribe to this view. Here is his friend Francesco Guicciardini stating his position in *Dialogue on the Government of Florence*: "I say that by nature all men are inclined toward the good . . ." There may be a few who are pleased more by evil than good, but "even if one found some, and they are most rare, they deserve to be called beasts rather than men, for they lack that inclination that is natural to almost all men."

Seneca, the Roman statesman and philosopher, is sometimes named as a precursor of the Christian doctrine of the Fall. He presents an idyllic state of nature and subsequent alienation from it through man's possessiveness, self-seeking, and greed. Our author does not seem to be acquainted with Seneca's Ninetieth Letter, where the idyll is drawn.

Niccolò's fulminations against human nature often seem to come from the pulpit, and this may be a clue. Chapter 4 above noted their bearing on the first and second of the Ten Commandments and on the seven deadly sins. Where we are more apt to find men as wicked as he conceives them is in those homilies swept up in the strong Christian currents of Paul and Augustine.

Augustine's *City of God* does most to elaborate the implications for human nature of the expulsion from the Garden of Eden. The enormity of Adam and Eve's offense provoked God to change human nature permanently for the worse. The punishment of the first humans passes on to their issue as something natural and congenital. By divine sentence, posterity became not man as first made, but what he became after his sin and condemnation, man as second made, man by God's post-creation intervention. Human nature was vitiated and altered: man experienced the rebellion and disobedience of desire in his body and was bound to sin and dying. Quoting scripture, Augustine writes that man had been brought to the level of animals without understanding, and made like them. He insists that what Paul means by works of the flesh are the works of man.

When we first begin to observe Niccolò in the habit of moralist, we noted that he does not deny original sin. He summons up the Garden of Eden in his poetry. Whether and how—literally, allegorically, symbolically, figuratively—he believes in the rendition in Genesis of the serpent, Eve, the apple, and Adam the rebel, cannot be said with certainty. His mind does return to the idea of fall, not as in the upsets by Fortuna or in the downs of the ups and downs of history, not of just *a* fall, but of one great fall. Several of his accounts convey that a break in the world occurs soon after man's creation and that men subsequently acquire an inferior nature fixed for all times. Elements of original sin—a good original nature and a permanently wicked second nature—indicate the theological sources of Niccolò's doctrine and lend it color, substance, and credibility.

Eve figures in one of his versions of original nature, but she did not, it would seem, transmit to womankind that wickedness natural to men. This we may keep in mind: here and almost everywhere that Niccolò makes general statements about the nature of men, he does not include women. He is writing of men's relations with men. Not woman, but man, is the wolf to man. Not women, but "men eat one another." Not even when our author writes of the world of human things does he mean to include women. He offers some general and comparative remarks and sayings about women and about women and men; they appear mainly in his plays and verse, and are nowhere so nasty, so brutish, so sweeping and serious, as those about men.

There seems to have been a span of time, then, in an Eden, a golden age, when man was not wicked. In a split second something happened—Adam and his woman exited from Paradise, a hidden power sent two Furies to earth, and the vices swarmed—and man became what men are now and forever—prone to these vices. Several of Niccolò's accounts sketched earlier convey that a break in the world occurred soon after man's origin. Thenceforth, the proclivity of men in their freedom to direct themselves toward the evils of the seven deadly sins type, the abundant choice that tempts them to relapse in times of ozio or indo-

Adam and his woman exited from Paradise . . .

lence, the insatiability of their appetites, the deceptiveness of memory, desires, and passions, all go to work on their senses and prudence, and together aggravate their wickedness.

For political philosophy, we conclude, Niccolò uncovers men's nature, baring a Christian, more specifically a Pauline and Augustinian, anthropology.

Another of his contributions concerns the common good. Holding to this goal places him in a dominant tradition of political philosophy and theology. But he does revamp the theory.

In the orthodox version, the knowledge that the common good is the highest earthly good is linked to God or nature, indirectly, by a certain belief or assumption or argument, to wit, that man is a special kind of animal whose constitution bends him toward the common good. Because God or nature gave this animal a special disposition for the common good, by inference, the common good must also be desired by God or by nature.

Niccolò does not go through men's nature to find the good favored by God. He treats the common good as the direct desire of God—'the greatest good that one can do is that which one does for one's country', which is the good most 'gratifying to God', and that one can only be one that served the common good. We have located this position at the heart of Niccolò's credo. Men's knowledge of the supremacy of the common good, he treats as universal: all men know that they should put the common above the private good. (Otherwise, his censures of them would not make sense.) But they are not so inclined.

Such differences move Niccolò away from mainline doctrine of the common good and constitute the second of his services to political philosophy: the affirmation that God treasures political community and the common good without reference to or reliance on a special, natural proclivity for it as a particular kind of animal.

What part of man's nature as an animal, according to conventional theory, disposes him to the common good? Greece and Rome, the Holy Roman empire and the communes, juridical as well as post-Thomist ecclesiastical circles, and the consensus of the learned, literary and political, all maintain that the worldly end of the state is the common good or some differently worded equivalent.

An earlier chapter of this book hinted at the past of this ancient political idea. It travels with the baggage of Aristotle and the Stoics from Greece to Rome, where it is rewrapped, taken up by Thomas Aquinas, and distributed among Christians everywhere. We did not pause to ask the question, What kind of human nature explains men's alleged attraction to the common good? The answer can be attended to now: Man is a state animal or political animal, by nature meant to live in the polis, which itself, therefore, exists by nature.

If this denotes little more than that man is by nature a sociable animal preferring to live with others rather than alone, or that man by nature is so constructed as to be a generator of mental and bodily force or energy useful to other men in the fulfillment of their desires, or that only in the state can men attain to the common good, Niccolò might not stubbornly disagree. In both cases, his and the Aristotelian-Thomistic, the argument proceeds from the biological or corporeal nature of men. For both, men are nonfur-bearing, rational bipeds. But only in the latter case are they also political and social animals with senses, reason, and will turned by a natural impulsion toward political community (Aristotle) and the common good (Thomas). Aristotle, with whom this doctrine originates in the early pages of the *Politics*, in the same breath with which he says that man is a political animal, speaks of there existing "in all men an inherent impulse" toward political community. It may still take some human will and action to maintain a polis, but will and action already are naturally so inclined. Ineluctably, natural impulse moves through couples, families, households, and villages to the culmination of the political animal in the state.

Thomas Aquinas takes over the conception from Aristotle, modifying it somewhat, repeating every so often that man is naturally a political and social animal, as the Philosopher (Aristotle) says or as the Philosopher proves in Book 1 of the *Politics*. To hold to this conception, Aquinas has to lighten Augustine's heaviness about original sin. Aquinas, the good doctor, makes leaving Eden, or as he prefers to call it, the state of innocence, more of a transition than a break, speculating that political relationships of authority and obedience existed there and would still exist had the state of innocence continued. The state cannot be merely a remedy for the sinfulness acquired after the Fall. The particular nature of men disposes them to politics, and this pre- and post-Fall nature must be God-given and inclined to good.

The advantage of this one expression, the political animal, is that it leads into a theory of the state as a body with an independent positive purpose. The state's role would not need to be confined to the sword, to helping keep some wicked and unruly men on the path to salvation. A goal exists, a goal one arrives at and enjoys *before* the possibility of beatitude—the common good, a life men are intended by nature to attain and enjoy together, civilly, that is, as a political community or state.

There is, however, a disadvantage to the theory: it is untrue. A conduit running straight from man's inborn nature to his final worldly end? No. Unable to see it, Niccolò cannot claim it. He has his own method of truth finding, which the next chapter will consider as part of his theory of how to know the things of this world. Enough to mention here that the first truth to emerge from that method is that a man who vows goodness in all things goes to his ruin among so many who are not good.

In our philosopher's world men do not have an inherent impulse toward the common good. Quite the reverse. These wicked and unruly men are not just a few: they comprise mankind. Their nature originates in some kind of fall, and they are henceforth set in motion by appetites or passions, abetted by mind or reason, and directed toward various evils in all extensions and forms. In turning "against God," Niccolò declaims in the "Exhortation," man "transforms himself from rational animal into brute animal . . . from angel into devil, from master into servant, from man into beast." We can characterize this new human nature as that of rational brutes. The greatest mistake is to think that men will arrive at the common good guided by such a nature. It leads only to ruin. They must arrive by some other way.

This is Niccolò's third major contribution to political philosophy: the vision of a world in which rational brutes must reach the common good.

Binding a permanent, state-prone, or political and social, human nature to the end of a good-in-association, or the common good, was a triumph of ancient political philosophy. Niccolò snaps the link of nature and end. The common good is still the goal but no longer do men reach it naturally. To join, as he does, an evil-disposed human nature with that same end is unique, not in its two terms of sinful genesis and God-favored goal but in their relationship or lack thereof. Men have a chance to correct the things of this world, all right; evidently they do not will or want to.

No philosopher, no theologian either, has presented such a doctrine of the human things of this world. It offers a radically new political philosophy. Contrasted with the model political animal of the philosophers, for whom human nature and final end are made for each other and for whom men and the common good come together like filings to a magnet, it may at first look like an incongruous combination. This does not indicate that Niccolò is wrong or confused. He might have arranged his doctrine differently. He might have seen, as he does, that there is no positive connection between men's origins and the state's end, and further sustained, as he does not, that human nature is good but not innately oriented toward the state, that man is a good-prone and rational, but not necessarily political, animal. Or he might have retained men's evil-disposed nature while ignoring an earthly goal like the common good, focusing instead on a nonpolitical, eremitic, or contemplative thisworldly life and an otherworldly end like salvation or beatitude. Our political and moral philosopher knows differently. First, men are rotten-hearted by nature. Second, either they will move toward the common good of the state or they are lost.

The truth about this world out of joint is that it is inhabited by rational brutes hell-bent for ruin. That being the case . . .

Chapter 11

THE MIRROR OF THE PRINCE NEW

> . . . a man of low and mean status
> dares to discuss and make
> rules for the conduct of princes.
> —*The Prince*

. . . THAT BEING the case, all statecraft falls in place. One better understands now why Niccolò's political philosophy is different; why he stresses the correction by law and punishment; why he prescribes strong medicine and the extraordinary man in crisis and opportunity, enlists the help of true religion, counts on the fear and favor of God, and looks to constraints from necessity, poverty, and adversity; why he insists on oaths and ceremony, on eternal vigilance over the appetites and passions of men, over their discontent and cunning, their weakness for indolence and luxury; why he militates with force and fraud against the designs of other states, relies on his own troops alone, gropes for a brighter image with which to animate country, and, to the point of tedium, urges love of that country; why he relives the bygone days when citizens loved one another and rails against personal ambition, greed, envy, ingratitude, and their outcome—civil division, weakness, war, defeat, loss of freedom and the common good, in short, a world out of joint. With the discovery that rational brutes roam the city of man, all the separate perspectives of Niccolò's political reasonings come together and constitute his political science.

Aristotle and Thomas Aquinas use the term political science. The phrase from the *Discourses* quoted at the beginning of the previous chapter, claiming knowledge and learning in 'the things of the world', refers to the affairs of men more broadly than the 'things of the state' or of politics, although the subject matter of *The Prince* is almost as far-ranging as that of the *Discourses*. Late in 1500 when the Florentine Secretary spoke to Cardinal George d'Amboise in France about the self-defeating moves of Louis XII, the cardinal, obviously nettled, remarked that the

Italians did not understand about war, 'and I replied to him that the French did not understand about the state'.

Niccolò rarely uses the word *science*. The most notable instance appears in the 10 December 1513 letter to Vettori where he gives a reason for writing *The Prince*, ". . . Dante says that one does not do science without retaining what one understands." *Science* here designates a body of knowledge, and Beatrice and Niccolò are concerned with preserving it. Beatrice, in the *Paradisio*, remarks to Dante, "Open your mind to what I shall reveal to you and hold it there inside." She talks on in the jargon of moral philosophy and theology.

Niccolò's concern is with another body of knowledge. When in his writing room composing *The Prince* he says he is in the ancient courts, speaking with ancient men, and reports, 'I noted down what I made capital of in their conversation'. If we combine these remarks with a felicitous phrase that appears in a later moment of the Vettori letter—that he has been fifteen years "at the study of the art of the state"—we find expressed an equivalent, in his terms, of political science. Scientific storage of fifteen years of study rests within him. "And anyone ought to appreciate availing himself of someone who at the expense of others is full of experience." Once he turns the studying into writing, it is reduced, more accessible, and more securely retained. It is also an advertisement for someone, though not anyone, to avail himself of our author's services, who, although he says he has written down all he knows, has a lot more retained in personal scientific deposit, as yet unwritten, available to recall when needed.

THE PROXIMATE AND THE REMOTE

Though we have only this one instance of the phrase 'art of the state', given Niccolò's skimpy use of the term science, one should construe the word *art* to denote craft or technique. A closer equivalent than political science, then, would be statecraft. Among the other arts are those of wool and silk, for which he claimed he was not cut out. There is also an "art of peace," which one should profit by if one is not cast in the mold of warrior. Solomon knew about it; Castruccio on his death bed counseled its use to his son. But demanding far more attention is the art of war; a prince ought "not have other object or other thought for, or take anything for his art outside of war . . . for it is the sole art that one expects of he who commands." The author will devote a whole book to the subject.

Rules of craft Niccolò sometimes refers to as general rules. After he makes the riposte to Cardinal George d'Amboise, he writes: "From which one derives a general rule that never or rarely fails: that whoever is the cause that another becomes powerful comes to ruin." Another example: "For which one must note that men must be either caressed or extinguished." (The obviously figurative language here can be nicely compared to the choice between using love or force, both pairs of terms not untypical of Chancery lingo.) Another: "From which one can draw another noteworthy [thing]: that princes should have others administer burdensome things; they themselves, [things] of favor." The author knows he is in the habit of making generalizations or rules; he sometimes refers to rules as *his*: "the which goes against one of my rules, which says . . ."

Often these rules are drawn or born or arise out of material he has just presented. And often they are followed by a *because* that generally gives a further reason for the rule, based on human nature or ways of thinking and acting. The stable side to Niccolò's political philosophy, to be sure, makes prediction possible, but only roughly possible, as we have grasped, for human nature is constant in its volatility and the mundane world that is changing is unchanging in its flux. Thus he might say, "But of this [particular historical recurrence] one cannot speak broadly, because it varies according to the subject." The world of human things is like the deck of cards Niccolò and his pals play with up at the tavern, continually reshuffled and redealt, but the same cards.

Granted things we have already seen—a world out of joint harassed by a capricious Fortuna—the uncertainty of predictive rules should come as no surprise. There are many things that prudence can foresee and art overcome, and this makes causal action possible and worthwhile. Nonetheless, Niccolò is the first to admit that many schemes go awry and not for want of care in preparation, "so uncertain and false are our plans."

He makes the last remark in the *Florentine Histories*, in connection with the Pazzi conspiracy. Surely conspiracies constitute a special case of risky planning. That is the reason he is so much against them. But in the *Discourses* he spreads uncertainty over the whole face of politics and war. "And because one cannot give a certain solution to similar disorders that are born in republics, it follows that it is impossible to set up a perpetual republic, because its ruin is caused in a thousand unexpected ways." Philosophers would agree with him: the subject of politics and ethics is human action; human action evinces regularities or probabilities, but not certainties.

The bulk of words in our author's serious works is dedicated to lessons and rules aimed at proximate ends, of which these above on retaining a preponderance of power, on rewards and punishments, and on administration are not untypical, and which are themselves proximate means to more important, more distant ends. He does not spend too many words on the common good: it is the ultimate end of the state and known to all. He spends fewer words on God, as remote cause of men's nature, occasional intervener in worldly affairs, friend of certain men, legislator of free choice and glory, benefactor of lovers of country, inspirer of fear, et cetera. He might have written more about these things had he, like his brother, Totto, or like Thomas Aquinas, been a priest. He knows about 'the things of the world' and specializes in 'the things of state'. "A wise and kind master of our human life," he calls himself, not without irony, in the final song of *Clizia*. He is concerned with the moral end of aiding men to attain the common good, the best possible life together in this world.

In the up-and-down motion of the things of the world, Niccolò breaks in at the point of ozio, or even a little later. If men are to be saved from the downward plunge, there are a thousand things to learn and to put in practice immediately. The thousand things take the form of lessons and rules, complete with commentary, ancient and modern, domestic and foreign examples, illustrations from history and recent experience, and praise for the good, blame for the bad. When mentioned at all, the aim of these rules is usually phrased as preserving, maintaining, ordering, or revitalizing the state or one's country, or simply as avoiding ruin. Sometimes the author takes the next step up in his short hierarchy of ends; he mentions subsidiary ends (like independence and liberty) of the ultimate good, to wit, the common good itself. More often, he implies or elides them. Clear or well-known premises need not be explicit. The reader can supply them on his own.

Niccolò's pages of words, then, were they put on the scale and weighed numerically, would tip the balance heavily on the side of discourse about means to proximate ends. This discourse comprises his statecraft, as contrasted with his political philosophy, part of which the previous chapter focused on, and with his moral philosophy, which the next chapter shall take up.

CHOOSING A PRINCELY CANDIDATE

To accommodate the real human world, Niccolò proposes a different statecraft. Chapter 8 above uncovered the distinction between ordinary and extraordinary political measures and related them to the prince new and one-man-alone conceptions. Ordinary measures are harsh enough. A letter of The Ten to the Florentine emissary in Pisa on 27 November 1507 reads:

We having understood yesterday by yours of the twenty-fourth and by one from the commissioner of Libbrefacta in confirmation of yours, that Volteranno was cut in pieces in the house of those of the Chiostra after being made prisoner in Pisa; the case gave us great displeasure both because we held Volteranno very dear and because we dislike the manner of his death, [it] seeming to us a cruel act and not conforming to the good treatment given by us to the Pisan prisoners we have always had in hand. And in order that every man might know that though we are not [ones] to be as cruel as our enemies, so we are not [ones] to let their cruelties go unpunished. This morning we had hanged from the window of our Captain's palazzo, Giovanni Orlandi and Miniato del Seppia. We give you this notice so that you may publish it, and that one understands in Pisa that their citizens have not been killed by us, but by the cruelty that has been used against ours; and that they may understand, since they misuse our humaneness, that one becomes of their nature.

Officially, this communication emanates from the magistrates, but the writing is in Niccolò's hand. As Secretary, he observes the event and carries out instructions to write the notice.

Extraordinary measures are worse. They make evil necessary for the prince new and the one-man-alone. We may recall them by looking at what Moses had to do. Moses was the lawmaker and savior of his people, the first and greatest of Niccolò's trio of heroes, the others being Cyrus and Theseus (plus, sometimes, Romulus). To illustrate that even men of religious renown may in the course of their political mission have to resort to mass violence and family extermination, our author writes: "And whoever reads the Bible sensibly will see that Moses was forced, were his laws and institutions to go forward, to kill numberless men." Exodus 32:27–29 and Numbers 31:13–18, 35 attest to the accuracy of the biblical reference. Three thousand brothers, friends, and neighbors were killed on orders of Moses.

Glancing at *The Life of Castruccio Castracani* for the treacheries and homicides this new prince had to commit, we see that he betrays and kills a peace-seeking mediator and all those who had relied on the old man's good faith; he liquidates under various pretexts all those in Lucca who might out of ambition aspire to be prince themselves, and of those who succeeded in escaping he confiscates all their property and builds a fortress with the materials of their houses; he kills at one blow the heads of the White and Black parties of Pistoia and kills or imprisons their supporters; through treachery he kills the lord of the strategic Castle of Serravalle. "He lived forty-four years and was in every kind of fortune a prince."

Our statecraftsman makes us face a sterner politics indeed.

Even in ordinary times the legal measures of execution and torture are necessary. Niccolò enters the scene when everything is starting the downward plunge, when the times cry out for a savior, 'a redeemer', a hero. Chapter 9 above already identified such a man as the prince new and the one-man-alone.

What do we know of this man? So far his dossier is slim. He is not necessarily or even typically a hereditary or born or natural prince. He may arise from a private or even humble station in life. Castruccio was found in the herbs and vines. Moses, the greatest of princes new, was found in the bulrushes. We have further found that the prince new is good—were he not good it would not be necessary for him 'to learn to be able to be not good'; that he works 'to do good for the generality of men'; that he will have greater moral choices to make than most men; that among these choices there often will be those of administering strong medicine or of carrying out extraordinary measures.

The qualification that he be good and yet accept that he will be 'forced to be not good' poses a problem of supply, or recruitment. Good men are few and will not want to become bad. Niccolò bares the problem in the *Discourses*, where distinguishing extraordinary from ordinary measures.

> And because to put a country back into good political life presupposes a good man, and becoming a prince of a republic by violence presupposes a bad man, for this one will find that most rarely does it happen that a good [man], through bad ways, even if his end is good, will want to become prince and that a wicked [man], once prince, will [ever] wish to work for the good and will ever have fall into his mind [the thought] of using that authority well that he has acquired badly.

Thence toward the conclusion that under circumstances of moral crisis, a country will need 'an almost regal power' or 'a regal hand' and not find it.

One can safely add that a prince new, in particular, for personal military leadership, cannot be as delicate as an apricot. He must have a strong body, able in war "to conduct the armies, to set up the battles," and in peace "to be always out on hunts and through them to harden his body to discomforts." He should have a good mind, also. For exercising his mind in military matters alone he will have to be literate, as we shall see in a moment. And for political matters he will have to be "a prudent prince" and intelligent. "Because this is a general rule that never fails: that a prince who is not wise himself cannot be well advised . . ."

Granted all this, it would seem that for the prince new and the *uno solo*, Niccolò has one task of recruitment and another of education in, among other things, moral justification and logic for the harsher politics. In each of his serious works, while specifying the qualifications for the one-man-alone, he is recruiting and educating him at the same time. He undertakes these tasks most directly in *The Prince*.

THE SHAPE OF *The Prince*

In political literature there is an ancient genre best identified as princely rulebooks (from the often-used title, *On Princely Rule*, in Latin, *De regimine principum*) and sometimes ambiguously called "Mirrors of Princes." Usually the genre embraces short works (but longer than political testaments or ad hoc memorials) of general advice and moral counsel and addresses the eldest sons of kings and princes, or more generally, an aristocratic readership. The genre has hundreds of practitioners, including the eminences of Plato, Aristotle, Plutarch, Cicero, and more recent, lesser figures like Poggio Bracciolini, almost all paying much attention to moral education. Among them also are Xenophon (*Cyropaeida*), Thomas Aquinas (*On Princely Rule*), and Johannes Jovannes Pontanus (*On the Prince*), to name but three known to our author, and Erasmus (*Education of the Christian Prince*), to name the most contemporary.

Niccolò knows the authors of the genre well. The *Discourses* contrasts ordinary biographers, "those [writers] that describe the life of princes," with these others, "those that ordain how they should live." Better yet is the designation a few pages later, "those that write on how a prince should conduct himself."

We may recall that when Niccolò announces he has 'composed a little work', he gives it the title *On Principalities*. In it, he declares, "I steep myself as much as I can in cogitations on this subject, discussing what a principality is, to what species they belong, how they are acquired, how they are maintained, why they are lost." As thus put, the work did not seem much to Vettori. Even after receiving a copy he reserved full judgment until he had seen the full manuscript, which indicates that a considerable portion was yet forthcoming.

The first chapter of the book serves, among other things, as a table of contents ("I shall go [ahead] weaving the above-written warps") and spells out more or less what Niccolò wrote Vettori, expressed more interestingly, however: republics versus principalities, hereditary versus new, all new versus new in part, used to living under a prince versus living free, acquired by arms of others versus of one's own, and acquired through virtue versus through fortune.

The headings of the first chapters support the title and subjects Niccolò mentions: "Of How Many Types Are Principalities and in What Way They Are Acquired," "On Hereditary Principalities," "On Mixed

Principalities," "For What Reason Darius's Kingdom ... Did Not Rebel ... after the Death of Alexander," "In What Way Cities or Principalities Must Be Governed, That Lived By Their [Own] Laws," and "On New Principalities."

In Chapter VIII there is a slight break. The title mentions not only a principality but also a type of person who succeeds in becoming ruler of it: "On Those Who Through Crimes Arrive at the Principality." He then returns to states exclusively: "On the Civil Principality," "In What Way the Strength of Principalities Should Be Measured," and "On Ecclesiastical Principalities."

As Niccolò is writing Vettori, he may only be up to this point. Somewhat later, Biagio Buonaccorsi, Niccolò's assistant and friend in the Chancery who was cashiered at the same time, has a copy of *The Prince* in his hands, too, which he sends to a friend, describing it as "a little work (*operetta*) on Principalities newly composed by our friend Niccolò Machiavelli, in which you will find described with greatest lucidity and brevity all the qualities of Principalities, all the ways of saving them, all their offenses, in an exact knowledge of ancient and modern history, and many other most useful documents." Here too we seem to have a little book on the order of that sent to Vettori.

The manuscript would have been just something more than a third of its final length. He says that Vettori may talk the work over with another friend (Filippo Casavecchia) who has seen it, "even though I am still fattening and cleaning it up." He can, if he desires, close the manuscript here with a peroration shorter but similar to that of Chapter XXVI, thus perhaps ending with the final sentence of Chapter XI, "His Holiness Pope Leo has thus found this pontificate most powerful: the which one hopes that if [his predecessors] made it great with arms, this one [Pope Leo] with his goodness and other infinite virtues will make it the greatest and revered." By enclosing a covering letter, then, our author would thus have an introductory letter hoping for greatness in one Medici (Giuliano) and a peroration hoping for greatness in another (Pope Leo).

Whether he intended to stop there forever or for a day, he ultimately switches at that point to a subject different from those he had announced either to Vettori or in the brief table of contents in the first chapter of the book itself. A three-chapter section on military matters follows, the titles of which do not refer to principalities: "On How Many Types of Militia There Are, and on Mercenary Soldiers," "On Troops, Auxiliary, Mixed, and One's Own," and "On What Pertains to a Prince in the Matter of the Militia."

The last of these chapters constitutes a bridge to another section.

While still dealing with military matters, it contains the word *prince* and discusses the place of the art of war in his training and education. War takes priority—'the one art'. The topic and its treatment are brief and forceful. The author then opens onto a broad, new avenue. Into this third section of the book (Chapters xv to xxiii preceded by the bridge of Chapter xiv) fits the Latin title he later gives the work in the *Discourses*—"our treatise 'On the Prince' "—which resembles the printed title of the work, *The Prince*. After Chapter xiv's first use of the word *prince* in its title, succeeding chapter titles keep on using it, expressed or implied, until the last two chapters, xxv and xxvi, which we identify as the metaphysical and theological chapters.

Niccolò does not wait until Chapter xiv however, to address himself to princes. Despite chapter titles, he begins to speak of them in Chapter ii and to them in iii: "you have as enemies all those that you have harmed . . ." (and, for that matter, in the *Discourses*, too: "You, prince, either wish to . . . or . . ."). But not only does he mention the prince in titles in and after Chapter xv, he also opens that chapter announcing a juncture in subject matter: 'It remains now to see what should be a prince's ways of conducting himself with subjects and friends'. This is a subject he mentioned neither in the Vettori letter nor in the first chapter of the book itself. Broadly speaking, this is the subject of books on princely rule, that is, how the ruler should treat those he rules over and those he deals with (the word *friends* in this context denoting presumably friendly or allied rulers and high state officials).

By the time of the writing of the covering letter the author probably had completed the section on princely rule, for he writes in the covering letter for Lorenzo that he 'dares to discuss and make rules for the conduct of princes' something he mentioned neither to Vettori nor in the first chapter of the book. These are the matters that in Chapter xv he says remain to be discussed. Now we may begin to see what education befits the harsher statecraft. In two paragraphs of this one and in quickly succeeding chapters, Niccolò's thoughts dance around excitedly and his pen races to keep pace, weaving in and out from one argument and perspective to another and back again. It is not easy to trace the strands as they rush to merge into a three-dimensional pattern of effective truth, rhetoric, and morality. He has original positions on all three subjects to communicate.

HOW TO KNOW

The previous chapter hinted at the question of how the political philosopher comes to his knowledge of the nature of men. Niccolò gives his own answer to that question, and at the same time takes a gigantic first step toward a theory of how to know about men and their affairs.

The magnitude of the change he is about to make does not escape Niccolò. He writes a singular opening paragraph in Chapter xv of *The Prince*, the chapter that takes the treatise on a new turn. 'It remains now to see . . .' The remarks to follow are new and different and important. "And because I know that many have written of this, I am afraid that writing of it myself, too, I may be held presumptuous, most of all for departing in discussing this material, from the principles of others." The others are numerous and evidently important, else why should differing from them seem presumptuous? Hence, Niccolò's assertions will bear on important new matters.

In the next clause Niccolò distinguishes his intention from theirs, and not only for writing this passage but for the whole work. "But it being my intent to write something useful for whoever may understand it . . ." He wants whoever understands that something to find his writing useful. That is why, "it has seemed to me more appropriate to follow the effective truth of the thing, than the imagination of it." One gathers that by *effective* he means *eminently useful*. To give a name to the kind of truth he is seeking he employs a rare word—*effettuale*. He does not coin it but is among the first few to put it to work.

These many other writers have succeeded only in imagining the truth. "And many have imagined republics and principalities that have never been seen or known in trueness." It seems to be a commonplace for men of affairs like Vettori and Guicciardini to characterize Plato's *Republic* or indeed all philosophy as imaginary, and our author here joins their company. They seem to have misplaced the edge of pride in Sophocles' voice. "Sophocles said that he drew men as they ought to be; Euripides, as they are." Thus quotes Aristotle in the *Politics*. Niccolò, in his sentence quoted above, has done something else: he has slipped from talking about effective, or useful, truth to generic *trueness*. His remarks now may be taken to show how to see or to know states truly.

The point about knowledge becomes this: to see or know states (or men or princes), you have to remove the distorting effect of imagination. He himself, he says, is therefore, "Leaving behind things about an imaginary prince and discussing those that are true . . ." The many other writers do not realize that "how one lives is so far away from how one ought to live that whoever leaves that which one does for that which one ought to do learns his ruin rather than his preservation."

Learning one's ruin is not useful, obviously; learning one's preservation certainly is. The other writers who visualize or imagine ideally or wishfully how men ought to live teach how to go to one's ruin. Niccolò thus rebuts criticism in advance by insinuating that previous writers, numerous and great as they are, have crafted out of imagination a 'how one lives' to fit the ideal of 'how one ought to live'.

The ought in the last phrase sounds few moral overtones. Niccolò is not opposing a moral perception to some other kind, but an imaginary or eyes-closed one to an extrinsic or open-eyed one. By removing the illusory effect of image, one can follow the effective truth, a truth about men that Niccolò reiterates varyingly over the next few chapters, from the first instance, "So many who are not good," to the briefest, "they are wicked."

Clearing our eyes of the imaginary glaze, we are ready to follow the effective truth of the thing and proceed to more particular levels of truth about "how one lives" and "how one acts." The author does not describe in any one place the steps he recommends. Because in other works, too, he stresses useful knowledge, the search for effective truth, we may assume, persists in them all and is our philosopher's particular emphasis in the study of how to know.

The twin procedures of knowledge, we soon find out, are reading and experience. Of these, Niccolò devotes most space to the need to read in order to know. The covering letter to *The Prince* states that the author has knowledge of the acts of great men that he "learned through a long experience of modern things and a constant reading of the ancient." The dedicatory letter of the *Discourses* confirms how our political philosopher comes to know about politics: "I have learned through a long practical experience and constant reading of the things of the world."

An important result of reading is the perspective of distance. Most people suffer a common limitation of living "from day to day." Pinned too closely to the ground, following 'the event of the thing', leads them to misjudge means and ends and other things. Niccolò, in the letter covering *The Prince*, employs the metaphor of high and low.

> As those who draw landscapes place themselves low to consider the nature of mountains and high places, and to consider that of low [places] they place themselves high above mountains, similarly, to know well the nature of people one must be a prince, and to know well that of princes one must be of the people.

This classification puts Niccolò himself, rhetorically, as a man of low station ('of the people', however, is not the bottom-most status), in a good position to know about princes but, to spin out the metaphor further than he might wish, leaves him at a disadvantage in knowing about people. Truth is, he knows about them both.

The use of high and low implies other metaphors. High and low connects with like and unlike, and also with near and far. The like/unlike metaphor does not appear frequently; the near/far one does. To be too near, like being too low, is generally unfavorable for knowing and learning. One gathers this by hearing the author reiterate that the proper perspective is that of distance. Early in *The Prince* he uses a medical analogy to introduce the point and then goes on: "Thus it happens in things of state, because knowing far off (which is granted only to someone prudent) the evils that are born in [the state], they are quickly healed; but when, for not having recognized them, they are allowed to grow so that while everyone knows them, there is no longer a remedy for them."

Niccolò uses the near/far perspective in relation both to time and to space. Whether temporal or spatial distance comes in focus, one gains distance, it appears, principally by knowing history and sometimes by learning that the ancients saw far ahead, too. "Therefore the Romans, seeing difficulties ahead, remedied them always . . ."

In the *Discourses* Niccolò transforms reading into past experience by another winsome simile of modern medicine, and also of law. For the legal cases men face or the illnesses they get, they always have recourse "to those decisions or those remedies that were judged or prescribed by the ancients, for civil laws are nothing but the sentences given by ancient juriconsults, which [having been] put in order, teach our present juriconsults to judge. Nor is medicine ever other than the experience had by ancient doctors, upon which present doctors found their judgment." *The Prince* and the *Discourses* are worth reading, Niccolò suggests, because they are written by someone who had tallied the many precedents of ancient readings to his account. To this, one may add that the reading and knowledge of these precedents enables the author to make his many universal generalizations, particularly those not simply about men that exist but about all men that have ever existed.

Reading has utility even for so active a subject as the art of war. To be a warrior prince one cannot just exercise the body, charge here and there, and sleep in campbeds.

> But as to the exercise of the mind, the prince must read histories, and in them consider the actions of excellent men, to see how they conducted themselves in wars; examine the causes of their victory and losses, to be able to escape the latter and to imitate the former; and above all to do as some excellent men have done in the past, who have taken to imitating anyone before them who has been lauded and glorified and have always kept his deeds and actions near them, as one says that Alexander the Great imitated Achilles; Caesar, Alexander; Scipio, Cyrus.

Here we have an indication of what to read—the accounts of Achilles, Alexander, Caesar, Cyrus, Scipio. The great ancient historians must find a place in our library. We can take as recommended those he names positively in his works, among whom are Livy, to start, Plutarch, Tacitus, Thucydides, Xenophon. Occasionally our educator pens a more specific advertisement. "And whoever reads the life of Cyrus written by Xenophon will recognize afterward in the life of Scipio how that imitation was [turned] by him to glory, and how much in chasteness, affability, humaneness, and generosity Scipio conformed with those things that were written of Cyrus by Xenophon."

Because the prince new and the one-man-alone are good men, the actions they cull from history to imitate will naturally be "the most virtuous works that history shows us, that have been done by kingdoms and by ancient republics, by kings, captains, citizens, lawgivers, and others who have wearied themselves out for their country . . ." A statement of guidance rather than a reading list is what Niccolò proffers the ruler. He may also classify personages to be imitated in whole or in part according to the princely reader's situation or circumstances, whether he is a new or a hereditary prince, whether a founder or a preserver of his country. Speaking of Roman emperors, "a new prince in a new principality cannot imitate the actions of Marcus, nor yet is it necessary to follow those of Severus; but he should take from Severus those parts that are necessary to found his state, and from Marcus those that are essential and glorious to preserve a state that is already established and firm."

He recommends his own writings, too, not alone in covering letters and proems but in cross-references from the *Discourses* to *The Prince*, from the *Florentine Histories* to the *Discourses*, and from *Clizia* to the *Mandragola*.

Niccolò remarks also on the how of reading. The covering letter to *The Prince* counsels that history be read "diligently." He himself has done his homework for the *Florentine Histories* on the work of previous historians of Florence, "having read their writings diligently." Twice in the *Discourses* he implies that the reader who finds out about the important things of the past is the one who reads with sense, with the application of the intellect. "And whoever reads sensibly all the pertinent histories will find . . ." The same holds true for biblical reading, where Niccolò encounters Moses, "And whoever reads the Bible sensibly will see . . ."

Diligently sets the requirement of reading with care; *sensibly*, of reading with intelligence, a rarer item.

Sensibly may also contain a hint at reading for the effective truth, the eminently useful. When reading history, one should not read for pleasure or even for admiration. The aim should be utility. One author sometimes reads for pleasure, but the works he then reads he calls minor: Ovid and Tibullus. At the villa, 'after everything was totally wrecked', he used to take books of poetry with him to the fountain in the morning and 'read of their amorous passions and of their loves, remembering mine, enjoying myself . . .' In the evening he went to visit the great ancients.

One may in reading history also put questions to history, as Niccolò did to these historical greats, but one may also put more specific questions, to search for things or fill a gap in knowledge. Whoever reads the history of "our city of Florence" knows that it has had dealings with barbarian Germans and French that showed them to be full of greed, pride, ferocity, and disloyalty, but whoever has not read it, suffers lack of pertinent ethnic knowledge. If Florence "had read and known the ancient customs of the barbarians, she would neither this nor other times have been fooled by them." Another example, this is a suggestion for the future, comes from a military man, the protagonist of the *Art of War*, who shows himself to be quite the music historian,

> . . . as one who dances proceeds with the same tempo of the music and, going with it, does not err, so an army obeying that sound in moving itself does not get disarrayed. And therefore [the ancients] varied the sound, according to whether they wanted to vary the motion and according to whether they wanted to enflame or quiet down or make firm men's courage. And as the sounds were various, so they named them variously. The Doric sound generated constancy, the Phrygian fury; whence they say that Alexander, while being at mess and hearing the Phrygian sound, his courage lit up so much that he immediately reached for his arms. All these modes it would be necessary to find again; and if this proved difficult, one would not like to leave behind at least those that taught the soldier to obey; which each one can vary and arrange to his mode, as long as with practice one habituates the ears of his soldiers to recognize them.

However rare this proposal for historical research may be, it fulfills the reading requirement of thrusting toward utility and the imitation of models. The knowledge sought aims at muscular reaction and reflects Niccolò's effective truth, true cognition and utility. He writes the *Discourses*, he says, to keep men away from error. They should not read history just for admiration or judge that imitating the deeds of the ancients is impossible. "Wishing to draw men away from this error, I have judged it necessary to write upon all those books of Titus Livy . . . that I, according to cognitions of ancient and modern things, shall judge necessary for greater understanding of them, so that those who will read these statements of mine may more easily draw from them that utility for which one should seek cognition of history."

As reading leads to cognition of ancient things, so practical experience leads to cognition of modern things. And to draw on the distancing metaphor, if reading the far-away ancients is best, experience teaches most if close to hand. Chapter XIV of *The Prince* treats of the ruler's training for military command. It recommends field workouts and hunting on battle terrain while posing oneself hypothetical tactical problems such as, if the enemy were up on that hill and we with our arms find ourselves here . . .

Experience must never be disregarded. In the abstract it is something that belongs to the present. The author, who presents himself as the model in the problems of knowledge, has 'a long experience of modern things' and a 'long practice . . . in the things of the world'. His signal letter to Vettori says as much, with an oblique reference to the defunct Republic that gave him political experience. Everyone should appreciate having the service of one who 'at the expense of others is full of experience'. But he also refers in the *Discourses* to his "weak news of ancient [things]," something that could never be correct, rhetorical modesty excepted. A few pages later in the proem, the disclaimer is set right: he speaks again of the knowledge he has as "cognitions of ancient and modern things."

There are some cases where only experience or simulated experience will do. A prince must "never in pacific times be idle (*ozioso*)" but must mount and take to hunting and simulated field maneuvers. Only in rare cases can experience not be counted on. One such case would seem to be the carrying out of assassinations in conspiracies, "where one has many times seen men expert in arms and soaked in blood lack the courage." Yet assassination is a most difficult task; expertness in arms and bloodletting count for as much as possible: "if ever in any undertaking one seeks great and firm courage, made resolute in life and death by many experiences, it is necessary to have it in this."

Fresh or modern examples for Niccolò are those that happen in contemporary history, sometimes in his ken or even with his participation, as in legations—"I presented myself immediately in horse-traveling dress to his Excellency, who received me most warmly; and I, presenting him with the letters of credential, disclosed to him the reason for my coming . . ."—and sometimes in the period between the present and the furthest extreme of memory, "within the memory of our fathers," he puts it. In reference to Alexander VI and his unexcelled ability for tricking men: "Of fresh examples there is one I do not wish to pass over in silence." The word *fresh* gives the requisite impression of temporal nearness.

As part of daily experience as Florentine Secretary, Niccolò had to do a lot of reading, but it was linked to the acts of live men. His superiors often gave him instructions orally, even for his legations, for security, convenience, and other reasons, and he in turn gave orders to his assistants viva voce. The mention of the memory span of fathers reveals that one of Niccolò's sources of experiences is an oral tradition. Thus, "the men who have governed the state of Florence from 1434 up to 1494 used to say . . ." He picks up a variety of information, not all of it grave, when sitting on the stone benches set into the façade of Palazzo Capponi or on those in front of his villa or the adjoining tavern. "I speak with those who are passing by, I ask about news of their countries, I understand varied things, and take note of varying tastes and diverse fancies of men." In the dialogue of the *Art of War* he praises conversation as a way "to understand the truth."

It is possible to get too close to experience. As imaginary truth and castles in the air may take the reader-observer too far off the ground, so 'the event of the thing' may hold the practical man's nose to running along a furrow. Reading and experience act, one presumes, as each other's corrective. Whether reading is active rather than contemplative is a question Niccolò does not broach. His doctrine of the imitation of models has roots in the Greek *mimesis* and the Christian *imitatio*; his particular concern is to graft imitation and reading. To his mind, reading if not active at least does not hamper the active man. The Florentine Secretary, as active a man as one can find, will ask to be sent books of ancient authors while on missions. In the *Life of Castruccio* he has the future prince as a youth lay "aside ecclesiastical books" but pick up and read "those that discussed wars and things done by the greatest men." True, in the case of honest ozio, he avers that letters and philosophy are not without danger to 'armed minds'. Let us say this, that the element of utility and imitation that Niccolò insists is essential to reading removes the contemplative or indolent dangers from the activity. A reader must read so that he jumps from the page to active experience. The two words, utility and imitation, applied to reading history relieve Niccolò from having to choose between a swashbuckling reader and a bespectacled prince.

KNOWLEDGE, DIFFICULT OR HIDDEN

The final chapter of the present book, touching on words versus deeds, will pick up this contrast. A few interesting phrases may still capture our attention here in the matter of how to know the things of the state. From these few phrases one ventures that there is an intuitive element to knowing and learning. In that draft of a letter meant to be sent to G. B. Soderini, our correspondent writes that he would marvel more at things had he not through both "reading and practical experiencing tasted the actions of man and their ways of proceeding." The word *tasted*, unusual in regard to reading and experiencing, crops up again much later in the *Discourses*. The first proem raises the problem of why one finds "neither a prince nor a republic to recur to the example of the ancients." The fault lies not so much in the lack of reading but in not having "a true cognition of history, because of not drawing from it, on reading it, that sense, and not tasting themselves that flavor that it has in itself."

If Niccolò by *tasting* merely wants to signify drawing sense out of reading history, he can put a period to the sentence some ten words earlier. Tasting that flavor is different from drawing that sense. Reading history involves the eyes, or sight; tasting the flavor of the actions of men, the gustatory buds. Another expression also involves one of the senses, this one related to experience alone, particularly to the judging of men: to *touch*. Our poet made powerful use of it in one of the sonnets addressed to Giuliano: 'Let opinions go / Your Magnificence, and feel and touch / and judge with your hands and not with your eyes.' The sense of palpating is opposed to the sense of seeing. *The Prince* presents another powerful usage of this sense: 'And men in general judge more with their eyes than with their hands'.

Like the ability to see ahead that is 'granted only to someone prudent', and the wisdom to see troubles as they are born that is "given to a few," and the intelligence that makes it possible to read sensibly, and the understanding that gives access to *The Prince*, and the tasting of the flavor of history and of the actions of men that so many have not done, and like the feeling and touching of Your Magnificence that fail all the others who can use only their eyes, and the judging with hands that is unavailable to the generality of men, these senses used in reading history or judging men seem to be faculties given to or inherited by only a few. What we seem to have here in embryo is a theory of the gifted. The passage from *The Prince* quoted at the end of the paragraph above continues thus: because to see belongs to everyone; to feel, to a few. "Everyone sees what you seem to be, few sense what you are."

Niccolò does not write often about the senses per se, a notable exception occurring in his reporting (transcribed in Chapter 4 above) of a dismemberment by a blood-smeared mob. When in connection with reading and experience he individuates the senses metaphorically, including that of sight (for, 'seeing difficulties ahead' is a metaphor of sight), he grants simple sight to everyone, while restricting the long sight, the touch, feel, or grasp, and the taste of history and experience to few. Reading and experience require an approach of superior sense or talent, likely metaphors for intuition, whose distribution among the population does not form a pattern of equality. But Niccolò's doctrine of equality never did include equality of intuition or intelligence and talent. 'I believe that as nature made men diverse faces, thus she made them diverse intellects and diverse imaginations'.

In brief, the formula for acquiring useful knowledge or effective truth or true cognition is experience plus reading. One should seek a lowly vantage point to observe princes and a high one to learn about people; a near one for modern events (preferably experience in war and politics) and a remote one for the vicarious experience and innumerable precedents obtained through diligent and sensible reading in ancient history. Reading is more than looking at the pages of an open book, experience is more than going through life day by day. One should approach reading and experience with the sensitivity and intuition intimated by phrases like *tasting* the flavor of history and *grasping* the nature of men. By imitating history's heroic models and applying its precedents to modern experience, a prince new will know how to comport himself. Thus, an open-minded approach to history and experience solves the problem of truth raised in the first paragraph of Chapter xv of *The Prince*.

With one proviso. There is a third part to the formula. For reading and experience to become cognition, they must pass first through thinking and reasoning, a process Niccolò calls cogitating. The covering letter to *The Prince* locates its proper place in the formula. The author's knowledge comes from his experience of modernity and his reading of antiquity, which "I [have] with great diligence for a long time cogitated and examined . . ."

There are three parts, then, to the formula for knowing or cognition: reading, experience, and cogitating. With another important proviso. Not all knowledge is of effective truth or true cognition. There is knowledge that cannot be arrived at. Its most elegant description is in the "Exhortation." "But let us detach ourselves from these earthly things, let us raise our eyes to the sky, let us consider the beauty of those things we see; of which [God] has made part of them for our use, part so that knowing the splendor and marvelous work of these things the thirst and desire may come upon us to possess those others that are hidden from us." A more prosaic statement appears in *The Prince*'s discourse on ecclesiastical principalities. The reason for their security and happiness is that they are "sustained by superior causes to which the human mind does not reach . . ." The context for both of these remarks is religious: the knowledge our author is referring to is part of what is customarily considered religious knowledge. Because it is religious, however, does not mean it is accessible to men of religion. The human mind, whether that of the humblest friar or the highest bishop, does not reach that knowledge. Nor does it mean that a prince new or *uno solo* like Numa, who takes recourse to the authority of God when his own is not enough, has access to it. He may feign access to it, "because many are the [public] goods known by a wise man that do not have in themselves reasons evident [enough] to be able to persuade others of them." Such men, whether of the church or state, fall in the category of the exceptionally wise we have just spoken of; their minds, though gifted, are human. The knowledge in point, however, is knowledge that God has made inaccessibl· to all men, to all reason. Hidden to us, yet we know it to exist and thirst after it.

A RHETORICAL STRATEGY

So much for the methods of how to know the things of the world. What of the findings they reveal? Chapter XV of *The Prince* reports on them immediately. The first fruit of the tree of effective truth, appearing just after its identification, is the knowledge that there are 'so many [men] who are not good'. (This affirmation we earlier scrutinized as a major orientation of Niccolò's political philosophy.) Chapters XV to XXIII have more to offer. For one thing, they reveal the importance of rhetoric to the prince, and for another, the outlines of a rhetorical strategy directed more to the people than to external potentates. These topics are different from Niccolò's own rhetoric targeting the reader, princely or not: a matter that arises in the present book at various intervals. Niccolò's pressure as a rhetorician is broad and constant: he seeks to persuade prospective leaders to specific courses of action for Florence, Rome, and Italy, to arouse in Italians the sentiment of love of country, and in the process to praise and blame the particular deeds of men, past and present.

We may recall that when the poet Petrarch pleads for the liberation of Italy, he appeals to the rulers of Italy, whereas Niccolò declares that if military virtue is spent in Italy, the reason lies in the "weakness of leaders." His metaphors in *The Prince*'s final chapter reveal the people to be "the matter that is not lacking"; they are the limbs: 'Here there is great virtue in the limbs, were it not lacking in the heads'. We may recall also that in our political philosopher's definition of the state there appears the dramatic phrase 'imperium over men'. Be they citizens or subjects, without them there is no state. In his scheme of things, a prince has "to live always with that same people." In comparison, "he can well do without those same grand ones, being able to make them and unmake them every day . . ." People are the state's reason for being, those for whose common good the state exists. Any state that does not so benefit them is a bad state, a tyranny. Men have grievous faults, God knows, but they have certain merits too—in comparison to princes and grandees.

Niccolò, we must bear in mind, is a republican. To support the people he will go against common opinion, as in *The Prince*, "And let no one contradict this opinion of mine with the trite proverb that 'whoever founds himself on the people founds himself on mud'." He will also go against the great ancient historian on whom he founds the *Discourses*, "our Titus Livy, as well as all the other historians," for their saying that "nothing is more vain and inconstant than the multitude." A noble passage articulates his stand: "I do not know whether I shall be taking a field [that is] hard and full of so much difficulty that it might be better either to abandon it with shame or sustain it with energy, wishing to defend a cause that as I said, is disparaged by all the writers. But however it may be, I do not judge nor will I ever judge it a defect to defend any opinion with reasons, without wishing to use for it either authority or force." To depart from the ancients is a serious step. His open break indicates strength of conviction.

The bad reputation of the people comes from having to judge them, or what is written about them, under the distorting influence of power. "But opinion against the people arises because about people everyone speaks ill without fear and freely even when they [themselves] rule, [that is, in a republic]; about princes one speaks always with a thousand fears and a thousand concerns."

Were someone to blame "the peoples and princes together, he could be telling the truth"—about both of them being shifty, changing, and ungrateful—"but by subtracting princes from this [statement] one fools oneself." For men and princes possess the same nature. Differences in their actions "do not arise out of their diverse nature," because "in everyone there is the one pattern."

Apart from their political virtues and vices, men taken as a whole are invaluable. They not only constitute the state, they also comprise, or should comprise, its military force. We have seen the importance Niccolò attaches to arms. He attaches importance also to size of population. He measures the strength of a principality by its capacity for battle in the field. "I say that I judge those to be able to rule themselves by themselves that are able through either an abundance of men or of money to put together an adequate army and to do battle with whoever comes to assault them." If in the times of the Roman emperors it was necessary "to satisfy the soldiers more than the people . . . now it is more necessary for all princes . . . to satisfy the people more than the soldiers because the people can do more than they [can]."

Soldiers for Niccolò must come from people, citizens, or subjects, all the more so because in his view cavalry, the military base of the rich and aristocratic, is not the critical armed force. Our military expert gives credit to the services cavalry can render—light cavalry were indeed useful for scouting, skirmishing, and mobile but brief attacks—but considers its prestige overrated: "the foundation and nerve of the army, and that which one must esteem most, must be infantry." At this very time the art of war in Europe is altering. Niccolò realizes this and watches carefully the progress of Spanish military experiments. The heavily armed horseman begins to take leave of the battlefield, put out of the fight by thickets of pike squares and by the newer armor-penetrating missiles: the long and cross bows, cannon, and handguns.

In armed forces, when one speaks of infantry, one signifies men in numbers. In their numbers is their power: "against a hostile people a prince can never assure himself because they are too many." He concludes "to a prince it is necessary to have the people as a friend: otherwise in adversity he has no remedy." And again later: "when the people are [the prince's] enemy and hold him in hate, he must fear everything and everyone."

We have also appreciated much earlier the significance of the militia, which is to be composed of a prince's own subjects or a republic's own citizen and subject levies. You, prince, "cannot stay unarmed . . ." Disarming your subjects and building fortresses to protect yourself will not save you if they hate you. "Therefore, the best fortress that exists is not to be hated by the people . . ." *The Prince* states categorically: "It never happened, then, that a new prince disarmed his subjects; actually, if he found them disarmed, he always armed them; because arming them, those arms become yours . . ." The *Discourses* sees the people as the heart of the state: "the heart and vital parts of a body must be kept armed . . . [if] injured it dies." Niccolò's republican doctrine, throughout all his writings, is based on an expanded body of people politically active and militarily participant.

Strongly pro-militia though he is, Niccolò is no fool: one does not arm a multitude indiscriminantly or in a hurry, but "in a certain order and certain way." We have seen earlier with what religious care he enrolls the militia. Men make up the country, they can defend and engrandize it, they can topple a prince within it; the prince must pay them attention.

Chapter xv begins to advance a particular strategy for dealing with subjects, a rhetoric of imposture or of seeming to be, and a new ethics with which to commit oneself to affairs of state.

TO BE OR TO SEEM TO BE

> As far as the act goes, that it may
> be a sin, is a fable, because
> what sins is the will, not the body.
> —*Mandragola*

THE TYPICAL work on princely rule speaks of what the prince's conduct should be. Similarly, *The Prince* begins Chapter xv by announcing that it will now consider what a prince's conduct should be with subjects and rulers. But there is a difference. Whereas the typical mirror of princes holds up a standard enjoined by God, however transcribed by moral philosophers, confessors, or conscience, *The Prince* holds up the standard of the people.

A prince should conduct himself so as to be praised by his own subjects and friendly rulers. Parts of chapter titles in this section of *The Prince* indicate as much, beginning with Chapter xv's "Of Those Things for Which Men, and Especially Princes, Are Praised or Blamed." The following titles specify some of these things—liberality and parsimony, cruelty and compassion. Later ones discuss the finer points of praise and blame. A most general title is Chapter xxi's "What Is Necessary for a Prince to Be Esteemed."

Looking at the people for the standard of a prince's conduct is a unique twist. Searching for the effective truth evidently has revealed what this standard consists of. People have an image of princes good and bad, and in talking about them or about any other newsworthy persons, they praise or censure them in terms of facets of this image. "I say that all men, when one speaks of them, and most of all princes, for being placed up higher, are noted for some of these qualities that bring them either blame or praise." Conduct, apparently, is going to be measured in terms of qualities:

And this is that one is held generous, one miserly . . . ; one is held to be gift giving, one rapacious, one cruel, one compassionate, the one word breaking,

the other word keeping, the one effeminate and pusillanimous, the other ferocious and spirited, the one humane, the other proud, the one lascivious, the
other chaste, the one sincere, the other tricky, the one rigid, the other easy to
reach, the one serious, the other light, the one religious, the other unbelieving, and similars.

He also offers four- and five-item short lists like, "to be compassionate,
word keeping, humane, sincere, religious."

The image Niccolò sees in this mirror for princes is remarkably solid.
Imaginary though it be, he has found it in the minds of the prince's
subjects and friends and described it to be constructed of qualities. As it
contains the beliefs people hold about right and wrong conduct in the
men they talk about, he has described, at least in substantial part, conventional moral ideas. One notes that he does not arrange them with all
the goods to the right and all the bads to the left. He mixes the order,
sometimes giving the good first, sometimes the bad. The reader may be
supposed to know or intuit on which side the presumed bad or good
lies in such pairs as generous/miserly, word keeping/word breaking,
cruel/compassionate.

Our moral philosopher knows that "everyone would confess that it
would be a most praiseworthy thing were a prince to find in himself
those of all the above-written qualities that are held to be good." There
seems no doubt in Niccolò's mind that man, though evil-disposed by
nature, can tell good from bad conduct in their rulers and notable men.
Not only can they tell it, but their knowledge is uniform among themselves.

The mirror reflects what everyman holds to be the ideal prince or fully
praiseworthy notable person: except that by everyman the moral philosopher includes the good prince new, and himself as well. Niccolò's certainty of these qualities, of their universality, uniformity, and content,
relate them to his own morality as depicted in Chapter 4 above. The
negative qualities of being miserly, cruel, word breaking, pusillanimous,
proud, lascivious, and unbelieving bear on the vices found there in ab-
horrence: greed, cruelty, deceit, sloth, pride, ambition, and man's greatest offense, the ungrateful disobedience to God. The vices appear now
more sharply in these qualities as elements of moral judgment common
to all men, and though Niccolò has shifted the standard from God to
men, it is not much different from what the many writers of mirrors-of-
princes were dealing with.

How men got this knowledge is another matter. The explanation our
author gives in the *Discourses* is but lip service to Polybius's ideas about

the origin of mankind. The certainty with which he encases moral knowledge in *The Prince* suggests ideas implanted or innate, self-evident, intuited, or natural. Their uniformity among men precludes their acquisition through diverging family, religious, legal, or social transmission. For whatever reasons men hold them, these constant and uniform ideas of what constitutes bad or good in a leader's conduct are reflected in the mirror the prince must look into.

Having argued the importance of people—they can save or sink the prince and the state; they constitute the state—and listed the qualities around which they praise or blame men of note, Niccolò, it would seem, might either seek to recruit or select leaders who fit the popular image or urge that leaders strive to be what people look to them to be, and might then send each off with a word of counsel: Be yourself, Prince, or, Be the man your people wish you to be, or, Seek to have, Prince, the qualities they hold dear.

So it might appear, were one to forget that the search for effective truth also reveals that the nature of men is bad. Though they may be quick to praise the good qualities of a man in the public's eye, they themselves are not good. "A man who wishes to make a vow of goodness in all parts," that is, in all the qualities, as a matter of course goes to his ruin 'among so many who are not good'. Alas, Prince, you cannot be the man they wish you to be; their praising you does not guarantee that they will behave well, will do what is necessary to save the state or serve the common good.

If the prince matches the image in the mirror, he cannot hold the state together; if he holds the state together, he will not match the mirror. What then is the prince to do?

THE RHETORIC OF IMPOSTURE

Our counselor of princes devotes a chapter or more to each of the pairs of qualities he considers "the most important": generosity/miserliness, cruelty/compassion, and word breaking/word keeping. He lays out one main line of princely conduct. The plan is simple: to seem to be a prince that people will praise. "To a prince, therefore, it is not necessary to have the above-written qualities, but it is surely necessary to seem to have them"—Assume a virtue, Prince, if you have it not! He must modify his persona to reflect the image held by his subjects and friends.

The strategy is based on a weakness already revealed: men's vulnerability to deception and to whatever seems to be. A statement from the

Discourses: "The generality of men feed on what seems, as [much as] they do on what is." A statement in *The Prince*: 'the common people are taken in by what seems to be . . . and in the world there is nothing if not the common people'. Successfully to seem to have the good qualities should not be hard.

The prince's conforming to the mirror model does not merit being called deceit, trickery, or fraud. Niccolò prefers variants of seeming to be. At most, it involves representing oneself as something one is not, putting on a disguise, dissembling, modifying a persona to fit an image, activities calling for the skills of an actor or an ambassador. We may call it a rhetoric of imposture.

Because of defects in their nature and condition, people in extraordinary times cannot be easily persuaded to the truth; at other times, as Fra Savonarola discovered to his loss, "it is easy to persuade them of a thing, but it is difficult to keep them in that persuasion." People see politics and the prince in a certain light. That light is wrong. The prince cannot govern as they idealize his governing. Yet he must appear in that light to them if he is to secure their support and work successfully for their good. This is the justification for the rhetoric of imposture, if justification is needed.

Step one, then, is the rhetoric of imposture: a prince new in his conduct with subjects and friends must keep his mirror image burnished for all to see. "A prince therefore should take great care that not a thing ever comes out of his mouth that is not full of the above five qualities and that does not seem to be, to see him and hear him, all compassion, all true to his word, all humaneness, all religion." Following his thesis of the importance of religion to the state, he adds, "And there is nothing more necessary to seem to have than this last quality." Ferdinand of Aragon owed much of his success to operating "under the same mantle."

At the same time, the prince has to get down to the actual governing of men. Here begin the moral difficulties. Step two is the business of ruling. The prince new, in his conduct, must apply a statecraft to fit the nature of men as rational brutes. This kind of work is distinct from the rhetoric of imposture. Its dirty aspects, especially in extraordinary times, are what make the imposture necessary. We are talking about a prince's breaking his word deceitfully, acting inhumanely and cruelly, and being irreligious. Niccolò states again, this time in terms of the negative qualities of the mirror, the necessity for the prince to enter evil, "And one has to understand this, that a prince, and most of all a new prince, cannot observe all the things for which men are held good, being often necessitated in order to maintain the state, to operate against keeping one's word, against charity, against humaneness, against religion."

DIRTY WORK: WORD BREAKING

Take now the instance of breaking one's word. We can with Niccolò's blessing locate it, as we cannot the prince's mirror posturing, in the camp of deceit. Chapter XVIII entitled, "What Manner Princes Have of Keeping Their Word," is devoted to deceit and begins with the sentence, "How praiseworthy it may be in a prince to keep his word, and live with sincerity and not with cunning, everyone understands." ('Everyone' again.) To word breaking, add the notions of fraud, trickery, and cunning, and we will have a fair span of Niccolò's idea of deceit. (In his version of the seven deadly sins, one of his two insertions was deceit. The other was cruelty, to which we shall return shortly).

To get a fuller idea of deceit, we shall have to go from *The Prince* to the *Discourses*, and back to *The Prince*, as our author himself has done. Chapter XVIII of *The Prince*, more than the preceding and following chapters on princely rule, treats less of the conduct of the prince with his subjects than with his friends, so-called, namely, friendly rulers, allies, and, in general, rulers of nonhostile states. Here appear, for the first time in this section of the book, forms of the words *cunning, trickery* or *deceit, simulating* and *dissimulating*. The subject of the chapter deals not with word breaking, fraud, or deceit in general, but with word breaking against external powers. In this, it resembles the chapters on fraud in the *Discourses*, where the subject matter is tricking the military or political enemy, who already expects trickery. The initial expedition of Cyrus "against the king of Armenia is full of fraud," and he occupies the kingdom "with trickery and not with force."

First, Niccolò takes a stand on fraud: "to use fraud in any action is detestable." How can this be? Cyrus is one of Niccolò's greatest heroes. The author goes on: "Nonetheless, in conducting war it is a praiseworthy and glorious thing, and the one who overcomes the enemy with fraud is praised equally as much as he who overcomes him with forces." Our author clarifies his stand: "I shall say only this, that I do not intend that fraud to be glorious that makes you break your given word and concluded pacts, because this, even though it may sometimes acquire you state and kingdom . . . will never acquire you glory. I am speaking of that fraud that one uses against that enemy that does not trust you, and that consists actually in conducting warfare."

The distinction that Niccolò makes is one moral philosophers insist

[297]

on. A fraud or a trick, say, an ambush, does not involve a promise, pledge, or given word, whereas breaking a treaty or a pact does. Niccolò continues to subject deceit to moral considerations. He tackles the tougher question of breaking one's word. In affairs of state, breaking the faith is justified if the pledge given was forced. (This proposition, too, would find support among moral philosophers, although he does not mention them, except for one reference early in Chapter xv of *The Prince*.) He has already said in his comparison with fraud that word breaking may win you political objectives, but it will never bring you glory. This we may remember, was Niccolò's condemnation of Agathocles (in *The Prince*) for, among other things, being 'without faith' to his word. It won him "imperium but not glory."

In the *Discourses*, Niccolò informs us of a current practice. "And not only are forced promises not observed among princes when the force is lacking, but all the other promises are not observed when the reasons that made them promise are lacking." We can see that military fraud and word or promise breaking among princes are different kinds of moral acts, and that Niccolò has led us to an important case of infraction, for he refers us now to *The Prince*, and the subject matter of Chapter 18 therein, word breaking. (The author makes a cross-reference to the book at another point in the *Discourses*, but the topic at hand there is on how to enter other countries, indicating as a source the early part of the work, Chapters III and V, and he calls the book there, "our treatise on principalities.") Here he refers to the princely conduct section and, to our knowledge, for the first time calls the book explicitly a work about the prince: "whether [not keeping promises] is a praiseworthy thing or not, or whether by a prince such methods ought to be observed or not, is broadly argued by us in our treatise 'On the Prince'; therefore, at present we will not speak on it." Early in *The Prince* itself, the author makes a cross-reference to what "one will say below about the faith of princes and how one should observe it." From this we may gather that Chapter XVIII of *The Prince* contains his deliberated word on the subject (and also that manuscript copies of the treatise are in circulation).

Back to *The Prince*, then, where we left off. There we learn that breaking one's word with other princes and living with cunning is not a praiseworthy thing. Everyone understands that. Yet we know (Niccolò has already said it) that the prince new is going to have to operate against keeping his word. And against charity, against humaneness, against religion, too. These comprise almost the full bill of charges for which he denied glory to Agathocles: 'It cannot still be called virtue to kill one's citizens, betray one's friends, be without faith [to one's word], without compassion, without religion', and more, to be of 'bestial cruelty and inhumanity'. Yet nowhere does Niccolò hint that the prince new will not be 'celebrated among the most excellent men', nowhere does he deny him the glory he denied Agathocles.

Simultaneously as he enjoins a rhetoric of imposture and a statescraft tarred with deceit and cruelty, he is easing moral conflict. His princely candidate is a good man, and 'most rarely does it happen that a good man through bad ways, even if his end is good, will want to become prince'. Niccolò wishes to encourage him. He urges him "to let [the infamy of the bad qualities] go with less concern" and "not care about incurring the reputation of those vices . . ." Ever since Chapter xv, we have noticed, his writings are edging over beyond moralism into moral philosophy.

He devises the rhetoric of imposture to protect the prince from the conscience of his subjects and friends. He must now invent a moral philosophy to protect the prince new from his own conscience.

To offset or resolve the difficulties, Niccolò introduces in these several chapters after Chapter xv two moral novelties. Although they apply to acts involving any of the negative qualities, one evolves particularly in keeping with deceit or breaking of faith, the other in keeping with cruelties.

CONSCIENCE EASING: THE UN-GOLDEN RULE

The first novelty is an injunction the terms of which resemble a norm found, with variants, in such ancient authors as Plato, Aristotle, Diogenes Laertius, and in scriptural books including Matthew and Luke. For its distinguished history and universal applicability, at least in its idea of exchanging moral acts, we may refer to the norm as the Golden Rule and select as our text Matthew 7:12 and Luke 6:31, paraphrased as, "Do unto others as you would have them do unto you." Niccolò's norm, too, lends itself to paraphrase. "Do unto others as they would do unto you." The two rules resemble each other in urging reciprocated conduct: the scriptural one basing itself on wished-for conduct in others, Niccolò's on effective truth about others (founded on grasping observed behavior and on tasting the flavor of history). The doctrine of men's evil disposition—reiterated several times in the qualities chapters of *The Prince*—prevents him from dreaming that they would do unto him what he or you would have them do. In the *Florentine Histories* the deposed leader, Giorgio Scali, as he awaits beheading, reproaches his honorable opponent: "And you . . . you consent to their doing to me what I in your place would never have permitted them to do?" Believing that others would do unto you what you would have them do, is a forlorn hope, is imagining men as they ought to be, far from men as they live, and leads to ruin.

The precept is implicit in many of Niccolò's pages. Witness the quoted passage above to the effect that the prince cannot be good 'among so many who are not good'. And witness the many other passages testifying to the everyday unfaithfulness of French, German, Italian, Spanish, and all other princes, ancient and modern. The most explicit statement of the norm appears in Chapter XVIII where the counselor enjoins the prince to adopt a strategy of deception, or, as he later illustrates with the emperor Settimius Severus, "the persona of the fox": "Therefore a prudent lord cannot and should not observe his word when such observance would turn against him, and the causes that made him promise it are out of existence. And if men were all good, this precept would not be good, but because they are bad and would not keep [their word] with you, you also do not have to observe it with them." The harm men would do you lays the moral basis for the harm you must do them.

To stress the importance of word breaking and deceit, our author takes a page from the book of beasts. We looked at it in Chapter 5 above in the context of law. Though garbled, the passage still has interest. You should know, he says, that "there are two types of combat: one with laws, the other with force; the first is proper to men, the second to beasts, but because the first often does not suffice, it is necessary to recur to the second . . . so that a prince needs to know how to use the one and the other nature, for one without the other does not last." Of the various beasts whose nature a prince might take on, the choice falls to the fox and the lion: "because the lion cannot defend himself from traps, the fox cannot defend himself from wolves."

The choice of the lion as a symbol of force is clear—if one is talking about types of combat. At this juncture of the book, however, our counselor is talking about keeping and breaking one's word with subjects and friends, and not about fighting openly. The fox is out of place as a fighter; rather, he is a symbol of cunning, and Niccolò uses him thus. Instead of two types, our author might have said there are three ways, of dealing with subjects and allies (or three types of combat)—law, force, and deception. What the fable of beasts conveys nonetheless is that force is not enough and may at times be saved by cunning. The *Discourses* goes so far as to claim that resorting to deceit may sometimes avoid a resort to force altogether. At all events, you can often get more with a club and a deceitful word than with a club alone. Deciding not to depend any longer on the military aid of others, Duke Valentino "turned to trickery . . ."

"Those that take their stand simply on the lion do not understand [that the fox is also needed]." The fox remains the symbol for a word breaker, deceiver, dissimulator, one who knows how "to color well" his nature; and the lion (not to mention the predatory wolves) remains in the background to suggest that force can never be absent and that the lion and the fox live in symbiosis.

The fable seems mixed up, true, but it has not to lose sight of the necessity for fox, prince, citizen, and country to keep well armed and strong as the lion. Yet, to characterize force as beastly and not appropriate to man seems awkward in our counselor's broad thesis of good arms and good laws, and seems to put his 'things of the state', with its icon of sword and scales, on the side of the beasts.

Deception, we realize more and more, is also a broad thesis. Fraud in war may be glorious, trickery in love is supreme. It warrants a song. Our playwright composes a laud to deceit to be sung after act 3 of the *Mandragola*, and later places it to be sung again, word for word, after act 4 of *Clizia*, perhaps not because he likes it so much but because he is in a hurry to provide songs for his sweet friend Barbera.

> So suave is deceit
> brought to its imagined and dear purpose
> that divests another of effort
> and makes every bitter taste sweet.
> O remedy high and rare,
> you show the straight path to erring souls;
> you with your great valor,
> in making another blessed, make Love rich:
> You conquer, with your saintly counsels,
> stones, poisons, and charms.

Playwright as well as ex-Secretary, Niccolò has both a light and a serious appreciation of deceit. The spectacle of cheats cheated and of disguise and transvestism is central to the *Mandragola* and *Clizia*. In *Clizia* the wife arranges to put a male servant in the bed where her husband plans on lying with the fair young maiden. She then says in an aside, "Go on ahead there, Nicomaco, you will find [your] counterpart, because your woman will be like the pitchers of Santa Maria in Pruneta." These pitchers from the nearby terracotta-producing town have a peculiarity hard to miss: the spout sticks out straight from the vessel's belly.

In sum, and rounded off, what is Niccolò's position on deceit? Because of the nature of men, the prince new will, under certain conditions, have to do things that do not conform to the ideal of the good ruler held by people generally and elaborated by princely rule books in particular. As a day-to-day procedure, the prince should adopt a rhetoric of imposture to make him seem to conform to the mirror ideal. In truth, he does conform as much as possible. This rhetoric is not deceit. Deceit is a true vice. Only in the form of fraud against military enemies is it glorious; only in the tricks of lovers is it fun. Against other princes it is legitimate because of Niccolò's Un-Golden Rule.

The rhetoric of imposture, of seeming to be, like the tricks of lovers, requires no excuse; fraud in warfare needs but a conventional justification, trickery and word breaking demand more than the conventional excuses. The Un-Golden Rule is some small gift to moral philosophy. Near antecedents can be found in the legal and military language of self-defense and preemptive strike. Niccolò scoops his precept from human nature and lifts it onto a pedestal of statecraft. Speaking of the law, this time as man-made necessity, he writes: "men will always succeed in being wicked to you if they are not by a necessity made good." In the *Discourses* he pronounces a rule for the legislator: "As all those who reason about civil life demonstrate, and as every history is full of examples of it, it is necessary for whoever disposes a republic and institutes laws in it, to presuppose all men criminal, and that they will always use the malignity of their spirit whenever they may have free occasion; and when some malice stays hidden a while . . . time, which they say is the father of every truth, uncovers it." He propels the Un-Golden Rule to the heights of constitution making and asks the legislator to strike first with the law.

DIRTY WORK: CRUELTIES

Niccolò does not underestimate the power of a kind word or rewards and honors, of a policy sometimes referred to as love or sweetness, in contrast to force or punishment. From the moment of Niccolò's earliest short prose one can detect his grappling with the dilemma of 'either force or love' in foreign affairs or "to benefit or extinguish" in domestic affairs. Such colorful language, we have already noted, is not unusual in the behind-the-scenes chatter of the Chancery. Particularly among the younger members below the grade of Secretary, a sometimes trenchant, sometimes cynical idiom takes hold, much like that among students in medicine. For the princely rule part of *The Prince*, our author has chosen to use the forceful word *cruelty*.

Cruelty calls for a stronger defense in moral philosophy. The Un-Golden Rule is not enough. Other sins speak, cruelty shrieks. Without doubt, this is the quality, or vice, that disturbs Niccolò most. To cope with it he spreads a mosaic over these pages of *The Prince*—and over these pages alone—depicting a new approach to the morality of political conduct. Part and parcel of the innovation are the qualities, but the story of Niccolò's creation is bound up with the vice of cruelty and with a certain man who for over three years filled the thoughts and slimmed the purses of Florentines. The man is Caesar Borgia.

❧

I N June of 1502, Niccolò (thirty-three years old and having been on the job of Secretary for four years or so) and the ambassador he is assisting, Cardinal Francesco Soderini, send back to the government in Florence their opinion of the man to whose court they have been dispatched, the one who in a short time had grown into a menace.

> This Lord is very splendid and magnificent, and so spirited at arms that there is no great thing that does not seem small to him; and [in striving] for glory and for acquiring [new] state [dominions] he never rests, nor recognizes fatigue or danger. He arrives at a place before one can find out from where he is taking his departure; he makes himself well-liked by his soldiers; he has got the best men in Italy: which things make him victorious and formidable, with a perpetual [good] fortune in addition.

This man, "who already made you Florentines tremble and Rome cry," versifies our poet later in his *First Decennial*, this man, a Spaniard and the son of Pope Alexander VI, threatens and obliges the Florentine republic to pay out money for so-called protection by his troops. His plan, to form a central Italian kingdom strong enough to hold off other states and to deal with France and Spain as an equal, would have required making himself or his father, as Niccolò says, "lord of Tuscany."

There are admirable sides to Caesar Borgia. As envoy to his court on several occasions, Niccolò carries out his orders and reports as best he can. Back in Florence, however, hatred and fear of the duke is great. Our envoy comes under suspicion of siding with him. One of his office pals, Biagio Buonaccorsi, warns him of being bird-trapped. "Niccolò, you will drink white wine," which in the area around Greve in Chianti means, "you will be disillusioned." One rumor would have him seeking bribes from Caesar Borgia. Undoubtedly untrue. The duke does present Niccolò with at least one costly gift, a lovely rug from the Orient pieced in the form of a cross, and perhaps with some minor objects, but this could not be other than princely largesse, at most contributing to the quality, "generous," that the author adds to his description of the duke.

One rumor would have him seeking bribes from Caesar Borgia . . . The duke does present Niccolò with at least one costly gift . . .

His weaknesses do not escape Niccolò's sharp eye. Niccolò asks to return home. He is newly married. His superiors refuse.

Although he describes merciless traps, ambushes, and killings by the duke, he does not write of him as cruel by nature. In the *First Decennial*, the poet writes of him with moral disfavor, calling him a 'rebel against Christ' who, to cap his now-suppressed arrogance, was sent to Spain "bound and conquered." This verse chronicle was sure to circulate in the Palazzo, where belief still lingered that Niccolò harbored admiration for the duke. Our poet alludes unequivocally to cruelty, but to that of the duke's father. "To have rest, the spirit of Alexander was brought glorious among the blessed souls" (sarcasm dripping). Following in "the Pope's sainted footsteps" were "his three familiars and dear handmaidens, luxury, simony, and cruelty."

. . .

Now back to *The Prince*. There, in Chapter VII, we first meet with cruelty as a problem—a problem for Caesar Borgia, not for his own cruelty but that of his lieutenant, Ramiro de Lorqua, 'a cruel and expeditious man'. "And because [Borgia] knew that past rigors had generated some hatred, to purge the minds of those peoples [of Romagna] and win them over completely, he wanted to show that if any cruelty had been carried out, it did not issue from him but from the bitter nature of his minister." Thereupon Borgia executed his lieutenant in the spectacular manner described in Chapter 4 above. Worthy of note: Ramiro's cruelty issued from his 'bitter nature'. And the duke, whom Niccolò describes as "severe" and magnanimous (but not as cruel), wished to disassociate himself from his lieutenant's cruelty and hatefulness.

The next chapter of *The Prince*, devoted to "those who arrive at the principality through crimes," puts Agathocles the Sicilian, a truly cruel character, on stage. Niccolò rules, in the same absolute way that he regards ingratitude, envy, ambition, greed, and so forth, that successful though Agathocles is, he cannot be celebrated among the most excellent men because of his bestial cruelty.

But the case ushers in a puzzle. "Someone could wonder how it might happen that Agathocles and anyone similar, after infinite betrayals and cruelties, can live a long time secure in his country and defend himself from external enemies; and by his citizens he was never conspired against, whereas many others were not able to maintain the state through cruelty even in pacific times, much less in the uncertain times of war."

Niccolò has thought out the solution. "I think that this depends on cruelties badly used or well used." Not only that, he has a well-considered definition ready, too. "Well used can be called those (if of evil it is permissible to say good) that are done in a swoop, for the necessity of assuring one's security, and afterward one does not persist in them, but they are converted into the greatest utility to [one's] subjects that can be."

As we shall shortly see, Caesar Borgia fulfilled all parts of this definition. In contrast to what the author says of Agathocles, of Borgia he writes, "I should not know which better precepts myself to give to a new prince than the example of his actions."

If cruelties can be used or not used, and used well or badly, it may follow that any quality can be so used. This turns out to be the case: every prince "must be advised not to use badly this compassion," "[t]o use generosity . . . and miserliness," or "to use the one and other nature" of man and beast.

To be able to use or not to use qualities implies some measure of control. Niccolò points out that the prince ought to be able to "change to the contrary" of any of the given qualities. Though every prince ought to desire to be held compassionate, he may need at times to act cruelly, for example, when in command of armies. Another example: a prince should be both loved and feared, but if he cannot be both he should at least be feared. To be feared, he will have to use cruelties. Yet, in order to avoid the worst forms of blame—hatred and contempt—he has to steer a course between cruelty and compassion.

To write of using qualities well or badly, emphasizes their possible utility toward some end and their use according to some judgment. They become means, tools, instruments, detachable from the person using them. Each tool, each quality, and its opposite, too, can be picked up and plied or left lying on the ground.

Progressing from qualities as imputed traits of behavior to qualities as means to ends, that is, as kinds of acts that give rise to imputed traits of behavior and that can be of use for political ends, Niccolò further detaches the actor from his acts or qualities. This becomes clear as we notice that his talking about qualities as traits of behavior breathes an air of insubstantiality. He speaks little of their existence or being, and instead almost always of their seeming to be or being held to be; he speaks not of one's being generous or miserly, but of one's being "held to be generous, another miserly."

CONSCIENCE EASING: VICE AT FIRST BLUSH

Not only is the person merely held to have certain qualities, but the goodness or badness of the qualities themselves, despite the consensus over their goodness or badness, is also merely held to be the case. True, there is a consensus on their positive or negative value, but this is a human judgment after all, not a divine ordinance. Glancing back, we see that Niccolò never intended the qualities to promise anything but an apparent plus or minus value. He writes of 'all the above-written qualities' as being 'held to be good' or bad.

All through the chapters on qualities, Niccolò tries, and for the most part succeeds, in keeping the specifications of 'held to be' or 'seem to have' in front of any quality whether he happens to be talking about it as a trait of behavior or as an act instrumental to an end. Thus, in the assertion, "I say that every prince should desire to be held to be compassionate and not cruel," that 'held to be' cannot be excised. Throughout, 'held to be' is consistent and never to be confused with 'to be'. Uncertainty, one concludes, applies not only to whether the person has the quality imputed but also to the actual positive or negative value of the quality.

The reason for the uncertainty of a quality as a trait of behavior is that it is merely imputed to the prince and not truly known of him, particularly if he is employing a rhetoric of imposture; whereas the reason for the uncertainty about the positive or negative value of a quality employed as means is that, when it is thus put to use, its consequences are uncertain.

In application, or use, or performance, the various qualities may belie the blameworthiness or praiseworthiness their names associate them with. Acts that everyone holds to be cruel may reveal themselves capable of being used compassionately. Friar Timoteo may be permitted here to speak a word on the semblance of good and evil in the same simple way he instructs Lucrezia in the *Mandragola*: "There are many things that, far off, seem terrible, unbearable, strange; and when you approach them, they turn out to be human, bearable, comfortable; and therefore it is said that the fears are greater than the evils [thereof]." Niccolò writes a more prosaic version in *The Prince*: "if one considers everything well, one will find something that seems virtue, and following it would bring one's ruin, and something else that seems vice, and following it there results security and one's welfare."

Until one can calculate according to given criteria, these various acts or qualities that are associated with good or bad are but held to be or seeming or apparent or first blush or prima facie goods or bads. Henceforth, no quality is to be taken without question or at face value. One needs to apply the standard of *well used*.

The one requirement of all qualities employed as means is that they further the common good. As proximate goals Niccolò in these chapters specifies saving the state of the prince or keeping or losing control of the state, or "to keep subjects united and faithful," and leaves relation of such goals to the remote goal of the common good as taken for granted or elided or understood and retained from previous statements. *The Prince* first phrases the remote goal (we have just read it again in the case of Agathocles above) as the greatest possible utility to one's subjects.

The *Discourses* restates it in the case of Romulus's killing of Remus. There, we remember from our look at ends and means in Chapter 10 above, Niccolò handles Romulus's act as a violent means and sets the standard to be met if such an act is to be justifiable: the sequel must quickly indicate that the consequences redound to the common good. The standard for well-used cruelties and always excusable means are the same: accrual to the common good. In the first instance, 'well-used' is extended to any quality, in the second instance, 'always excusable' is extended to 'any extraordinary action'.

For well-used cruelties two other criteria must be met. Our moral philosopher in Chapter XVIII of *The Prince* shows how Caesar Borgia satisfied all parts of the definition. The duke's alleged cruelty had "restored the Romagna, united it, reduced it to peace and loyalty." Thus does he meet the overall standard of the common good. A prince following his example will attain the same end "with the fewest examples" and without "harming the whole community." Thus does he meet the other two criteria for well-used cruelties—"in a swoop" and 'not persist[ing] in them'—and he will be more compassionate than those who "out of too much compassion let disorders follow, out of which is born killings and plunder."

The duke's cruelties, one must admit from the definition and given facts, were well-used. Now Niccolò can take revenge for all the times the Florentines sniped at him for admiring anything at all about the man. So, "if one considers it well, one will see [the duke] to have been more compassionate than the Florentine people who, to avoid the name of cruel, [permitted factional quarrels to sweep the city and] let Pistoia be destroyed." The Florentines crueler than Caesar Borgia!

The Florentines who were cruel to Pistoia were Florentines of the republic. The Medici of the time thought the duke might help restore them to power. But while the author is writing *The Prince*, they are in power, and the days of Caesar Borgia are dead and gone. Duke Valentino is already a figure of history.

INTENT, KNOWLEDGE, AND REASON

In judging whether a leader is dedicated to the common good, two approaches are possible: to have access to his innermost thoughts or intent, or to determine this intent from the course of his acts. When considering the acts of historical figures like Agathocles, our author does not try to uncover the intent privy to the actors themselves, to their confessors or to God. History books tell him what he needs to know. Of some contemporaries he does make a statement of their intent as well as of their acts. Piero Soderini, the Gonfalonier-for-life and Niccolò's former friend and superior for one: "judging his works and his intent from his end . . . everyone could certify that what he had done was for the health of his country and not for his [own] ambition." Generally, it suffices Niccolò to examine whether the actor's acts march in the direction of the common good.

For ordinary people, an examination of intent is better left to confessors like Fra Timoteo. (Our playwright uses him to enunciate moral rules precisely and to misapply them grossly.) The friar cites the story of Lot and his daughters in order to identify evil with will rather than with the act: "The Bible says that the daughters of Lot, believing themselves the sole ones left in the world, had relations with their father; and because their intent was good, they did not sin." Confessors are in a good position to ascertain will or intent. As Ligurio remarks, 'they know our sins as well as their own'.

Niccolò does not deny the criterion of intent, but he has established as a premise that the prince new is a good man, bent on the common good. The problem of trying to unveil his will and intent need not arise. The prince new's conscience does not have to undergo examination. Rather, the danger against which our moral philosopher is trying to protect him is that he might subject himself to too much self-examination and be crippled by conscientious doubts.

The position of the prince new, we recall, has another requirement: he must be intelligent. He will have to use his head; he has much to learn and weigh. He must learn something of this world; he must be able to estimate, basing himself on historical record, what results his acts may have in the present or future. The recommended program of reading and experience, outlined in Chapter II above, will meet these objectives. There is something else that he must learn: the ethics of the prince new. Only our moral philosopher can teach him what to do about the evil acts he will have to perform and about the qualities such acts impute to him.

The prince new must learn to regard the traditional qualities as virtue or vice merely at first blush, as good or bad prima facie, as only seemingly good or bad. To do so would be to act prudently, for whenever the prince uses them as means they may prove to be the reverse of what they are traditionally classified. He may adopt them as useful, and therefore good, if on examination no bad effect is likely to follow, and drop them if they endanger the chosen end.

Here something else new, it seems, is being required. Whereas acceptance or rejection of an act was presumed immediate under the old system of regarding these eleven or four or five qualities as intrinsically good (an act either fell, pro or con, within the ambit of one of these qualities or it did not), the new system requires an act of reason. The qualities or, better, the acts comprising them, are generally perceived to be, but are not virtues or vices until stamped true on examination by reason or cogitation. What is now required is a process of the intellect utilizing the related standards of true cognition, utility, and useful contextual consequence. Niccolò sometimes alludes to this scrutiny by adding a phrsae about 'a prudent lord' or about being prudent: "it is necessary [for a prince] to be so prudent . . ." or 'if one considers everything well'.

Chapter XVI of *The Prince* takes the first pair of qualities—generosity/miserliness—and applies them to budget balancing and fiscal management, arguing primarily that a reputation for parsimony is the better choice if, while being generous, you lose the ability to continue being generous "and become poor and contemptible or, to escape poverty, [you become] rapacious and hated." The infamy brought by some of the qualities may "take the state away" from the prince. The quality of miserliness is not often a losing-the-state vice, whereas that of rapacity is. Rapacity is the negative quality of the gift giving/rapacious pair, and "gives birth to infamy with hate."

Our moral reasoner has explained not so much that one quality may be worse than another in the abstract, as that, under certain conditions, one may more likely lead to another quality more dangerous or infamous still. In any given case, prudence before a decision will dictate the ranking of qualities. One proceeds from an instrumental quality that seems good at first blush, to one that is truly good via the proximate goal it effectuates. Thus, 'one will find something that will seem virtue . . . and another that will seem vice . . .' Between the two, our moral philosopher inserts the knife-edge of reason: 'if one will consider everything well', he will realize that ruin would follow the first course, while security and good would follow the second.

THE LIMITS OF CRUELTIES

We have seen that reason or prudence will decide the prince's conduct on the basis of his immediate or proximate goals. Reason will also have to be the judge in case of possible conflict between proximate goals and the remote goal of the common good, where the most pressing case is that between cruelty as a usable quality and as an undeniable evil. Is there a limit to the use of cruelties for the sake of country or the common good? Are they at some extreme point transformed into the cruelty of Chapter 4 above, a full-blown evil? The questions may be handled in two ways, the first, theoretically, the second by judging the condemnation of cruelty in the author's writings.

By Niccolò's standards of well-used cruelties and proper means, the quality of cruelty cannot be well-used when the required acts exterminate, mutilate, or exile a great part of the community, falling out of all proportion and becoming self-defeating as a means to the common good. This conclusion follows from the common good requirement of well-used qualities and proper means.

Chapter 4 above, which puts in evidence Niccolò's uncompromising view of cruelty, corroborates the theoretical conclusion just made. We may glance now at some forms of cruelty and some borderline cases not included there. Torture according to law, the kind to which the author was subjected for the extraction of information, draws no protest from him except that in his case it was wrongly applied to a presumably exempt class, that of poets. Torture done for the pleasure of the torturer—the duke of Athens cutting out a citizen's "tongue with so much cruelty that [the man] died of it"—or unusual torture—the duke's torturing citizens "with new methods"—leads not just to the worst danger of statecraft, that is, hatred of the prince, but classifies the duke not as one who *acts* cruel but one who *is* cruel. "This duke, as his governing demonstrated, was miserly and cruel . . . he deserved to be hated." Deserving of hatred too was Galeazzo Maria Sforza, duke of Milan, whom our historian condemns with the line: "nor was he content with putting men to death unless he could kill them in some cruel way."

Chapter 4 observes that cruelty to, or the killing of, large numbers of men seems to trouble Niccolò most. If cruelties destroy the bulk of the citizenry or population, the possibility of their being imposed for the common good is excluded. Executions by Caesar Borgia, or any prince, should involve particular persons or only those in command—the ruling of a state is in the hands of a relatively few men, of a defeated enemy army, even fewer—and should not be of the kind that "injure an entire community."

In Chapter 41 of the third book of the *Discourses* Niccolò urges that when the safety of one's country is imperiled one must give no thought to whether a policy is just or unjust, kind or cruel, praiseworthy or ignominious: 'instead [one must] follow that policy that saves her life and maintains her liberty'. A cruel consideration in a deliberation or decision would refer to the advisability of performing a cruelty or cruel act. Taking the example Niccolò gives from Livy, the Roman army, faced with disaster at the Caudine Forks, had the choice of hopelessly fighting to the last man or of accepting the enemy's shameful terms of passing under the symbolic yoke and being sent back to Rome disarmed. The Roman legate decided the day by reminding the Romans that "the life of Rome [consisted] in the life of that army" and that "one's country is well defended in whatever way one defends it, whether with ignominy or with glory." Without the army "Rome, even if it died gloriously, was lost and its liberty [too]."

The example shows a fine sense of proportion, arguing from an ignominious means to a proximate end of saving the army intact, thence to the remote end of saving one's country—the common good—and a considerable part of the male population. The chapter, however, throws little light on how cruel an act a prince can avail himself of without passing the limit and becoming himself cruel.

The Prince's early recommendation that in conquering and annexing a hereditary state the prince new cannot rest secure unless he exterminates the blood line of the ruling family, implicates not the entire community but more or less a relatively few persons; as for the community itself, it is to be left intact, with its customs as far as possible undisturbed. The conquering prince has two concerns: "one, that the blood[line] of their hereditary prince be extinguished; the other, to alter neither their laws nor their taxes." The *Discourses* asserts both these concerns more vigorously: "one can warn every prince that he never lives secure of his principality so long as those who were despoiled of it are alive." And, 'May princes know then that they begin to lose [their] state at that hour in which they begin to break the laws and those customs and usages that are ancient and under which men have lived for a long time'.

A more directly pertinent case is the problem of having to execute "multitudes of errants." In Rome there were plots in which hundreds or even thousands of persons, men and women, were found implicated and then executed or imprisoned. "The poisoners and Bacchanalians were punished as their sins deserved." The number of errants involved began to reach the 'infinite men', Niccolò reminds us, that Moses had to kill.

The difficulty of large-scale punishment appears most critical in armies. In the *Art of War*, apropos of military discipline, our author writes of the frightful punishment of a cohort or legion by decimation, "in order not to kill all of them." The subject arises also in the *Discourses*: "But of all other executions the [one that was] terrible was decimating the armies, where by lot, of a whole army, one man out of every ten was killed."

As the *Art of War* maintains, "to brake armed men" is not easy. Niccolò's motto there for a captain is "to keep his soldiers punished and paid." In *The Prince* he writes that "when the prince is with armies and has under rule a multitude of soldiers, then it is wholly necessary [for him] not to care about the name of cruel, for without this name one never kept an army united or disposed to battle whatever." To note well: even with armies, Niccolò does not counsel the prince to *be* cruel but to take the *name* of cruel and not to worry about it, that the name is necessary if one commands armies.

By the time Niccolò reaches Chapter XIX of *The Prince*, to discourse on the soldiers and rulers of the Roman empire, he drops the justification of cruelties as a means and cruelty as a reputation and exposes the genuine "cruelty and greed" and "greed and cruelty" of the soldiers and the string of 'most cruel and rapacious' Roman emperors from Commodus to Maximus. 'Held to be' or 'seem to be' has no place here.

There is a limit, then, to the concept of well-used cruelties and held-to-be-cruel reputations. Difficult as the limit is to state in numbers of deaths or by manner of punishment, Niccolò abandons concepts of relative and reasonable morality the moment that acts of cruelty begin to cut into the populace or violate the customs of the community.

THE SECOND MIRROR

The cruel Roman emperors are not the rulers the prince new must imitate. These emperors had the "extraordinary vices" that Niccolò mentions early in *The Prince*, that make even a hereditary prince hated. Nor are they to imitate the low-level lives of ordinary people, whose image of princes the prince now seeks to project. Instead, he is to take "the paths trod by grand men" and "to imitate the most excellent," the category from which Agathocles is excluded. Encouragement to this kind of imitation occurs throughout our author's writings, and as the previous chapter showed, plays a large role in his theory of how to know. Although the exhortation to imitation quoted above precedes the mirror section of *The Prince*, it nonetheless offers, in effect, a second mirror in which the prince must also see himself. Niccolò confirms this in the *Discourses*. Princes "need not endure other effort than to take as their mirror the life of the good princes, as would be Timoleon the Corinthian and Aratus the Sicyonian, in the life of whom they would find such security and such satisfaction of the one who rules and the one who is ruled that they ought to be seized with desire to imitate them."

The people governed by these two rulers "constrained them to be princes as long as they lived, even though several times [the princes] tried to reduce themselves to private life." Here we see Niccolò's reverse ideal, to be followed when times are no longer extraordinary: to go from prince to private.

So, the prince new has two mirrors, one to preen himself in before going out for a walk; the other to inspire and guide him before he gets down to business; one for the rhetoric of imposture, the other for statecraft.

A VOCABULARY OF THE NEW ETHICS

In the mirror-of-princes chapters of *The Prince*, the author is at his most technical. He never repeats this style and vocabulary elsewhere in his writings. Here he develops less than a handful of words into technical terms—cruelties, well-used, and qualities—each complementing and reinforcing the other. Though Niccolò puts these few words to heavy duty from Chapter XV on, the germinal chapter is VIII of *The Prince*, where two of the three technical concepts first appear and where the inspiration may have come for the third or for all three.

For some reason not immediately apparent, our author chooses in Chapter VIII to write of cruelties (plural). Had we noticed this, we might have realized that he was breaking up the trait *cruel* into *acts of cruelty*. And at the same time, by denying Agathocles a place among the most excellent men of history, our author was not relinquishing his view of cruelty (singular) as the absolute vice he castigates in the numerous other passages that have come to our attention. After Chapter XV *The Prince* fixes on this word to the detriment of related terms like force, violence, harshness, hardness, severity, terror, ferocity, or brutality, all of which he distributes elsewhere with discrimination.

As for the phrase well or badly used, it appears commonly in the sense of matters well or badly performed, managed, or handled. In Chapter VIII our author couples it systematically with a vice or a trait of behavior (cruelty) giving the coupled phrase the function of a means and simultaneously implying standards of judgment (well or badly). The text in Chapter VIII is thus able to go from Agathocles as a bestially cruel and inhuman man to Agathocles as a manipulator of cruelties (plural) that are divorced from any essential characteristic of Agathocles and used by him as a means, as "mediating through cruelty," and defined as well-used cruelties. Niccolò thus detaches acts of cruelty from the nature of the person who commits the acts: a compassionate as well as a cruel person may perform cruel acts or, using the form Niccolò prefers, cruelties.

The text in the princely rule section of *The Prince* picks up and incorporates this usage of 'well-used cruelties', extending and complicating it in the noun *qualities*. The author's many writings display the term in many senses. The *Discourses* uses the term to discuss the mixture of three basic elements of a state or the classes underlying its constitution or its distribution of powers: "mixed only of two qualities of the three above-written, that is, of principate and of optimates;" and the third is, of the people. *The Prince* uses the term also, simply to signify characteristics: "to examine the qualities of these principalities." The *Mandragola* employs a meaning verging on the sense about to be considered. Ligurio belittles Lucrezia's husband, "He is a man of the qualities that you know, of little prudence, of less courage."

The books of most writers on princely conduct urged virtues or good qualities on a prince as permanent parts of a good character. Their ethics was one of being, rather than of doing or of consequences. For them, What ought I to be? comes prior to, What ought I to do?, or to, What ought my acts achieve? The inculcation of virtue was typically to begin when the prince was young. Virtues and vices implied rules of conduct that were rigidly to be observed, that time and place did not alter, that were unconditionally obligatory. Their counsel in a capsule was: Be good till you die, Prince. That the virtues may prove disastrous in practice was not supposed to be the good prince's business. If he did not have and hold to the virtues, worse than disaster was in store. His personal salvation was at stake.

The broader history of the term *qualities*, moreover, is more intricate. It bears on the terms ethos, character, habitude, and attributes, as employed in rhetoric, the theater, allegory, and philosophy to distinguish and represent stable, temporary, and shifting traits of men's makeup. In rhetoric, for instance, one man may be used to represent or bear the judgment of all common or ordinary men, much as Niccolò's prince does through the mirror of people, or in the theater, one individual may represent a single quality, much as in Niccolòs plays we encounter one man exemplifying stinginess, another cunning, or lust, or piety, and so on.

We begin to get a sense of why Niccolò chooses and adheres to the word *qualities*. As befits the word's Latin origin, he can use it to signify something special about persons or things, their peculiar and essential characteristics. He can also use it as a pivot, going from signifying a stable trait to signifying a shifting trait. He takes the sense familiar to princely rule-book writers, that of permanent qualities, virtues, moral attributes, and traits of character, and swings it around to his idea of a prince's using qualities as put-on-and-off, held-to-be, shiftable traits. Then he may pivot back to reattach the word to its sense of permanent quality or virtue; "not being able to use this virtue of generous," for example, or, the quality of miserliness is "one of those vices that enable him to reign." Slipping back and forth from permanent qualities or virtues to shiftable qualities or behaviors, Niccolò destabilizes the conventional morality of the mirror-of-princes writers.

Under the old ethics this could not be done. Cruelty was only and always an evil. "O cruel souls," Dante cries out in the *Inferno*, "so great that to you is given the last place." The new ethics offers the name of cruelty as something the prince can use rather than as something that condemns him for what he is, it offers him an acitivity rather than a being.

The new ethics will better fit the exigencies of the new, harsher statecraft. With it, the prospective prince new can face the future with greater moral confidence. It liberates him from the hobbling morality of the princely rule-book writers. Viewing the good qualities as merely apparent goods and as means to an end, he will learn to choose the proper good. He will be more truly religious than the sanctimonious. Though nothing but compassion, good faith, and religion pass his lips, in truth he is not playing false.

For Niccolò, the linking of the qualities to well-used cruelties creates a dazzling double discovery: first, the idea that any of a series of traits of behavior (the qualities) may be treated as means; thence to the idea that the whole series of those virtues and vices (also called qualities) of the many princely rule-book writers may be disposed of in the same way. The excitement of this discovery may have affected the content and structure of *The Prince*, leading the author to fatten the latter part of the book as a mirror-of-princes. The first sentence in Chapter xv echoes: What should be a prince's way of conducting himself?

Niccolò's achievement in moral philosophy could not have been made without the technical exploitation of *cruelties*, of *well-used*, and of the ethos-pathos faces of *qualities*. Simply and briefly: cruelties breaks up cruelty, a vice attached to a person, into cruelties or cruel acts free of personal attachment. The *used* of *well-used* turns these detached acts into means, while the *well* imposes worldly standards (principally, the common good) with the help of reason. The *qualities* embrace cruelty in a comprehensive list of moral attributes and apply *well-used* to them as a whole, thus converting them all into means and sliding into a different sense of qualities: groups of acts with uncertain or first-impression moral attributes.

In brief, what can we say to be Niccolò's position on cruelty? Cruelty is a true vice, compassion a true virtue. People judge a prince or other notable person to be cruel because of his cruel acts, his cruelties. Yet such cruelties reveal but a first-blush vice, a seemingly blameworthy quality. The ruler who uses them well lightens the cruelties necessary for the common good, especially in new states or in extraordinary times, and deserves praise as a compassionate and prudent prince.

The question now arises: The evil that a prince new or one-man-alone must often do, is that an absolute evil or a first-blush evil? The answer is: That evil is a first-blush evil. Our moral philosopher knows what he is saying with all those held-to-be, thought-to-be, and seem-to-be's; he knows what he is doing with that provocative: 'if of evil it is permissible to say good'. Absolute and seeming evil differ as high noon from midnight; yet to shock the shockable, to appease his own irrepressible irreverence, of which we shall soon hear more, Niccolò keeps the reader's tension alive by playing on the resemblance effected by his leaving the noun, *evil*, unqualified. It *is* permissible to say good of evil if that evil is but seeming evil and converts to a true good.

As Niccolò defines it in the case of well-used cruelties, entering into that class of evil has a distinctively temporary aspect. Because it is not part of the commands or compulsions of the actor's true nature, it can be temporary. It is to be used only when necessitated by the common good, and then done with dispatch, directed toward the common good, and ceased: 'and afterward one does not persist'. This from Chapter VIII of *The Prince*. And this again from Chapter XVIII: a new prince should 'not depart from the good [as long as] being able to, but [he should] know how to enter evil [for whenever he is] necessitated'.

The temporary aspect of first-blush evil acts go far to explain Niccolò's unusual turn of phrase 'to enter evil'. Entering implies exiting. If cruelty is stable, a fixed tendency of your nature, your cruel acts are truly evil, and you can no more exit from them than could the Emperor Commodus, who was 'of cruel and bestial spirit', or Duke Galeazzo Sforza, who was not content with putting men to death 'unless he could kill them in some cruel way'.

The bad prince will find it hard to desist or exit from evil acts. The prince new will find it hard to perform or enter into evil acts—until he learns and follows Niccolò's moral logic and all it implicates of double mirrors, the rhetoric of imposture, qualities possessed and imputed, qualities used, badly and well, the Un-Golden Rule, first-blush vice, reason and true virtue, the divorcing of acts from the actor, of acting from being, and the destabilizing of conventional ethics.

THE REFORM OF HELL

They would like a preacher that
might teach them the way to paradise, and I should like to find one
that might teach them the way to
get to the devil's house.
                    —Letter to Guicciardini

B ECAUSE H E writes like an angel, few have noted Niccolò's interest in hell and his new thesis that as a preview may be condensed in an analect: Heaven for the climate, hell for the company.

Niccolò may be the most original easer of hell since Origen, the church father who taught that in the end the devil himself would be saved. His popularity is greater than Origen's. He discusses and refers to the inferno in letters, speeches, plays, short stories, verse, and songs. These writings, consisting more in comic and satirical pieces than in political, moral, and historical ones, quickly revamp the devil and hell in the literature of entertainment.

Among the first literary signs that Niccolò is going to poke fun at hell are those that appear in *The Ass*, perhaps Niccolò's most ambitious, though unfinished, verse work. Often referred to as *The Golden Ass* because of its patent resemblance to Apuleius's *Metamorphoses* (also known as *The Golden Ass*), the plot deals with the hero's stumbling onto the territory of Circe, the goddess who turns men into various kinds of animals. Ulysses in his wanderings was the first to encounter her. Niccolò's poet-hero never meets Circe; instead, he becomes attached to a damsel or maid-in-waiting (a creature told of by Homer, Apuleius, and Ovid, too). From Circe's damsel he learns that he will have to go through the "infernal portals." He will then be changed into an ass: "that providence that maintains / the human species wants you to sustain / this discomfort for your greater good." His guide, like Dante's in the *Paradise*, is a woman. Beatrice, we know, is untouchable. On Circe's damsel ("my duchess," Niccolò calls her) we have feasted our eyes more than once.

She made him her slave, but unlike Beatrice, violating the code of love service and following instead the inspiration of Apuleius, and the other poets mentioned, she takes him to bed, making him feel like a blushing young bride. "Shame almost painted my face."

Before he is to turn into an ass, however, the damsel dines him by firelight on chicken. Not one of Circe's own fowl, let us hope. Among "so many beasts," she does keep "some birds." They sup also on salad and bread, and a wine that seems to be like "that the Valley of Greve and Poppi offers." In bed together, consoling themselves of the morrow, she puts her cool hand between the sheets and he begins to touch her. 'Not in one place did my hand stay; / but running over her limbs, / the lost virtue came back firm'. No longer timid, "Blessed be your beauties," he ejaculates. What does Dante, without benefit of bed, sing in *Purgatory*? "Blessed in eternity may your beauties be." Dante's reward is to be guided to Paradise. Niccolò's reward is not about to end with his and his duchess's lying abed. While he is an ass, he is to stay with her: "with me you among the other beasts will come to pasture." Later "the heavens will show themselves benign / times will return happier than ever." Kissing him ten times she says, "Fair soul / this journey of yours, this hardship of yours, / let it be sung by historian or poet."

Niccolò while imitating Apuleius parodies Dante. Throughout the poem Niccolò purloins from the *Inferno* and *Purgatory*, using their lines without quotes to describe the presence and condition of animals, to represent persons and states and states of mind in Circe's herds. Where a phrase of Dante is carnal, "wrapped up in the delight of the flesh," Niccolò's version may be reverent, "wrapped up in these angelic beauties."

Our poet hesitates before crossing over into the unknown world of beastdom. At the beginning of the seventh chapter, he writes, "we were with our foot already on the threshold / of this door, and to pass there inside / my woman had made me desire." But he holds tight to his beautiful guide. At the chapter's end he writes, "my woman moved her foot / and not to separate myself from her an iota, / I took her by the hand she gave me . . ."

THE NEW MODEL

The topography of Circe's domain is simple: dark woods, shady and thick, ditches, waters, caverns, and "a great building of wonderful height," where the animals are installed for the night. None of the complicated circles and ingenious punishments Dante describes. All in all, Niccolò's topography, as disclosed in other works too, presents a four-story cosmos: hell or inferno, sometimes called the nether regions, sometimes apparently designating a lateral zone, difficult of mortal access; the region above it, limbo, for the souls of the unbaptized; then earth, or the region of mundane things; and high above, heaven or paradise. Purgatory, if it exists, is hard to locate on Niccolò's maps. In the *Mandragola* a widow asks the priest about her late husband: 'But do you believe he is in Purgatory?' 'Without doubt', the answer issues. Purgatory is for venial sinners.

We noted early that Niccolò is an habitué of the otherworld. He often sets up reports, communications, and journeys between this world and that one beyond the tomb. Devils can leave hell for long periods, as we shall see, gods and spirits can descend to earth, beatific beings can be cast out of heaven as devils and come to earth from hell on special occasions, lovers in hell (again, in certain seasons) can lament their beloved on earth who, in turn, can reply.

Nowhere in these writings are the pains of hell comparable to their description from the pulpit and in contemporary art. They are comparable, rather, to the pains of lovers spurned. To listen to the lovers in "About Desperate Lovers and Women," a carnival song, they would and did give themselves up "to the deep center, fearful and ugly," because they were "tormented by so many pains." Now they can judge from their new servitude in the "cursed kingdom" that "one does not find cruelty greater than [that of women]."

The fable of *Belfagor*, the short story about a devil who took a wife, begins with recognition of a fact by the infernal authorities: that, of the infinite souls dying in hell, "all or the greater part complained that for no other reason except to have taken wives were they led to such unhappiness." The punishment these miserable mortals find in hell, it appears, is unhappiness. When Belfagor himself goes on earth with an entourage of lesser devils as his servants, he takes a wife who proves of so insolent a nature that the subdevils desert in a body: "they elected rather to return to hell and stay in the fire than live in the world under the imperium of that [woman]." The flames of hell are not red-hot if the pain they cause is but an unhappiness, an unhappiness less than that suffered by lovers and married men on earth.

The new model hell also is better governed than earthly states. The carnival song, "About the Devils Cast Out of Heaven," opens with a brief statement apropos:

> We were once, now we are no longer, blessed Spirits:
> for our pride
> we have all been cast from heaven;

and in this city of yours [Florence]
we have taken over the government,
because here is shown
confusion, pain greater than in hell.

A more detailed description of afterworld government comes from *Belfagor*. The judges there, among them the famous Minos and Rhadamantus, were all puzzled "And unable to believe these calumnies that these [men] brought [before the bench] as true of the female sex, and with the accusations growing everyday and having made the necessary report of all of it to Pluto, it was decided by him to have a mature examination of this case with all the infernal princes and to take afterward that step that was judged best to uncover this falseness or know the whole truth of it." Pluto then called them together in a council for a judicial review. Clearly he takes his responsibilities seriously.

Niccolò always says that a ruler should obey the law. Pluto goes further. Possessing his kingdom by an irrevocable decree, he does not have to account "to any judge, celestial or mundane, yet . . . it is wiser for those that can, to put themselves more under the laws [than they are bound to] and to esteem more the advice of others."

Also, though an "irremovable ruler," Pluto shows as much concern for public opinion as Niccolò thinks a prince always should. What men arriving in hell say about their wives seems impossible. To believe these damned men without further ado, Pluto deliberates, would lay his own empire open to infamy. "We could be calumniated as too credulous . . . or else as not severe enough and slight lovers of justice. And since the one sin is that of frivolous [men] and the other of unjust [men], and wishing to avoid these burdens [of low opinion], . . . we have called you [in council] . . . so that the realm in the past as in the future will live without infamy."

All agreed that it was necessary to discover the truth, but disagreed on the method. If, as seems to be the case, there are no women in hell, a problem in judicial fact finding arises. "Because to some it seemed that someone should be sent to the world; to others, more than one [should be sent], who in the form of man might know personally this truth; to many others it seemed possible to do it without such trouble [by] constraining various souls to reveal it under various tortures." (Pain cannot be so severe in hell if torture is resorted to so exceptionally.) The majority (hell is majoritarian and its majority humane) were for sending someone, and not finding anyone to volunteer to undertake this enterprise, they decided that the selection be made by lot. (The lot is the most democratic method of choice.) The choice "fell on Belfagor, [now an]

archdevil, but in the past, before he fell from heaven, an archangel." He
accepts the task reluctantly.

Just as in the Florentine Chancery the envoy is given instructions for
his mission, so Belfagor gets his orders cut: he is to be "consigned
100,000 ducats [a lot of money!] with which to come to the world, and
in the form of man to take a wife and live with her for ten years and
then, faking his death, to return and on the basis of experience testify to
his superiors on the burdens and discomforts of marriage." Changing
his name to Rodrigo, the archdevil, with his escort and horses, decides
to go to Florence, because it of all the others seemed the city "most apt
to support one who invested his money according to the usurer's art."
(Here in Niccolò's manuscript two lines are completely canceled: they
may have contained remarks even more critical of Florence.)

A further stipulation of Rodrigo's mission was that during the ten-
year stay he was to be "exposed to all the discomforts and evils that men
are exposed to, and had to bring along poverty, prison, illness, and every
other misfortune that men run into, unless by trick or shrewdness he
might free himself of them." This last clause reveals that hell, though
insulated, is not completely unaware of the nature of men's world.

The result of this requirement was that after choosing a most beautiful young girl of a most noble family (unfortunately burdened with
three other marriageable daughters as well as three grown sons, not to
mention father- and mother-in-law) Rodrigo—being, by the law given
him on leaving the inferno, exposed to all human passion—begins immediately "to take pleasure in the honors and pomp of the world and to
desire to be praised among men, the which brought him no little expense. Besides this, he had not lived long with his lady Onesta when he
fell in love with her beyond measure."

Once Onesta learns her husband is head over heels in love with her,
she begins to treat him villainously. Soon she and her family sink him
in debt, creditors hound him, prison beckons. Onesta has brought to
his house "more pride than Lucifer ever had, and Rodrigo, who had
experienced the one and [now] the other, judged his wife's to be superior." With creditors at his heels, he flees.

The story of what happens to him afterward, in his attempts to serve
out his ten years by entering into people's bodies and possessing them,
of how in the end he is outwitted by a farmer and in fear of his wife's
discovering him, flies back to hell to give account of his action and to
report on the "matrimonial yoke"—all this part of the tale we listened
to in Chapter 3 above. But Belfagor, as we shall shortly hear, has not yet
departed this earth.

The climate in hell is not so hot as reported, and its government is better than that of any on earth that comes to mind. Also, the company one finds there is select. A scene appropriate to the society to be found in hell takes place in the *Mandragola*. The lover Callimaco soliloquizes: "At times I try to conquer myself, to bring myself back out of this frenzy, and I say to myself: 'What are you doing? have you gone crazy? . . . the worst that can come to you is to die and go to hell; and so many others are dead! And there are so many good men in hell!'" The self-interrogation continues, "Are you ashamed of going there yourself?" This is a new note: ashamed of going to hell! Pull yourself together, Callimaco. "Turn your face to fate, flee evil and [if] unable to flee it, bear it like a man; do not prostrate yourself, do not get depressed like a woman."

Hell is an exclusive club. For real men only. Piero Soderini, the former chief executive of Florence, elected for life, a man with whom Niccolò had had the closest working relationship, fled Florence when the Republic toppled in 1512. There must have been something, possibly his fright at personal danger or his underestimating the envy in men's breasts, that suggested he was less than manly. He died in 1522. Niccolò writes an epigram.

> The night that Piero Soderini died
> his soul went to the mouth of hell.
> Pluto shouted: "What hell? silly soul.
> Go up to limbo with the other children."

Niccolò is referring to the limbo of infants, where unbaptized children remain without chance of paradise but also without punishment. Once limbo was a section of hell reserved for unbaptized pre-Christian adults, mainly Old Testament figures, and the great pagan poets and philosophers, including Homer and Socrates. Jesus Christ, in harrowing limbo, leapt out with many virtuous souls, including patriarchs, prophets, and martyrs.

In the first age of mankind men were so good, we have heard, that the gods used "to descend from heaven to come together with them and inhabit the earth." With the decline of virtue and rise of vice, "the gods little by little began to return to heaven." This is a story of deities journeying to earth from heaven and back. *Belfagor* is a fable of an archdevil's journeying to earth from hell and back. "The Devils Cast Out of Hell" journey to earth from hell and back, too, at carnival times. In *The Ass*, the poet has his damsel's word that he shall return and his journey be celebrated. "Perhaps you will even take vainglory / recounting to these people and those / the long history of your hardships."

There is also a story about Niccolò's going to the otherworld and back himself. He tells it when he is without a job and reduced to living in the country. His friend Vettori has invited him to Rome and described his life there. But Niccolò cannot go; so he responds with the description of his own daily routine at the villa narrated in Chapter 1 above. 'When evening comes I return to the house and enter my writing-room . . .'

The most famous travels to the dead available to Niccolò in literature in one form or another would include Odysseus's in Homer, Er's in Plato, Orpheus and Aeneas's in Virgil, and Dante's guided by Virgil in Dante. All of these journeys are drawn out in lengthy sections of long works, cast with unhappy scenes. Niccolò's journeys are short, described in a paragraph, and anticipated with delight. The conversations he finds there are what he was born for, they banish all trouble and fear. Each night he looks forward to them. He wins a reward, too, from his evening seances with those *antiqui huomini*. 'I took note of what I profited from in their conversation and composed a little work, *De principatibus* . . .' Thus does he first reveal where he got his material for *The Prince*. The passage makes otherworld society even more select, reserving it to the great luminaries of the ancient world.

These various writings lighten the burden of hell. The weather there is not so steamy, the government and men are good, and the company better. For prospective princes new, and for great leaders, this may be good news, but before the rejoicing begins, we had better look to see what happened to hell, old model. The question is of utmost importance. Hell is the chief instrument of the fear of God. There is nothing Niccolò insists on more than that the fear of God is necessary to any country. Political unity, oaths, promises, arms, and religion itself depend on it. The dread is of negative post mortem judgment and consignment to hell for punishment.

If, to quiet the fears of the prince new, Niccolò has to deprive God of the fearfulness of post-mortem judgment, he has at the same time to deprive the prince of any possibility of a virtuous people, a strong religion, a staunch militia, good custom, and enforceable law. Widespread belief in the new model hell would shear away the four pillars of civil life—state, religion, law, and arms—and make life on earth more hellish than it is.

No reason to expect consistency in a man's writings, one can say easily enough. No reason for a writer to be aware of his contradictions or to worry about them; no reason not just to drop them off and leave them there as paradoxes. Up to now, however, Niccolò has shown himself to be a writer who is bothered by contradictions in himself and others, and who likes to resolve them. How it happens, he says, "that different approaches sometimes equally help or equally harm I do not know, but I should greatly like to know."

What hangs on the resolution of the present problem is whether Niccolò speaks with forked tongue and whether a contradiction shows up to flaw his political philosophy. To examine the problem, one should take into account, among other things, the literary forms he uses, the traditions he feels close to, the times he finds himself in, and those particularities of his nature he gives expression to.

BEFORE THE COMEDY BEGINS . . .

The congenial hell we have been looking at is portrayed in story, play, and song. To Niccolò they are part of light, as opposed to serious, literature. Perhaps light works have different audiences from serious works, and thus Niccolò can rest assured that license will never bump into loftiness. But no, they are all written in the same language, and though understanding them does not need knowledge of Latin, it does require considerable schooling. Those works—songs and plays—that are meant to be sung and spoken rather than read, they too have the same audience. If Niccolò is thinking of Giuliano and Lorenzo de' Medici for *The Prince*, he is thinking of Alessandro and Ippolito de' Medici for *Clizia*.

Quite possibly, too, lighter works have lesser aims than the serious. The unusual prologue to the *Mandragola* treats the play as light material, all the more so because composed by a man who wants to appear 'wise and serious'. The play and its characters are but "your entertainment this day." Light and entertaining versus wise and serious. That comedy is entertaining does not exclude it from being moral or educational simultaneously. The prologue to *Clizia* says comedies have two purposes: "comedies are made to help and delight the spectator . . . to delight it is necessary to move the spectators to laughter, which one cannot do [by] keeping speech serious and severe; because the words that make for laughter are either silly or harmful or amorous. It is thus necessary to represent silly, ill-spoken of, or enamored persons."

And comedy may also *help* the spectator. Niccolò gives a list of concrete examples and a summary flick: "It helps greatly to any man, and most of all to the young, to know the avarice of an old man, the frenzy of a lover, the tricks of a servant, the gluttony of a parasite, the misery of a poor man, the ambition of a rich, the flatteries of a harlot," and then the flick of the whip, "the little faith of all men." Comedies can "represent all these things with great honesty." If comedy can teach 'the little faith of all men' then it, too, can do what serious works of politics and moral philosophy do.

THEORY OF STAGING

Theater does not always take place in a fabric called a theater. It may occur in a house and garden, as did Niccolò's comedies at first, or in a church or a square. We can consider the theory of comedy more broadly as part of a theory of spectacle or of staging, where serious purpose appears more sharply. The dramaturgy of spectacle, pageant, pomp, games, and ceremony uses real, not 'fictive names' and finds its way into serious works.

Our dramatist shows great interest in spectacle, staged or unstaged, in all public displays or representations, for their rhetorical and educational possibilities. Should Niccolò come across a spectacle inadequately staged, he may restage it in his own words. As history, his report of the beseiging of the duke of Athens in the palace ranks as a closet drama. In it, Niccolò describes the mob that tore a man and his not yet eighteen-year-old son to pieces and thus satiated itself: 'the multitude [having] vented itself on the blood of these two' forgot about the blood of the other man, whose death they had demanded, and concluded a pact with the duke. The concepts Niccolò uses implicate the satisfying and satiating of inner and outer senses, and the venting of blood. In Aristotelian terms, one can extract from the report the effect of purging on the rioters, and of pathos (for the innocence of the youth) and terror (at the cannibalism) on the readers.

We have seen Niccolò, in drafting legislation for the militia, create political and religious ceremony for ritual enlistment and solemnization of oaths. In taking 'solemn oath', the recruits one by one had to lay hand on the Sacred Gospels. He expresses the effect of the ceremonies in terms of solemnity and the conserving and confirming of union and loyalty. *The Ass* gives an overall evaluation of ceremony using similar terms: the achieving of unity and good order.

The *Discourses* yearns for reform of Christian sacrificial rites along the lines of those of the pagan Roman. Rites should change from those 'more delicate than magnificent' into those 'full of blood and ferocity'. Here the dramaturge specifies a new effect of terror. The ancient spectacle, 'being terrifying, made men similar to it'. The emotions aroused by rites turn the nature of a participant to their likeness. This would seem to work against the theory of purgation, whereby a savage ceremony may purge men of savagery. In fact, Niccolò credits Numa's religion with taming the savagery of the early Romans, ". . . the heavens, judging that the institutions of the Romans were not enough for so great an imperium, inspired the breast of the Roman senate to elect Numa Pompilius as successor to Romulus. Finding a ferocious people and wishing to reduce it to civil obedience with the arts of peace, Numa turned to religion as a thing wholly necessary in wishing to maintain a civilized life." He formed religion in such a way that for centuries 'there was never so great a fear of God as in that republic'.

Both theses, of purging savagery and of instilling it, can be reconciled if we view religious ceremony as it was in Rome, as pertinent to both war and peace. Ceremony can strike fear in men's breasts while arousing savagery in their hearts. Numa's rites kept the Romans disciplined to internal civil life and channeled their ferocity outward toward military enterprises. Niccolò attributes considerable refinement to Rome's leaders in manipulating the effects they needed from ceremony. In truth, one cannot help recalling, Cato the Censor could not see how in Rome two diviners could pass each other on the street without grinning.

Niccolò often looks to dramaturgy for its rhetorical effect. One paragraph in particular, in Chapter VII of *The Prince*, discloses his attraction to spectacle and his skill in restaging it in words. In composing the tableau in the square of Cesena, referred to in an earlier chapter, Caesar Borgia's purpose was 'to purge the minds of those people and win them over completely'. So (and here follow the staging instructions) he had his officer placed one morning 'in the square at Cesena in two pieces with a piece of wood and a bloody knife alongside. The ferocity of such a spectacle . . .' To estimate the ferocity one has to decipher the phrase *in two pieces* and the symbolism of the piece of wood and the bloody knife. Chapter 4 above raised a number of questions about this scene, some of which we may attempt to answer now. The piece of wood is not a block or a trunk, either of which words Niccolò would have chosen if proper, as they would have been in the case of an execution by axe. A short, oblong piece of wood is sometimes part of the iconography before the judges' bench in deciding capital offenses. Originally, it was a small block on which the condemned's neck was placed in readiness for braining with a mallet or beheading with an axe. Both mallet and axe also figure before the bench as judicial symbols of death dealing. The phrase 'in two pieces' indicates that the man was quartered. The adjective 'bloody knife' may indicate that the quartering was done or deserved to be done by a butcher. A bloody knife is not a judicial symbol. Quite possibly Caesar turned Ramiro de Lorqua over for strangling to a lieutenant who then turned the cadaver over to the butcher for splitting. Pope Alexander VI alleged that Ramiro was plotting treachery. The punishment of quartering in certain parts of Italy is reserved

". . . the symbolism of the piece of wood and the bloody knife."

for heinous crimes like treason and revolt. A pathetic sentence of the *Florentine Histories* praising the firmness of the twenty-three-year-old assassin of the duke of Milan describes him as standing "naked and with the executioner in front [of him], who was holding in hand the knife [with which] to cut him." The fate of this man, whose flesh was pinched off with pincers piece by piece and who was quartered alive, indicates that the knife may be associated with quartering. In the official dispatch describing the spectacle at Cesena, the Florentine Secretary uses the same phrase, which suggests that his superiors would understand it. It is not a common expression, nonetheless. The only other similar to it is the phrase "in two parts," appearing in a translation Niccolò once made of a Latin history of A.D. 500 dealing with the persecution of Christians in Africa. There the phrase is explained: "innumerable children torn from the breasts of their mothers were taken up by the legs and [with the sword] divided up to the head in two parts."

In the case of Caesar Borgia's staging, so absorbing is the latter half of the paragraph in *The Prince* that one forgets the first half, and when

". . . worthy of notice and of being imitated by others . . ."

we think of Niccolò's insisting that the duke's actions are "worthy of notice and of being imitated by others," our minds immediately revert to this execution and no one remembers the duke's more important accomplishments described in the first half—ridding Romagna of thieves and brigands and of the lordlings who had more readily "despoiled than corrected their subjects," the achieving of peace and unity, and the setting up of "a civil tribunal in the center of the region, with a most excellent president, in which every city had its advocate." The fury of writing carries Niccolò away with the drama and lets it almost bring to a stop the rest of the discourse.

What Niccolò is learning in his observation of staging he puts to work in law. We saw in the previous chapter above how the legislator could use the Un-Golden Rule by creating constitutional law on the premise that all men were criminal, a premise Niccolò purposely extends beyond his own finding, which is that men are not all criminal as the law should put it, but that they are *ready* for wickedness. What our jurist now proposes is to make the law alive. The expression, to give the law life or to turn it into "live deeds," has an ironical twist. To make the law alive, someone has to be made dead. But Niccolò has in mind the humane purpose stated in *Justinian's Institutes*: "that the punishment may reach a few but the fear of it affect all." For our jurist, the objective is all the more valuable: so much of his statecraft is designed for a country that is fast sinking into corruption, 'when so many delinquents quickly get together that they cannot be punished without danger', and must, in order that the country find 'new life and new virtue', recover not only "the observance of religion" but also "of justice." One cannot, therefore, leave the law in a condition of inert writing; one has to make the word flesh, transform the laws into 'live deeds'. This can be done by dramatic public executions, an example of which is the satisfying and stupefying open-air tableau above, arranged by Caesar Borgia. More generally, Niccolò holds that not alone punishment but rewards, too, deserve staging. When someone in civil life has done something extraordinary, "for good or for bad," the prince new should "take a way of rewarding him or punishing him" that will give people "much to talk about."

In addition to staging reward and punishment, another, complementary method of vivifying the law is by personification. The personifier or model, typically a man of consequence, can take an unyielding stand in support of the law, even though as in the ancient Roman examples given in the *Discourses*, the stand condemns members of one's own family. The laws are "made live by the virtue of a citizen" who spiritedly fights to keep the law "against those who transgress it." Or the personifier can lead a life of example: of the "simple virtue of a man, without depending on any law . . ." Men of the latter kind are "of such reputation and of such example that good men desire to imitate [their virtues], and the bad are ashamed to lead a life contrary to them." In religion, we know, the exemplars are Saint Francis and Saint Dominic; in the state, the examples are Roman: Horatius Cocles, Scaevola, the two Decii, and several others. A great and virtuous man is a live law. Not only must justice be done, it must appear to be done. Agreed. For our jurist, the more clearly it appears to be done, and followed—through the rhetoric of imposture and staging, if necessary—the less it will have to be done.

The execution of Ramiro de Lorqua is exceptional in that it was unscheduled. Executions, processions, pageants, games, meals, rites, ceremonies in all shapes and forms are typically scheduled or repetitive, or both. In reporting conspiracies (another kind of historical event that Niccolò stages in words), he often records the conspirators' reasoning about "the time and place." The scheduled or repetitive quality of ritual makes it a frequent choice of assassins. The Pazzi tried to kill the Medici brothers at mass; the conspirators against the duke of Milan selected St. Stephen's Day, on which the duke traditionally went "to visit with great pomp the temple of that martyr." They had discarded as possibilities the castle ("it did not seem sure to them"), the hunt ("uncertain and dangerous"), a banquet ("doubtful"). "So they finally decided to suppress him at some pomp and public festivity where they might be certain he would come and they might under various guises join with their friends." Surely enough: "Those who preceded the duke were already entering the temple when he came in surrounded by a great multitude, as befitted the solemnity of a ducal pomp."

Fear and the impression of power are effects Niccolò ascribes to the pomp and majesty of state. Among the things that defend a prince internally is 'the majesty of the state' and of his person. A prince must keep "always firm the majesty of his dignity because this must never be lacking in anything." This he says in *The Prince*, while similarly in the *Discourses* he appraises "the majesty and reverence that trails the presence of a prince . . ." Majesty can paralyze a would-be assassin even if the intended princely victim were in a prison. "How much greater can one hold [the effect] to be in an unimpeded prince [then, surrounded] by the majesty of the decorations, the pomp, and his entourage!"

One who is not impressed by mundane pomp is Belfagor. In *Belfagor*, Niccolò uses pomp and music in the climax of the fable. (The music of pomp and circumstance is a subject in itself. Our author, we recall, shows an acquaintance with the effects of musical modes on heart and mind.) Gianmatteo, the farmer protagonist, instructs the king on what to do as "a last experiment" to rid his daughter of the devil possessing her. (That devil, of course, is none other than Rodrigo, who has fled Florence and is hiding out inside the daughter of Ludwig, seventh king of France.) "Sire, . . . you will make a raised platform in the square of our Lady, huge and capable of [holding] all your barons and all the clergy of this city; you will cover the platform with drapes of silk and gold; you will build in the middle of it an altar; and I want on the next Sunday morning, after first celebrating a solemn mass . . ." He then asks

(That devil of course, is none other than Rodrigo, who has fled Florence and is hiding out inside the daughter of Ludwig, seventh king of France.)

for a band of twenty persons with trumpets, horns, drums, cornamuses, several kinds of cymbals, "and every other quality of noises," who when he raises his hat will come toward the stand. "On Sunday the possessed girl was led by the hand by two bishops and many lords to the stand." When Rodrigo saw so many people together and so much apparatus, he was almost stupefied and said to himself: " 'What does he think of doing, this poltroon of a villain? Does he think to scare me with this pomp? Does he not know that I am used to seeing the pomp of heaven and the furies of hell? I shall punish him in any case. . . . Ribald villain, I shall have you hanged no matter what'." Gianmatteo decided he had better not lose more time, and signaled with his hat. At the sign, all the musicians and noisemakers marched toward the stand "with noises that were going up to heaven." At the clamor, Rodrigo raised his ears; not knowing what to make of it, and wonder-struck, completely stupefied, asked Gianmatteo what it was. At which Gianmatteo, all agitated, said: "Oh dear, Rodrigo! It's your wife coming to find you again . . ."

The sudden pomp had briefly stupefied Rodrigo; the clamor stupefied him again, more effectively. The people of Cesena who got up the morning after Christmas day and went to the square, came upon the body of Ramiro de Lorqua cut in two pieces. Niccolò, an eye-witness to the scene, reports in *The Prince* that the spectacle made them 'satisfied and stupefied at the same time'. Close equivalents of purging and terror.

The word *satisfied* fits the effect of purging. If Duke Valentino's intent was to purge their hate, he succeeded; they were satisfied. The word *stupefied* inclines toward the effects of terror and of awe of power. If the duke wished to win them over completely, the spectacle succeeded in that also, at least to the extent of satisfying the people and dazing and aweing them with the demonstration of his power.

Were one to gather up the possible aims and effects of plays, spectacles, rites, and stagings in general that Niccolò recognizes, they would embrace delighting, instructing, developing selected traits of men's nature, purging, and stupefying or terrorizing. Chapter XXI of *The Prince* offers other pertinent suggestions, both general and specific. "Nothing makes a prince more esteemed than do great enterprises and giving rare examples of himself. . . . He should, beyond this, keep people occupied in the proper times of the year with feasts and spectacles . . . join in with [different groups], set examples of humaneness and munificence, keeping always firm, nevertheless, the majesty of his dignity . . ."

The art of staging is part of rhetoric. The prince new must learn a rhetorical strategy that comprehends staging because he more than a 'born prince' lacks hereditary roots and independence of popular opinion. Proper staging of punishments and rewards, of processions, spectacles, pageants and games, ceremonies and rites, and the enabling efforts of the arts of building, painting, poetry, music, and sculpture will help build his foundations and meliorate the harshness his rule might otherwise find necessary. But all this does not help much in taking the precise weight of earnestness in Niccolò's fictitious writings about hell.

SENATORIAL VERSUS LAURENTIAN

Drama moves in and out of true and 'fictive names', heavy poetry and light prose, the sober and the funny. The tableau Caesar Borgia set up for the denizens of Cesena, as the Secretary depicts it, could as well have been a *tableau mort*, but it was not. Let us put our author's distinction between light and serious literature and its relation to his writings about hell back into focus. He claims that comedy can teach many things 'with great honesty'. The fable of *Belfagor*, though not a comedy, is a comic novella, and a similar claim for it, one presumes, would apply.

In satirizing life on earth, *Belfagor* suggests that a hell exists, that hell and devils are not as black as they are painted, and that, in some significant respects, life there is superior to life on earth. Why does our author not tell us this in direct, serious style where the aim 'to help' is not complicated or confused by the aim 'to delight'? One might adduce many reasons; the reason Niccolò gives for his unworthy efforts is that, in effect, his serious works were duds. Therefore he turned to light genres.

A chronology of his light and serious works more or less confirms his statement. *The Prince* is not a rousing success. He puts it to bed and starts tucking in the *Discourses*, too. In the period roughly from 1515 to 1518, our writer is experimenting with various light literary forms. He turns his hand to other materials, beginning to move away from concentrated doses of things of the state, toward private, even antipolitical, writings. The subject of public affairs keeps intruding, to be sure, but he has already begun to pay more and more attention to the drafting and polishing of personal letters; he tries short verse: carnival songs; writes a fable: *Belfagor*; a fancy: *The Ass*. While composing *The Ass* he reads Ariosto's *Orlando Furioso* and compares the two. He puts *The Ass* aside; it remains unfinished. Comedies seem to be in fashion. Possibly in this period he translates a comedy by Terence into the vernacular: *Andria*. He decides to craft a play of his own: out comes the *Mandragola*. A hit.

Certainly, without his serious works on our table we should be forgiven for classifying him as a derider of church, clergy, hell, family, women, and country, as an Epicurean, a ribald, a hedonist. Even while Secretary, before he wrote his great light works, he had difficulty suppressing his reputation for ribaldry among the wrong people in the Palazzo.

Conversely, without his plays, stories, letters, and verse, we should have no notion of the humor and fun of this man; a whole side of his nature would escape us. We should know only Niccolò the heavy moralist and pedagogue of *The Prince*, the *Discourses*, the *Art of War*, the *Florentine Histories*, and the minor political works and correspondence where not a smile cracks his face. We can bear the heaviness only because of the light, fast, dramatic lines that flash throughout. We should not know the Niccolò who does not go to church unless he has to, whose letters break everybody up in laughter, who falls headlong in love, who promises his friends he will show up soon to plunk himself down with a "Here I am," who pokes fun at and holds dear and sympathizes with men and fools, the one who in spite of death and taxes, and "the thousand hardships" of writing, can say, "I come joyous onto the field."

Believe it or not, with the lighter side of his nature Niccolò has difficulty himself. A youthful reader of Livy, an admirer of the *gravitas* of ancient senators, a lover of "men grave and full of reverence," he is irreverent. His ideal is a "grave man and of authority," or 'wise and grave', the model Roman senator. Yet a few seconds later he is saying that "he has respect for nobody."

Our author recognizes the mixture in his makeup. (Come to think of it, we did notice once that the phrase 'God more a friend' seemed an odd passage in a not particularly religious man.) The contrast of the Niccolò of Chapter 1 above with the Niccolò of Chapter 3 and 4, of the irreverent with the moralist, is noticeable, and at the time of reading may have left us somewhat uncertain, as if reading about two curiously different persons: either one or the other Niccolò should be the true one, but not the twain together. Writing to Vettori, he himself puzzles over the mixture of levity and seriousness in their correspondence. After delivering some observations on love in response to his friend's letter about lust, Niccolò writes,

> Whoever might see our letters, honorable godfather [of one of Niccolò's children], and might see the diversity in them, would greatly wonder because it would seem first that we were grave men all turned to grand things and that in our breasts no thought could fall that did not have in itself honesty and greatness. But afterward, turning the page, it would seem to him [that] our same selves, light, inconstant, lascivious, were turned to vain things. . . . And though we are used to arriving at this variety in more than one letter at a time,

I want this time to do this about-face in one [letter], as you will see if you read the other side [of the sheet].

The other side gets most serious, bringing up Giuliano and Pagolo's project for a new state.

Niccolò justifies his two-sided character tritely, it would seem, attributing it to the variety of nature. "If this way of proceeding seems to some to be vituperous, to me it seems praiseworthy, because we imitate nature, which is various; and he who imitates nature cannot be reproved." But perhaps by referring to his imitating nature, he was using the phrase in the sense of unavoidably following or being part of, rather than unconsciously imitating nature. Men 'cannot command their nature'. About his nature, after all, he did in effect confess something when explaining in the prologue to the *Mandragola* why he shifted from wise and serious to light and vain, writing that he would stay to laugh at men, once he could not correct them.

In the *Florentine Histories*, Niccolò makes a practice, after narrating the political and military events in the life and death of a given personage, of appending a postscript adumbrating the man's personal idiosyncrasies. He discovered the practice in the Roman historian Suetonius and first experimented with it himself in the *Life of Castruccio*. Here in the *Histories* are a few sentences from the postscript to Lorenzo the Magnificent: "Nor can vices be adduced about him that might stain his so many virtues, even though he was astonishingly wrapped up in the things of Venus and delighted in facetious and mordant men and in childish games to the extent that for so great a man it did not seem right: so that many times he was seen among his sons and daughters, mixing in with their games. So that to consider in him both the voluptuous and the grave life, one saw in him two different persons conjoined in an almost impossible conjuction." We may refer to this as the Laurentian model.

In the season before Lent, certain things are permitted that are forbidden the rest of the year. The hell and devils that Niccolò sings about in carnival songs, one may assume, are not the real ones of the other fifty-odd weeks of the year. Nights more than days are times for revelry. Our author quotes what seems to be a saying he likes, describing and justifying his own light and serious alternation. He uses it twice, once as a retort made by Castruccio Castracani to a friend who found fault with his dancing, cavorting, and making merry with the women at a party.

"He who is held to be wise by day will never be held to be crazy by night." But years before, in a letter to Vettori, Niccolò had written the same words as his own.

To review in two paragraphs: There is an afterworld; in it the wicked are punished in hell. This punishment is not as terrible as Dante chants it, the painters paint it, and the friars preach it, but Niccolò is willing to represent it by 'sempiternal fire'. He does not detail this hell, preferring to speak of the fear of God and its indispensability to civil life. The Romans feared God, Italians do not fear God enough.

After things are 'totally wrecked', *The Prince* is written and set aside. The days of the Florentine Secretary and his republic are past. Moved by the times and his antipolitical humor, Niccolò swings to light and private as opposed to serious and political literary forms, to pieces for carnivals, betrothals, festivals. The devil and hell are not the only things one can poke fun at, but the irreverent, facetious strain in him erupts and attaches itself to the derisory tradition to satirize a world out of joint and the small faith of all men.

The derisory tradition has respectable ancestors. They appear centuries before Niccolò, in the art and sculpture of churches themselves, making fun of the devil. At the same time, people unquestionably feared him as the Prince of Darkness. Dante only once, Niccolò never, calls him Satan. As for pagan times, the derisory tradition goes back as far as one wishes to go. Without tapping Epicurean and Lucretian sources: Cicero thought fears of the infernal regions were old womanish; Seneca childish; Plutarch, nursery tales. The tradition in Christianity is different, yet often aligns itself with anticlericalism. It pops up conspicuously in the festivities of Saturnalia and Carnival, times of Bacchanalian revelry. Florence is well-known for the licentiousness of Carnival. The carnival songs of Lorenzo the Magnificent set its tone.

Carnival lasts but several days and when over, Lent is here. The *Art of War*, the "Exhortation to Penitence," and the *Florentine Histories* reaffirm the sober side, the gravity of writing, and the fear of God. "In everyone religion and the fear of God is spent," laments a statesman of the fourteenth century in the *Florentine Histories*. But shortly thereafter in that same *Florentine Histories* our historian reveals that even the lowest orders of the population, the downtrodden wool-carders of the city, feel the force of hell and conscience and have to overcome it before being persuaded to action. "It saddens me greatly," their bold leader says, "that I hear that many of you repent in conscience of the things done [burnings and robberies] and want to abstain from [doing] new things." The speaker first diminishes the extent of their wrongdoing and urges them on to political deeds: "the small misdeeds are punished, the great and serious [ones] are rewarded." He then allays their fears of hell. "And of conscience we should not take account, because where there is, as in us, the fear of hunger and of prison, that of hell neither can nor should find room."

The argument is Niccolò's legalistic one of necessity and choice. If men do evil acts out of hunger and fear of prison, they are, to use his language, 'necessitated'. The speaker does not deny hell's existence. But when one has no choice but hunger or prison—the phrasing is admirably delicate—the fear of hell neither can nor should 'find room'.

Niccolò's reckoning of hell in the "Exhortation" is not a mockery. Whoever has not charity shall not be introduced to the 'celestial wedding of the emperor our Jesus Christ in the celestial kingdom' but shall be chased from the banquet and put 'in the sempiternal fire!' Fabrizio, the Spanish captain and protagonist of the *Art of War*, Niccolò's spokesman, as discourse rolls on gets more and more wound up, until practically he alone is speaking and the dialogue in the Gardens turns into a monologue. In the long last paragraph of the book, he speaks again of God and soldiers, having in mind contemporary Italy. "By what god, or by what Saint, can I have them swear? For those they worship or for those they curse? Of those they adore I know not one; but I know well they curse them all." Niccolò relates keeping one's promise to the mutual trust of citizens and soldiers and to the love of neighbor, as Captain Fabrizio continues his series of rhetorical questions: "How can I believe that they will keep their promise to those that they scorn?" Then, briefly, as befits a soldier, he asks the broadest question. 'How can those who scorn God respect men?' Our author, it seems, is not about to fracture the fear of God.

The seesawing of light and serious genres, of the irreverent and the moral, of the facetious and grave sides to Niccolò's nature, of Laurentian and Senatorial models, of Carnival and Lent, of night and day—has no fixed arc. There are seesaws of minutes within the seesaws of years. If you want to see the other face to his nature, turn the page and 'read the other side'.

Doctrinally, we must confess, if Niccolò's political philosophy has need of the fear of hell for everyone and of the consignment to hell of the truly wicked, so has it need of special consideration for great men, the prince new and the one-man-alone. Simple and too neat though it may have appeared at the start of this chapter, the idea of a corresponding lightening of hell to balance the lightening of evil, after more complex examination, cannot be discarded. Niccolò wants prospective heroes not to love their soul more than their country, not to think of the evil they must enter as true evil, not to be hesitant out of fear of hell.

. . . the fear of God.

For whatever motives, he has sketched a congenial club for real men alone, approaching the need for a more appropriate and select post mortem treatment.

His light, vain, and unworthy efforts may have produced something worthy: a hell greatly different from the composite model of Dante, Traini, Giotto, Fra Bartolomeo, Signorelli, and the pulpit. If the congenial hell is not to supplant this other, it is certainly mocking it, with its supposed climate, administration, and population.

Is the one hell to be exchanged for the other? Or are there to be two hells? Is one hell to be shut down? Should we then revise Niccolò's topography? Where do we locate each? He has left us with some uncertainty.

Niccolò, we see, has a political philosophy, a statecraft, and a moral philosophy to go with it. Further, he has revamped hell to make it less hot, well-governed, and pleasantly populated. What more does he need? Well, suppose the moral philosophy is but a sleight of hand and the revamped hell but whistling in the dark?

But now, time to be quiet. Niccolò is dying. As he lies in bed, his brigade gathered round . . .

Chapter 14

THE GOODLY COMPANY

> . . . not excepting even his soul . . .
> [for] the good of his country.
> —*Art of War*

. . . H E S E E S a long file of people, ragged, sick, weak, and weary. Asking who they are, he is told that they are the blessed of paradise whom one reads about in scripture: "Blessed are the poor for theirs is the kingdom of heaven." As they fade from sight he sees gathering a group of impressive persons in courtly attire, walking and gravely discussing matters of state. Among them he recognizes Plato, Plutarch, Livy, Tacitus, and other famous men of antiquity. These, he is told, are the damned of hell, because it is written: "The wisdom of this world is the enemy of God." As they stroll off, Niccolò hears himself being asked: "With whom would you rather go?" "Me?" he said, "I am not tagging along with those ragbags to go to paradise. I am staying with that other company, to talk about the state and go to hell."

From his letters and from letters to and about him, Niccolò emerges as a storyteller much in demand. Unfortunately there exist only two stories qua stories attributed to this great, mostly unpublished storyteller. Both talk about hell—*Belfagor*, to which we have already been introduced, and the other just recounted, which he narrated, it is told, on his deathbed.

It is easy to understand how this latter story could have been made up about him. If not true, it ought to be true, but whoever made up or reported Niccolò's telling of it botched it. An earlier version is better told, and is not Niccolò's. In it the lover's name is Aucassin. He registers a protest.

> What do I have to do with paradise? I do not want to enter there unless I have with me Nicolette, my so sweet friend whom I love so much, for in

paradise go only those people I shall number for you. There go the priests so old and those old cripples and the maimed who all day and all night cough before those altars and in old crypts, and those who wear old tattered capes and old clothes, who are naked, without shoes or breeches, who are dead of hunger and thirst, and of cold and misery. Such are the people who go to paradise: with them I have nothing to do. But it is to hell that I want to go, because it is to hell where the fine scholars go, and the fine cavaliers killed in the tournament and the brilliant wars, the valiant men of arms and the knights. It is with these that I want to go. And there go too the fair ladies so courteous for having two or three friends besides their wedded lords; and there go also the gold and silver, the furs of miniver and vair; and there go the harpers, the minstrels, the kings of this world.

Whose story this is we do not know, nor how much older it is than the version above, which is a few centuries older than Niccolò's. The one who reported the story or started the rumor about Niccolò on his deathbed not only botched it, he left out something interesting, for Aucassin continues: "It is with these I want to go, as long as I have with me Nicolette, my very sweet friend."

❧

THE determination to go to hell rather than give up something precious, whether it is Niccolò's goodly company or Aucassin's Nicolette, refers us to Chapter 6 above, the one on Niccolò's loves. That chapter brought up a comparison that our author used in his next to last letter (16 April 1527) to his old correspondent, Vettori. In it he expresses the affection and gratitude in which he holds Guicciardini for the hard fight he is putting up as the Pope's lieutenant in the fight against the imperial foe descending on Italy. "I love Francesco Guicciardini . . ." This personal outburst, most unusual in itself, prefaces the even more passionate declaration: 'I love my country more than my soul'.

Chapter 6 also touched on the relation of this avowal to going to hell. A description of its background will now take in more of its significance and tell us as well something of the last year or so of Niccolò's life. But why, at this time, love of one's country should imperil one's soul does not seem obvious, for Machiavelli and Guicciardini are both Florentines and are both fighting for Florence and Rome as allies.

1526–1527

Foreign invasions threaten Italy anew. Niccolò's fury of writing has conferred on him an intriguing double reputation: military theorist, as well as playwright. The Pope and Florence put him on horseback on foreign and military missions once again. In the end as in the beginning he 'always ran'.

But all is not the same. He is older and feels the travel more. Invasions are not new to him; in his lifetime they had begun when he was a young man of twenty-five. Now he begins to sense something worse—impending catastrophe.

In 1519 with the death of the Emperor Maximilian I, the existing European equilibrium had broken up into the fierce Valois-Hapsburg feud between Francis I of France and the new emperor and king of Spain, Charles V. In 1521 Charles opened hostilities for supremacy in Italy. In 1525 Francis is defeated at Pavia, badly wounded, captured, taken to Madrid, and imprisoned in the Alcazar. The Spaniards occupy all Milan.

In October of that year, Niccolò, advising Guicciardini about dowries, changes the subject and writes a brief paragraph of foreboding: "the dukedom of Milan is swept away . . . there is no longer a way out." Then he quotes a Latin saying. "So is it given down from on high," and follows it with a few words from Dante's *Purgatory*: "And in his vicarage, etc." He returns to Latin to say, "You know the verses, read the rest yourself." The rest of the letter is in the vernacular again: "Let us for once have a happy carnival, and you order lodgings for Barbera [who is to be there in Faenza for a performance of the *Mandragola*] with those friars, who, if they do not go crazy, I shall not ask for money . . ." He does not forget a female admirer of his in Guicciardini's entourage: "and remember me to Maliscotta." Finally he turns to his literary efforts, to the history of Florence he is still working on: "I am beginning to write again now . . ." He signs this disjointed, entranced letter, Niccolò Machiavelli, "historico, comico, et tragico."

As for the rest of Dante's lines Niccolò alluded to but did not quote, they refer to the humiliation of Pope Boniface VIII in 1303 when Guillaume de Nogaret and Sciarra Colonna, acting for Philip the Fair, penetrated the papal apartment, seized the Pope in his bed, demanded his resignation, and threatened to kill him.

> In his vicarage . . .
> . . . Christ is captured,
> I see him scorned and mocked at once again;
> I see the vinegar, the gall, renewed,
> And him between living malefactors slain.
> I see the second Pilate's cruel mood
> grow so insatiate . . .

No subsequent pope ever repeated Boniface's declaration: "I am Pope. I am Caesar."

Niccolò's meaning is not obvious: something to do with the pope's being captured, made to suffer as Christ, and the scenario's being decreed 'on high'?

Emperor Charles, after taking Francis prisoner and getting him to sign a document called the Treaty of Madrid on 14 January 1526, sets him free. Hardly able to believe the news, Niccolò strikes off an epigram: ". . . and so it happens that the daft / Charles King of the Romans and the Viceroy [of Naples] / for not [having eyes] to see have let the King go."

The crisis deepens. Niccolò writes to Guicciardini on 15 March 1526 predicting that Italy will have war; there is no alternative. "I estimate that in whatever way things proceed, there has to be war, and soon, in Italy."

His mind runs ahead. What one-man-alone can he find in this emergency? "You know," he continues, "and everyone knows it that knows how to reason about this world, that people are various and foolish; yet, made as they are, what they say to do many times [is] what one ought to do." This praise of the voice of the people comes by way of preamble to Niccolò's idea. "Some days ago they were saying in Florence that Signor Giovanni de' Medici was raising a banner [of his military company called the Bande Nere, the Black Bands] to make war wherever it might present itself better [to his efforts]. This rumor encouraged me to think that the people might have been saying what one [actually] ought to do." Niccolò begins to reason as he did in the last chapter of *The Prince*.

> Everyone I think believes that among the Italians there is no leader [to be found] whom soldiers would follow more willingly, whom the Spaniards would hesitate more [over confronting] and respect more; everyone holds besides that Signor Giovanni is audacious, impetuous, of great concepts, a seizer of great risks; one can therefore, enlarging [his force] secretly, make him raise this banner, putting under him as many horse and infantry as one can . . . it would quickly indeed spin the brain of the Spaniards and change their plans, [they] who have thought perhaps to ruin Tuscany and the Church without obstacle. It could change the opinion of the king [of France, too] . . . And if there is not this solution, [and given our] having to make war, I do not know what [other] there is; nor for me is anything more needed.

Guicciardini, to whom he is writing, does what he can to carry out 'what [people] say to do'.

Florence finally girds for war. In the spring of 1526, Niccolò is given the job of inspecting and recommending changes in the city walls and fortifications, a matter he discusses with Pope Clement VII in Rome. There is still time to pay court to Barbera and to help Guicciardini marry off one of his four daughters, but his head is beginning to get "so full of bulwarks that nothing else could enter it." The most urgent, imperative, and fierce of his letters to Guicciardini carries the date of 17 May 1526.

> For the love of God may one not lose this occasion, and do remember that fortune, our bad counsel, and worse officials have led not the king but the Pope into prison; the bad counsel of others and the same fortune have taken him out. See to it now, for the love of God, in such a way that His Holiness will not return in the same perils, of which you will never be sure until the Spaniards in some way are pulled out of Lombardy so that they cannot come back . . . and remember that the Duke of Sessa [the Emperor's ambassador to the Holy See] used to go about saying that that pontiff began too late to be afraid of Caesar. Now God has brought things back to term, so that the Pope is in time to hold off [the Emperor] . . .

On 22 May 1526, Francis I repudiates the Treaty of Madrid (anyone reading Chapter XVIII of *The Prince* could have predicted that he would do so) and forms the League of Cognac with the Pope, Milan, Venice, and Florence as allies against Charles V. Niccolò now rides here and there on various missions for Florence, for the Pope, for Guicciardini. He dashes off letters to friends who read and relay them along a line of sympathizers where they are avidly consumed—"all your friends are well and greatly desire your letters," writes one of them—even by the Pope who, handed them by Filippo Strozzi, "not only reads them but rereads and thinks them over." So reports Vettori to Niccolò on 24 August 1526.

The Pope, as we heard in an earlier chapter above, on the basis of a truce had disbanded his forces in Rome. On the night of 20 September, surprised by an attack of the Colonna clan at the head of a horde of peasants, Clement VII has to flee to shut himself up in Castel Sant'Angelo. Later the Pope offers Niccolò the post of papal commissioner for the punitive expedition he plans against the Colonna. The letter of offer reaches Niccolò too late, the expedition was already on its way, fortunately, thinks Guicciardini who writes him, "to tell you the truth you would have stayed with [but] small satisfaction in those outposts of the Colonna [family]." Niccolò blames the Pope for having disbanded his infantry, thus, "taken like a baby," making possible "the disorders in Rome," the foretaste of disaster to come.

"Magnificent Lords, etc., I arrived here [Modena] at a late hour and went immediately to his Lordship the lieutenant [Guicciardini] . . . The

Niccolò's last hero expires before he can 'raise the banner'.

landsknechts . . . today have crossed the river . . . These Germans number fifteen or sixteen thousand . . . 2 December 1526." The letter from Niccolò to his superiors in Florence carries a brief postscript: "Your Lordships will have heard of the death of Signor Giovanni, who is dead to everyone's sorrow." Giovanni, advancing with his troops to prevent fourteen thousand Germans from crossing the Po, had fallen mortally wounded. Niccolò's last hero expires before he can 'raise the banner'.

An apocalyptic miasma settles over people in the path of invading forces. It was around this time that Niccolò reported to Guicciardini the prophetic mood of Modena. Through his dispatches of this his last year, flickers the presentiment that things are out of human control. On 18 March 1527 he informs his superiors that "the [bad] weather began Saturday night and up to now . . . it has always either rained or snowed, so that the snow is an arm deep in every part of the city, and it snows still. And thus that impediment that we were not able or did not know how to give the enemy, has been given and [given] by God," and then adds, "and if God loves us at all, he would have deferred this weather until . . . they had entered those mountains . . ." A few days later he writes to his superiors again. "Nor do I think anyone does not know about [the keeping of the treaty]. But the heavens when they wish to color their designs lead men to the point where they cannot take any sure decision." (In the *Discourses* it was Fortuna that colored her designs.) After another couple of days: "And so my magnificent Lords, it seems to everyone that the treaty is done for, and that one has to think of war, so much that may God help in such a way that [the parties] become more humble." The following day: "Therefore the lieutenant [Guicciardini] lives in great anxiety, and reorganizes and remedies all those things he can, and may, God wish that he can do as much as will be enough."

A few weeks pass and Niccolò's last letter to Vettori is as imperative and fierce as that above to Guicciardini. "And for the love of God . . . cut negotiations immediately . . . and if Count Guido [Rangoni, the field commander of pontifical forces] says otherwise, he is a prick . . . But whoever enjoys war, as these soldiers do, would be crazy to praise peace. But God will manage that they will have to make more war than we would want."

The letter to Vettori preceding the one above is where 'I love my country more than my soul' appears. That letter had concluded: "And I tell you this by that experience that sixty years have given me [his fifty-eighth birthday had just been reached a month and a half earlier], that I do not believe that more difficult articles were ever suffered through than these, where peace is necessary and war cannot be abandoned, and to have on hand a prince [Clement VII] who can barely see to peace alone or war alone."

Niccolò and Guicciardini are working together hand in glove. Niccolò reports occasionally instead of regularly to his Florentine superiors, thinking it enough for them to get Guicciardini's dispatches second-hand from the papal legate in Bologna, Cardinal Cibo, cousin of the Pope. "Magnificent Lords, etc. If your Lordships had not been kept up to date every day of everything of these events by the Signor Lieutenant by letter to the most reverent legate, they might . . . reasonably accuse me of negligence: but I judged it superfluous to say the same things that were said and written by said Signor Lieutenant." The Eight of Affairs, Niccolò's superiors in Florence, at the moment terrified by events at the front and yet wishing to show a degree of independence of Rome, are not satisfied by this channeling of intelligence, "especially your judging . . . for the aforesaid causes, writing us to be superfluous; it seems to us wholly useless and beyond question, not only your having been there idle up to the present, but also for the future to go on [as you have been doing] . . . it displeases us greatly." Niccolò idle! They go so far as to hint at "insubordination." To all of which Niccolò seems to pay small heed: he seems well-protected by the Pope and papal supporters including the above-mentioned papal legate, Cardinal Cibo, about whom he will shortly write his son, Guido, 'I have made a new friendship . . .'

Caught in the churning danger and struggle and helplessness, Niccolò is proud of himself and Guicciardini. Buoyed by their fighting side by side to save Italy, Niccolò bursts with passion, 'I love . . .'

An exclamation of love, then, in the highest degree, and a pledge to risk the soul for that love.

. . .

With this particular background the comparison of love of country with love of soul accents the greatness of Niccolò's love of Italy rather than the peril of going to hell for it. He is not here entering evil, whether absolute, true, or apparent. He is never surer of the justness of his cause than at this moment. To enflame Guicciardini the more, Niccolò reverts to the Latin of his master, Livy: "Free Italy from day-after-day anguish, extirpate those terrible beasts that except for face and voice have nothing of men about them."

We hear again the powerful call of Dante and Petrarch and Julius II— Out the barbarians!—and of the last chapter of *The Prince*: "See how Italia prays God to send someone to redeem her from these barbaric cruelties and insolences; see her further, all ready and disposed to follow a banner if only there were someone to seize it . . . To everyone this barbarian domination stinks!"

Niccolò wrote these lines of *The Prince* more than a dozen years earlier, in the aftermath of other barbarian invasions and sackings—Ravenna, Prato, and Brescia, where the horses finding no place to put their hooves down had to tread on the fresh corpses covering the streets, when Italia was "raced over by Charles, preyed on by Louis, forced by Ferdinand, and vituperated by the Swiss." Chapter 5 above reported the Secretary's traveling then to Lombardy, Blois, and Pisa to get the

French-convoked, anti-papal council moved away from Pisa, and riding all over Florentine territory in an effort to organize a military defense. It mentioned also his frenzied horsebacking in this later period and the events culminating in the horrific sack of Rome of 6 May 1527. It touched on his prophecy in the *Discourses* that the church faces ruination or a scourge and on the relation of the *landsknechts* to Lutheranism. In the sequel to the struggle, Florence loses its republican constitution forever. As for Italy . . . the Pope crowns Charles V, king of Italy.

NO GREATER LOVE

Niccolò shows no doubt whatever that Italia is worth entering evil for, risking one's soul for, going to hell for, or that God wants her saved. He gives not a second's thought to the empire. Charles V has proclaimed goals that Niccolò too desires with all his heart—to reform the church and bring peace to Europe. The emperor's proposed reforms of the church are simply not the important ones, and his peace would bring a unity in which Florence, Rome, and surely Italy would not be free. Nor does Niccolò give thought to the Frenchman, the Spaniard, the German, or the Swiss who also may love his country more than his soul. He has paraded history before us, and marches country after country on and off the world stage: Sparta and Rome, Assyria and Persia, strutted their course. On and off: it happened to them, it can happen to Italy. Florence, a weak state, and Italy—corrupt above all others—are being pierced by swords coming from all points of the compass.

Still Niccolò writes as if God were on Italy's side. His attitude reminds one of Nicomaco in *Clizia*.

NICOMACO: I thought it might be a good idea to get out of this confusion by drawing lots for whom Clizia shall belong to. My wife will not be able to get away from that.

PIRRO: But if the draw goes against you?

NICOMACO: I have trust in God it will not happen.

PIRRO: (*Aside*) Oh, crazy old man! He wants God to hold hands with his dishonesties! (*to Nicomaco*) I believe that if God gets involved in such things, Sofronia too might trust in God.

NICOMACO: Let her trust!

Italy is the only country in the world that is not barbarian. How could God not wish her salvation. Yet God has been chastising that weak state, Florence, and that Rome with her disbelieving prelates, and that Italy 'corrupt above all others'. There is a sword, as on the back of the medallion of Savonarola, that may transfix Italy from above, too. Niccolò calls it a scourge. In the "Words to Speak," back in 1503, we recall, he wrote 'I am persuaded that God has not yet chastised us to his manner, and that he is reserving us a greater scourge.' A decade or more later he concludes in *The Prince* that Italy has taken enough blows: "it was necessary that Italy be reduced to the terminal condition that she is [in] at present, and that she be more slave than the Hebrews, more dispersed than the Athenians . . . that she has borne every sort of ruin."

Like Dante and Petrarch, Niccolò believes that Italy's sufferings constitute the preparation for her redemption. But, for him, while Italy may be the apple of God's eye, God will not save her if Italians do not act to save her themselves. Italic favoritism has a divine limit. God judges single persons as well as nations and churches. God's judgment would not fall on Italy. It would be a judgment on men, on Italians, and particularly their leaders. We are back to the sins of princes.

From *The Prince* to the *Florentine Histories* and beyond, our moralist points the finger of shame to one group—the princes old. He has already presented the *Florentine Histories* to Pope Clement VII in Rome and received the extra one hundred ducats approved by the Pope for his work when he tells Guicciardini that he is beginning to write again. "I vent myself by blaming those princes who have all done everything to bring us here [to this pass]." He portrays most fully in the *Art of War* the product of existing princely education.

> They thought, our Italian princes, before they tasted the blows of transalpine wars, that it sufficed for a prince in the writing-rooms of palaces to think up a sharp reply, to write a beautiful letter, to demonstrate wit and readiness in sayings and words, to know how to weave a fraud, to decorate oneself with gems and gold, to sleep and eat with greater splendor than others, to keep many lascivious women around, to conduct himself avariciously and proudly, to rot in idleness, to give military rank by favor, to be scornful if anyone might show them any praiseworthy path, to want their words to be oracular responses, nor did these no-accounts realize that they were preparing themselves to be the prey of whoever assaulted them. Born out of these, then, in one thousand four hundred ninety-four, were the great frights born, the immediate flights and the miraculous defeats; and thus three most powerful states [Florence, Milan, and Venice] were time and again sacked and wrecked.

And 'the one [namely, Savonarola] who said that our sins were the reason [for King Charles of France's being able to 'take Italy with chalk'] spoke the truth', writes Niccolò in *The Prince*, 'but they were not those that he believed, but those that I have narrated; and because they were sins of princes, they too have suffered the punishment for them'.

The sins of the old princes, like those of monarchs and tyrants, have earned them the hell of the ancients. Few escape a bad end, Niccolò writes in the *Discourses*, and to the point quotes the Roman poet Juvenal: To the infernal regions "few kings descend without mortal wounds and tyrants with a bloodless death." In taking over and holding a hereditary principality, Niccolò recommends early in *The Prince*, "it is enough to extinguish the [blood] line of the prince," and then just take care not to violate old customs, the implication being that the justification of princes to rule by right or by performance is not worthy of consideration. It is their fault, as well as those of the disbelieving prelates of the Roman court, that a strong central Italian state has not been forged.

But blaming them is not enough. Italy must yet have a great leader or a prince new. Italia "left for lifeless awaits whoever might be the one to heal her wounds." Now is the time, here the occasion, "to follow those excellent men [Moses, Cyrus, and Theseus] who redeemed their lands," and for "one prudent and virtuous to introduce a form [of civil life] that would bring honor to himself and good to the universality of men [of Italy]," for that one "to make himself head of this redemption."

Dante and Petrarch also seek the redemption of Italia, but Niccolò is the only one to point out that the agent of that redemption must enter evil and risk his soul.

TRADING SOUL FOR COUNTRY

There is the possibility that Niccolò considers the great leader's damnation to be a sacrifice for the common good, or is asking him to walk down that dubious lane to immolate himself. The self-sacrifice of a hero to purify a nation or a people is an institution familiar to the ancients long before there were Christians. But we have seen that our moralist lays the guilt not on country or people but on leaders. The prince, the one-man-alone that Italia awaits, will be judged alone.

The phrase "my country more than my soul" has flowed from Niccolò's pen in expressions similar to those whose significance we are presently exploring. The author's eulogy of Cosimo Rucellai in the first book of the *Art of War* reads thus: "I do not know what thing could be so much his (not excepting even his soul) that would not be spent by him willingly for his friends; nor do I know what undertaking would [ever] have dismayed him once he knew it to be for the good of his country." The expression as used for Cosimo is hypothetical. Cosimo is dead, and although he was all a friend could desire of a friend and all a country could desire of its citizen, he was to die "unhonored," as he himself lamented. The implication, the pledge, is there nonetheless, that though he had not occasion to do so, he would have given his soul—something uniquely his—for his friends and for his country. It is not unheard of, then, that good men will risk anything for country, even going to hell. Niccolò uses the phrase here as he does for himself later, to express the greatest depth of affection.

The *Florentine Histories* shows by example how the phrase applies to great men who indeed put their soul at risk for country. Our historian indicates the origin of the expression: the time of the War of the Eight Saints, referred to in Chapter 6 above, who led the war against Gregory XI, the Pope in Avignon. These eight citizens were called saints even though they thought little of excommunication, stripped the churches of their goods, and forced the clergy to celebrate offices: 'so much did those citizens then value [their] country more than [their] soul'. (In the expressions used for Cosimo Rucellai and for himself Niccolò changes the value of 'so much . . . more than' to 'love . . . more than'.) Though these men did most unsaintly things against the church and the Pope, thereby risking their souls, they were deemed saints because they counted their country for so much more.

Aucassin wants to go to hell to stay in the company of his sweet Nicolette; Niccolò and Cosimo Rucellai and the Eight Saints would go to hell to keep their country from suffering and ruin, from what in terrestrial affairs is the greatest evil. And as the Eight Saints did, so may the one-man-alone have to do. Our moral philosopher gives notice in *The Prince* that the prince new may find it necessary to operate 'against religion', namely, against the Christian church.

If God consigns the prince new to the same hell as the prince old, then that prince will have sacrificed himself, for he knew that by his use of strong medicine or extraordinary measures he was trading his soul for country and was slated for hell. Against this very possibility Niccolò painted a new hell and provided a new moral philosophy. Chapter 13, however, left us suspended with the thought that Niccolò may sometimes wonder whether in this world's 'brief dream' he may be whistling in the dark, whether his new moral reasoning and revamped hell may fit effective truth well enough and yet not fit that truth that exists but is hidden or not available to reason. If so, the evil acts of men of state are the absolute evil they were always taken to be, acts that signal death of the soul, and the hell God consigns them to is the inferno, old style. As a counselor of evil, then, Niccolò has a place reserved for himself not in heaven but in the eighth circle of the eighth chasm of hell. The slightest acquaintance with the topography of the inferno conjures up this vision. One can imagine it occurring to one of Niccolò's intelligent, prospective candidates for prince-newship or Eight Sainthood.

CANDIDATE: Yes, but what if you are wrong about well-used cruelties and separating evil acts from the actor? You might be wrong, you know.

NICCOLÒ: Wrong? Yes, of course. You are really asking about risking your soul then for your country. Let me tell you something about it.

God is a friend to certain men: to the prince new or the one-man-alone, or to those few 'most excellent men', 'beloved of heaven', or 'ordained by God'. Chapter 2 above first posed the question of why it was important for them to have God as a friend. The answer lies in the threat contained in this saying about country versus soul. If the great leader must risk his soul, the friendship of God makes a difference.

What does God do with his friends? He has no need to judge them. He is prejudiced. For them he bears unjudging affection. When these princes new and great leaders die, if God is their friend, it is not likely that their soul would be in danger or that they must wait in purgatory or anywhere else for the end of the world and the final assize. They would receive special post-mortem treatment.

Niccolò's study of great religious, political, and military leaders—past, present, and future—his wish to see them extolled in history and religion reflects a form of hero-exaltation, and as such, pertains to the phenomenon of

APOTHEOSIS: the elevation of a mortal to the rank of a god and his placing among the gods.

Hero-cults, to be sure, stretch beyond Roman paganism to embrace the Pharaohs and great public figures of ancient Egypt, the Hellenistic kings of Syria and Asia Minor, and the Caesars of later Rome, first in the East and then in the rest of the empire. Niccolò is too republican for this kind of immortality. In his villa there is a copy of Ovid's *Metamorphosis*; his son Guido has read it too; therein appears an account of Julius Caesar's apotheosis. The title of Caesar or Emperor or King spells no magic for the political philosopher. Nearer to his heart are the Greek and Roman city-state heroes—founders of cities, constitution-makers, great captains. Nearer still are Cicero's republican heroes. Cicero, who bows here to the myth of Er in Plato's *Republic*, gave apotheosis a different literary cast by hedging great men of state with the divinity of republicans. Petrarch features the dream in his epic poem *Africa*. And we remember Niccolò's father once lending his copy of the *Dream of Scipio* to a chaplain. No question that Niccolò made capital of it. Here

And we remember Niccolò's father once lending his copy of the Dream of Scipio *to a chaplain . . . Here in the sixth book of Cicero's* On the Republic *is the dream.*

in the sixth book of Cicero's *On the Republic* is the dream. The elder Scipio is speaking.

> But Africanus, know from me, so that you may be even more eager to defend the Republic that all those who have preserved, helped, or enlarged their country have a special place assigned to them in heaven where they enjoy an endless life of happiness. For nothing of all that is done on earth is more pleasing to that Supreme God who rules the whole universe than the assemblies and gatherings of men associated in justice, which are called states. Their rulers and preservers come from that place, and to that place they return.

The immortals are more or less the same as those in Niccolò's dream and as those he converses with in his writing room when evening falls, but Scipio locates them in the heavens. The life they have led "is the way to heaven, to this gathering of those who have already completed their earthly lives and been relieved of the body and inhabit the place that you now see [a circle of light blazing most brightly among the other fires] and which you, learning from the Greeks, call the Milky Way."

APOTHEOSIS AND ASCENSION

The Christian resurrection and ascension can be looked on as a religious manifestation of apotheosis, no less than apotheosis can be considered the political version of religious ascension. Augustine, speaking in the *City of God* of the resurrection of Christ, says that it is incredible that the world would believe so incredible an event. In Niccolò's day artists are depicting the ascension of Christ. Raphael's *Transfiguration* is a well-known example. Other earlier representations of such levitation are close by. These express better the marvel of rising straight to heaven. In Santa Croce, where Niccolò's family tomb is located, one finds Giotto's *Ascension of St. John*, and in the Old Sacristy of the basilica of San Lorenzo, Donatello has modeled a rondel in colored stucco of the same saint in an even more wondrous levitation.

For these works to affect Niccolò, he does not have to be looking to them as models. Even had he never looked at them, others did look and did listen as well to preachings about resurrection and ascension, and contemporary linguistic usage would reflect this experience of theirs. One pertinent expression, not of our author's own coinage, of course, but one he resorts to in light and serious works is to 'rise to heaven'.

Niccolò's accounts in song and story of communication between the worlds note the direction of movement involved in going from one life to another. There are blessed spirits who descend and devils who rise to earth, and "infinite souls of miserable mortals who in the disfavor of God" go to hell. In two of his extant speeches, also, transport between the worlds occurs, of another variety: select men rise to heaven, there to be seated among God's elect. There are traces of stylistic similarity in the two discourses, but in the main the idiom of each fits its occasion. The first one, the "Allocation Made to a Magistrate," written while he was Secretary, was assuredly not drafted for his own delivery but for that of a superior official at a solemn ceremony of "ancient usage." The second, a long sermon written at a later date, the "Exhortation," reveals his acquaintance not with the pagan sources of the first speech but with scripture. Both speeches speak of God's saving of great men from hell by direct final judgment.

Trajan, though a pagan and infidel, was through the intercession of St. Gregory received by God for his statesmanship and justice and placed "among the number of His elect." Peter, against whom the gates of the underworld shall not hold out, "denied [Christ] not only one time, but three." David, a special hero of Niccolò, whom the *Discourses* hails as "a man in arms, learning, judgment most excellent" and whom the relatively small Florentine republic reveres as the giantslayer, committed adultery and murder. God not merely forgave them, "He honored them among the first elect of heaven."

The lesson seems to be that whether Jew or pagan, political or religious leader, God does not let such men burn in hell. Like the prophets and martyrs of Islam, they will gain immediate access to heaven. Certain Christians, present and future, may not need await final judgment either; they may get direct post-mortem dispensation for all eternity; they may rise straight to heaven and take their place amid God's elite.

In these speeches Niccolò does not specify how the three men saved are transported or transport themselves to heaven. In other writings, ascension is sometimes specified, sometimes not. About Belfagor all our author reveals is that "he came to the world." The *Art of War* claims that when the Venetians hired a captain to fight on land instead of on the sea, where they were practiced, they adopted "a sinister policy that cut their legs off," thus preventing them from enlarging their country and "from rising to heaven." But this is an example of our writer's free and easy way with metaphors rather than an indication of the pedestrian path to heaven. The phrase, 'rising to heaven', occurring in frequent slight variants, is one he uses on occasion to designate also the glorious ascent of men and states. Thus, in the *Discourses*, "if two princes one after the other are of great virtue . . . they go with fame up to heaven."

The expression has currency. A Florentine may write, for example, that friends go up to a fatherland in heaven together. Niccolò's friend Buonaccorsi, advising him that the Secretary's letters are to be read from that afternoon on in council and committee, suggests in a typical, half-serious manner, "one thing I want you to remember and this is, when you write, speak of every little incident . . . because these particulars satisfy and fill the brigade up a lot, and they are those [things] that will bring you to heaven." The heaven he intends is satiric, namely, the esteem of top government magistrates.

The most explanatory use of the phrase appears as the singing finale of Clizia: "You . . . so intent and quiet, / Fair souls . . . ," the playwright takes leave of his select audience, ". . . an honest example, humble, / a maestro wise and kind / of our human life have you heard, / And through him you know / what thing one must shun and what [one must] follow / to rise straight to heaven." The words 'rise' and 'straight' together make sure that there are no layovers on the way.

*In Santa Croce, where Niccolò's family tomb is located,
one finds Giotto's* Ascension of St. John . . .

NICCOLÒ'S HEROES AND GOD'S

At the back of Niccolò's mind, to gather from what he has said about
the prince new, lingers the idea of a mythological hero who has a miraculous but humble birth (Moses, Romulus, Castruccio Castracani) offset
by strong guardians or preceptors (Moses had God; Theseus, Connidas;
Achilles, Charon) and who is marked by early demonstration of talent
and strength (Castracani), a swift rise to power (from private to public),
and the triumph over evil (Moses, Theseus, and Cyrus as saviors of their
people, Theseus as savior also of Ariadne, and St. George who as Perseus saves Andromeda). A composite picture of the hero.

Sometimes the hero goes through a stage of pride and fall. Niccolò does not warn of the possibility of pride in his heroes after their rise from private to public station—except obliquely, perhaps, in his republican notations on the cult of personality or in remarking how fortune-hubris or men's ingratitude can break men of rank. In any case, Niccolò's heroes in the abstract, we know, are the one-man-alone, the great fundamental or constitutional legislator, the giver of religion, and the prince new who has more in him of a blend of the political with the religious, the redeeming or messianic prince.

So far, in the concrete we have in paradise as God's elect by direct confirmation, the Emperor Trajan, Peter, and David; as God's friends, Moses, Cyrus, and Theseus. We should include Scipio Africanus, "by heaven sent, a divine man." Also, there should be there the men 'most gratifying to God' mentioned in Niccolò's constitution, the *Discursus*, the men who did 'the greatest good' for country, including those who have reformed republics and kingdoms with laws and institutions. So, to paradise we must add these four—Solon, Lycurgus, Aristotle, and Plato. Then there are those found in the proem to the second book of the *Discourses*. We do not know them by name, nor does he, except to say, "some one of those more loved by heaven." We may presume that some are the candidates he finds in the Gardens—young, moneyed, of good family, bright, energetic. These patricians are not born poor and did not, as he did, 'learn to stint before enjoying' themselves. They live in a different world from our political philosopher. Their background resembles that of the optimates who so tenaciously and for so long opposed the Florentine Secretary. A number of the regulars of the gardens, though, are young and out of politics now that Florence and Rome are both ruled by the Medicean papacy. They listen to Niccolò as a maestro of republicanism, past and present. "I will be courageous in saying openly what I understand of these and those times so that the spirit of the young who will read these writings of mine can flee [the vice that rules now] and prepare themselves to imitate [the virtue that ruled in antiquity] whenever fortune gives them occasion for it ... [T]here being many able ones, some one of those more loved by heaven might put in operation [that good work that another good man could not carry out himself]." We can name, if desired, those to whom Niccolò dedicates the *Discourses*—Zanobi Buondelmonti and Cosimo Rucellai— and those others he mentions in the *Art of War* as being present at that colloquy—Luigi Alamanni and Batista della Palla and the dedicatee of the book itself, Lorenzo di Filippo Strozzi. Lorenzo the Magnificent, too, so the *Florentine Histories* remarks, 'was loved by fortune and God to the highest degree'. Of the rest of the Medici house, not all gain admittance, but perhaps Cosimo the Elder, the Magnificent Giuliano, Leo X, and certainly Clement VII, despite his faults.

A long way from suckling wolves and bulrushes now, yet we are still in the camp of those who might or did rise from private to public station. There are also the 'ancient men of the ancient courts of antiquity' who treat Niccolò with such courtesy on his nightly visits while he is writing *The Prince*. Besides the numerous heroes of Greece and Rome, including "Themistocles, a most excellent man," Xenophon, biographer of Cyrus, whose treatise "On Tyranny" Niccolò recommends, Cicero whom he calls Tullius, and "Marcus philosopher" Aurelius, others worth imitating are "the good historians, as is ours" (namely, Livy), Plutarch, Thucydides, and Cornelius Tacitus of the "golden precept." Then there are Dante and Petrarch, "Symmachus and Boethius, most saintly men," the eloquent Boccaccio, the philosophers Marsilio Ficino, "second father of Platonic philosophy," and Pico della Mirandola, "an almost divine man." Among religious personages, Numa is present and Augustine, "a man worthy of every praise," Saints Francis, Dominic, and Jerome, restorers of the Christian religion.

All these may be the greatest, expressly connected as so many of them are, to God's favor, but they are not the only great-souled ones. We may enlarge Niccolò's troupe to include those for whom he bestows highest praise, all those who resemble the gatherings of Scipio, and the men in Aucassin's hellward-bound file, and the "excellent men" who by deliberation can separate opinion from truth, and "the good men" and "the liberal minds" that wish to follow the best of antiquity. All in all, a goodly company.

AND GREAT SHALL BE THEIR REWARD

I think that this would be the true
way to go to paradise: to learn the
way to hell in order to flee it.
    —Letter to Guicciardini

HOW BEAUTIFUL is love in a young heart." So begins a song
from *Clizia*.

In the last years the span of life criss-crosses Niccolò's mind. Still traveling much but resting more, still in health but troubled by stomach
pains, he writes Cardinal Giulio as early as 1521: "I found that I cannot
ride in haste, owing to some indisposition of mine." He seems always
to have believed that God sets the limits of one's health and life.

Writing about his coming personally for the opening of the *Mandragola* in Faenza he promises Guicciardini that "nothing can stop me except an illness, from which may God keep me." About fifty pages from
the end of the *Florentine Histories* he reveals that he plans to write therein
about his patron, Pope Clement VII, "God giving life for it."

From the time of his retreat to the country Niccolò begins to think of
himself as old. He is then not yet forty-five. In grading his age he typically adds a few years. A couple of years under fifty, he considers himself
fifty; just over fifty—in the battle dress of the protagonist of the *Art of
War*—he considers himself "old" and "beyond in years." Just turned
fifty-eight, he considers himself sixty.

Both the *Mandragola* (written when he is forty-nine) and *Clizia*
(when he is fifty-five) are stories of conflict between an old and a young
man for the favors of a young woman, with the palm going to youth.
The song from *Clizia* ends by advising the "amorous old" to leave the
field to "ardent young men." The husband in the play, "an old man all
full of love," actually the playwright's namesake, Nicomaco (Nico-maco

*"I think that this would be the true way to go to paradise:
to learn the way to hell in order to flee it."*

Both the Mandragola *(written when he is forty-nine) and* Clizia
(when he is fifty-five), are stories of conflict between an old and a young man,
for the favors of a young woman . . .

= Nicco-Macchia), drinks a tonic that as he claims, would rejuvenate "a man of ninety [and] much more the man of seventy that I am."

At the chronological age of fifty-three, Niccolò falls head over heels in love with Barbera.

> But because not equal
> in strength to desire
> arise all the evils
> that I feel, O my lord,
> nor can I complain
> of you but of myself,
> I see and confess
> how so much beauty
> loves a greener age.

So ends the short verse, "To Barbera."

The thought of death is no stranger to him. In times when war and pestilence rage all around, the dread of death is in the air. To someone who has been so often so close to the battlefields as Niccolò has over the years, the dead in ditches give off a familiar stench. His verse has told us of the horrors of war. As for plagues, we have heard of them, too. In the great letter to Vettori, he says that while he is conversing with the ancient men of antiquity 'death does not dismay me', leaving the suspicion that at other times it does dismay him. In *The Ass* when the hero is lost in the forest, out of "great fear and the dark night" he dares not move. "And I thought I saw Death around with his scythe." On 3 December 1526 he writes his superiors in Florence that he will leave Modena the next day to return "day by day so as not to get too tired without need to." In the letter to his son wherein he hopes God will lend the boy and himself life, Niccolò warns his family to prepare to hide their stores but not to worry, that he will be back before trouble can strike. Three weeks later he does return to Florence, but time is soon to run out. He has run the course.

In the grotesquely funny letter about the two hags of Verona, Niccolò seemed to count on his place in heaven: 'I bet that place of mine in heaven . . .' That was an expression of youthful spirit from one young man to another (Luigi Guicciardini). Niccolò was not thinking of death. As Secretary he had not yet worked and written out the theology of political action. He likely felt, though, that his work for Florence made him a good citizen and that this entitled him to a place in heaven automatically. He had, moreover, a taste of glory in his militia's conquest of Pisa but he had also a share of shame in its rout at Prato. As part of his job Niccolò wrote thousands of letters, notices, orders, drafts, dispatches, and as if this were not enough, he wrote things not strictly required for business: notes, short political papers, and political chronicles in verse. So long as he had the post, Niccolò had no problem of identifying himself. He is Niccolò Machiavegli, Florentine Secretary and Citizen. Once defenestrated he could sign himself as neither. He was cut off from things of the state and deprived of a palpable relation to heaven. He then wanted to do something, almost anything, for the Medici, not because he could not live without them as company; rather because they ruled Rome and Florence, and to work for them might have restored action-for-country to him in all its exalted significance.

In one of the "Prison Sonnets" he pretended to resign himself to his fate, 'for this is the way poets are treated!' A poet is more than someone who writes mainly in verse: he is a literary man generally. By this standard Niccolò could certainly have claimed to be a poet, even in a strict definition by virtue of his verse chronicles. In the other prison sonnet the poet reveals that the Muses have maltreated him and denied him identity. 'Niccolò you are not'. Here begins, we know, the crisis of identity and spirit. Does a conception of himself as justifiable to men and God ever return? How, and in what form?

So much of Niccolò's life—as the Florentine Secretary dealing with state secrets, as the envoy showing himself, if need be, to this court or that, to be "discontented . . . by words and gestures," as the teller of tales, the matchmaker, the ghostwriter, the dramatist mounting the boards himself, the devisor of solemn public ceremonies, the advocate of a statecraft of imposture and faith-breaking, the military expert discoursing on deceptions and spies, the inventor of historical speeches, equaling those of Thucydides—so much of his life has been spent in such acting roles that one relishes the response he once made to his friend Francesco Guicciardini. The government and wool guild of Florence had sent Niccolò on missions, we have noted before, to a meeting of the Chapter General of Minorite Friars at the convent and town of Carpi north of Florence, above Modena. Guicciardini had jokingly written that he was afraid the air there would turn his friend into a liar. Niccolò, in the manner of the paradoxical Cretan who declared, "All Cretans are liars," reassures him: "As for the lies of the Carpigians . . . for some time up to now I never say what I believe, nor believe what I say, and even if sometimes the truth is told me, I hide it among so many lies that it is difficult to find it again."

THE WRITER AS HERO

While Niccolò was staying those few days in May of 1521 with the friars at Carpi, he again mentioned his place in heaven, this time in the correspondence he was having not with Luigi Guicciardini, but with Luigi's brother, the super-anticlerical Francesco above. "Your Lordship knows what these friars say, that when one is confirmed in grace, the devil has no power to tempt him. So I have no fear that these friars might hang the name of hypocrite on me, because I believe [myself] to be very well confirmed." He does not have to pretend to be religious, thereby succumbing to the devil's temptation, because he is already in a state of grace. Niccolò is no longer a young man but obviously he is still full of spirit.

Throughout this book we have referred to Niccolò variously as Niccolò Machiavegli, as author, as Florentine Secretary, citizen, envoy, poet, playwright, military theorist, prophet, moralist, sermonizer, jurist, counselor, historian, political and moral philosopher, depending usually on the particular responsibilities he has while writing or on the subject he is dealing with or on the genre he is writing in. We applied these names also because at some point or other he makes use of most of them himself and of one or two we have not yet encountered. We might speculate more about which if any of the titles or activities of his career might in his mind have confirmed him in grace and entitled him to join the goodly company.

First let us exclude the fleeting roles he voices in song and story, like shepherd, pitchman, hermit, blessed spirit, and fallen devil, and the titles he has or assumes for various short offices like Ambassador of the Florentine Republic to the Minor Brothers, or Procurator of the City Walls. As Secretary he had to make written reports. In addition he had to mount horses, ride places, and do things—follow orders, spend money, lead troops, negotiate with people high and low, give bribes, order others about, leave tips. Once the Secretary has to write a note of instruction for an ambassador about to set off for France: "[G]ive the first porter a ducat. To the second, two ducats . . . To the trumpeters do not give anything, but you would do well to invite them to drink . . . Your servants, in all the lodgings you will take, must take care of your things; and they must watch your clothes and boots from mice, that is, attach your boots up high: which though it may be a minimal and ridiculous thing, yet I speak from experience . . . [T]he morning on leaving the inn, a little tip to the chambermaid and to the groom . . ."

'After everything is totally wrecked' he calls or signs himself in several ways, chronologically as follows: poet, quondam secretary, composer, author, historian, writer of comedy, and writer of tragedy, all of them identities we have already come across. *Poet* as a minimum encompasses writing in verse, *composer* and *author* refer to his plays, *historian* takes in the *Florentine Histories*. *Writer of comedy* alludes principally to his comic plays again, whereas *writer of tragedy*, we suppose, refers to the grave works embracing the plight of Italy in what we denominated moral and prophetic language and political and moral philosophy. (The poet of the *First Decennial* had accurately identified himself as a "reciter of [Italy's] troubles.") The chief portentous works are *The Prince*, the *Discourses*, and the *Art of War*, and because he takes the same stance throughout the *Florentine Histories*—'those bad seeds began to be born that after not a long time, there being no one alive who might know how to exterminate them, ruined and still ruin Italy'—that work, too, falls in the same category.

The Prince and *Discourses* are works of things of the state and, strictly speaking, not history. Circe's damsel in *The Ass* intimates that the hero's journey will one day be 'sung by historian or poet'. She is probably basing the prediction on Niccolò's verse chronicles. *The Prince* and *Discourses*, however, may be loosely classified as historical works; they make use and recommend making use of history. Writing these many works, no matter how disparate in form, is in all events merely writing, and much less active than the many doings of the Secretary on horseback. A writer writes sitting, standing, or lying down. Niccolò's aim we may guess, from what we heard earlier of action-stressed reading, will be to make writing as spirited as an Arabian charger.

At a low point in morale after losing his post, Niccolò imagines to Vettori that he will be forced one day to leave his family, go out, and if nothing else works, 'stick himself in some deserted land to teach reading to youths . . .' The idea of being a teacher seems to grow on him. He removes to no deserted land but sets off to teach youths, yes, a little older than those he then entertained, and to teach them reading, yes too, because one avenue to effective truth as we learned is reading, especially the diligent, imitative sort of reading he insists on. The author of a princely rule book may, moreover, regard himself as a teacher to princes. *The Prince* takes on more and more the color of the prince new and approximately midway begins to look like a mirror for princes. This makes the author not merely the writer of a treatise on forms of states;

he is also (via the written word, of course) a counselor to princes or rather a counselor unassumed. Given the history of the genre, he is likely to consider himself a maestro of morals as well as statecraft.

The conviction that he is a teacher of the young appears in each of the four great serious works of our writer of tragedy. The final page of the *Art of War* offers an illustration of his attitude toward younger frequenters of the Orti: "I have been generous with [my knowledge] with you who being young and qualified will be able, if the things said by me please you, at the right times, in support of your princes, to help them and advise them." Niccolò, a teacher, an intermediary of knowledge, teaches other intermediaries, the princely advisors of the future.

Those students do not belong, we already noted, to the bulrushes type he generalizes about in the *Life of Castruccio*, and his books, though penned in the vernacular, would not have been that semi-illiterate hero's dish. Still, some of the students can be thought to be candidates for the private-to-public persuasion of prince or else for counselors of a prince. Indeed the Rucellai Gardens seem to have a tradition of being the place where those congregate who by family and wealth should be in politics but are not, and may be waiting to catch the hair of the Goddess Occasion as she flashes by.

At various times Niccolò states what a teacher's relation to pupils should be and what his own are, and by luck they are both one. The *Art of War* may serve to illustrate again. "I shall appreciate your asking me questions; because I can learn thus from you through your asking me, as you from me in [my] responding to you; because often a wise questioner makes one consider many things and know many others, that without having been asked, could never have been known."

Also, one remembers, Niccolò assigns serious pedagogic purpose even to his comedies. The farewell song of *Clizia*, sung by Barbera and her troupe of singers, with histrionic exaggeration, one imagines, calls the playwright 'a wise and gentle maestro of this human life'. He teaches through laughter as well as through sorrow, and his pupils, the spectators of the comedies and readers of the books, come from the same public.

Niccolò as moralist and exhorter everywhere in his writings is a teacher. Teaching can better men; virtue can be taught. Chapter 5 discussed Niccolò's views of the clergy as teachers, as well as of other factors in moral education such as law and adversity. So he needs no persuasion that teaching, whether through reading or oral discourse, can help men to moral improvement.

The occupations of poet, playwright, historian and others above, all involve writing, and teaching, too. The informal teaching that goes on in the Orti involves speaking or oral teaching as well, an activity that implicates the vocal chords, at least. In speaking, Niccolò must have been skilled, too, not only with his brigade of friends but also in negotiations, public and private. Without him his friends lack the flame to light up their get-togethers. Fathers with marriageable daughters on their hands seek his skill in matchmaking and dowry negotiations. When no longer Secretary and no longer ostracized by the Medici, his persuasive skills are sought by businessmen, judicial officials, and clergy. "The whole people of Florence, subtle interpreters of all things," have a reputation for a sharpness in criticism encroaching on meanness. As a critic or responder to criticism Niccolò himself boasts of quickness and a biting tongue. Taking a page from the prologue style of the Roman playwright Terence, he warns away any likely critic of the *Mandragola* by claiming that bad-mouthing others was "his first art." We have felt the force of Niccolò's sharp tongue several times: when telling the minister of Louis XII that the French did not know about the state, for instance, and when consigning Piero Soderini to limbo, not to except when calling the Pope a baby.

Niccolò often distinguishes words from deeds. Surely the reading, writing, and speaking of words are acts; yet their muscular involvement is slight when compared to lifting, pulling, pushing, copulating, walking, running, riding, strangling, cutting down, or coming to blows. Especially in a military context does our writer's contrast between words and deeds result in the discomfiture of the first and the radiance of the second, and prompts a caution about relying too much on words. A good example is Niccolò's remark about Pope Clement VII who laid himself open to attack by disbanding his troops as part of an agreement. The Pope believed "more in a stroke of the pen than in the thousand infantrymen that suffice to guard him." The king of France, on the other hand, would change his mind if he saw "he had to deal with live troops and that they, [going] beyond counsels, show him accomplished deeds." Another remark of his is that 'to hold states, studies and books are not enough'; in exchange for the book, 'a sword in hand'. Prayers, typically composed of words, can also be contrasted with deeds, whereupon he opines, 'I think that persuasions and prayers may help but believe that the [military] facts would help much more'. This much we already learned from the saying that states are not held with paternosters in hand. Nor did hearing twenty first masses of the morning help Lucrezia, heroine of the *Mandragola*, become pregnant. All she needed, she afterward sighed, was to taste Callimaco's lovemaking.

Getting back around to the comedy itself, the playwright says, "But let us let whoever wants to, to go ahead and bad-mouth. / Let us return to our case, / so that the hour does not get too far ahead. / One should not take words into account / . . ." He equates oral criticism and backbiting with mere words, while the representation of the comedy is more in the line of deeds, of something to take more into account.

Writing or producing words for plays, he conveys, is more active exercise than most other forms of word production, and not simply because the author can mount the stage and recite a prologue. The actualizing of a play, if not real action, is acting, a performing, a live, in motion representation of acts, of word-acts plus others. This may have helped dispose Niccolò to writing the *Art of War* (a serious work appearing between two plays, the *Mandragola* and *Clizia*) as a dialogue. The vast topic of staging, as surveyed in Chapter 13 above, opens up new avenues of power. Writing may set the stage, as it does in drama; staging may put writing on set, as in the ceremonial signing of law.

Printing may further enhance the power and energy of writing. In Florence printing is born about the time when Niccolò's dark eyes first see the light of day. Even as a young man, as he begins to write, he thinks of his works being printed. He has an early success with the *First Decennial*. *The Prince* and *Discourses* are not published while he is alive, although manuscript copies are circulating. Niccolò's cross-references in the one and the other indicate he thinks both are being read and would circulate in manuscript or in print for some time to come. The *Mandragola*'s full text appears, is performed and printed within a year. The first edition, a poor one, is put out by an unknown small Florentine typographer. Within a few years, the *Art of War* is printed in the neat type of the heirs of Filippo Giunta, the transaction speeded along by the young patricians of the Orti. Our playwright and military expert, and his printers, can look forward with optimism to the historian: the *Florentine Histories*, subsidized through the benevolence of Clement VII, should have no trouble being published either and being "understood better and by every [period of] time."

The process of printing, the bustle of print shops, the stamping of sheets, the hangers-on of authors and the curious—all impart a stirring air to pen-pushers and their products. Writing transformed into the printed page travels farther and with greater authority.

Our writer reposes great faith in reading, specifically in the active kind of careful, non-fanciful, intelligent reading that has imitation and usefulness in mind, and that embraces the most worthy examples and imparts experience vicariously. But, to faith in reading we must add another: the faith in writing. To stage, to exhort, and to enact—these are the great activating powers of the writing of words. Niccolò approaches the act of writing with an attitude bordering on reverence. Writing leads to reading, reading leads to action, and action is what God wants.

THE CHAMBER OF IMAGINATION

Little is known of Niccolò's writing practice or habits, but that little is interesting. Its main source is the momentous letter to Vettori, as quoted in the scene laid out in Chapter 1 above. That passage is strangely attractive. It describes Niccolò's wooing of inspiration just at the moment that he is inspired.

A home or a place of making one's living can be looked on as a repetitive if not constant context to other contexts, and Niccolò seems to employ his writing room at night as an asylum or chamber of vision. Leaving aside the interesting antecedents in workshop and monastic cell and in the pictorial representations of the indoor ambiance of saints Augustine and Jerome as they read or contemplate, we may take a closer look at Niccolò's use of the room. During the day he transacts business there: it is a writing room not a study. At night he converses there, he tells us, with the men of ancient courts.

To enter that room, one opens the door and, following his habit, steps on the threshold. Closed at the other end by another door, more than a threshold, it is a passage. The letter gives it a certain significance. Measurement would show it to be extraordinarily deep, two or three times as deep as one might expect, a space of disengagement creating specially at nightfall a passageway effect, on a minuscule scale something like that of the series of entrances and thresholds to the land of the dead in Egyptian pyramids, and a sense of going from the real to the imaginary, if you will, or from one world to another. The unusual depth may have prompted Niccolò's choice of the threshold-crossing figure of speech, a case of the architectural structure of the house affecting the metaphorical structure of his prose.

In the passageway there is a door on either side. Opening the door to the left, you discover an old stone washbowl fixed on the wall; opening the door to the right, you find a closet deep enough to accommodate a change of clothing and footgear and little more. On this door, cut into and through it, is the Machiavegli coat of arms.

Before crossing the threshold to this special room, Niccolò stops. Chapter 1 above described the sequence of his acts at that juncture. Given the notion gaining currency in Florence that a poet or even an

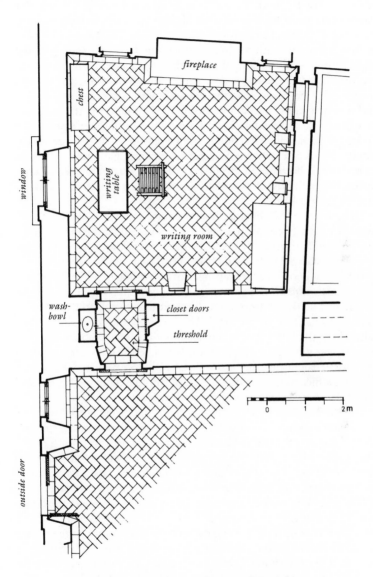

fireplace

chest

window

writing table

writing room

wash-bowl

closet doors

threshold

0   1   2 m

outside door

. . . one opens the door and . . . steps on the threshold.

artist or artist-engineer (Leonardo is an instance) should not dirty his hands while at his art, Niccolò should clean up before writing and per-haps, occasionally, change from soiled into cleaner clothes. Nothing out of the ordinary in washing up before settling down to handle pen and paper, nor even in changing from outdoor to indoor clothing, or from the very soiled to the less soiled. Any clothes should do, but Niccolò specifies that he changes on the threshold into court and curial robes and that he is thus "properly re-clothed." He has put on the garments he would wear as Secretary on mission. While writing *The Prince*, he is no longer Secretarius Florentinus. Yet he remains in the Palazzo and in foreign courts as Florentine Secretary . . . in imagination. Once in that room Niccolò becomes all spirit—no weariness, no trouble, no poverty, no fear of death. Loss of physicality enables him to transfer all of himself into his ancient heroes.

To be able to cross that threshold over into another world night after night confirms Niccolò's prestige. He has gained admittance already. 'Affectionately received by them', he has approval, too. And so has his work. He takes notes there and from them composes *The Prince*.

We do not know exactly how much of his writing between *The Prince* and the *Florentine Histories* occurs in that room in the villa. His journeys as a mythic hero start from there. "I pasture on that food that alone is mine and for which I was born." This ambrosia that he is destined or called forth to nibble, and to nibble on nothing else, is study, contem-plation, and writing of the great words and deeds of his heroes, but in less prosaic language (and at this point Niccolò's language soars) it is life on another plane, the destination of spiritual flight, or release and ascent. He departs his body.

The Ass reveals Niccolò in another heroic moment. His voyage, we have heard his duchess hint to him, will be 'sung by poet and historian'. In the *Discourses* the heroic vision invokes a new metaphor for himself. The author takes a path "no less dangerous than unknown lands and seas." In the age of great navigators, Niccolò has become a navigator of uncharted seas. Although he never calls himself a military man, the *Art of War* gives him the opportunity to speak also as an experienced cap-tain. With that voice at the end of the book he confesses to a penchant for a glorious role. Had fortune conceded him a country large enough to enable him to become "lord of this province [of Italy]," he believes he would "in the shortest time have shown the world . . ." Once he begins to go down to the Gardens and after that to the Kilns-man's, he stays more and more in the city. By then the great letters to Vettori, certainly, and the *Discourses*, and *Belfagor*, *The Ass*, and the *Mandragola* almost certainly are in great part complete and the *Art of War*, too, and they begin to show the world what the writer can do.

When at work on the *Florentine Histories*, laying into the princes who have ruined Italy, he writes Guicciardini that, "I have stayed and am staying in the villa to write the history." The date of the letter (30 August 1524) indicates that he is at the time composing modern parts of the work. The earlier parts, going back to Roman history and then forward, had put him in touch again with earlier historians and with the 'ancient courts of the men of antiquity'. So, all these works, and we cannot firmly exclude the *Art of War*, may have been written in the same place and with the same attitude shown in his ritualistic preparation for other-worldly journeys at eventide, with their preliminary ablutions, changes in vestments, and threshold crossings.

On the other hand it is possible that his metabolism has changed, he gets sleepy at night, does his best writing in the morning, and a new ritual evolves.

One presumes that he does not take so reverential an attitude toward business and family writing. The only other informative passage about Niccolò's writing practice and habits, an amusing one, demonstrates the subject's importance while treating it irreverently. He is on mission to the meeting of Minorite friars at Carpi, and describes to Guicciardini, present governor of Modena, the awe with which they regard his writing practice. The governor's mounted messenger is waiting outside for Niccolò's reply. (This was part of the joke they were carrying out: to impress the friars with Niccolò's rank by having messengers ride back and forth with apparently vital documents.) As Niccolò sets down to write out a reply for the mounted courier waiting outside, the friars gawk with cap in hand. "And while I write I have a circle of them about, and seeing me write at length they marvel, and watch me as though I were possessed; and to make them marvel more I sometimes stop with the pen and blow myself up [by holding in breath] . . ." The friars "gape" in awe; "if they knew what I am writing you, they would marvel at it [even] more."

One senses the respect in which our author holds writing also by the absence of scurrilous language from his works, from all of the serious and most of the light works as well. In the one or two of the slight pieces written for carnivals there is unsubtle play on obscenity, and in the comedies a few salty piazza expressions, but they make up the sum total.

Only from his correspondence with friends do we harvest dirty words, and out of hundreds of letters we may find about a dozen such words. Not that our author does not know others. If one of the stiff-necked lords in the Palazzo calls him 'that ribald' we need not return so much as a nod of agreement. But if his friend Buonaccorsi can correspond in a friendly, scurrilous way and if even his patrician, 'more religious than you', friend Vettori can do the same on occasion, we must assume that their expressions were neither new nor shocking nor repulsive to our author, 'young prick' that he is or may have been at one time. Yet we have no letters from him as foul as theirs. And though he writes in the vernacular (Tuscan has never been noted for a shortage of swear words and blasphemous expressions) he is able to make a promise and keep it, that his language will be plain and clean.

The covering letter of *The Prince* to the Magnificent Lorenzo states, 'I have not decorated this work with blown-up cadences or turgid and magnificent words or any other preciousness or extrinsic ornamentation'. It informs the reader that the book will be written in a plain and simple style so as not to interfere with the variety of the material and the gravity of the subject.

In plays real enough to capture language of the streets, a promise of decorum may be harder to maintain. The prologue to *Clizia* reassures the audience "the author of this comedy is a very well-mannered man, and he would take it badly if it seemed to you in seeing it recited that there might be some impropriety." He fully recognizes that moving people to laughter cannot be done by 'keeping the speaking grave and severe'. Nonetheless, "if there might be anything improper, it will be said in such a way that these women [indicating them in the audience] will be able to hear it without blushing."

As for the *Florentine Histories*, a grave work, the author announces before the book begins: "In all places I flee odious words as hardly necessary to the dignity and truth of history."

Here above are three examples from three genres—a political treatise, a comedy, and a history—in each of which the author promises plainness and purity of language and holds to the bargain.

THE GLORY OF WRITING

Thus one glimpses several tendencies in Niccolò's writing practice and reasoning about words and deeds: to assign deeds greater force than words, to favor combining words with action (as in ceremony, plays, laws, and so on), to view the use of words in teaching (and in reading) as initiators of action, and throughout to treat the process of writing as an act set apart. Writing's active potential and the role played in immortalizing heroes by its revered, ancient practitioners lead our author to prepare himself ceremonially for writing. Ritually composed, the work issues forth simple, flexible, and pure, worthy of allowing its author to converse with the great ancients.

An apparently small related matter. When Niccolò crosses the threshold to speak with the men of the ancient courts, he remains somewhat in a position of inferiority. He acts as their pupil: he asks them questions and they respond. He does not truly participate in the give-and-take of dialogue. In the activating of language a step seems to be missing: our writer has not as yet found a place for writing as an heroic act. He takes this step in 1520 by composing the "Discursus," an absorbing lesson (so we found it in Chapter 5) in constitution drafting.

There a change seems to have come in the value Niccolò puts on writing in general and on writing of imaginary countries in particular. When writing to his friend Vettori that out of his visits with the men of ancient courts he wrote a little work "On Principalities," he discloses that by saving dusk and nightfall for composing it he has selected the time of day widely acknowledged as a stimulant to fantasy. Yet he seems never to have thought of it as a work of spirit or imagination. Indeed, in the treatise he disapproves of the imagination of things, having in mind the imagining of states and leaders that have 'never been seen or known in trueness'. (His allusion to unnamed writers of such figments we know to be a common reference to Plato.) Niccolò's own proposal now for a new constitution of Florence treats undeniably of a republic, 'this republic of mine' veritably of 'a perfect republic' that has never been seen or known in trueness. This time our author makes a different assessment of the writers who have written of such a non-thing.

The "Discursus" is Niccolò's proposal for a new constitution for Florence. Addressed to Pope Leo X at the request of Cardinal Giulio, later Clement VII, our political philosopher will add something that applies to himself. First, he makes a general remark touching on the subject of apotheosis: "Beyond this, no man is exalted so much in any of his actions as are they that have with laws and institutions reformed republics and kingdoms; these have been the highest praised, second only to those who have been Gods." The next words are for the Pope: If Leo X enacts Niccolò's imaginary republic into law, "among the many felicities that God has given your house [of the Medici] and to the person of Your Holiness, this [will be] the greatest, to give him the power and the subject to make himself immortal, and in this way surpass paternal and ancestral glory by far."

Now our political philosopher adds words that apply to himself. "And because they have been few, those who have had occasion to do it, and most few those who knew how to do it, the number of those is small that [actually] did do it. And this glory has been so much esteemed by men that have never awaited anything but glory, that not being able to make a republic in deed they have made it in writing."

Finally, the laurel can be placed on Niccolò's brow. (Not to mention Plato's.) "As Aristotle, Plato, and many others who wanted to show the world that if they were not able to found a civil way of life as [did] Solon and Lycurgus, it was left lacking [to them] not because of their ignorance, but from their impotence to put it into actuality." There still remains a small step down between those who found a state in deed and those who found it in writing, but both go to glory. "Heaven does not give to a man nor can it show him a more glorious path than this."

By this line about the glory of writing, Niccolò shows that he has learned to avoid the commonplace and to think of Plato as a writer of model constitutions, something akin to the great legislator. He puts the writing of imaginary republics, now called states-founded-in-writing, next to the greatest deeds. Superior to all ordinary acts, this writing becomes res gestae, and Niccolò a member in good standing of the goodly company.

After this, Niccolò's crown of laurel only gets thicker, greener, more redolent. The *Art of War* makes him the country's foremost military writer and the *Florentine Histories*, the official historian of Florence, servant of 'the dignity and truth of history'.

GOD'S SECULAR PARTIALITY

As apotheosis is related to ascension, so to *glorify* is related to *sanctify* or *beatify*, the one political, the other religious.

We have heard Niccolò criticize Christianity, in its evolution, for coming to favor the weak and contemplative over the strong and active, for celebrating saints and martyrs, the specialists in praying and in being killed, instead of lauding the specialists in politics and killing, those without whom one's country goes into servitude or anarchy. Seeking reform of Christianity's rites, Niccolò reveals how terms like *beatify* and *glorify* can be interchanged in order to arrive at a more political sainthood. Ancient religion he says, "did not beatify men unless they were full of mundane glory," as were captains of armies and princes of republics. Our religion has glorified humble and contemplative men more than the active and thus most men in order to go to paradise think more of suffering the blows of the world than of avenging them . . .'

Our religion, he insists, 'permits us the defense and exaltation of [our]

"... second only to those who have been Gods"

country'. It permits us also to glorify, as God does, those men who have done great deeds for country. Our political philosopher wants not only to modify the Christian rites but also to change the objects of veneration of those rites, wants to pass from saints to heroes.

The literature of heroes bathes them in a misty light. We remarked earlier that glory is both mundane and heavenly, and spoke of the military and political components of earthly glory. Heroes win glory not by mere derring-do, but by deeds that redound to country and the common good. A man may have to defend his country by feats of ignominy rather than by feats of fanfare. True glory may or may not be recognized mundanely but it is recognized in heaven.

Sometimes it seems that the glory of heroes was won by themselves and then recognized and authenticated in heaven; more often it seems that a spark of the divine or the grace or form of God was always in them. Dante's idea that one's soul remains in the infernal regions until one's mundane glory has reached a certain peak, whereupon the soul goes to paradise, fits the first possibility. Niccolò inclines toward this vision but offers a double benefit and does not mention hell. The way of good princes "makes them live secure and after death makes them glorious." For a prince to enjoy glory 'after' he leaves this life indicates that he may enjoy it in "the heavens" that gave him the "occasion for glory."

Cicero's conclusion in his work on the *Nature of the Gods* follows the second and more common tradition. "There is," he writes, "no great man without divine afflatus." Niccolò's expressions of 'God more a friend' and 'most gratifying to God' and 'beloved of heaven' seem to lean toward this tradition. If we glance again, however, at his stress on the value of deeds over words, the pointer of divine inspiration shifts.

Action is not just a matter of our Secretary's and author's sheer physical energy, nor is activism just one of his maxim's for success in politics and love. Behind Niccolò's insistence on political action stands God. He grants His grace when it is earned—in political coin. To be judged virtuous, to be worthy of salvation, you must show you prefer high-intentioned political action to words and prefer words that lead to such deeds or that share in them. For God, faith—'while you stay otiose on your knees'—is not enough. If you believe that while you genuflect and mutter words of prayer God will fight for you, you are mistaken.

Our political philosopher relates glory and grace with virtuous political action in his metaphysical statement in *The Prince* on the relation of glory and free will. If God grants us free will in order not to take away the share of glory that is our due, it would seem that by the gift of free will God has done his part, and 'the rest you must do yourself'. God does not want to do everything, Niccolò affirms. What He does not want to do himself gives us the chance for our share of glory, the chance to govern ourselves, and by extension, relieves God from piddling in the affairs of mortals.

Niccolò's chief figure in the relation of grace, glory, and virtue is Moses. Moses became the successful leader of the people of Israel, not alone because he was 'a sheer executor of the things ordained by God'. Niccolò does not skirt the issue: he admits that Moses was indeed ordained by God. But Moses must also be admired if only 'for that grace that made him worthy of speaking with God'. Here is where other prophets fail: they do not, or cannot take the action that Moses and other of Niccolò's heroes did to earn God's friendship, of making their constitutions obeyed for a long time through armed action. Hence the reflection: "all the armed prophets won, the disarmed went to their ruin."

By associating virtuous political action with grace and glory, our political philosopher argues that through this kind of active and political virtue men conform to God's desire.

The matter of earning grace borders on the thorny theological question of justification by faith or by works: *faith* in this case typified by the words of prayer; *works* equated with virtuous political leadership. We have heard our author say that those who want to deprive people of prayers and ceremonies are crazy; we have also heard that there is nothing more dangerous to a country 'than to see the divine cult scorned' and that cult Niccolò supports is a reformed cult that encourages the very virtue that wins men glory and earns them God's grace and friendship. The position is consistent.

Niccolò is not an advocate of aristocratic or dynastic rule. As an incitement to glorious action he does not flourish the benefit that may accrue to one's descendants or add to the power, glory, and honor of the family, the illustrious house. The family and paterfamilias, so important in Roman law, religion, commerce, and politics, the pattern of all discipline and education, get scant attention in Niccolò's serious works except for cases of family-country conflict.

Aristocratic descendants hold that the glorious memory of ancestors requires celebration. Moreover, the fact of their glory attests to favor by God or by family gods. Niccolò's republican glory, too, attaches to God's favor: first, in the divine grant to men of free will, second, in men's use of that free will (virtuous participation in the republic, for the many; heroic deeds for the common good, for the few), and third, in post-mortem preferment.

If a great man dies without his glory being recognized, great shall be his reward. If another happens to reap glory on earth, his reward is double, mundane and heavenly. But they are both there when God takes up his jewels.

REVOLUTIONS

One can take it as a rule, that if there are new things in heaven, there will be new things on earth. A new hierarchy in the first will bring about a new one in the second. The rumblings of heavenly innovations grow thunderous as we approach the path of otherworldly glory and become more aware of God's partiality.

The present book concerns itself less with mutations in states than in ideas about states. Niccolò, we have discovered, makes major contributions to political and moral philosophy and to statecraft. There remain another few radical implications to be drawn, related more closely to the theological base of his political philosophy.

To signify turnovers and revolvings of times and circumstances Niccolò once in *The Prince* in Chapter XXVI uses the word *revolutions*: "if in so many revolutions of Italy . . . it seems that military virtue is spent." But when he wishes to signify more radical, specifically civic change, change greater than disorders and tumults, a turnover in the form of government, he may speak of "a mutation of state." Occasionally, he will use with similar significance the term *alteration* or *rebellion*, or both, as in "its laws have not been altered up to these times because . . . one cannot do so without the danger of a certain and dangerous rebellion." Most often he employs terms coming from the Latin *res novae*, new political things, as in "men take the courage to attempt new political things." In a similar sense he will use *innovation* (political) or *newness* (political): "among those who wished to make a newness in Florence." The closing line of the "Discursus" boasts of Niccolò's proposal for a constitution under which "no citizen of whatever rank either out of fear for himself or out of ambition would have to desire innovation."

The overarching superiority of a republic—'the free way of life', the only form of government that approaches the common good and the one that God therefore favors—makes any attempt at a mutation of state (when one does not have a republic) ethically just. The mechanics of plots and similar efforts at political innovation is another matter; the long chapter on conspiracies in the *Discourses* exposes their dangers. Niccolò is chiefly concerned there with keeping would-be innovators from taking foolish risks, whether out of stupidity, hatred, or exaltation. He quotes the great Roman historian Tacitus's resigned conclusion: "And that sentence of Cornelius Tacitus is golden that says: that men ought to honor the things of the past and obey those of the present, and must wish for good princes, and however [their prevailing princes] are made, tolerate them. And truly, whoever does otherwise, most of the time destroys himself and his country." But other chapters therein show different possibilities. There is no question where Niccolò's sympathies lie. He is for the man who rather than live in servitude, dies with sword in hand.

But first of all, confining oneself to ideas, one can point out, that heredity and hereditary claims to rule have no divine support. In the beginnings of civil life hereditary succession flew in like a bird of evil; good government is not possible until it is driven off. If among the hereditary princes a virtuous ruler appears, it is by accident. God and fortune favor the Medici house, true, but not every member of that house. God favored none of them because of the principle of blood, but because they had virtue. The Medici do not and cannot use the grounds of superior heredity; they are not natural or born princes.

The hereditary principle gives princes a claim of authority to rule and, when widely accepted, does make ruling easier. It happens to be a false principle and claim.

A leader's rise from a private person to a prince new is justifiable in part because it shows the irrelevance of hereditary claims, in part because it has a chance of moving the country toward a republic. The lives of princes, like those of popes, are short. In the "Discursus" our constitutionalist pre-sets his republic, looking ahead to the lamentable but unavoidable death of the existing Pope and the decline of the Medici house.

Chapter 5 above first examined some of the changes in church-state relations presaged by Niccolò's credo (as expressed in the "Discursus"), but at that point could do little more than remark its significance in going beyond church-state relations to implicate God Himself in matters of state. 'I believe', Niccolò there affirmed, 'that the greatest good that one can do and the most gratifying to God, is that which one does for one's country'.

Thus, second of all, not spiritual or pastoral activity but secular or civic political action pleases God most. The statement does not say that God holds the work of the bishop to be unimportant; it simply points out that God is partial to secular or political action. Princes of republics outstrip princes of the church.

Just as our political philosopher blends citizenry and congregation together in ceremony and education, so would he draw spiritual and temporal rulers together. Niccolò's hope, naturally, would be that the church reform itself and in its own language adapt to his doctrines. Until then, until the church can tell, as our maestro's students can, what seems to be real from what is really real, it will be of little help to the virtuous ruler.

The high priest may reprove the ruler for his acts; the ruler is under no obligation to take heed. Buoyed up by Niccolò's new moral philosophy he will be confident that his knowledge in the political world is superior. The position of the Vicar of Christ will be reduced to something like what Gregory the Great settled for in his letters to the emperor. While he may remonstrate with the ruler on spiritual matters, he does not try to secure obedience, but leaves him to risk damnation, to risk his soul by learning the way to the devil's house.

Already we have seen that Niccolò's moral philosophy lessens the need that political rulers might have for spiritual counselors in the mundane world. Moreover, by giving great men of state, saints, and scholars direct post-mortem access to God, Niccolò has removed their need for ecclesiastical keys to heaven. The great and good political leader, as friend of God, more beloved of God, ordained by God, or most gratifying to God, needs no introduction to the Deity. He may have God as his preceptor as did Moses, he may invoke God like David, please God like Solon and Lycurgus, Plato and Aristotle, be loved by God like Lorenzo the Magnificent, and be ordained by God as Moses and Scipio were and Caesar Borgia was not. After his death he rises to heaven.

The prince new or the one-man-alone reaches God independently. So do bishops, presumably. Niccolò's writings do not reveal a belief in or defense of a papal relation to God. Several of his theological pronouncements have a papal presence in the background, Leo X, in *The Prince*, for example, or the future Clement VII in the "Discursus." We might expect to find, therefore, a few nice remarks on papal benevolence, and we do find them. We might expect also to find some appreciation of the divine work of pope and bishop. Not at all. God has a definite preference for politics. These pronouncements reduce God's interest in ecclesiastical affairs and make the persons most worthy of his favor those who sweat for the common good. The implications of God's secular favoritism are profound.

In the mundane hierarchy to come the bishop is down, the prince new is up, the prince old is out, the people are in.

So far, for a politics joined to divine agency, a flexible politics where great leaders and virtuous people play complements, Niccolò's eschatology rests incomplete. His political philosophy envisions a virtuous people who maintain a republic—"where the people are the princes"—and rule themselves in a free way of life. In that country's beginnings are God-related leaders to found its religion, enact its fundamental laws, establish and protect its boundaries. Later, when the people are corrupted by vice and on the last downhill slide, these great leaders gather them up to restore the country's founding principles.

The great leaders have God for their friend, but what of the virtuous people? Their dignity, Chapter 8 above concluded, comes from the glory that belongs to them and that they attain by serving the common good. The virtuous citizen wins glory, too. "And not without reason does the voice of a people resemble that of God, so that it seems that by an occult virtue it foresees its [own] harm and its [own] good." A prince after all is no more virtuous than anyone else. When unregulated by law he becomes "ungrateful, changeable, and imprudent more than a people." The prince or one-man-alone may save or found a state but it takes the people to preserve it: 'people are so much superior in maintaining the things set in order that they without doubt reach the glory of those [princes] that set them in order'.

In this comprehensive, fervent statement Niccolò has left implicit the role of future citizens in the defense of their country. He wants to enlarge the size of the Grand Council of citizens. What will ensure its enlargement will be the inevitable increases in the size of the militia. For political reasons Niccolò in his recruiting has to limit his levy to the subjects, those in Florence's outlying territory, rather than to its citizens, but "you must understand this, that the best armies that there are, are those of armed populations," that is, formed of all citizens, "nor can [anything] stand in their way except armies similar to them." The larger the militia, the larger the Grand Council will grow, and so the entire body of citizens.

Virtuous citizens use free will in politics in the exaltation and defense of their country as God wishes it to be used, and the glory of great leaders and an ennobled country embraces them. And they too die. Shall not their reward also be great? Shall the only face they turn to God be one of fear?

This cannot be the answer for Niccolò, lover of republics, believer in *vox populi, vox dei*, upholder of the people's virtues against the claims of the old princes and oligarchs, and the comrade (once on the threshold of the tavern) of butcher, baker, candlestickmaker. His view of the deceptiveness of the world and the fuller portion of error and of political vices in sin diminishes the rigors of hell for the people, even for the multitude, and prepares a logic for universalism, the doctrine that all men will eventually be saved: ". . . the streets will be / of heaven open . . ." But in the matter of salvation he must, we judge, hold on to a word meaning *eventually*. The fear of God is what keeps evil-disposed men in that minimum of mutual trust essential to community. *The Prince* puts it succinctly: "no fear of God, no faith with men."

It would be rash to begin at this point to try to distinguish the varieties, stages, names, and routes of afterlife consignment of various divisions of the population, women, the militia, or the plebs. "The service is long . . ." Friar Timoteo warns us, and we must try to keep distinctions at a minimum.

THE MAPS

It may have been Aucassin's doing: the road signs seem to have been reversed. If hell is what the pulpit says it is, God's friends and Niccolò's will have to rise directly to heaven or to reach it somehow else. If it is an elect of noble spirits, then it must be Elysium or Cicero's heaven or a special retreat or garden on God's right hand, within paradise, and the fair company is already there.

That the road signs are confusing is not unheard of in the eschatological history of Greece and Rome. Take the tale that Socrates heard and believed, and Plato retold in the *Gorgias*. Pluto and the authorities from the Islands of the Blessed came to Zeus and said that souls were finding their way to the wrong places. (Shades of Belfagor!) Zeus said, "I shall put a stop to this." Then Plato changed the map in the *Republic*, in his myth of Er the Pamphylian, and relayed it to Cicero for the *Dream of Scipio*.

We cannot be sure of these maps. As final destination there is also Parnassus to think of. Raphael illustrates it for us in his painting of *The Council of the Gods*. It is Niccolò's exhorting the imitation of great men and connecting them with divinity that leads to thinking along these paths. Anyway, gathering his brigade up like this, 'to rise to heaven', has enabled us to see them almost all on parade. "Come on out here all of you," the playwright-captain commands the cast before the comedy begins, "so that the people might see you."

Most of the goodly company are the kinds of people with whom our political philosopher and playwright would like to eat, drink, and talk, to pasture with them on that food that once was his alone and for which he was born. When he makes dialogue or conversing the principal activity of the otherworld, when he asserts that the distinguishing feature of man is reason and that he prefers the use of reason to that of force or authority, he tugs on the tradition of Socrates in the gymnasium, Plato under the plane trees, Aristotle in the Stoa, and Epicurus in the garden, and draws it all the way up to Niccolò in the Orti. Lucian of Samosata, like Niccolò a designer of ritualistic journeys to the afterworld, wrote that Socrates as a special reward was given a place to himself in the outskirts of the Isles of the Blessed where he founded a Post-Mortem Academy.

What Niccolò believes in or would like to be true or what turns up in his writings as expressions of belief or of attempts to convince himself or convert others, is a new or reformed redemptive system, a true religion in which the master deity is God, the saints on earth are few, poor, and honest, the beloved of God are makers of states in deed and in writing, great legislators, founders of religion, warriors, and saviors of country who, their entering and exiting evil divinely comprehended, go postmortem by God's immediate and final judgment directly to the dwelling place of heroes. With them—wherever they go, he has cast his lot—is Niccolò Machiavegli, whose nature is bent to the 'common benefit of each [one]', a fascinating man, citizen, poet, political and moral philosopher, official and theorist of the state, historian, author of tragedy and comedies, teacher of the young and worthy, and a state-founder in writing.

The place jokingly called hell by those who know is a corner of paradise, a garden for God's elect, well presided over not by a fallen angel but by Pluto the Rich One, the brother of Zeus and Poseidon, the Giver of Wealth, possessor of a beautiful wife—"woman beautiful above any woman in the world"—traveller to earth and back, and benign spirit of an academy, a garden of delights, a place for the society and conversation of liberal spirits.

As for Niccolò, he laughs and says that on earth his friends have composed an epitaph for him.

Niccolò Machiavegli

for love of country

"pissed in many a snow"

Notes

I have translated all texts from the following editions: For *The Prince*, the *Discourses*, the *Art of War*, and minor political writings: Sergio Bertelli's editions of *Il Principe e Discorsi sopra la prima deca di Tito Livio* (Milan: Feltrinelli, 1961), and *Arte della guerra e scritti politici minori* (Milan: Feltrinelli, 1961). For the *Florentine Histories*, the letters, and the theater and literary writings: Franco Gaeta's editions of the *Istorie fiorentine* (Milan: Feltrinelli, 1962), *Lettere* (Milan: Feltrinelli, 1961), *Lettere* (Turin: Unione Tipografico-Editrice Torinese, 1984), and *Il Teatro e tutti gli scritti letterari* (Milan: Feltrinelli, 1965). For official correspondence from 1498 to 1504: Fredi Chiappelli's four volumes of *Legazioni, commissarie, scritti di governo* (Bari: Gius, Laterza & Figli, 1971–1985), and for official correspondence from 1505 to 1527: volumes II and III of Sergio Bertelli's three volumes of *Legazioni e commissarie* (Milan: Feltrinelli, 1964). Occasional translations from other editions are separately identified.

In the Notes, when numbers appear *before* the title of a work, they refer to the book or chapter number of the work itself; references to correspondence carry addressee and date; plays show act and scene numbers; poetry shows chapter and line numbers where pertinent. These indications in each case are followed by the volume and page numbers of the Bertelli, Gaeta, or Chiappelli editions, italicized and numbered thus: *1* equals *Il Principe e Discorsi*, *2* equals *Arte della querra*, *3* equals *Istorie fiorentine*, *4* equals *Il Teatro*, *5* equals *Lettere*, *5a* equals *Lettere* 1984, *6–9* equals the four Chiappelli volumes above of *Legazioni*, and *10–11* equals the two Bertelli volumes of *Legazioni*, numbered consecutively.

Other abbreviations used in the Notes are as follows:

P	*Il Principe*
D	*Discorsi sopra la prima deca di Tito Livio*
Arte	*Arte della guerra*
IF	*Istorie fiorentine*
L	Lettere
M	*La Mandragola*
"Discursus"	"Discursus florentinarum rerum post mortem iunieris Laurentii Medices"
"Esortaz"	"Esortazione alla penitenza"
Vita	*La Vita di Castruccio Castracani da Lucca*

2 e poi, chi vede il diavolo daddovero, / lo vede con meno corna e manco nero ("De' romiti" *4.335*)

CHAPTER I Irreverent and on the Go

3 La predica io non la udii, perché io non uso simili pratiche (L to Francesco
   Vettori, Dec. 19, 1513: *5.309*)

   Nicomaco: E' non si può andare ad altri che a frate Timoteo, che è nostro
   confessoro di casa ed è uno santarello, ed ha già fatto qualche miracolo.
   Sofronia: Quale?
   Nicomaco: Come, quale? Non sai tu che per le sue orazioni monna Lucrezia di messer Nicia Calfucci che era sterile ingravidò?
   Sofronia: Gran miracolo, un frate ingravidare una donna! Miracolo sarebbe se una monaca la facessi ingravidare ella! (2.3 *Clizia 4.131*)

4 sotto il mantello della religione (L to Francesco Guicciardini, May 17, 1521:
   5.403)

   de' pochi, per dare principio a quello governo con terrore ch'eglino
   avieno cominciato con forza, confinorono messer Girolamo Machiavelli (7.3 *IF 3.455*)

   andando circuendo Italia, sollevando i principi contro alla patria . . . condotto a Firenze fu morto in carcere (7.3 *IF 3.456*)

5 un dottore / che 'mparò in sul Buezio legge assai (Prologo *M 4.56*)

6 Tito Livio nostro (1.58 *D 1.261*)
   istorico nostro (1.58 *D 1.265*)

   gl'importa assai che un giovanetto da' teneri anni cominci a sentire dire
   bene o male d'una cosa, perché conviene di necessità ne faccia impres-
   sione, e da quella poi regoli il modo del procedere in tutti i tempi della
   sua vita (3.46 *D 1.501*)

   soleva essere uno uomo, grave, resoluto, rispettivo. Dispensava el tempo
   suo onorevolmente. E' si levava la mattina di buon'ora, udiva la sua
   messa, provedeva al vitto del giorno: di poi s'egli aveva faccenda in
   piazza, in mercato a' magistrati, e' la faceva, quando che no, o e' si
   riduceva con qualche cittadino tra ragionamenti onorevoli [o] e' si ri-
   tirava in casa nello scrittoio, dove ragguagliava sue scritture, riordinava
   suoi conti: dipoi piacevolmente con la sua brigata desinava, e desinato
   ragionava con el figliuolo, ammunivalo, davagli a conoscere gli uomini,
   e con qualche esemplo antico e moderno gl'insegnava vivere (2.4 *Clizia
   4.132*)

7 venuta la sera, sempre l'Avemaria lo trovava in casa: stavasi un poco con
   esso noi al fuoco s'egli era di verno, dipoi se n'entrava nello scrittoio a
   rivedere le faccende sue: alle tre ore si cenava allegramente. Questo ordine della sua vita era un esempio a tutti gli altri di casa, e ciascuno si
   vergognava non lo imitare, e così andavano le cose ordinate e liete. Ma
   dapoi che gli entrò questa fantasia di costei . . . (2.4 *Clizia 4.133*)

   Nicomaco: Ove si va?
   Sofronia: Alla messa.

Nicomaco: Ed è pur carnesciale: pensa quel che tu farai di quaresima! (2.3 *Clizia 4.128*)

né dell'arte della seta, né dell'arte della lana, né de' guadagni né delle perdite (L to Francesco Vettori, April 9, 1513: *5.239*)

quanto alla mercanzia infelicissimo: . . . onde che quella . . . lasciate da parte le mercantili industrie, alle possessioni come piú stabili e piú ferme ricchezze si volse (8.36 *IF 3.574*)

9 Lorenzo di Filippo Strozzi Patrizio Fiorentino (Proemio *Arte 2.325*)

con brevità passarla (8.1 *IF 3.508*)

Erano i Pazzi in Firenze per ricchezza e nobilità allora di tutte l'altre famiglie fiorentine splendidissimi (8.2 *IF 3.510*)

si ristrinse in modo lo stato tutto a' Medici; i quali tanta autorità presono che quelli che ne erano mal contenti conveniva o con pazienza quel modo del vivere comportassero o, se pure lo volessero spegnere, per via di congiure e secretamente di farlo tentassero (8.1 *IF 3.508*)

Giuliano de' Medici molte volte con Lorenzo suo fratello si dolfe, dicendo come e' dubitava che, per volere delle cose troppo, che le non si perdessero tutte (8.2 *IF 3.511*)

caldo di gioventú e di potenza (8.3 *IF 3.511*)

conclusono che non fusse da differire il mandarla ad effetto: perché gli era impossibile, sendo nota a tanti, che la non si scoprisse. E perciò deliberorono nella chiesa cattedrale di Santa Reparata ammazzargli, dove sendo il cardinale, i duoi frategli secondo la consuetudine converrebbono" (8.5 *IF 3.516*)

non gli basterebbe mai l'animo commettere tanto eccesso in chiesa e accompagnare il tradimento con il sacrilegio. Il che fu il principio della rovina della impresa loro (8.5 *IF 3.517*)

10 quando si comunicava il sacerdote che nel tempio la principale messa celebrava (8.5 *IF 3.517*)

Sendo adunque preparati gli ucciditori, quelli accanto a Lorenzo dove, per la moltitudine che nel tempio era, facilmente e sanza sospetto potevono stare, e quegli altri insieme con Giuliano, venne l'ora destinata (8.6 *IF 3.518*)

dopo pochi passi cadde in terra (8.6 *IF 3.518*)

obcecato da quel furore (8.6 *IF 3.518*)

con l'arme sua si difese (8.6 *IF 3.518*)

la maggior parte de' quali nella cancelleria per sé medesimi si rinchiusono, perché in modo era la porta di quella congegnata che serrandosi non si poteva se non con lo aiuto della chiave, cosí di dentro come di fuora, aprire (8.7 *IF 3.520*)

tutta la città era in arme. . . . per tutta la città si gridava il nome de' Medici, e le membra de' morti, o sopra le punte delle armi fitte o per la città strascinate si vedevano; e ciascheduno con parole piene d'ira e con fatti pieni di crudeltà i Pazzi perseguiva. Già erano le loro case dal popolo occupate, e Francesco cosí ignudo fu di casa tratto, e al Palagio condotto, fu a canto all'arcivescovo e agli altri appiccato (8.9 *IF 3.522*)

Non fu cittadino che armato o disarmato non andasse alle case di Lorenzo in quella necessità, e ciascheduno sé e le sustanze sue gli offeriva (8.9 *IF 3.522*)

11 E perché questo caso non mancasse di alcuno estraordinario esempio, fu messer Iacopo prima nella sepultura de' suoi maggiori sepulto, di poi, di quivi come scomunicato tratto, fu lungo le mura della città sotterrato; e di quindi ancora cavato, per il capestro con il quale era stato morto, fu per tutta la città ignudo strascinato, e da poi che in terra non aveva trovato luogo alla sua sepultura, fu da quelli medesimi che strascinato l'avevono, nel fiume d'Arno che allora aveva le sue acque altissime gittato. Esempio veramente grandissimo di fortuna, vedere uno uomo da tante ricchezze e da sí felicissimo stato, in tanta infelicità, con tanta rovina e con tale vilipendio cadere! (8.9 *IF 3.523*)

13 gravi e tumultuosi accidenti . . . tanti terribili che pareva che il tempio rovinasse (8.6 *IF 3.519*)

uno figliuolo naturale il quale, dopo a pochi mesi che fu morto, nacque e fu chiamato Giulio; il quale fu di quella virtú e fortuna ripieno che in questi presenti tempi tutto il mondo cognosce e che da noi, quando alle presenti cose perverremo, concedendone Iddio vita, sarà largamente dimostro (8.9 *IF 3.524*)

14 i soldati del re di preda e i Fiorentini di spavento (8.16 *IF 3.537*)

nel voltare uno cavallo o la testa o la groppa dava la perdita o la vittoria (8.16 *IF 3.537*)

tutti i cittadini per fuggire la morte per le loro ville si erano ritirati (8.16 *IF 3.537*)

subito, come meglio poterono, non solamente con i figliuoli e robe loro, ma con i loro lavoratori a Firenze corsono (8.16 *IF 3.537*)

in una felicità grandissima (8.36 *IF 3.573*)

tutti i [suoi] cittadini e tutti i principi di Italia (8.36 *IF 3.577*)

pigliare la Italia col gesso (12 *P 1.54*)

16 insolenzie barbare (26 *P 1.102*)

primo motor (*Decennale Primo 4.238*)

le genti barbariche (*Decennale Primo 4.236*)

corsa da Carlo, predata da Luigi, sforzata da Ferrando e vituperata da' Svizzeri (12 *P 1.57*)

mille / e quattrocen novanta quattro . . . / dal tempo che Iesú le nostre ville / vicitò prima e col sangue che perse / estinse le diaboliche faville (*Decennale Primo 4.236*)

ruinò (6 *P 1.32*)

18 Segretario, io non ho nimicizia né con el Papa, né con alcuno (Legation of July 18, 1510: *11.1242*)

20 mille rimedi di mille ragioni (1 *Asino 4.270*)

ch'in ogni luogo per la via correva / e d' ogni tempo sanza alcun rispetto (1 *Asino 4.270*)

Ed ei gli fe' cento profumi al naso / trassegli sangue de la testa, e poi / gli parve aver il correr dissuaso (1 *Asino 4.271*)

21 Ma giunto un dí nella via de' Martelli, / onde puossi la via Larga vedere, / cominciaro arricciarglisi i capelli (1 *Asino 4.271*)

Qui non mi terrà Cristo e corse via (1 *Asino 4.271*)

abitazioni . . . opere e azioni . . . regie (7.5 *IF 3.459*)

nuove strade da empiersi di nuovi edifizi (8.36 *IF 3.575*)

la mente nostra (1 *Asino 4.271*)

abito o natura (1 *Asino 4.271*)

tra l'uno e l'altro corno / il sol fiammeggia del celeste bue (2 *Asino 4.273*)

corse sempre mentre visse (1 *Asino 4.271*)

trovare modi ed ordini nuovi (1. Proemio *D 1.123*)

non altrimenti periculoso (1. Proemio *D 1.123*)

cercare acque e terre incognite (1. Proemio *D 1.123*)

26 entro nelle antique corti degli antiqui huomini, dove, da loro ricevuto amorevolmente, mi pasco di quel cibo, che solum è mio, et che io nacqui per lui; dove io non mi vergogno parlare con loro, et domandarli della ragione delle loro actioni; et quelli per loro humanità mi rispondono; et non sento per quattro hore di tempo alcuna noia, sdimenticho ogni affanno, non temo la povertà, non mi sbigottisce la morte: tucto mi trasferisco in loro (L to Francesco Vettori, Dec. 10, 1513: *5.304*)

27 composto uno opuscolo (L to Francesco Vettori, Dec. 10, 1513: *5.304*)

nostro trattato "De Principe" (3.42 *D 1.496*)

el componitor (Prologo *M 4.57*)

lo autore (Prologo *Clizia 4.117*)

perch'altrove non have / dove voltare el viso: / che gli è stato interciso / monstrar con altre imprese altra virtue, / non sendo premio alle fatiche sue (Prologo *M 4.57*)

delle città grandi (L to Francesco Guicciardini, May 18, 1521: *5.410*)

E se questa materia non è degna, / per esser pur leggieri, / d'un uom che voglia parer saggio e grave, / scusatelo con questo, che s'ingegna / con questi van pensieri / far el suo tristo tempo piú suave (Prologo *M 4.57*)

28 una grande e continua malignità di fortuna (Lettera *P 1.14*)

CHAPTER 2 God's Friends and Machiavelli's

30 né fu a loro Dio piú amico che a voi (26 *P 1.103*)

Exhortatio ad capessendam Italiam in libertamque a barbaris vendicandam (26 *P 1.101*)

La quale opera io non ho ornata né ripiena di clausole ample, o di parole ampullose e magnifiche, o di qualunque altro lenocinio o ornamento estrinseco (*P 1.13*) io ho voluto, o che veruna cosa la onori, o che solamente la varietà della materia e la gravità del subietto la facci grata (*P 1.14*)

31 Oh Dio, che sarà poi? (4.7 *Clizia 4.154*)

Dio m'aiuti (3.11 *M 4.90*)

Mal che Dio li dia! (3.5 *M 4.84*)

Oh Dio, questa vecchiaia . . . ! (2.1 *Clizia 4.127*)

per l'amor di Dio! (5.2 *Clizia 4.161*)

al presente in quale lei possa piú sperare . . . nella illustre casa vostra, quale con la sua fortuna e virtú, favorita da Dio e dalla Chiesia, della quale è ora principe (26 *P 1.102*)

32 io lo indirizzo alla M.tia di Giuliano (L to Francesco Vettori, Dec. 10, 1513: *5.304*)

de' piú nobili di questa città . . . armati a palazzo . . . per sforzare il gonfaloniere a partire, furno da qualche cittadino persuasi a non fare alcuna violenzia, ma lasciarlo partire d'accordo. E cosí il gonfaloniere accompagnato da loro medesimi se ne tornò a casa (L to a noblewoman, post Sept. 16, 1512: *5.226*)

33 li amici di V.S. Ill.ma et patroni miei (L to a noblewoman, post Sept. 16, 1512: *5.222*)

spera non vivere meno honorata con l'aiuto loro che si vivesse ne' tempi passati, quando la felicissima memoria del magnifico Lorenzo loro padre governava (L to a noblewoman, post Sept. 16, 1512: *5.228*)

34 Io ho, Giuliano, in gamba un paio di geti / con sei tratti di fune in su le spalle: / l'altre miserie mie no vo' contalle, / poiché cosí si trattano e poeti! (1. 1–4 "A Giuliano di Lorenzo de' Medici" *4.362*)

di quindici dí . . . mi [è] in simili ozi concesso (Lettera *Decennali*, *4.235*)

Menon pidocchi queste parieti / bolsi spaccati che paion farfalle, / né fu mai tanto puzzo in Roncisvalle / o in Sardigna fra quegli alboreti, / quanto nel mio sí delicato ostello; / con un romor che proprio par che 'n terra / fulgori giove e tutto Mongibello. / L'un si incatena e l'altro si disferra / con batter toppe, chiavi e chiavistello: / un altro grida è troppo alto da terra! (1. 5–14 "A Giuliano di Lorenzo de' Medici" *4.362*)

36 E di nuovo vi replico che, sanza forze, le città non si mantengono ("Parole da dirle sopra la provisione del danaio, fatto un poco di proemio e di scusa" *2.58*)

timore è tenuto da una paura di pena che non ti abbandona mai (17 *P 1.70*)

voglio che habbiate di questi miei affanni questo piacere, che gli ho portati tanto francamente, che io stesso me ne voglio bene (L to Francesco Vettori, March 18, 1513: *5.234*)

38 Questa vostra lettera mi ha piú sbigottito che la fune (L to Francesco Vettori, April 9, 1513: *5.239*)

Dubiterei che alla tornata mia io non credessi non scavalcare a casa, et scavalcassi nel Bargiello. . . . Pregovi mi solviate questa paura, et poi verró infra el tempo detto a trovarvi a ogni modo (L to Francesco Vettori, Dec. 10, 1513: *5.305*)

Quel che mi fe' piú guerra / fu che dormendo presso a la aurora / cantando sentii dire: "per voi s'ora (1. 15–17 "A Giuliano di Lorenzo de' Medici" *4.362*)

è piuttosto miracolo che io sia vivo, perché mi è suto tolto l'uffitio, et sono stato per perdere la vita (L to Giovanni Vernacci, June 26, 1513: *5.262*)

Or vadin in buon ora; / purché vostra pietà ver me si voglia, / buon padre, e questi rei lacciuol ne scioglia (1. 18–20 "A Giuliano di Lorenzo de' Medici" *4.363*)

39 In questa notte, pregando le Muse / che con lor dolce cetra e dolci carmi / dovesser visitar, per consolarmi, / Vostra Magnificenzia e far mie scuse, / una comparse a me che mi confuse / dicendo: "Chi se' tu ch'osi chiamarmi?" / Dissigli il nome, e lei per straziarmi / mi batté al volto e la bocca mi chiuse / dicendo: "Niccolò non se' . . . / poiche ha' legato le gambe e i talloni, / e sta'ci incatenato come un pazzo." / Io gli volevo dir le mie ragioni: / lei mi rispose e disse: "Va al barlazzo / con quella tua commedia in guazzeroni." / Dátegli testimoni, / Magnifico Giulian, per l'alto Iddio, / come io non sono il Dazzo ma sono io (2. "A Giuliano di Lorenzo de' Medici" *4.363*)

Lasci l'opinioni / vostra Magnificenzia, e palpi e tocchi / e giudichi a le mani e non agli occhi (3. 15–17, "A Giuliano di Lorenzo de' Medici" *4.364*)

spiccon pur di me di buon bocconi (3. 14, "A Giuliano di Lorenzo de' Medici" *4.364*)

La M.tia di Giuliano verrà costà, et troverretela volta naturalmente a farmi piacere (L to Francesco Vettori, April 16, 1513: *5.244*)

40 io sono uscito di prigione con la letizia universale di questa città (L to Francesco Vettori, March 13, 1513: *5.232*)

darlo o non lo dare; et sendo ben darlo, se gli era bene che io lo portassi, o che io ve lo mandassi. El non lo dare mi faceva dubitare che da Giuliano e' non fussi, non ch'altro, letto, e che questo Ardinghelli si facessi honore di questa ultima mia faticha. El darlo mi faceva la necessità che mi caccia, perché io mi logoro, et lungo tempo non posso star cosí che io non diventi per povertà contennendo . . . harei che questi signori Medici mi cominciassino adoperare, se dovessino cominciare a farmi voltolare un sasso (L to Francesco Vettori, Dec. 10, 1513: *5.305*)

42 Io non voglio lasciare indreto di darvi la notizia del modo del procedere del magnifico Lorenzo, che è suto fino a qui di qualità, che egli ha ripieno di buona speranza tutta questa città; et pare che ciascuno cominci a riconoscere in lui la felice memoria del suo avolo. Perché sua M. Tia è sollecita alle faccende, liberale et grato nell'audienzia, tardo et grave nella risposta. Il modo del suo conversare è di sorta . . . che non vi si conosce dentro superbia; né si mescola in modo che per troppa familiarità generi poca reputazione. Con i giovani suoi eguali tiene tale stile, che né gli aliena da sé, né anche dà loro animo di fare alcuna gio-

vanile insolenza. Fassi insomma et amare et riverire, piuttosto che temere; . . . assai magnificenzia et liberalità, nondimeno non si parte della vita civile (L to Francesco Vettori, Feb.–March, 1514: *5.331*)

mi è parso descrivervelo, perché col testimonio mio ne prendiate quel piacere che ne prendiamo tutti noi altri . . . et possiate, quando ne abbiate occasione, farne fede per mia parte alla S.tà di N.S. (L to Francesco Vettori, Feb.–March, 1514: *5.331*)

fratelli et nipoti senza stato (L to Francesco Vettori, June 20, 1513: *5.260*)

Desiderando io adunque offerirmi alla vostra Magnificenzia con qualche testimone della servitú mia verso di quella, non ho trovato intra la mia suppellettile cosa, quale io abbia piú cara, o tanto esistimi, quanto la cognizione delle azioni delli uomini grandi . . . le quali avendo io . . . in uno piccolo volume ridotte, mando alla Magnificenzia vostra. . . . Pigli adunque vostra Magnificenzia questo piccolo dono con quello animo che io lo mando; il quale se da quella fia diligentemente considerato e letto, vi conoscerà drento uno estremo mio desiderio, che Lei pervenga a quella grandezza che la fortuna e le altre sue qualitè li promettano. E, se vostra Magnificenzia dallo apice della sua altezza qualche volta volgerà li occhi in questi luoghi bassi, conoscerà quanto io indegnamente sopporti una grande e continua malignità di fortuna (*P 1.13–14*)

43 sogliono sempre le loro opere a qualche principe indirizzare (D 1.121)

Passiamo al Papa e al duca suo . . . ogni uomo sa la natura e l'appetito loro quale e' sia ("Parole" *2.60*)

aspiri allo imperio di Toscana, come piú propinquo ed atto a farne un regno con gli stati che tiene ("Del modo di trattare i popoli della Valdichiana ribellati" *2.75*)

quando nel principio la fosse governata bene. Et a volerla governare bene, bisogna intendere bene la qualità del subbiecto. Questi stati nuovi, occupati da un signore nuovo, hanno . . . infinite difficultà . . . Debbe pertanto chi ne diventa principe pensare di farne un medesimo corpo . . . l'opere del quale io imiterei sempre quando io fossi principe nuovo (L to Francesco Vettori, Jan. 31, 1515: *5.374–375*)

44 signoria . . . bella et forte (L to Francesco Vettori, Jan. 31, 1515: *5.374*)

Io ne parlai seco; piacquegli, et penserà d'aiutarsene (L to Francesco Vettori, Jan. 31, 1515: *5.375*)

Tenetemi, se è possibile, in memoria di N.S. (L to Francesco Vettori, March 13, 1513: *5.232*)

45 ella è passata (L to Francesco Vettori, March 13, 1513: *5.232*)

Proemio di Niccolò Machiavegli, cittadino e segretario fiorentino sopr' al libro dell'arte della guerra (Proemio *Arte 2.325*)

quondam segretario (L to Francesco Vettori, April 9, 1513: *5.240*)

perché un po' del pover Machiavello / Vostra Magnificenzia si ricordi (3.3–4 "A Giuliano di Lorenzo de' Medici" *4.364*)

46 tutto quello che mi avanza di vita riconoscerlo dal magnifico Giuliano e
da Pagolo vostro (L to Francesco Vettori, March 18, 1513: *5.234*)

e cosí andiamo . . . godendoci questo resto della vita, che me la pare so-
gnare (L to Francesco Vettori, March 18, 1513: *5.236*)

riconosco tutto quello che mi è restato (L to Francesco Vettori, April 16,
1513: *5.244*)

post res perditas (Marginalia, foglio di coperta "La cagione
dell'ordinanza," *2.91*)

io non posso credere che essendo maneggiato il caso mio con qualche
destrezza, che non mi riesca essere adoperato a qualche cosa, se non per
conto di Firenze, almeno per conto di Roma e del pontificato; nel qual
caso io doverrei essere meno sospetto . . . se la S.tà di Nostro Signore
cominciasse a adoperarmi (L to Francesco Vettori, April 16, 1513: *5.244*)

però se alcuna volta io rido o canto, / Follo perché non ho se non quest-
'una / Via da sfogare il mio acerbo pianto (L to Francesco Vettori, April
16, 1513: *5.243*)

Starommi dunque cosí tra' miei pidocchi, senza trovare huomo che della
servitú mia si ricordi, o che creda che io possa essere buono a nulla. Ma
egli è impossibile che io possa stare molto cosí . . . et veggo . . . che
sarò un dí forzato ad uscirmi di casa, et pormi per ripetitore o cancel-
liere di un connestabole, quando io non possa altro, o ficcarmi in
qualche terra deserta ad insegnare leggere a' fanciulli, et lasciar qua la
mia brigata, che facci conto che io sia morto; la quale farà molto meglio
senza me, perché io le sono di spesa . . . Io non vi scrivo questo, perché
io voglia che voi pigliate per me o disagio o briga, ma solo per sfogar-
mene, et per non vi scrivere piú di questa materia, come odiosa quanto
ella può (L to Francesco Vettori, June 10, 1514: *5.343*)

47 non credo mai piú potere far bene né a me né ad altri (L to Francesco
Vettori, Dec. 20, 1514: *5.368*)

i tempi, i quali sono stati e sono di sorte che mi hanno fatto sdimenticare
di me medesimo (L to Giovanni Vernacci, Aug. 18, 1515: *5.376*)

la fortuna non mi ha lasciato altro che i parenti et gli amici (L to Giovanni
Vernacci, Nov. 19, 1515: *5.377*)

quanto ad me, io sono diventato inutile ad me, a' parenti et alli amici (L
to Giovanni Vernacci, Nov. 19, 1515: *5.378*)

Ma sendomi io ridotto a stare in villa per le adversità che io ho havute et
ho, sto qualche volta un mese che io non mi ricordo di me (L to Giovanni Vernacci, June 8, 1517: *5.379–380*)

Scusimi lo essere io alieno con l'animo da tutte queste pratiche . . . ridutto
in villa (L to Francesco Vettori, April 29, 1513: *5.516*)

48 Et benché io sia botato non pensare piú ad cose di stato né ragionarne,
come ne fa fede l'essere io venuto in villa, et havere fuggito la conversazione, non di manco, per rispondere alle domande vostre, io sono
forzato rompere ogni boto (L to Francesco Vettori, April 29, 1513: *5.250*)

Ho lasciato dunque i pensieri delle cose grandi et gravi; non mi diletta piú leggere le cose antiche, né ragionare delle moderne . . . io non ci ho mai trovato se non danno, et in queste sempre bene et piacere. Valete (L to Francesco Vettori, Aug. 3, 1514: *5.347*)

Io ho letto a questi dí Orlando Furioso dello Ariosto, et veramente il poema è bello tutto, et in di molti luoghi è mirabile. Se si truova costí, raccomandatemi a lui, et ditegli che io mi dolgo solo che, avendo ricordato tanti poeti, che m'habbi lasciato indietro come un cazzo, et ch'egli ha fatto a me quello in sul suo Orlando, che io non farò a lui in sul mio Asino. (L to Lodovico Alamanni, Dec. 17, 1517: *5.383*)

Io canterò l'italiche fatiche (*Decennale Primo 4.236*)
un de' suoi primi membri (Lettera *Decennale Primo 4.235*)

49 Spero non incorrere piú, sí perché sarò piú cauto, sí perché i tempi saranno piú liberali, et non tanto sospettosi (L to Francesco Vettori, March 13, 1513: *5.232*)

50 se vi piacque mai alcuno mio ghiribizo, questo non vi doverrebe dispiacere; et a un principe, et maxime a un principe nuovo, doverrebbe essere accetto. (L to Francesco Vettori, Dec. 10, 1513: *5.304*)

51 amato dagli dii (5. Scena Ultima *Andria 4.51*)

52 piú amato dal cielo (2.Proemio *D 1.274*)
Fu dalla fortuna e da Dio sommamente amato (8.36 *IF 3.575*)
non vorrà essere de' malvagi uomini amico (6.20 *IF 3.419*)
piú suo amico . . . maggiore giustizia (6.21 *IF 3.420*)

53 parranno non discrepanti da quelli di Moisé (6 *P 1.31*)
non gli fu necessario dell'autorità di Dio (1.11 *D 1.161*)

54 Voglio ancora ridurre a memoria una figura del Testamento Vecchio (13 *P 1.60*)
legge la Bibbia sensatamente (3.30 *D 1.468*)
non di manco furono uomini (26 *P 1.102*)

56 [Il] popolo di Firenze . . . da frate Girolamo Savonarola fu persuaso che parlava con Dio. Io non voglio giudicare s'egli era vero o no, perché d'uno tanto uomo se ne debbe parlare con riverenza: ma io dico bene che infiniti lo credevono (1.11 *D 1.163*)
PADRE DELLA PATRIA (7.6 *IF 3.463*)
debbe essere ammirato solum per quella grazia che lo faceva degno di parlare con Dio (6 *P 1.31*)
estraordinarii sanza esemplo, condotti da Dio: el mare s'è aperto; una nube vi ha scòrto el cammino; la pietra ha versato acqua; qui è piovuto la manna (26 *P 1.103*)

CHAPTER 3 The Heavenly Host

58 Sta' bene con Cristo e fatti beffe de' santi! (3.6 *Clizia 4.143*)
ebbe sí gran precettore (6 *P 1.31*)

quella sua corte sanza rispetto della Chiesa o di Dio, tutta di carne si cibava (7.28 *IF 3.495*)

tutta i miseri sogliono sperare (1.5 *IF 3.82*)

timore di Dio, non fede con li uomini (12 *P 1.53*)

59 Dell'Ambizione ("Ambiz."*4.319*)

Di poco aveva Dio fatto le stelle, / il ciel, la luce, gli elementi e l'uomo / dominator di tante cose belle ("Ambiz." *4.319*)

Esortazione alla penitenza ("Esortaz." *4.207*)

onorandi padri e maggiori frategli ("Esortaz." *4.209*)

i beneficii che noi abbiamo ricevuti da Dio ("Esortaz." *4.210*)

Non vedete voi quanta fatica dura il sole per farci parte della sua luce, per fare vivere con la sua potenza e noi e quelle cose che da Dio sono state create per noi? Adunque ogni cosa è creata per onore e bene dello uomo, e l'uomo è solo creato per bene e onore d'Iddio ("Esortaz." *4.210*)

Allocuzione fatta ad un magistrato ("Allocuz." *2.131*)

Giustizia ("Allocuz." *2.135*)

Questa sola virtú è quella che infra tutte le altre piace a Dio ("Allocuz." *2.136*)

60 quanto Iddio ama la giustizia e la pietà ("Allocuz." *2.136*)

tornerà ad abitare in questa città ("Allocuz." *2.137*)

o sacro Apollo ("Capitolo Pastorale" *4.351*)

o Giove dio ("Capitolo Pastorale" *4.351*)

Sottili, arcati e neri erano i cigli, / perch'a plasmargli fur tutti gli dei, / tutti i celesti e superni consigli. / . . . Io non so già chi quella bocca fesse: / se Giove con sua man non la fece egli (4 *Asino 4.283–284*)

che non la riducerebbe Christo (L to Bartolomeo Cavalcanti, Oct. 6, 1526: *5.491*)

li pose per la soma / che meritava un rebellante a Cristo (*Decennale Primo 4.255*)

lo esemplo della vita di Cristo (3.1 *D 1.383*)

61 Sopra questa è fondata la fede di Cristo ("Esortaz." *4.211*)

el piú onorato santo che sia in Francia (4.10 *M 4.102*)

Dio m'aiuti e la Nostra Donna (3.11 *M 4.90*)

né quello potette altro fare che, cadendo, una volta sola il nome della Nostra Donna in suo aiuto chiamare (7.34 *IF 3.50*)

intervennono molti segni della sua futura morte (7.34 *IF 3.505*)

Priega Iddio ch' . . . (2.5 *Clizia 4.134*)

Iddio vi salvi (Prologo *M 4.56*)

O Dio, fa' questo miracolo . . . (3.7 *Clizia 4.145*)

Al nome di Dio (2.3 *Clizia 4.131*)

62 O vecchio impazzato! Vuole che Dio tenga le mane a queste sue disonestà! (3.6 *Clizia 4.143–144*)

Christo ti guardi (L to Giovanni Vernacci, Jan. 5, 1518: *5.385*)

Al nome di Dio (L to Giovanni Vernacci, April 15, 1520: *5.386*)

Christo vi guardi da dovere (L to Francesco del Nero, Aug. 31, 1523: *5.416*)

che Idio ti conduca (L to Giovanni Vernacci, Oct. 9, 1519: *5a.503*)

Ihesus Maria (L to Francesco Vettori, April 29, 1513: *5.250*)

Il nostro arcivescovo a questa hora debbe esser morto; che Iddio habbi l'anima sua et di tutti e' sua (L to Francesco Vettori, April 9, 1513: *5.240*)

Christo vi guardi tutti (L to Guido Machiavelli, April 2, 1527: 5.500)

per grazia di Dio, ella è passata (L to Francesco Vettori, March 13, 1513: *5.232*)

priego Iddio . . . di potervene essere grato, perché io posso dire che tutto quello che mi avanza di vita . . . (L to Francesco Vettori, March 18, 1513: *5.234*)

et sono stato per perdere la vita, la quale Iddio et la innocentia mia mi ha salvata (L to Giovanni Vernacci, June 26, 1513: *5.262–263*)

63 io sto bene del corpo, ma di tucte l'altre cose male. Et non mi resta altra speranza che Idio che mi aiuti, et in fondo ad qui non mi ha abandonato ad fatto (L to Giovanni Vernacci, Aug. 4, 1513: *5.271*)

il savio comandasse alle stelle et a' fati. . . . di questi savi non si truova (L to Giovan Battista Soderini c. Sept. 13–21, 1506: *5a.244*)

E per non mi discostare da casa nel provare questo, sa ciascuna quanto da frate Girolamo Savonerola fusse predetta innanzi la venuta del re Carlo VIII di Francia in Italia (1.56 D *1.259*)

E' si trova in questa nostra città, calamita di tutti i ciurmatori del mondo, un frate di S. Francesco, che è mezzo romito, el quale, per haver piú credito nel predicare fa professione di profeta; et hier mattina in Santa Croce, dove lui predica, dixe multa magna et mirabilia. Che avanti che passassi molto tempo, in modo che chi ha novanta anni lo potrà vedere, sarà un papa iniusto, creato contro ad un papa iusto, et harà seco falsi profeti, et farà cardinali et dividerà la Chiesia. Item, che il re di Francia si haveva ad nichilare, et uno della casa di Raona ad predominare Italia. La città nostra aveva a ire a fuoco et a sacco, le chiese sarebbono abbandonate et ruinate, i preti dispersi, et tre anni si haveva a stare senza divino offitio. Moria sarebbe et fame grandissima; nella città non haveva a rimanere dieci huomini, nelle ville non harebbe a rimanere dua. Era stato diciotto anni un diavolo in uno corpo umano, et detto messa. Che bene dua milioni di diavoli erano scatenati per essere ministri della sopraddetta cosa, et che egli entravano in di molti corpi che morivano, e non lasciavano putrefare quel corpo, accioché falsi propheti et religiosi potessono fare risuscitare morti et essere creduti (L to Francesco Vettori, Dec. 19, 1513: *5.308–309*)

64 ma la ho sentita recitare cosí da tutto Firenze" (L to Francesco Vettori, Dec. 19, 1513: *5.309*)

praticai con un profeta che disse con testimoni havere predetto la fuga del papa, et la vanità della inpresa, et di nuovo dice non essere passati tutti li cattivi tempi, ne' quali il papa et noi patireno assai (L to Francesco Guicciardini, Nov. 5, 1526: *5.496*)

Avevano gli antichi capitani una molestia della quale i presenti ne sono quasi liberi, la quale era di interpretare a loro proposito gli auguri sinistri; perché, se cadeva una saetta in uno esercito, s'egli scurava il sole o la luna, se veniva un tremuoto, se il capitano o nel montare o nello scendere da cavallo cadeva, era da' soldati interpretato sinistramente, e generava in loro tanta paura che, venendo alla giornata, facilmente l'arebbero perduta. E però gli antichi capitani, tosto che uno simile accidente nasceva, o e' mostravano la cagione di esso e lo riducevano a cagione naturale, o e' l'interpretavano a loro proposito. Cesare, cadendo in Africa nello uscire di nave, disse: "Affrica, io t'ho presa." E molti hanno renduto la cagione dello oscurare della luna e de' tremuoti; le quali cose ne' tempi nostri non possono accadere, sí per non essere i nostri uomini tanto superstiziosi, sí perché la nostra religione rimuove in tutto da sé tali opinioni (6 *Arte 2.487*)

65   Favola (*Belfagor 4.167*)

donne graziose e belle ("De' romiti" *4.334*)

ogni astrologo e 'ndovino / v'han tutti sbigottiti ("De' romiti" *4.334*)

a quegli van rumori ("De' romiti" *4.335*)

che un tempo orrendo e strano / minaccia a ogni terra / peste, diluvio e guerra, / fulgor, tempeste, tremuoti e rovine, / come se già del mondo fussi fine ("De' romiti" *4.334*)

Innanzi che seguino i grandi accidenti in una città o in una provincia, vengono segni che gli pronosticono o uomini che gli predicano (1.56 *D 1.258*)

Donde ei si nasca io non so, ma ei si vede per gli antichi e per gli moderni esempli che mai non venne alcun grave accidente in una città o in una provincia che non sia stato, o da indovini o da rivelazioni o da prodigi o da altri segni celesti, predetto (1.56 *D 1.258–259*)

Pure, potrebbe essere, che sendo questo aere, come vuole alcuno filosofo, pieno di intelligenze, le quali per naturali virtú, preveggendo le cose future ed avendo compassione agli uomini, acciò si possino preparare alle difese gli avvertiscono con simili segni (1.56 *D 1.259*)

66   Spiriti beati siàno / che da' celesti scanni / siàn qui venuti a dimostrarci in terra, / . . . sí come al Signor nostro al tutto piace / che si ponghin giú l'arme e stieno in pace ("Degli spiriti beati" *4.332*)

Conoscessi questo benissimo per questo testo, come la fortuna per fare maggiore Roma e condurla a quella grandezza venne, giudicò fussi necessario batterla . . . ma non volle già in tutto rovinarla (2.29 *D 1.367*)

Quanto alle cause che vengono dal cielo, sono quelle che spengono la umana generazione e riducano a pochi gli abitatori di parte del mondo. E questo viene o per peste o per fame, o per una inondazione d'acque: e la piú importante e questa ultima, sí perché la è piú universale . . . quando tutte le provincie sono ripiene di abitatori, in modo che non possono vivervi né possono andare altrove per essere occupati e ripieni tutti i luoghi; e quando la astuzia e la malignità umana è venuta dove la può venire, conviene di necessità che il mondo si purghi per uno de' tre modi: acciocché gli uomini, sendo divenuti pochi e battuti, vivino piú comodamente e diventino migliori (2.5 *D 1.293–294*)

quella providenza che mantiene / l'umana spezie (3 *Asino 4.281*)

della umana generazione (2.5 *D 1.293*)

67 potenzia occulta che 'n cielo si nutrica / tra le stelle che quel girando serra, / a la natura umana poco amica, / per privarci di pace e porne in guerra, per torci ogni quiete e ogni bene, / mandò duo furie ad abitare in terra ("Ambiz." *4.319–320*)

mente umana ("Ambiz." *4.320*)

istinto natural ("Ambiz." *4.321*)

68 parve che Iddio le volessi prendere Egli, tanta fu grande una tempesta di venti . . . spinta da superiori forze, o naturali o soprannaturali . . . Volle sanza dubbio Iddio piuttosto minacciare che gastigare la toscana: perché se tanta tempesta fusse entrata in una città . . . faceva quella rovina e fragello che si può con la mente conietturare maggiore. Ma Iddio volle per allora che bastasse questo poco di esempio a rinfrescare intra gli uomini la memoria della potenzia sua (6.34 *IF 3.442–444*)

E come dalla sua morte ne dovesse nascere grandissime rovine ne mostrò il cielo molti evidentissimi segni; intra i quali, l'altissima sommità del tempio di Santa Reparata fu da uno fulmine colpito con tanta furia percossa che gran parte di quel pinnacolo rovinò, con stupore e maraviglia di ciascuno (8.36 *IF 3.576–577*)

subito morto Lorenzo, cominciorono a nascere quegli cattivi semi i quali . . . rovinorono e ancora rovinono la Italia (8.36 *IF 3.577*)

Sa ciascuno ancora come poco innanzi che Piero Soderini, quale era stato fatto gonfalonieri a vita dal popolo fiorentino fosse cacciato e privo del suo grado, fu il palazzo medesimamente da uno fulgure percosso (1.56 *D 1.259*)

Di qua non ci è che dirvi, se non prophezie et annunzii di malanni: che Iddio, se dicono le bugie, gli facci annullare; se dicono il vero, gli converta in bene (L to Francesco Vettori, Feb 4, 1514: *5.323*)

69 E benché fino a qui si sia monstro qualche spiraculo in qualcuno da potere iudicare che fussi ordinato da Dio per sua redenzione, tamen si è visto da poi come, nel piú alto corso delle azioni sua, è stato dalla fortuna reprobato (26 *P 1.102*)

una estraordinaria et estrema malignità di fortuna (7 *P 1.35*)

infinita bontà ("Esortaz." *4.209*)

CHAPTER 4 The Way of Evil

71 Oh buono! Come se Dio facessi le grazie del male come del bene! (4.2 *M 4.94*)

inviluppati ne' lacci del peccato ("Esortaz." *4.212*)

Vivete lieti, et spendete meno che voi potete (L to Guido Machiavelli, April 2, 1527: *5.500*) se ne va con l'acqua benedetta (3.11 *M 4.89*)

Saluta mona Marietta, et dille che . . . non hebbi mai tanta voglia di essere ad Firenze, quanto hora . . . Solo dirai che . . . stia di buona voglia . . . Bacia la Baccina, Piero et Totto, se vi è, il quale harei havuto caro intendere se gli è guarito degli occhi. . . . Et ricorda a Bernardo che attenda a fare bene, al quale da 15 dí in qua ho scritto due lettere et non ne ho risposta. Christo vi guardi tutti (L to Guido Machiavelli, April 2, 1527: *5.500*)

72 della fede mia non si doverrebbe dubitare, perché, havendo sempre osservato la fede, io non debbo imparare hora a romperla; et chi è stato fedele et buono quarantatré anni, che io ho, non debbe poter mutare natura (L to Francesco Vettori, Dec. 10, 1513: *5.305–306*)

che è buono ("Memoriale a Raffaello Girolami" *2.283*)

Considerato adunque tutto quello che vi si è scritto, gli uomini prudenti che si trovano qua, giudicano che ne abbia a seguire il tale effetto e il tale ("Memoriale" *2.285*)

il giudizio vostro nella bocca vostra sarebbe odioso ("Memoriale" *2.285*)

io credo che l'uffizio di un prudente sia in ogni tempo . . . il bene favorire et al male opporsi a buon'hora . . . (L to Francesco Vettori, June 20, 1513: *5.259*)

73 spinto da quel naturale desiderio che fu sempre in me di operare sanza alcuno respetto quelle cose che io creda rechino comune benefizio . . . (1. Proemio *D 1.123*)

gli è offizio di uomo buono, quel bene che per la malignità de' tempi e della fortuna tu non hai potuto operare, insegnarlo ad altri (2. Proemio *D 1.274*)

e l'uomo è solo creato per bene e onore d'Iddio, al quale dié il parlare che potessi laudarlo, gli dette il viso non volto alla terra come a li altri animali ma volto al cielo perché potessi continuamente vederlo, diegli le mani perché potessi fabbricare i tempii, fare i sacrifici in onore suo, diegli la ragione e lo intelletto perché potesse speculare e cognoscere la grandezza d' Iddio ("Esortez." *4.210*)

pensate pertanto come tutte le cose fatte e create sono fatte e create a beneficio dell'uomo ("Esortez." *4.210*)

74 piú pronti al male che al bene (7.30 *IF 3.498*)

cognobbe lo altissimo Iddio quanto era facile l'uomo a scorrere nel peccato ("Esortez." *4.209*)

la sua donna pe 'l gustar del pomo ("Ambiz." *4.319*)

l'albergo di Adam ("Ambiz." *4.320*)

75 quella lingua fatta per onorare Iddio lo bestemmia, la bocca donde si ha a nutrire la fa diventare una cloaca e una via per sodisfare allo appetito e al ventre con dilicati e superflui cibi, quelle speculazioni d'Iddio in speculazioni del mondo converte, quello appetito di conservare la umana spezie in lussuria e molte altre lascivie diventa ("Esortaz." *4.210–211*)

di moto, di ordine e di potenza da quello che gli erano antiquamente (1. Proemio *D 1.124*)

i tempi e le cose universalmente et particularmente si mutano spesso (L to Giovan Battista Soderini, c. Sept 13–21, 1506: *sa.244*)

in tutte le città e in tutti i popoli sono quegli medesimi desideri e quelli medesimi omori, e come vi furono sempre (1.39 *D 1.222*)

Credo che come la natura ha fatto all'huomo diverso volto, cosí gli habbia fatto diverso ingegno et diversa fantasia (L to Giovan Battista Soderini, c. Sept. 13–21, 1506: *sa.244*)

comandare alla natura loro (L Giovan Battista Soderini, c. Sept. 13–21, 1506: *sa.224*)

non si può deviare da quello a che la natura l'inclina (25 *P 1.100*)

si vede li uomini, nelle cose che li 'nducono al fine, quale ciascuno ha nanzi, cioé glorie e ricchezze, procedervi variamente: l'uno con resin-petto, l'altro con impeto; l'uno per violenzia, l'altro con arte; l'uno per pazienzia, l'altro con il suo contrario (25 *P 1.99–100*)

76   altri appetiti, altri diletti, altre considerazioni nella vecchiezza, che nella gioventú (2.Proemio *D 1.273*)

gli appetiti umani insaziabili, perché avendo dalla natura di potere e volere desiderare ogni cosa . . . (2.Proemio *D 1.274*)

disposto a volgersi secondo ch'e' venti e le variazioni della fortuna li comandono (18 *P 1.73–74*)

quello è felice che riscontra il modo del procedere suo con il tempo, et quello, per opposito, é infelice che si diversifica con le sue actioni dal tempo e dall'ordine delle cose (L to Giovan Battista Soderini, c. Sept. 13–21, 1506: *sa.244*)

gli uomini operono o per necessità o per elezione (1.1 *D 1.127*)

el nostro libero arbitrio non sia spento (25 *P 1.99*)

ci torre il libero arbitrio (26 *P 1.103*)

77   la prima morte violenta / nel mondo e la prima erba sanguinosa ("Ambiz." *4.321*)

dispersi a similitudine delle bestie (1.2 *D 1.131*)

dispersi in molte e piccole parti (1.1 *D 1.125*)

nimico (1.1 *D 1.125*)

maggiore autorità (1.1 *D 1.125*)

nel principio del mondo, sendo gli abitatori radi . . . per potersi meglio difendere cominciarono a riguardare infra loro quello che fusse piú robusto e di maggiore cuore, fecionlo come capo e lo ubedivano (1.2 *D 1.131*)

78   Da questo nacque la cognizione delle cose oneste e buone, differenti dalle perniziose e ree: perché, veggendo che se uno noceva al suo benifica-tore ne veniva odio e compassione intra gli uomini, bisasimando gl'ingrati ed onorando quelli che fussero grati, e pensando ancora che quelle medesime ingiurie potevano essere fatte a loro, per fuggire simile

male si riducevano a fare leggi, ordinare punizioni a chi contrafacessi: donde venne la cognizione della giustizia (1.2 *D 1.131*)

piú prudente e piú giusto (1.2 *D 1.131*)

79   tutti i mali, tutti gli errori degli uomini; i quali, ancora che sieno molti e in molti e varii modi si commettino, non di meno si possono largo modo in due parti dividere: l'uno è essere ingrato a Dio, l'altro essere inimico al prossimo ("Esortaz." *4.209–211*)

la natura degli uomini . . . ambiziosa e sospettosa (1.29 *D 1.198*)

Fu d'Avarizia figlia e di Sospetto ("Ingratitudine" *4.305*)

questo vizio della ingratitudine nasce o dall'avarizia o da il sospetto (1.29 *D 1.197*)

sospetto (1.29 *D 1.197*)

incesto e publico parricida (1.27 *D 1.195*)

[n]el viver vostro che stimate tanto (8 *Asino 4.302*)

80   Gli uomini salgono da un'ambizione a un'altra (1.46 *D 1.235*)

sormontare, opprimendo or quello or questo ("Ambiz." *4.321*)

e tanto potente ne' petti umani che mai, a qualunque grado si salgano, gli abbandona (1.37 *D 1.215*)

nobilissimi scrittori . . . se ne ingannorono, e mostrorono di cognoscere poco l'ambizion degli uomini (Proemio *IF 3.70*)

regnando in ogni loco Ambizione ("Ambiz." *4.321*)

d'Ambizion sono quelle ferite / ch'hanno d'Italia le provincie morte ("Ambiz." *4.323*)

l'uom mai non ricorda / né premia il ben ma . . . / il suo benfattor laceri e morda ("Ingratitudine" *4.306*)

de' principi e de' re vive nel petto ("Ingratitudine" *4.305*)

piú si diletta nel cor del popul quando egli é signore ("Ingratitudine" *4.307*)

questo comun vizio / armato contro a sé . . . lo 'ngrato ospizio ("Ingratitudine" *4.307*)

solo a la patria sua lasciar non volse / quell'ossa che d'aver non meritava. . . . il cerchio di sua vita . . . fuor del suo patrio nido ("Ingratitudine" *4.309*)

81   questo vizio della ingratitudine (1.29 *D 1.197*)

Per quale cagione i Romani furono meno ingrati contro agli loro cittadini che gli Ateniesi (1.28 *D 1.196*)

Quale sia piú ingrato, o uno populo o uno principe (1.29 *D 1.197*)

Quali modi debbe usare uno principe o una republica per fuggire questo vizio della ingratitudine; e quali quel capitano o quel cittadino per non essere oppresso da quella (1.30 *D 1.201*)

i popoli non mai per avarizia la usarono, e per sospetto assai manco che i principi, avendo meno cagione di sospettare (1.29 *D 1.200*)

davanti a quel popolo che poco tempo innanzi lo aveva adorato (3.20 *IF 3.204*)

né fede né gratitudine alcuna (3.20 *IF 3.254*)

alle sue buone operazioni la sua patria poco grata (3.22 *IF 3.256*)

L'ossa . . . furono condotte in Firenze, e da coloro con grandissimo onore sepolte, che vive, con ogni calunnia ed ingiuria avevono perseguitate (3.23 *IF 3.259–260*)

di qualunque principe degni (3.23 *IF 3.258*)

assai invidia (3.23 *IF 3.258*)

cagione della sua rovina (3.23 *IF 3.258*)

la già cominciata divisione . . . per l'ambizione de' Ricci e degli Albizzi . . . seguirono in vari tempi dipoi effetti gravissimi (3.18 *IF 3.250*)

82 di tanta vile e infame condizione che crebbe il desiderio agli uomini di liberarsi di tanta infamia (3.18 *IF 3.249*)

né io mi maraviglio né voi vi dovete maravigliare: perché sempre cosí avvenne a coloro i quali intra molti cattivi vogliono essere buoni (3.23 *IF 3.259*)

degli uomini si può dire questo generalmente: che sieno ingrati, volubili, simulatori e dissimulatori, fuggitori de' pericoli, cupidi di guadagno (17 *P 1.69*)

l'ingratitudine contro a Dio è grandissima ("Esortaz." *4.212*)

Questi che sono ingrati a Dio è impossibile che non sieno inimici al prossimo ("Esortaz." *4.211*)

Come possono coloro che dispregiano Iddio, riverire gli uomini? (7 *Arte 2.517*)

l'uno e l'altro di questi due rovinarono, e la rovina loro fu causata da non avere saputo o potuto vincere questa invidia (3.30 *D 1.468*)

forzato . . . ad ammazzare infiniti uomini, i quali non mossi da altro che dalla invidia (3.30 *D 1.468*)

prediche sono piene di accuse de' savi del mondo . . . perché chiamava cosí questi invidi (3.30 *D 1.468*)

spegnere questa invidia (3.30 *D 1.468*)

dal cor tòrre / e frenar quel dolor de' casi avversi / che drieto a l'almo mio furioso corre ("Ingratitudine" *4.305*)

come infra rena si semini ed acque ("Ingratitudine" *4.305*)

né dormiti né giuocati (L to Francesco Vettori, Dec. 10, 1513: *5.305*)

83 prigione, esilio, vilipendio e morte ("Ingratitudine" *4.309*)

Onde che spesso servendo si stenta, / e poi del ben servir se ne riporta / misera vita e morte violenta. / Dunque non sento Ingratitudo morta, / ciascun fuggir le corti e' stati debbe: / che non c' è via che guidi l'uom piú corta / a pianger quel che volle, poi che l'ebbe ("Ingratitudine" *4.311*)

Tra la gente moderna e tra l'antica— / cominciò ella—alcun mai sostenne / piú ingratitudin né maggior fatica (3 *Asino 4.280*)

io voglio che tu lo sciolga. . . . gli cavi la briglia e il capestro, et lascilo andare dove vuole ad guadagnarsi il vivere et ad cavarsi la pazzia. Il paese è largo, la bestia è piccola, non può fare male veruno (L to Guido Machiavelli, April 2, 1527: *5.500*)

Mi faccio aiutare da un mio figliuolo (L to Francesco Guicciardini, May 17, 1526: *5.465*)

84 Pur se credessi alcun, dicendo male, / tenerlo pe' capegli / . . . io lo ammunisco e dico a questo tale / che sa dir mal anch'egli . . . / ma làscian pur dir male a chiunche vuole (Prologo *M 4.58*)

solamente l'uomo / l'altr'uom amazza, crocifigge e spoglia (8 *Asino 4.302*)

uomo crudele et espedito (7 *P 1.37*)

a Cesena in dua pezzi in sulla piazza, con un pezzo di legno et uno coltello sanguinoso a canto (7 *P 1.37*)

La ferocità del quale spettaculo fece quelli populi in uno tempo rimanere satisfatti e stupiti (7 *P 1.37*)

per purgare li animi (7 *P 1.37*)

quelli che non poterono ferirgli vivi gli ferirono morti, né saziati di straziarli col ferro, con le mani e con i denti gli laceravano. E perché tutti i sensi si sodisfacessero nella vendetta, avendo udito prima le loro querele, veduto le loro ferite, tocco le loro carni lacere, volevono ancora che il gusto le assaporasse, acciò che come tutte le parti di fuora ne erano sazie, quelle di dentro ancora se ne saziassero. . . . perché, stracca la moltitudine nelle crudeltà di questi duoi, di quello non si ricordò (*2.37 IF 3.203*)

85 sfogare la loro avarizia e crudeltà (19 *P 1.79*)

crudelissimi e rapacissimi (19 *P 1.80*)

principe nuovo (19 *P 1.80*)

molte crudeltà (19 *P 1.83*)

d'animo crudele e bestiale (19 *P 1.82*)

ferocia e crudeltà . . . tanta e sí inaudita (19 *P 1.82*)

né . . . esemplo piú miserabile né piú raro (21 *P 1.90*)

pietosa crudeltà (21 *P 1.90*)

Sono questi modi crudelissimi e nimici d'ogni vivere non solamente cristiano ma umano; e debbegli qualunque uomo fuggire, e volere piuttosto vivere privato che re con tanta rovina degli uomini (*1.26 D 1.194*)

basta spegnere solo coloro che comandano (*2.8 D 1.297*)

conviene spegnere ciascuno, perché vogliono vivere di quello che altri viveva (*2.8 D 1.297*)

crudelissima e paventosissima (*2.8 D 1.297*)

86 la sua ferocia e crudeltà fu tanta e sí inaudita, per avere, dopo infinite uccisioni particulari, morto gran parte del populo di Roma, e tutto quello di Alessandria (19 *P 1.82*)

infiniti tradimenti e crudeltà (8 *P 1.44*)

De his qui per scelera ad principatum pervenere (8 *P 1.40*)

scellerata e nefaria (8 *P 1.40*)

uno anno dopo el commisso parricidio, fu insiemo con Vitellozzo, il quale aveva avuto maestro delle virtú e scelleratezze sua, strangolato (8 *P 1.43*)

efferata crudeltà et inumanità (8 *P 1.42*)

li sua cittadini (8 *P 1.42*)

Non si può ancora chiamare virtù ammazzare li sua cittadini, tradire li amici, essere sanza fede, sanza pietà, sanza relligione (8 *P 1.42*)

via del bene (1.26 *D 1.194*)

una potestà assoluta, la quale dagli autori è chiamata tirannide (1.25 *D 1.193*)

CHAPTER 5 Clergy and Country

88 Oh frati! Conoscine uno e conoscigli tutti (4.4 *M 4.98*)

89 la nostra religione . . . la verità e la vera via (2.1 *D 1.282*)

capo della religione nostra (1.12 *D 1.165*)

per gli esempli rei . . . ha perduto ogni divozione e ogni religione . . . Abbiamo adunque con la Chiesa e con i preti noi italiani questo primo obligo: di essere diventati sanza religione e cattivi (1.12 *D 1.165*)

piú propinqui alla Chiesa romana, capo della religione nostra, hanno meno religione (1.12 *D 1.165*)

mandasse ad abitare [la corte romana] . . . in le terre de' Svizzeri (1.12 *D 1.166*)

che in poco tempo farebbero piú disordine in quella provincia i rei costumi di quella corte che qualunque altro accidente che in qualunque tempo vi potesse surgere (1.12 *D 1.166*)

Di modo che tutte le guerre che dopo questi tempi furono da' barbari fatte in Italia, furono in maggior parte dai pontefici causate, e tutti e' barbari che quella inondorono furono il piú delle volte da quegli chiamati (1.9 *IF 3.90*)

90 potente da potere occupare la Italia, né avendo permesso che un altro la occupi (1.12 *D 1.166*)

Né mai staranno quiete . . . qualunque volta abbino cardinali, perché questi nutriscono in Roma e fuora, le parti . . . e cosí dalla ambizione de' prelati nascono le discordie e li tumulti infra baroni (11 *P 1.52*)

capi della religione (3.1 *D 1.383*)

e cosí quegli fanno il peggio che possono, perché non temono quella punizione che non veggono e non credono (3.1 *D 1.383*)

oltre alle grandi amicitie che io ho, io ho fatto nuova amicitia con il cardinale Cibo, et tanta grande, che io stesso me ne maraviglio, la quale ti tornerà a proposito; ma bisogna che tu impari . . . (L to Guido Machiavelli, April 2, 1527: *5.499*)

92 ed ho atteso a consumare el tempo in varie cose: io dissi matutino, lessi una vita de' Santi Padri, andai in chiesa ed accesi una lampana che era spenta, mutai uno velo a una Madonna che fa miracoli. Quante volte ho io detto a questi frati che la tenghino pulita! E si maraviglino poi se la divozione manca. Io mi ricordo . . . Ora non si fa nulla di queste cose, e po' ci maravigliamo se le cose vanno fredde! Oh quanto poco cervello è in questi mia frati! (5.1 *M 4.105*)

E' son ben necessarie l'orazioni: / e matto al tutto è quel ch'al popol vieta / le cerimonie e le sue divozioni: / perché da quelle in ver par che si mieta / unione e buono ordine, e da quello / buona fortuna poi dipende e lieta (6 *Asino 4.290*)

De principatibus ecclesiasticis (II *P 1.50*)

principi . . . spirituali ("Ritratto delle cose della Magna" *2.212*)

principi ecclesiastici ("Rit. Magna" *2.212*)

soli hanno stati, e non li difendano; suddITI, e non li governano; e li stati, per essere indifesi, non sono loro tolti; e li suddITI, per non essere governati, non se ne curano, né pensano né possono alienarsi da loro (II *P 1.50*)

è simile al pontificato cristiano (19 *P 1.84*)

come se fussi (19 *P 1.84*)

non . . . alcune di quelle difficultà (19 *P 1.84*)

93   la Chiesia nel temporale (II *P 1.51*)

uno re di Francia ne trema (II *P 1.51*)

grandezza (II *P 1.51*)

e' Franzesi non si intendevano dello stato (3 *P 1.25*)

con l'armi insieme, mescolate con le indulgenzie (1.9 *IF 3.90*)

La cagione dell'ordinanza (Marginalia, foglio di coperta *2.91*)

arme proprie ("Provisione prima per le fanterie," Dec 6, 1506: *2.101*)

mescolarsi qualche cosa di religione ("Discorso dell'ordinare lo stato di Firenze alle armi" *2.99*)

94   cinque provveditori della mura ("Provisione per la istituzione dell'ufficio de' cinque provveditori della mura della città di Firenze" *2.303*)

buon fanti fedeli (Legation of July 21, 1499: *6.213*)

95   La cagione dell'ordinanza, dove la si trovi, e quel che bisogna fare (Marginalia, foglio di coperta, "La cagione dell'ordinanza," *2.91*)

quelli preti e quelli altri cittadini usi a non conoscere arme cominciorono a soldare forestieri (12 *P 1.57*)

96   col nome dell'onnipotente Iddio e della sua gloriosissima madre madonna Santa Maria sempre vergine, e del glorioso precursore di Cristo Giovanni Battista, avvocato, protettore e padrone di questa repubblica fiorentina ("Provisione prima" *2.101–102*)

udito prima la messa dello Spirito Santo, di tempo accettare e giurare detto ufficio in quel modo che accettono e giurano l'ufficio loro ("Provisione prima" *2.103*)

una messa solenne dello Spirito Santo in luogo che tutti i ragunati la possino udire; e dopo la detta messa, il deputato debba far loro quelle parole che in simile cerimonia si convengono; dipoi leggere loro quello e quanto per loro si debba osservare, e darne loro solenne giuramento, facendo ad uno ad uno toccar con mano il libro de' Sacri Vangeli; e debba leggere loro innanzi a tale giuramento tutte le pene capitali a che sono sottoposti, e tutti quelli ammonimenti che saranno ordinati da detti ufficiali in conservazione e fermezza della unione e fede loro; aggravando il giuramento con tutte quelle parole obbligatorie dell'anima e del corpo, che si potranno trovare piú efficaci: e fatto questo sieno licenziati, e ritornino tutti alle case loro ("Provisione prima" *2.III*)

Valeva assai nel tenere disposti gli soldati antichi, la religione e il giuramento che si dava loro quando si conducevano a militare . . . La quale cosa, mescolata con altri modi religiosi, fece molte volte facile a' capitani antichi ogni impresa, e farebbe sempre, dove la religione si temesse e osservasse (4 *Arte 2.441*)

98 un poco da alto ("Discorso" *2.95*)

ognuno sa che chi dice imperio, regno, principato, republica ; chi dice uomini che comandano, cominciandosi dal primo grado e descendendo infino al padrone d'uno brigantino, dice iustitia e armi ("Discorso" *2.95*)

possono nuocere in dua modi, o fra loro, e contro alla città ("Discorso" *2.99*)

la viltà che si era veduta in Prato ne' soldati nostri (L to a noblewoman, post Sept. 16, 1512: *5.226*)

99 avere perduto una volta . . . rimediare alla cagione della perdita (1 *Arte 2.347*)

Voi della iustizia ne avete non molta, e dell'armi non punto ("Discorso" *2.95*)

la repubblica vostra è di buone e sante leggi bene instituta e ordinata circa alla amministrazione della giustizia, e che gli manca solo il provedersi bene dell'arme ("Provisione prima" *2.101*)

Quali pericoli si portano nel farsi capo a consigliare una cosa, e quanto ella ha piú dello istraordinario, maggiori pericoli vi si corrono (3.35 D *1.481*)

tutto il male che ne risulta s'imputa allo autore del consiglio; e se ne risulta bene, ne è commedato; ma di lunge il premio non contrappesa a il danno (3.35 D *1.481*)

È cosa adunque certissima che quegli che consigliano una republica e quegli che consigliano uno principe sono posti intra queste angustie: che se non consigliano le cose che paiono loro utili o per la città o per il principe sanza rispetto, e' mancano dell'ufficio loro; se le consigliano, e' gli entrano in pericolo della vita e dello stato (3.35 D *1.481*)

100 E pensando in che modo ei potessono fuggire o questa infamia o questo pericolo, non ci veggo altra via che pigliare le cose moderatamente, e non ne prendere alcuna per sua impresa, e dire la opinione sua sanza passione e sanza passione con modestia difenderla: in modo che se la città o il principe la segue, che la segua voluntario, e non paia che vi venga tirato dalla sua importunità. Quando tu faccia cosí non è ragionevole che uno principe ed uno popolo del tuo consiglio ti voglia male, non essendo seguito contro alla volglia di molti: perché quivi si porta pericolo dove molti hanno contradetto, i quali poi nello infelice fine concorrono a farti rovinare. E se in questo caso si manca di quella gloria che si acquista nello essere solo contro a molti a consigliare una

cosa, quando ella sortisce buono fine, ci sono a rincontro due beni: il primo, del mancare di pericolo; il secondo che se tu consigli una cosa modestamente, e per la contradizione il tuo consiglio non sia preso e per il consiglio d'altrui ne seguiti qualche rovina, ne risulta a te gloria grandissima. E benché la gloria che si acquista de' mali che abbia o la tua città o il tuo principe non si possa godere, nondimeno è da tenerne qualche conto (3.35 *D1.482–483*)

101 simulò (1.11 *D 1.161*)

atti a perturbare ogni ordine buono (1.12 *D 1.164*)

trovando un popolo ferocissimo, e volendolo ridurre nelle obedienze civili con le arti della pace, si volse alla religione come cosa al tutto necessaria a volere mantenere una civiltà, e la constituí in modo che per piú secoli non fu mai tanto timore di Dio quanto in quella republica (1.11 *D 1.160*)

temevano piú assai rompere il giuramento che le leggi, come coloro che stimavano piú la potenza di Dio che quella degli uomini (1.11 *D 1.160*)

perché dove è religione facilmente si possono introdurre armi (1.11 *D 1.161*)

E veramente mai fu alcuno ordinatore di leggi straordinarie in uno popolo che non ricorresse a Dio . . . (1.11 *D 1.161*)

hanno sopra a ogni altra cosa a mantenere incorrotte le cerimonie della loro religione, e tenerle sempre nella loro venerazione; perché nessuno maggiore indizio si puote avere della rovina di una provincia che vedere dispregiato il culto divino (1.12 *D 1.163*)

religione se ne' principi della republica cristiana si fusse mantenuta secondo che dal datore d'essa ne fu ordinato, sarebbero gli stati e le repubbliche cristiane piú unite, piú felici assai che le non sono (1.12 *D 1.165*)

La nostra religione ha glorificato piú gli uomini umili e contemplativi che gli attivi. Ha dipoi posto il sommo bene nella umiltà, abiezione, e nel dispregio delle cose umane: quell'altra lo poneva nella grandezza dello animo, nella fortezza del corpo e in tutte le altre cose atte a fare gli uomini fortissimi. E se la religione nostra richiede che tu abbi in te fortezza, vuole che tu sia atto a patire piú che a fare una cosa forte (2.2 *D 1.282*)

piú delicata che magnifica (2.2 *D 1.282*)

pieno di sangue e di ferocità . . . aspetto, sendo terribile, rendeva gli uomini simili a lui (2.2 *D 1.282*)

102 E chi considerasse i fondamenti suoi, e vedesse lo uso presente quanto è diverso da quelli, giudicherebbe essere propinquo sanza dubbio o la rovina o il fragello (1.12 *D 1.165*)

103 in le terre de' Svizzeri, i quali oggi sono solo popoli che vivoni, e quanto alla religione e quanto agli ordini militari, secondo gli antichi (1.12 *D 1.166*)

Io sarò costí prima che venga travaglio alcuno (L to Guido Machiavelli, April 2, 1527: *5.500*) sia la diversità della educazione nostra dalla antica, fondata nella diversità della religione nostra dall'antica (2.2 D *1.282*)

104 sanza dubbio dalla viltà degli uomini, che hanno interpretato la nostra religione secondo l'ozio e non secondo la virtú (2.2 D *1.283*)

educazioni e sí false interpretazioni (2.2 D *1.283*)

E pensando io come queste cose procedino, giudico il mondo sempre essere stato ad uno medesimo modo, ed in quello essere stato tanto di buono che di cattivo; ma variare questo cattivo e questo buono di provincia in provincia come si vede per quello si ha notizia di quegli regni antichi, che variavano dall'uno all'altro per la variazione de' costumi, ma il mondo restava quel medesimo. Solo vi era questa differenza, che dove quello aveva prima allogata la sua virtú in Assiria, la collocò in Media, dipoi in Persia, tanto che la ne venne in Italia ed a Roma; e se dopo lo imperio romano non è seguito imperio che sia durato né dove il mondo abbia ritenuta la sua virtú insieme; si vede nondimeno essere sparsa in di molte nazioni dove si viveva virtuosamente; come era il regno de' Franchi, il regno de' Turchi; quel del Soldano; ed oggi i popoli della Magna; e prima quella sètta Saracina che fece tante gran cose ed occupò tanto mondo, poiché la distrusse lo imperio romano orientale (2.Proemio D *1.272–273*)

Questa virtú e questo vizio che io dico trovarsi in un uomo solo, si truova ancora in una republica (3.31 D *1.470*)

dalla educazione nella quale ti se' nutrito (3.31 D *1.472*)

quello che si dice d'uno solo si dice di molti che vivono in una republica medesima (3.31 D *1.472*)

perché le amicizie che si acquistono col prezzo e non con grandezza e nobiltà d'animo si meritano (17 P *1.70*)

Li uomini alli universali iudicano piú alli occhi che alle mani; perché tocca vedere a ognuno, a sentire a pochi (18 P *1.74*)

105 mentre fai loro bene (17 P *1.69*)

quando il bene è discosto; ma quando ti si appressa . . . (17 P *1.69–70*)

né posso esprimere con quale amore e' fussi ricevuto in tutte quelle provincie . . . (26 P *1.105*)

buone arme (12 P *1.53*)

non può essere buone legge dove non sono buone arme, e dove sono buone arme conviene siene buone legge (12 P *1.53*)

Talché se si avesse a disputare a quale principe Roma fusse piú obligata, o a Romolo, o a Numa, credo piú tosto Numa otterrebbe il primo grado (1.11 D *1.161*)

piú perfetta (1.3 D *1.135*)

gli uomini non operano mai nulla se non per necessità; ma dove la elezione abonda, e che vi si può usare licenza, si riempie subito ogni cosa di confusione e di disordine. Però si dice che la fame e la povertà fa gli uomini industriosi, e le leggi gli fanno buoni. E dove una cosa per sé medisima sanza la legge opera bene, non è necessaria la legge. Ma quando quella buona consuetudine manca, è subito la legge necessaria (1.3 *D 1.136*)

107 cosí come gli buoni costumi per mantenersi hanno bisogno delle leggi, cosí le leggi per osservarsi hanno bisogno de' buoni costumi (1.18 *D 1.179–180*)

io stimerò sempre poco vivere in una città dove possino meno le leggi che gli uomini: perché quella patria è desiderabile nella quale le sustanze e gli amici si possono sicuramente godere, non quella dove ti possino essere quelle tolte facilmente, e gli amici per paura di loro propri nelle tue maggiori necessità t'abbandonono (4.23 *IF 3.323–324*)

È cosa di malo esemplo non osservare una legge fatta e massime dallo autore d'essa (1.45 *D 1.233*)

io non credo che sia cosa di più cattivo esemplo che fare una legge e non la osservare; e tanto piú quanto non la è osservata da chi l'ha fatta (1.45 *D 1.233*)

108 obligati a infinite leggi (1.16 *D 1.176*)

non ne potessono altrimenti disporre che le leggi si ordinassero (1.16 *D 1.176*)

nessuno ei rompa tali leggi, comincerà in breve tempo a vivere sicuro e contento (1.16 *D 1.176*)

109 dua generazione di combattere: l'uno con le leggi, l'altro con la forza: quel primo è proprio dello uomo, quel secondo delle bestie (18 *P 1.72*)

fece dipoi nascere in quella tanti animali . . . a beneficio suo ("Esortaz." *4.210*)

Noi a natura siam maggiori amici (8 *Asino 4.301*)

è caso da Otto: io non ci voglio capitare sotto male (2.6 *M 4.76*)

ma, sopra a tutto, che non si sappia, per amore degli Otto! (2.6 *M 4.76*)

110 fra gli uomini privati, le leggi, le scritte, e' patti, fanno osservare la fede, e fra e' signori la fanno solo osservare l'armi ("Parole" *2.60*)

Parole da dirle sopra la provisione del danaio, fatto un poco di proemio e di scusa ("Parole" *2.49*)

uno freno in bocca che li correggessi (19 *P 1.77*)

si vede quivi essere maggior virtú dove la elezione ha meno autorità (1.1 *D 1.127*)

111 Descrizione del modo tenuto dal Duca Valentino nello ammazzare Vitellozzo Vitelli, Oliverotto da Fermo . . . ("Descrizione" *2.33*)

mandorno Niccolò Machiavegli loro secretario ("Descrizione" *2.42–43*)

non fu usato da alcuno di loro parole degne della loro passata vita, perche Vitellozzo pregò che si supplicassi al papa che gli dessi de' suoi peccati indulgenza plenaria; e Liverotto, tutta la colpa delle iniurie fatte al duca, piangendo rivolgeva addosso a Vitellozzo ("Descrizione" *2.48*)

Questi frati son trincati, astuti; ed è ragionevole, perché e' sanno e peccati nostri e loro (3.2 *M 4.80*)

Ho chiamato a te, o Signore, misericordia ("Esortaz." *4.209*) sanza dubbio fu un uomo per arme, per dottrina, per giudizio eccellentissimo (1.19 *D 1.184*)

112　Miserere mei, Deus ("Esortaz." *4.213*)

discreto e savio (6 *Asino 4.289*)

non basti (6 *Asino 4.289*)

qualche peccato carnale (6 *Asino 4.289*)

perché se considerassono come la ci permette la esaltazione e la difesa della patria, vedrebbono come la vuole che noi l'amiamo ed onoriamo, e prepariamoci a essere tali che noi la possiamo difendere (2.2 *D 1.283*)

tempi piú che mai felici (3 *Asino 4.281*)

So che vi trovate costí tutto el giorno insieme . . . et vi ricordate poco di noi qui, poveri graziati, morti di gelo et di sonno. Pur, per parere vivi ci troviamo qualche volta . . . et ragioniano di quella gita di Fiandra con tanta efficacia, che ci pare essere in cammino, in modo che de' piaceri vi habbiano ad havere li habbiano già consumati mezzi (L to Lodovico Alamanni, Dec. 17, 1517: *5.383*)

113　mi avete forzato a scrivere quello ch'io mai per me medesimo non arei scritto (Letter 9 *D 1.121*)

per anni ecc. con salario ogni anno ecc. con obligo che debba et sia tenuto scrivere gli annali o vero la istoria delle cose fatte dallo stato et città di Firenze, da quello tempo gli parrà piú conveniente, et in quella lingua o latina o toscana che a lui parrá. Nicholaus Machiavelli (L to Francesco del Nero, Sept. 10–Dec. 7, 1520: *5.397*)

114　Discursus florentinarum rerum post mortem iunioris Laurentii Medices ("Discursus" *2.245*)

desiderarebbe trovare un ordine dove l'autorità sua rimanesse in Firenze grande, e gli amici vi vivessino securi ("Discursus" *2.268*)

la Santità Vostra e monsignore reverendissimo . . . avendo a mancare, e volendo che rimanga una repubblica perfetta ("Discursus" *2.272*)

questa mia repubblica ("Discursus" *2.268*)

è cosa difficile, inumana e indegna di qualunque desidera essere tenuto pietoso e buono ("Discursus" *2.268*)

credo che il maggiore bene che si faccia, e il piú grato a Dio, sia quello che si fa alla sua patria ("Discursus" *2.275*)

116　ad tenere ad freno un papa, non bisogna tanti Imperadori, né fare tanto romori; perché li altri che per lo addreto li hanno fatto guerra, o e' l'hanno ingannato, come fece Filippo Bello, o e' l'hanno fatto rinchiudere in Castello Sant'Angiolo da' suoi Baroni, li quali non sono sí spenti che non si potessi trovar modo ad raccenderli (*Legation of* Aug. 9, 1510: *8.1284*)

tutte le cose che sono state io credo che possano essere; e io so che si son visti de' pontefici fuggire, exiliare, perseguitare, et extrema pati, come e' signori temporali, e ne' tempi che la Chiesa nello spirituale haveva piú riverenza che non ha hoggi (L to Francesco Vettori, Dec. 20, 1514: *5.365*) ma molto piú per eccellenza di animo (6.29 *IF 3.433*)

trarre la patria sua delle mani de' prelati (6.29 *IF 3.433*)

in sé nel pensarle alcuna ombra di gloria, hanno nello esequirle quasi sempre certissimo danno (6.29 *IF 3.435*)

disarmato (1.27 *D 1.195*)

sarà per sua buona natura e umanità (*Legation of* Sept. 13, 1506: *10.980*)

117 si fusse astenuto o per bontà o per coscienza (1.27 *D 1.195*)

sendo col papa tutti li cardinali con tutte le loro delizie (1.27 *D 1.195*)

memoria eterna (1.27 *D 1.195*)

il primo che avesse dimostro a' prelati quanto sia da stimare poco chi vive e regna come loro (1.27 *D 1.195*)

perché la brevitá della vita de' papi, la variazione della successione, il poco timore che la Chiesa ha de' principi, i pochi rispetti che la ha nel prendere i partiti, fa che uno principe seculare non può in uno pontefice interamente confidare, nè può securamente accomunare la fortuna sua con quello. Perché, chi è nelle guerre e pericoli, del papa amico, sarà nelle vittorie accompagnato e nelle rovine solo, sendo il pontefice dalla spirituale potenza e reputazione sostenuto e difeso (8.17 *IF 3.539–540*)

118 perseguiterallo nello stato e nella persona, e crederà essere scusato e con tutto il mondo e con Dio (*Legation of* July 21, 1510: *8.1246*)

119 Et chi replicasse che il papa, per la reverenzia della persona e per l'autorità della Chiesa, è in un altro grado, et harà sempre refugio a salvarsi, risponderei che tal replica merita qualche consideratione, et che vi si può fare su qualche fondamento: non di manco e' non è da fidarsene, anzi, credo che, a volersi consigliar bene, non sia da pensarvi . . . (L to Francesco Vettori, Dec. 20, 1514: *5.365*)

ire in Svizzería a morirsi di fame, o nella Magna a vivere disperato, o in Spagna ad essere espilato et rivenduto (L to Francesco Vettori, Dec. 10, 1514: *5.367*)

Magnifici Domini. Adviso col nome di Dio le Signorie vostre come questa mattina el Cardinale di San Piero in Vincula è stato pronuntiato nuovo Pontefice. Che Iddio lo facci utile pastore per la Christianità. Valete. Die prima Novembris 1503. Servitor Nicholò Machiavegli. Secretarius. Romae (*Legation of* November 1, 1503: *8.99*)

sono sustentati dall'ordini antiquati nella relligione (II *P 1.50*)

120 Debbono adunque i principi d'una republica o d'uno regno, i fondamenti della religione che loro tengono, mantenergli; e fatto questo, sarà loro facil cosa mantenere la loro republica religiosa, e per conseguente buona e unita (1.12 *D 1.164*)

CHAPTER 6 The Fool of Love

122 Il soldato muore in una fossa, lo amante muore desperato (1.2 *Clizia 4.124*)

'i sento l'alma / arder nel foco ov'io / lieta arsi ("A stanza della Barbera" *4.359*)

Se col tuo valor santo / far puoi, Amor, che sempre / a lui vivuta paia in questo foco, / io sarò lieta tanto / che in le piú crude tempre / il viver mi fie gioia e 'l morir gioco: e sempre il canto mio / lui chiamerà signor e te mio Dio ("A stanza della Barbera" *4.359*)

124 io scriverrei una lettera . . . et fatto un simil preambulo, io gli mostrerrei quale è lo stato vostro, et come vi trovate senza figlioli maschi, ma con quattro femmine, et come vi pare tempo di maritarne una . . . et qui strignerlo et gravarlo con quello piú efficaci parole che voi saprete trovare, per mostrarli quanto voi stimiate la cosa . . . (L to Francesco Guicciardini, Oct. 21, 1525: *5.442–443*)

125 non facessino il debito loro ("Capitoli per una compagnia di piacere" *4.204*)

126 Affogaggine, Luigi; et guarda quanto la fortuna in una medesima faccenda dà ad li huomini diversi fini. Voi, fottuto che voi avesti colei, vi è venuta voglia di fotterla et ne volete un'altra presa; ma io, stato fui qua parecchi dí, accecando per carestia di matrimonio, trovai una vecchia che m'imbucatava le camicie, che sta in una casa che è piú di meza sotterra, né vi si vede lume se non per l'uscio. Et passando io un dí di quivi, la mi riconobbe et, factomi una gran festa, mi disse che io fussi contento un poco andar in casa, che mi voleva mostrare certe camicie belle se io le volevo comperare. Onde io, nuovo cazzo, me lo credetti, et, giunto là, vidi al barlume una donna . . . Questa vecchia ribalda mi prese per mano et menatomi ad colei dixe: "Questa è la camicia che io vi voglio vendere, ma voglio la proviate prima et poi la paghrete." Io, come peritoso che io sono, mi sbigottí tucto; pure, rimasto solo con colei et al buio (perché la vecchia si uscí subito di casa et serrò l'uscio) (L to Luigi Guicciardini, Dec. 8, 1509: *5.204–205*)

127 alla sfuggiasca (L to Francesco Vettori, Feb. 4, 1514: *5.323*)

Questi savi, questi savi, io non so dove si stanno a casa (L to Francesco Vettori, Feb. 4, 1514: *5.323*)

qualche fanciulla per rihavere le forze (L to Francesco Vettori, March 18, 1512: *5.236*)

le menono la coda piú che mai (L to Francesco Guicciardini, May 18, 1521: *5.409*)

128 avendo ella, oltre alle vere ragione, gustato che differenzia è dalla iacitura mia a quella di Nicia (5.4 M *4.109*)

ad ogni ora e sanza sospetto (5.4 M *4.110*)

a' segni ed a' vestigi / l'onor di gentilezza (Prologo M *4.57*)

io ci sto poco su, perché da ogni parte mi assalta tanto desio d'essere una volta con costei che io mi sento, dalle piante de' pie al capo, tutto alterare: le gambe triemono, le viscere si commuovono, il core mi sbarba del petto, le braccia s'abandonano, la lingua diventa muta, gli occhi abbarbagliono, el cervello mi gira (4.1 M *4.92–93*)

amore (1.1 M *4.63*)

leggo quelle loro amorose passioni et quelli loro amori, ricordomi de' mia
... (L to Francesco Vettori, Dec. 10, 1513: *5.303*)

129   già vicino a ... né le vie aspre mi straccano, né le obscurità delle notti mi
sbigottiscano. Ogni cosa mi pare piano, et a ogni appetito, etiam diverso et contrario a quello che doverrebbe essere il mio, mi accomodo.
Et benché mi paia essere entrato in gran travaglio, tamen io ci sento
dentro tanta dolcezza (L to Francesco Vettori, Aug. 3, 1514: *5.347*)

tanto gentile, tanto delicata, tanto nobile (L to Francesco Vettori, Aug. 3,
1514: *5.346*)

reti d'oro tese tra fiori (L to Francesco Vettori, Aug. 3, 1514: *5.347*)

io credo, credetti, et crederrò sempre che sia vero quello che dice il Boccaccio: che egli è meglio fare et pentirsi, che non fare et pentirsi (L to
Francesco Vettori, Feb. 25, 1514: *5.330*)

131   Carissimo Giovanni. Tu non mi scrivi mai di non havere haute mia lettere,
che tu non mi dia d'un coltello ... Io ho inteso per piú tua e' tuoi
travagli: ringratio Iddio, che li hanno posato in modo che tu rimani
vivo ... Sono tuo. Christo ti guardi. A' dí 15 di Febbraio 1515. Niccoló
Machiavegli in Firenze (L to Giovanni Vernacci, Feb. 5, 1516: *5.377–378*)

comanda l'amore e reverenza che io vi porto (L to Francesco Guicciardini, Jan. 3, 1525: *5.451*)

tutto lo amore ... che era grande, considerata la novità (L to Francesco
Vettori, Jan. 31, 1515: *5.375*)

Che uno buono cittadino per amore della patria debbe dimenticare le ingiurie private (3.47 *D 1.503*)

Tanto v'inganna il proprio vostro amore / che altro ben non credete che
sia / fuor de l'umana essenza e del valore (8 *Asino 4.299*)

Questa, padri e fratelli miei, è quella sola che conduce l'anime nostre in
cielo, questa è quella sola che vale piú che tutte le altre virtú degli uomini, questa è quella di cui la Chiesa sí largamente parla: che chi non
ha la carità non ha nulla ("Esortaz." *4.211*)

e tanto a me parver maravigliose / che meco la cagion discorrer volli / del
variar de le mondane cose (5 *Asino 4.287*)

132   lungamente escogitate (Lettera *P 1.13*)

ragione delle (L to Francesco Vettori, Dec. 10, 1513: *5.304*)

per quattro hore di tempo (L to Francesco Vettori, Dec. 10, 1513: *5.304*)

di questo subbietto (L to Francesco Vettori, Dec. 10, 1513: *5.304*)

studio all'arte dello stato (L to Francesco Vettori, Dec. 10, 1513: *5.305*)

io non giudico né giudicherò mai essere difetto difendere alcuna opinione
con le ragioni, sanza volervi usare o l'autorità o la forza (1.58 *D 1.262*)

non sapendo ragionare né dell'arte della seta, né dell'arte della lana, né de'
guadagni né delle perdite, e' mi conviene ragionare dello stato, et mi
bisogna o botarmi di stare cheto, o ragionare di questo (L to Francesco
Vettori, April 9, 1513: *5.239–240*)

Come per cagione di femine si rovina uno stato (3.26 *D 1.459*)

133   vedendo messer Buondelmonte che solo veniva verso la sua casa, scese da

basso e dietro si condusse la figliuola; e nel passare quello se gli incontra dicendo: Io mi rallegro veramente assai dello avere voi preso moglie, ancora che io vi avesse serbata questa mia figliuola'; e sospinta la porta, gliene fece vedere. Il cavaliere, veduta la bellezza della fanciulla . . . si accese in tanto ardore di averla, che, non pensando alla fede data, né alla ingiuria che faceva a romperla, né ai mali che dalla rotta fede gliene potevano incontrare, disse: 'Poiché voi me la avete serbata, io sarei uno ingrato, sendo ancora a tempo, a rifiutarla (2.3 *IF 3.142*)

La Barbera si trova costí . . . la mi dà molto piú da pensare che lo inperadore (L to Francesco Guicciardini, March 15, 1526: *5.458*)

Questa mattina io ricevetti la vostra, per la quale mi avvisavi in quanta grazia io ero con la Maliscotta: di che io mi glorio piú che di cosa che io abbia in questo mondo (L to Francesco Guicciardini, Aug. 3, 1525: *5.425*)

ch'ogn'altra cosa fosse vana / fuor di colei di cui fui servo fatto (6 *Asino 4.290*)

134 E s'alcuno infra gli uomin ti par divo, / felice e lieto, non gli creder molto, / che 'n questo fango piú felice vivo, / dove sanza pensier mi bagno e vólto (8 *Asino 4.302*)

non ti invilire come una donna (4.1 *M 4.92*)

135 io non credo sia nel mondo el piú sciocco uomo di costui . . . lei bella donna, savia costumata e atta a governare un regno (1.3 *M 4.66*)

136 Io son contento / morire ("Serenata" *4.348*)

Callimaco: . . . Io ho morire per l'allegrezza.

Ligurio: Che gente è questa? Or per l'allegrezza, or pel dolore, costui vuol morire in ogni modo (4.2 *M 4.94*)

donne . . . non gli mandate al regno maledetto: ché chi dannazion provoca altrui, / a simil pena il ciel condanna lui ("Di amanti e donne disperati" *4.331*)

137 una celeste disposizione che abbi voluto cosí, e non sono sufficiente a recusare quello che 'l cielo vuole che io accetti (5.4 *M 4.109*)

io mi truovo el piú felice e contento uomo che fussi mai nel mondo, e se questa felicità non mi mancassi o per morte o per tempo, io sarei piú beato ch'e beati, piú santo che e santi (5.4 *M 4.110*)

Chi non prova, Amore, / della tua gran possanza, indarno spera / di far mai fede vera / qual sia del cielo il piú alto valore (1. Canzona *Clizia 4.126*)

una donna piena di beltate, / ma fresca e frasca, mi si dimostrava / con le sue trecce bionde e scapigliate (2. *Asino 4.274*)

Sare' io d'ortica o pruni armata? (4. *Asino 4.285*)

Sian benedette le bellezze tue. / Sia benedetta l'ora quando io missi / il pié nella foresta (4 *Asino 4.285*)

tutto prostrato sopra il dolce seno (4 *Asino 4.286*)

Chi giammai donna offende, / a torto o a ragion, folle è se crede / trovar per prieghi o pianti in lei merzede. / Come la scende in questa mortal vita, / con l'alma insieme porta / superbia, sdegno e di perdono oblio: / inganno e crudeltà le sono scorta / e tal le dànno aita / che d'ogni impresa appaga el suo desio; / e se sdegno aspro e rio / la muove o gelosia, adopra e vede: / e la sua forza, mortal forza eccede (3. Canzona *Clizia* *4.146*)

138 non fia mai ricordato da me sanza lagrime, avendo conosciute in lui quelle parti le quali, in uno buono amico dagli amici, in uno cittadino dalla sua patria si possono disiderare (1 *Arte 2.328*)

non si trova chi voglia andare ad una certa morte (3.6 *D 1.393*)

che per tuo amore si mettino alla morte . . . uno o due (3.6 *D 1.396*)

il piú delle volte dello amore che tu giudichi che uno uomo ti porti (3.6 *D 1.396*)

139 o la forza o l'amore, come sarebbe il ricuperarla per assedio, o che ella vi venga nelle mani volontaria ("Discorso fatto al magistrato dei dieci sopra le cose di Pisa" *2.13*)

Nasce da questo una disputa: s'elli è meglio essere amato che temuto, o e converso (17 *P 1.69*)

amando li uomini a posta loro (17 *P 1.71*)

140 tocco et attendo a femmine . . . Ambasciatore, voi ammalerete; e' non mi pare che voi pigliate spasso alcuno; qui non ci è garzone, qui non sono femmine; che casa di cazzo è questa? (L to Francesco Vettori, Jan. 5, 1514: *5.315*)

Donna: . . . Ma credete voi che sia in Purgatorio?

Timoteo: Sanza dubio!

141 *Donna*: Io non so già, cotesto. Voi sapete pure quello che mi faceva qualche volta. Oh, quanto me ne dolsi io con esso voi! Io me ne discostavo quanto io potevo; ma egli era si importuno! Uh, Nostro Signore!

Timoteo: Non dubitate, la clemenzia di Dio è grande; se non manca a l'uomo la voglia, non gli manca mai el tempo a pentirsi.

Donna: Credete voi che 'l Turco passi questo anno in Italia?

Timoteo: Se voi non fate orazione, sí.

Donna: Naffe! Dio ci aiuti, con queste diavorie! io ho una gran paura di quello impalare. (3.3 *M 4.81–82*)

tu medesimo ti giudicherai degno di quella pena che i parricidi hanno meritata (6.20 *IF 3.418–419*)

Dunque questa nostra patria ci ha dato la vita perché noi la togliamo a lei? Ci ha fatti vittoriosi perché noi la destruggiamo? ci onora perche noi la vituperiamo? (7.23 *IF 3.488*)

patrio nido ("Ingratitudine" *4.309*)

paterno solo ("Ambiz." *4.323*)

142 sí forte catene, che io sono al tutto disperato della libertà né posso pensare via come io habbia a scatenarmi; et quando pure la sorte o altro aggiramento humano mi aprisse qualche cammino ad uscirmene, et per avventura non vorrei entrarvi, tanto mi paiono hor dolci, hor leggeri, hor

gravi quelle catene, et fanno un mescolo, di sorte che io giudico non potere vivere contento senza quella qualità di vita (L to Francesco Vettori, Jan. 31, 1515: *5.373*)

Credi a me ch'il conosco: costui t'ama / piú che la vita sua e te sol vuole, / sol te disia in questo mondo e brama / e non cerca altra cosa sotto il sole: / costui tuo servo per tutto si chiama, / sol di te parla, sol ti onora e cole: / tu se' il suo primo amor, e se tu vuoi / t'ha dedicati tutti gli anni suoi ("Serenata" *4.346*)

battuta, spogliata, lacera (26 *P 1.102*)

143 Io vi potrei addurre in exemplis cose greche, latine, hebraiche, caldee, et andarmene sino nel paese del Sophi et del Prete Janni, et addureveli, se li esempli domestichi et freschi non bastassino (L to Francesco Vettori, Jan. 5, 1514: *5.314*)

amore . . . io sono tuo servo (L to Francesco Vettori, Feb. 4, 1514: *5.322*)

145 in ogni parte / del mondo ove el sí suona (Prologo *M 4.58*)

unita come era al tempo de' Romani ("Ritratto di Cose di Francia" *2.272*)

148 perché questa provincia pare nata per risuscitare le cose morte, come si è visto della poesia della pittura e della scultura (7 *Arte 2.519*)

tutti superbi e regii . . . al tutto maggiore che alcuno altro che da privato cittadino infino a quel giorno fusse stato edificato (7.4 *IF 3.457*)

adornare la loro città (5.15 *IF 3.350*)

uno eccellentissimo architettore chiamato Filippo di ser Brunellesco, delle opere del quale è piena la nostra città, tanto che meritò dopo la morte che la sua immagine fusse posta di marmo nel principale tempio di Firenze, con lettere a pié che ancora rendono a chi legge testimonianza delle sue virtú (4.23 *IF 3.303–304*)

per maggiore magnificenza della città e del tempio e per piú onore del pontefice, si fece un palco da Santa Maria novella, dove il papa abitava, infino al tempio che si doveva consecrare . . . coperto tutto di sopra e d'attorno di drappi ricchissimi, per il quale solo il pontefice con la sua corte venne, insieme, con quelli magistrati della città e cittadini i quali ad accompagnarlo furono diputati; tutta l'altra cittadinanza e popolo per la via, per le case e nel tempio a vedere tanto spettacolo si ridussono (5.15 *IF 3.51*)

voi non siete uso a perdere la Cupola di veduta (1.2 *M 4.65*)

Credo pertanto che sempre fusse chiamata Florenzia per qualunque cagione cosí si nominasse; e cosí, da qualunque cagione si avesse la origine, la nacque sotto lo imperio romano, e ne' tempi de' primi imperadori cominciò dagli scrittori ad essere ricordata (2.2 *IF 3.140*)

149 servo (1.49 *D 1.242*)

Vero è . . . sono contrario, come in molte altre cose, all'oppinione di quelli cittadini (L to Francesco Guicciardini, May 17, 1521: *5.403*)

in grande venerazione el loro re ("Ritratto di Cosa di Francia" *2.173*)

la corona, andando per successione del sangue ("Ritratto di Cose di Francia" *2.164*)

nelli stati ereditarii et assuefatti al sangue del loro principe . . . basta solo
non preterire l'ordine de' sua antenati (2 *P 1.16*)

ordini antiquati nella relligione . . . sono suti tanto potenti e di qualità,
che tengono e' loro principi in stato, in qualunque modo si procedino
e vivino (11 *P 1.50*)

150 Le cose soprascritte, osservate prudentemente, fanno parere uno principe
nuovo antico, e lo rendono subito piú sicuro e piú fermo nello stato,
che se vi fusse antiquato dentro (24 *P 1.97*)

tutte le cose del mondo (3.1 *D 1.379*)

misti (3.1 *D 1.379*)

conviene che abbiano in sé qualche bontà, mediante la quale ripiglino la
prima riputazione ed il primo augumento loro (3.1 *D 1.379*)

fare piú conto della loro virtú (3.1 *D 1.380*)

Sappino adunque i principi come a quella ora ei cominciano a perdere lo
stato, che cominciano a rompere le leggi e quelli modi e quelle consue-
tudini che sono antiche e sotto le quali lungo tempo gli uomini sono
vivuti (3.5 *D 1.389*)

nostra lingua (15 *P 1.65*)

151 lingua . . . toscana (L to Francesco del Nero, Sept. 10–Nov. 7, 1520: *5.397*)

noi Italiani (1.12 *D 1.165*)

noi altri di Italia (L to Francesco Vettori, Aug. 26, 1513: *5.292*)

per l'italico sito . . . canterò io (*Decennale Secondo 4.258*)

non si può avere né piú fidi né piú veri né migliori soldati (26 *P 1.104*)

quelli che sanno non sono obediti, et a ciascuno pare di sapere (26 *P 1.103–104*)

152 la prega Dio che le mandi qualcuno che la redima da queste crudeltà et
insolenzie barbare. . . . tutta pronta e disposta (26 *P 1.102*)

mi pare concorrino tante cose in benefizio d'uno principe nuovo, che io
non so qual mai tempo fussi piú atto a questo (26 *P 1.102*)

sotto l'imperio del papa, Viniziani, Re di Napoli, duca di Milano e Fiorentini. Questi potentati avevano ad avere dua cure principali: l'una che
uno forestiero non intrassi in Italia con le arme, l'altra che veruno di
loro occupassi piú stato (11 *P 1.51*)

Carlo re di Francia, passassi in Italia (11 *P 1.51*)

Virtú contro a furore / prenderà l'arme; e fia el combatter corto: / che
l'antico valore / nelli italici cor non è ancor morto (26 *P 1.105*)

153 li capi senza coda si spengono presto (L to Francesco Vettori, Aug. 26,
1513: *5.296*)

Né posso esprimere con quale amore e' fussi ricevuto in tutte quelle provincie che hanno patito per queste illuvioni esterne; con che pietà, con
che lacrime. Quali porte se li serrerebbano? quali popoli li negherreb-
bano la obedienzia? quale invidia se li opporrebbe? quale italiano li
negherebbe l'ossequio? (26 *P 1.105*)

capo (26 *P 1.102*)

qui è virtú grande nelle membra, quando non la mancassi ne' capi (26 *P*
1.103)

uno prudente e virtuoso, di introdurvi forma (26 *P 1.102–103*)

l'amore della patria è causato dalla natura (4 *Arte 2.442*)

154 È necessario, pertanto, prepararsi a queste arme, per potere con la virtú
italica defendersi dalli esterni (26 *P 1.104*)

volendo conoscere la virtú d'uno spirito italiano, era necessario che la
Italia si riducessi nel termine che ell'è di presente (26 *P 1.102*)

Non si debba adunque lasciar passare questa occasione, acciò ché l'Italia,
dopo tanto tempo, vegga uno suo redentore (26 *P 1.105*)

intenzione alta (7 *P 1.39*)

156 le non hanno altro amore né altra cagione che le tenga in campo, che un
poco di stipendio, il quale non è sufficiente a fare che voglino morire
per te (12 *P 1.54*)

qualunque cittadino si truova a consigliare la patria sua . . . dove si deli-
bera al tutto della salute della patria non vi debbe cadere alcuna consi-
derazione né di giusto né d'ingiusto, né di piatoso né di crudele, né di
laudabile né d'ignominioso (3.41 *D 1.495*)

in quale uomo debbe ricercare la patria maggiore fede che in colui che le
ha a promettere di morire per lei? (Proemio *Arte 2.326*)

tanto quelli cittadini stimavano allora piú la patria che l'anima (3.7 *IF 3.225*)

amo la patria mia piú dell'anima (L to Francesco Vettori, April 16, 1527:
5.505)

CHAPTER 7 The Point of It All

157 al perfetto e vero fine (1.2 *D 1.130*)

grave e severo (Prologo *Clizia 4.117*)

questa metaphora piú non mi serve (L to Francesco Vettori, Feb. 25, 1514:
5.328)

158 da qualunque cittadino si truova a consigliare la patria sua (3.41 *D 1.495*)

si divise la Italia in piú stati (12 *P 1.57*)

Tutti li stati, tutti e' dominii che hanno avuto et hanno imperio sopra li
sono stati uomini, e sono o republiche o principati (1 *P 1.15*)

159 Se io potessi sbucare del dominio (L to Francesco Vettori, April 9, 1513:
5.240)

compartita in Svizzeri, republiche che chiamano terre franche, principi ed
imperadore. E la cagione che intra tante diversità di vivere non vi nascano, o se le vi nascano non vi durano molto le guerre, è quel segno
dello imperadore; il quale, avvenga che non abbi forze, nondimeno ha
infra loro tanta riputazione ch'egli è un loro conciliatore, e con l'autorità sua interponendosi come mezzano spegne subito ogni scandolo
(2.19 *D 1.335–336*)

E' principali fondamenti che abbino tutti li stati . . . sono le buone legge
e le buone arme (12 *P 1.53*)

[420]

160 egli era rimaso primo capitano d'Italia e, non avendo stato, qualunque era
in stato doveva temerlo, e massimamente il duca (7.7 *IF 3.465*)

questo partito che voi pigliate farà alla patria nostra perdere la sua libertà,
a voi lo stato e le sustanze, a me e agli altri la patria (7.15 *IF 3.477*)

I ghibellini . . . solo aspettavano la occasione di ripigliare lo stato (2.6 *IF
3.146*)

mutare lo stato in Firenze (2.27 *D 1.362*)

la conservazione dello stato suo (2.27 *D 1.362*)

uomini che non avevano stato ma erano come capitani di ventura (2.18 *D
1.330*)

per la ignoranza di coloro che tenevano stato (2.18 *D 1.330*)

quegli che hanno governato lo stato di Firenze dal 1434 infine al 1494 (3.1
D 1.381–382)

chi acquista imperio e non forza insieme, conviene che rovini (2.19 *D 1.336*)

chi non ha lo stato . . . non truova cane che gli abbai (2.3 *M 4.72*)

161 Dicevano . . . come egli era necessario ripigliare ogni cinque anni lo stato;
altrimenti era difficile mantenerlo: e chiamavano ripigliare lo stato,
mettere quel terrore e quella paura negli uomini (3.1 *D 1.381–382*)

Ai Palleschi. Notate bene questo scripto ("Ai Palleschi" *2.217*)

questa calca ("Ai Palleschi" *2.226*)

bene a questo stato . . . a loro proprii ("Ai Palleschi" *2.225*)

162 né per chi vuole stare con loro al bene ed al male ("Ai Palleschi" *2.226*)

di nuovo dico che trovare e' difetti di Piero non dà reputazione a lo stato
de' Medici ("Ai Palleschi" *2.226*)

al bene de' Medici ("Ai Palleschi" *2.227*)

nimici di Piero ("Ai Palleschi" *2.226*)

che puttaneggiono infra el popolo ed e' Medici ("Ai Palleschi" *2.226*)

universalità di cittandini ha cagione evidentissima di contentarsi. ("Discursus" *2.268*)

163 (che Dio guardi) ("Discursus" *2.277*)

io voglio fare un pronostico; . . . pensi Vostra Santità, quante morti,
quanti esilii, quante estorsioni ne seguirebbe, da fare ogni crudelissimo
uomo, non che Vostra Santità, che è pietosissima, morire di dolore
("Discursus" *2.276–277*)

cambiare gli abitatori da un luogo a un altro (1.26 *D 1.19*)

164 Tucidide istorico greco (3.16 *D 1.436*)

gravissimo scrittore (2.1 *D 1.275*)

sanza forze le città non si mantengono, ma vengono al fine loro. El fine è
o per desolazione o per servitú ("Parole" *2.58*)

Uscitevi ora di casa e considerate chi voi avete intorno: voi vi troverrete
in mezzo di dua o tre città che desiderano piú la vostra morte che la
loro vita. Andate piú là, uscite di Toscana, e considerate tutta Italia: voi
la vedrete girare sotto el re di Francia, Viniziani, papa e Valentino ("Parole" *2.59*)

165 è stata governata molti anni dalle arme mercennarie (12 *P 1.56*)

serva de' forestieri (2.18 *D 1.330*)

alla fine si aperse di nuovo la via a' barbari e riposesi la Italia nella servitú di quegli (5.1 *IF 3.326*)

cominciasti a sentire e' meriti della durezza vostra; vedesti ardere le vostre case, predare la roba, ammazzare e' vostri sudditi, menarli prigioni, violare le vostre donne, dare el guasto alle possessioni vostre, sanza posservi fare alcun rimedio ("Parole" *2.61*)

Rivolga gli occhi in qua chi veder vuole / l'altrui fatiche e riguardi se ancora / cotanta crudeltà mai vidde il sole. / Chi 'l padre morto e chi 'l marito plora, / quell'altro mesto del suo proprio tetto, / battuto e nudo trar si vede fora. / O quante volte, avendo il padre stretto / in braccio il figlio, con un colpo solo / è suto rotto a l'uno e l'altro il petto! / Quello abbandona il suo paterno sòlo / accusando gli Dei crudeli e ingrati / con la brigata sua piena di dolo. / O esempli mai piú nel mondo stati! / Perché si vede ogni dí parti assai / per le ferite del loro ventre nati. / Drieto a la figlia sua piena di guia / dice la madre: 'A che infelici nozze, / a che crudel marito ti serva!' / Di sangue son le fosse e l'acque sozze, / piene di teschi, di gambe e di mani / e d'altre membra laniate e mozze. / Rapaci uccei, fere silvestri cani / son poi le lor paterne sepolture: / O sepulcri crudei, feroci e strani! . . . Dovunque gli occhi tu rivolti, miri / di lacrime la terra e sangue pregna, / e l'aria d'urla, singulti e sospiri ("Ambiz." *4.323–324*)

166   Questo a Dio non è grato ("Degli spiriti beati" *4.332*)

da uno armato a uno disarmato non è proporzione alcuna (14 *P 1.62*)

ogni città, ogni stato debbe reputare inimici tutti coloro che possono sperare di poterle occupare el suo, e da chi lei non si può difendere ("Parole" *2.58*)

io credo al frate che diceva Pax, Pax, et non erit pax (L to Francesco Vettori, Aug. 26, 1513: *5.292*)

in uno certo modo bilanciata (20 *P 1.86*)

167   la guerra non si lieva . . . si differisce a vantaggio di altri (3 *P 1.21*)

fuggire [una guerra] (3 *P 1.21*)

S'egli è meglio, temendo si essere assaltato, inferire o aspettare la guerra (2.12 *D 1.307*)

Io stimo che in qualunque modo le cose procedino, che gli habbia ad essere guerra, et presto, in Italia (L to Francesco Guicciardini, March 15, 1526: *5.456–457*)

E' si debbe molti di voi ricordare quando Gonstantinopoli fu preso dal Turco. Quello imperadore previde la sua ruina. Chiamò i suoi cittadini, non potendo con le sue armate ordinarie provedersi; espose loro e' periculi, monstrò loro e' rimedii; e se ne feciono beffe. La ossedione venne. Quelli cittadini che avéno prima poco stimato e' ricordi del loro signore, come sentirno sonare le artiglierie nelle lor mura e fremer lo esercito de' nimici, corsono piangendo allo 'mperadore con grembi pieni di danari; e' quali lui cacciò via, dicendo: Andate a morire con cotesti danari, poi che voi non avete voluto vivere sanza essi ("Parole" *2.60–61*)

el tempio . . . a Marte (*Decennale Primo 4.257*)

con il ferro e non con l'oro (2.10 *D 1.303*)

l'oro non è sufficiente a trovare i buoni soldati, ma i buoni soldati sono bene sufficienti a trovare l'oro (2.10 *D 1.304*)

Gli uomini, il ferro, i danari e il pane sono il nervo della guerra; ma di questi quattro sono piú necessari i primi due, perché gli uomini e il ferro trovano i danari e il pane, ma il pane e i danari non truovano gli uomini e il ferro (7 *Arte 2.512*)

168   Sarebbe lungo raccontare quante terre i Fiorentini ed i Viniziani hanno comperate; di che si è veduto poi il disordine e come le cose che si acquistano con l'oro non si sanno difendere con il ferro (2.30 *D 1.369*)

mai acquistarono terre con danari, mai feciono pace con danari, ma sempre con la virtú dell'armi (2.30 *D 1.368*)

de' loro propri cittadini (Proemio *IF 3.370*)

Debbe adunque uno principe non avere altro obietto né altro pensiero, né prendere cosa alcuna per sua arte, fuora della guerra (14 *P 1.62*)

quando non avessi il nimico fuora, lo troverrebbe in casa, come pare necessario intervenga a tutte le gran cittadi (2.19 *D 1.335*)

Quegli mali che sogliono nella pace il piú delle volte generarsi (7.28 *IF 3.494*)

quando il Cielo le fusse sí benigno che la non avesse a fare guerra, ne nascerebbe che l'ozio la farebbe o effeminata o divisa; le quali due cose insieme, o ciascuna per sé, sarebbono cagione della sua rovina (1.6 *D 1.145*)

170   è impossibile che ad una republica riesca lo stare quieta e godersi la sua libertà e gli pochi confini: perché se lei non molesterà altrui, sarà molestata ella; e dallo essere molestata le nascerà la voglia e la necessità dello acquistare (2.19 *D 1.334–335*)

Stette Roma libera quattrocento anni . . . era armata (1 *Arte 2.348*)

Egli fu sempre, e sempre sarà, che gli uomini grandi e rari in una republica ne' tempi pacifichi sono negletti (3.16 *D 1.436*)

mantenere i cittadini poveri . . . non potessino corrompere né loro né altri (3.16 *D 1.437*)

ordinarsi in modo alla guerra che sempre si potesse fare guerra (3.16 *D 1.437*)

faccia volentieri la guerra per avere pace, e non cerchi turbare la pace per avere guerra (1 *Arte 2.340*)

capitani, contenti del trionfo, con disiderio tornavano alla vita privata; e quelli che erano membri, con maggior voglia deponevano le armi che non le pigliavano, e ciascuno tornava all'arte sua, mediante la quale si avevano ordinata la vita (1 *Arte 2.337*)

subito, non solamente cangia abito, ma ancora ne' costumi, nelle usanze, nella voce e nella presenza da ogni civile uso si disforma (Proemio *Arte* 2.325)

a quello che con la barba e con le bestemmie vuole fare paura agli altri uomini (Proemio *Arte* 2.325)

171 d'una republica o d'uno principe, come è avvenuto alla Francia ed alla Spagna (1.12 *D 1.165*)

nel presente giorno / ciascaduna città vive sicura, / per aver manco di sei miglia intorno. / A la nostra città non fe'paura / Arrigo già con tutta la sua possa, / quando i confini avea presso alle mura; / e or ch'ella ha sua potenza promossa / intorno, è diventata e grande e vasta, / teme ogni cosa, non che gente grossa. / Perché quella virtute che soprasta / un corpo a sostener quando egli è solo / a regger poi maggior peso non basta (5 *Asino 4.288*)

da virtú . . . o da necessitate (5 *Asino 4.289*)

uno principe ha tanto stato che possa, bisognando, per sé medesimo reggersi (10 *P 1.48*)

La eccellenzia di Teseo (26 *P 1.102*)

172 iustum enim est bellum quibus necessarium, et pia arma ubi nulla nisi in armis spes est (26 *P 1.103*)

si erano fatte per riempiere i cittadini e non per necessità (4.14 *IF 3.290*)

pax servientibus gravior, quam liberis bellum esset (3.44 *D 1.499*)

173 questi principi oziosi o repubbliche effeminate (3.10 *D 1.420*)

sopra ogni cosa si guardi dalla zuffa (3.10 *D 1.420*)

amare la pace e saper fare la guerra (1 *Arte 2.342*)

e veramente alcuna provincia non fu mai unita o felice (1.12 *D 1.365*)

sicuri e felici (11 *P 1.51*)

nobilitata e . . . felicissima (6 *P 1.31*)

per allor felice e buona ("Fortuna" *4.315*)

la religione introdotta da Numa fu intra le prime cagioni della felicità di quella città, perché quella causò buoni ordini, i buoni ordini fanno buona fortuna, e dalla buona fortuna nacquero i felici successi delle imprese (1.11 *D 1.162*)

se Firenze avesse avuto tanta felicità che . . . ella avesse preso forma di governo che l'avesse mantenuta unita, io non so quale republica o moderna o antica le fusse stata superiore (Proemio *IF 3.70*)

174 quello è felice che riscontra il modo del procedere suo con il tempo . . . Et veramente . . . harebbe sempre buona fortuna (L to Giovan Battista Soderini, c. Sept. 13–21, 1506: *sa.244*)

Credo, ancora, che sia felice quello che riscontra el modo del procedere suo con le qualità de' tempi; e similmente sia infelice quello che con il procedere suo si discordano e' tempi. . . . Concludo, adunque, che, variando la fortuna, e stando li uomini ne' loro modi ostinati, sono felici mentre concordano insieme, e, come discordano, infelici (25 *P 1.99, 101*)

Talché felice si può chiamare quella republica la quale sortisce uno uomo si prudente che gli dia leggi ordinate in modo che, sanza avere bisogno di ricorreggerle, possa vivere sicuramente sotto quelle. . . . e pel contrario tiene qualche grado d' infelicità quella città che non si sendo abbattuta a uno ordinatore prudente, è necessitata da se medesima riordinarsi. E di queste ancora è piú infelice quella che è piú discosto dall'ordine; e quella ne è piú discosto che co' suoi ordini è al tutto fuori del diritto cammino che la possa condurre al perfetto e vero fine (1.2 *D 1.129–130*)

se una republica fusse sí felice (3.22 *D 1.450*)

175 perfezione d'ordine (1.2 *D 1.130*)

quando vi è uno principe dove il piú delle volte quello che fa per lui offende la città e quello che fa per la città offende lui. Dimodoché subito nasce una tirannide . . . E se la sorte facesse che vi surgesse uno tiranno virtuoso, . . . non ne risulterebbe alcuna utilità a quella republica, ma a lui proprio (2.2 *D 1.280*)

una potestà assoluta, la quale dagli autori è chiamata tirannide (1.25 *D 1.193*)

avendo gli uomini il fine buono (1.17 *D 1.178*)

a proposito del bene comune (1.9 *D 1.154*)

176 questo bene alla sua patria (1.9 *D 1.155*)

non a sé ma al bene comune, non alla sua propria successione ma alla comune patria (1.9 *D 1.153*)

invidia natura degli uomini (1.Proemio *D 1.123*)

fastidio e difficultà (1.Proemio *D 1.123*)

non essendo suta ancora da alcuno trita (1.Proemio *D 1.123*)

spinto . . . a ciascuno (1.Proemio *D 1.123*)

bene alla università delli uomini (26 *P 1.102*)

un cavalier che Italia tutta onora, / pensoso piú d'altrui che di se stesso (6.29 *IF 3.433*)

amare l'uno l'altro, a vivere sanza sétte, a stimare meno il privato che il publico (1 *Arte 2.332*)

dico come molti per avventura giudicheranno di cattivo esempio che uno fondatore d'un vivere civile, quale fu Romolo, abbia prima morto un suo fratello, dipoi consentito alla morte di Tito Tazio Sabino, eletto da lui compagno nel regno (1.9 *D 1.153*)

177 La quale opinione sarebbe vera, quando non si considerasse che fine lo avesse indotto a fare tal omicidio (1.9 *D 1.153*)

assoluto e tirannico (1.9 *D 1.154*)

nella morte del fratello e del compagno meritasse scusa (1.9 *D 1.154*)

il desiderio di liberare la patria (3.6 *D 1.392*)

padre della romana libertà (3. *D 1.384*)

tutto è in favore del publico (3.22 *D 1.452*)

ambizione privata (3.22 *D 1.452*)

mostrandosi sempre aspro a ciascuno ed amando solo il bene comune (3.22 *D 1.452*) chiudervi gli occhi, turarvi gli orecchi, legarvi le mani, quando voi abbiate a veder nel giudizio amici o parenti . . . ("Allocuz." *2.137*)

quelli cittadini stimata la comune utilità che la privata amicizia (2.22 *IF 3.170*)

mossi dallo amore della patria (3.5 *IF 3.218*)

amore delle parti (3.5 *IF 3.220*)

non per alcuna publica utilità, ma per loro propria ambizione (3.5 *IF 3.218*)

per bene e utilità publica (3.5 *IF 3.218*)

non per publica ma per propria utilità (3.5 *IF 3.218*)

el bene esser (7 *P 1.36*)

buon governo (7 *P 1.37*)

Spogliateci tutti ignudi, voi ci vedrete simili; rivestite noi delle vesti loro ed eglino delle nostre; noi sanza dubbio nobili ed eglino ignobili parranno (3.13 *IF 3.238*)

178   alcuno de piú arditi e di maggiore esperienza (3.13 *IF 3.236–237*)

Gli uomini plebei (3.13 *IF 3.236*)

popolo minuto (3.13 *IF 3.236*)

Né vi sbigottisca quella antichità del sangue che ei ci rimproverano; perché tutti gli uomini avendo avuto uno medesimo principio sono ugualmente antichi, e dalla natura sono stati fatti a uno modo (3.13 *IF 3.237–238*)

posponendo ogni loro commodo alla commune utilità, e le cose private e le publiche con somma diligenzia governavano e conservavano (1.2 *D 1.132*)

figliuolo . . . contenti alla civile equalità (1.2 *D 1.132*)

dove è grande inequalità di cittadini non si può ordinare repubblica ("Discursus" *2.267*)

quelle republiche dove si è mantenuto il vivere politico ed incorrotto . . . mantengono intra loro una pari equalità . . . a quelli signori e gentiluomini che sono in quella provincia sono inimicissimi; e se per caso alcuni pervengono loro nelle mani . . . gli ammazzano (1.55 *D 1.256*)

tutti quelli che possono avere amministrazione si chiamano Gentiluomini (1.6 *D 1.142*)

E per chiarire questo nome di gentiluomini quale e' sia, dico che gentiluomini sono chiamati quelli che oziosi vivono delle rendite delle loro possessioni abbondantemente, sanza avere cura alcuna o di coltivazione o di altra necessaria fatica a vivere. . . . Trassi adunque di questo discorso questa conclusione: che colui che vuole fare dove sono assai gentiluomini una republica, non la può fare se prima non gli spegne tutti; e che colui che dove è assai equalità vuole fare uno regno o uno principato, non lo potrà mai fare . . . di quella equalità (1.55 *D 1.257, 258*)

179   Io mi lievo la mattina con el sole et vommene in un mio boscho che io fo tagliare, dove sto dua hore a rivedere l'opere del giorno passato (L to Francesco Vettori, Dec. 10, 1513: *5.302*)

Questi tali sono perniziosi in ogni republica ed in ogni provincia; ma piú perniziosi sono quelli che oltre alle predette fortune comandano a castella, ed hanno sudditi che ubbidiscono a loro (1.55 *D 1.256*)

Credo che a questa mia opinione, che dove sono gentiluomini non si possa ordinare republica, parrà contraria la esperienza della Republica viniziana, nella quale non possono avere alcun grado se non coloro che sono gentiluomini. A che si risponde come questo esemplo non ci fa alcuna oppugnazione, perché i gentiluomini in quella republica sono piú in nome che in fatto: perché loro non hanno grande entrate di possessioni, sendo le loro ricchezze grandi fondate in su la mercanzia e cose mobili (1.55 *D 1.258*)

180 il numero de' Gentiluomini o egli è equale al loro o egli è superiore (1.6 *D 1.142*)

che vi venissono ad abitare di nuovo (1.6 *D 1.142*)

181 plebe minuta (3.18 *IF 3.249*)

nate tante genti nuove che le cominciavano avere tanta parte ne' suffragi (3.45 *D 1.505*)

Ordinando cosí lo stato, quando la Santità Vostra e monsignore reverendissimo avesse a vivere sempre, non sarebbe necessario provvedere ad altro; ma avendo a mancare, e volendo che rimanga una republica perfetta . . . ("Discursus" *2.272*)

Resta ora da satisfare al terzo et ultimo grado degli uomini, il quale è tutta la universalità dei cittadini: a' quali non si satisferà mai (e chi crede altrimenti non è savio), se non si rende loro o promette di render la loro autorità. . . . giudico che sia necessario di riaprire la sala del Consiglio de' mille o almeno de' seicento cittadini ("Discursus" *2.271*)

Senza satisfare all'universale non si fece mai alcuna repubblica stabile. Non si satisferà mai all'universale dei cittadini fiorentini, se non si riapre la sala: però, conviene al volere fare una republica in Firenze, riaprire questa sala, e rendere questa distribuzione all'universale, e sappia Vostra Santità, che qualunque penserà di torle lo stato, penserà innanzi ad ogni altra cosa di riaprirla. E però è partito migliore che quella l'apra con termini e modi sicuri, e che la tolga questa occasione a chi fussi suo nemico di riaprirla con dispiacere suo, e destruzione e rovina de' suoi amici ("Discursus" *2.272*)

182 le divisioni (20 *P 1.86*)

le parte (20 *P 1.86*)

le sètte (20 *P 1.86*)

sotto vari nomi (1.55 *D 1.258*)

perché in ogni città si truovano questi dua umori diversi . . . e da questi dua appetiti diversi nasce . . . (9 *P 1.45*)

ragunatosi Castruccio assai umore in bocca, lo sputò tutto in sul volto a Taddeo (*Vita 3.38*)

legge o maggior forza ("Ambiz." *4.321*)

sendo gli appetiti umani insaziabili, perché avendo dalla natura di potere e volere desiderare ogni cosa, e dalla fortuna di potere conseguitarne poche, ne risulta continuamente una mala contentezza . . . delle cose che si posseggono (2.Proemio *D 1.274*)

di dominare . . . di non essere dominati (1.5 *D* 1.139)

183 comandare . . . non ubbidire (3.1 *IF* 3.212)

temono di non perdere l'acquistato (1.5 *D* 1.140)

chi sforza . . . chi è sforzato (1.55 *D* 1.257)

desidera mantenere l'onore già acquistato . . . desidera acquistare quello che non ha (1.5 *D* 1.140)

184 perdere . . . acquistare . . . chi possiede . . . voglia di possedere (1.5 *D 1.141*)

Dove dice che sempre o il Popolo o la Nobilità insuperbiva quando l'altro si umiliava (1.46 *D 1.235*)

e prima si cerca non essere offeso, dipoi si offende altrui (1.46 *D 1.235*)

dal 1378 allo '81 (3.21 *IF 3.256*)

per la arroganza sua l'aveva soggiogata (3.20 *IF 3.253*)

il popolo . . . e di quello la parte piú ignobile (3.5 *IF 3.210*)

qualunque piú al nome fiorentino crudele nimico si sarebbe di tanta rovina vergognato (3.5 *IF 3.210*)

per esperienza (3.5 *IF 3.221*)

la superbia e l'ambizione de' grandi non si spense, ma da' nostri popolani fu loro tolta (3.5 *IF 3.221*)

non basta ricuperare il loro, che vogliono occupare quello di altri e vendicarsi (3.11 *IF 3.232–233*)

la superbia de' grandi . . . il puzzo della plebe (3.17 *IF 3.248*)

in una republica piú nocivi, o quelli che desiderano d'acquistare, o quelli che temono di non perdere l'acquistato (1.5 *D 1.140*)

l'uno e l'altro appetito può essere cagione di tumulti grandissimi. Pur nondimeno il piú delle volte sono causati da chi possiede, perché la paura del perdere genera in loro le medesime voglie che sono in quelli che desiderano acquistare: perché non pare agli uomini possedere sicuramente quello che l'uomo ha, se non gli acquista di nuovo dell'altro. E di piú vi è, che possedendo molto, possono con maggiore potenza e maggiore moto fare alterazione. E ancora vi è di piú, che gli loro scorretti e ambiziosi portamenti accendano, ne' petti di chi non possiede, voglia di possedere, o per vendicarsi contro di loro spogliandoli, o per potere ancora loro entrare in quelle ricchezze e in quegli onori che veggono essere male usati dagli altri (1.5 *D 1.140*)

et vi prego che voi consideriate le cose degl'huomini come l'esser creduto et le potentie del mondo, et maxime delle repubbliche, come le creschino; et vedrete come agl'huomini prima basta potere difendere se medesimi et non esser dominato da altri; da questo si sale poi a offendere altri et a volere dominare altri (L to Francesco Vettori, Aug. 10, 1513: *5.279–280*)

la dolcezza del dominio (L to Francesco Vettori, Dec 10, 1513: *5.281*)

delle civili discordie e delle intrinseche inimicizie (Proemio *IF 3.68*)

descriverrò particularmente, insino al 1434, solo le cose seguite drento alla città, e di quelle di fuora non dirò altro che quello sarà necessario per intelligenzia di quelle di drento (Proemio *IF 3.71*)

Firenze, non contenta di una, ne ha fatte molte (Proemio *IF 3.69*)

si divisono intra i nobili, di poi i nobili e il popolo, e in ultimo il popolo e la plebe; e molte volte occorse che una di queste parti, rimasa superiore, si divise in due. Dalle quali divisioni ne nacquero tante morti, tanti esili, tante destruzioni di famiglie, quante mai ne nascessero in alcuna città di quale si abbia memoria. . . . Se Firenze . . . avesse preso forma di governo che l'avesse mantenuta unita, io non so quale republica o moderna o antica le fusse stata superiore (Proemio *IF 3.69–70*)

185 i tumulti . . . rade volte partorivano esilio, e radissime sangue (1.4 *D 1.137*)

il popolo insieme gridare contro al Senato, il Senato contro al popolo, correre tumultuariamente per le strade, serrare le botteghe, partirsi tutta la plebe di Roma, le quali cose tutte spaventano non che altro chi le legge (1.4 *D 1.137–138*)

alcuno esilio o violenza in disfavore del commune bene, ma leggi e ordini in beneficio della publica libertà (1.4 *D 1.137*)

anzi giovorono alla Republica (1.17 *D 1.178*)

sfogarsi (1.7 *D 1.147*)

offesa da privati a privati, la quale offesa genera paura, la paura cerca difesa, per la difesa si procacciano partigiani, da' partigiani nascono le parti nelle cittadi, dalle parti la rovina di quelle (1.7 *D 1.147–148*)

che il populo desidera non essere comandato né oppresso da' grandi, e li grandi desiderano comandare et opprimere el populo: e da questi dua appetiti diversi nasce nelle città uno de' tre effetti, o principato o libertà o licenzia (9 *P 1.145*)

io non credo che le divisioni facessino mai bene alcuno (20 *P 1.86*)

uno tiranno virtuoso . . . non ne risulterebbe alcuna utilità a quella republica, ma a lui proprio . . . Talché de' suoi acquisti solo egli ne profitta e non la sua patria. E chi volessi confermare questa opinione con infinite altre ragioni legga Senofonte del suo trattato che fa De tyrannide (2.2 *D 1.280–281*)

186 non il bene particulare ma il bene comune è quello che fa grandi le città. E sanza dubbio questo bene comune non è osservato se non nelle republiche . . . Non è maraviglia adunque che gli antichi popoli con tanto odio perseguitassono i tiranni ed amassino il vivere libero, e che il nome della libertà fusse tanto stimato da loro (2.2 *D 1.280–281*)

quelle leggi che dipoi si creavano non a comune utilità, ma tutte in favore del vincitore si ordinavano (3.1 *IF 3.213*)

le leggi . . . non secondo il vivere libero ma secondo la ambizion di quella parte che è rimasa superiore (3.5 *IF 3.220*)

187 onori e premii mediante alcune oneste e determinate cagioni, e fuora di quelle non premia né onora alcuno; . . . comune utilità che del vivere libero si trae, non è da alcuno . . . conosciuta: e di poter godere libera-

mente le cose sue sanza alcuno sospetto, non dubitare dell'onore delle donne, di quel de' figliuoli, non temere di sé (1.16 *D 1.174*)

animare li sua cittadini di potere quietamente esercitare li esercizii loro, e nella mercanzia e nella agricultura et in ogni altro esercizio delli uomini, e che quello non tema di ornare le sua possessione per timore che li siano tolte, e quell'altro di aprire uno traffico per paura delle taglie (21 *P 1.92–93*)

sopra a tutto, astenersi della roba d'altri . . . li uomini sdimentican piú presto la morte del padre che la perdita del patrimonio (17 *P 1.70*)

tutte le terre e le provincie che vivono libere in ogni parte . . . fanno profitti grandissimi. Perché quivi si vede maggiori popoli, per essere e' connubii piú liberi, piú desiderabili dagli uomini: perché ciascuno procrea volentieri quegli figliuoli, che crede potere nutrire; non dubitando che il patrimonio gli sia tolto, e ch'ei si conosce non solamente che nascono liberi e non schiavi, ma ch'ei possono mediante la virtú loro diventare principi. Veggonvisi le ricchezze multiplicare in maggiore numero, e quelle che vengono dalla cultura e quelle che vengono dalle arti. Perché ciascuno volentieri multiplica in quella cosa e cerca di acquistare quei beni che crede acquistati potersi godere. Onde ne nasce che gli uomini a gara pensano a' privati e publici commodi e l'uno e l'altro viene maravigliosamente a crescere. Il contrario di tutte queste cose segue in quegli paesi che vivono servi: e tanto piú scemono dal consueto bene, quanto piú è dura la servitú (2.2 *D 1.284*)

188   quindici o ventimila giovani (7 *Arte 2.515*)

perché sanza gran numero di uomini e bene armati non mai una republica potrà crescere (1.6 *D 1.144*)

quella memorabile pestilenzia da messer Giovanni Boccaccio con tanta eloquenzia celebrata, per la quale in Firenze piú che novantaseimila anime mancorono (3.42 *IF 3.211*)

189   una equale povertà (1.6 *D 1.143*)

ricco il publico povero il privato (2.19 *D 1.334*)

tutte l'arti che si ordinano in una civiltà per cagione del bene comune degli uomini, tutti gli ordini fatti in quella per vivere con timore delle leggi e d'Iddio, sarebbono vani, se non fussono preparate le difese loro (Proemio *Arte 2.325*)

di gemme e d'oro . . . che dalla pioggia le difendesse (Proemio *Arte 2.325*)

190   duoi eccellentissimi istorici . . . avendo io diligentemente letto (Proemio *IF 3.68*)

191   o per straccurataggine delle monache o per cervellinaggine della fanciulla, la si truova gravida di quattro mesi (3.4 *M 4.83*)

dare trecento ducati per l'amore di Dio (3.4 *M 4.83*)

. . . persuadere alla badessa che dia una pozione alla fanciulla per farla sconciare.

Timoteo: Cotesta è cosa da pensarla.

Ligurio: Guardate, nel fare questo, quanti beni ne risulta: voi mantenete

l'onore al monistero, alla fanciulla, a' parenti, rendete al padre una figliuola, satisfate qui a messere, a tanti sua parenti, fate tante elemosine
quante con questi trecento ducati potete fare; e dall'altro canto voi non
offendete altro che un pezzo di carne non nata, sanza senso, che in mille
modi si può sperdere; e io credo che quello sia bene che facci bene ai
piú e che e piú se ne contentino. (3.4 *M 4.83–84*)

193   Dio fa gli uomini, e' si appaiano! (1.3 *M 4.66*)
anzi, posposto ogni altro rispetto, seguire al tutto quel partito, che le salvi
la vita e mantenghile la libertà (3.41 *D 1.495*)
una republica perfetta (1.2 *D 1.135*)
tutto il corso . . . ordinato dal cielo (3.1 *D 1.379*)

CHAPTER 8 Can Men Govern?

194   Dio non vuole fare ogni cosa (26 *P 1.103*)
E' non mi è incognito come molti hanno avuto et hanno opinione che le
cose del mondo sieno in modo governate dalla fortuna e da Dio, che li
uomini con la prudenzia loro non possino correggerle, anzi non vi abbino remedio alcuno, e, per questo, potrebbono iudicare che non fussi
da insudare molto nelle cose, ma lasciarsi governare alla sorte. . . . A
che pensando io qualche volta, mi sono in qualche parte inclinato nella
opinione loro (25 *P 1.98*)

197   in tutte le città ed in tutti gli popoli sono quegli medesimi desideri e quelli
medesimi omori, e come vi furono sempre. In modo che gli è facil cosa
a chi esamina con diligenza le cose passate, prevedere in ogni republica
le future e farvi quegli rimedi che dagli antichi sono stati usati, o non
ne trovando degli usati, pensare de' nuovi per la similitudine degli accidenti. . . . queste considerazioni . . . non sono conosciute da chi go-
verna, ne seguita che sempre sono i medesimi scandoli in ogni tempo
(1.39 *D 1.222*)
la imitazione non solo difficile ma impossibile (1.Proemio *D 1.124*)
rari e maravigliosi (26 *P 1.102*)

198   la quale cosa fa testimonianza a quello che di sopra ho detto, che gli uomini non operano mai nulla se non per necessità; ma dove la elezione
abonda, e che vi si può usare licenza, si riempie subito ogni cosa di
confusione e di disordine (1.3 *D 1.136*)
necessità fa virtú, come . . . abbiamo detto (2.12 *D 1.309*)
a quante necessitadi le leggi fatte da Romolo, Numa e gli altri la constrin-
gessono . . . e la mantennero piena di tanta virtú, di quanta mai fusse
alcuna città o republica ornata (1.1 *D 1.129*)

199   Altre volte abbiamo discorso quante sia utile alle umane azioni la necessità, ed a quale gloria sieno sute condutte da quella e come da alcuni
morali filosofi è stato scritto, le mani e la lingua degli uomini, duoi
nobilissimi instrumenti a nobilitarlo, non arebbero operato perfetta-

mente né condotte le opere umane a quella altezza si veggono condotte, se dalla necessità non fussero spinte (3.12 *D 1.425*)

200 che hanno scritto delle republiche (1.2 *D 1.130*)

Alcuni altri e, secondo la opinione di molti, piú savi, hanno opinione che siano di sei ragioni governi: delle quali tre ne siano pessimi; tre altri siano buoni in loro medesimi, ma sí facili a corrompersi che vengono ancora essi a essere perniziosi. Quelli che sono buoni sono e' sopra-scritti tre: quelli che sono rei sono tre altri i quali da questi tre dipen dano e ciascuno d'essi è in modo simile a quello che gli è propinquo, che facilmente saltano dall'uno all'altro: perché il Principato facilmente diventa tirannico; gli Ottimati con facilità diventano stato di pochi; il Popolare sanza difficultà in licenzioso si converte. Talmente che . . . nessuno rimedio può farvi a fare che non sdruccioli nel suo contrario (1.2 *D 1.130–131*)

e questo è il cerchio nel quale girando tutte le republiche si sono gover-nate (1.2 *D 1.133*)

ma rade volte ritornano ne' governi medesimi, perché quasi nessuna re-publica può essere di tanta vita che possa passare molte volte per queste mutazioni e rimanere in piede. . . . Dico adunque che tutti i detti modi sono pestiferi, per la brevità della vita che è ne' tre buoni e per la mali-gnità che è ne' tre rei (1.2 *D 1.133*)

201 perché l'uno guarda l'altro (1.2 *D 1.133*)

rimanendo mista fece una republica perfetta (1.2 *D.1.135*)

Ed è cosa verissima come tutte le cose del mondo hanno il termine della vita loro . . . il corso che è loro ordinato dal cielo (3.1 *D 1.379*)

ciascuno pregava Dio che ci dessi tempo ("Parole" *2.61*)

mi persuado che Iddio non ci abbi ancora gastigati a suo modo, e che ci riserbi a maggior fragello ("Parole" *2.57*)

202 Avresti tu mai visto in loco alcuno / come una aquila irata si trasporta / cacciata da la fame e dal digiuno? / e come una testudine alto porta, / acciò che 'l corpo del cader la 'nfranga / e pasca sé di quella carne morta? / Cosí Fortuna non ch'ive rimanga / porta una in alto, ma che, ruinando / lei se ne goda e lui cadendo pianga ("Fortuna" *4.317–318*)

203 o per fortuna o per virtú (1 *P 1.15*)

amica alle discordie (4. *IF 3.313*)

204 questa inconstante dea e mobil diva ("Fortuna" *4.313*)

un Palazzo d'ogni parte aperto ("Fortuna" *4.313*)

la sua forza sente ("Fortuna" *4.312*)

andando . . . per vie traverse ed incognite (2.29 *D 1.367*)

in alto sopra tutti . . . comandi e regni impetuasamente ("Fortuna" *4.312*)

E la diva crudel rivolga intanto / ver di me gli occhi sua feroci, e legga / quel ch'or di lei e del suo regno canto ("Fortuna" *4.312*)

La fortuna acceca gli animi degli uomini, quando la non vuole che quegli si opponghino a' disegni suoi (2.29 *D 1.365*)

E se alcuno fusse che vi potesse ostare, o la lo ammazza o la lo priva di tutte le facultà da potere operare alcuno bene (2.29 *D 1.367*) il cielo (2.29 *D 1.365*)

i cieli (2.29 *D 1.365*)

205 Questa da molti è detta omnipotente / perché qualunche in questa vita
viene, / o tardi o presto la sua forza sente ("Fortuna" *4.312*)

ben si sa certo / ch'infino a Giove sua potenzia teme ("Fortuna" *4.313*)

vuole essere arbitra di tutte le cose umane (*Vita 3.33*)

le cose del mondo ("Fortuna" *4.317*)

Potenzia, onor, ricchezza e sanitate / stanno per premio: per pena e dolore, / servitú, infamia, morbo e povertate ("Fortuna" *4.314*)

Costei spesso gli buon sotto i pié tiene, / gl'improbi innalza ("Fortuna"
4.312–313)

206 comanda agli huomini, e tiengli sotto il giogo suo (L to Giovan Battista
Soderini, c. Sept. 13–21, 1506: *sa.244*)

E sottosopra e regni e stati mette / secondo ch'a lei pare, e giusti priva /
del bene che agli ingiusti larga dette ("Fortuna" *4.313*)

i cieli, dandogli occasione o togliendogli (2.29 *D 1.366*)

Quelle occasioni che la gli porge (2.29 *D 1.366*)

Moisè, Ciro, Romulo, Teseo e simili . . . che la occasione, la quale dette
loro materia a potere introdurvi drento quella forma parse loro; e sanza
quella occasione la virtú dello animo loro si sarebbe spenta, e sanza
quella virtú la occasione sarebbe venuta invano (6 *P 1.30-31*)

Come conviene variare co' tempi, volendo sempre avere buona fortuna
(3.9 *D 1.416*)

E' si ottiene con l'impeto e con l'audacia molte volte quello che con modi
ordinari non si otterrebbe mai (3.44 *D 1.498*)

207 Perché tutto quel mal ch'in voi procede / s'imputa a lei, e s'alcun ben
l'uom truova, / per sua propria virtude averlo crede ("Fortuna" *4.314*)

aveva pensato a ciò che potessi nascere morendo el padre, et a tutto aveva
trovato remedio, eccetto che non pensò mai, in su la sua morte, di stare
ancora lui per morire (7 *P 1.39*)

errò . . . fu cagione dell'ultima ruina sua (7 *P 1.40*)

Nel primo loco colorato e tinto / si vede come già sotto l'Egitto / il mondo
stette subiugato e vinto, / . . . veggonsi poi gli Assiri ascender sue / ad
altro scettro, quand'ella non volse / che quel d'Egitto dominassi piue; /
poi come a' Medi lieta si rivolse, / da' Medi a' Persi: e de' Greci la
chioma / ornò di quello onor ch'a' Persi tolse. / . . . quivi si mostran
quanto furon belle, / alte, ricche, potenti e come al fine / Fortuna a' lor
nimici in preda diella ("Fortuna" *4.316*)

208 per sua stella / a quanto è possibile, ogni ora / accomodarsi al variar di
quella ("Fortuna" *4.316*)

che ruota al suo voler conforme piglia ("Fortuna" *4.315*)

perché mentre girato sei dal dorso / di ruota per allor felice e buona, / la
suol cangiar le volte a mezzo il corso; / e non potendo tu cangiar persona / né lasciar l'ordin di che 'l ciel ti dota, / nel mezzo del cammin la
t'abbandona ("Fortuna" *4.315*)

se si mutassi di natura con li tempi e con le cose, non si muterebbe fortuna (25 *P 1.100*)

avendo sempre uno prosperato camminando per una via, non si può persuadere partirsi da quella (25 *P 1.100*)

ne' di nostri e nella nostra patria memorabile (3.3 *D 1.386*)

Come conviene variare co' tempi volendo sempre avere buona fortuna (3.9 *D 1.416*)

procedeva in tutte le cose sue con umanità e pazienza. Prosperò egli e la sua patria mentre che i tempi furono conformi al modo del procedere suo; ma come e' vennero dipoi tempi dove e' bisognava rompere la pazienza e la umiltà, non lo seppe fare; talché insieme con la sua patria rovinò (3.9 *D 1.418*)

uno nappo d'ariento pieno di confetti (3.19 *IF 3.251*)

scoperto e veduto da tutti i convivanti, fu interpretato che gli era ricordato conficcasse la ruota; perché avendolo la fortuna condotto nel colmo di quella, non poteva essere che, se la seguitava di fare il cerchio suo, che la non lo traesse in fondo. La quale interpretazione fu, prima dalla sua rovina, dappoi dalla sua morte, verificata (3.19 *IF 3.251*)

209 Nicholaus Maclavellus Cancellarius (Legation of April 29, 1499: *6.175*)

E quelle ruoton sempre notte e giorno, / perché il cielo vuole (a cui non si contrasta) / . . . Però se questo si comprende e nota, / sarebbe un sempre felice e beato / che potessi saltar di rota in rota ("Fortuna" *4.314–315*)

210 Ma perché il pianto a l'uom fu sempre brutto / si debbe a' colpi della sua fortuna / voltar il viso di lagrime asciutto (3 *Asino 4.280*)

Le republiche forti e gli uomini eccellenti ritengono in ogni fortuna il medesimo animo e la loro medesima dignità (3.31 *D 1.469*)

se la fortuna mi avesse conceduto per lo addietro tanto stato quanto basta . . . sanza dubbio o io l'arei accresciuto con gloria o perduto sanza vergogna (7 *Arte 2.520*)

la fortuna vuol fare ogni cosa . . . stare quieto e non le dare briga . . . la lasci fare qualche cosa agl'huomini (L to Francesco Vettori, Dec. 10, 1513: *5.301*)

Né sempre mai preme / colui che 'n fondo di sua rota giace ("Fortuna" *4.313*)

Affermo bene di nuovo questo essere verissimo, secondo che per tutte le istorie si vede, che gli uomini possono secondare la fortuna e non opporsegli; possono tessere gli orditi suoi e non rompergli. Debbono bene non si abbandonare mai; . . . hanno sempre a sperare e sperando non si abbandonare in qualunque fortuna ed in qualunque travaglio si truovino (2.29 *D 1.367*)

io indegnamente sopporti una grande e continua malignità di fortuna (Lettera *P 1.14*)

211 iudico potere essere vero che la fortuna sia arbitra della metà delle azioni nostre, ma che etiam lei ne lasci governare l'altra metà, o presso, a noi.

Et assomiglio quella a uno di questi fiumi rovinosi, che, quando s'adirano allagano e' piani, ruinano li arberi e li edifizii, lievono da questa parte terreno, pongono da quell'altra: ciascuno fugge loro dinanzi, ognuno cede allo impeto loro, sanza potervi in alcuna parte obstare. E benché sieno cosí fatti, non resta però che li uomini, quando sono tempi quieti, non vi potessino fare provvedimenti e con ripari et argini, in modo che, crescendo poi, o egli andrebbono per uno canale, o l'impeto loro non sarebbe né sí licenzioso né sí dannoso. Similmente interviene della fortuna: la quale dimonstra la sua potenzia dove non è ordinata virtú a resisterle, e quindi volta li sua impeti dove la sa che non sono fatti li argini e li ripari a tenerla. . . . E questo voglio basti quanto allo avere detto allo opporsi alla fortuna in universali (25 *P 1.99*)

questa antica strega ("Fortuna" *4.313*)

212 Io iudico bene questo, che sia meglio essere impetuoso che respettivo, perché la fortuna è donna; et è necessario, volendola tenere sotto, batterla et urtarla. E si vede che la si lascia piú vincere da questi, che da quelli che freddamente procedono. E però sempre, come donna, è amica de' giovani, perché sono meno respettivi, piú feroci, e con piú audacia la comandano (25 *P 1.101*)

non sapendo la via quanto era aperta (4 *Asino 4.284*)

quel che 'n virtú sua non ispera (4 *Asino 4.284*)

poi che virtude hai sí poca che questi / panni che son fra noi ti fanno guerra, / e da me sí discosto ti ponesti (4 *Asino 4.285*)

Non in un loco la man si ritenne; / ma discorrendo per le membra sue, / la smarrita virtú tosto rinvenne (4 *Asino 4.285*)

a chi lei porta amore ("Fortuna" *4.315*)

214 la è amica de' giovani (L to Giovan Battista Soderini, c. Sept. 13–21, 1506: *sa.242*)

l'offesa che si fa all'uomo debbe essere in modo che la non tema la vendetta (3 *P 1.20*)

a questa volta tu se' stata amica de' vecchi (4.1 *Clizia 4.146*)

Annibale in Italia giovane e con una fortuna fresca (3.9 *D 1.417*)

audacia e gioventú fa miglior pruova ("Fortuna" *4.314*)

quanto a costei piaccia / quanto grato le sia si vede scorto, / chi l'urta, chi la pigne o chi la caccia ("Fortuna" *4.317*)

215 Dio non vuole fare ogni cosa, per non ci torre el libero arbitrio e parte di quella gloria che tocca a noi (26 *P 1.103*)

CHAPTER 9 The Prince New, and Other Sinners

217 quanto era facile l'uomo a scorrere nel peccato ("Esortaz." *4.209*)

218 È notissima la storia di Orazio (1.24 *D 1.191*)

219 Ma spicchiamoci da queste cose terrene, alziamo gli occhi al ceilo, consideriamo . . . quelle altre chi ci sono nascoste ("Esortaz." *4.210*)

delle cose del mondo (Lettera *D 1.121*)

le cose degli uomini (1.6 *D 1.145*)

mondane cose (5.1 *IF 3.325*)

le cose del mondo in ogni tempo hanno il proprio riscontro con gli antichi tempi (3.43 *D 1.496*)

sendo tutte le cose degli uomini in moto (1.6 *D 1.145*)

come procedono le cose umane (2.29 *D 1.365*)

conoscitori delle cose naturali (1.12 *D 1.164*)

220 coloro che sono stati padroni del mondo ("Del modo di trattare" *2.73*)

e pentirsi e cognoscer chiaramente / che quanto piace al mondo è breve sogno ("Esortaz." *4.213*)

gli soldati antichi (4 *Arte 2.441*)

non solamente di quelli mali che potessono temere dagli uomini, ma di quegli che da Dio potessono aspettare (4 *Arte 2.441*)

intercessione di San Gregorio ("Allocuz."*2.136*)

pagano ed infedele ("Allocuz." *2.136*)

insieme con gli altri infernali giudici (*Belfagor 4.169*)

Questa, quella celestiale veste della quale noi dobbiamo vestirci se vogliamo essere intromessi alle celestiale nozze dello imperadore nostro Cristo Iesú nel celeste regno! questa, quella della quale chi non sia ornato sarà cacciato dal convito . . . ("Esortaz." *4.211*)

221 clementissimo Iddio ("Esortaz." *4.209*)

vidde che avendo a stare in sul rigore della vendetta era impossibile che niuno uomo si salvasse ("Esortaz." *4.209*)

222 cresciuta poi questa mala sementa / multiplicata la cagion del male, / non c'è ragion che di mal far si penta ("Ambiz." *4.321*)

grazia o miglior ordin di Dio ("Ambiz." *4.324*)

sendole detto da una sua vicina che, s'ella si botava di udire quaranta mattine la prima messa de' Servi che la impregnerebbe, la si botò e andovvi forse venti mattine. Ben sapete che un dí que' fratacchioni li cominciò a 'ndare d'atorno, in modi che la non si volse piú tornare. Egli è pure male però, che quelli che ci arebbono a dare buoni essempli sien fatti cosí. Non dich'io el vero! (1.2 *M 4.79–80*)

Callimaco: Oh benedetto frate! Io pregherrò sempre Dio per lui

Ligurio: Oh buono! Come se Dio facesse le grazie del male come del bene! El Frate vorrà altro che preghi!

Callimaco: Che vorrà?

Ligurio: Danari! (4.2 *M 4.93–94*)

224 gli stati non si tenevono co' paternostri in mano (7.6 *IF 3.462*)

non potendo fare uno papa a suo modo, poteva tenere che uno non fussi papa; e non doveva mai consertire al papato di quei cardinali che lui aveva offesi (7. *P 1.40*)

mostrò quanto uno papa, e con il danaio, e con le forze, si poteva prevalere (11 *P 1.52*)

le forze temporali (11 *P 1.52*)

Papa Iulio secondo, andando nel 1515 a Bologna per cacciare di quello stato la casa de' Bentivogli, la quale aveva tenuto il principato in quella città cento anni (1.27 *D 1.194–195*)

si era dimostro lupo e non pastore (8.11 *IF 3.528*)

in compagnia di traditori e parricidi . . . tanto tradimento in nel tempio, nel mezzo del divino officio, nella celebrazione del Sacramento, e da poi, perché non gli era successo ammazzare i cittadini, mutare lo stato della loro città e quella a suo modo saccheggiare, la interdiceva e con le pontificali maledizioni la minacciava e offendeva. . . . Non mancavano ancora al papa ragioni da giustificare la causa sua. E perciò allegava appartenersi a uno pontefice spegnere la tirannide, opprimere i cattivi, esaltare i buoni: le quali cose ei debbe con ogni opportuno rimedio fare, ma che non è già l'ufficio de' principi seculari detenere i cardinali, impiccare i vescovi, ammazzare, smembrare e strascinare i sacerdoti, gli innocenti e i nocenti sanza alcuna differenzia uccidere (8.11 *IF 1.529–530*)

225   molti il loro mobile per i munisteri e per le chiese nascondevano (3.10 *IF 3.230*)

Costui . . . non avendo altro rimedio che nascondersi o fuggire, prima in Santa Croce si nascose, di poi vestito da frate in Casentino se ne fuggí (3.10 *IF 3.231*)

all'omicidio (3.6 *D 1.403*)

che per pratica e per natura erano a tanta impresa inettissimi (8.6 *IF 3.517*)

furono vituperosamente morti e per tutta la città strascinati (8.6 *IF 3.519*)

alcuni cittadini . . . si guastava la città e facevasi contro a Dio a cacciare di quella tanti uomini da bene (7.6 *IF 3.461*)

226   materia a' nimici di calunniarlo come uomo che amasse piú sé medesimo che la patria e piú questo mondo che quell'altro (7.6 *IF 3.462*)

e' ficca el capo in quante chiese e' truova e va a tutti gli altari a borbottare uno paternostro (1.1 *Clizia 4.120*)

credo che le persuasioni e i prieghi potrieno giovare, ma io credo che molto piú gioverebbono i fatti (L to Francesco Guicciardini, March 15, 1526: *5.456*)

San Marco a le sue spese, e forse invano / tardi conosce come li bisogna / tener la spada e non il libro in mano ("Ambiz." *4.324*)

dipingere un San Marco, che in scambio di libro ha una spado in mano . . . ad loro spese che ad tenere li stati non bastano li studj e e' libri (Legation of Dec. 7, 1509, *11.1202*)

227   il piú reputato e nomato cittadino, di uomo disarmato (7.5 *IF 3.458*)

l'Italia quasi che nelle mani della Chiesia e di qualche Republica, et essendo quelli preti e quelli altri cittadini usi a non conoscere arme, cominciorono a soldare forestieri (12 *P 1.57*)

228   il papa per non gli stare bene le armi indosso sendo religioso, e la reina Giovanna di Napoli per essere femmina, . . . i Fiorentini . . . avendo per le spesse divisioni spenta la nobilità e restando quella republica nelle mani di uomini nutricati nella mercanzia (1.39 *IF 3.135*)

il desiderio del popolo fiorentino era ingiurioso e ingiusto (3.1 *IF 3.213*) al sangue e allo esilio de' cittadini (3.1 *IF 3.213*)

molti di loro intra popolare moltitudine mescolorono (1.42 *IF 3.210–211*)

di qui nasceva le variazioni delle insegne le mutazioni de' tituli delle famiglie, che i nobili, per parere di popolo, facevano: tanto che quella
virtú dell'armi e generosità de animo che era nella nobilità si spegneva,
e nel popolo dove la non era non si poteva raccendere; tale che Firenze
sempre piú umile e piú abbietto divenne (3.1 *IF 3.213*)

si spogliasse (2.41 *IF 3.211*)

229 subietto allo animo sacerdotale al tutto disforme (*Vita 3.11*)

dolore e noia inestimabile (*Vita 3.11*)

Lo esercizio del quale era la guerra (*Vita 3.11*)

una autorità regia (*Vita 3.12*)

dove piú volentieri starebbe: o in casa d'uno gentile uomo che gli insegnasse cavalcare e trattare armi, o in casa d'uno prete dove non si udisse
mai altro che uffizii e messe (*Vita 3.12*)

è cosa straordinaria a pensare in quanto brevissimo tempo ei diventò
pieno di tutte quelle virtú e costumi che in uno vero gentile uomo si
richieggono (*Vita 3.12*)

Venere (6 *Arte 2.478*)

Sí, s'elle fussono abitate da donne (2.24 *D 1.355*)

che le donne, i vecchi i fanciugli e i deboli si stieno in casa e lascino la
terra libera a' giovani e gagliardi (7 *Arte 2.501*)

né a donne né a luoghi pii si perdono (7.30 *IF 3.498*)

230 donne in casa . . . stanno come bestie (5.6 *M 4.111*)

riempiere una sedia in paradiso, contentare el marito vostro (3.11 *M 4.89*)

e come si è veduto in questra nostra istoria, l'eccesso fatto contro a Lucrezia tolse lo stato ai Tarquinii, quell'altro fatto contro a Virginia, privò
i dieci dell'autorità loro. Ed Aristotile intra le prime cause che mette
della rovina de' tiranni e lo avere ingiuriato altrui per conto delle
donne, con stuprarle o con violarle o con rompere i matrimoni; . . .
Dico adunque come i principi assoluti ed i governatori delle repubbliche non hanno a tenere poco conto di questa parte (3.26 *D 1.459–460*)

231 E' pare che Alessandro di Mariano di costí che al presente si trova nelle
stinche di Firenze a istanza degli spettabili Otto di Guardia e Balia della
città nostra, abbia usato con una sua serva di età di anni 11, per ogni
verso, in modo che l'abbia guasta, e che di questa cosa ne hanno notizia
la donna di Cristofano Messo costí della sua corte, e la donna di Lazzaro Magnano, ed un'altra donna che si chiama la Parvola, che si ritro-
varono, per quello ne è riferito, con detta fanciulla a lavare panni a una
fonte fuora della porta Passerina di Colle. Ora perché noi desideriamo
d'avere piena notizia di tutta questa cosa, vogliamo e' comandianti facci
d'avere a te dette tre donne di sopra nominate, e similmente della fanciulla, et medio earum iuramento ciascuna di per sé le farai esaminare
per tuo cavaliere, e Notajo diligentemente sopra questo caso, con piú
riguardo e onestà ti sarà possibile; purché noi abbiamo la stretta e

semplice verità della cosa; ed esaminate saranno, ce ne manderai una copia de' detti loro, chiusa e sigillata del tuo sigillo, e per persona fidata; e insieme ci manderai la fanciulla predetta accompagnata in modo che l'onestà sia preservata. Fa quanto ti comandiamo con la celerità possibile, dando per tuo onore avviso per chi mandi detti testimoni, e chi verrà con la fanciulla predetta ("Lettere di Niccolò Machiavelli Scritte sopra differenti affari di Governo a nome della Repubblica Fiorentina" in *Opere di Niccolò Machiavelli* [no named editor(s)] 10 vols., Genoa: Domenico Porcile & C., 1798, VIII, 26–27 [second enumeration])

per quello che noi intendiamo buona e de' primi parentadi di costí, ed halla in tal modo trattata e tratta con tenere una femina in casa e in su gli occhi sua . . . ella è stata necessitata . . . uscirsene di casa e tornare co' parenti sua, e non la provvede di cosa alcuna, in modo che la povera donna ha carestia del boccone dal pane, e lui colla femmina si gode e la dote della donna, e l'eredità sua . . . Tu intendi la mente nostra ("Affari di Governo," in *Opere di Niccolò Machiavelli*, Genoa, 1798, VIII, 37–38)

fa quanto ti comandiamo, non manchi ("Affari di Governo," in *Opere di Niccolò Machiavelli*, Genoa, 1798, VIII, 38)

232 De Principatibus . . . et a un principe, et maxime a un principe nuovo, doverrebbe essere accetto (L to Francesco Vettori, Dec. 10, 1513: *5.304*)

233 ma nel principato nuovo consistono le difficultà (3 *P 1.16*)

sempre bisogni offendere quelli di che si diventa nuovo principe, e con gente d'arme, e con infinite altre iniurie che si tira drieto el nuovo acquisto; in modo che tu hai nimici tutti quelli che tu hai offesi in occupare quello principato, e non ti puoi mantenere amici quelli che vi ti hanno messo, per non li potere satisfare in quel modo che si erano presupposto e per non potere tu usare contro di loro medicine forti, sendo loro obbligato (3 *P 1.17*)

el principe naturale (2 *P 1.16*)

non preterire l'ordine de' sua antinati, e di poi temporeggiare con li accidenti (2 *P 1.16*)

uno che . . . diventi principe (9 *P 1.46*)

quelli che sono nuovi (20 *P 1.87*)

nato principe (24 *P 1.97*)

234 che io farò de' principati al tutto nuovi e di principe e di stato (6 *P 1.30*)

di privato principe (6 *P 1.30*)

dico che li piú eccellenti sono Moisé, Ciro, Romulo, Teseo e simili (6 *P 1.30*)

in su le arme mercennarie (12 *P 1.54*)

e chi diceva come e' n'erano cagione e' peccati nostri, diceva el vero; ma non erano già quelli che credeva, ma questi che io ho narrati: e, perché elli erano peccati di principi, ne hanno patito la pena ancora loro (12 *P 1.54*)

Quod principem deceat circa militiam (14 *P 1.62*)

Considerato, adunque, tutte le cose di sopra discorse e pensando meco medesimo se in Italia al presente correvano tempi da onorare uno nuovo principe, e se ci era materia che dessi occasione a uno prudente e virtuoso, di introdurvi forma che facessi onore a lui e bene alla università delli uomini di quella, mi pare concorrino tante cose in benefizio d'uno principe nuovo, che io non so qual mai tempo fussi piú atto a questo. (26 *P 1.101–102*)

235   uno principe, e massime uno principe nuovo (18 *P 1.73*)
necessitato (18 *P 1.73*)

E debbesi pigliare questo per una regola generale: che mai o rado occorre che alcuna republica o regno sia da principio ordinato bene, o al tutto di nuovo fuora degli ordini vecchi riformato, se non è ordinato da uno; anzi è necessario che uno solo sia quello che dia il modo e dalla cui mente dependa qualunque simile ordinazione (1.9 *D 1.153*)

ha subito a fare infra sé medesima uno capo (1.57 *D 1.261*)

236   non è cosa piú difficile a trattare né piú dubia a riuscire, né piú pericolosa a maneggiare, che farsi capo a introdurre nuovi ordini. Perché lo introduttore ha per nimici tutti quelli che delli ordini vecchi fanno bene, et ha tepidi difensori tutti quelli che delli ordini nuovi farebbano bene. La quale tepidezza nasce, parte per paura delli avversarii, che hanno le leggi dal canto loro, parte dalla incredulità delli uomini; li quali non credano in verità le cose nuove, se non ne veggono nata una ferma esperienza (6 *P 1.31–32*)

non è . . . ordinata per durare molto quando la rimanga sopra le spalle d'uno, ma sí bene quando la rimane alla cura di molti e che a molti stia il mantenerlo . . . cosí come molti non sono atti a ordinare una cosa . . . cosí conosciuto che lo hanno non si accordano a lasciarlo (1.9 *D 1.154*)

E se i principi sono superiori a' popoli nello ordinare leggi, formare vite civili, ordinare statuti ed ordini nuovi, i popoli sono tanto superiori nel mantenere le cose ordinate ch'egli aggiungono sanza dubbio alla gloria di coloro che l'ordinano (1.58 *D 1.265*)

di corta vita (1.11 *D 1.162*)

la salute d'una republica o d'uno regno avere uno principe che prudentemente governi mentre vive, ma uno che l'ordini in modo che morendo ancora la si mantenga (1.11 *D 1.162*)

per il modo dello eleggere non solamente due successioni ma infiniti principi virtuosissimi che sono l'uno dell'altro successori: la quale virtuosa successione fia sempre in una republica bene ordinata (1.20 *D 1.186*)

237   numerati tra' principi di una città (1 *Arte 2.332*)

uno prudente ordinatore . . . debbe ingegnarsi di avere l'autorità solo; né mai uno ingegno savio riprenderà alcuno di alcuna azione straordinaria, che per ordinare un regno o per constituire una republica usasse (1.9 *D 1.153*)

non basta usare termini ordinari essendo modi ordinari cattivi; ma è necessario venire allo straordinario, come è alla violenza e all' armi . . . (1.18 *D 1.182*) modi estraordinari di procedere . . . perfettamente (4.27 *IF* 3.309)

il primo al quale non piacevano le vie straordinarie (4.27 *IF* 3.309)

eccessive e notabili (3.1 *D* 1.381)

estraordinaria et eccessiva (2 *P* 1.16)

mano regia . . . potenza assoluta ed eccessiva (1.55 *D* 1.257)

sarebbe necessario ridurla piú verso lo stato regio che verso lo stato popolare, acciocché quegli uomini, i quali dalle leggi per la loro insolenzia
non possono essere corretti, fussero da una podestà quasi regia in
qualche modo frenati (1.18 *D* 1.182)

238 braccio regio (7 *P* 1.37)

pienissima potestà (7 *P* 1.37)

maestà del principato (19 *P* 1.76)

maestà dello stato (18 *P* 1.74)

la maestà degli ornamenti, della pompa, e della comitiva sua! Talché ti
può questa pompa spaventare, o vero con qualche grata accoglienza
raumiliare (3.6 *D* 1.403)

uno principe e massime uno principe nuovo . . . bisogna che . . . non partirsi dal bene, potendo, ma sapere entrare nel male, necessitato (18 *P*
1.73–74)

imparare a potere essere non buono, et usarlo e non usare secondo la
necessità (15 *P* 1.65)

239 sendo spesso necessitato, per mantenere lo stato, operare contro alla fede,
contro alla carità, contro alla umanità, contro alla relligione. (18 *P* 1.73)

inimici al prossimo che mancano della carità. . . . Non può essere pieno
di carità quello che non sia pieno di religione ("Esortaz." 4.211)

posto nel sempiterno incendio ("Esortaz." 4.211)

240 Io spero e lo sperar cresce 'l tormento, / io piango e il pianger ciba il lasso
core, / io rido e el rider mio non passa drento, / io ardo e l'arsion non
par di fore, / io temo ciò che io veggo e ciò che io sento, / ogni cosa mi
dà nuovo dolore: / cosí sperando, piango rido e ardo, / e paura ho di
ciò che io odo e guardo ("Strambotto" I, 4.357)

CHAPTER 10 The Truth about Human Things

241 in questo guasto mondo (5.1 *IF* 3.327)

Pensate pertanto come tutte le cose fatte e create sono fatte e create a
beneficio dell'uomo. Voi vedete in prima lo immenso spazio della terra,
la quale perché potessi essere dagli uomini abitata non permesse che la
fusse circundata tutta da le acque ma ne lasciò parte scoperta per suo
uso. Fece di poi nascere in quella tanti animali, tante piante, tante erbe,
a qualunque cosa sopra quella si genera, a beneficio suo: e non solo
volle che la terra provedessi al al vivere di quello, ma comandò ancora
alle acque che nutrissino infiniti animali per il suo vitto. Ma spicchiamoci da queste cose terrene, alziamo gli occhi al cielo, consideriamo la

bellezza di quelle cose che noi vediamo . . . splendore e la mirabile opera ("Esortaz." *4.210*)

Vedete adunque con quanta ingratitudine l'uomo contro a tanto beneficatore insurga! ("Esortaz." *4.211*)

essendo le cose umane sempre in moto (2.Proemio *D 1.272*)

non essendo dalla natura conceduto alle mondane cose il fermarsi . . . (5.1 *IF 3.325*)

242 tutte le cose del mondo . . . operate dagli uomini (3.43 *D 1.496*)

o le salgono o le scendano (2.Proemio *D 1.272*)

alla loro ultima perfezione, non avendo piú da salire conviene che scendino (5.1 *IF 3.325*)

ad ultima bassezza . . . conviene che salghino (5.1 *IF 3.325*)

e cosí sempre da il bene si scende al male, e da il male si sale al bene (5.1 *IF 3.325*)

243 la virtú partorisce quiete, la quiete ozio, l'ozio disordine, il disordine rovina; e similmente dalla rovina nasce l'ordine, dall'ordine virtú, da questa, gloria e buona fortuna (5.1 *IF 3.325*)

Questo modo di vivere adunque pare che abbi renduto il mondo debole, e datolo in preda agli uomini scelerati; . . . E benché paia che si sia effeminato il mondo e disarmato il Cielo, nasce piú sanza dubbio dalla viltà degli uomini, che hanno interpretato la nostra religione secondo l'ozio e non secondo la virtú (2.2 *D 1.282–283*)

La virtú fa le region tranquille; / e da tranquillità poi ne risolta / l'ocio: e l'ocio arde i paesi e le ville (5 *Asino 4.289*)

non si può la fortezza degli armati animi con piú onesto ozio che con quello delle lettere corrompere, né può l'ozio con il maggiore e piú pericoloso inganno che con questo nelle città bene institute ertrare (5.1 *IF 3.325*)

244 veggendo come la gioventú romana cominciava con ammirazione a seguitargli, e cognoscendo il male che da quello onesto ozio alla sua patria ne poteva risultare, provvide che niuno filosofo potesse essere in Roma ricevuto (5.1 *IF 3.325*)

le republiche bene ordinate hanno a tenere ricco il publico e gli loro cittadini poveri (1.37 *D 1.216*)

dopo quattrocento anni che Roma era stata edificata, vi era una grandissima povertà . . . Durò questa povertà infino a' tempi di Paulo Emilio che furono quasi gli ultimi felici tempi di quella Republica, dove uno cittadino, che col trionfo suo arricchí Roma, nondimeno mantenne povero sé (3.25 *D 1.457–459*)

a uno uomo buono e valente quale era Cincinnato, quattro iugeri di terra bastavano a nutrirlo (3.25 *D 1.458*)

Potrebbesi con un lungo parlare mostrare quanto migliori frutti produca la povertà che la ricchezza, e come l'uno ha onorato le città, le provincie, le sétte, e l'altra le ha rovinate, se questa materia non fusse stata molte volte da altri uomini celebrata (3.25 *D 1.459*)

NOTES

245 che me ne vo l'anno in 40 fiorini et ne ho 90 d'entrata o meno (L to Francesco Vettori, April 16, 1514: *s.334*)

246 Degl'altri cavalli (L to Guido Machiavelli, April 2, 1527: *s.500*)

248 questa povera villa e paululo patrimonio (L to Francesco Vettori, Dec. 10, 1513: *s.303*)

sendo avezzo a spendere . . . senza spendere (L to Francesco Vettori, June 10, 1514: *s.343*)

povero e contennendo (16 *P 1.68*)

intra tutte le cose di che uno principe si debbe guardare, è lo essere contennendo et odioso (16 *P 1.68*)

Mangiato che ho, ritorno nell'hosteria: quivi è l'hoste, per l'ordinario, un beccaio, un mugnaio, dua fornaciai. Con questi io m'ingaglioffo per tutto dí giuocando a cricca, a triche-tach, et poi dove nascono mille contese et infiniti dispetti di parole iniuriose, et il piú delle volte si combatte un quattrino et siamo sentiti non di manco gridare da San Casciano (L to Francesco Vettori, Dec. 10, 1513: *s.303*)

249 Cosí, rinvolto entra questi pidocchi traggo el cervello di muffa . . . (L to Francesco Vettori, Dec. 10, 1513: *s.303*)

In casa Antonio Guicciardini . . . certi altri cittadini (L to Francesco Vettori, Dec. 10, 1513: *s.302*)

in un mio boscho che io fo tagliare dove sto dua hore a rivedere l'opere del giorno passato et a passar tempo con quegli tagliatori, che hanno sempre qualche sciagura alle mane o fra loro o co' vicini. (L to Francesco Vettori, Dec. 10, 1513: *s.302*)

250 Partitomi del boscho io me ne vo a una fonte e di quivi in un mio uccellare. Ho un libro sotto, o Dante o Petrarca, o un di questi poeti minori, come Tibullo, Ovvidio e simili: leggo quelle loro amorose passioni et quelli loro amori, ricordomi de' mia, godomi un pezzo in questro pensiero (L to Francesco Vettori, Dec. 10, 1513: *s.303*)

Quanto al cavallo, voi mi fate ridere al ricordarmelo (L to Francesco Vettori, April 9, 1513: *s.240*)

Occorre . . . molte volte, che uno uomo animoso sarà sopra uno cavallo vile e uno vile sopra uno animoso; donde conviene che queste disparitadi d'animo facciano disordine. Né alcuno si maravigli che uno nodo di fanti sostenga ogni impeto di cavagli, perché il cavallo è animale sensato e conosce i pericoli e male volentieri vi entra. E se considererete quali forze lo facciano andare avanti e quali lo tengano indietro, vedrete sanza dubbio essere maggiori quelle che lo ritengono che quelle che lo spingono; perché innanzi lo fa andare lo sprone, e dall'altra banda lo ritiene o la spada o la picca. Tale che si è visto per le antiche e per le moderne esperienze, un nodo di fanti essere securissimo, anzi insuperabile da' cavagli. E se voi arguisti a questo che la foga, con la quale viene, lo fa piú furioso a urtare chi lo volesse sostenere, meno stimare la picca che lo sprone, dico che, se il cavallo discosto comincia a vedere di avere a percuotere nelle punte delle picche, o per se stesso egli raffrenerà il corso, di modo che come egli si sentirà pugnere si fermerà affatto, o, giunto a quelle, si volterà a destra o a sinistra. Di che se volete fare esperienza, provate a correre un cavallo contro a un muro . . . (2 *Arte 2.369–370*)

251   ho infino a qui uccellato a' tordi di mia mano. Levatomi innanzi dí, inpaniavo, andavone oltre con un fascio di gabbie addosso, che parevo el Geta quando e' tornava dal porto con i libri d'Anphitrione; pigliavo el meno dua, el piú sei tordi. Et cosí stetti tutto Settembre; di poi questo badalucco, ancora che dispettoso e strano, è mancato con mio dispiacere (L to Francesco Vettori, Dec. 10, 1513: *5.302*)

nacqui povero et imparai prima a stentare che a godere (L to Francesco Vettori, March 18, 1513: *5.235*)

non dispregiare la povertà (1 *Arte 2.332*)

252   della fede et bontà mia ne è testimonio la povertà mia (L to Francesco Vettori, Dec. 10, 1513: *5.306*)

Vedi le stelle e 'l ciel, vedi la luna, / vedi gli altri pianeti andare errando / or alto or basso sanza requie alcuna (3 *Asino 4.280*)

Sa ciascuno . . . come avanti la morte di Lorenzo de' Medici vecchio fu percosso il duomo nella sua piú alta parte con una saetta celeste (1.56 *D 1.259*)

254   il mondo fu sempre ad un modo abitato da uomini che hanno avuto sempre le medesime passioni ("Del modo di trattare" *2.73*)

tutte le cose del mondo in ogni tempo hanno il proprio riscontro con gli antichi tempi. Il che nasce essendo quelle operate dagli uomini che hanno ed ebbono sempre le medesime passioni, conviene di necessità che le sortiscono il medesimo effetto (3.43 *D 1.496*)

Che direte voi che questo medesimo caso, pochi anni sono, seguí ancora in Firenze? (Prologo *Clizia 4.116*)

Se nel mondo tornassino i medesimi omini come tornano i medesimi casi, non passerebbono mai cento anni che noi non ci trovassino un'altra volta insieme a fare le medesime cose che ora (Prologo *Clizia 4.117*)

255   quelli cittadini parlavono in Greco, e voi quella lingua non intenderesti (Prologo *Clizia 4.117*)

256   La cagione è perché la natura ha creato gli uomini in modo che possono desiderare ogni cosa e non possono conseguire ogni cosa: talché essendo sempre maggiore il desiderio che la potenza dello acquistare, ne risulta la mala contentezza di quello che si possiede, e la poca sodisfazione d'esso (1.37 *D 1.215*)

Perché qualunque volta è tolto agli uomini il combattere per necessità, combattono per ambizione; la quale è tanto potente ne' petti umani che mai, a qualunque grado si salgano, gli abbandona (1.37 *D 1.215*)

ci mena / per proprio moto e propria passione ("Ambiz." *4.321*)

un asin voli (2.Canzone *M 4.78*)

egli è tanta la voglia estrema che è in loro di ritornare a casa, che ei credono naturalmente molte cose che sono false (3.31 *D 1.372*)

257 Et facto che io l'hebbi, venendomi pure voglia di vedere questa mercatan-
tia, tolsi un tizone di fuoco d'un focolare che v'era et accesi una lucerna
che vi era sopra; né prima el lume fu apreso che 'l lume fu per cascarmi
di mano. Omè! fu' per cadere in terra morto, tanto era bructa quella
femina. . . . la bocca somigliava quella di Lorenzo de' Medici, ma era
torta da un lato e da quello n'usciva un poco di bava. . . . io le recé
addosso. Et cosí, pagata di quella moneta che la meritava, mi partí (L
to Luigi Guicciardini, Dec. 8, 1509: *5.205–206*)

ma noi siamo ingannati dalla libidine ("Esortaz." *4.212*)

Et per quel cielo che io darò, io non credo, mentre starò in Lombardia,
mi torni la foia (L to Luigi Guicciardini, Dec. 8, 1509: *5.206*)

Perché, mancando gli uomini, quando gl'invecchiano, di forze e crescendo di giudizio e di prudenza, è necessario che quelle cose che in
gioventú parevano loro sopportabili e buone, rieschino poi invec-
chiando insopportabili e cattive (2.Proemio *D 1.273–274*)

biasimare i presenti tempi, laudare i passati e desiderare i futuri, ancora
che a fare questo non fussono mossi da alcuna ragionevole cagione.
Non so adunque se io meriterò d'essere numerato tra quelli che s'ingan-
nano, se in questi mia discorsi io lauderò troppo i tempi degli antichi
Romani e biasimerò i nostri (2.Proemio *D 1.274*)

e sono tanto semplici li uomini, e tanto obediscano alle necessità presenti,
che colui che inganna troverrà sempre chi si lascerà ingannare (18 *P 1.73*)

258 Quanto siano false molte volte le opinioni degli uomini nel giudicare le
cose grandi (2.22 *D 1.342*)

aprire gli occhi a' popoli (1.47 *D 1.240*)

discendere a' particulari (1.47 *D 1.240*)

Il popolo molte volte disidera la rovina sua ingannato da una falsa spezie
di beni (1.53 *D 1.249*)

E se nel descrivere le cose seguite in questo guasto mondo non si narrerà
o fortezza di soldati o virtú di capitano o amore verso la patria di cittadino, si vedrà con quali inganni, con quali astuzie e arti i principi, i
soldati, i capi delle republiche . . . si governavano (5.1 *IF 3.327*)

non fece mai altro, non pensò mai ad altro che ad ingannare uomini, e
sempre trovò subietto da poterlo fare . . . perché conosceva bene questa
parte del mondo (18 *P 1.73*)

Firenze, città . . . che le cose dai successi . . . giudica (8.22 *IF 3.549*)

259 el vulgo ne va preso con quello che pare e con lo evento della cosa; e nel
mondo non è se non vulgo (18 *P 1.74*)

la cagione del male era la febbre e non il medico (1.39 *D 1.223*)

tutti gli uomini in questo ciechi (3.35 *D 1.482*)

Conviene bene che, accusandolo il fatto, lo effetto lo scusi; e quando sia
buono come quello di Romolo, sempre lo scuserà (1.9 *D 1.153–154*)

colui che è violento per guastare, non quello che è per racconciare, si
debbe riprendere (1.9 *D 1.154*)

quello che fece fusse per il bene comune e non per ambizione propria (1.9 *D 1.154*)

260 spenta che fu quella generazione che l'aveva ordinato (1.2 *D 1.132*)

gli uomini cominciano a variare con i costumi e trapassare le leggi (3.1 *D 1.381*)

A volere che una sétta o una republica viva lungamente, è necessario ritirarla spesso verso il suo principio (3.1 *D 1.379*)

quella riputazione ch'egli aveva ne' principi suoi (3.1 *D 1.383*)

ritirare verso il segno (3.1 *D 1.381*)

i palagi publici, i luoghi de' magistrati, le insegne de' liberi ordini la ricordono (2.34 *IF 3.193*)

e se non nasce cosa per la quale si riduca loro a memoria la pena, e rinnuovisi negli animi loro la paura, concorrono tosto tanti delinquenti che non si possono più punire sanza pericolo (3.1 *D 1.381*)

261 che la rinascesse, e rinascendo ripigliasse nuova vita e nuova virtú ripigliasse la osservanza della religione, e della giustizia (3.1 *D 1.380*)

la prima riputazione ed il primo augumento loro (3.1 *D 1.379*)

corpi misti come sono le republiche e le sétte (3.1 *D 1.379*)

hanno il termine della vita loro; ma quelle vanno tutto il corso che è loro ordinato dal cielo generalmente, che non disordinano il corpo loro ma tengonlo in modo ordinato, o che non altera o s'egli altera è a salute e non a danno suo (3.1 *D 1.379*)

spesso rinnovare (3.1 *D 1.379*)

Ed è cosa più chiara che la luce, che non si rinnovando questi corpi non durano (3.1 *D 1.379*)

E questi dottori di medicina dicono, parlando de' corpi degli uomini: "Quod quotidie aggregatur aliquid, quod quandoque indiget curatione" (3.1 *D 1.379–380*)

questa bontà e questa religione ancora in quelli popoli essere grande; la quale fa che molte republiche vi vivono libere, ed in modo osservano le loro leggi che nessuno di fuori né di dentro ardisce occuparle (1.55 *D 1.255*)

262 cosí si godono questa loro rozza vita e libertà ("Magna" *2.210*)

non è cosa alcuna che gli ricomperi da ogni estrema miseria, infamia e vituperio . . . non è osservanza di religione, non di leggi, non di milizia, ma sono maculati d'ogni ragione bruttura (2.Proemio *D 1.273*)

veramente dove non è questa bontà non si può sperare nulla di bene; come non si può sperare nelle provincie che in questi tempi si veggono corrotte, come è la Italia sopra tutte l'altre (1.55 *D 1.255*)

accecato da uno poco d'ambizione (1.42 *D 1.230*)

facilmente gli uomini si corrompono e fannosi diventare di contraria natura, quantunque buoni e ben ammaestrati (1.42 *D 1.230*)

ma la fa poi scoprire il tempo (1.3 *D 1.135*)

Il tempo . . . essere padre di ogni verità (1.3 *D 1.135*)

li abbiano sempre a usare la malignità dello animo loro qualunque volta ne abbiano libera occasione (1.3 *D 1.135*)

263 ritornorono i cittadini al loro consueto modo di vivere, pensando di godersi sanza alcuno sospetto quello stato che si avevano stabilito e fermo. Di che ne nacquono alla città quegli mali che sogliono nella pace il piú delle volte generarsi, perché i giovani, piú sciolti che l'usitato, in vestire, in conviti, in altre simili lascivie sopra modo spendevano, ed essendo oziosi, in giuochi e in femmine il tempo e le sustanze consumavano; e gli studi loro erano apparire con il vestire splendidi e con il parlare sagaci e astuti, e quello che piú destramente mordeva gli altri era piú savio e da piú stimato. Questi cosi fatti costumi furono da' cortigiani del duca di Milano accresciuti, il quale insieme con la sua donna e con tutta la sua ducale corte, per sodisfare, secondo che disse, a uno boto, venne in Firenze; dove fu ricevuto con quella pompa che conveniva un tanto principe e tanto amico alla città ricevere. Dove si vide, cosa in quel tempo nella nostra città ancora non veduta, che sendo il tempo quadragesimale, nel quale la Chiesa comanda che sanza mangiare carne si digiuni, quella sua corte, sanza rispetto della Chiesa o di Dio, tutta di carne si cibava. E perché si feciono molti spettaculi per onorarlo, intra i quali nel tempio di Santo Spirito si rappresentò la concessione dello Spirito Santo agli Apostoli, e perché per i molti fuochi che in simile solennità si fanno quel tempio tutto arse, fu creduto da molti Dio indegnato contro di noi avere voluto della sua ira dimostrare quel segno. Se adunque quel duca trovò la città di Firenze piena di cortigiane delicatezze e costumi a ogni bene ordinata civiltà contrari, la lasciò molto piú (7.28 *IF 3.494–495*)

264 pendé piú verso il principato che verso la republica ("Discursus" *2.262*)

ambizioso ozio (1.Proemio *D 1.124*)

licenzia ambiziosa (1.47 *D 1.239*)

O mente umana insaziabil, altera, / subdola e varia e sopra ogni altra cosa / maligna, iniqua, impetuosa e fera ("Ambiz." *4.320*)

265 proni al male (1.9 *D 1.154*)

266 gli uomini mangiono l'uno l'altro (3.13 *IF 3.238*)

269 contro a Dio ("Esortaz." *4.211*)

di animale razionale in animale bruto si transforma. . . . di angelo diavolo, di signore servo, di uomo bestia ("Esortaz." *4.211*)

CHAPTER 11 The Mirror of the Prince New

271 uno uomo di basso et infimo stato ardisce discorrere e regolare e' governi de' principi (Lettera *P 1.14*)

272 Dante dice che non fa scienza senza lo ritenere lo havere inteso, io ho notato quello di che per la loro conversazione ho fatto capitale (L to Francesco Vettori, Dec. 10, 1513: *5.304*)

et doverrebbe ciascheduno haver caro servirsi d'uno che alle spese d'altri fussi pieno di experientia (L to Francesco Vettori, Dec. 10, 1513: *5.305*)

arte della pace (1.19 *D 1.184*)

non avere altro obietto né altro pensiero, né prendere cosa alcuna per sua arte, fuora della guerra . . . perché quella è sola arte che si aspetta a chi comanda (14 *P 1.62*)

Di che si cava una regola generale, la quale mai o raro falla: che chi è cagione che uno diventi potente, ruina (3 *P 1.25*)

273 per il che si ha a notare che li uomini si debbono o vezzeggiare o spegnere (3 *P 1.19*)

Di che si può trarre un altro notabile: che li principi debbono le cose di carico fare sumministrare ad altri, quelle di grazia a loro medesimi (19 *P 1.78*)

il che fu contro ad una mia regola che dice . . . (L to Bartolomeo Cavalcanti, c. Oct. 6, 1526: *5.490*)

Ma di questa cosa non si può parlare largamente, perche la varia secondo el subietto (20 *P 1.87*)

tanto sono i disegni nostri incerti e fallaci (8.2 *IF 3.510*)

E perché a simili disordini che nascano nelle republiche non si può dare certo rimedio, ne seguita che gli è impossibile ordinare una republica perpetua, perché per mille inopinate vie si causa la sua rovina (3.17 *D 1.439*)

274 mastro saggio e gentile / di nostra umana vita udito avete (5.Canzona *Clizia 4.166*)

275 E chi legge la Bibbia sensatamente vedrà Moisé essere stato forzato, a volere che le sue leggi e che li suoi ordini andassero innanzi, ad ammazzare infiniti uomini (3.30 *D 1.468*)

Visse quarantaquattro anni, e fu in ogni fortuna principe (*Vita 3.40–41*)

276 E perché il riordinare una città al vivere politico presuppone uno uomo buono, e il diventare per violenza principe di una republica presuppone uno uomo cattivo; per questo si troverrà che radissime volte accaggia che uno buono, per vie cattive, ancora che il fine suo fusse buono, voglia diventare principe; e che uno reo, divenuto principe, voglio operare bene, e che gli caggia mai nello animo usare quella autorità bene che gli ha male acquistata (1.18 *D 1.182*)

condurre li eserciti, ordinare le giornate (14 *P 1.63*)

debbe stare sempre in su le caccie, e mediante quelle assuefare el corpo a' disagi (14 *P 1.63*)

uno principe prudente (23 *P 1.95*)

Perché questa è una regola generale che non falla mai: che uno principe, il quale non sia savio per sé stesso, non può essere consigliato bene (23 *P 1.96*)

277 quelli che descrivano la vita de' principi, e . . . quegli che ordinano come ei debbano vivere (3.20 *D 1.445*)

quegli che scrivono come uno principe si abbia a governare (3.22 *D 1.451*) io mi profondo quanto io posso nelle cogitationi di questo subbietto, disputando che cosa è principato, di quale spetie sono, come e' si acquistono, come e' si mantengono, perché e' si perdono (L to Francesco Vettori, Dec. 10, 1513: *5.304*)

andrò tessendo li orditi soprascritti (2 *P 1.16*)

Quot sint genera principatum et quibus modis acquirantur (1 *P 1.15*)

De principatibus hereditariis (2 *P 1.15*)

De principatibus mixtis (3 *P 1.16*)

278   Cur Darii regnum . . . post Alexandri mortem non defecit (4 *P 1.25*)

Quomodo administrandae sunt civitates vel principatus, qui antequam occuparentur, suis legibus vivebant (5 *P 1.28*)

De principatibus novis (6 *P 1.30*)

De principatu civili (9 *P 1.45*)

Quomodo omnium principatuum vires perpendi debeant (10 *P 1.48*)

De principatibus ecclesiasticis (11 *P 1.50*)

anchor che tuttavolta io l'ingrasso et ripulisco (L to Francesco Vettori, Dec. 10, 1513: *5.304*)

Ha trovato adunque la Santità di papa Leone questo pontificato potentissimo: il quale si spera , se quelli lo feciono grande con l'arme, questo con la bontà e con infinite altre sua virtú lo farà grandissimo e venerando (11 *P 1.52–53*)

Quot sint genera militiae et de mercenariis militibus (12 *P 1.53*)

De militibus auxiliariis, mixtis et propriis (13 *P 1.58*)

279   nostro trattato "De Principe" (3.42 *D 1.496*)

tu hai inimici tutti quelli che tu hai offesi . . . (3 *P 1.17*)

O tu, principe vuoi . . . o tu . . . (3.24 *D 1.351*)

280   resta ora a vedere . . . (15 *P 1.64*)

E, perché io so che molti di questo hanno scritto, dubito, scrivendone ancora io, non essere tenuto prosuntuoso, partendomi, massime nel disputare questa materia, dalli ordini delli altri. Ma,sendo l'intento mio scrivere cosa utile a chi la intende, mi è parso piú conveniente andare drieto alla verità effettuale della cosa, che alla immaginazione di essa. E molti si sono immaginati repubbliche e principati che non si sono mai visti né conosciuti essere in vero (15 *P 1.64–65*)

Lasciando adunque indrieto le cose circa uno principe immaginate, e discorrendo quelle che sono vere . . . (15 *P 1.65*)

elli è tanto discosto da come si vive a come si doverrebbe vivere, che colui che lascia quello che si fa per quello che si doverrebbe fare, impara piú tosto la ruina che la preservazione sua (15 *P 1.65*)

281   tanti che non sono buoni (15 *P 1.65*)

sono tristi (18 *P 1.73*)

imparata con una lunga esperienza delle cose moderne et una continua lezione delle antique (Lettera *P 1.13*)

Io ho imparato per una lunga pratica e continua lezione, delle cose del mondo (Lettera *D 1.121*) dí per dí (L to Francesco Vettori, August 10, 1513: *5.280*)

cosí come coloro che disegnono e' paesi si pongano bassi nel piano a considerare la natura de' monti e de' luoghi alti, e per considerare quella de' bassi si pongano alto sopra monti, similmente a conoscere bene la natura de' populi bisogna esser principe, et a conoscere bene quella de' principi bisogna esser populare (Lettera *P 1.14*)

282   Cosí avviene nelle cose di stato; perché conoscendo discosto (il che non è dato se non a uno prudente) e mali che nascono in quello si guariscono presto; ma quando, per non li avere conosciuti, si lasciono crescere in modo che ognuno li conosce, non vi è piú remedio. Perciò e' Romani, vedendo discosto e' inconvenienti, vi rimediorono sempre (3 *P 1.21*)

a quelli iudizii o a quelli remedii che dalli antichi sono stati iudicati o ordinati perché le leggi civili non sono altro che sentenze date dagli antiqui iureconsulti, le quali, redutte in ordine, a' presenti nostri iureconsulti a iudicare insegnano. Né ancora la medicina è altro che esperienze fatte dagli antiqui medici, sopra la quale fondano e' medici presenti e' loro iudizii (Proemio *D 1.124*)

Ma, quanto allo esercizio della mente, debbe el principe leggere le istorie, et in quelle considerare le azioni delli uomini eccellenti vedere come si sono governati nelle guerre, esaminare le cagioni della vittoria e perdite loro, per potere queste fuggire e quelle imitare; e sopra tutto fare come ha fatto per l'adrieto qualche uomo eccellente, che ha preso ad imitare se alcuno innanzi a lui è stato laudato e gloriato, e di quello ha tenuto sempre e' gesti et azioni appresso di sé: come si dice che Allessandro Magno imitava Achille, Cesare Alessandro, Scipione Ciro (14 *P 1.64*)

283   E qualunque legge la vita di Ciro scritta da Senofonte, riconosce di poi nella vita di Scipione quanto quella imitazione li fu di gloria, e quanto nella castità, affabilità, umanità, liberalità, Scipione si conformassi con quelle cose che di Ciro da Senofonte sono sute scritte (14 *P 1.64*)

le virtuosissime operazioni che le istorie ci mostrono, che sono state operate da' regni, e da republiche antique, dai re, capitani, cittadini, latori di leggi ed altri che si sono per la loro patria affaticati (Proemio *D 1.124*)

uno principe nuovo, in uno principato, non può imitare le azioni di Marco, né ancora è necessario seguitare quelle di Severo; ma debbe pigliare da Severo, quelle parti che per fondare el suo stato sono necessarie, e da Marco quelle che sono convenienti e gloriose a conservare uno stato che sia già stabilito e fermo (19 *P 1.84*)

con . . . diligenzia (Lettera *P 1.13*)

avendo io diligentemente letto gli scritti loro (Proemio *IF 3.68*)

E chi leggerà sensatamente tutte le istorie, troverrà . . . (1.23 *D 1.190*)

E chi legge la Bibbia sensatamente vedrà . . . (3.30 *D 1.468*)

284   nostra città di Firenze (3.43 *D 1.497*)

avesse letti e conosciuti gli antichi costumi de' barbari, non sarebbe stata né questa né molte altre volte ingannata da loro (3.43 *D 1.497*)

come chi balla procede con il tempo della musica e, andando con quella, non erra, cosi uno esercito, ubbidendo nel muoversi a quel suono, non si disordina. E però variavano il suono secondo che volevano variare il moto e secondo che volevano accendere o quietare o fermare gli animi degli uomini. E come i suoni erano varii, cosí variamente gli nominavano. Il suono dorico generava costanzia, il frigio furia; donde che dicono che, essendo Alessandro a mensa, e sonando uno il suono frigio, gli accese tanto l'animo che misse mano all'armi. Tutti questi modi sarebbe necessario ritrovare; e quando questo fusse difficile, non si vorrebbe almeno lasciare indietro quegli che insegnassero ubbidire al soldato; i quali ciascuno può variare e ordinare a suo modo, pure che con la pratica assuefaccia gli orecchi de' suoi soldati a conoscergli (2 *Arte* 2.*392*)

Volendo pertanto trarre li uomini di questo errore, ho guidicato necessario scrivere sopra tutti quelli libri di Tito Livio . . . quello che io, secondo le cognizione delle antique e moderne cose, iudicherò essere necessario per maggiore intelligenzia di essi, a ciò che coloro che leggeranno queste mia declarazioni, possino piú facilmente trarne quella utilità per la quale si debba cercare la cognizione delle istorie (1.Proemio *D.124–125*)

285 debole notizia delle antique (1.Proemio *D 1.123*)

cognizione delle antiche e moderne cose (1.Proemio *D 1.125*)

mai ne' tempi pacifici stare ozioso (14 *P 1.64*)

se mai in alcuna faccenda si ricerca l'animo grande e fermo, e nella vita e nella morte per molte esperienze risoluto, è necessario averlo in questa, dove si è assai volte veduto agli uomini nelle arme esperti e nel sangue intrisi lo animo mancare (18 *IF 3.517*)

mi presentai subito cosí cavalchereccio a sua Eccellenza, la quale mi accolse amorevolmente; e io, presentategli le lettere di credenza, gli esposi la cagione della mia venuta (Legation of Oct. 7, 1502: *7.195*)

alla memoria dei nostri padri (19 *P 1.77*)

io non voglio delli esempli freschi tacerne uno (18 *P 1.73*)

286 dicevano . . . quegli che hanno governato lo stato di Firenze dal 1434 infine al 1494 . . . (3.1 *D 1.381–382*)

parlo con quelli che passono, domando delle nuove de' paesi loro, intendo varie cose, et noto varii gusti et diverse fantasie d'uomini (L to Francesco Vettori, Dec. 10, 1513: *5.303*)

per intendere . . . la verità (1 *Arte 2.331*)

e' libri ecclesiastici da parte (*Vita 3.11*)

quelle che di guerre o di cose fatte da grandissimi uomini ragionassino (*Vita 3.11*)

287 leggendo né praticando le actioni delli uomini et i modi del procedere loro (L to Giovan Battista Soderini, c. Sept. 13–21, 1506: *5a.242*)

principe né republica che agli esempli delli antiqui ricorra (1.Proemio *D 1.124*) vera cognizione delle storie, per non trarne leggendole quel senso né gustare di loro quel sapore che le hanno in sé (1.Proemio *D 1.124*)

dato a pochi (13 *P 1.61*)

perché tocca a vedere a ognuno, a sentire a pochi. Ognuno vede quello che tu pari, pochi sentono quello che tu se' (18 *P 1.74*)

288   avendo io con gran diligenzia lungamente escogitate et esaminate (Lettera *P 1.13*)

Ma spicchiamoci da queste terrene, alziamo gli occhi al cielo, consideriamo la bellezza di quelle cose che noi vediamo: delle quali, parte ne ha fatte per nostro uso, parte perché, cognoscendo lo splendore e la mirabile opera di quelle ci venga sete e desiderio di possedere quelle altre che ci sono nascoste ("Esortaz." *4.210*)

289   retti da cagione superiore alla quale mente umana non aggiugne (11 *P 1.51*)

perché sono molti i beni conosciuti da uno prudente, i quali non hanno in sé ragioni evidenti da poterli persuadere a altrui (1.11 *D 1.161*)

debolezza de' capi (26 *P 1.103*)

non manca la materia (26 *P 1.103*)

290   vivere con quello medesimo populo (9 *P 1.46*)

può ben fare sanza quelli medesimi grandi potendo farne e disfarne ogni dí (9 *P 1.46*)

E non sia alcuno che repugni a questa mia opinione con quello proverbio trito, che chi fonda in sul popolo, fonda in sul fango (9 *P 1.47*)

Tito Livio nostro, come tutti gli altri istorici (1.58 *D 1.261*)

Nessuna cosa essere più vana e più incostante che la moltitudine (1.58 *D 1.261*)

Io non so se io prenderò una provincia dura e piena di tanta difficultà che mi convenga o abbandonarla con vergogna o seguirla con carico; volendo difendere una cosa, la quale, come ho detto, da tutti gli scrittori è accusata. Ma comunque si sia, io non giudico né giudicherò mai essere difetto difendere alcuna opinione con le ragioni, sanza volervi usare o l'autorità o la forza (1.58 *D 1.262*)

ma la opinione contro ai popoli nasce perché de' popoli ciascuno dice male sanza paura e liberamente ancora mentre che regnano; de' principi si parla sempre con mille paure e mille sospetti (1.58 *D 1.266*)

i popoli ed i principi insieme, potrebbe dire il vero; ma traendone i principi s'inganna (1.58 *D 1.263–264*)

nasce non dalla natura diversa . . . in tutti è a uno modo (1.58 *D 1.264*)

Dico come io iudico coloro potersi reggere per sé medesimi, che possono, o per abundandi uomini, o di danari, mettere insieme un esercito iusto, e fare una giornata con qualunque li viene ad assaltare (10 *P 1.48*)

291   satisfare piú a' soldati che a' populi . . . ora è piú necessario a tutti e' principi . . . satisfare a' populi che a' soldati, perché e' populi possono piú di quelli (19 *P 1.83*)

il fondamento e il nervo dello esercito e quello che si debbe piú stimare, debbano essere le fanterie (2.17 *D 1.330*)

del populo inimico uno principe non si può mai assicurare (9 *P 1.46*)

a uno principe è necessario avere el populo amico: altrimenti non ha nelle avversità remedio (9 *P 1.47*)

quando li sia nimico et abbilo in odio, debbe temere d'ogni cosa e d'-ognuno (19 *P 1.77*)

non puoi stare disarmato (20 *P 1.85*)

la migliore fortezza che sia, è non essere odiato dal populo (20 *P 1.88*)

non fu mai adunque che uno principe nuovo disarmasse e' sua sudditi; anzi, quando li ha trovati disarmati, li ha sempre armati; perché, ar-mandosi, quelle arme diventono tua (20 *P 1.85*)

il cuore e le parti vitali di uno corpo si hanno a tenere armate . . . offeso questo si muore (2.30 *D 1.370*)

con certo ordine e certo modo (3.30 *D 1.469*)

CHAPTER 12 To Be or To Seem to Be

293 Quanto all'atto, che sia peccato, questa è una favola, perché la volontà è quella che pecca, non el corpo (3.11 *M 4.89*)

De his rebus quibus homines et praesertim principes laudantur et vitu-perantur (15 *P 1.64*)

Quod principem deceat ut egregius habeatur (21 *P 1.89*)

Dico che tutti li uomini, quando se ne parla, e massime e' principi, per essere posti piú alti, sono notati di alcune di queste qualità che arrecano loro o biasimo o laude (15 *P 1.65*)

E questo è che alcuno è ritenuto liberale, alcuno misero . . . alcuno è te-nuto donatore, alcuno rapace; alcuno crudele, alcuno pietoso; l'uno fedi-frago, l'altro fedele; l'uno effeminato e pusillanime, l'altro feroce e ani-moso; l'uno umano, l'altro superbo; l'uno lascivo, l'altro casto; l'uno intero, l'altro astuto; l'uno duro, l'altro facile; l'uno grave, l'altro leg-gieri; l'uno relligioso, l'altro incredulo, e simili (15 *P 1.65*)

294 parere pietoso, fedele, umano, intero, relligioso (18 *P 1.73*)

ciascuno confesserà che sarebbe laudabilissima cosa che uno principe tro-varsi di tutte le soprascritte qualità (15 *P 1.65*)

295 uno uomo che voglia fare in tutte le parte professione di buono (15 *P 1.65*)

piú importanti (19 *P 1.73*)

A uno principe, adunque, non è necessario avere tutte le soprascritte qua-lità, ma è bene necessario parere di averle (18 *P 1.73*)

296 lo universale degli uomini si pascono di quel che pare come di quel che è (1.25 *D 1.192*)

è facile a persuadere loro una cosa, ma è difficile fermarli in quella persua-sione (6 *P 1.32*)

Debbe adunque avere uno principe gran cura che non li esca mai di bocca una cosa che non sia piena delle soprascritte cinque qualità, e paia, a verderlo et udirlo, tutto pietà, tutto fede, tutto integrità, tutto umanità, tutto relligione. E non è cosa piú necessaria a parere di avere, che questa ultima qualità (18 *P 1.74*)

sotto questo medesimo mantello (21 *P 1.90*)

Et hassi ad intendere questo, che uno principe et massime uno principe nuovo, non può osservare tutte quelle cose per le quali li uomini sono tenuti buoni, sendo spesso necessitato, per mantenere lo stato, operare contro alla fede, contro alla carità, contro alla umanità, contro alla relligione (18 *P 1.73*)

297   Quomodo Fides a principibus sit servanda (18 *P 1.72*)

Quanto sia laudabile in uno principe mantenere la fede, e vivere con integrità e non con astuzia, ciascuno lo intende (18 *P 1.72*)

contro al re di Armenia è piena di fraude . . . con inganno e non con forza (2.13 *D 1.311*)

lo usare la fraude in ogni azione sia detestabile, nondimanco, nel maneggiare la guerra è cosa laudabile e gloriosa e parimente è laudato colui che con fraude supera il nimico, come quello che lo supera con le forze. . . . Dirò solo questo, che io non intendo quella fraude essere gloriosa che ti fa rompere la fede data ed i patti fatti: perché questa, ancora che la ti acquisti qualche volta stato e regno . . . la non ti acquisterà mai gloria. Ma parlo di quella fraude che si usa con quel nimico che non si fida di te, e che consiste proprio nel maneggiare la guerra (3.40 *D 1.493*)

298   imperio ma non la gloria (8 *P 1.42*)

E non solamente non si osservano intra i principi le promesse forzate, quando e' manca la forza; ma non si osservano ancora tutte le altre promesse quando e' mancano le cagioni che le feciono promettere. Il che se è cosa laudabile o no, o se da uno principe si debbano osservare simili modi o no, largamente è disputato da noi nel nostro trattato "De Principe"; però al presente lo tacereno (3.42 *D 1.496*)

nostro trattato de' Principati (2.1 *D 1.278*)

di sotto si dirà circa la fede de' principi e come la si debbe osservare (3 *P 1.24–25*)

299   con meno rispetto lasciare andare . . . non si curi di incorrere nella fama di quelli vizii (15 *P 1.67*)

E tu . . . consenti che a me sia fatta quella ingiuria che se io fossi costí non permetterei mai che la fusse fatta a te? (3.20 *IF 3.254*)

300   la persona della golpe (19 *P 1.80*)

Non può pertanto uno signore prudente, né debbe osservare la fede, quando tale osservanzia li torni contro, e che sono spente le cagioni che la feciono promettere. E, se li uomini fussino tutti buoni, questo precetto non sarebbe buono; ma, perché sono tristi e non la osservarebbano a te, tu etiam non l'hai ad osservare a loro (18 *P 1.72–73*)

sono dua generazione di combattere: l'uno con le leggi, l'altro, con la forza: quel primo è proprio dello uomo, quel secondo delle bestie, ma perché el primo molte volte non basta, conviene ricorrere al secondo . . . che bisogna a uno principe sempre sapere usare l'uno e l'altra natura, e l'una sanza l'altra non è durabile . . . perché il lione non si defende da' lacci, la golpe non si defende da' lupi (18 *P 1.72*)

si volse alli inganni (7 *P 1.36*)

301 coloro che stanno semplicemente in sul lione non se ne intendano (18 *P 1.72*)

bene colorire (18 *P 1.73*)

Sí suave è l'inganno / al fin condotto imaginato e caro, / ch'altrui spoglia d'affanno / e dolce face ogni gustato amaro. / O rimedio alto e raro / tu mostri il dritto calle all'alme erranti; / tu, col tuo gran valore, / Nel far beato altrui, fai ricco Amore: / tu vinci, sol co' tuoi consigli santi, / pietre veneni e incanti (4.Canzona *Clizia 4.157*)

Va pur la, Nicomaco, tu troverrai riscontro; perché questa tua donna sarà come le mezzine da Santa Maria in Prunéta (4.11 *Clizia 4.157*)

302 li uomini sempre ti riusciranno tristi se da una necessità non sono fatti buoni (23 *P 1.96*)

Come dimostrano tutti coloro che ragionano del vivere civile, e come ne è piena di esempli ogni istoria, è necessario a chi dispone una republica ed ordina leggi in quella, presupporre tutti gli uomini rei e che li abbiano a usare sempre la malignità dello animo loro qualunque volta ne abbiano libera occasione; e quando alcuna malignità sta occulta un tempo . . . la fa poi scoprire il tempo, il quale dicono essere padre d'ogni verità (1.3 *D 1.135*)

o beneficare o spegnere (*Del modo 2.74*)

303 Questo signore è molto splendido e magnifico; et nelle armi è tanto animoso che non è sí gran cosa che non li paia piccola; et per gloria et per adquistare stato mai si riposa, né conosce faticha o periculo. Giugne prima in un luogo che se ne possa intendere la partita donde si lieva; fassi benevolere a' suoi soldati; ha cappati e' migliori huomini d'Italia: le quali cose lo fanno victorioso et formidabile, adgiunto con una perpetua fortuna (*Legation of* June 26, 1502: *7.125*)

che già fe' tremar voi e pianger Roma (*Decennale Primo 4.255*)

signore di Toscana (3 *P 1.23*)

liberale (7 *P 1.39*)

304 legato e vinto (*Decennale Primo 4.255*)

per aver riposo / portato fu tra l'anime beate / lo spirto d'Alessandro glorioso / . . . le sante pedate / tre sue familiari e care ancelle, / lussuria, simonia e crudeltate (*Decennale Primo 4.252–253*)

305 E perché conosceva le rigorosità passate averli generato qualche odio, per purgare li animi di quelli populi e guadagnarseli in tutto, volle monstrare che, se crudeltà alcuna era seguita, non era nata da lui, ma dalla acerba natura del ministro (7 *P 1.37*)

severo (7 *P 1.39*)

Potrebbe alcuno dubitare donde nascessi che Agatocle e alcuno simile, dopo infiniti tradimenti e crudeltà, posse vivere lungamente sicuro nella sua patria e defendersi dalli inimici esterni, e da' sua cittadini non li fu mai conspirato contro: con ciò sia che molti altri mediante la crudeltà non abbino, etiam ne' tempi pacifici, possuto mantenere lo stato, non che ne' tempi dubbiosi di guerra. Credo che questo avvenga dalle crudeltà male usate o bene usate. Bene usate si possono chiamare quelle (se del male è lecito dire bene) che si fanno ad un tratto, per necessità dello assicurarsi, e di poi non vi si insiste dentro, ma si convertiscono in piú utilità de' sudditi che si può (8 *P 1.44*)

io non saprei quali precetti mi dare migliori a uno principe nuovo, che lo esemplo delle azioni sua (7 *P 1.34–35*)

306 debbe avvertire di non usare male questa pietà (17 *P 1.68*)
usare liberalità . . . e miseria (16 *P 1.67*)
usare l'una e l'altra natura (18 *P 1.72*)
mutare el contrario (18 *P 1.73*)
tenuto liberale, alcuno misero (15 *P 1.65*)

307 dico che ciascuno principe debbe desiderare di essere tenuto pietoso e non crudele (17 *P 1.68*)
E' sono molte cose che discosto paiano terribile, insopportabile, strane, e quando tu ti appressi loro, le riescono umane, sopportabile, dimestiche; e però si dice che sono maggiori li spaventi ch'e mali (3.11 *M 4.89*)
se si considerrà bene tutto, si troverrà qualche cosa che parrà virtú, e seguendola sarebbe la ruina sua, e qualcuna altra che parrà vizio, e seguendola ne riesce la securtà et il bene essere suo (15 *P 1.66*)
tenere e' sudditi . . . uniti et in fede (17 *P 1.69*)

308 aveva racconcia la Romagna, unitola ridottola in pace et in fede (17 *P 1.68*)
con pochissimi esempli (17 *P 1.69*)
offendere una universalità intera (17 *P 1.69*)
ad un tratto (8 *P 1.44*)
per troppa pietà, lasciono seguire e' disordini, di che ne nasca occisioni o rapine (17 *P 1.69*)
Il che, se si considerrà bene, si vedrà quello essere stato molto piú pietoso che il populo fiorentino, il quale, per fuggire el nome di crudele, lasciò destruggere Pistoia (17 *P 1.68–69*)
a giudicare l'opere sue e la intenzione sua dal fine . . . poteva certificare ciascuno come quello che aveva fatto era per salute della patria e non per ambizione sua (3.3 *D 1.387*)

309 Dice la Bibbia che le figliuole di Lotto, credendosi essere rimase sole nel mondo, usorno con el padre; e, perché la loro intenzione fu buona, non peccorno (3.11 *M 4.89*)

310 è necessario essere tanto prudente (15 *P 1.65–66*)
diventi o povero o contennendo, o, per fuggire la povertà, rapace e odioso (16 *P 1.68*)
li torrebano lo stato (15 *P 1.66*)
partorisce una infamia con odio (16 *P 1.68*)

311 la lingua con tanta crudeltà . . . che se ne morí (2.36 *IF 3.198*)
nuovi modi (2.36 *IF 3.196*)
Fu questo duca, come i governi suoi dimostrorono, avaro e crudele . . . di essere odiato meritava (2.37 *IF 3.203–204*)

né era contento fare morire gli uomini se con qualche modo crudele non gli ammazzava (7.33 *IF 3.503*)

consistendo la vita di Roma nella vita di quello esercito ... la patria è bene difesa in qualunque modo la si difende, o con ignominia o con gloria: ... ancora che gloriosamente morisse, era perduto Roma e la libertà sua (3.41 *D 1.494–495*)

312   l'uno, che il sangue del loro principe antiquo si spenga; l'altro di non alterare né loro legge né loro dazii (3 *P 1.18*)

si può avvertire ogni principe che non viva mai sicuro del suo principato, finché vivono coloro che ne sono stati spogliati (3.4 *D 1.387*)

le moltitudini degli erranti (3.49 *D 1.505*)

Furono punite adunque le venefiche e le Baccanali, secondo che meritavano i peccati loro (3.49 *D 1.505*)

per non gli fare morire tutti (6 *Arte 2.477*)

Ma di tutte le altre esecuzioni era terribile il decimare gli eserciti, dove a sorte di tutto uno esercito era morto di ogni dieci uno (3.49 *D 1.505*)

a frenare gli uomini armati (6 *Arte 2.478*)

quando el principe è con li eserciti et ha in governo moltitudine di soldati, allora al tutto è necessario non si curare del nome di crudele; perché sanza questo nome non si tenne mai esercito unito, né disposto ad alcuna fazione (19 *P 1.70*)

313   crudeltà e avarizia (19 *P 1.78*)

avarizia e crudeltà (19 *P 1.79*)

estraordinarii vizii (2 *P 1.16*)

vie battute da uomini grandi ... eccellentissimi imitare (6 *P 1.30*)

non hanno a durare altra fatica che pigliare per loro specchio la vita de' principi buoni; come sarebbe Timoleone Corintio, Arato Sicioneo e simili: nella vita de' quali ei troveria tanta sicurtà e tanta sodisfazione di chi regge e di chi è retto, che doverrebbe venirgli voglia di imitargli (3.5 *D 1.389*)

gli costrinsono ad essere principi mentre che vissono, ancora che da quegli piú volte fosse tentato di ridursi in vita privata (3.5 *D 1.390*)

314   mediante la crudeltà (8 *P 1.44*)

solo a essere mista di due qualità delle tre soprascritte, cioé di Principato e di Ottimati (1.2 *D 1.134*)

esaminare le qualità di questi principati (10 *P 1.48*)

egli è un uomo della qualità che tu sai, di poca prudenzia, di meno animo (1.3 *M 4.66*)

315   non potendo usare questa virtú del liberale (16 *P 1.67*)

perché questo è uno di quelli vizii che lo fanno regnare (16 *P 1.67*)

CHAPTER 13 The Reform of Hell

318   eglino vorrieno un predicatore che insegnasse loro la via del paradiso, et io vorrei trovarne uno che insegnassi loro la via di andare a casa il diavolo (L to Francesco Guicciardini, May 17, 1521: *5.403*)

infernal porte (4 *Asino* *4.282*)

quella providenza che mantiene / l'umana spezie, vuol che tu sostenga / questo disagio per tuo maggior bene (3 *Asino* *4.281*)

la mia duchessa (3 *Asino* *4.278*)

319 vergogna alquanto il viso mi dipinse (6 *Asino* *4.291*)

tante bestie qualche uccello (7 *Asino* *4.295*)

di quel che Val di Grieve e Poppi mena (4 *Asino* *4.283*)

meco tra l'altre bestie a pascer venga (3 *Asino* *4.281*)

benigni i ciel si mostreranno / torneran tempi piú che mai felici (3 *Asino* *4.281*)

Alma discreta, / questo viaggio tuo, questo tuo stento, / cantato fia da istorico o poeta (3 *Asino* *4.282*)

rinvolto in quelle angeliche bellezze (4 *Asino* *4.286*)

Noi eravam col pié già 'n su la soglia / di questa porta, e di passar la drento / m'avea fatto venir la donna voglia (7 *Asino* *4.294*)

mosse la mia donna il piede, / e per non separarmi da lei punto, / la presi per la man ch'ella mi diede (7 *Asino* *4.298*)

un gran palazzo di mirabil altura (3 *Asino* *4.278*)

320 al basso centro pauroso e brutto ("Di Amanti e Donne Disperati" *4.330*)

di tante pene tormentati ("Di Amanti" *4.330*)

crudeltà fuor di lor non si truova ("Di Amanti" *4.330*)

tutte o la maggior parte si dolevano non per altro che per avere preso moglie essersi a tanta infelicità condotte (*Belfagor* *4.169*)

piú tosto elessono di tornarsene in inferno a stare nel fuoco che vivere nel mondo sotto lo imperio di quella (*Belfagor* *4.173*)

Già fummo, or non siam piú, Spirti beati: / per la superbia nostra / siàno stati dal ciel tutti scacciati: / e in questa città vostra / abbian preso il governo, / perché qui si dimostra / confusion, dolor piú che in inferno ("De' Diavoli iscacciati di cielo" *4.329*)

321 E non potendo credere queste calunnie che costoro al sesso femmineo davano essere vere, e crescendo ogni giorno le querele, e avendo di tutto fatto a Plutone conveniente rapporto, fu deliberato per lui di avere sopra questo caso con tutti gl'infernali principi maturo esamine, e pigliarne di poi quel partito che fussi giudicato migliore per scoprire questa fallacia o conoscerne in tutto la verità (*Belfagor* *4.169*)

alcuno iudicio o celeste o mondano, nondimeno, . . . gli è maggiore prudenza di quelli che possono piú sottomettersi piú alle leggi e piú stimare l'altrui iudizio (*Belfagor* *4.169–170*)

inrevocabile (*Belfagor* *4.169*)

possiamo essere calunniati come troppo creduli, e non ne dando come manco severi e poco amatori della iustizia. E perché l'uno peccato è da uomini leggieri, e l'altro da ingiusti, e volendo fuggire quegli carichi . . . vi abbiamo chiamati acciò . . . ché questo regno, come per lo passato è vivuto sanza infamia, cosí per lo advenire viva (*Belfagor* *4.170*)

Perché a chi pareva che si mandassi uno, a chi piú, nel mondo, e sotto forma di uomo conoscessi personalmente questo vero: a molti altri occorreva potersi fare sanza tanto disagio costringendo varie anime con varii tormenti a scoprirlo (*Belfagor 4.170*)

cadde sopra Belfagor arcidiavolo, ma per lo adietro, avanti che cadessi dal cielo, arcangelo (*Belfagor 4.170–171*)

322 consegnati centomila ducati, con i quali doveva venire nel mondo, e sotto forma di uomo prender moglie e con quella vivere X anni e di poi fingendo di morire tornarsene e per esperienza fare fede a i suoi superiori quali sieno i carichi e le incommodità del matrimonio (*Belfagor 4.171*)

piú atta a supportare chi con arte usuraie esercitassi i suoi danari (*Belfagor 4.171*)

sottoposto a tutti quegli disagi e mali che sono sottoposti gli uomini, e che si tira drietro la povertà, le carcere, la malattia e ogni altro infortunio nel quale gli uomini incorrono, eccetto se con inganno o astuzia se ne liberassi (*Belfagor 4.171*)

a pigliare piacere degli onori e delle pompe del mondo e avere caro di essere laudato intra gli uomini, il che gli arrecava spesa non piccola. Oltra di questo non fu dimorato molto con la sua monna Onesta che se innamorò fuori di misura (*Belfagor 4.172*)

tanta superbia che non ne ebbe mai tanta Lucifero: e Roderigo che aveva provata l'una e l'altra giudicava quella della moglie superiore (*Belfagor 4.172*)

giogo matrimoniale (*Belfagor 4.179*)

323 Talvolta io cerco di vincere me stesso, riprendomi di questo mio furore, e dico meco: 'Che fai tu? se' tu impazzato? . . . el peggio che te ne va è morire e andarne in inferno; e' son morti tanti degli altri! E sono in inferno tanti uomini da bene! Ha'ti tu a vergognare d'andarvi tu? Volgi el viso alla sorte; fuggi el male, e non lo potendo fuggire, sopportalo come uomo, non ti prosternere, non ti invilire come una donna' (*4.1 M 4.92*)

La notte che morí Pier Soderini / l'anima andò de l'inferno a la bocca: / gridò Pluton: "Ch'inferno? anima sciocca, / va su nel limbo fra gli altri bambini" ("Epigramma" *4.365*)

Di discendere di cielo e venire insieme con loro ad abitare la terra ("Allocuz." *2.135*)

cominciarono appoco appoco a ritornarsene in cielo ("Allocuz." *2.135*)

Forse ch'ancor prenderai vanagloria / a queste genti raccontando e quelle / delle fatiche tue la lunga istoria (3 *Asino 4.281*)

325 che le diverse operazioni qualche volta equalmente giovino o equalmente nuochino, io non lo so, ma desiderrei bene saperlo (L to Giovan Battista Soderini, Sept. 13–21, 1506: *sa.239–240*)

avanti che la comedia cominci (Prologo *Clizia 4.116*)

questo giorno il vostro badalucco (Prologo *M 4.57*)

Sono trovate le comedie per giovare e per dilettare alli spettatori. . . . volendo dilettare è necessario muovere li spettatori a riso, il che non si può fare mantenendo il parlare grave e severo; perché le parole che fanno ridere sono o sciocche o iniuriose o amorose. È necessario pertanto rappresentare persone sciocche, malediche o innamorate (Prologo *Clizia 4.117*)

Giova veramente assai a qualunque uomo, e massimamente a' giovanetti conoscere l'avarizia d'un vecchio, il furore d'uno innamorato li inganni d'uno servo, la gola d'uno parassito, la miseria d'un povero, l'ambizione di un ricco, le lusinghe d'una meretrice, la poca fede di tutti li uomini (Prologo *Clizia 4.117*)

tutte queste cose con onestà grandissima rappresentare (Prologo *Clizia 4.117*)

326   giudicando i cieli che gli ordini di Romolo non bastassero a tanto imperio, inspirarono nel petto del Senato romano di eleggere Numa Pompilio per successore a Romolo ... trovando un popolo ferocissimo, e volendolo ridurre nelle obedienze civili con le arti della pace si volse alla religione come cosa al tutto necessaria a volere mantenere una civiltà (1.11 *D 1.160*)

328   ignudo e con il carnefice davanti, che aveva il coltello in mano per ferirlo (7.34 *IF 3.507*)

infiniti fanciulli erano da' petti delle madri divelti ... presi per le gambe e divisi infino al capo in dua parti (Traduzione, *Libro delle persecuzioni d'Africa 4.228*)

329   e degna di notizia e da essere imitata da altri (7 *P 1.37*)

avevano spogliato e' loro sudditi che corretti (7 *P 1.37*)

uno iudicio civile nel mezzo della provincia, con uno presidente eccellentissimo, dove ogni città vi aveva lo avvocato suo (7 *P 1.37*)

330   mantenere la religione e la giustizia (3.1 *D 1.380*)

o in bene o in male ... pigliare uno modo circa premiarlo o punirlo, di che s'abbia a parlare assai (21 *P 1.90*)

fatti vivi dalla virtú d'uno cittadino ... contro ... quegli che trapassano (3.1 *D 1.381*)

semplice virtú d'un uomo, sanza dependere da alcuna legge (3.1 *D 1.382*)

sono di tale riputazione e di tale esemplo che gli uomini buoni desiderano imitarle, e gli cattivi si vergognano a tenere vita contraria a quelli (3.1 *D 1.382*)

331   del tempo e del luogo (3.33 *IF 3.504*)

con pompa grande vicitare il tempio di quello martire (7.34 *IF 3.504*)

non pareva loro sicuro (7.33 *IF 3.504*)

incerto e pericoloso ... dubbio ... Pertanto deliberarono in qualche pompa e publica festivitate opprimerlo, dove fussero certi che venisse, ed eglino sotto vari colori vi potessero loro amici ragunare (7.33 *IF 3.504*)

entravano già nel tempio quelli che precedono al duca; di poi entro egli circondato da una moltitudine grande, come era conveniente in quella solennità a una ducale pompa (7.34 *IF 3.506*) ferma . . . la maestà della dignità sua, perché questo non vuol mai mancare in cosa alcuna (21 *P 1.93*)

la maestà e la riverenza che si tira dietro la presenza d'uno principe . . . (3.6 *D 1.403*)

quanto si può tenere che la sia maggiore in uno principe sciolto, con la maestà degli ornamenti della pompa e della comitiva sua! (3.6 *D 1.403*)

una ultima sperienza (*Belfagor 4.178*)

Sire . . . farai pertanto fare in su la piazza di Nostra Dama un palco grande e capace di tutti i tuoi baroni e di tutto il clero di questa città; farai parare il palco di drappi di seta e d'oro; fabbricherai nel mezzo di quello uno altare; e voglio che domenica mattina prossima . . . celebrata prima una solenne messa . . . (*Belfagor 4.178*)

333   e d'ogn'altra qualità romori (*Belfagor 4.178*)

venne la spiritata condutta in sul palco per le mani di dua vescovi e molti signori. Quando Roderigo vide tanto popolo insieme e tanto apparato rimase quasi che stupido e fra sé disse: "Che cosa ha pensato di fare questo poltrone di questo villano? Crede egli sbigottirmi con questa pompa? non sa egli che io sono uso a vedere le pompe del cielo e le furie dello inferno? Io lo gastigherò in ogni modo" . . . "Villano ribaldo, io ti farò impiccare in ogni modo" (*Belfagor 4.178–179*)

con romori che andavano al cielo (*Belfagor 4.179*)

Oimé, Roderigo mio! Quella è mogliata che ti viene a ritrovare (*Belfagor 4.179*)

Nessuna cosa fa tanto stimare uno principe quanto fanno le grande imprese e dare di sé rari esempli (21 *P 1.89*)

Debbe oltre a questo, ne' tempi convenienti dell'anno, tenere occupati e' populi con le feste e spettaculi . . . raunarsi con loro . . . dare di sé esempli di umanità e di munificenzia, tenendo sempre ferma non di manco la maestà della dignità sua (21 *P 1.93*)

335   eccomi (L to Francesco Vettori, Dec. 10, 1513: *5.301*)

mille . . . disagi (Prologo *M 4.58*)

io vengo allegro in campo (Lettera *IF 3.67*)

uomini gravi e pieni di riverenza (1.54 *D 1.254*)

uomo grave e di autorità (1.54 *D 1.253*)

non istima persona (Prologo *M 4.58*)

Chi vedesse le nostre lettere, honorando compare, et vedesse la diversità di quelle, si maraviglierebbe assai, perché gli parrebbe hora che noi fussimo huomini gravi, tutti volti a cose grandi, et che ne' petti nostri non potesse cascare alcuno pensiere che non havesse in sé honestà et grandezza. Però dipoi, voltando carta, gli parrebbe quegli noi medesimi essere leggieri, inconstanti, lascivi, volti a cose vane. . . . Et benché questa varietà noi la solessimo fare in piú lettere io la voglio fare questa volta in una, come vedrete, se leggerete l'altra faccia (L to Francesco Vettori, Jan. 31, 1515: *5.374*)

336   Questo modo di procedere, se a qualcuno pare sia vituperoso, a me pare

laudabile, perché noi imitiamo la natura, che è varia; et chi imita quella non può essere ripreso (L to Francesco Vettori, Jan. 31, 1515: *5.374*)

Né di quello si possono addurre vizi, che maculassero tante sue virtú, ancora che fusse nelle cose veneree maravigliosamente involto e che si dilettasse di uomini faceti e mordaci, e di giuochi puerili piú che a tanto uomo non pareva si convenisse: in modo che molte volte fu visto, intra i suoi figliuoli e figliuole, intra i loro trastulli mescolarsi. Tanto che a considerare in quello e la vita voluttuosa e la grave, si vedeva in lui essere due persone diverse, quasi con impossibile congiunzione congiunte (8.36 *IF 3.576*)

337 Chi è tenuto savio di dí, non sarà mai tenuto pazzo di notte (*Vita 3.38*)

in tutti la religione e il timore di Dio è spento (3.5 *IF 3.219*)

duolmi bene che io sento come molti di voi delle cose fatte, per coscienza si pentono, e delle nuove si vogliono astenere (3.13 *IF 3.238*)

i falli piccoli si puniscono, i grandi e gravi si premiano (3.13 *IF 3.237*)

338 e della coscienza noi non dobbiamo tenere conto, perche dove è, come è in noi, la paura della fame e delle carcere, non può né debbe quella dello inferno capere (3.13 *IF 3.238*)

Per quale Iddio, o per quali santi, gli ho io a fare giurare? Per quei ch'egli adorano, o per quei che bestemmiano? Che ne adorino non so io alcuno; ma so bene che li bestemmiano tutti. Come ho io a credere ch'egli osservino le promesse a coloro che ad ogni ora essi dispregiano? Come possono coloro che dispregiano Iddio, riverire gli uomini? (7 *Arte 2.516–517*)

CHAPTER 14 The Goodly Company

341 non eccettuando, non ch'altro, l'anima . . . il bene della patria (1 *Arte 2.328*)

342 Io amo messer Francesco Guicciardini . . . (L to Francesco Vettori, Apr. 16, 1527: *5.505*)

343 il ducato di Milano è spacciato . . . non ci è piú rimedio. Sic datum desuper. . . . Et nel vicariato suo, etc. Nosti versus, caetera per te ipsum lege. Facciamo una volta un lieto carnesciale, et ordinate alla Barbera uno alloggiamento tra quelli frati che, se non inpazzano, io non ne voglio danaio . . . Et raccomandatemi alla Mariscotta . . . Comincio hora a scrivere di nuovo . . . Niccolò Machiavelli historico, comico e tragico (L to Francesco Guicciardini, Oct. 21, 1525: *5.443–444*)

344 e quinci avvien che 'l matto / Carlo re de' Romani e' l Vicere / per non vedere hanno lasciato il Re ("*Epigramma*" *4.365*)

voi sapete e sallo ciascuno che sa ragionare di questo mondo, come i popoli sono varii e sciocchi; nondimeno, cosí fatti come sono, dicono molte volte che si fa quello che si doverrebbe fare. Pochi dí fa si diceva per Firenze che il signor Giovanni de' Medici rizzava una bandiera di ventura per fare guerra dove gli venisse meglio. Questa voce mi destò l'animo a pensare che il popolo dicesse quello che si doverrebbe fare.

Ciascuno credo che creda che fra gli Italiani non ci sia capo, a chi li soldati vadino piú volentieri dietro, ne di chi gli Spagnuoli piú dubitino, et stimino di piú: ciascuno tiene ancora il signor Giovanni audace, inpetuoso, di gran concetti, pigliatore di gran partiti; puossi adunque, ingrossandolo segretamente, fargli rizzare questa bandiera, mettendoli sotto quanti cavalli e quanti fanti si potesse piú. . . . ben presto farebbe aggirare il cervello agli Spagnuoli, et variare i disegni loro, che hanno pensato forse rovinare la Toscana et la Chiesa senza ostacolo. Potrebbe far mutare opinione al re . . . Et se questo rimedio non ci è, havendo a far guerra, non so qual ci sia; né a me occorre altro (L to Francesco Guicciardini, March 15, 1526: *5.457–458*)

345 sí pieno di baluardi che non vi è potuta entrare altra cosa. . . . Questa occasione per l'amor di Dio non si perda, et ricordatevi che la fortuna, i cattivi nostri consigli, et peggior ministri harieno condotto non il re, ma il papa in prigione: hannonelo tratto i cattivi consigli di altri et la medesima fortuna. Provvedete, per l'amor di Dio, hora in modo che Sua Santità ne' medesimi pericoli non ritorni, di che voi non sarete mai sicuri, sino a tanto che gli Spagnuoli non siano in modo tratti di Lombardia, che non vi possino tornare . . . et ricordatevi che il duca di Sessa andava dicendo, quod pontifex sero Caesarem coeperat timere. Hora Iddio ha ricondotto le cose in termine, che il papa è a tempo a tenerlo (L to Francesco Guicciardini, May 17, 1526: *5.464–465*)

preso come un binbo (L to Bartolomeo Cavalcanti, Oct. 6, 1526: *5.491*)

i disordini di Roma (L to Bartolomeo Cavalcanti, Oct. 6, 1526: *5.491*)

Magnifici Domini, etc. Io arrivai qui oggi a grand'ora, e subito fui alla Signoria del luogotenente. . . . I Lanzichenét . . . oggi sono passati il fiume . . . sono questi Tedeschi in numero di quindici o sedicimila . . . A dí 2 di dicembre 1526. Aranno vostre Signorie inteso della morte del signor Giovanni, il quale morto con dispiacere di ciascuno (*Legation of* Dec. 2, 1526: *11.1601–1603*)

347 il qual tempo cominciò il sabato notte, ed infino ad ora . . . è sempre piovuto o nevicato; tale che la neve è alta uno braccio in ogni parte di questa città, e tuttavia nevica. E cosí quello impedimento, che noi non portavamo o non sapevamo dare agli inimici, lo ha dato e da Iddio. . . . E se Dio ci avesse voluto bene affatto, egli arebbe differito questo tempo quando fussino . . . entrati intra quelli monti (*Legation of* March 18, 1527: *11.1634–1635*)

Né credo sia alcuno che non conosca questo medesimo. Ma i cieli quando vogliono colorire i disegni loro, conducono gli uomini in termine, che non possono pigliare alcun partito sicuro (*Legation of* March 17, 1527: *11.1641*)

Onde magnifici Signori miei, pare ad ognuno qui la tregua sia spacciata, e che si abbia a pensare alla guerra, tanto che Iddio ne aiuti in modo che diventino piú umili (*Legation of* March 29, 1527: *11.1642*)

Per il ché il luogotenete vive in angustie grandi, e riordina e rimedia a tutte quelle cose che può, e Dio voglia che possa fare tanto che basti (*Legation of* March 30, 1527: *11.1643*)

Et, per l'amor di Iddio . . . tagliate subito subito la pratica . . . et se il conte Guido dice altrimenti, egli è un cazzo . . . Ma chi gode nella guerra, come fanno questi soldati, sarebbono pazzi se lodassino la pace. Ma Iddio farà che gli haranno a fare più guerra che noi non vorremo (L to Francesco Vettori, April 18, 1527: *5.507–508*)

et vi dico questo per quella esperienza che mi hanno data sessanta anni, che io non credo che mai si travagliassino i più difficili articuli che questi, dove la pace è necessaria, et la guerra non si può abbandonare, et havere alle mani un principe, che con fatica può supplire o alla pace sola o alla guerra sola (L to Francesco Vettori, April 16, 1527: *5.505*)

Magnifici Domini, etc. Se le vostre Signorie non fussino state tenute ragguagliate ogni giorno di ogni cosa di queste occorrenze da il signore luogotenente per lettere ad il reverendissimo legato; quelle si potrebbero . . . ragionevolmente di negligenza accusarmi: ma io ho giudicato superfluo dire quelle medesime cose che da detto signore luogotenente erano dette e scritte (*Legation of* March 4, 1526: *11.1628*)

348 Liberate diuturna cura Italiam, extirpate has immanes belluas, quae hominis, praeter faciem et vocem, nihil habent (L to Francesco Vettori, May 17, 1526: *5.465*)

Vedesi come la prega Dio che le mandi qualcuno che la redima da queste crudeltà et insolenzie barbare. Vedesi ancora, tutta pronta e disposta a seguire una bandiera, pur che ci sia uno che la pigli . . . a ognuno puzza questo barbaro dominio (26 *P 1.102, 104*)

è suta corsa da Carlo, predata da Luigi, sforzata da Ferrando e vituperata da' Svizzeri (12 *P 1.57*)

349 *Nicomaco*: Io ho pensato che sarà bene, per uscire una volta di questo farnetico, che si getti per sorte di chi sia Clizia; da che la donna non si potrà discostare.

Pirro: Se la sorte vi venisse contro?

Nicomaco: Io ho speranza in Dio che la non verrà.

Pirro: (Oh, vecchio impazzato! Vuole che Dio tenga le mane a queste sue disonestà!) Io credo che se Iddio s'impaccia di simili cose che Sofronia ancora speri in Dio.

Nicomaco: Ella si speri! (3.6 *Clizia 4.143–144*)

350 era necessario che la Italia si riducessi nel termine che ell' è di presente, e che la fussi più stiava che li Ebrei . . . più dispersa che li Ateniesi . . . avessi sopportato d'ogni sorte ruina (26 *P 1.102*)

mi sfogo accusando i principi, che hanno fatto tutti ogni cosa per condurci qui (L to Francesco Guicciardini, Oct. 21, 1525: *5.444*)

Credevano i nostri principi italiani, prima ch'egli assaggiassero i colpi delle oltramontane guerre, cha a uno principe bastasse sapere negli scrittoi pensare una acuta risposta, scrivere una bella lettera, mostrare ne' detti e nelle parole arguzia e prontezza, sapere tessere una fraude,

ornarsi di gemme e d'oro, dormire e mangiare con maggiore splendore
che gli altri, tenere assai lascivie intorno, governarsi co' sudditi avara-
mente e superbamente, marcirsi nello ozio, dare i gradi della milizia per
grazia, disprezzare se alcuno avesse loro dimostro alcuna lodevole via,
volere che le parole loro fussero responsi di oraculi; né si accorgevano
i meschini che si preparavano ad essere preda di qualunque li assaltava.
Di qui nacquero poi nel mille quattrocento novantaquattro i grandi
spaventi, le subite fughe e le miracolose perdite; e cosí tre potentissimi
stati che erano in Italia, sono stati piú volte saccheggiati e guasti (7 *Arte*
2.518)

351 sine caede et vulnere pauci descendunt reges et sicca morte tiranni (3.6 *D*
1.392)

rimasa come sanza vita, espetta qual possa esser quello che sani le sua
ferite (26 *P 1.102*)

seguitare quelli eccellenti uomini che redimirno le provincie loro (26 *P*
1.104)

uno prudente e virtuoso, di introdurvi forma che facessi onore a lui e bene
alla università delli uomini (26 *P 1.101–102*)

farsi capo di questa redenzione (26 *P 1.102*)

io non so quale cosa si fusse tanto sua (non eccettuando, non ch'altro,
l'anima) che per gli amici volentieri da lui non fusse stata spesa; non so
quale impresa lo avesse sbigottito, dove quello avesse conosciuto il
bene della patria sua (1 *Arte 2.328*)

355 infinite anime di quelli miseri mortali che nella disgrazia di Dio morivano
all'inferno (*Belfagor 4.169*)

antica consuetudine ("Allocuz." *3.135*)

356 nel numero degli eletti suoi ("Allocuz." *3.136*)

non solo una volta ma tre negato ("Esortaz." *4.212*)

un uomo per arme, per dottrina, per giudizio eccellentissimo (1.19 *D 1.184*)

li onorò intra i primi eletti nel cielo ("Esortaz." *4.212*)

ne venne nel mondo (*Belfagor 4.171*)

partito sinistro che tagliò loro le gambe del salire in cielo (1 *Arte 2.349*)

se dua l'uno dopo l'altro sono di gran virtú . . . ne vanno con la fama fino
in cielo (1.19 *D 1.183*)

Voi . . . sí intente e quiete, / anime belle, esemplo onesto, umile / mastro
saggio e gentile / di nostra umana vita udito avete, / e per lui conoscete
/ qual cosa schifar diesi, e qual seguire / per salir dritti al cielo
(5.Canzona *Clizia 4.166*)

358 da ciel mandato, un uom divino ("Ingratitudine" *4.307*)

alcuno di quelli piú amato dal cielo (2.Proemio *D 1.274*)

sarò animoso in dire manifestamente quello che io intenderò di quelli e di
questi tempi, acciocché gli animi de' giovani che questi mia scritti leggeranno, possino fuggire questi e prepararsi ad imitare quegli, qualunque volta la fortuna ne dessi loro l'occasione . . . sendone molti ca-

paci, alcuno di quelli piú amato dal Cielo possa operarlo (2.Proemio *D* *1.274*)

359   Themistocle, uomo eccellentissimo (2.31 *D 1.372*)

Marco filosofo (19 *P 1.78*)

istorici buoni, come è questo nostro (3.30 *D 1.468*)

sentenzia . . . aurea (3.6 *D 1.390*)

Simmaco e . . . Boezio uomini santissimi (1.4 *IF 3.81*)

secondo padre della platonica filosofia (7.6 *IF 3.462*)

uomo quasi che divino (8.36 *IF 3.575*)

uomo degno di ogni laude (Traduzione, *Libro delle persecuzioni d'Africa* *4.229*)

uomini eccellenti (2.22 *D 1.342*)

uomini da bene (4.33 *IF 3.323*)

i liberali animi (5.1 *IF 3.327*)

CHAPTER 15 And Great Shall Be Their Reward

360   io credo che questo sarebbe il vero modo ad andare in Paradiso: inparare la via dello Inferno per fuggirla (L to Francesco Vettori, March 17, 1521: *5.402*)

Quanto in cor giovenile è bello amore (2.Canzona *Clizia 4.135*)

ho provato che il cavalcare in pressa non mi riesce per qualche mia indisposizione (*Legation of* c. May 18, 1521: *11.1559*)

né mi può impedire altro che una malattia, che Iddio ne guardi (L to Francesco Guicciardini, Jan. 3, 1526: *5.449*)

vecchi amorosi . . . giovinetti ardenti (2.Canzona *Clizia 4.135*)

un vecchio tutto pieno d'amori (Prologo *Clizia 4.117*)

363   un uomo di novanta anni non che di settanta come ho io (2.4 *Clizia 4.149*)

ma perché non uguali / son le forze al desío, / ne nascon tutti mali / ch'io sento o signor mio, / né doler mi poss'io / di voi ma di me stesso, / poi ch'i' veggio e confesso / come tanta beltade / ama piú verde etate ("Barbera" *4.360*)

timor grande e per la notte oscura (2 *Asino 4. 273*)

e mi parea veder intorno Morte / con la sua falce (2 *Asino 4.274*)

a giornate per non prendere affanno senza bisogno (*Legation of* Dec. 3, 1526: *11.1605*)

364   malecontento . . . con parole e con gesti (*Legation of* July 24, 1499: *6.218*)

Quanto alle bugie de' Carpigiani . . . da un tempo in qua, io non dico mai quello che io credo, né credo mai quel che io dico, et se pure e' mi vien detto qualche volta il vero, io lo nascondo fra tante bugie, che è difficile a ritrovarlo (L to Francesco Guicciardini, May 17, 1521: *5.405*)

365   Vostra signoria sa che questi frati dicono, che quando uno è confermato in gratia, il diavolo non ha piú potentia di tentarlo. Cosí io non ho paura che questi frati mi appicchino lo ippocrito, perché io credo essere assai ben confermato (L to Francesco Guicciardini, May 17, 1521: *5.404*)

A' primi portieri, un ducato. A' secondi, due ducati. . . . A' Trombattieri non date niente, ma ben li fate invitare a bere. . . . I vostri servitori abbino cura, per tutti li alloggiamenti farete, alla roba; e guardino i panni e gli stivali da' topi, cioè appicchino alto i vostri stivali: ché, benché questa sia cosa minima e ridicula, pure expertus loquor. . . . La mattina, al partire dall'osteria, una favola di beneandata alla ciambrereria ed al varletto di stalla ("Notula per uno che va ambasciadore in Francia" *2.162–163*)

366   delle sue fatiche recitatore (Lettera *Decennali 4.235*)

367   io ne sono stato con voi liberale, che, essendo giovani e qualificati, potrete, quando le cose dette da me vi piacciano, ai debiti tempi, in favore de' vostri principi aiutarle e consigliarle (*7 Arte 2.519*)

E mi sarà grato mi domandiate; perché io sono per imparare cosí da voi nel domandarmi, come voi da me nel rispondervi; perché molte volte uno savio domandatore fa a uno considerare molte cose e conoscerne molte altre, le quali, sanza esserne domandato, non arebbe mai conosciute (*1 Arte 3.331*)

368   popolo universale di Firenze, sottile interpetre di tutte le cose (8.20 *IF 3.545*)

la sua prim'arte (Prologo *M 4.58*)

il papa ha creduto piú ad una inpennata d'inchiostro che a mille fanti che gli bastavano a guardarlo (L to Francesco Guicciardini, Nov. 5, 1526: *5.495*)

veggendo di havere a convenire con genti vive, et che, oltre alle persuasioni, gli mostrano i fatti (L to Francesco Guicciardini, March 15, 1526: *5.458*)

369   Ma lascian pur dir male a chiunche vuole. / Torniamo al caso nostro, / acciò che non trapassi troppo l'ora. / Far conto non si de' delle parole (Prologo *M 4.58*)

meglio e d'ogni tempo . . . sia intesa (Proemio *IF 3.71*)

372   rivestito condecentemente . . . mi pasco di quel cibo, che solum è mio et che io nacqui per lui (L to Francesco Vettori, Dec. 10, 1513: *5.304*)

cantato fia da istorico o poeta (*4 Asino 4.282*)

non altrimenti periculoso . . . acque e terre incognite (1.Proemio *D 1.123*)

signore di questa provincia (*7 Arte 3.519*)

in brevissimo tempo avere dimostro al mondo (*7 Arte 3.520*)

373   Ho atteso et attendo in villa a scrivere la historia (L to Francesco Guicciardini, Aug. 30, 1524: *5.417*)

E mentre che io scrivo, ne ho un cerchio d'intorno, et veggendomi scrivere a lungo si maravigliano, et guardonmi per spiritato; et io, per farli maravigliare piú, sto alle volte fermo sulla penna, et gonfio . . . egli sbavigliano; che se sapessino quel che io vi scrivo, se ne maraviglierebbono piú (L to Francesco Guicciardini, May 17, 1521: *5.404*)

374   lo autore di questa comedia è uomo molto costumato e saprebbegli male se vi paresse nel vederla recitare che ci fussi qualche disonestà. . . . Dove

se fia cosa alcuna non onesta, sarà in modo detta che queste donne potranno sanza arrossire ascoltarla (Prologo *Clizia 4.117*)

Fuggo bene in tutti i luoghi i vocaboli odiosi, come alla verità e dignità della istoria poco necessari (Lettera *IF 3.66*)

375 Oltre di questo non è esaltato alcuno uomo tanto in alcuna sua azione, quanto sono quegli che hanno con leggi e con istituti reformato le repubbliche e i regni: questi sono, dopo quegli che sono stati Iddii, i primi laudati ("Discursus" *2.275*)

E infra tante felicità che dato Iddio alla casa vostra e alla persona di Vostra Santità, è questa la maggiore, di darle potenza e subietto da farsi immortale, e superare di lunga per questa via la paterna e la avita gloria ("Discursus" *2.276*)

E perché e' sono stati pochi che abbino avuto occasione di farlo, e pochissimi quelli che lo abbino saputo fare, sono piccolo numero quelli che lo abbino fatto: ed è stata stimata tanto questa gloria dagli uomini che non hanno mai atteso ad altro che a gloria, che non avendo possuto fare una republica in atto, l'hanno fatta in iscritto; come Aristotile, Platone, e molti altri: e' quali hanno voluto mostrare al mondo, che se, come Solone e Licurgo, non hanno potuto fondare un vivere civile, non è mancato dalla ignoranza loro, ma dalla impotenza di metterlo in atto ("Discursus" *2.275–276*)

376 Non da . . . il cielo maggiore dono ad uno uomo, né gli può mostrare più gloriosa via di questa ("Discursus" *2.276*)

non beatificava se non uominini di mondana gloria (2.2 *D 1.283*)

378 li fa vivere sicuri e dopo la morte li rende gloriosi (1.10 *D 1.159*)

i cieli . . . occasione dì gloria (1.10 *D 1.159*)

379 tutt'i profeti armati vinsono, e li disarmati ruinorono (6 *P 1.32*)

380 se in tante revoluzioni di Italia . . . e' pare . . . che . . . la virtú militare sia spenta (26 *P 1.103*)

una mutazione di Stato (3.3 *D 1.386*)

legge sue . . . infino a questi tempi non sono state alterate perché . . . non si può sanza pericolo di una certa e pericolosa ribellione, alterarle (8.29 *IF 3.562*)

gli uomini prendono ardire di tentare cose nuove (3.1 *D 1.382*)

intra coloro che desideravano fare novità in Firenze (1.8 *D 1.152*)

nessuno grado di cittadino, o per paura di sé o per ambizione, abbi a desiderare innovazione ("Discursus" *2.77*)

381 E . . . quella sentenzia di Cornelio Tacito è aurea, che dice: che gli uomini hanno ad onorare le cose passate e ad ubbidire alle presenti, e debbono desiderare i buoni principi, e comunque ei si sieno fatti, tollerargli. E veramente chi fa altrimenti, il più delle volte rovina sé e la sua patria (3.6 *D 1.390*)

383 dove i popoli sono principi (1.58 *D 1.265*)

E non sanza cagione si assomiglia la voce d'un popolo a quella di Dio:

... talché pare che per occulta virtú ei prevegga il suo male ed il suo bene (1.58 *D 1.264*)

ingrato vario ed imprudente piú che un popolo (1.58 *D 1.264*)

havete a intendere questo, che gli migliori exerciti che sieno, sono quelli delle populationi armate, né a loro puo obstare se non exerciti simili a loro (L to Francesco Vettori, Aug. 26, 1513: *5.295*)

fien le strade / del ciel aperte ("Degli spiriti beati" *4.333*)

384   non timore di Dio, non fede con li uomini (12 *P 1.53*)

l'uficio è lungo (5.6 *M 4.112*)

uscite qua fuori tutti che il popolo vi vegga (Prologo *Clizia 4.117*)

385   donna sopra ogni donna al mondo bella ("De' diavoli iscacciati di cielo" *4.329*)

[ha] pisciato in tanta neve (1.2 *M 4.65*)

Acknowledgments

For help, encouragement, readings in whole or in part, and many good conversations about Niccolò and related matters I bow to Morton White, Dolf Sternberger, Felix Gilbert, Rosario Villari, Paul Oskar Kristeller, Sergio Bertelli, Donald Weinstein, and Pendleton Herring.

Concerning more particular kindnesses, I thank Franco Aversa for help with Niccolò's wills, Paolo A. Rossi for the floor plan of the writing room of Niccolò's country house, Eugenio Garin for guidance into the dense literature of astrology, M. Gary Dickson (and Denys Hay for leading me to him) for prized comment on my notes to the text of "God more a friend," and Luigi Sensi for setting in order the notes to the book with remarkable understanding and dedication.

For help with the illustrations that form part of the book I thank first Samuel Edgerton, Jr., and as well Fiorella Superbi Gioffredi of I Tatti, William Connell, Denile Sensi, Eliane Heilbronn (and her firm of Salans Hertzfeld Heilbronn Beardsley & van Riel, Paris), Alessandra Corti and Emanuela Sesti of the Alinari Archives, Florence, and Theodore H. Feder of Art Resource, New York.

The Eagleton Institute of Politics of Rutgers University comes in for a large share of thanks. Alan Rosenthal, its director, facilitated the study in many ways and was always appreciative of its import for statecraft. Christine Lenart stepped in whenever necessary with administrative dispatch. Edith Saks, sometimes under conditions that would try the patience of saints, saw to it that the manuscript never failed to meet its many deadlines and did it with characteristic efficiency and good cheer. To C. Fred Main and the Research Council of Rutgers I am grateful for concrete instances of material assistance.

The Institute for Advanced Study, Princeton, invited me to visit at a most appropriate time in the history of the manuscript. I have ever since enjoyed the fellowship the Institute affords. The members of the Institut International de Philosophie Politique, Paris, comprised a small, select forum for several of the major theses of the book. I treasure their company.

To the Harvard Center for Italian Renaissance Studies at Villa I Tatti, Florence, I am indebted for bringing me together with international scholars. I am grateful to the Istituto Nazionale di Studi sul Rinascimento, Florence, for access to its library. Librarians, archivists, and curators in Florence were almost without exception courteous and knowledgeable. I am grateful, too, for the helpfulness and library facilities of the Istituto Italiano di Cultura, New York.

The manuscript found its way bright and early to Princeton University Press through the good offices of Marjorie Sherwood, then literature editor, and R. Miriam Brokaw, then associate director and editor. In time the pages reached the care, energy, and quick mind of Joanna Hitchcock, my editor, executive editor for the humanities. My art designer, Michael Burton, production director, demonstrated in the book his immediate and sure grasp of artistic values. I am indebted to Charles Ault, manuscript editor, not for the routine planting of commas but for many suggestions and queries that improved the manuscript. It was a pleasure to work with the able staff of the Press. Their interest in the book was gratifying.

Margreta, my daughter, cast her literary gaze over the whole manuscript, and my sons Alfred Joseph and Sebastian dipped into it, with feigned enthusiasm. My sons Marc and Tancredi, on stopover visits, joined in the explication of certain longtailed Tuscanisms, with gusto. My brother Edward was living near enough to give the benefit of his scrutiny to large parts of the work. To my wife Lucia Heffelfinger de Grazia we, producers and public alike, owe the perfection of a manuscript word processed from start to finish.

SEBASTIAN DE GRAZIA

January 1988
The Great Road
Princeton, New Jersey

Illustrations

[473]

Index of Persons

Index of Subjects

Note: Italicized numbers indicate illustrations.